INDUSTRIAL
RELATIONS
IN CANADA

INDUSTRIAL
RELATIONS
IN CANADA

THIRD EDITION

FIONA A. E. McQUARRIE
University of the Fraser Valley

John Wiley & Sons Canada, Ltd.

Permission Acknowledgements

Statistics Canada information is used with the permission of Statistics Canada. Users are forbidden to copy this material and/or redisseminate the data, in an original or modified form, for commercial purposes, without the expressed permission of Statistics Canada. Information on the availability of the wide range of data from Statistics Canada can be obtained from Statistics Canada's Regional Offices, its World Wide Web site at http://www.statcan.gc.ca, and its toll-free access number 1-800-263-1136.

Material from the Canadian Labour Relations Boards Reports (CLRBR) is reprinted with permission of LexisNexis Canada Inc.

Data from tables 4-1, 5-5, 5-6, 6-1, 6-3, 6-4, 7-4, 9-2, 9-4, 10-1, and 10-3 are reproduced with the permission of the Minister of Public Works and Government Services, 2006.

Library and Archives Canada Cataloguing in Publication

McQuarrie, Fiona Anne Elizabeth, 1958-
    Industrial relations in Canada / Fiona A.E.
McQuarrie. — 3rd Canadian ed.

ISBN 978-0-470-67887-9

1. Industrial relations—Canada—Textbooks.   I. Title.
HD8106.5.M29 2011   331'.0971   C2010-905812-7

Production Credits

Acquisitions Editor: Darren Lalonde
Vice President and Publisher: Veronica Visentin
Vice President, Publishing Services Director: Karen Bryan
Art Director: Ian Koo
Editorial Manager: Karen Staudinger
Marketing Manager: Aida Krneta
Media Editor: Channade Fenandoe
Senior Production Editor: Joyce Poh

Developmental Editor: Gail Brown
Editorial Assistant: Laura Hwee
Typesetting: Thomson Digital
Cover Artwork: *Radium Mine, Great Bear Lake*, 1938, oil on wood by A.Y. Jackson. Courtesy of the Estate of the late Dr. Naomi Jackson Groves
Printing & Binding: Edwards Brothers

Printed & bound in the United States
1 2 3 4 5 EB 15 14 13 12 11

John Wiley & Sons Canada Ltd.
6045 Freemont Blvd.
Mississauga, Ontario L5R 4J3
Visit our website at www.wiley.ca

ABOUT THE AUTHOR

Fiona A. E. McQuarrie is a faculty member in the School of Business at the University of the Fraser Valley (UFV). She received her Ph.D. in organizational analysis from the University of Alberta, and also has a bachelor's degree in business administration and English and an MBA from Simon Fraser University. She has taught industrial relations at Simon Fraser University, the University of Prince Edward Island, and UFV, and has experience in industrial relations processes in both union and management roles.

Her current research interests include organizational histories and images, and employer support for employee leisure. Her articles on these and other topics have appeared in such journals as the *Academy of Management Executive, Business Horizons, Leisure/Loisir, the Journal of Management Education, the Journal of Career Development, Management and Organizational History, Relations Industrielles/Industrial Relations,* and the *Canadian Journal of Administrative Sciences.*

In addition to her academic interests, she is also a competitive figure skater and enjoys reading all types of books and listening to all kinds of music.

PREFACE

INTRODUCTION

Industrial Relations in Canada, Third Edition, is a comprehensive introduction to the theories, issues, and processes that characterize contemporary Canadian industrial relations. It is significantly different from other Canadian industrial relations textbooks in that it uses a process-oriented approach to the topic and makes every effort to minimize the amount of technical and legal jargon. This approach was born out of many years of classroom experience, and is intended to go beyond the jargon and demonstrate practical, real-world applications of industrial relations in Canada. Since only about 14% of Canadians aged 15–24—the age group including most college and university students—belong to a union, it is not uncommon for industrial relations classes to include students who have no prior industrial relations experience because they have never belonged to a union themselves or known anyone who has. These students' experiences with industrial relations may therefore be limited to being inconvenienced by a strike or lockout or to hearing second-hand information about what unions do in a workplace.

This book is intended to introduce students to the main features of the Canadian industrial relations system, the processes that operate within that system, and the forces that shape it. After finishing this book, students should be able to continue on to further studies in industrial relations or human resource management, and will have the information they need to function more effectively in a unionized workplace as a union member, a management representative, or a business partner.

NEW TO THIS EDITION

Industrial Relations in Canada has established itself as a market-leading textbook, receiving praise for its accessible and student-friendly approach from students and instructors from across the country. The goal of the third edition was to enhance and refine this approach while updating the latest research findings and developments in the field. Specific changes to this edition that support this goal include:

- Discussion of recent research findings and industrial relations events in Canada, such as the Supreme Court decision on the right to collective bargaining, and various high profile strikes and lockouts from across Canada

- Discussion of new developments in the union-management environment including the use of social media for communication and/or support in organizing campaigns and strikes

- Updated statistics and data and summaries of legislation from each Canadian jurisdiction

- New Chapter News Stories, highlighting the real-world significance of the topics covered in the chapter; new Chapter-Opening Vignettes; and new End-of-Chapter Cases

- New and updated instructor and student resources

FEATURES OF THE TEXT

Industrial Relations in Canada, Third Edition, is intended to be as reader-friendly and accessible as possible. Achieving this goal is something of a challenge when dealing with material that can be quite complex and legalistic. Thus, this book has several features intended to help students gain a complete understanding of the material more easily.

Chapter-Opening Vignettes   Each chapter opens with a feature story on an aspect of industrial relations in Canada pertaining to that chapter. These stories provide insight into how various parts of the system function in day-to-day operations.

Chapter News Stories   Each chapter includes a news article that illustrates one of the issues discussed in that chapter. These stories have been chosen to represent all regions in Canada and to demonstrate contemporary, real-life applications of industrial relations principles.

Chapter Objectives   A set of chapter objectives is included to indicate what students should know after completing each chapter.

Key Terms   Throughout each chapter, important terms are identified with boldface type and explained in the textbook. The key terms are also listed at the end of each chapter with page numbers indicating where they can be found within the textbook.

Chapter Summary   Each chapter concludes with a summary of the major points covered. Students can read the summary prior to reading the chapter to get a sense of what lies ahead, or can read the summary after reading the chapter to enhance their understanding of the material they have just covered.

Discussion Questions   A set of discussion questions is included at the end of each chapter. These can be used for review to ensure that the student is familiar with the concepts discussed. The discussion questions also challenge students to explain the material in their own terms and present their own opinion on an issue based on their interpretation of the chapter material.

Cases and Exercises   Each chapter also includes exercises or cases that build on the concepts discussed. The exercises challenge students to learn more about industrial relations in their own area or region. The cases are adapted from actual labour relations board cases from across Canada, and put the student in the position of a labour relations board member who must assess the evidence and render a decision. The book also includes a collective bargaining simulation exercise and a grievance arbitration simulation exercise.

Glossary   A full glossary of key terms, cross-referenced by chapter, is included at the end of the textbook.

INSTRUCTOR AND STUDENT RESOURCES

Resources for both instructors and students are available on the textbook's companion website, *www.wiley.com/canada/mcquarrie*.

For Instructors

PowerPoint Slides   A full set of PowerPoint slides for each chapter with accompanying lecture notes is available for *Industrial Relations in Canada* Third Edition.

Instructor's Manual   The instructor's manual for *Industrial Relations in Canada* Third Edition includes:

- *PowerPoint Slides Lecture Notes* with a thumbnail picture of each chapter's PowerPoint slides accompanied by summary notes for the material covered by each slide.

- *Teaching Notes* to facilitate the use of the textbook's cases and exercises in class, including questions related to the case or exercises that can be used to guide class discussions.

- *Suggested Answers to Discussion Questions* found at the end of each chapter.

- *List of Websites* related to the material in that chapter for further reference.

Test Bank   The comprehensive test bank contains questions in four formats: true-false, multiple choice, short essay, and critical thinking. The test bank and other resources can be easily added to your course on your institution's Learning Management System to create resources such as a Respondus-formatted test bank.

CBC Videos   These videos provide relevant real-world examples of some of the issues covered in the textbook and are accompanied by questions to help generate discussion and analysis.

For Students

On-line Quizzes   These quizzes and question material, which are provided for each chapter, allow students to receive instant response and feedback as they test their understanding of material covered in the textbook.

Web Links   Links to websites relevant to material covered in the textbook are provided and are organized according to the relevant chapter and by type.

News Updates Website   This site includes relevant news articles and videos with accompanying questions to generate discussion and analysis. The site will keep both instructors and students informed about the very latest news in industrial relations.

Online Glossary   An online glossary with links to key terms from the textbook is available.

ACKNOWLEDGEMENTS

A book such as this could not be created singlehandedly. It is a pleasure to acknowledge the contributions of the many individuals whose work has helped create the final product.

I would especially like to acknowledge the textbook's reviewers who have given extensive, detailed, and very thoughtful comments for this and previous editions. Their invaluable insight is greatly appreciated.

Jean-Louis Castonguay, *McGill University*

Timothy DeGroot, *McMaster University*

Claude Dupuis, *Athabasca University*

Geoffrey England, *University of Lethbridge*

Edward G. Fisher, *University of Alberta*

Isabelle Gaétan, *University of Ottawa*

Eleanor Gallant, *University of Prince Edward Island*

Gary Gannon, *Durham College*

Linda M. Gaudet, *University of Prince Edward Island*

Richard Guerin, *McGill University*

Larry Haiven, *University of Saskatchewan*

Terry Hercus, *University of Manitoba*

Gerald Hunt, *Ryerson University*

Thomas R. Knight, *University of British Columbia*

Maurice Mazerolle, *Ryerson Polytechnic University*

Frédéric Potok, *Université de Moncton*

Paula Pyne, *Humber College*

Joseph B. Rose, *McMaster University*

Basu Sharma, *University of New Brunswick*

Andrea Soberg, *Trinity Western University*

Mark Thompson, *University of British Columbia*

A. Tarik Timur, *University of Calgary*

Johanna Weststar, *Saint Mary's University*

J. David Whitehead, *Brock University*

Jeffrey D. Young, *Mount Saint Vincent University*

Dr. Robert Rogow, now sadly deceased, taught industrial relations for many years in the Faculty of Business Administration at Simon Fraser University. His passionate commitment to the study, teaching, and practice of industrial relations was a strong influence, and his perspectives shaped the presentation of the material in this textbook in numerous places.

The students in BUS 305 at the University of the Fraser Valley willingly offered honest feedback on what a student-friendly industrial relations textbook should look like. They also served as guinea pigs for test runs of cases and exercises. Their input and their generous participation was very helpful.

The textbook and supplemental materials benefited from the work of Alison Arnot (chapter-opening vignettes writer and copyeditor), Sanchari Sil (photo researcher), Laura Hwee (permissions), Georgina Montgomery (proofreader), Tom Barrett (website news updates), and Kenda Murphy (PowerPoint slides and test bank contributor).

The staff at John Wiley & Sons Canada Ltd. deserve special recognition for their commitment to every part of this project. Darren Lalonde, Acquisitions Editor, was responsible for getting the third edition underway; Karen Staudinger guided the manuscript's progress to publication; Joyce Poh managed the production process; and Aida Krneta oversaw the marketing for the book at various phases. Particular thanks to the Wiley sales representatives for getting the book "out there."

I also extend my personal thanks to a number of individuals who contributed to this project in both direct and indirect ways. My colleagues in the School of Business at the University of the Fraser Valley, and Dr. Rosetta Khalideen, UFV Dean of Professional Studies, have been a source of motivation and inspiration. I am also grateful to the UFV Research Option Program for facilitating my work on this project.

I could not have accomplished my work on this book without the enthusiastic support of my family. Thanks to my mother, Carol; my father, Mike; and my brother, Michael.

Tom Barrett, my husband, was a constant source of encouragement throughout this entire project, and sometimes his belief made all the difference. My appreciation for his patience and love is boundless.

Finally, suggestions and comments from users of this book are encouraged. Feedback from users will help improve future editions and ensure that the material remains user-friendly, contemporary, and relevant. We have done our best to produce an error-free textbook, but if any mistakes have slipped through, please let us know so that corrections can be made to subsequent printings.

Fiona A.E. McQuarrie
December 2010

BRIEF TABLE OF CONTENTS

CONTENTS

INDUSTRIAL RELATIONS

IN CANADA

The Employer-Union Relationship

The types of relationships between an employer and union can be as varied as the number of employers and unions out there.

"Every employer has their own approach to labour relations," says Natalie Wiley, legal counsel with the United Food and Commercial Workers (UFCW) Locals 175 and 633 in Toronto. The UFCW deals with as many as 450 different employers, and they all have different ways of approaching labour relations. "Where some employers may work toward developing a working relationship with the union, others will not. Some are more conciliatory in their approach, while others are more aggressive," says Wiley.

A number of employers and unions have adopted a more relationship-based approach to labour relations, says Michael Fitzgibbon,

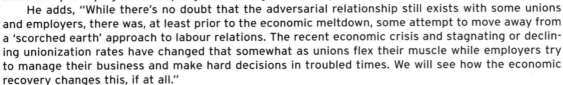

founder and partner at Watershed LLP, a management-side labour and employment specialized law firm. "They're trying to develop a good working relationship."

He adds, "While there's no doubt that the adversarial relationship still exists with some unions and employers, there was, at least prior to the economic meltdown, some attempt to move away from a 'scorched earth' approach to labour relations. The recent economic crisis and stagnating or declining unionization rates have changed that somewhat as unions flex their muscle while employers try to manage their business and make hard decisions in troubled times. We will see how the economic recovery changes this, if at all."

Fitzgibbon's practice is devoted to the management side of labour relations. He represents private sector employers in a variety of industries, in wrongful dismissal litigation, unfair labour practice complaints, and in unlawful strike proceedings, as well as with respect to other issues brought before the Ontario Labour Relations Board, such as union applications for certification.

Wiley represents the UFCW in similar situations. "With the recent downturn of the economy, we did see an increase in certain grievances," she agrees. "However, you typically see the same types of individual grievances time and time again."

In Ontario, the parties often resolve grievances and other disputes without going to a formal hearing. "This is part of the relationship-building," says Fitzgibbon. "They are working to resolve things informally."

Wiley, however, believes that unions still have an important place in today's workplace. "As the gap between rich and poor widens, and the gap between those with formal education and those without increases, the need for unions is even greater," she says. "With the global economy driving markets to be more competitive, more is asked of employees and the need for union representation is increased."

AN INTRODUCTION TO INDUSTRIAL RELATIONS IN CANADA

objectives

In this chapter, we will introduce the subject of industrial relations, describe the legislative framework that Canadian industrial relations operate within, give a brief overview of various Canadian industrial relations facts, and provide an overview of the structure and content of this book. By the end of the chapter, you should be able to:

- identify the various terms used to describe union-management relationships
- describe how other academic subjects might address industrial relations issues
- identify the major pieces of legislation that regulate Canadian industrial relations and explain the common elements among these laws
- understand how other kinds of Canadian legislation affect industrial relations
- identify some of the major demographic and statistical features of Canadian union membership

INTRODUCTION

Many people believe that unionization protects job characteristics such as fair pay rates and decent working conditions. However, others believe that unions serve only to preserve outdated privileges for an elite few. These conflicting views arise from a complex interaction of internal forces (such as job classification and worker training) and external elements (such as competitive product markets and labour markets) that affect both the individual and the organization. Gaining an understanding of this interaction and its effects is one of the major aims of the study of industrial relations. The two news stories later in this chapter illustrate these differing perspectives, which make industrial relations such an interesting topic of study.

The term "industrial relations" generally conjures up an image of greedy union members continually on strike for excessive salaries. Throughout this text, we will show that industrial relations encompasses much more than that. The scope of industrial relations as a topic of study includes fundamental issues of work control, the structure of work, the value of work, and the balance between the conflicting goals of workers and management. Understanding how industrial relations works is very important to anyone who participates in a workplace, whether as a worker or manager, or whether the workplace is unionized or non-unionized.

WHAT DOES THE TERM "INDUSTRIAL RELATIONS" MEAN?

The term "industrial relations" is generally used to refer to the relationship between a **union** (an organization run by and for workers) and the **employer** (the organization or organizations the workers in the union work for). The employer is also referred to as "management", the "company", or the "organization", although "employer" is the most commonly used term, since it reflects the employer-employee relationship that is the basis of the connection between the union and the company. As we will see in subsequent chapters, the union's primary role in the workplace is to represent the workers or employees in interactions with the employer. The union is able to carry out this role because Canadian provincial and federal law gives it the formal power to negotiate mutually acceptable workplace rules and working conditions with the employer.

Actors and miners both belong to unions, though "blue collar" workers like miners were the first ones to seek union representation, in the 19th century.

The term "labour relations" is sometimes used to describe the union-employer relationship. This term is derived from the definition of unions as organized labour (that is, as workers who have formally joined together to advocate for work-related issues). Legislation governing industrial relations is usually referred to as labour law or labour legislation. However, "industrial relations" is the preferred term for union-employer interactions in the Canadian context; it has been used by the Canadian federal government since 1919, when the Royal Commission to Enquire into Industrial Relations in Canada issued its report. In our opinion, "industrial relations" is a more appropriate descriptive of the union-employer relationship than "labour relations," since it emphasizes that there are two parties in the relationship and does not focus only on "labour." It also indicates that the relationship exists within the context of an industry or workplace. Hence, we have chosen to use "industrial relations" as the primary descriptive term in this book.

One part of the debate over the appropriate usage of the term "industrial relations" questions whether the term should also be used to describe workplace relationships between employers and non-unionized workers. According to one widely used definition, "industrial relations" is "a broad, interdisciplinary field of study and practice that encompasses all aspects of the employment relationship."[1] This definition clearly implies that the study of industrial relations includes both non-unionized and unionized workplaces, and, in fact, in recent years, the scope of industrial relations research has expanded to include studies of non-unionized workplaces. We would argue, however, that the term "industrial relations" is more appropriate as a descriptor of union-employer relationships than of employer-employee relationships in non-unionized workplaces. We offer three reasons for this contention:

1. The term "industrial relations" is generally used to refer to interactions in unionized rather than workplaces.

2. The field of study of non-unionized workplaces is already clearly defined as "employment relations" or "human resource management" (although the latter field of study can, and does, include overviews of the main characteristics of unionized workplaces).

3. A considerable amount of industrial relations research on non-unionized workplaces focuses on how non-unionized organizations replicate or adopt structures found in unionized workplaces; therefore, non-union industrial relations research is still closely related to the study of unionized organizations.

Throughout this book, the focus will be on union-employer relationships, although, where appropriate, reference will be made to how employer-worker relationships are conducted in non-unionized workplaces.

Before proceeding, we should take a moment to examine how industrial relations differs from human resource management. This is an important issue because many post-secondary institutions do not have courses devoted solely to the study of industrial relations, and instead address the subject only in the context of human resource management courses, or in courses dealing with employment relationships. The simplest way to explain the difference between the terms "human resource management" and "industrial relations" is to say that the former has a broader range and is generally applied to employment-related issues of importance to all organizations. One Canadian human resource management textbook defines human resource management as "the policies, practices and systems that influence an employee's behavior, attitude and performance in the attainment of organizational goals."[2] This definition is applicable to both unionized and non-unionized workplaces, since human resource policies, practices, and systems occur in any organization that has employees, whether those employees are unionized or not. This definition could even be applied to organizations whose "workers" may not be in an employment relationship with the organization (e.g., volunteers donating their time or labour to not-for-profit organizations).

Thus, the distinction between human resource management and industrial relations can be summed up as follows: "industrial relations," as we have defined the term, deals primarily with employee-employer relationships in unionized organizations, while "human resource management" deals with employer-employee or organization-worker relationships in all types of organizations. The two fields certainly have issues in common, but the focus of industrial relations is more specific and less generalized than that of human resource management.

INDUSTRIAL RELATIONS AS AN ACADEMIC SUBJECT

In most academic settings, as elsewhere, "industrial relations" is the term used to refer to the study of union-employer relationships. As an academic subject, industrial relations draws on a number of different academic fields,[3] because many of the topics of interest to industrial relations researchers have also been addressed in the context of other disciplines of study. Union-management relationships and, more broadly, conflict between workers and employers are not new topics of interest. A quick examination of any database of academic publications will show that industrial relations topics were and are addressed in many other academic fields. Here are some examples of how researchers in other academic areas could address industrial relations issues:

- A historian might be interested in the events that led to the formation of a union or to a particular industrial relations conflict.

- A psychologist might be interested in how individual attitudes toward unions or employers develop or change.

- An economist might be interested in how negotiated wage rates in a unionized organization affect wage rates in non-unionized organizations or the cost of living in a particular geographic area.

- A political scientist might be interested in how or why a governing political party changes labour legislation.

- A lawyer might be interested in how the wording of labour legislation affects unions' ability to represent their membership effectively.

- A sociologist might be interested in how group or cultural dynamics affect the actions of a union or an employer.

It is clear from reviewing this list of the approaches of different academic disciplines to union-employer issues that the field of industrial relations draws its ideas and theories from a broad spectrum of subjects. While industrial relations courses at colleges and universities are most commonly found in economics or business administration departments, this list demonstrates why they might also be found in several other academic areas.

It can be frustrating for new students of industrial relations to find that there is no single unifying theory or perspective underlying their field of study. How do we know what is "right" when various disciplines offer multiple and sometimes conflicting theories to explain a single event? However, as is true in many other areas of study, it is unrealistic to expect to find one industrial relations theory that explains everything. Union-employer relationships involve complex human interactions, and these occur within many different types of work, work structures, and workplaces.[4] Therefore, no single theory or solution could explain every possible situation. A more realistic approach is to recognize the rich contributions that different perspectives make toward an understanding of the union-employer relationship, and to appreciate how these contributions create a broader, rather than narrower, understanding of that relationship.

WHY STUDY INDUSTRIAL RELATIONS?

As we have mentioned, many post-secondary institutions in Canada do not offer courses devoted specifically to industrial relations, but instead address industrial relations only as a secondary topic in another course, such as one on human resource management. Students enrolled in industrial relations courses or in broader courses that touch on the subject often argue that the study of industrial relations is irrelevant. This argument can take a number of different forms:

- "Unions have achieved everything they set out to do because workers are now treated fairly, so there is no reason for unions to exist any more and no reason to study them."

- "Only part of the workforce in Canada is unionized, so I can go through my entire career working in non-unionized firms; there's no point to learning about unions if I'm never going to have to join one."

- "I personally don't believe in unions and would never vote to join one, so I'm not interested in learning about them because I'm never going to be a union member."

Many instructors of industrial relations have encountered these arguments from students of all ages and backgrounds. We acknowledge that there is a great deal of validity to each of these arguments. As we show in Chapter 2, unions emerged in response to working conditions that are almost unknown today, at least in most industrialized First World countries. In several chapters, we address the fact that only about 30 percent of the Canadian workforce is unionized, and much of that unionization is concentrated in a few sectors of the labour market. And we certainly would not argue against an individual's right to hold the beliefs or attitudes he or she personally considers meaningful. However, let us present our arguments in favour of industrial relations as a relevant topic worthy of in-depth study.

First, in many unionized workplaces or occupations, union membership is a prerequisite to employment. Therefore, attaining a desired job or career may require joining a union, regardless of one's own feelings about unions. If one has to belong to an organization, it is better to be informed about the organization's purpose and operations than to run the risk of making mistakes out of ignorance or misunderstanding.

Second, even if only part of the Canadian workforce is unionized, people who are not union members sometimes have to interact with a unionized organization or with unionized workers. For example, during the 2009 Toronto municipal workers' strike, the direct conflict was between the unionized workers and their employer (the City of Toronto). However, the impact of that conflict was felt by many other individuals, such as residents of the city who watched their uncollected garbage pile up on the streets, and children whose city-run daycare facilities were closed. Because of the likelihood of this sort of interaction occurring, it is important to have some understanding of unions and the activities unions might undertake, even if one is never personally involved in a union.

Third, in every jurisdiction in Canada, legislation makes unionization an option for workers who are dissatisfied with their treatment and want their employer to formally address their concerns. While the horrific working conditions described in Chapter 2 that motivated the formation of the first unions are relatively uncommon in modern Canada, not every workplace in Canada is a model of perfect employer-employee relationships. It is important to know about unions because Canadian law makes unionization an option for nearly every kind of worker, and because unions have the potential to influence employee satisfaction and working conditions.

Fourth, learning about the history of unionization in Canada helps one understand how the modern Canadian workplace, both unionized and non-unionized, has reached its current form. The influence of unions is apparent in the existence of legislation that affects every Canadian worker and workplace. Minimum wage legislation, occupational health and safety regulations, and the Labour Day statutory holiday are some obvious examples.

Fifth, for people considering human resource management as a career, a working knowledge of industrial relations is a definite asset. Aspiring human resource managers who are familiar with industrial relations issues are much more employable than those who are experienced only in non-unionized workplaces. Also, in many organizations, human resource functions are no longer the sole responsibility of the human resource management department. Managers of all kinds and at all organizational levels may be expected to participate in human resource management activities such as maintaining discipline, determining wage levels, appraising performance, and interviewing job candidates.[5] Anyone considering managerial work of any sort should be familiar with how human resource management activities are conducted in both unionized and non-unionized firms.

Finally, an individual may be so opposed to unions that he or she wishes to actively resist their presence, either as an unwilling potential union member or as a manager or employer. Opposing a union is much easier if one has some knowledge about what a union is, what legal requirements underlie a union's existence, and what an employer or employee can or cannot legally do to counteract unionization.

By writing this textbook, we are not attempting to change the attitudes of individuals who are fundamentally opposed to unions. We also do not intend to try to convince people to join or support unions. And we do not want to present unions as perfect organizations that act appropriately in every situation. A union, like any organization, is the product of the individuals who belong to it, and individuals in unions, as in any organization, can make poor decisions or act unfairly. Unions are no more perfect and no less flawed than other organizations. They do, however, influence the lives of most

Canadians, directly or indirectly, and Canadian legislation enshrines the right of unions to exist and the right of employees to join unions if they so desire. Thus, we believe it is important to learn about union-employer relationships in order to be a better-informed worker or manager and, more generally, a better-informed member of Canadian society.

Collective Bargaining: Democracy in the Workplace

VANCOUVER—With a civic strike that has been needlessly prolonged in Vancouver, and a major stoppage in the forestry sector that seems destined to last even longer, British Columbians might ask why they have to be inconvenienced by labour disputes.

This question is best answered in the context of Canadian democracy.

The place of collective bargaining is debated in primarily economic terms. The parties focus on the costs of demands and concessions. Third parties estimate the financial losses caused by work stoppages. Economists study the wage benefits that unionized workers receive. Employers are concerned about the costs of restrictions on their right to manage.

Little attention is directed at the aspirations, frustrations, satisfactions or fears of workers represented in bargaining.

What recourse do they have if their employer wants to terminate them because it believes that a service can be delivered less expensively by an outside contractor?

How can they respond to a supervisor who treats them unfairly in a job they fundamentally enjoy? If workers are dissatisfied with their conditions, must they resign and start another career to obtain relief?

Democratic societies address these issues through collective bargaining.

Collective bargaining is our form of workplace democracy. Canadians rightly pride ourselves for our political freedoms. We can express our views, however unpopular, with little fear of official retribution.

Citizens form groups to promote their political or social views. They lobby government and the media to persuade others to their opinions. The justice system protects them from abuses of authority.

For most Canadians, these freedoms end at the door to the workplace. The employer can restrict expressions of their views on working conditions or any other subject, with only modest limits imposed by the law. Management can impose terms and conditions of employment without effective challenge.

Collective bargaining introduces elements of democracy into the workplace. Workers form interest groups to advance their position and elect their representatives to meet with management. Worker organizations negotiate procedures to resolve disputes over the conduct of work through a neutral decision-maker.

Source: Thompson, Mark. "Collective Bargaining: Democracy in the Workplace." *Vancouver Sun*, September 3, 2007, p. A11.

Do Unions Still Matter?

TORONTO—The percentage of Canadian private-sector workers in unions fell from 26% in 1977 to 18% in 2003.

Canada's overall "union density" numbers remain high only because of our bloated public sector. Socialists regard this as a sign of Canada's superior "class consciousness," but what it really represents is the existence of a coterie of over-entitled, super-secure public servants whose position relative to the real-world worker (who pays for his master's generous pensions, conference trips, and stress leaves) grows even stronger.

Since the Canadian union movement is dominated by the public sector, most of its leaders are decades away from perceiving this as a problem. Those that do, if any, will say that the answer is to get serious about organizing the unorganized. (They'd never turn against their comfortable government comrades in the interests of the taxpayer.)

But the deep question is whether unions have any chance of regaining power in a world of computerization and globalization. It's no coincidence that private-sector unions are strongest in classic industrial enterprises where trained people are needed in a particular place—those precise places where workers would enjoy the most leverage even without a union. It's also awfully hard to sell old-time class war in a world of broad middle-class stock ownership. And even the future of the traditional corporation—the despised twin on which the union's existence depends—is questionable in a world of emergent auctioneering, outsourcing, and modular self-employment.

So are unions capable of delivering real value to postmodern workers, or are they just gangs of conspiratorial spongers who smother the occasional business to death as a means of clinging to relevance? This is the question that has to be answered, credibly, for today's skeptical young worker. If it isn't, any effort to revive organized labour will be a sheer waste of energy.

Source: Cosh, Colby. "Do Unions Still Matter?" *National Post*, August 3, 2005, p. A16.

INDUSTRIAL RELATIONS LEGISLATION IN CANADA

To begin our introduction to the topic of industrial relations in Canada, we will review the legal framework that regulates the union-employer relationship. We will introduce the legal framework first in order to give students a general understanding of what laws in Canada affect industrial relations, and to provide some context for our subsequent discussions of the activities that these laws regulate. At this point, we will provide a general overview of the relevant legislation. The detailed provisions of many of these pieces of legislation will be discussed in subsequent chapters in relation to particular topics.

The Question of Jurisdiction

In Canada, legislation relating to labour relations is found in every province and territory as well as at the federal level. The conflict over the division of **jurisdiction**, or legal responsibility for an issue, between federal and provincial legislatures has been ongoing throughout Canadian history. The question of jurisdiction over industrial relations arises because of the question of whether a union-employer relationship should be governed by federal or provincial labour relations legislation.

As Chapter 3 describes, up until the mid-1920s, all Canadian industrial relations issues fell under federal labour relations legislation, and industrial relations was considered to be solely within the federal jurisdiction. This concentration of labour legislation in the federal jurisdiction reflected the strong federal focus of other Canadian legislation at the time. The concentration of Canadian legislative power at the federal level was a deliberate choice of the authors of the 1867 *British North America Act* (the act that established the first federal Canadian government); they had seen how the United States' system of decentralized "states' rights" had contributed to the American Civil War.[6] However, the outcome of a 1925 legal case, *Snider v. Toronto Electrical Commission*, established that jurisdiction over industrial relations in Canada was mostly, but not completely, a provincial responsibility. As a result of this ruling, each province eventually developed its own labour relations legislation. However, there is still also a federal labour relations act to govern employer-union relationships that are deemed to be under federal jurisdiction.

How, then, do we know whether a union-employer relationship is regulated by federal or provincial law? The answer is quite simple. If an employer's business has an **interprovincial component**—that is, if the employer's activities regularly cross

CN is an interprovincial company, and its union-employer relationships are federally regulated.

provincial boundaries—then the union-employer relationship is federally regulated. This means that industries such as banking, telecommunications, broadcasting, and interprovincial transport, which all involve business transactions across provincial boundaries, are governed by federal labour relations legislation. Federal labour relations legislation also applies to employees of the federal government and some Crown corporations. But if most of an employer's activities take place within the boundaries of a single province or territory, the union-employer relationship is governed by the labour relations legislation of that province or territory. In practice, this means that approximately 90 percent of union-employer relationships in Canada are under provincial jurisdiction and approximately 10 percent are federally regulated.

In both federal and provincial jurisdictions, there are a number of pieces of legislation that affect industrial relations. The most obvious are the labour relations laws, but other laws also affect the union-employer relationship. We will outline each of these types of legislation in turn.

Labour Relations Laws

Table 1-1 lists the names of the major provincial and federal labour relations acts. These are the primary pieces of legislation that govern industrial relations in each Canadian jurisdiction. Although, as we will see, there are variations in the terms and conditions of these different acts, they also have common characteristics.[7] Every one of these pieces of legislation includes the following:

- The establishment of procedures to legally recognize the union as the workplace representative for the employees. This procedure is called "certification" and is discussed in detail in Chapter 5.

- A requirement that collective agreements between the union and the employer have a minimum term. In most Canadian jurisdictions, this term is one year.

- The establishment of procedures that must be followed for a legal strike or lockout to take place. Most jurisdictions also have some regulations governing activity that might take place during a strike or lockout, such as picketing or the use of replacement workers. These procedures are discussed in detail in Chapter 9.

- The establishment of procedures that must be followed to resolve disputes while the collective agreement is in effect. These procedures are usually referred to as

TABLE 1-1 Labour Relations Laws in Canadian Jurisdictions[i]	
Jurisdiction	Name of Primary Labour Relations Law
Federal	*Canada Labour Code*
Alberta	*Labour Relations Code*
British Columbia	*Labour Relations Code*
Manitoba	*Labour Relations Act*
Ontario	*Labour Relations Act*
New Brunswick	*Industrial Relations Act*
Newfoundland and Labrador	*Labour Relations Act*
Nova Scotia	*Trade Union Act*
Prince Edward Island	*Labour Act*
Quebec	*Labour Code/Code du travail*
Saskatchewan	*Trade Union Act*

[i] The Northwest Territories, the Yukon, and Nunavut do not yet have their own laws governing industrial relations in the private sector. Instead, the federal *Canada Labour Code* is considered the applicable private sector labour relations law in these jurisdictions.

grievance resolution procedures. Some jurisdictions simply require that collective agreements contain a grievance resolution procedure, while others detail the terms that must be contained in these procedures. These procedures are discussed in detail in Chapter 11.

• The definition of legal behaviour by union and management in situations such as a campaign for certification. Usually, these definitions take the form of identifying so-called unfair labour practices. These practices are discussed in more detail in Chapter 6.

• The establishment of a **labour relations board** to administer and enforce labour relations legislation. The specific name of the board varies by jurisdiction, but its purpose is similar in all jurisdictions. It resolves disputes relating to the application of the legislation and also provides specific services, such as assistance in resolving grievances. The labour relations board has a **quasi-judicial** status; like a civil or criminal court, it rules on cases brought before it and issues interpretations of the law. In addition, as with a civil or criminal court, the government funds the costs of running a labour relations board, but the board operates independent of government influence or control. However, a labour relations board does not have the same legal status as a civil or criminal court, since it has the option of suggesting remedies as well as imposing solutions. It also has slightly broader guidelines than civil or criminal courts regarding what evidence can be submitted when a case is heard.

In most jurisdictions, the labour relations board is composed of an equal number of union and employer representatives. These appointed representatives are then selected to sit on panels to make decisions on specific cases. Usually, a panel consists of one union representative, one employer representative, and a third party chosen by the first two parties, although in most jurisdictions a panel can also consist of a single member. Most labour relations boards have a chair and a number of vice-chairs who are appointed by the government, as well as staff members who assist the board members in their work and provide other services to unions, employers, and the public.

Public Sector Labour Relations Legislation

Most Canadian jurisdictions have separate labour relations acts to govern **public sector** employees—employees of the government itself or of organizations affiliated with the government, such as Crown corporations. Some jurisdictions also have separate labour legislation for **para-public** or **quasi-public sector** employees—employees who work for organizations funded by the government but who are not directly employed by the government. Examples of para-public sector employees are court workers, health care workers, and employees of colleges, technical institutes, and universities.

There are several reasons for having separate labour legislation for these types of employees. One is that the government and its employees have a unique employment relationship. The government is the employer, but it is also the body that sets the rules under which all employees and employers operate. Separate public sector labour legislation is intended to recognize that the government holds considerably more power than an ordinary employer. Thus, public sector labour legislation may contain terms and conditions designed to address this larger-than-usual power imbalance between employer and employee. Another reason for separate public sector labour legislation is that public and para-public sector employees often provide services that are needed for communities and provinces to function effectively, such as fire protection, social services, and health care. Public sector labour legislation recognizes this reality by, for example, stipulating specific conditions under which public sector employees may strike or otherwise withdraw their services, or by implementing dispute-resolution procedures that minimize or avoid service disruptions.

In some Canadian jurisdictions, disputes over the interpretation or application of public sector labour relations legislation are taken to the labour relations board that administers all labour legislation. In other Canadian jurisdictions, the public sector labour relations legislation establishes a public sector labour relations board. While this board is similar in structure and function to the "regular" labour relations board, its mandate is limited to the administration and enforcement of public sector labour laws.

Occupation-Specific Labour Relations Legislation

Some Canadian jurisdictions have additional labour relations legislation that applies only to particular occupations or industries. This type of legislation usually exists to address specific conditions in an occupation or industry that would not be adequately covered under the regular labour relations legislation. Table 1-2 on the following page provides examples of public sector, para-public sector, and occupation-specific labour relations legislation in Canada.

The types of legislation that will be discussed next are not usually identified as labour relations legislation, but are included in this section because their contents can directly or indirectly affect workplace conditions or the relationship between unions and employers.

Employment Standards Legislation

In every Canadian jurisdiction, there is an employment standards act or code that establishes minimum standards for working conditions in all workplaces. Employment standards legislation usually covers such matters as working hours, minimum wage rates, holiday time, and the minimum time needed for a notice of termination or layoff to be legal.

TABLE 1-2 Examples of Public Sector, Para-Public Sector, and Occupation-Specific Labour Relations Laws in Canadian Jurisdictions[i]

Jurisdiction	Names of Laws
Federal	Public Sector Staff Relations Act
Alberta	Public Service Employee Relations Act, Police Officers Collective Bargaining Act
British Columbia	Public Sector Labour Relations Act, Fire and Police Services Collective Bargaining Act
Manitoba	Civil Service Act
Ontario	Public Sector Act, Hospital Labour Disputes Arbitration Act, Colleges Collective Bargaining Act
New Brunswick	Public Service Labour Relations Act
Newfoundland and Labrador	Public Service Collective Bargaining Act, Fishing Industry Collective Bargaining Act, Teachers' Collective Bargaining Act
Northwest Territories	Public Service Act
Nova Scotia	Public Service Act, Teachers' Collective Bargaining Act, Highway Workers Collective Bargaining Act
Nunavut	Public Service Act
Prince Edward Island	Civil Service Act, Health Authorities' Employees Act
Quebec	Public Service Act/Loi de la fonction publique, An act respecting the process of negotiation of the collective agreements in the public and para-public sectors
Saskatchewan	Public Service Act, Construction Industry Labour Relations Act
Yukon	Public Service Staff Relations Act

[i] Public sector industrial relations in the Yukon are governed by the federal public sector legislation.

Employment standards legislation applies to all workplaces, whether unionized or non-unionized. Its terms and conditions are important to unions and management because their mutually negotiated collective agreements must not contain terms that are inferior to those outlined in employment standards legislation. It would, for example, usually be illegal for a collective agreement to include wage rates that are less than those in the relevant employment standards law, even if the union and the employer had agreed to those rates.

Human Rights Legislation

Every Canadian jurisdiction has some form of human rights legislation that forbids discrimination against individuals on the basis of personal attributes such as gender, ethnic origin, or sexual orientation. Discrimination in the context of these laws is defined as the refusal to grant someone access to accommodation, contracts, goods and services, or employment opportunities because they possess one of the identified personal attributes (called **protected grounds** or **prohibited grounds** in the legislation).[8] It would be illegal, for example, for a landlord to refuse to rent an apartment to anyone who is Aboriginal, or for an employer to deny a woman a job promotion because the employer believes that all women eventually quit work to take care of their children. However, if there is an important part of a job that requires the exclusion of members of a particular group, refusing to hire members of that group would not be considered discrimination. For example, it might be inappropriate to hire male correctional officers for a women's prison, since officers might have to conduct full-body searches of the prisoners. Thus, it would likely be considered acceptable for a job advertisement or hiring committee to recruit only female candidates for correctional officer jobs in women's prisons.

It is important to note that Canadian human rights legislation identifies two kinds of discrimination. One is **intentional discrimination**; this type of discrimination involves direct and deliberate refusal based on the prohibited grounds. The other is **systemic discrimination** (also called unintentional, constructive, or adverse impact discrimination); this type of discrimination occurs when an organization or individual uses policies or practices that have the effect of discriminating against groups of individuals. Systemic discrimination can occur even if the individual or organization, when adopting the policy or practices, did not intend to discriminate. An example of systemic discrimination would be a policy that required applicants for a job to be a minimum height, say five feet, eight inches (or 173 centimetres) tall. If it were not essential for the individual to be that height or taller to perform the job successfully, such a requirement would be systemic discrimination because it would exclude many women and also individuals from ethnic groups whose average heights are shorter than the Canadian norm.

Human rights legislation has two major implications for unions and employers. The first is that collective agreements must not contain any terms that intentionally or systematically discriminate (unless, as noted above, certain restrictions are imposed because of legitimate job requirements). The second is that unions and employers, as organizations in and of themselves, must not act in a discriminatory fashion. A union, for example, could not refuse to support an employee in a complaint against the employer simply because the employee was of Asian origin.

If an individual feels that he or she has been discriminated against on the basis of one or more of the protected grounds, he or she can file a complaint with the relevant human rights commission. A human rights commission is similar to a labour relations board in structure and function; however, its mandate is to administer and enforce only human rights legislation. The human rights commission will investigate the complaint and suggest or impose a remedy if the complaint is substantiated. In addition, employees who feel their union has discriminated against them can file a complaint with a labour relations board, alleging that the union has breached its "duty of fair representation." The concept of duty of fair representation is discussed in more detail in Chapter 11.

The Charter of Rights and Freedoms

The *Charter of Rights and Freedoms* is contained in the federal *Constitution Act*, which became law in 1982. It guarantees certain basic rights and freedoms to all Canadians and is considered to take precedence over all other laws, with two exceptions. The first is laws that "can be demonstrably justified as reasonable limits in a 'free and democratic society.'"[9] An example of the use of these limits is when the Supreme Court of Canada decided to uphold mandatory retirement laws in several provinces. The reasoning behind the court's decision was that, while mandatory retirement was clearly discrimination on the basis of age (individuals were forced to retire when they reached a certain age, regardless of whether they were still capable of performing their job satisfactorily), the objectives of mandatory retirement were "of sufficient significance" to justify such discrimination.[10] The second kind of laws that can override the superior status of the

Charter are those that provincial legislatures pass by invoking the so-called "notwithstanding" provision. This provision prevents the challenge of a law passed by a provincial legislature if the basis for the challenge is the law's perceived infringement of Charter rights. The purpose of this provision is to permit individual provinces some flexibility in applying the Charter to conditions in their particular jurisdiction.

The *Charter of Rights and Freedoms* defines a number of fundamental rights. Because these rights are broadly defined, without much specific guidance on their practical application, numerous court cases have tested the applicability of these rights in certain situations. To date, the following rights have been the subject of major cases involving industrial relations issues:

Prime Minister Pierre Elliott Trudeau watches Queen Elizabeth II sign the *Constitution Act* in Ottawa in 1982. The *Constitution Act* contains the *Charter of Rights and Freedoms*. © Government of Canada. Reproduced with the permission of the Minister of Public Works and Government Services Canada (2010).

- freedom of association
- freedom of peaceful assembly
- freedom of thought, belief, opinion, and expression

Three particular early "Charter cases" involving these issues have important implications for industrial relations, and each will be briefly described here.[11] In the first, the 1982 *Dolphin Delivery case*,[12] employees involved in a dispute with their employer wanted to set up a picket line at a company that did business with the employer but was not directly involved in the dispute. The company successfully applied for a court injunction to stop the picket line, and the union appealed the injunction on the grounds that the inability to picket restricted the union members' freedoms of expression, association, and assembly. The Supreme Court of Canada ruled in this case that a court order like an injunction could not be considered "the type of government action that would attract the application of the Charter."[13] In other words, the Charter provisions were not considered applicable to court orders resolving common-law-based disputes between private parties.

The second set of cases occurred in 1987 and is referred to as the "labour trilogy."[14] A decision in a subsequent case in 1990 reinforced the general direction of the judgements in this set of cases.[15] The basic question in each of these cases was whether the Charter provisions outlining the rights to freedom of association also protected the right to bargain collectively and strike. The Supreme Court of Canada ruled in these cases that the rights to establish, belong to, and maintain an association, along with the right to participate in the association's lawful activities, were protected under the Charter. However, the rights to strike and to participate in collective bargaining were, in the court's view, rights created by law and not fundamental freedoms protected by the Charter.

The third Charter case is the 1991 *Lavigne* case.[16] A college instructor claimed that the mandatory union dues he had to pay as part of his employment contract violated his freedom of association. His complaint was not primarily about the mandatory dues payment, but more about his union spending part of his dues to support organizations that he personally objected to and would not voluntarily donate money to. The question in this case, then, was whether freedom of association also implied the freedom not to associate. The Supreme Court of Canada narrowly ruled that mandatory dues payment did not violate the provisions of the Charter, since all individuals in the workplace benefited from the union's representation of their interests and that unions had the right to spend dues in support of political and social causes. The reasoning behind this decision was that distribution of funding raised through dues payment would be determined by the wishes of the membership, and that each member of the union had the opportunity to influence the distribution of those funds through voting or other participation in union activities.

Three later cases may also have important implications for the union-employer relationship in Canada. In many Canadian jurisdictions, specific groups of workers are not permitted to unionize for a variety of reasons. In Ontario in 1995, the provincial government repealed a law that permitted agricultural workers to unionize. The government excluded farm workers from the jurisdiction of labour law by arguing that unionization of these workers would cause excessive labour costs for small family farms, many of which were already experiencing financial difficulty. This decision was appealed in a series of court cases, and the issue eventually reached the Supreme Court of Canada in the case of *Dunmore v. Ontario (Attorney-General)*.[17] The Supreme Court ruled that the right to freedom of association was violated if an entire class of workers was excluded from protection under labour legislation. Steven Barrett, a lawyer who represented labour organizations in the case, predicted that this ruling would encourage other groups currently excluded from collective bargaining (such as domestic workers, professionals, and some classifications of public servants) to undertake similar challenges to the laws excluding them from participating in this activity.[18] The Ontario government responded to the *Dunmore* decision by passing a law that allowed agricultural workers to unionize but not to engage in collective bargaining. This subsequent law is the subject of another legal challenge that the Supreme Court has agreed to hear.[19]

More recently, several British Columbia health care unions brought a case before the Supreme Court which challenged the legality of Bill 29, a British Columbia law. The collective agreement between these unions and the British Columbia government specified that the government could not end unionized jobs and assign the work to non-unionized subcontractors. Bill 29 removed those parts of the collective agreement and also stated that these conditions would not be reinstated in future negotiations. The unions argued that collective agreements could not be changed by one party without consulting the other party. The government argued that the changes were necessary to improve the delivery of health care services. In June 2007, the Supreme Court ruled that Bill 29 was unconstitutional, on the basis that the right to collective bargaining was part of the freedom of association guaranteed by the Charter. The court gave the British Columbia government and the unions one year to renegotiate their collective agreements, which eventually resulted in the government agreeing to pay $85 million to retrain employees who had lost their jobs as a result of the legislation.[20] One commentator on this decision explains that it is important because "labour's hard-won collective bargaining rights are now considered worthy of constitutional protection ... [which] provides a halo of much needed legitimacy to one of organized labour's core activities."[21]

In another recent case, some former employees of a Walmart in Jonquière, Quebec, brought a case to the Supreme Court in 2009 arguing that they had lost their jobs as a result of union activity, and that this affected their right to freedom of association. The employees at the store unionized in 2004 and were not able to reach a collective agreement with their employer. The Quebec minister of labour notified the union and the employer in early 2005 that the bargaining dispute would be sent to a third party for a decision. On the day this information was communicated, the employer announced that it would be permanently closing the store because the store was not profitable. The Supreme Court ruled that the employer was within its rights to close the store and dismissed the workers' complaints; however, the workers have indicated that they plan to continue to pursue their case under other sections of Quebec's labour laws.[22]

The rulings in these cases give some idea of how the general principles expressed in the Charter may have practical applications in the workplace. However, it is still difficult to specify the implications of the Charter provisions for union-employer relationships at the workplace level, since many issues remain untested by court challenges. The identified fundamental freedoms have the potential for very broad application, but the extent of many practical applications of those freedoms will not be clarified until cases involving particular situations are addressed by the Supreme Court of Canada. In the meantime, unions and employers should be aware of the Charter's provisions and keep in mind the applications that the Supreme Court has outlined to date.

THE UNIONIZED WORKPLACE IN CANADA

To conclude our introductory overview of Canadian industrial relations, we will provide in Tables 1-3, 1-4, and 1-5, statistics that outline the characteristics of the unionized workplace in Canada. From these statistics, we can observe a number of distinctive characteristics of unionized workplaces in Canada. Unionized workplaces are more likely to be in the public sector and to be relatively large in size. The rates of unionization are quite similar across broad industrial categories, but there are wide variations in unionization rates across different occupations. Certain demographic characteristics also distinguish Canadian union members. Union membership is slightly higher among women than among men and higher among older workers than among younger workers. Union members are relatively well educated, and they usually hold full-time rather than part-time jobs.

We will revisit these statistics throughout the book and discuss in more depth some of the reasons behind the characteristics of Canadian unionization. In Chapter 13, we will assess what these statistics indicate for future workplace trends in Canada.

TABLE 1-3 Unionization Rates by Province, 2009

Province	Number of Unionized Workers (in thousands)	Number of Workers Covered by a Collective Agreement as Percentage of Total Provincial Workforce[i]
Alberta	376	24.8
British Columbia	527	30.6
Manitoba	184	37.4
New Brunswick	88	29.1
Newfoundland and Labrador	71	39.3
Nova Scotia	114	30.8
Ontario	1,446	28.1
Prince Edward Island	17	32.6
Quebec	1,189	40.0
Saskatchewan	145	36.3

[i] This figure includes union members as well as workers who are not union members but who are covered by the terms of a collective agreement (the "coverage-only" group of workers as defined by Statistics Canada). In 2009, there were approximately 300,000 Canadian workers in this group.

Source: Adapted from Statistics Canada, *Perspectives on Labour and Income* (Statistics Canada catalogue number 75-001-XIE), August 2009, vol. 10 no. 8.

TABLE 1-4 Demographic Indicators of Union Membership in Canada, 2009

Gender	Total Number of Union Members (in thousands)	Union Coverage as a Percentage of Total National Workforce in This Category*
Male	2,116	30.4
Female	2,343	32.9

TABLE 1-4 Demographic Indicators of Union Membership in Canada, 2009 (Continued)

Work Status	Total Number of Union Members (in thousands)	Union Coverage as a Percentage of Total National Workforce in This Category*
Full time	3,784	33.2
Part time	675	25.1

Age	Total Number of Union Members (in thousands)	Union Coverage as a Percentage of Total National Workforce in This Category*
15 to 24	383	16.5
25 to 44	2,027	31.6
45 to 54	1,313	38.8
55 and over	733	37.3

Education	Total Number of Union Members (in thousands)	Union Coverage as a Percentage of Total National Workforce in This Category*
Less than Grade 9	76	27.2
Some high school	290	21.6
High school graduation	750	26.9
Some post-secondary education	286	23.3
Post-secondary certificate or diploma	1,781	35.6
University degree	1,274	37.1

* These percentages include workers who are not union members but who are covered by the terms of a collective agreement (the "coverage-only" group as defined by Statistics Canada). In 2009, there were approximately 300,000 Canadian workers in this group.

Source: Adapted from Statistics Canada, *Perspectives on Labour and Income* (Statistics Canada catalogue number 75-001-XIE), August 2009, vol. 10 no. 8.

TABLE 1-5 Sectoral, Industrial, Occupational, and Workplace Union Coverage in Canada, 2009

Sector	Number of Union Members (in thousands)	Union Coverage as a Percentage of Total National Workforce in This Category*
Public	2,570	75.1
Private	1,887	17.7

Industry	Number of Union Members (in thousands)	Union Coverage as a Percentage of Total National Workforce in This Category*
Goods producing	846	28.5
Service producing	3,613	32.5

Occupation	Number of Union Members (in thousands)	Union Coverage as a Percentage of Total National Workforce in This Category*
Management	114	11.2
Business, finance, and administrative	774	26.7
Natural and applied sciences	258	24.9
Health	585	62.4
Social and public service	807	58.2
Art, culture, sport, and recreation	99	30.9
Sales and service	815	22.3
Trades, transport, and equipment operators	740	37.6
Unique to primary industries	40	15.9
Unique to processing, manufacturing, and utilities	255	34.3

TABLE 1-5 Sectoral, Industrial, Occupational, and Workplace Union Coverage in Canada, 2009 (Continued)

Workplace Size	Number of Union Members (in thousands)	Union Coverage as a Percentage of Total National Workforce in This Category*
Under 20 employees	700	14.9
20 to 99 employees	1,533	32.4
100 to 500 employees	1,242	43.1
Over 500 employees	983	55.4

* These percentages include union members as well as workers who are not union members but who are covered by a collective agreement (the "coverage-only" group as defined by Statistics Canada). In 2009, there were approximately 300,000 Canadian workers in this group.

Source: Adapted from Statistics Canada, *Perspectives on Labour and Income* (Statistics Canada catalogue number 75-001-XIE), August 2009, vol. 10 no. 8.

AN OVERVIEW OF THE BOOK

After surveying the legislation that forms the framework for Canadian industrial relations and outlining some of the statistics that describe unionization in Canada, we now turn to a description of the framework of this book. We have placed the material in an order that replicates as closely as possible the process that a union and employer would go through in starting a relationship, carrying out their mandated duties and roles once the relationship is established, and altering that relationship in response to internal or external forces.

In this first chapter, we have introduced some theoretical and historical background to explain how modern Canadian workplaces and legislation have evolved into their present form. We also reviewed the legislation that provides a framework for union-employer relations in Canada, and presented some of the current data on unionized workers and workplaces in Canada. In Chapter 2, we explain the reasons for the creation of unions and how unions' purposes have changed over time. The emergence of craft guilds, the significant shifts in work and production that occurred with the Industrial

Revolution, and the development of the first modern trade unions are described. We then examine the origins of the modern trade union, the functions of unions, and the future challenges unions may face.

In Chapter 3, we focus on the events and forces that have created the unique circumstances of Canadian labour relations. We begin with an overview of some of the characteristics of Canada that have affected the history of unions. We then discuss the early years of the Canadian union movement in the 1800s, the industrial age in the early 1900s, and the advent of the First World War. We describe the forces that led to increased unionization before and during the Second World War and the start of modern-day federal and provincial labour legislation. We outline the growth of unionization in the public sector, the effects of unemployment and inflation in the 1970s, and more recent events such as the passage of free trade legislation.

In Chapter 4, we describe the structure of Canadian unions, which roughly parallels the three levels of government in Canada. At the federal level, the Canadian Labour Congress (CLC) and several other bodies represent organized labour nationally. In each of the provinces and territories, the federations of labour are the coordinating bodies for the labour movement. At the municipal level, the labour movement operates through labour councils. Finally, the local union is the base level for the regional, national, or international unions. We describe the structure of local unions and the activities that they engage in.

After examining the structure of unions, we turn in Chapter 5 to a discussion of why employees may (or may not) wish to join a union. After looking at the personal, workplace, economic, and societal factors that explain why employees do (or do not) support a union, we consider the dynamics of an organizing campaign itself. To succeed, an organizing campaign requires the support of a specific number of employees. We explore the definitions of "employee," "trade union," and "employer," and describe the criteria that are used to determine the bargaining unit that the union wishes to represent. The outcome of a successful organizing campaign is the establishment of the union's status as the employee's exclusive bargaining agent.

In Chapter 6, we explain how a labour relations board assesses a certification application. This explanation includes a description of a representation vote and the circumstances under which a labour relations board may hold a hearing into a certification application. We also explore special circumstances of certification, such as a certification application for a previously unionized workplace. As a final consideration in the certification process, we discuss various "bars" to certification—these determine when and under what circumstances an application for certification may be filed. We then outline unfair labour practices and the legislative provisions used to balance the rights of the various parties involved in the certification process. We end this chapter with a description of the remedies for unfair labour practices.

Once a certification order is issued, the union and the employer are compelled to commence collective bargaining. In Chapter 7, we discuss the effects of a certification order. As well as directing the parties to start bargaining, the certification order also implements provisions requiring all union members to pay union dues, provisions for union dues check-off, and an exemption from paying union dues on religious grounds. We also examine the concept of a "union shop." We then discuss the actual structure of collective bargaining. The simplest bargaining structure is a single union negotiating with a single employer at a single location. We also review more complex structures, including structures in which groups of unions or groups of employers bargain as a single unit. Next, we discuss the individuals who participate in collective bargaining on behalf of the union and of the employer. We conclude by outlining what the parties can bargain for and what is implied by the expectation of bargaining in good faith.

In Chapter 8, we outline the stages in union-management negotiations, subprocesses, strategies, and tactics in collective bargaining. We discuss the four stages that can be observed in the bargaining process and identify the subprocesses within each stage that influence the parties' behaviour. We also outline the strategies and tactics used in each subprocess and discuss the factors that affect how much power each side might hold or be perceived to hold at any time. Finally, we explore two alternative models of union-management negotiations.

If the parties are unable to reach a collective agreement, or if collective bargaining breaks down, a strike or lockout may occur. In Chapter 9, we define strikes and lockouts and describe their use as part of the collective bargaining process. We also review some of the factors and motivators that would lead unions or employers to consider striking or locking out. Canadian labour legislation specifies several conditions that must exist before a strike or lockout can be considered legal, and we examine these preconditions in this chapter. If a strike or lockout occurs, two major factors affect how it will proceed: picketing and the use of replacement workers. We explore the major functions of picketing and whether the employer should be permitted to use or hire replacement workers. Finally, we examine the ways a lockout or strike can end and, if a collective agreement results, the ratification process. We conclude Chapter 9 with a comparison of Canada's strike record to that of other industrialized countries.

In Chapter 10, we examine the use of third-party intervention in collective bargaining. These interventions can help the parties to resolve their differences without having to resort to a strike or lockout. The main types of third-party intervention are conciliation, mediation, and arbitration. To conclude Chapter 10, we discuss the advantages and disadvantages of using mediation/arbitration as a form of third-party dispute resolution, differences between disputes in the private sector and public sector, and other methods of resolving bargaining disputes.

Once a collective agreement is achieved, Canadian labour legislation provides for a method of settling disputes between the employer and the union during the term of a collective agreement. In Chapter 11, we discuss the grievance arbitration process. The term "grievance" is defined and the various types of grievances are explained. We describe the steps in the grievance procedure as well as procedural issues such as timelines, and we also provide an explanation of who is involved at the various steps in the procedure. A union's duty of fair representation is defined and explained.

The remainder of Chapter 11 focuses on the arbitration process. We begin by discussing the appointment of an arbitrator and how an arbitration hearing is arranged. We then discuss the arbitration procedure itself, including issues such as preliminary steps, procedural onus, standard of proof, order of proceeding, and issuing of the award. We then turn to alternatives to the traditional arbitration process, first examining the complaints about the arbitration process and then exploring the processes of expedited arbitration, grievance mediation, and mediation/arbitration.

In Chapter 12, we discuss the changes that may take place during the life of the collective agreement and that can affect the status of the union-employer relationship. Successorship usually involves some form of change of employer, while raiding and union mergers may change the union that represents the employees. Decertification significantly changes the union-employer relationship by removing the union from the workplace. Finally, both technological change and workplace restructuring may cause changes to work structure or content that need to be addressed by the union, the employer, or both.

In Chapter 13, we address some recent trends that are changing the Canadian workplace and look at their implications for unions and employers. Changes in workplace demographics have caused unions to examine their certification and representation strategies in order to maintain membership levels. Changes in work arrangements, such as telecommuting, involve new structures of work that do not always lend themselves to the standard model of union-employer relationships; the same issue arises with changes to organizational structures that are characterized by flatter hierarchies and fewer distinctions between workers and employers. We discuss some of the actions that unions and employers have taken in response to these trends. We also outline some of the recent Canadian industrial relations trends and discuss their implications for the future of union-employer relationships.

SUMMARY

In this chapter, we have presented some reasons why industrial relations is an exciting and relevant subject. Understanding industrial relations is essential to understanding how the Canadian workplace has evolved and how it currently operates. To begin that process of understanding, we have outlined the major components of Canadian labour legislation and presented some statistics on Canadian unionization rates. Finally, we have presented an overview of the rest of the textbook to convey some sense of the discussion that is yet to come.

KEY TERMS FOR CHAPTER 1

employer (p. 4)
intentional discrimination (p. 19)
interprovincial component (p. 13)
jurisdiction (p. 12)
labour relations board (p. 15)
para-public/quasi-public sector (p. 16)
protected/prohibited grounds (p. 19)
public sector (p. 16)
quasi-judicial (p. 16)
systemic discrimination (p. 19)
union (p. 4)

DISCUSSION QUESTIONS FOR CHAPTER 1

1. What are some of the arguments for and against using the term "industrial relations" to describe union-management relationships?

2. Why could the field of industrial relations be characterized as multidisciplinary? Do you see this characteristic as a positive or a negative attribute?

3. Distinguish between industrial relations and human resource management.

4. Outline the common features of the different pieces of Canadian labour legislation.

5. What is the importance of the "interprovincial component"?

6. Describe some of the characteristics of Canadian union members and unionized workplaces. Choose at least one of these characteristics and explain how or why you think it has evolved (e.g., why more women than men are union members).

EXERCISES FOR CHAPTER 1

1. Describe your experiences with unions, either as a member or as a non-member. Have your experiences been positive or negative? How have your experiences affected your attitudes toward unions and toward industrial relations in general? Compare your experiences and attitudes with those of other students in your class to see if there are similarities or differences. If differences exist, try to identify the reasons why.

2. Explain what you, at this point in the course, see as the benefits and drawbacks of a unionized workplace, both for the workers and for the employer. As in the previous exercise, compare your explanation with those of other students in the class to see if there are similarities or differences. If differences exist, try to identify the reasons why.

References

[1] Kochan, T., & Katz, H. (1988). *Collective bargaining and industrial relations: from theory to policy and practice* (2nd edition). New Homewood, IL: Richard D. Irwin.

[2] Zinni, D.M., Mathis, R.L., & Jackson, J.H. (2011). *Human resource management* (2nd Canadian edition). Toronto: Nelson.

[3] Dunlop, J. (1958). *Industrial relations systems*. New York: Holt.

[4] Dabscheck, B. (1989). A survey of theories of industrial relations. In Barbash, J., & Barbash, K. (Eds.), *Theories and concepts in comparative industrial relations*. Columbia, SC: University of South Carolina Press.

[5] Dessler, G., Cole, N. & Sutherland, V.L. (1999). *Human resources management in Canada* (7th Canadian edition). Scarborough, ON: Prentice-Hall.

[6] Creighton, D. (1970). *Canada's first century, 1867–1967*. Toronto, ON: Macmillan.

[7] This summary is based on the discussion in Dessler, Cole & Sutherland, *op. cit.*

[8] Dessler, Cole, & Sutherland, *op. cit.*

[9] Dessler, Cole, & Sutherland, p. 75.

[10] Dessler, Cole, & Sutherland, p. 76.

[11] The summaries of these cases are based on Alter, S. (1993). *The courts, the Charter, and labour relations*. Ottawa, ON: Research Branch, Library of Parliament. Background paper BP-305E.

[12] *Retail, Wholesale and Department Store Union, Local 580 v. Dolphin Delivery Ltd.* [1986] 2 S.C.R. 573 at 583.

[13] Alter, *op. cit.*, p. 6.

[14] *Reference Re Public Service Employee Relations Act* [Alberta] [1987] 1 S.C.R. 313; *Public Service Alliance of Canada v. R.* [1987] 1 S.C.R. 424; *Government of Saskatchewan v. Retail, Wholesale and Department Store Union, Local 544 et al.* [1987] 1 S.C.R. 460.

[15] *Professional Institute of the Public Service of Canada v. Northwest Territories* [1990] 2 S.C.R. 367.

[16] *Lavigne v. Ontario Public Service Employees Union* [1991] 2 S.C.R. 211.

[17] Makin, K. (2001). "Farm workers win right to unionize." *The Globe and Mail*, December 21, 2001, A6.

[18] Quoted in Makin, *op. cit.*

[19] *Fraser v. Ontario (Attorney General)* [2008] ONCA 760; "Epic fight for farm workers reaches Supreme Court." National Union of Public and General Employees, December 17, 2009. <http.www.nupge.ca/node/2832>

[20] *Health Services and Support—Facilities Subsector Bargaining Assn. v. British Columbia* [2007] SCC 27; Sandborn, T. (2007, June 8). Campbell government violated Charter rights: Supreme Court. <http://thetyee.ca/news/2007/06/08/Bill29Dies>; "B.C. and health care unions settle 6-year dispute." <http://www.cbc.ca/canada/british-columbia/story/2008/01/28/bc-bill29dealreached.html>

[21] Fudge, J. (2008). The Supreme Court of Canada and the right to bargain collectively: the implications of the *Health Services and Support* case in Canada and beyond. *Industrial Law Journal*, 37(1), pp. 25-48.

[22] *Plourde v. Walmart Canada Corp.* [2009] SCC 54, and *Desbiens v. Walmart Canada Corp.* [2009] SCC 55; "Walmart wins at Supreme Court," CBC News, November 27, 2009. <http://www.cbc.ca/canada/story/2009/11/27/supreme-court-walmart-union.html>

Where Canada's Unions Are Today

With an average of approximately 30 percent union density, Canada's workforce appears to be highly unionized compared to the United States' workforce, which has a density rate of around 12 percent. However, this discrepancy is due in part to high unionization rates in Canada's public sector, says Judy Haiven, PhD, chair of the Department of Management at Saint Mary's University in Halifax.

Canada's private sector hasn't fared so well. "As a result of free trade, we have lost a lot of our industrial jobs," says Haiven. "Corporations no longer have an incentive to keep jobs here, so are moving them either home to the U.S. or to low-wage developing countries." Haiven points out that free trade was likely responsible for the closure of the 135-year-old railcar plant TrentonWorks near New Glasgow, Nova Scotia. The parent company, Oregon-based Greenbrier Companies, shut down the company in 2007, laying off 330 workers. As recently as 2006, TrentonWorks had been a major employer of up to 1,200 semi-skilled and skilled tradespeople. "These were 'good' union jobs, with decent pay and benefits, plus full-time hours," says Haiven. "Workers at Greenbrier's railcar plant in Mexico earn about $3 per hour, in comparison to its Nova Scotia workers who earned about $19 per hour."

In addition, privatization has had a big impact on industrial towns. For example, when Nova Scotia Power was privatized in 1992, the company, which traditionally had bought coal from Nova Scotia mines, started buying it cheaper offshore. "The mining and industrial jobs in Cape Breton simply evaporated, and with that went the unionized workforce," says Haiven.

Haiven describes this reduction in unionization in the private sector as "the new face of work," but stresses that the need for unions still exists. She points to the call centre environment, in which employees have few rights, and management electronically monitors their work. For the most part, these jobs are low paying, unrewarding, and offer little job security.

The retail sector is another area that would benefit from unionization, and various groups of retail employees are beginning to organize. Haiven points out that in Alberta and Saskatchewan, a large proportion of supermarket employees are unionized, while in Nova Scotia few are—and the difference in wage rates is striking. "Many Nova Scotians who work in supermarkets earn around $10.00 per hour (minimum wage is $9.20). Out west, supermarket employees earn on average $12.40 per hour, some as much as $22 per hour," she says.

So why have unions failed to make significant inroads in industries that clearly need them? "When you have about a third of working people unionized, you can't easily point to their success," Haiven says. "You must show that people are better off because of unions."

THEORIES OF INDUSTRIAL RELATIONS

objectives

In this chapter, we will introduce and discuss the ideas of some of the theorists who have attempted to explain the reasons for the creation of unions and the purposes that unions serve in the workplace and for their members. By the end of the chapter, you should be able to:

- describe how the structure of work changed from the 15th to the 19th century
- identify the functions of early forms of unionism
- outline the conditions that gave rise to the modern trade union
- describe the theories of authors who discuss trade union origins, functions, and futures

INTRODUCTION

As unions have emerged and developed as a force in the workplace, a number of authors and researchers have attempted to explain the reasons for the continued existence of unions and to identify the purposes unions serve. A review of the work of these individuals is important for two reasons. First, such a review demonstrates how, over time, opinions about unions have evolved alongside the evolution of unions themselves. Second, the different perspectives that these authors and researchers bring to the study of unions illustrate that unions have not served just one function throughout their history, but instead have played multiple roles for their members, responding to changes in work and in the workplace.

To create a context within which we can assess the work of these authors, we will begin our discussion with a brief outline of the general historical origins of unions. (We will discuss the specific history of the Canadian union movement in Chapter 3.) We will then present the authors' works in roughly chronological order to show how theories about unionism have evolved over time.

THE ORIGIN OF UNIONS

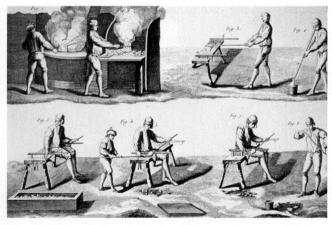

Pre-industrial craftspeople, such as this glassblower, completed an entire product from start to finish.

The earliest organizations that can be identified as similar to the modern trade union are the craft guilds that emerged in Europe during the 14th century and in North America during the 17th century. The members of craft guilds were usually workers involved in a single trade, such as weaving, woodworking, metalwork, or pottery. In order to understand the reasons for the existence of craft guilds, we must understand how work and production were structured during those pre-industrial times.[1] Most craftspeople worked at home or in a small, shared workshop located in the community where they lived. Craftspeople usually owned their business and, in effect, worked for themselves (much like the self-employed do today). Production of goods was on a custom basis; work would be generated by an order from a customer and each unit would be produced to the customer's requirements. The craftsperson was usually responsible for the production of an entire unit from start to finish, although some tasks might be given to apprentices, who learned their craft by working alongside an experienced practitioner. If part of the job required a skill that the craftsperson did not have (for example, a leatherworker might not have the skills or equipment to produce the metal parts of a horse's bridle), the craftsperson would commission the needed materials from another craftsperson. If the skills of a different craftsperson were required on a regular basis, the two craftspeople could arrange to work cooperatively.

The lack of mass transportation and the poor quality of most roads in that era meant that transporting goods was slow and expensive. Because of this, the market served by individual craftspeople did not usually extend far beyond their own community. There was no intermediary such as a distributor or wholesaler between the producer and the consumer. Furthermore, craftspeople had to do their own marketing; they were responsible for identifying and reaching the markets and customers they served.

This method of structuring work offered some degree of freedom and independence to craftspeople, since they worked at their own pace on projects of their own choosing. They were also responsible for deciding how the work was to be carried out and how their business would be administered. However, succeeding within this structure required the craftsperson to have good health, the ability to work, and up-to-date skills to meet the market's demands. Since craftspeople were self-employed, there was usually no backup or support if they became injured, ill, or otherwise unable to work. As well, there was little opportunity for craftspeople to develop or expand their skills because of the ongoing demands of maintaining their business. It was because of these weaknesses in the craft system that craft guilds emerged.

The craft guild served several important functions for the craftsperson. One function was to supply insurance. Many guilds had schemes similar to modern unemployment insurance or workers' compensation plans. Craftspeople would regularly pay a fee to the guild, and if they were injured or otherwise unable to work, the guild would make payments to the craftsperson to offset their lost income. Some guilds provided the services of another craftsperson to keep the business in operation during the owner's absence, so that the owner would not lose customers while they were inactive. Another function of the guild was to ensure an adequate supply of trained practitioners of the craft. This function was present in those occupations where the guild had exclusive control over apprenticeships and other forms of education. A person wanting to become, for example, a goldsmith or a carpenter would contact the appropriate craft guild, which would then arrange for the individual to serve as an apprentice with various craftspeople so that he or she could learn all aspects of the craft from experienced practitioners. At the end of the apprenticeship, usually after completing a test intended to demonstrate mastery of the craft, the individual would be declared a full member of the craft guild and was permitted to operate their own business.

The apprenticeship and training function of the craft guild provided a form of quality control for products. To maintain the guild's control over the labour market, guild members would usually refuse to work or to share skills with craftspeople who were not affiliated with their guild. This ensured a shared body of knowledge among guild members that was not accessible to non-guild members. Thus, a customer purchasing a product from a member of the guild could be assured that the craftsperson had been adequately trained in making an acceptable product. Guilds were also able to maintain something of a monopoly over the price of goods by encouraging guild members to charge similar prices for their products and to refrain from undermining other members' businesses by undercharging for goods.

In providing a forum for the exchange of information and knowledge among the craft's practitioners, guilds also served an educational function for their members. Guild members could share information about new techniques, expanding markets, or new products. Some guilds in more populated and accessible areas reduced production costs for their members by purchasing supplies or raw materials in bulk.

The initial challenges to the craft guild system surfaced in Italy during the 14th century, when merchants created the Wool Guild to displace the clothmakers' guild. The Wool Guild acted much like an employers' association, using the collective knowledge and influence of the producers and sellers to counteract the power of the craft guild. It succeeded in reducing the power of the clothmakers' guild by controlling the supply of raw materials and distribution of finished products. This permitted the Wool Guild to change the predominant method of production from a single craftsperson creating a product from start to finish to a method in which different steps in production were divided among different craftspeople. Instead of a single craftsperson spinning fleece into wool, weaving the wool into fabric, and then dying the fabric, for example, one craftsperson would spin the wool, another would weave, and another would dye. The Wool Guild was able to enforce this division of labour because the Wool Guild controlled the supply of raw materials, and was thus able to ensure that each craftsperson received only the materials needed for his or her part of the production process.

This division of labour allowed for faster production, since individual craftspeople became specialists in their part of the production process and thereby developed more efficient methods of carrying out their task. However, a more significant change instigated by the Wool Guild was in the way that the craftspeople were paid. Rather than being paid directly by the customer for the completed product—a price that would cover the costs of labour, raw materials, and production tools—the craftspeople were instead paid a standard piecework rate by the producer who coordinated their work. The producer would then sell the completed product to the market or consumer.

This method of compensation reduced wage and production costs for the producer, since the producer was not obligated to compensate the craftspeople for their time or skill. Rather, the producer simply paid a set rate based on how many finished pieces the craftspeople were able to produce, regardless of how long it took them to generate those pieces or what skills were needed to carry out the work. The producer also did not have to carry the costs of purchasing the tools for production, since the craftspeople were expected to provide their own tools. Since craftspeople usually worked at home, the producer did not have to carry the overhead costs associated with operating a production facility or workplace. The popularity of this system of production soon expanded beyond Italy; by the 18th century, the so-called "putting-out system" was prevalent throughout Europe.[2]

The Toronto Rolling Mills was typical of many 19th-century factories. Centralized production brought new concerns about working conditions and safety.

The next major shift in the structure of work and production occurred with the Industrial Revolution in the mid-18th century. The degree of change that mechanization and industrialization brought to the work of craftspeople was immense; in England, nearly 1,000 patents for new inventions were issued in one 30-year period.[3] These new inventions, such as the flying shuttle (for weaving) and the spinning jenny (for spinning wool), meant great increases in production capacity, since the people using them could produce output more quickly and in greater quantities than craftspeople could. Mechanization also reduced the demand for skilled workers, since machines rather than human workers could now carry out many of the complex steps of production. Relatively low prices for land facilitated the establishment of large-scale factories, and improvements in transportation and communication meant that raw materials and finished goods could easily be marketed in areas far from their place of origin.

These changes, however, meant substantial changes in the structure of work and of workplaces. These are summarized in Table 2-1. Because factories were centralized places of production, workers were required to travel to the workplace rather than working from home as before. In addition, because factories were generally located in urban

TABLE 2-1 Pre- and Post-Industrial Revolution Work Structure		
	Pre-Industrial Revolution	**Post-Industrial Revolution**
Work location	Home or workshop in home community	Factory in urbanized centre
Work division	Responsible for entire production process	Individual part of production process
Work training	Apprenticeship with established craftsperson or worker	Minimal because tasks were specialized and simplified
Ownership of business	Craftsperson owed own business	Employer
Market for goods	Local/regional	National/international
Type of goods	Custom	Mass produced
Design/control of work	By individual craftsperson/worker	By employer

areas, many workers had to leave their rural communities to find employment in cities. And, as mentioned, the work itself substantially changed due to mechanization. Where previously a worker would participate from start to finish in producing an item, industrialization resulted in production being broken down into distinct stages, some or most of which were handled by machinery. A worker would perform only one or a few of the steps in production. The production process was divided so these steps usually required minimal skill and, if necessary, workers could easily be replaced without any significant loss of production time for training.

More importantly, however, control over work also changed. In the pre-Industrial Revolution economy, the individual craftsperson was both worker and business owner. The craftsperson designed his or her product, produced it, sold it, and received the financial rewards directly. In the factories, control of the workplace and ownership of the business rested solely with the factory owner. The owner decided what the factory would produce, designed the production process, and purchased the necessary machinery and raw materials. The owner also controlled how labour was used in the process, decided who would or would not work in the factory and how they would do their work, and paid the workers whatever wage rates he or she deemed appropriate.

These major changes in work and production initially resulted in generally horrific working conditions. The focus in the new economy was on increased production and consumption, which meant that factories operated continuously in order to produce sufficient goods for expanding consumer markets. Because of the pressure to maintain competitive retail prices, goods were produced at the lowest cost possible, which resulted in little consideration for the safety or job satisfaction of workers. Women and children worked alongside men in the factories—the "dark Satanic Mills"[4]—since the high cost of living in an urban centre usually meant that more than one family member had to work to provide sufficient household income. Another factor compelling as many family members as possible to earn an income was the decline in wage rates caused by industrialization. One writer visiting a major British cloth-manufacturing region in 1830 reported that weavers who formerly earned 20 to 30 shillings per week as craftspeople earned five shillings or less per week working in clothmaking factories.[5]

The use of child labour was commonplace in factories. In fact, for tasks requiring delicate manual work, such as stripping tobacco leaves from plants, children were preferred because their small fingers allowed them to work more neatly and with less waste than adults did. Not all children worked alongside their parents in factories; some were sent to work alone in factories by impoverished parents who could not afford the fees for trade apprenticeships in their home communities.[6] Children living away from their parents were often housed in sheds near the factory and forced to work shifts that lasted for as long as they could stay awake. In Britain, it was not until 1819 that laws were passed forbidding the employment of children younger than nine years old and prohibiting older children from working more than 12 hours per day. Although this legislation protected child labourers, there was almost no legal protection for adult workers, and the few laws that did exist were rarely enforced because of a lack of factory inspectors. If workers were injured on the job or became ill after prolonged exposure to unsafe working conditions, the usual remedy was to fire them and hire new workers. New workers could easily replace the injured (or deceased) workers because factory jobs were standardized and simplified.

The negative impact of these working conditions on workers was the major reason that the first modern trade unions developed. Our discussion of trade union theories will begin with authors who addressed the origins of the modern trade union, and will then proceed to authors who analyze the historical evolution of unions' functions. We will conclude with a review of more recent authors who address the role that unions might play in the future.

THEORIES OF UNION ORIGINS

The Webbs: The Effects of Industrialization

Sidney and Beatrice Webb were English authors whose interest in trade unions developed through their co-founding of the Fabian Society, a socialist group dedicated to large-scale social reform. The Webbs and their colleagues advocated the reform of working conditions like those found in the industrialized factories; however, they believed that these conditions were not simply problems in the workplace, but were also manifestations of larger societal problems such as the division between rich and poor. In their opinion, the immediate problems in the workplace could only be meaningfully addressed if the larger societal problems were also solved. The Webbs were interested in how trade unions emerged in response to industrialized work structures. They researched the origins of trade unions and published their results in two important books.[7]

The results of the Webbs' research identified the primary purpose of trade unions as improving the conditions of their members' working lives. The Webbs suggested that unions emerged primarily because of the separation between capital and labour caused by industrialization. In the pre-Industrial Revolution economy, labour and capital were both controlled by the worker, who invested in his or her own work and subsequently gained all the financial benefits from the sale of that work. In the factory-based economy, the worker provided labour but the factory owner provided capital. The factory owner also controlled how labour would be used in the production process.

A child coal miner in 1912. The effects of industrialization, as documented by the Webbs and their colleagues, caused reformers to demand legal protection for child and adult workers.

In the Webbs' analysis, this division between capital and labour led owners and businesspeople to exploit labour for their own gain, since owners and businesspeople would want to maximize return on their investment. One method of maximizing return was to minimize production costs, including wages; owners and businesspeople would therefore attempt to keep wages as low as possible, regardless of the financial needs of the workers. The pressures to maximize return and minimize cost were even greater in competitive markets, where the owner or businessperson had less freedom to adjust selling prices if costs changed in other areas of the business. Thus, according to the Webbs, one important objective of unions was to "regulate the conditions of employment" to protect workers' interests against the pressures caused by the owner or businessperson's financial situation. Unions also served the larger purpose of representing workers' interests at a level beyond that of the individual workplace or particular trade; for example, they lobbied governments or regulatory authorities for legislation that would serve the interests of working people.

The Webbs identified three instruments, or "methods," that unions employed to achieve these purposes and objectives. The first was the **method of mutual insurance**. This method involved unions accumulating funds from union membership fees and then using those funds to make payments to workers unable to work. These payments took two forms: (1) "benevolent" or "friendly" payments for workers who were sick, injured, or laid off and (2) "out-of-work" payments for workers whose tools were lost or whose factories were temporarily or permanently closed. This method helped achieve the objective of improving union members' working lives by providing support for workers who were sick or hurt, or whose source of income had disappeared through no fault of their own. The second was the **method of collective bargaining**. This method involved unions acting as the workers' representative in negotiating terms and conditions of work with the employer. By ensuring fair and consistent rules in the workplace and adequate wage rates, this method also helped achieve the objective of improving union members' working lives. The third was the **method of legal enactment**, whereby unions lobbied governments to enact laws guaranteeing basic minimum employment standards. This method helped achieve the goal of representing workers' interests at a higher level, since it ensured that the interests of all workers, not just union members, were brought to the attention of decision-makers and other influential individuals.

The Webbs described two internal mechanisms, or "devices," that unions used to ensure that the unions themselves were democratic and were truly representative of their members' interests. The first of these was the **device of the common rule**, whereby unions would ensure their survival by fighting for better conditions for all workers (not just their own membership). The use of this device would increase support for unions, since non-union members would be impressed by the work that unions had done on their behalf and would thus be interested in joining a union themselves. The second device was the **device of restriction of numbers**, whereby unions limited their membership through qualifying requirements such as apprenticeships. Unions argued that the device of restriction of numbers allowed them some control over conditions in the labour market. Employers would have to depend on unions for a supply of workers guaranteed to have a certain level of training, and unions would have more power to negotiate wages and working conditions with employers, since they could threaten to cease supplying skilled labour if their demands were not met. However, the Webbs felt that the system of restriction of numbers caused injustice and exploitation in the labour market; under this system, access to certain kinds of work was limited, since only those who were approved or accepted by the union would have access to the training needed for particular jobs. In the Webbs' opinion, these limitations kept many workers out of jobs with relatively decent rates of pay and good working conditions, and unfairly condemned them to the dismal life of industrialized factory work.

Selig Perlman: Unions and the Class System

Born in Poland in 1883, Selig Perlman immigrated to the United States in 1918 where he joined the University of Wisconsin–Madison. The university would subsequently become a renowned centre for teaching and research on unionism. The contrasts Perlman observed between the Marxist system of labour and the North American system were at the centre of his major work, *A Theory of the Labor Movement*.[8]

Like the Webbs, Perlman identified the emergence of capitalism as one of the catalysts for the emergence of unions; his reasoning was that the capitalist system was based on a separation between capital and labour that did not exist in the pre-Industrial Revolution economy. However, he also argued that if unions' support came solely from the working class, they would not be successful in representing workers' concerns to capitalists, since the working class was only one part of society, and part that historically had limited power and influence. He suggested that unions needed the support of the middle class, and that, in order to gain this support, they had to respect some of the basic tenets of capitalism, such as ownership of private property. If unions had a broader base of support in society, their concerns would be more widely circulated and noticed. Also, if they supported some of the principles of capitalism and did not reject it outright, they would appear to be cooperative rather than radical and thus be more acceptable to parts of society beyond the working class.

That did not mean, though, that unions should be dominated or controlled by the middle class or by capitalists. Perlman stated that unions would be most effective if they were motivated by what he called the **psychology of the labourer**. Labourers, unlike middle- or upper-class individuals, had the experience of scarcity of work: of not being able to find work at all, or of having difficulty obtaining jobs in a highly competitive labour market. This experience would affect unions' goals and objectives, because the issue of employment security would be uppermost in the minds of their members. In addition, because their views would be shaped by practical realities, labourers would not be distracted by socialist or intellectual idealism. Perlman's concern was that while middle- or upper-class individuals might be sympathetic to the goals of unionism, their personal experience would not be the same as that of the labourer and they would thus not be as sensitive to workers' concerns. Allowing those individuals to dominate unions would ultimately mean that unions would not reflect the needs or concerns of the labourers they were intended to represent. Also, because middle- or upper-class individuals' actual experience with unions would tend to be limited to intellectual or theoretical discussions of unionism, these individuals would have more theoretical than practical ideas of how a union should function. The problem Perlman anticipated was that these ideas might not reflect the needs or concerns of the working-class union members and that, again, unions would not function in a way that would serve the members they were intended to support.

While the Webbs proposed that one of the purposes of unions was to promote large-scale social change, Perlman suggested that the primary purpose of unions was to provide "collective mastery" over employment opportunities and standards. He did not believe that unions should be concerned with gaining ownership of businesses, but instead proposed that they should focus on creating economic security and opportunity for their members. He felt that this strategy—in contrast to one that entailed entering the volatile area of business ownership—would create a stable, long-term basis for union existence.

John Commons: The Effects of the Market

Like Perlman, John Commons was a professor at the University of Wisconsin-Madison. In much of his work on unions, he investigated the emergence of unions as a response to changes in the economic system and the subsequent changes in the structure of work.[9] However, unlike Perlman and the Webbs, Commons focused his research on unions in the United States, seeing them as part of a larger economic, industrial, and political framework.

In an article that he wrote which described the evolution of the shoemaking industry, Commons identified the development of competitive markets as a force driving the emergence of unions. In competitive capitalist markets, workers were separated from the distribution and sale of their work; workers created a product but were not responsible for transporting it to buyers or for determining a competitive selling price. Unions, Commons believed, would serve as a means to ensure that competition in markets was based on product quality and not on wages paid to workers. A competitive product would not be the product that was sold at the lowest price (a condition that would exert downward pressure on wages); rather, it would be the product that was the best made and would thus give the greatest value to the consumer. If unions were able to organize workers in a majority of organizations in a single industry, or if they could organize significant numbers of workers in the same occupation, they would influence competitiveness by ensuring that skilled workers received wages that represented their contribution to the making of a quality product. Commons called this perspective "taking [wages] out of competition."

TABLE 2-2 Theories of the Origins of Unions	
Sidney and Beatrice Webb	– separation between capital and labour
	– method of mutual insurance
	– method of collective bargaining
	– method of legal enactment
	– device of common rule
	– device of restriction of numbers
Selig Perlman	– unions needing support of middle class
	– emphasis on "psychology of the labourer"
John Commons	– influence of competitive markets on wages
	– influence of expanding markets; unions able to use better communication and travel to broaden membership

Commons also noted that the broadening of markets through improved transportation and communication provided opportunities for unions as well as for capitalists. No longer would unions be confined to representing workers in a restricted geographic area; instead, workers could organize workers in other areas who were engaged in the same trade or occupation. By allowing workers in different areas to share common concerns more easily, communication and travel improvements, Commons suggested, led to the development of national and even international unions.

Table 2-2 presents a summary of the theories dealing with the origins of unions.

THE FUNCTIONS OF UNIONS

Robert Hoxie: Union Types

Robert Hoxie, an economist, was interested in identifying the actions that unions undertook to serve their members' interests. He had a somewhat different perspective on the emergence of unions than the authors previously discussed. While those authors focused on the role of unions as unifiers of the working class, Hoxie believed that unions would not be confined to the working class but could emerge in any workplace where the workers had a "class consciousness."[10] In other words, a union could be created by any group of individuals in a workplace or organization who shared interests and common goals.

Hoxie's major contribution to theories of unionism was his identification of four "functional types" of unionism. He stated that unions were established to serve different purposes for their members, and that the structure and actions of any individual union would be shaped by the function the union was established to fulfill. Thus, in order to understand why a union acted as it did, it was important to understand what type of union it was.

The first type of unionism Hoxie identified was **business unionism**. The role of a business union was to protect workers in a particular occupation or trade. Business unions would achieve their goals primarily through collective bargaining, and would be less concerned with larger social issues or with alternative means of resolving workplace issues.

The second type of unionism was **friendly or uplifting unionism**. This type of union acted as a mechanism to improve standards of living for workers and thereby improve society at large. Friendly unions, like business unions, engaged in collective bargaining, but they also used the Webbs' mechanism of mutual insurance and political action to gain desired outcomes. Friendly unions provided a means for workers to interact socially and develop a sense of membership or belonging that might not emerge in other workplace situations.

The third type of unionism that Hoxie identified was **revolutionary unionism**. Unions of this kind would attempt change either through large-scale political action or through direct action such as sabotage or violence. Hoxie noted that revolutionary unions were extremely class-conscious; they were concerned with the long-term objective of changing the class structure of society, as well as with the short-term goal of gaining power for workers.

Finally, Hoxie identified **predatory unionism**. Here, unions were mainly concerned with increasing their own power by whatever means possible—sometimes through unethical or illegal activity. Hoxie noted that predatory unionism was distinct from business unionism in that predatory unions often operated in partnership with employers.

Predatory unions would, for example, take bribes from employers to accept collective agreements with little value for workers (so-called sweetheart agreements). Business unions, on the other hand, would maintain an arm's-length relationship with the employer and not agree to anything that would compromise the workers' interests.

It is important to note that Hoxie did not present these four functional types of unionism as mutually exclusive. He argued that one union could serve more than one of these functions at the same time and that many unions simultaneously engaged in, for example, business and friendly unionism. Hoxie also suggested that a union might move from one form of unionism to another as the union developed or as the workplace or the attitude of employers changed. A union that was newly certified might be more concerned with business unionism in order to establish favourable workplace conditions, but as the union became more skilled in that role, it might acknowledge larger social issues and develop the ability to engage in friendly or even revolutionary unionism.

E. Wight Bakke: Choosing to Join a Union

Like Hoxie, E. Wight Bakke, a professor at Yale, was also interested in how unions served the interests of their members. His primary interest, however, was why workers chose to join or reject unions and how the role a union played for its members affected this decision. Bakke researched these questions through extensive interviews with workers, and presented his results in a series of articles and books.[11]

Bakke stated that workers' main reasons for joining unions were to reduce their frustration and anxiety in the workplace and to improve their opportunity to achieve specific "standards of successful living." If workers perceived that joining a union would be a means to attain these goals, they would join; if workers did not see that a union would assist them in reaching these outcomes, they would not join.

Bakke elaborated on these findings by identifying five factors that constituted the standards of successful living, and explaining how workers perceived that unions might help them attain these standards. The first factor is **social status**. Union membership—more specifically, holding a designated position in a union (e.g., being an executive member or shop steward)—may provide a means for a worker to gain the respect of others in the workplace or in society. Such respect may not be attainable through other means if the worker is perceived to belong to a lower-ranked social or economic class.

The second factor is **creature comforts**. Union membership may allow a worker to enjoy a similar standard of living to that of his or her peers, because the union negotiates on behalf of the workers for competitive wages and benefits. Non-unionized workers may not have enough formal influence in the workplace to obtain these conditions.

The third factor is **control**. The presence of a union in a workplace gives workers a formal voice in operations through negotiation, the presence of a collective agreement, and the opportunity to file grievances. These mechanisms guarantee that the individual worker will have influence over his or her working conditions; a non-unionized worker may or may not have this influence, depending on the attitude of the employer.

The fourth factor is **information**. Unions serve as a source of information on companies, the economy, and society at large; they also run programs to educate workers on labour-related matters. This means that unionized workers may be better informed and better educated than non-unionized workers.

The final factor is **integrity**, which, according to Bakke, would include self-respect and fairness. A worker's decision to join a union would be partly based on whether union membership would enhance his or her sense of integrity.

Bakke concluded that a decision about whether to join a union would be based on a worker's perception of whether the union was able to provide the factor or factors of importance to him or her. If, for example, a worker perceived creature comforts to be a high priority, he or she would only join a union that seemed to promise a means through which creature comforts could be obtained.

John Dunlop: The Industrial Relations System

John Dunlop, a professor at Harvard, created one of the most influential theories of union functions with his "systems theory" of industrial relations.[12] Dunlop attempted to explain how unions functioned by looking at how unions fit into larger social systems. He analyzed how unions interacted with other organizations and what guidelines existed to regulate or shape those interactions.

In its general form, systems theory explains why an organization functions as it does by depicting it as a system with three interdependent components: inputs, processes, and outputs. At the simplest level, the processes are the means by which inputs (e.g. resources and raw materials) are converted into outputs (e.g. products and services).

"We Are Tired of Being Cheap Labour"

MONTREAL—Montreal's army of home-based daycare operators has begun to organize under the umbrella of one of Quebec's biggest unions.

But many still aren't sure how it will help improve working conditions or what it will mean long-term for parents or Quebec's $7-a-day child-care system.

"Will we get paid for Christmas? Sick days? What it means, I don't know," said Rachel Funderburk, the owner of Northview Home Daycare in Pointe Claire.

"It can't make things any worse though," she added.

Numbering more than 14,000 across Quebec, home-based daycare operators provide 44 per cent of the province's $7-a-day daycare spots, and care for nearly 90,000 children.

However, unlike child-care educators working in government-run $7-a-day centres, home-based daycare operators are considered self-employed rather than government employees.

They are not covered by workers' compensation. They don't receive vacation pay, paid sick days, or statutory holidays.

When you factor in 10-hour shifts and the cost of running a home-based day care like heating, materials and food (two snacks and one meal a day), hourly wages come in at less than $5 an hour, according to one union organizer.

"We are tired of being cheap labour," said Marie Mady, a former kindergarten teacher who now runs Young Explorers Daycare out of her home in Dollard des Ormeaux. "The provincial government is saving money on us.

"The last time I had a sick day was April 3, 2000," said Mady. "I remember because I was in the hospital."

She said her day begins at 7 a.m. and ends at 6 p.m., five days a week.

Source: Cornacchia, Cheryl. "'We are tired of being cheap labour': fed-up home-based daycare operators are organizing under a union banner." *The Gazette* [Montreal], December 4, 2008, p. A6.

The type of input affects the choice of processes, and the choice of processes affects the output. To illustrate this idea, think of a manufacturing plant that produces cars. The model of car being produced will determine which inputs are needed. A plant producing minivans, for example, would not need materials to make convertible tops, or workers with the skills to produce convertible tops. Similarly, the production process would be organized to produce minivans in the most efficient manner. If the plant changes its product to two-door economy sedans, the production process has to be altered. However, the outputs may also be affected or constrained by the components used in the production process. The manufacturer may want to offer minivans in four different colours, but the painting machinery may only allow three colours of paint to be available at any given time. Either the manufacturer will have to revise its expectations, or the production process will have to be redesigned to permit four paint colours to be used during production.

We can see from this example that systems theory emphasizes not only the existence of distinct parts of the organization, but also the interrelationships between those parts. What happens in one part of the organization may directly or indirectly affect other parts of the organization because of these linkages. Because systems theory explores the effect of interrelationships, it can be used to analyze social and cultural activity in the organization in addition to more tangible processes. Understanding the social and cultural interrelationships between individuals, groups, or departments can be crucial to understanding how an organization really functions. Systems theory can also be used to analyze the interactions of the organization with the external environment and thus help us to understand how events or forces in the external environment affect events within the organization.

Dunlop took the principles of systems theory and used them to explain how industrial relations systems operate on two levels: within the framework of the individual organization and with other organizations in the external environment. His "framework" is depicted in Figure 2-1.

In Dunlop's framework, unions are one of three actors in the industrial relations system. The other two actors are management (the employer) and government and/or private agencies. The definition of "actors" may be expanded to include external stakeholders, such as customers or other businesses. Dunlop argued that each of these actors has a distinct ideology—a set of values and beliefs that determines how they will act

FIGURE 2-1 Dunlop's Industrial Relations System		
Actors	**Contexts**	**Web of Rules**
Unions	Technologies	Procedures for determining substantive rules
Management/employer	Markets	Substantive rules
Government and other third parties	Budgets, power	Procedures for applying substantive rules

within the system. For example, management may believe that it is their right to control the workplace because they represent the individuals who have made financial invest-ments to create and sustain the organization. This belief would lead managers to under-take actions consistent with maintaining or increasing that control. On the other hand, unions may believe that they have a right to "have a say" in the workplace because they represent the workers whose labour makes it possible for management to earn profits. This belief would lead them to undertake actions intended to counteract or balance the control exerted by management, if they perceived that management's actions would neg-atively affect the workers.

It is apparent that the ideologies of the actors within the industrial relations system are often in conflict over fundamental issues. What, then, keeps the system functioning? Dunlop proposed that, despite their different beliefs on certain issues, the actors share a belief about the value of the system itself and each actor's role. It is this shared belief that maintains stability within the system, even if the representatives of the actors or the actors themselves change. While the actors may have ideological disagreements over par-ticular issues, they are committed to participation in the system as a method of interac-tion and conflict resolution. This commitment allows the system to function even when there are disputes between the actors, because they share a belief in the system itself.

The interactions that occur among the actors include, for example, collective bar-gaining and grievance resolution procedures. These are processes to which the actors bring their inputs (general ideologies and positions on specific issues), and it is through these interactions that the inputs are converted into outputs (generally, the collective agreement and the resolution of grievances). The actors also have guidelines, either informal or legislated, for how the interactions will occur (e.g. a mutually agreed upon series of steps the parties will follow in resolving a grievance after a collective agreement is in effect).

Dunlop's framework also identifies the contexts within which the interactions occur. These contexts both shape the interactions and influence the eventual outputs: the col-lective agreement, which can include outputs related to the negotiation of the agreement (e.g., strikes or lockouts), and the general quality of the ongoing relationships between the parties. Dunlop identified four contexts: the technological context (such as the skill level of the workers, degree of flexibility within the workplace, and job content), the mar-ket context (labour, product, and geographical), the budgetary context, and the power context (the amount of power the actors have or are able to generate). An example of contexts influencing outputs would be a situation where an employer wants to negotiate lower wage rates as a means of lowering prices to stay competitive. In this situation, the market context influences the employer's desired output because the perceived basis of competition in the market is pricing. However, the union could argue that the workers are highly skilled, and that reducing wages would cause workers to seek better-paying employment elsewhere, which would lead to a shortage of trained labour for the employer. This argument would reflect the influence of the technological context. The power context would come into play if the government, as another actor in the system, passes legislation forbidding employers to cut wage rates below a certain level; the employer will then lose negotiating power, since it can no longer threaten to lower wages beyond that level.

Finally, Dunlop's framework recognized a "web of rules" that governs the interactions between the parties within the system. There are three general types of rules in this "web." The first type includes the rules in the workplace that are created through negotiation; these are usually contained in the collective agreement. The second type of rules determines how disputes such as grievances will be governed; these rules are also contained in the collective agreement, but they may be influenced by other actors or contexts, such as government legislation. The third type of rules govern the processes underlying how rules themselves will be determined; these are usually legislative guidelines determining such matters as when management and unions must meet to commence collective bargaining, or when a strike or lockout can legally be used as a bargaining tactic. Dunlop speculated that the web of rules and the processes the rules govern are themselves influenced by feedback. Once a process or a rule is in place, the actors monitor its success or failure and, depending on the result, can alter subsequent processes or rules to build on successes or avoid repeating failures.

Dunlop also contributed to industrial relations theory through his research with Clark Kerr, Frederick Harbison, and Charles Myers. The work of these four authors focused on similarities and differences between industrial relations systems in different countries.[13] They contended that the emergence of unions was not a response to capitalism but a response to industrialization. The process of industrialization was consistent across different countries, while markets and economies in different parts of the world differed substantially. The consistency in the process of industrialization, they argued, explained the similarity of union functions and actions in many countries, even if economic structures and markets were different.

They noted that the major exception to this theory existed in Communist countries, where unions were controlled by the ruling Communist Party and were thus not completely independent in representing workers' interests. They argued, however, that as industrialization spread throughout the world, and as workers and managers grappled over universal issues like job security and technological change, there would be a "convergence" of industrial relations systems among developed nations. Industrial relations systems around the world would gradually come to resemble each other rather than remaining distinct.

Table 2-3 presents a summary of the theories of the functions of unions.

TABLE 2-3 Theories of the Functions of Unions	
Robert Hoxie	– class consciousness as a cause of union formation
	– business unionism
	– friendly/uplifting unionism
	– revolutionary unionism
	– predatory unionism
E. Wight Bakke	– factors affecting the decision to join a union:
	– social status
	– creature comforts
	– control
	– information
	– integrity
John Dunlop	– systems theory of industrial relations
	– parties as actors
	– actors operating within contexts
	– web of rules
	– eventual similarity of industrial relations systems in industrial countries

THE FUTURE OF UNIONS

Karl Marx and Friedrich Engels: Unions and the Class Struggle

A cartoon from the anti-Communist "Red Scare" in Canada in 1919. Unions were linked with the Communist ideology espoused by Marx, though most worked hard to quell radical opinions among their members.

If strict chronological order had been followed, Karl Marx and Friedrich Engels would have been placed earlier in our discussion, and in fact their writings did deal with many of the issues relating to the origins of unions. However, these authors also discussed how unions would develop and function after their establishment, and hence we have placed them at the start of our discussion about the future of unions.

In a number of different works, Marx and Engels identified the emergence of unions as one symptom of an ongoing class struggle. Like some of the other authors we have discussed, Marx and Engels saw unions as a means by which the working class could avoid exploitation by the upper classes. Unions would serve as a countervailing force to the power exerted by the upper classes, because they would unite the members of the working class in a single body that would be powerful simply because of its great size. Unions would also enlighten the working class about the injustice of the working class's position in society, and this knowledge would help inspire workers to take action to improve their circumstances.

However, Marx and Engels also believed that unions in and of themselves would not be sufficient to offset the ongoing exploitation of workers, which they viewed as an inherent part of the capitalist system. They proposed that the continued operation of the capitalist system needed a large class of workers who would work (willingly or otherwise) for substandard wages. Keeping wages low created greater profits for the upper classes, and those profits gave the members of the upper class a continual source of wealth that could be reinvested or retained to maintain the upper classes' economic dominance. Marx and Engels argued that unions would need to have a larger purpose beyond gaining increased control of the workplace if unions were to continue to survive, given the inherent oppression that workers faced in the capitalist system. Once unions had satisfied the work-related demands of their members, there would be no reason for them to exist if their only focus was the workplace.

Thus, Marx and Engels argued, unions had to have a larger political purpose as well. They predicted that, in the future, unions would be a vehicle of class discontent, and that discontent would eventually contribute to the overturning of capitalism and the development of a "classless society." This process would, ironically, be aided by means developed by the upper classes: "[T]he ever-expanding union of the workers ... is helped on by the improved means of communication that are created by modern industry. ... [T]his contact was needed to centralize the numerous local struggles, all of the same character, into one national struggle between classes."[14] Marx and Engels contended that once workers recognized the power that they could exert through a collective mechanism such as a union, they would turn their attention to using that collective power to break down larger structures in society. Eventually, classes in society would disappear because all individuals would be equally represented and have equal amounts of power in decision-making.

Harry Braverman: The Effect of Deskilling

While Harry Braverman's theories do not always deal directly with unionism, his work is included in this section because of its ongoing implications for union-related issues like wages and workplace control.

In his book *Labor and Monopoly Capital*,[15] Braverman discusses the enduring popularity of management techniques such as industrial engineering and scientific management, despite the demoralizing effects these techniques have on workers. While industrial engineering and scientific management were developed in the early 1900s, their principles are still used in the design of production processes: for example, in assembly lines and fast-food restaurants. Work is broken down into small, simple, repetitive components that are designed to maximize production output and minimize the skill requirements of the workers. Rather than praising these techniques as innovative and efficient, Braverman identifies them as part of the ongoing attempt by management to increase control over workers and workplaces.

Braverman distinguishes two general methods of achieving the goal of increased management control. The first method is **deskilling**, where tasks are specialized or subdivided to such a degree that there is very little need for highly skilled labour. Deskilling means that management can reduce the number of skilled workers and instead use unskilled and semi-skilled workers, who are in greater supply and who can be paid less. For example, rather than using a highly trained chef to produce a burger from start to finish, a restaurant could employ workers who only know how to operate a grill or a toaster or a chopping knife, and collectively use all of their limited skills to produce the burger. The second method of increasing management control is controlling the methods by which work is done and the pace at which work is conducted. In the restaurant example, management could increase its control over burger production by producing guidelines for how each step in the burger production process is to be performed and/or by setting a maximum time that can elapse between an order being submitted and the customer receiving the burger. Implementing methods of control like these has the effect of increasing production output since the predetermined steps of production are designed for efficiency; it also decreases worker resistance since the worker has little or no say in determining how work will be conducted. The combined use of these two methods of control has resulted, Braverman argues, in more production for less pay.

Braverman suggests that the effect of this managerial orientation has been, and will continue to be, to encourage managers to select workplace technologies not on the basis of quality of service or output, or even of overall technical efficiency. Instead, managers will make their selections based on which technologies permit them to continue to exercise the greatest amount of control over their workers and the workplace, even if the technologies are more costly or inefficient in other ways. For example, management might have to choose between a machine whose price exceeds the organization's capital budget but which allows standardization of a significant part of the production process, and a machine whose price is within budgetary guidelines but whose operation gives more autonomy to the workers. Braverman's argument suggests that management will select the more expensive machine because it gives management greater control of production, even though its purchase will result in inefficiencies in other parts of the organization where budgets will have to be altered to compensate for the excessive cost of the machine. Braverman suggests that a managerial orientation favouring this kind of choice will result in continuous downward pressure on wages and reduced opportunity for workers to develop advanced or varied skills. Although he does not explicitly address the role of unions in this process, it is logical to assume that unions would likely attempt to counteract these restrictions, or arise as a response to excessive management control.

Thomas Kochan, Robert McKersie, and Peter Cappelli: New Union and Employer Roles

Thomas Kochan, Robert McKersie, and Peter Cappelli, all professors at American universities,[16] build on Dunlop's systems theory of industrial relations. They believe that Dunlop's proposed industrial relations system would be a more accurate reflection of industrial relations reality if it included the larger societal and international framework that the employer operates within. They contend that this larger framework ultimately affects the relationship between the employer and the union at the level of the individual workplace, since events in this larger framework, such as international trade agreements, may affect the terms of individual workplace-level collective agreements.

Kochan, McKersie, and Cappelli also point out that earlier industrial relations theories portrayed the employer's role in industrial relations as that of a reactor to the union. In earlier conceptualizations of the union-employer relationship, the employer did not actively attempt to manage the relationship with the union, but instead simply responded to whatever the union brought to its attention. In their view, the employer's role in the union-employer relationship is no longer passive; employers are now sophisticated and active, rather than reactive, participants in industrial relations. Kochan, McKersie, and Cappelli support this assertion by pointing to a number of events in the United States. American employers have lobbied for legislative changes to reduce the power of unions or even outlaw them entirely. Professional strikebreaking firms can legally provide labour to organizations whose regular workers are on strike; there are also cases of non-unionized firms harassing or intimidating individuals attempting to organize unions. These events are all evidence that employers are actively trying to manage their relationship with unions and to shape the framework that guides that relationship.

Kochan, McKersie, and Cappelli argue that if unions are to continue to be effective worker representatives, they need to recognize this fundamental change in the nature of employer participation in industrial relations. The authors do not suggest that all employers undertake actions as extreme as the examples they cite, but they do note that it is essential for unions to realize the change of the employer's role from passive responder to active intervenor, because of the implications this change has for the quality of the union-employer relationship. More importantly, Kochan, McKersie, and Cappelli suggest that industrial relations and the entire human resource management function of an organization are now, more than ever, integrated into the organization's overall strategy. The effect of this integration is that decisions made at the organizational strategic level could ultimately affect the workplace-level union-employer relationship. For example, if an organization decides to outsource part of its production process to another country or another organization, this decision will have a direct impact on the number of workers on the payroll and will, quite possibly, exert downward pressure on wage levels because of the cost savings generated by the outsourcing. These are outcomes that would clearly be of concern to the union as well as the employer.

Thus, Kochan, McKersie, and Cappelli argue, for unions to continue to survive and to be effective worker representatives, they must attempt to be included in decisions at the highest strategic levels of the organization, and not to be too narrowly focused on workplace rules and regulations. This inclusion could take many forms, ranging from informal consultations with management to a worker representative having a formal role on the board of directors or the executive planning committee. This change in direction may mean that unions will have to rethink their traditionally adversarial attitudes toward management, and instead attempt to develop a more cooperative relationship focusing on positive outcomes for all parties. It is unlikely that unions would be considered for participation in strategic planning if they were perceived as hostile or opposed to management's intentions, so unions must emphasize goals, like the long-term survival and health of the organization, which will benefit both unions and management. The authors suggest that cooperative high-level union-management relationships, rather than the traditional adversarial bargaining-level relationships, are more suitable for addressing the potentially wide-ranging impact of strategic-level issues.

Richard Chaykowski and Anil Verma: The Distinctive Canadian Context

Richard Chaykowski and Anil Verma, both Canadian industrial relations professors, address some of the same issues as Kochan, McKersie, and Cappelli, but do so in the context of the Canadian industrial relations system.[17] Chaykowski and Verma acknowledge the shortcomings of the workplace-level, short-term focus of most industrial relations interactions. However, their findings differ from those of the American authors in that they do not see as extensive changes in Canadian management practices or attitudes as the American authors see in the American counterparts. While Canadian employers have experimented with different innovative forms of human resource management practices, the resulting changes have not been as lasting or as wide-ranging as those in the United States. Furthermore, Canadian employers have not engaged in the extreme anti-union activity practised by some American employers, although this may be because Canadian labour legislation places stronger restrictions on employer activity than American legislation does. For example, many Canadian jurisdictions prohibit or restrict the use of replacement workers during legal strikes or lockouts, while such regulations are rare in the United States.

Chaykowski and Verma thus characterize the Canadian industrial relations system as relatively stable in comparison to the American system. They attribute this stability in large part to higher levels of unionization in Canada; since Canadian unions represent a greater proportion of the workforce, they have more power than American unions to resist changes they see as detrimental to their members' interests. While Chaykowski and Verma generally support Kochan, McKersie, and Cappelli's opinion that cooperative union-management relationships are potentially more productive than confrontational relationships, they note that Canadian unions are likely to resist cooperative relationships with management, for fear that cooperation will weaken the unions' ability to oppose unwanted change in the future. If unions compromise on smaller issues, management may expect that unions will then be willing to compromise on larger issues in the future. In other words, unions could find it difficult to maintain an adversarial position if they have cooperated on earlier issues. Union members may also perceive union-management cooperation as "selling out" to management and as an indication that the union is not representing their interests strongly enough.

More recently, Verma and Chaykowski[18] have identified several unique trends in the Canadian context that they speculate will affect the Canadian industrial relations system. The most prominent is a technologically driven shift in economic activity away from traditional production industries and toward service provision. This shift has reduced workforces because of flatter organizational structures and more efficient operations, and has threatened union membership in Canada because of unions' past focus on membership in production rather than service industries. Verma and Chaykowski note that Canadian unions have been more successful than American unions in organizing workers in service-based organizations. Another important trend relates to the implementation of the North American Free Trade Agreement, which may have two effects on the Canadian industrial relations system. First, if employers use the provisions of the agreement to transfer work to other countries, there may be further job loss in Canada and further declines in union membership. Second, Canadian unions may see their influence reduced because it might seem excessive in contrast to the relatively weak power of American unions.

Other Canadian researchers have subsequently identified other factors that may affect the future of the Canadian industrial relations system. As noted in this chapter's opening story, the relatively high rate of unionization in Canada, in comparison to the United States, is partly due to the extensive unionization of Canadian public sector workers.[19] However, since the 1990s, the number of jobs in the public sector has stabilized or shrunk, and governments have become more willing to use legislation and other tactics (such as outsourcing work or jobs) to counteract public sector unions' power.[20]

It has also been noted that Canadian unions have not been as active as they might have been in internally restructuring and in developing new strategic directions to respond to changing work realities and changing workforce demographics. This inactivity might also limit their potential for future growth.[21]

Table 2-4 summarizes the theories of the future of unions.

SUMMARY

As unions have developed over time, so have the perspectives on unions offered by the authors and researchers reviewed in this chapter. Significant changes in the structure, content, and control of work occurred with the Industrial Revolution, and early writers on unions suggested that unions began as a response to these changes and the poor

TABLE 2-4 Theories of the Future of Unions	
Marx and Engels	– unions as a means of worker resistance to exploitation by upper classes
	– unions serving a larger political purpose
	– unions as a method of achieving a classless society
Harry Braverman	– management theories promoting control by management in the workplace rather than efficiency or job satisfaction
	– deskilling
	– control of work methods and control of the pace of work
Kochan, McKersie, and Cappelli	– societal and international framework in the industrial relations system
	– employers changing from passive to active participants in the industrial relations system
	– industrial relations as part of an overall organizational strategy
Chaykowski and Verma	– distinct features of the Canadian industrial relations system
	– stability of Canadian managerial practices and attitudes in comparison to the United States
	– Canadian unions resisting cooperation with employers
	– Decreasing influence of Canadian public sector unions

working conditions they caused. However, as workplaces further evolved and some of the early concerns of unions were addressed, such as workplace safety and pay rates, the functions of unions expanded to include more comprehensive attention to workers' concerns and to social issues outside the workplace. More recent authors have addressed the question of whether the historically adversarial union-management relationship is still viable in a changing workplace and economy, and have suggested issues that unions need to address in the future to remain viable.

KEY TERMS FOR CHAPTER 2

business unionism (p. 50)

control (p. 52)

creature comforts (p. 52)

deskilling (p. 60)

device of restriction of numbers (p. 46)

device of the common rule (p. 46)

friendly or uplifting unionism (p. 50)

information (p. 52)

integrity (p. 52)

method of collective bargaining (p. 46)

method of legal enactment (p. 46)

method of mutual insurance (p. 45)

predatory unionism (p. 50)

psychology of the labourer (p. 47)

revolutionary unionism (p. 50)

social status (p. 51)

DISCUSSION QUESTIONS FOR CHAPTER 2

1. Describe the functions of craft guilds and identify how these are similar to the functions of modern unions.

2. How did industrialization change workers' personal and workplace conditions?

3. Identify common themes among the writers who discuss the origin of unions. Are these themes still applicable to unions being formed in the 21st century?

4. Which of the four functions of unions do you see as being most relevant to current unions? Why?

5. Use Dunlop's theory of industrial relations systems to describe the relationship between a specific union and employer that you are familiar with.

6. Provide arguments for and against the validity of Braverman's theories of management control.

7. Do you agree with the assertion that unions and management need to be cooperative, not confrontational, in the modern economic system? Why or why not?

EXERCISES FOR CHAPTER 2

1. Read the news story in this chapter. Which of the theories discussed in this chapter do you think best explain(s) this situation? Choose the theories that you think are most relevant, and use them to analyze the situation and to suggest what the outcomes of this conflict might be.

2. Choose a union that you are personally familiar with or one that you can research. From the information available to you, can you see evidence that supports a theory or theories presented in this chapter? You can look at the reasons for the origin of the union, the functions the union currently serves, its future plans, its relationship with employers, or any other area that you think is relevant. Explain how the theories you have chosen are illustrated or explained by the information you have collected. Also identify where or how the theories do not address or explain your information, and suggest why these apparent discrepancies might exist.

References

[1] This discussion is based on Commons, J. (1909, November). American shoemakers, 1648–1895: a sketch of industrial evolution. *The Quarterly Journal of Economics*, Vol. 24.

[2] Marsden, R. (2000). Labour history and the development of modern capitalism. In Gunderson, M., Ponak, A., & Taras, D.G. (Eds.), *Union-management relations in Canada* (4th edition). Toronto: Addison-Wesley Longman.

[3] Hibbert, C. (1988). *The English: a social history, 1066–1945*. London: Paladin Books.

[4] Blake, W. (ca. 1804). Jerusalem. Anthologized in Palgrave, F.T. (1861), & Williams, O. (1961), *The golden treasury of the best songs and lyrical poems*. New York: Mentor Books.

[5] Thompson, E.P. (1963). *The making of the English working class*. London: Victor Gollancz/Penguin Books.

[6] Hibbert, *op. cit.*

[7] Webb, S. & B. (1894). *The history of trade unionism*. New York: Longmans Green and Co.; Webb, S. & B. (1897). *Industrial democracy*. New York: Longmans Green and Co.

[8] Perlman, S. (1928). *A theory of the labor movement*. New York: reprinted in 1949 by Augustus M. Kelley.

[9] Commons, *op. cit.*

[10] Hoxie, R.F. (1919). *Trade unionism in the United States*. New York: D. Appleton and Co.

[11] Among others, Bakke, E.W. (1945). Why workers join unions. *Personnel, 22(1)*, 2–11.

[12] Dunlop, J. (1958). *Industrial relations systems*. New York: Holt.

[13] Dunlop, J.T., Harbison, F.H., Kerr, C., & Myers, C.A. (1975). *Industrialism and industrial man reconsidered: some perspectives on a study over two decades of the problems of labor and management in economic growth*. Princeton: Inter-University Study of Human Resources in National Development.

[14] Marx, K., & Engels, F. (1888; reprinted 1985). *The Communist manifesto* [translation by Samuel Moore]. London: Penguin Books.

[15] Braverman, H. (1974). *Labor and monopoly capital*. New York: Monthly Review Press.

[16] Kochan, T., McKersie, R., & Cappelli, P. (1984). Strategic choice and industrial relations theory. *Industrial Relations, 23(1)*, 17–39.

[17] Chaykowski, R., & Verma, A. (Eds.) (1992). *Industrial relations in Canadian industry*. Toronto: Dryden Press.

[18] Verma, A., & Chaykowski, R.P. (Eds.) (1999). *Contract and commitment: employment relations in the new economy*. Kingston, ON: IRC Press, Industrial Relations Centre, Queen's University.

[19] Rose, J.B. (2007). Canadian public sector unions at the crossroads. *Journal of Collective Negotiations*, *31(3)*, 183–198.

[20] Rose, *op.cit.*

[21] Yates, C.A.B. (2002). Expanding labour's horizons: union organizing and strategic change in Canada. *Just Labour*, *1(1)*, 31–40.

A Meeting Place to Remember Workers

A new pavilion and exhibit centre focusing on the history of the labour movement in Saint John, New Brunswick have found a place in a lakeside park setting, fulfilling the final wishes of Warren Franklin Hatheway, a community, business, and political leader during the late nineteenth and early twentieth centuries.

Described as a "visionary who was ahead of his time," W. Franklin Hatheway gave his employees at W.F. Hatheway and Company a share of the profits and allowed some to become active partners in the wholesale grocery business. As president of the Saint John Board of Trade, he advocated for workers' rights and influenced key pieces of legislation. As a member of the New Brunswick legislature, he was behind the Workmen's Compensation Statutes, commonly known as "The Hatheway Act."[1]

Before his death in 1923, Hatheway established a trust for the working people of Saint John, bequeathing more than 70 acres of land for a labour park or to construct a "Labour Temple." "Over the years, a lot of that land was sold off and the money banked," explains Pat Riley, Chair of the W. Franklin Hatheway Trust Board. The trust became inactive, with the trustees meeting perhaps once a year. But in the 1990s, a new volunteer board was set up and plans for the pavilion and exhibit centre soon took shape.

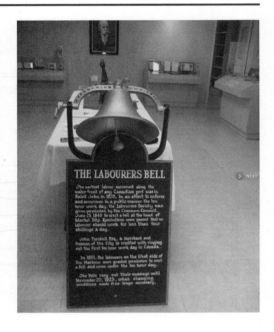

The board reached an agreement with the Saint John Horticultural Society to renovate the Lily Lake Pavilion in Rockwood Park. "The proposal to renovate was a perfect fit in terms of fulfilling the request of Franklin Hatheway," says Mr. Riley. The renovations cost $1.75 million, of which the trust provided $350,000; the remainder was funded by the federal and provincial governments, as well as community donors.

The Hatheway Pavilion and the W. Franklin Hatheway Labour Exhibit Centre officially opened in 2007. The Pavilion complies with Mr. Hatheway's vision of providing a place for the "recreational, moral, and mental betterment" of workers and their families and friends. The facility rents space for weddings, meetings, and fundraising dinners, and includes a popular restaurant. All profits are donated for charitable purposes, such as running day camps out of the lakeside Pavilion.

The Exhibit Centre displays labour memorabilia, photographs, and documents, and includes the Labourers Bell, which dates back to 1849, when the first trade union in Canada was established at the Saint John waterfront. Saint John area unions will showcase their history at the Exhibit Centre on a revolving basis.

A 17-foot monument in front of the centre will have its official unveiling on April 28, 2011, the International Day of Mourning for workers who have been killed or injured on the job. This memorial day was established in Canada in 1984 and is now observed worldwide.

---

[1] Jane Barry, "W. Franklin Hatheway Trust A Friend of Labour," The Greater Saint John Community Foundation

HISTORY OF THE CANADIAN UNION MOVEMENT

objectives

In this chapter, we will discuss the origins and historical development of the Canadian union movement. By the end of the chapter, you should be able to:

- describe the geographic, cultural, economic, and political factors that are relevant to Canada
- identify the major events in Canadian labour history
- understand the role of craft and industrial unionism in shaping Canadian union structure
- discuss how American unions have influenced Canadian unions
- identify some of the regional differences in Canadian labour history

INTRODUCTION

In Chapter 2, we reviewed some of the general history and theories of unions. Our focus in this chapter will be specifically on events and forces that have affected union history in Canada. Union history in Canada has been marked by conflict between different cultures, classes, and regions. Many of the forms of conflict in earlier years would be almost unknown in most 21st-century workplaces.

We will begin with an overview of some of the characteristics of this country that have affected the history of unions, and then turn to a chronologically organized discussion of significant events in the history of organized labour in Canada.

CANADA AS A COUNTRY: DISTINCT CHARACTERISTICS

Before embarking on our discussion of Canadian union history, we will first identify some distinct characteristics that have formed the framework within which this history has occurred. While some of these characteristics may seem, at first glance, rather obvious or simplistic, they are nevertheless important because of their effect on the development of industrial relations in Canada.

The first characteristic is the physical geography of this country. Canada is a large country, and it has expanded greatly since its beginnings in the 1867 merger of modern-day Ontario and Quebec with Nova Scotia and New Brunswick.[1] It currently encompasses 10 provinces and three territories within a total area of almost 10 million square kilometres.[2] Its borders reach from the Atlantic Ocean in the east to the Pacific Ocean in the west, and from the United States in the south to above the Arctic Circle in the north. This vast expanse of land contains climates and physical landscapes ranging from desert to tundra; however, Canada's location in the Earth's northern hemisphere means that most regions in Canada have distinct seasons accompanied by severe weather conditions in at least one of those seasons. The extreme conditions in the northern part of the country make much of the land within Canada unsuitable for agricultural and other primarily resource-based activities; as a consequence, the majority of Canadians live in the southern part of the country, close to the U.S. border.

The physical characteristics of Canada have affected the history of Canadian industrial relations in several ways. As we will see, most early Canadian unions were local or regional because of the difficulty of communicating with or travelling to other parts of such a large country. Canadian climate and land conditions have forced much of Canadian industry to be either seasonal or resource-based; these circumstances have made successful union organizing difficult because of the isolation and lack of permanent employment in these industries. (The story later in the chapter illustrates the challenges faced by union organizers in such industries.) Proximity to the United States has also meant, at various times in Canadian history, that American workers have competed with Canadian workers in the Canadian labour market, and that American unions have exerted an influence on Canadian workers.

Another distinct characteristic of Canada is its cultural mix. The history of Canada as a whole has been influenced by immigration from other parts of the world. First Nations inhabitants were joined by British and French settlers at the time the country was formed, and much of Canada's early history was shaped by struggles between these founding groups for authority and dominance. The early influence of the French settlers is still strongly apparent in the distinct identity of Quebec and in the existence of francophone communities throughout Canada; many of these communities were influenced not only by settlement from Quebec but also by French-speaking immigrants from other countries. Immigrants from Europe, Asia, Central America, South America, and other regions around the world have also been attracted to Canada. These immigrants have settled throughout the country and brought the influence of their own cultures to their new homes. Canada's proximity to the United States has also allowed the pervasive influence of American culture.

This mix of multiple cultural influences has had both positive and negative effects on Canadian union history. Immigrants who had had experience with union or union-like organizations in their countries of origin assisted in the development of some early Canadian unions. However, Canadian unions have not always been successful in addressing the challenges of organizing or representing a culturally diverse workforce; in fact, some Canadian unions have a sad history of racial or cultural discrimination. And, as noted above, Canadian unions and workers have been affected by American unions and workers' easy access to this country.

Canada's economic system is the third characteristic we will discuss. Because of Canada's vast land mass and the rich stores of resources that can be taken from the land, the Canadian economy was historically based on activity in **primary** and **secondary industries**. Primary industries are resource-based industries such as forestry, fishing, and mining, and secondary industries are those industries that process or use the products of resource-based industries, such as construction and steel production. Agriculture has also been an important industry in Canada in those parts of the country where the land is suitable for farming. Toward the end of the 20th century, however, the importance of these industries declined, and the role of **tertiary industries** (service industries) increased in the Canadian economy. Another important sector of the Canadian economy is international trade, particularly with the United States. This reliance on trade with other countries means that Canada's economy is more susceptible to the influence of external events than the economy of a country less dependent on external trading relationships. Canadian unions have historically focused on organizing workers in resource-based industries and have only been partly successful in organizing workers in tertiary industries. International trade has also challenged Canadian unions by providing employers with the opportunity to move jobs outside the country and by pressuring Canadian unions and employers to establish work conditions that are competitive internationally. In Canada, the latter has often implied a reduction in existing standards.

Our fourth and final characteristic is Canada's political structure. Canada's historical relationship with Britain is still recognized by the presence of a federal head of state, the Governor-General, and a lieutenant-governor in each province and territory. These individuals act as the British monarch's representatives and must give "royal assent" to legislation passed by provincial or federal governments. In practice, however, Canada is formally governed by a federal Parliament and by provincial or territorial legislative assemblies. Canadians elect both federal and provincial representatives. Unlike other countries, such as the United States, Canadians do not vote directly for a prime minister or premier. Instead, the prime minister or premier is the leader of the political party that has the most elected members in the House of Commons or regional legislative assembly.

The importance of this division between federal and provincial jurisdictions will become more apparent as we discuss how Canadian labour legislation has developed. We will note at this point that, while there are both federal and provincial labour codes, labour relations is considered to be primarily a provincial responsibility, as outlined in Chapter 1. In contrast, labour relations in the United States is considered primarily a federal responsibility. The basis for this allocation in the United States was the desire to provide a single law that would create identical frameworks for union-employer relationships across the country and ensure the same basic rights for all workers.[3] However, some evidence suggests that this decision has seriously hindered the growth of the American union movement, since a single piece of legislation may not fully address different regional conditions. The Canadian structure of different jurisdictions in each province, while causing difficulties for employers and unions that operate in more than one province, has allowed for experimentation and reform to meet the particular needs of each jurisdiction.[4]

EARLY CANADIAN UNIONISM: THE 1800s

The early years of the Canadian union movement have been called the "period of local unionism."[5] The earliest attempts to organize trade unions in Canada were limited to specific geographic areas and small groups of workers, usually those in a particular trade or occupation. This model of organizing is known as the **craft union** model. The popularity of this organizing model in Canada in the 1800s can be attributed to two main factors.

One factor was the size of Canada. The difficulties of transportation and communication over long distances made organizing at the local level much more practical than attempting to organize a regional or national union. In fact, as we will see, different unions representing the same types of workers emerged at roughly the same time in different parts of Canada. The focus on organizing workers in a specific geographic area also meant that issues specific to that group could be the main focus of the union's activity; the union did not have to attempt to balance the varied concerns that would have emerged in a union encompassing workers in different regions.

The second main factor contributing to the popularity of the craft union model of organizing was the need to protect wage rates for workers in skilled trades. This factor was particularly important in areas where tradespeople's expertise could not easily be replaced by the work of unskilled immigrant labourers.[6] Forming a union was a means for tradespeople to control the market for their skills and thus to control wage rates.

Canada's economic role as an exporter, rather than importer, of goods has been identified as another factor in the predominance of the craft union model of organizing. Many of the skilled craftspeople involved in Canada's first unions were employed in trades such as shipbuilding and carpentry, which "benefited from the economic strategy of export-led growth."[7] The international market for exported Canadian-made goods created domestic production demand, which in turn increased the demand for skilled tradespeople's work and gave those tradespeople increased bargaining power with employers.

Informal workers' groups that undertook collective action such as strikes were formed in Canada as early as 1827. These groups protested poor wages and working conditions on large public works projects, and their structure may have been modelled on the social or fraternal societies to which many of the workers already belonged.[8] Experience with these societies gave the workers the skills and knowledge needed to create informal workers' groups, and these informal alliances quite naturally operated on democratic and structural principles similar to those of the societies.

The first formal unions emerged at roughly the same time as the informal alliances. One historian identifies the first union in Canada as being either a printers' union in Quebec City in 1827 or a shoemakers' or tailors' union in Montreal in 1830.[9] Other authors point out that the Nova Scotia government of 1816 was sufficiently concerned about groups of "journeymen workmen" in Halifax who had joined together to regulate wages for their work that it attempted to outlaw such groups.[10] Still others claim that the earliest unions emerged in Saint John, New Brunswick, which in the early 1800s was a major port and shipbuilding centre. By 1840, Saint John had 10 different trades associations with a total of 1,200 members.[11]

The emergence of regionally based craft unions is understandable given the geographic and occupational difficulties that would have occurred if other forms of organizing had been used, but the prevalence of craft unionism initially inhibited any wider growth of unions in Canada. While craft unions were able to control the regional labour market for the particular skills of their members, as well as ensuring consistent quality of work by controlling training, their membership was restricted to practitioners of the craft. This model of organizing did not encourage unionization of larger numbers of less-skilled workers or workers in non-trade occupations[12]—the alternative organizing model of **industrial unionism**. This form of unionism focuses on "strength in numbers" and maximizing power by recruiting as many members as possible, regardless of occupation, rather than concentrating solely on representation of a particular occupational group. In contrast, several early Canadian craft unions, such as the early miners' unions in British Columbia, were deliberately established along craft lines to exclude workers who were seen as threats to their members' living standards (e.g., immigrant Chinese labourers who were perceived to be undercutting miners' wage rates in British

Columbia). As we will see, conflicts between different regional interests and conflicts between craft and industrial unionism have reoccurred throughout Canadian labour history.

Because of the dominance of craft unions, the next major expansion of the Canadian labour movement came through affiliation with **international unions**—"international" in this case usually meaning based in the United States. International influences were informally present in many of the early Canadian unions. Immigrant workers from Britain brought their experience in the British trade union movement to Canadian workplaces, and there is evidence that the first international unions in Canada were British unions of engineers and carpenters that established affiliated locals in southern Ontario in the mid-1800s.[13] However, because of the easy mobility of skilled workers between Canada and the United States, it made sense for Canadian craft unions to affiliate with American unions representing workers in similar occupations. The mid- and late 1800s saw the **continental movement**[14] of American-based international unions entering central Canada. These unions either formally affiliated with existing Canadian unions or recruited members into new Canadian locals of the American unions. However, the continental movement was restricted primarily to Ontario and other regions with trade links to the United States. Few Quebec unions saw any commonalities with the American unions, and most chose to remain independent to preserve their distinct regional culture. Most of the Maritime unions also continued to be regional and craft-based. The first regional unions in British Columbia—representing typographers, shipwrights, and miners—emerged at approximately the same time.[15]

In the late 1800s, several events further solidified the existence of Canadian unions. During this period, unions began to realize that it was better to work together for common issues rather than simply to concentrate on their own concerns and activities. They thus began to cooperate in campaigns and joint action. One example of this sort of cooperation was the **Nine-Hour Movement** in 1872. The standard working day in most trades at this time was 10 to 12 hours, and in Britain and the United States, a movement was underway to pass legislation restricting the working day to nine hours. It was argued that a shorter working day would produce better quality work because workers would not be exhausted, and society as a whole would benefit by freeing up time that workers could spend with their families and communities. A Nine-Hour Movement similar to the American and British movements emerged in Hamilton and spread across southern Ontario and Quebec.[16] "Nine-Hour Leagues" held public meetings to promote the benefits of a shorter working day. Employers, however, resisted the idea, and this resistance eventually resulted in a major strike in the spring of 1872 involving typesetters and printers in Toronto. Even though a rally of 10,000 workers and citizens expressed their support for the strikers, 24 union executive members were arrested and charged with conspiracy.[17]

It is important to note that at this point there was almost no Canadian legislation specifically addressing industrial relations issues. Around the time that unions started to emerge in Canada, British legislators, attempting to stop the growth of unions in Britain, used existing "criminal conspiracy" or **monopoly laws** against union organizers. These laws were originally designed to stop merchants or traders from colluding with each other for the purpose of controlling or dominating a product market. British legislators expanded the application of the laws, defining unions as a method of monopolizing the labour market. Thus, under the monopoly laws, unions could be considered a means to restrain trade, and "criminal conspiracy" charges could be laid against union organizers. This use of the British law was eliminated by the passage of a new *Trades Union Act* in 1871, which established the right of workers to organize a union (although there were still severe penalties against striking and picketing). Even though the Canadian legal system was dominated by the British legal system at this time, the Canadian Parliament did not choose to adopt its own version of the British *Trades Union Act*. Canadian employers could therefore still use monopoly laws to resist organizing attempts. It was under the Canadian version of the monopoly laws that the Toronto union organizers were charged in the 1872 Toronto strike.

A rather unusual set of circumstances led to the repeal of the Canadian monopoly laws. The person who laid the charges against the leaders of the Toronto strikers was George Brown, the publisher of the *Globe* newspaper. The *Globe* had been a persistent and vocal critic of the federal government led by Prime Minister Sir John A. Macdonald. Macdonald identified the "criminal conspiracy" charges against the Toronto strikers as providing an excellent opportunity to strike back against Brown and his newspaper. He promptly presented Canadian versions of the revised British legislation to the Canadian Parliament, and these proposals were adopted as law.[18] The charges against the Toronto strikers were dropped, but the incident had had the effect of "[breaking] the momentum" of the Nine-Hour Movement[19] and the desired reforms to the length of the working day were not gained.

The Nine-Hour Movement did, however, have one lasting effect. The inter-union networks established by participation in the movement inspired the formation of the first federations of trade unions. The Canadian Labour Union was established in 1873, although the "Canadian" part of the name was somewhat misleading, since the first non-Ontario delegate did not attend an annual meeting until 1878.[20] A more representative group, the **Trades and Labour Congress** (TLC), formed in 1883. Although at this point only about 2 percent of the Canadian workforce was unionized,[21] the TLC was effective in lobbying for reforms to labour legislation that would benefit all workers. As we will see, the TLC remained a national force in the Canadian labour movement for the next 70 years.

Another event that significantly expanded the scope of the Canadian union movement was the entry of the first international industrial union into Canada in 1881. Several unions in the United States, recognizing the limitations of organizing on the craft-based model, were promoting the idea that all workers, regardless of occupation or employer, should belong to unions. The first union to bring this idea to Canada was the **Knights of Labor**, which had successfully organized railway workers in the United States. The Knights' entry into the Canadian union movement began with the organization of a small group of workers in Hamilton. Eventually, the Knights had 400 "local assemblies" in Canada and over one million members worldwide.[22] The Knights of Labor had a significant impact on the Canadian labour movement because they organized workers in occupations that most existing Canadian unions considered too challenging to organize, such as railway work, mining, and employment in the resources sector. They even succeeded in organizing workers in "company towns," where simple matters such as getting access to the town itself were challenging, since the employer who controlled the town would usually forbid even a preliminary visit from a union organizer. The Knights of Labor also

The Knights of Labor march down the main street of Hamilton, 1881. Such processions were seen as a symbol of order and respectability rather than militancy.

organized workers—such as women and minorities—who had previously been excluded, intentionally or otherwise, from other unions' organizing efforts.[23]

The Knights' influence in Quebec was such that the province's "hierarchy" (the elite members of churches and government) obtained a letter from the Vatican that was read aloud in all Roman Catholic churches in the province in June 1886. The papal letter declared membership in the Knights of Labor a "grievous sin," because the organization supposedly required "unswerved obedience to occult chiefs" and thus allegedly required members to renounce their religious beliefs and loyalty to the church. Members of the Knights of Labor who belonged to the Roman Catholic Church were banned from taking communion, and had to file declarations with their parish priest that they had left the Knights if they wished to regain the privilege.[24] The letter caused some decline in the Knights' membership in Quebec, but it also caused a controversy in the province because of its perceived interference with union organizing and membership. The "General Master Workman" of the Knights, a position roughly parallel to president, met with American and Canadian Roman Catholic bishops to lobby against the letter's pronouncements. The bishops intervened with the church authorities on the Knights' behalf, and the letter was rescinded in mid-1887. After the letter was withdrawn, Quebec membership in the Knights promptly increased.

Table 3-1 presents a timeline of events in the 1800s.

THE INDUSTRIAL AGE: THE EARLY 1900s

In the late 1800s and early 1900s, the structure of work in Canada continued to undergo the process of transformation outlined in Chapter 2, evolving from rural-based individually controlled work to urban centralized factory-based work. An additional complication in the Canadian scenario was American ownership of Canadian organizations and industries. While foreign investment brought new industries to Canada, such as nickel mining and pulp and paper processing, many companies in these and other Canadian industries were controlled or owned outright by American financial interests.[25] Thus, the owners were not only separate from the workers in the factory but also located in another country, exacerbating the effects of the separation between capital and labour described in Chapter 2. While Canadian workers appreciated the employment that the new industries created, particularly since many of these industries operated in rural or remote areas with otherwise limited job opportunities,

TABLE 3-1 Canadian Industrial Relations Events in the 1800s

Early 1800s	Some evidence of craft unions in Saint John, New Brunswick
1816	Nova Scotia legislation involving "journeymen workmen" groups
1827	Informal worker groups formed in several regions
1827/1830	First recorded Canadian unions formed
Mid-1800s	Some British craft unions create international affiliates in Southern Ontario
Mid-/late 1800s	Continental movement
1872	Nine-Hour Movement
1872	Toronto typesetters' strike and use of monopoly laws to arrest strikers
1872	First federal industrial relations legislation passed
1873	First labour federation formed (Canadian Labour Union)
1881	First international industrial unions formed
1883	Trades and Labour Congress formed
1886	Papal letter in Quebec denouncing Knights of Labor

they resented the American management that too often seemed to favour options that would maximize the amount of profits flowing to the United States, and too rarely considered the circumstances of the workers or the communities where the industries were located.

A somewhat more positive form of American influence was evident in the Canadian union movement as more American union organizers arrived in Canada to recruit new members. While there were concerns about American unions being unsympathetic to Canadian workers' issues, it was also felt that the greater goal of increasing unionization in Canada was more important than the issue of where the union was based. Generally, the American organizers were welcomed. In 1898, the American Federation of Labor (AFL), the federation of craft unions headed by the influential leader Samuel Gompers, sent its first "fraternal delegate" to Canada to organize workers. By 1900, the AFL had over 10,000 members in its Canadian locals. Another significant event in 1900 was the passage of the federal **Conciliation Act**. This legislation created a federal department of labour and gave it the ability to appoint third-party intervenors or commissions of inquiry to assist in resolving labour disputes.[26]

The AFL's most active organizer in Canada, a carpenter from Hamilton named John Flett, was elected president of the TLC at its 1902 convention. The election of a craft union member as the president of the largest Canadian labour federation further reinforced craft unionism as the dominant model of organizing in Canada.[27] The influence of the American union movement in Canada was further solidified at the same convention by a motion restricting TLC membership. The delegates voted to forbid any national Canadian union from joining the TLC if an international union represented workers in the same occupation or with the same employer. The TLC delegates also decided to accept membership from only one central labour organization or federation in any given region of Canada. As a result of these decisions, the Knights of Labor locals and several national unions—totalling about one-fifth of the TLC's membership—were expelled.[28]

Much union organizing, however, took place independent of American or international unions in the early 1900s. An active economy created a high demand for workers, giving them greater power to advocate for better wages and working conditions. Workers often perceived unionization as necessary to ensure that wage rates matched the cost of living.[29] Economists who have studied wage levels during this period have noted that while the dollar amounts of wages increased, there was no increase in real wages (purchasing power) and that, during some periods, real wages actually decreased. Achieving a steady income was also important to the ever-increasing number of immigrants arriving in Canada to seek a better life, although many of these "cheap labour" immigrants were brought to the country specifically to work for substandard wages.[30]

One major industry that saw a good deal of union activity was the railway. Railways were expanding rapidly across Canada during this time and carrying increasing amounts of goods and passengers. Several major railway strikes took place, either to gain union recognition or to support demands for wage increases in light of hefty government subsidies to the industry. Workers felt that the government should subsidize not only expanded service but also better wages since the expansion of service was only possible because of the workers' efforts. Several of the major unions representing Canadian railway workers were international unions based in the United States, however, and the American unions were not totally sympathetic to the Canadian cause. In some of the strikes, the American-based railway unions, attempting to avoid conflict with American employers, sided with the railway owners and insisted that the Canadian workers accept less than desirable contract terms.[31] These events may be seen as some of the first indications that the Continental Movement might have negative, rather than positive, implications for Canadian workers.

As a result of the railway strikes, the federal government, with the encouragement of then-Deputy Minister of Labour William Lyon Mackenzie King, passed the **Industrial Disputes Investigation Act** in 1907. This legislation required that industrial disputes under federal jurisdiction be submitted to a neutral third party, who then would either make recommendations or, by prior agreement of the parties, impose a binding decision to solve the dispute. This act was later supplemented and replaced by other legislation, but it introduced principles that are still present in many current Canadian labour laws, such as the prohibition of strikes and lockouts during the time of a third-party intervention in a dispute and requirements for conciliation before a strike or lockout takes place.[32] (Conciliation and other forms of third-party intervention in collective bargaining disputes are described in detail in Chapter 10.)

During the early 1900s, there was significant strike activity in Atlantic Canada, where unions had been much more active in organizing less-skilled and non-craft workers than unions in central Canada. The majority of these strikes were undertaken by coal miners, who were represented mainly by the regionally based and locally controlled Provincial Workmen's Association.[33] But coal miners were not the only eastern workers going on strike. A total of 411 strikes were recorded in Atlantic Canada between 1901 and 1914, and 140 of these strikes were attributed to associations of unskilled labourers.[34] This statistic indicates that organizing and collective action in this region was not restricted to tradespeople and that it was much more broadly based than in the rest of the country.

The period of economic growth that began in the early 1900s lasted until about 1914, when American-based unions accounted for approximately 80 percent of the total Canadian union membership.[35] Part of this American domination in the union movement was due to extensive organizing in western Canada by the **Industrial Workers of the World** (IWW), nicknamed the "Wobblies." (The origin of the nickname is unclear, although the most common explanation is that it resulted from a pronunciation of the "IWW" acronym by an IWW organizer who had emigrated from China.) The American-based IWW was similar in philosophy and strategy to the Knights of Labor, although the

TABLE 3-2 Canadian Industrial Relations Events in the Early 1900s	
Early 1900s	American investment in Canadian industries
Early 1900s	Extensive organizing in Canada by American unions
Early 1900s	Strike activity in many regions and industries
1900	Federal *Conciliation Act* passed
1901	Knights of Labor and several national Canadian unions expelled from Trades and Labour Congress
1907	*Industrial Disputes Investigation Act* passed
1910s	International Workers of the World organize extensively in western provinces

Wobblies were more explicitly socialist in orientation, advocating general strikes as a means not only of achieving workers' demands, but also of bringing about a new egalitarian society.[36]

Table 3-2 presents a timeline of events in the early 1900s.

THE FIRST WORLD WAR ERA

The advent of the First World War, following a short economic depression, had a dramatic effect on the growth of Canadian unions. Three simultaneously occurring factors made unionization more attractive to Canadian workers. The first factor was the increased production needed to supply the war effort. Dissatisfaction in the workplace grew as workers were pressured to improve their rate of production without any corresponding improvement in wages. The second factor was the continuing mechanization of production that further reduced the market value of skilled craftspeople, as tasks formerly performed by workers were taken over by machines. And, finally, the federal government expanded the jurisdiction of the *Industrial Disputes Investigation Act* to include munitions industries. This expanded jurisdiction limited the ability of workers in those industries to strike in support of their demands. As one historian states, "Resentments began to coalesce into a conviction that the whole system was stacked against workers."[37]

Many workers felt that the unions already established in Canada, both international and domestic, were not adequately addressing workers' concerns. A central focus for this discontent was the issue of conscription, or forced enrolment in the military. The federal government, led by Prime Minister Robert Borden, brought in conscription to meet the government's commitment to Britain to supply a certain number of troops for its war effort. Many Canadians were upset that individuals opposed to the war were being forced through conscription to go to war and to endanger their lives; they also objected to the fact that the conscription process was structured so that workers, rather than the businesspeople profiting from the war, were being sent to the battlefields of Europe.

Despite these protests against conscription, the large Canadian unions and labour federations did not formally oppose it. The response of the TLC to the implementation of conscription was "one of inaction and compromise,"[38] and at the 1918 TLC convention, motions opposing conscription were defeated. This rejection may have occurred because of the perception in some parts of Canadian society that opposition to conscription was either outright treason or a failure to support the Canadian troops already at war. Nevertheless, the refusal of the majority of TLC delegates to take action on this significant issue caused dissent within the federation's ranks. Many of those frustrated with the inaction of established labour unions on conscription and other issues turned to more radical unions, which they felt could better represent their interests. One of the larger unions these dissenters joined was the American-based **One Big Union** (OBU), an industrial union that by 1919 had nearly 30,000 members in British Columbia.[39]

Two major events in this period illustrate how extreme the divisions between workers, government, and employers had become. The first was the death of Albert "Ginger" Goodwin, a labour organizer in British Columbia. Goodwin worked in the province's coal mines, mills, and smelters and organized unions in several of those industries. Goodwin also ran for the British Columbia legislature in 1916 as a Socialist Party of Canada candidate.

When the First World War began, Goodwin actively opposed conscription. He hid in the woods of Vancouver Island to avoid being forced into military service, and when his hiding place was discovered, he was shot and killed. The Dominion Police officer who shot him claimed that Goodwin had pointed a rifle at him. The officer's version of events did not completely match some interpretations of physical evidence from the incident, and, as a consequence, many union supporters believed that the officer was

Workers topple a streetcar on June 21, 1919, at the height of protests during the Winnipeg General Strike. At the end of this protest march, two lay dead and thirty were injured.

under special military orders to shoot Goodwin because of his union organizing activity. (One account of these events refutes the physical evidence that supposedly supports the "government conspiracy" theory, but notes: "Government and business rarely need to operate in the shadows or illegally to suppress workers' resistance to capital. . . . [Goodwin] was the victim of a particular set of social relations and the institutions created to protect them.")[40] Goodwin's death caused a one-day general strike of protest in Vancouver, and he is still considered a martyr by many in the union movement.

The other major event that illustrated the widening of social divisions is the **Winnipeg General Strike**. The strike, which began in May 1919, is particularly significant in Canadian labour history because it was the first extended, large-scale general strike involving workers from different occupations and unions. Previous large strikes either had been short in duration or had involved workers from a single union, occupation, or employer. In the months prior to the strike, many unions across Canada had gone on strike for increased wages and the regulation of working hours, and many had been unsuccessful in reaching their demands. This general frustration boiled over in Winnipeg, where some workers, primarily in the metal and building trades, were being denied the right to collective bargaining because employers were refusing to respond to contract demands.[41]

On May 15, between 30,000 and 35,000 unionized and non-unionized workers walked off their jobs.[42] The resulting shutdown had a major impact on a city of 200,000 residents, and the reaction of the establishment was swift. A Citizens' Committee of 1000, representing most of the businessmen and employers in the city and all three levels of government, attempted to force the workers to return to work. Sympathy strikes in support of the Winnipeg strikers took place in Edmonton, Saskatoon, Toronto, and Vancouver, as well as in many smaller Canadian cities.[43]

As the strike continued, tensions increased. The mayor of Winnipeg fired the entire city police force, which supported the strikers but had agreed to remain on duty, and replaced them with volunteer "special constables." The special constables clearly had more commitment to the orders of the civic government than to respecting the civil rights of the strikers, and their presence was denounced and resented. At the same time, the federal government took action in response to the lobbying efforts of the Citizens' Committee of 1000. Parliament passed an emergency motion that altered the *Immigration Act* to allow for immediate deportation of any immigrant, broadened the Criminal Code to allow police to make arrests on suspicion rather than evidence, and placed the burden of proof of innocence on any accused who were arrested. These were highly exceptional alterations to some very basic principles of Canadian law, and it soon became clear what the purpose of the changes was.

In mid-June, eight of the strike leaders were arrested in a single night and charged with various conspiracy-related offences. As it happened, seven of the eight arrested were immigrants and thus were eligible for deportation under the newly altered *Immigration Act*. The acting minister of justice, Arthur Meighen, suggested that all of those arrested who were immigrants should be deported. This statement made it apparent that opposition to the Winnipeg strike was becoming entrenched at the highest levels of power in Canadian society. In response to the arrests, the strikers organized a protest march in Winnipeg on June 21. The Royal Northwest Mounted Police forcefully interrupted the relatively peaceful march, and at the end of the subsequent violence, two people were dead and 30 seriously injured.

The strike leaders gradually recognized that the objectives of the strike would not be accomplished in the face of organized opposition from such powerful forces as the government, businesses, and employers. The strike ended on June 25 with an agreement establishing limited collective bargaining rights for the metal and building trades workers. However, the divisions and resentments caused by the strike did not quickly dissipate, even after the strikers returned to work.

Many Canadian labour historians identify the Winnipeg General Strike as a turning point in the Canadian union movement. Even with extensive organizing and widespread worker support, the union movement was unable to achieve its demands when opposed by the power of the state and the capitalist system. The workers involved in the strike were also disadvantaged by the dominance of international craft unions in the union movement. As had previously happened in strikes involving the Canadian railway industry, the international craft unions were willing to compromise their members' demands in order to maintain their own exclusivity and control over groups of workers and their close relationship with employers.

The OBU had been involved in events leading up to the Winnipeg General Strike, but soon after the strike, its influence in Canada decreased dramatically. This was because many members, although enthusiastic supporters of the OBU in principle, were unable to pay their union dues. Infighting between various regions and industries represented within the membership distracted attention from more significant issues, such as the financial problems facing the union.[44] The departure of lumber industry members, who intended to establish their own union, severely threatened the OBU's survival, since these members constituted about one-quarter of the total OBU membership in Canada. (The lumber workers were not completely successful in establishing an independent union of their own.) The OBU was also hurt by its participation in the 1919 Crowsnest Pass coal miners' strike, which failed to achieve the workers' demands. Consequently, the OBU's reputation as an effective worker representative was damaged. Although the OBU continued to exist, it was never able to regain the influence it once exerted.[45]

The end of the decade saw a somewhat more positive trend with new levels of unification in the Quebec labour movement. The development of unions in Quebec followed a somewhat different pattern than in the rest of Canada because of the involvement of the Catholic Church, which played a highly influential role in Quebec society at the time. Initially, many unions in Quebec were founded with the encouragement of Catholic leaders, who saw involvement in unionization as one way to re-establish the church's influence over the "labouring poor."[46] Unionization by Quebec-based and-controlled unions was also perceived as a way to resist the influence of international unions, which might not be sensitive to issues of Quebec independence and autonomy.[47] In 1921, the so-called "Catholic unions" formed the Confédération des travailleurs catholiques du Canada (CTCC). This federation became extensively involved in organizing workers in Quebec, and, although its formal links with the Catholic Church gradually dissipated, it was increasingly militant in defending workers against the "practised ethnocentrism" of American-owned firms.[48] The CTCC was also involved in several high-profile strikes, such as the 1949 dispute involving mineworkers in the Quebec community of Asbestos. The outcome of this dispute—the achievement of most of the workers' demands—was seen as a victory both against American-based corporations and the "autocratic" government of Premier Maurice Duplessis.[49] In 1961, the CTCC became the Confédération des

TABLE 3-3	Canadian Industrial Relations Events During the First World War Era
1918	War effort increases pressure for production without wage increases
1918	*Industrial Disputes Investigation Act* expanded to include munitions industries
1918	Trades and Labour Congress convention refuses to oppose conscription
1918	One Big Union organizes extensively in western provinces
1918	"Ginger" Goodwin killed on Vancouver Island
1919	Winnipeg General Strike
1919	Crowsnest Pass miners' strike
1921	Formation of Confédération des travailleurs catholiques du Canada (CTCC)

syndicats nationaux (CSN), or, in English, the **Confederation of National Trade Unions** (CNTU), which continues to exist today.

Table 3-3 presents a timeline of events during the First World War era.

AFTER THE FIRST WORLD WAR

The conclusion of the Winnipeg General Strike was followed by the economic conse-quences of the end of the First World War: widespread unemployment and wage cuts. Promoting unionization was difficult when most workers were grateful just to have a job and did not want to threaten that status by antagonizing their employers. There was also disunity in the Canadian labour movement, with fighting between Canadian and inter-national unions, craft and industrial unions, and unions with different regional concerns. Such disharmony did not make unionization attractive to workers.[50] A poor agricultural market, the crash of the American stock market in 1929, and the subsequent Depression made life difficult for most Canadian workers and even more difficult for those who were unable to find or keep work that paid enough to live on.

There was, however, some positive activity for Canadian unions during this period of gloom.[51] First, skilled workers were still needed for many production functions in factories and workplaces, and many of these groups of workers were able to maintain their unity as craftspeople. Their ability to organize powerful unions was limited by their relatively small numbers in the workforce, but they at least were able to maintain unions that represented their own interests. Second, in some occupations (such as steelworking and longshoring), workers formed "industrial councils" (which included the less-skilled workers in the same organization) to support demands made to employers. Third, communities of ethnic immigrants within many occupations, such as Ukrainians in mining and Jews in the clothing and fabric industries, created support and information networks that could then be built upon for unionization efforts.

Unemployed workers in many parts of Canada banded together in associations to lobby for better "relief payments" (similar to modern-day employment insurance). These associations also demanded better conditions in the government-created "relief camps," where many individuals—mostly young single men—were forced to reside if they could not find employment. The relief camps were run by the federal Department of Defence, and were very strictly governed. Inmates were forced to perform manual labour for minimal wages and live in primitive conditions. Moreover, they were not permitted to undertake any actions that would publicize their plight, such as making speeches, circulating petitions, or writing letters.

Though government relief projects provided work for unemployed men in the 1930s, many objected to the harsh working conditions. This discontent culminated in the 1935 "On to Ottawa Trek".

Two major events demonstrated the extent of the resistance to the relief camps. In 1935, a group of unemployed workers undertook the "On to Ottawa Trek," a protest that was intended to mobilize opposition to relief camps and culminate in a massive demonstration at the Parliament Buildings. The trek originated in Vancouver and swelled in size as supporters joined it in its journey across the country, but it was violently halted by the Royal Canadian Mounted Police when it reached Regina. In May 1938, protestors occupied several government buildings in downtown Vancouver to attempt to force an end to the relief camp system. The RCMP forcibly evicted the protestors on "Bloody Sunday," June 19; this event came to be known as the "post office riots." Though neither of these events succeeded in persuading governments to dismantle the relief camps, the experience that participants gained in planning and generating support proved useful in subsequent union organizing campaigns.

Radical politics entered Canadian unionism during this period, most notably through the influence of the Communist Party.[52] The Communist Party was distrusted by many Canadians, particularly those who had immigrated to Canada to escape countries under the oppressive rule of Communist governments. Despite this distrust, the Canadian Communist Party became an attractive political alternative for workers disillusioned by the way that established parties dominated the federal and provincial governments. The Communist Party promoted unionism as one way through which economic and capitalist systems would be transformed—a prospect that appealed to workers suffering through the Depression and events like the Winnipeg General Strike. Communist Party members became active in a number of union-organizing efforts across Canada. The party also launched the All-Canadian Congress of Labour, the first major alternative to the TLC as a national federation for Canadian unions. The Congress was formed in 1927 with a membership composed primarily of industrial unions.

A significant legal event during this time was the resolution of the question of federal and provincial jurisdiction over labour relations. The case of *Snider v. Toronto Electrical Commission* raised the question of whether federal labour relations legislation—specifically, the *Industrial Disputes Investigation Act*—applied to provincially owned industries. The case went to the highest court of Canadian jurisdiction at the time, the British Privy Council. The Privy Council's ruling in 1925 determined that the federal government's jurisdiction over labour relations extended only to federally regulated industries and that all other labour relations matters were the responsibility of provincial governments. While this ruling was welcomed because it cleared up an area of longstanding confusion, it also hampered the development of Canadian unions by establishing separate provincial and federal jurisdictions for labour relations law. Organizing was thus more difficult because of the necessity to comply with multiple, and possibly varied, provincial and federal labour laws.

Although it was clear from the *Snider* ruling that provincial governments were responsible for regulation of most industrial relations in Canada, not every provincial government had labour legislation at this point. The next major development in Canadian labour legislation occurred, like several other innovations in Canadian labour relations, as a result of legislative changes in the United States. One of the ways in which American president Franklin Roosevelt attempted to counteract the effects of the Depression was by promoting legislation that encouraged worker-driven initiatives, including legislation that would protect workers' rights to unionize. Roosevelt believed that such legislation would increase productivity by reducing strikes and other time-consuming conflicts caused by American employers' refusal to recognize or to bargain with unions (such refusal was legal at the time).

Roosevelt introduced several pieces of legislation that improved conditions for American workers, including a social security plan guaranteeing pensions for retired workers and a set of basic employment standards. For the Canadian labour movement, however, the **Wagner Act** of 1935 was the most important of these laws. It guaranteed three basic rights to American workers: the right to organize, the right to collective bargaining, and the right to strike without employer harassment. Under the *Wagner Act*, employers could not refuse to acknowledge a union as the workers' representative if a vote indicated the union had majority support among the workers. Once a union was recognized, the employer was compelled to bargain with the union and could not refuse to meet with it or simply ignore its demands. Under certain conditions, the union also had the right to undertake strike action to pressure the employer to agree to its bargaining demands. While the *Wagner Act* was criticized for being too biased in favour of unions and workers, there was also recognition that formal legislation of these rights would do much to reduce union-employer conflict in the United States, some of which had resulted in very bloody and violent clashes.

The effect of enshrining these rights in legislation was powerful, and union membership in the United States increased substantially after the *Wagner Act* was passed. The *Wagner Act*'s influence on Canadian law was not immediate, but, within the space of a few years after its passage, several provinces adopted provincial labour codes that included the same basic principles as the *Wagner Act*, although in a form that was somewhat less binding on the employer. Thus, the *Wagner Act* is very important in Canadian labour legislation: it was the model on which many Canadian labour codes were based, and it contains principles that are still present in most Canadian labour law.

Another influential event in the United States in 1935 was the founding of the **Congress of Industrial Organizations** (CIO). This federation was founded for two reasons: to represent workers in mass-production industries (becoming increasingly important in the American economy) and to organize unorganized workers. The CIO immediately ran into jurisdictional conflicts with the existing American Federation of

Labor (AFL), whose member unions already represented workers in some of the industries the CIO had targeted for membership. The AFL did not want to see its own membership base weakened by CIO member unions taking away AFL members, and its response to this perceived infringement was to expel CIO-affiliated unions from its own membership. The AFL instructed the TLC in Canada, which was the AFL's Canadian affiliate, to expel the same unions that had been expelled from the AFL in the United States. The TLC was reluctant to do so, recognizing the loss this would mean to its own membership base; however, under pressure from the AFL, it expelled its member unions that were CIO affiliates. In doing so, the TLC lost about 22,000 members and a considerable amount of power.[53] The CIO opened a Canadian office in 1937 and was successful in organizing Canadian steelworkers, autoworkers, and other production workers. The newly formed Canadian affiliate of the International Woodworkers of America, representing forestry workers, also joined the CIO.

The year 1935 saw the election of the first federal members of Parliament from the Co-operative Commonwealth Federation (CCF). This party was the forerunner of the present-day New Democratic Party, the Canadian political party that has been most strongly identified with the interests of the labour movement.

Table 3-4 presents a timeline of events in the post–First World War period.

TABLE 3-4 Canadian Industrial Relations Events After the First World War

1920s	Communist Party involved in union organizing
1925	*Snider v. Toronto Electrical Commission* ruling
1929–early 1940s	Depression
1930s	Formation of associations for unemployed workers
1935	*Wagner Act* passed in United States
1935	"On to Ottawa Trek"
1935	Congress of Industrial Organizations (CIO) formed in United States; CIO-affiliated unions in Canada expelled from Trades and Labour Congress
1935	First Co-operative Commonwealth Federation members elected to Parliament
1938	"Post office riots" in Vancouver

The Organizing Boat

The following is a description by Al Parkin, a British Columbia labour historian and former union organizer, of how organizing campaigns were conducted in coastal British Columbia logging operations in the late 1930s.

It was obvious right from the beginning that we had to have an organizing boat. In those days most of the big camps were in isolated areas up and down the coast in various coves and places. You had to rely on the Union Steamship and the CPR [boats] for transportation to get organizers in. That didn't work because quite often an organizer would come down a gangplank and be met on the float or dock by a delegation of company people and he would just be manhandled right back on again. So in 1936 [the Lumber and Sawmill Workers' Union] bought an ancient old yacht [that] by this time had gone downhill a bit. The first trips were often accompanied by lots of breakdowns and layovers while they tried to get parts to get things going again.

I was on one trip where the camp was situated about 20 to 25 miles back from the beach where the office was and where the company officials stayed. We pulled in there about two o'clock in the morning and tied up for about five minutes—just long enough for us to get off with our little packsacks with a bite to eat, a spare blanket, and our [union] dues books in them, and a couple of bundles of [union newspapers]. We

sneaked along the edge of the dock, keeping well away from the offices until we got ourselves out of the camp area and started up the highway. We only walked halfway in and then lay around out of sight for the balance of the day, until about four o'clock. Then we continued our walk, planning it so that we could reach camp just after the men had left the cookhouses to go back to the bunkhouses. We would then hold our little meetings, covering all the bunkhouses but first of all going to the fallers' bunkhouses because the fallers were the Scandinavians and once you were in the fallers' bunkhouses you didn't have to worry about getting kicked out by any stooges of the boss; you felt secure. Then once having established, shall we say, a certain amount of confidence among these workers, we could go into the other bunkhouses and circulate, sell the paper, collect dues, and sort of carry the message of the union.

Then at nine o'clock the lights went out (they always used to turn the power off) and we had to walk all the way back to the beach, which was another 22 miles or so. We got back to the boat about five o'clock the next morning and we hadn't slept at all. But that was the sort of thing you had to do in those days. It couldn't have been done without the boat. It was simply the only thing that made it possible to establish the loggers' local. Oh no, there's no question about it.

Source: Smith, H., and Wejr, P. "Fighting for Labour: Four Decades of Work in British Columbia, 1910–1950." *Sound Heritage 7[4]*, 1978, pp. 63–64.

THE SECOND WORLD WAR

The start of the Second World War gave the same stimulus to the Canadian economy as the start of the First World War had done. Employment dramatically increased because of increased production in support of the war effort. However, governments feared that war-related production would be disrupted by political radicals and militant workers, such as Communists involved in the Canadian union movement and workers who had been politicized by the relief camp experience. Thus, the federal government was much more interventionist in regulating the economy than it had been during the First World War.[54] One indication of this increased desire for governmental control was the 1939 expansion of the jurisdiction of the *Industrial Disputes Investigation Act*. The act's jurisdiction now included all "essential" war-related industries, and the act itself was changed to require strike votes (a vote among the membership on whether to undertake strike action) for a strike to be legal. To provide some balance to these controls on unionized workplaces, the government introduced wage and price controls to quell workers' fear that businesses and entrepreneurs would "profiteer" from wartime shortages of goods.

Unionization rates increased significantly after the start of the war, and the divisions between industrial and craft unions became more formal at the national levels of the Canadian union movement. In 1940, the All-Canadian Congress of Labour and the CIO joined to form the **Canadian Congress of Labour** (CCL). This gave Canada two national labour federations: the CCL, which maintained its affiliation with the American industrial union-based CIO, and the Trades and Labour Congress (TLC), which, as we have seen, was historically affiliated with the American craft-union-based American Federation of Labour (AFL). The CCL's affiliation with the CIO was less rigid than the TLC's affiliation with the AFL. Most notably, the CIO did not try to direct the business of its Canadian affiliates, which was something that the AFL had actively done in the past.[55]

Despite the restrictions imposed by the newly expanded jurisdiction of the *Industrial Disputes Investigation Act*, strike activity increased in the first few years of the war. By 1943, one of every three union members was on strike, a number that exceeded the previous peak of strike activity in 1919.[56] This level of strike activity was attributable to the expertise and resources that were now available to Canadian unions through their international affiliations. The international unions provided guidance and leadership based on experience gained elsewhere, and offered financial support so that striking workers could continue their actions after other resources were exhausted. The high level of strike activity was also attributable to the organizing and political experience that many union members had gained in the pre-war years. The federal government, headed by William Lyon Mackenzie King, did not recognize this new reality. It was only after a long and bitter gold miners' strike in northern Ontario in 1941–42, during which the government was criticized for ineffectiveness, that the government took action and reworked the federal labour legislation to acknowledge the increased skills and resources that union members possessed. The government was also encouraged to be more supportive of workers by some significant provincial and federal electoral wins by the CCF: these wins clearly indicated that workers were prepared to vote for political parties friendly to labour and to vote against governments that did not support workers' interests.

In early 1944, the federal government passed **P.C. 1003**, a wartime order-in-council (similar in effect to a law passed by Parliament in peacetime) modelled on the American *Wagner Act*. The provisions of P.C. 1003 included compulsory collective bargaining and the right of "employee representatives" to be certified as bargaining agents by a labour relations board if the representatives could prove that they had sufficient support among employees in a workplace. The passage of P.C. 1003 led to further union organizing because of the legislative recognition of employee and union rights, and Quebec and British Columbia passed similar acts at the provincial level.

Table 3-5 presents a timeline of events during the Second World War.

TABLE 3-5   Canadian Industrial Relations Events During the Second World War

1939	*Industrial Disputes Investigation Act* expanded to cover "essential" war-related industries and to require strike votes
1940	Canadian Congress of Labour formed
1941-42	Gold miners' strike in Ontario
1943	Highest level of strike activity to that point in Canadian history
1944	P.C. 1003 passed

AFTER THE SECOND WORLD WAR

When the Second World War ended in 1945, there were fears that the experience of the post-war economic depression that had followed the First World War would be repeated.[57] The return of soldiers from the war and the gradual reduction of the war industry led to unemployment in large cities, especially among women workers who had worked in factories while male workers were serving in the armed forces. The Mackenzie King government attempted to offset this economic decline by giving gratuities and tax credits to the returning veterans. The government also subsidized retraining and education programs to keep the veterans temporarily out of the labour market and thus avoid massive increases in unemployment rates.

An important event for union-management relations during this time was the settlement of the first major Canadian post-war strike. In late 1945, workers at the Ford motor plant in Windsor went on strike over the issue of job security, motivated by concerns about post-war downsizing, and demanded a "closed shop," where union membership was a condition of employment—that is, workers would have to join the union if they wanted to work in the plant. The dispute over the issue of the closed shop went to arbitration, and Justice Ivan Rand was chosen to make a decision. Rand's settlement determined that union dues would be automatically deducted from every worker's paycheque. In exchange, the union would allow individuals to formally opt out of union membership if they so desired. The automatic deduction of union dues was awarded in recognition of the union's activities in representing the interests of all workers to management. The so-called **Rand Formula** was being used by 90 percent of Canadian unions by 1950.[58]

Other unions, however, were less concerned with the closed shop and job security issues and more concerned with immediate issues, such as ensuring that wage rates kept pace with inflation. Post-war price increases led unionized workers to demand matching wage increases. Despite the existence of legislation ensuring workers' rights to organize and bargain collectively, many employers were not responsive to these demands. Employers had assumed that the passage of P.C. 1003 had been a temporary necessity to keep operations going during the war and that they would not be compelled to recognize or to bargain with unions once the war was over.[59] This conflict led to a series of large, extended strikes in 1946 involving the lumber industry in British Columbia, the shipping industry on the Great Lakes, and the textile industry in Quebec. Further large-scale strikes occurred regularly across the country for the next four years. It was clear that the Canadian industrial relations system needed the same sort of permanent regulation that the *Wagner Act* had brought to the American system. Thus, the federal government enshrined the principles of P.C. 1003 in the *Industrial Relations and Disputes Investigation Act* of 1948 (the precursor to the current *Canada Labour Code*). By 1950, nearly every province had a provincial labour code with similar guidelines.[60]

Another significant event in this period was the previously mentioned strike in the Quebec community of Asbestos in 1949. This strike was notable both because of the level of conflict it generated and because of its repercussions for the Quebec union movement. The cause of the strike was a breakdown in negotiations between the asbestos workers' union and the management of the American-owned plant in the community. The workers chose to undertake an illegal strike, which was promptly declared as such by the Quebec government. However, the union had support from the local Catholic churches and also from the powerful archbishop of Montreal, Joseph Charbonneau.[61] The archbishop had spent several years working in impoverished communities in northern Ontario and was well aware of the problems faced by workers in isolated towns controlled by American-based companies. He ordered that collections of money to support the strikers be taken at every Catholic church in Quebec. The provincial government of Premier Maurice Duplessis responded to the strike by sending armed police to Asbestos; strikers retaliated against the police presence by beating company officials and dynamiting company property. In early May, strikers who were incensed that the company had hired replacement workers to operate the mines attacked the mines and their police guards. More police arrived and arrested over 200 strikers.

The strike lasted until late June, when a settlement was negotiated with the help of the archbishop of Quebec. The initial agreement was that the union would be recertified and the striking workers would receive a small raise and be reinstated (except for those who had been convicted of violent activity during the strike). Other issues would be sent to arbitration. However, after production resumed, approximately 100 strikers were not reinstated, and the arbitration did not produce many gains. Nevertheless, the continued existence of the union was considered a victory both against the employer and against the Duplessis government, which had not been supportive of the strikers or the strike.

The Asbestos strike "served notice to the world that the Catholic unions were no less militant than their secular counterparts."[62] It also marked the end of the formal relationship between the Catholic Church and the union movement in Quebec. Under pressure from more conservative elements in Quebec society, the church sent Archbishop Charbonneau to a new posting in British Columbia. A "pastoral letter" in early 1950 formally removed the church from involvement in Quebec's trade unions.

Table 3-6 presents a timeline of post-Second World War events.

TABLE 3-6 Canadian Industrial Relations Events After the Second World War	
1945	Post-war unemployment
1945	Ford strike in Windsor; resolution creates Rand Formula
1946	Major strikes in lumber, shipping, and textile industries
1947	*Industrial Relations and Disputes Investigation Act* passed
1950	Provincial labour codes in place in nearly every province
1949-50	Asbestos strike in Quebec

THE 1950s AND 1960s

Most Canadian labour historians view the 1950s and 1960s as a period of relatively strife-free growth and development for unions.[63] Many basic issues, like the ability of workers to organize and to bargain collectively, had been resolved by the passage of federal and provincial labour legislation. And by this time the post-war effects on the economy and unemployment had dissipated. Even the inter-union disputes within Canada were reduced somewhat when, in 1956, the TLC and the CCL followed the lead of their American affiliates and merged to form a single national Canadian labour federation, the **Canadian Labour Congress** (CLC). The CLC in turn affiliated with a Quebec counterpart, the Quebec Federation of Labour (QFL). (The QFL operates under a different affiliation agreement with the CLC than do other CLC components, one significant difference being that local unions in Quebec whose parent union is a CLC member can choose to be affiliated with either the CLC or the QFL. This relationship is outlined in more detail in Chapter 4.)

One issue of concern to many people in the labour movement during this period was the increasing bureaucratization and centralization of the predominantly international unions.[64] Most large unions had a centralized office and paid staff, usually located in Ottawa or in a provincial capital to facilitate interactions with government. But there was concern, particularly in unions that had membership across the country, that this form of bureaucratic structure did not facilitate operations in a country with significant regional differences. The centralization of major operations and paid staff in a single location was thought to make union bureaucrats less sensitive to regional issues. There was also concern that those at the top of the centralized union structures were more focused on formalizing and strengthening their own power than on addressing the needs of the membership.

The influence of "parent" American unions was another problematic issue. The American branches of international unions were much larger than most Canadian branches; Canadian membership in international unions was usually a relatively small percentage of the union's total membership. Some Canadian union members felt that American union leaders did not care about Canadian concerns, since there were not usually enough Canadian members to make Canadian issues a priority in the international union. There was also a perception that American union leaders simply expected Canadian union members to follow what American members were doing, without taking into consideration the distinct characteristics of the Canadian economy and Canadian working conditions. And the concerns about centralization of Canadian union operations were heightened in the international unions, whose offices were usually located in American cities.

Trade unionist and future Canadian Senator Jean Marchand (right) pitches in during the Murdochville Copper Strike in Quebec, 1957. The outcome of the strike helped pave the way for Quebec's "Quiet Revolution" reforms of the 1960s.

Despite the general climate of relative peace, there were some bitter industrial disputes during this time. In 1957, a disagreement over the legality of a denied certification led to a lengthy and violent strike in Murdochville, Quebec, involving the United Steelworkers and a copper mining firm.[65] A striker was killed in a dynamite explosion, and strikebreakers rolled boulders onto the cars of demonstrators who supported the union. The strike, which lasted nearly seven months and involved 1,100 workers, ended with the union conceding defeat. The company sued the union for damages in a court case that dragged on for nearly 13 years.

Although the union ended up having to pay over $2 million in damages, it later succeeded in certifying the mine.

Another major dispute occurred in 1958 and 1959, when a local of the International Woodworkers of America (IWA) succeeded in obtaining a certification for lumber industry workers in Newfoundland after a lengthy organizing campaign. The employer rejected a conciliator's suggestions for the terms of a first collective agreement, and the union went on strike on the last day of 1958.[66] Violence soon erupted on the picket lines when replacement workers were brought in, and many strikers and union leaders were arrested and jailed. The premier of Newfoundland, Joey Smallwood, was opposed to the presence of the IWA because he considered it a "foreign union." It has been suggested that he was more concerned about the possibility of having a strong union in the Newfoundland lumber industry, instead of the existing weak unions in the province that generally conceded to employers' demands.[67] Smallwood announced the formation of a new union to replace the IWA. He also pushed a bill through the Newfoundland legislature that gave the government the authority to dissolve any union whose leaders "have been convicted of any heinous crime such as trafficking in narcotics, manslaughter, extortion, embezzlement, or perjury."[68] Under this bill, the IWA was decertified, as were the Teamsters, even though the latter had no direct involvement in the lumber industry dispute.

Although Smallwood's actions were denounced across the country, the IWA's reputation was severely damaged by a March 11, 1959, fight between strikers, RCMP, and Royal Newfoundland Constabulary police in which a policeman, William Moss, was fatally injured. This turned the tide of public opinion in Newfoundland against the IWA. Smallwood's union, the Brotherhood of Woods Workers, was taken over by the carpenters' union and became part of the CLC. Eventually, the carpenters' union was given the certification that the IWA had originally been granted, and Smallwood's controversial amendments to the province's labour code were rescinded.

The start of the 1960s saw the beginning of an extended period of growth in the Canadian union movement, mostly due to extensive organizing in the public sector. Public sector unionization had been relatively minor up to this point because of the perception that employment in the public service was, as the name suggests, a form of service to the community or the country that implicitly required a long-term commitment. The concept of "service" included the intrinsic satisfaction of contributing to the successful functioning of a democratic society. Because of the intrinsic satisfaction and service orientation of the work, public sector workers were usually prepared to accept a lower standard of compensation than they would earn for similar work in the private sector.[69] However, public servants were aware that private sector wages and working conditions were increasingly better than those in the public sector. Although federal and most provincial public servants had previously been explicitly denied collective bargaining rights, public servants in some provinces, such as Saskatchewan and Quebec, were granted full bargaining rights by the early 1960s. This innovation led to demands from other public servants—federal, provincial, regional, and municipal—for the same conditions.

In 1965, two circumstances made public sector unionization more of a priority for the federal government. Drawing lessons from a national postal strike, the government realized that ignoring public sector bargaining issues would have negative consequences. A federal election around the same time as the postal strike resulted in the election of a Liberal minority government. The Liberals in Parliament were dependent on the parliamentary support of the New Democratic Party—labour's friend—to maintain their power to govern.[70] Since the minority government would benefit in several ways from satisfying labour's demands, the federal government passed the *Public Service Staff Relations Act*, which gave federal public servants the right to arbitration or strike action to settle bargaining disputes. This act served as the model for most provincial public service legislation, and, by 1975, every province and territory had some form of labour relations legislation governing public service employees.

During the same period, when federal public service labour issues were prominent, extensive organizing took place in the **para-public sector**. This sector, as noted earlier, consists of municipal or regional organizations that receive funding from governments but whose employees are not directly employed by the government; hospitals and schools, for example, are in the para-public sector. There was dissatisfaction among workers in this sector because of threatened funding cutbacks, which would likely result in job losses. There was also frustration, particularly among professionals, that the bureaucratic structures of para-public organizations did not respect or value employees' skills and judgement.[71] Disputes over pay equity for public servants eventually led to extensive public sector strikes in Quebec, some involving as many as 200,000 workers.[72] The pattern of unionization in the para-public sector was somewhat different from that in the public sector, where most workers joined a public sector union rather than a union specific to their occupation. Some para-public sector workers joined existing public sector unions; others joined the Canadian Union of Public Employees (CUPE), a newer public sector union that conducted extensive organizing campaigns among municipal and regional government workers. Other public and para-public sector workers, such as teachers and social workers, already belonged to professional associations representing their occupation. Some professional employees obtained certification by remaining in the same association but applying to have the association recognized as a union.

It was apparent during this period that changes in technology were having an impact on Canadian workplaces, as they had begun to reduce or eliminate entire occupations. As early as 1957, railway workers had gone on strike (and lost) over the issue of the replacement of coal-burning locomotives with diesel-powered locomotives. The introduction of diesel locomotives meant the loss of jobs for workers who handled coal for the railways. In 1964, typesetters at Toronto-area newspapers went on strike because technological changes in printing had eliminated the need for jobs such as theirs. Management was able to continue production of the newspapers, and the strike did not formally end until 1972, "although the union had lost long before then."[73]

Table 3-7 presents a timeline of events in the 1950s and 1960s.

TABLE 3-7 Canadian Industrial Relations Events in the 1950s and 1960s

1956	Canadian Labour Congress (CLC) forms and affiliates with Quebec Federation of Labour (QFL)
1957	Murdochville copper miners' strike
1957	Railway workers' strike over introduction of diesel locomotives
1958	International Woodworkers' strike in Newfoundland
1960s	Extensive public and para-public sector organizing
1964-72	Toronto typesetters' strike
1965	*Federal Public Service Staff Relations Act* passed

THE 1970s AND 1980s

By the early 1970s, several different factors were causing disruption in the Canadian economy.[74] Unemployment and inflation were both on the rise, and growth in North American markets was being overshadowed by the emergence of new economic powers in other parts of the world. Much discussion about this disruption focused on unions, especially the relatively new public sector unions. Unions' emphasis on wages in collective bargaining contributed to the perception that unions caused price inflation; the cost of higher wages, it was argued, led to higher prices. Unions were also blamed for lower productivity, since the workplace rules imposed by collective agreements supposedly reduced employers' ability to use workers in the most efficient fashion. In summary, union demands for better wages and working conditions were seen as a widespread cause of rising prices and, more simply, as "greed and selfishness."[75]

As a result of these perceptions, the federal government began to explore the possibility of imposing wage controls. The CLC and other labour organizations mounted strong opposition to this idea, believing that it would be unfair to restrict wages if there were no parallel controls on prices. Despite these concerns, in October 1975, the government implemented a three-year program of wage and price controls. The entire public sector workforce, workers in large private sector companies, and self-employed professionals were restricted to predetermined limits for annual wage increases. Collective agreements falling under the program had to be submitted to an Anti-Inflation Board in Ottawa, which would determine whether the agreements followed the guidelines and, would recommend or impose revisions if not. The board was also expected to regulate price increases, which were to match increases in costs, but "this stipulation was a good deal more flexible than the explicitly defined wage targets."[76]

Opposition to the wage and price controls was immediate and strong. The CLC pulled its representatives from all federal consultative committees and promoted the idea of a one-day national strike to protest the program. Strike activity rose significantly after the program was introduced, and the one-day national strike proposed by the CLC took place on October 15, 1976. More than one million workers across the country participated, although levels of participation were uneven across regions.[77] However, overall participation was high enough to set records for amounts of time lost due to industrial conflict.[78] The wage and price controls program ended as planned in 1978, but its effects were unclear. Prices increased sharply after the program ended, but, as several historians point out, controlling domestic prices and wages is a difficult task in an economy as dependent on international trade as Canada's. Thus, the fact that prices increased after the program was no longer in effect does not indicate that the program was a success.

By the start of the 1980s, Canadian government economic policy was much more interventionist than it had been in preceding years.[79] Interest rates were deliberately increased to combat high inflation, but the side effect was a recession that saw the worst unemployment levels since the 1930s. At the same time, eligibility for the established "safety net" of social programs was tightened, which meant that many Canadians who formerly relied on various forms of social assistance to carry them through periods of unemployment or underemployment were no longer eligible for such support. In addition, the amount of funding directed to social assistance programs was reduced in many Canadian jurisdictions, further restricting the support available for Canadians unable to find work.

Because the unionization of the public sector was still perceived as a cause of Canada's economic problems, both federal and provincial governments took action to reduce the bargaining power of public sector unions. Stricter penalties against public sector strikes were instituted in many jurisdictions, and back-to-work legislation was frequently used to end strikes. These deterrents, however, did not slow down strike activity in the public sector. In fact, there were numerous private and public sector strikes in the 1970s and 1980s, some resulting in jail terms for union leaders and financial penalties for unions that refused to obey back-to-work orders. These high-profile strikes included the 1972 Quebec public sector strike, which resulted in the jailing of several union leaders who defied a back-to-work order, and the 1978 nationwide postal worker strike, during which union leaders were arrested after refusing to honour Parliament's law forcing a return to work. There was also an eight-and-a-half-month-long strike by Ontario steelworkers in 1978, followed by another lengthy strike by the same workers in 1981.

The 1980s saw cutbacks in public service employment in many provinces owing to reduced government funding and the "contracting out" of functions previously performed by unionized public sector workers. Changes in legislation in several Canadian jurisdictions made organizing and bargaining more difficult than in the past; one such change was the federal government's 1982 suspension of public servants' bargaining rights for two years.

The passage of the federal ***Charter of Rights and Freedoms*** in 1982 provided a new set of guidelines for Canadian industrial relations, as the Charter included guarantees of such rights as the freedom of association. As outlined in Chapter 1, several cases tested the applicability of Charter provisions to questions such as whether the choice to belong to a union or the right to picket were protected; the decisions in most of these cases did not strengthen or protect unions' powers. The election of a federal Conservative government in 1984 and the emergence of major business alliances such as the Business Council on National Issues also created a hostile atmosphere for Canadian unions. This period also saw several major private sector strikes, such as the lengthy and occasionally violent 1984 strike at the Gainer's meat-packing plant in Edmonton—a conflict that indicated that unionized workers were not prepared to give up the standards they had previously achieved.

During this period, a fair amount of internal dissent within the union movement threatened solidarity on larger issues. In 1973, the **Confederation of Canadian Unions** (CCU) was formed as an alternative to the Canadian Labour Congress. The CCU was meant to be a national federation for Canadian-based unions that felt that the CLC's domination by American-controlled international unions did not serve Canadian interests. However, the CCU had difficulty challenging the CLC's established power and control. The CCU's position received some support from the construction workers' unions in the CLC, which shared the resentment of American dominance. This resentment was intensified when the CLC did not support the construction unions in a dispute between local and international unions in Quebec. (These unions broke away in 1982 to form a new Canadian Federation of Labour, which lasted until 1997.) However, the American dominance of the CLC was most severely challenged in 1985 when one of the largest constituencies within the CLC, the Canadian locals of the United Auto Workers, split with their American parent and formed the Canadian Auto Workers. This union has since merged with other unions and organized new locals to become one of the largest private sector unions in Canada.

The trend toward Canadian control of Canadian unions that developed during this period has continued to the present day. The demise of the CFL and CCU has left the CLC and the Quebec-based QFL and CNTU as the major national labour federations in Canada.

Table 3-8 presents a timeline of events in the 1970s and 1980s.

TABLE 3-8 Canadian Industrial Relations Events in the 1970s and 1980s

1973	Confederation of Canadian Unions (CCU) formed
1974	Federal wage and price controls program begins
1976	National one-day strike on October 15
1978	Postal workers' strike
1978	Federal wage and price controls program ends
1982	Canadian Federation of Labour (CFL) formed
1982	*Charter of Rights and Freedoms* becomes law
1984	Gainer's meat-packing plant strike in Edmonton begins
1985	Canadian Auto Workers formed

INTO THE 21st CENTURY

The major event affecting Canadian industrial relations in the late 1990s was the advent of liberalized international trade.[80] This included the signing of the **North American Free Trade Agreement** (NAFTA) in 1992, Canada's participation in worldwide tariff reductions under the 1994 General Agreement on Tariffs and Trade, and the 1995 creation of the World Trade Organization. A side agreement to NAFTA protects basic standards in each member country, such as minimum wages and the right to bargain collectively. However, NAFTA does not provide for the creation of common social and labour standards among participating countries, as do similar trade agreements such as the European Union agreement.

The effects of NAFTA and other agreements have been varied. Some employers have used NAFTA provisions to move formerly unionized jobs to regions where labour costs are lower and workers are not unionized. These movements have caused job losses in Canada and brought pressure on unions to agree to lower wage rates so products can remain cost-competitive. As will be outlined in Chapters 12 and 13, Canadian unions have been more reluctant to agree to such concessions than their American counterparts and have proposed increases in productivity and workplace structuring rather than wage reductions to keep product costs competitive.

Unionization rates in Canada did not drop significantly in the 1990s and the early part of the 21st century, although there has been a slow gradual decline since the 1970s. Chapter 13 outlines how unions are attempting to reverse this trend by targeting organizing campaigns at groups of workers traditionally under-represented in union membership: women, minorities, and workers in service industries, where the majority of new jobs in Canada are created. Unions in Quebec have tried other strategies to maintain their viability, including signing "social contracts" wherein unions guarantee labour peace in exchange for employment security and a formal role in administration of the collective agreement. This strategy has, at least initially, resulted in a dramatic drop in strike rates in Quebec, formerly one of the most strike-prone jurisdictions in Canada.[81]

A final trend of note in the 1990s, and one that is still playing itself out, is the reduced political influence of the New Democratic Party (NDP), historically, as noted previously, the Canadian political party most closely allied with union interests. The NDP has not had the same formal links with organized labour as the Labour Party in Britain has had with the Trades Union Congress (TUC), the British equivalent of the CLC (the TUC, for example, enjoys elected representation on the national Labour Party executive). But the NDP has still been the political party considered most sympathetic to Canadian workers' and unions' concerns. Although the NDP has never formed a federal government in Canada, in the 1960s and 1970s it had a sizeable number of members in the House of Commons, and NDP majorities were achieved in several provincial legislative assemblies. In the 2004 federal election, the NDP almost doubled its share of the popular vote from the previous election, gaining 19 seats in Parliament. In exchange for supporting the Liberal minority government in certain parliamentary votes, the party was able to negotiate support for its position on several issues. However, there have been very few provincial NDP majority governments in the past two decades. No feasible political alternative to the NDP has yet presented itself to the labour movement; it remains to be seen what this instability in union-friendly political representation will mean for future legislation and policy.

The start of the 21st century saw several major events in Canadian industrial relations. Some were structural changes, such as the federal government's review of the Canada Labour Code. This review was completed in 2006 and is now the subject of further discussion.[82] Also, two of Canada's largest unions, the United Steelworkers of America and the International Wood and Allied Workers of America, merged in 2004. This union, after several other mergers, is now known as the United Steel, Paper and Forestry, Rubber, Manufacturing, Energy, Allied Industrial and Service Workers International Union; it is the third-largest union in Canada with 280,000 members.[83] Also, as noted in Chapter 1, in 2007 the Supreme Court ruled in favour of several British Columbia unions that complained that the provincial government changed their collective agreement without consultation; this ruling may have significant implications for future union-management interactions in Canada.

However, the most visible events were several long-term large-scale labour disputes driven by financial issues and characterized by high levels of conflict. For example, the National Hockey League (NHL) lockout, which lasted nearly 300 days and resulted in the cancellation of the league's 2004–05 season, was caused primarily by a disagreement between players and the team owners and NHL administration over the imposition of salary caps, which would set a maximum amount for each team's payroll. The league and the team owners argued that salary caps were necessary to ensure that the league would be financially viable and that salary costs would not continue to grow to unaffordable levels, especially for teams in small markets. The players' union objected to the idea of salary caps, perceiving them as a restriction on the salaries of individual players; the union argued that salaries should be determined by the free market, and that the players should not suffer financially because the league chose to expand into markets where the viability of professional hockey was questionable. Ultimately, though, the union was unable to hold out against the combined strength of the team owners and the league, and the dispute was settled in July 2005 with the parties agreeing to a six-year collective agreement, including a salary cap provision. The parties are scheduled to start negotiating for a new agreement in 2010, although the union has the option of extending the existing collective agreement for an additional year if it chooses.

Other recent high-profile labour disputes in Canada have involved workers at a number of post-secondary institutions (e.g., the York University strike of 2008–0? the Université du Québec à Montréal strike in 2009), civic workers (e.g., the V city workers' strike of 2007 and the Toronto and Windsor city workers' str' other public sector workers (e.g., the Alberta teachers' strike in 20? Columbia paramedics' strike in 2009), and several groups of w' sector employers (e.g., the 2008 strike by workers at the

Saskatchewan, the 2006 lockout of workers at a Stora Enso plant in Nova Scotia, and the United Steelworkers strike against Vale Inco that started in 2009).

One feature of many of these disputes that represented a relatively new development on the Canadian labour scene was the use of technology. For example, during a dispute at TELUS in British Columbia in 2005, union members and locals created numerous websites carrying news about the conflict, blogs from picketers, and links to sites where union supporters could use express their dissatisfaction with the dispute or cancel their TELUS services. The company used technology as a tool in the dispute as well; in its role as an Internet service provider, one of TELUS' first actions when the dispute began was to bar all TELUS subscribers from viewing a union-run website that TELUS claimed contained proprietary and confidential information. The union agreed to remove the information, and TELUS restored access to the site, although not without enduring accusations of "arbitrary and unaccountable" behaviour.[84] Later in the dispute, the company also contracted out some customer service telephone work to call centres in India and the Philippines. None of these actions would have been feasible even a decade ago, but they indicate that technology may be an increasingly important factor in the progress or outcome of labour disputes, especially with the more recent introduction of other forms of social media such as YouTube, Facebook, and Twitter.

Another significant recent development in the Canadian labour movement has been the concentrated effort to unionize Walmart stores. Walmart has 241 stores in Canada with 60,000 employees, and the company earns U.S.$10.3 billion in annual worldwide profits.[85] There were several earlier attempts to unionize Walmart stores in the United States, but none were completely successful, in part, because of the company's considerable resources and its willingness to actively resist unionization campaigns. The United Food and Commercial Workers (UFCW), supported by several other large Canadian unions, identified Walmart as a prime target for unionization in Canada, not only because the company's workforce represented potential gains in union membership, but also because success in certifying locals at Walmart stores would be a foothold for unionizing workers at other "big-box" retailers, which are becoming a larger part of the Canadian economy. Canada's labour legislation is also considered more supportive of unionization than American labour legislation,[86] and thus there is the perception that Canadian organizing campaigns might succeed where American campaigns have failed. As noted in Chapter 1, the Supreme Court of Canada ruled that Walmart was justified in closing a recently unionized store in Quebec, which Walmart claimed had been unprofitable. However, the UFCW has not been deterred by these events and is continuing its campaign.

Finally, another development that may affect the face of Canadian unions in the future is some unions exploring different forms of worker representation, and different forms of cooperation with management. For example, the agreement that the Canadian Auto Workers union signed with auto parts manufacturer Magna International in 2007 allowed the union to represent Magna's employees, with Magna's consent, in exchange for the union agreeing not to go on strike to resolve contract disputes.[87] This agreement was criticized by other unions, who argued that giving up the right to strike deprived workers of a powerful way to support their bargaining demands. The Canadian Auto Workers were also heavily involved in the restructuring of the North American auto industry that resulted from the 2008 worldwide financial crisis. The historically powerful automobile workers' unions in the United States and Canada agreed to new contracts including concessions in such areas as wages and benefits: concessions which, in Canada, union bargainers had resisted for years.[88] It remains to be seen whether other Canadian unions will choose to, or be expected to, make similar changes.

SUMMARY

The history of industrial relations in Canada is long and varied. It contains manifestations of many of the forces that have shaped Canada as a whole: conflict between regions, conflict between economic and social classes, and conflict between different ideals. At the conclusion of this intricate story, and with the lessons of the past kept in mind, the future can be viewed negatively or positively. The negative perspective would include the power of internationalization, perhaps greater now than at any time in Canada's past, and the pressures it may exert on Canada's industrial relations system. The negative perspective might also view the slow decline in unionization rates and the weakening representation of unions' interests in the political arena as forces that will further erode the power of unions in Canada. On the other hand, the positive perspective would compare the Canadian industrial relations experience to the American industrial relations experience and note that Canada's unionization rates have remained steady while American rates have declined sharply and show little signs of recovering to previous levels. The positive perspective, after considering the history that this chapter has reviewed, would note how the actors in the Canadian industrial relations system have continually been successful in shaping the system to adapt to whatever challenges have developed. The positive perspective would suggest that the Canadian industrial relations system has continued to exist and function for well over a century and that there is no reason to expect that its adaptability will not continue. As with all histories, the story will continue to be written one way or the other.

KEY TERMS FOR CHAPTER 3

Canadian Congress of Labour (p. 95)
Canadian Labour Congress (p. 99)
Charter of Rights and Freedoms (p. 106)
Conciliation Act (p. 82)
Confederation of Canadian Unions (p. 106)
Confederation of National Trade Unions (p. 89)
Congress of Industrial Organizations (p. 92)
continental movement (p. 77)
craft union (p. 75)
Industrial Disputes Investigation Act (p. 83)
industrial unionism (p. 76)
Industrial Workers of the World (p. 83)
international unions (p. 77)
Knights of Labor (p. 79)
monopoly laws (p. 78)
Nine-Hour Movement (p. 77)
North American Free Trade Agreement (p. 107)
One Big Union (p. 85)
para-public sector (p. 102)
P.C. 1003 (p. 96)
primary industries (p. 73)
Rand Formula (p. 97)
secondary industries (p. 73)
tertiary industries (p. 74)

Trades and Labour Congress (p. 79)
Wagner Act (p. 92)
Winnipeg General Strike (p. 86)

DISCUSSION QUESTIONS FOR CHAPTER 3

1. Explain why the craft union model of organization was dominant in the early Canadian union movement.
2. What are the negative aspects of the craft union model?
3. How does a craft union differ from an industrial union?
4. What were the advantages and disadvantages for Canadians joining an international union rather than a Canadian-based union?
5. Describe and compare the effects that the two world wars had on the Canadian economy and on the union movement.
6. Describe the relationship between the *Wagner Act* and P.C. 1003.
7. How has the history of the union movement in Quebec differed from that in the rest of Canada?
8. Outline the reasons why union organizing occurred in the public and para-public sectors.
9. How have Canada's international trade linkages affected conditions for workers in Canada?
10. Do you agree with the negative or the positive perspectives outlined at the end of the chapter? Explain why.

EXERCISES FOR CHAPTER 3

1. Choose a union that you are familiar with or that you can research. (You can select either a local of a union or a union as a whole, although this exercise may be easier to conduct if you select a local.) Using the information available to you, describe the history of this union. You may want to answer such questions as:

- When was the union formed?
- What were the reasons for its formation?
- How has the union evolved or changed since its formation, and why?
- What would you see as the most significant events in the history of this union?
- Can you identify events or trends described in this chapter that have had an impact on the history of this union?
- What do you think will be important issues in the future for this union?

2. Using the information in this chapter and whatever additional material you can acquire, describe the history of industrial relations in your province or geographic area. You may want to address questions such as:

- What was the first union (or worker association) organized in your area, and how did it come into existence?
- How has labour legislation in your province or area evolved and changed?
- Who are some of the more significant individuals or groups in the industrial relations history of your province or area, and why are they important?
- Have any of the events or trends described in this chapter affected the industrial relations history of your province or area?
- What do you see as being important future issues for industrial relations in your province or area?

References

[1] Creighton, D. (1970). *Canada's first century, 1867–1967*. Toronto: Macmillan.

[2] The Atlas of Canada, <http://atlas.nrcan.gc.ca/site/english/index.html>.

[3] Downie, B.M. (1992). Industrial relations in elementary and secondary education: a system transformed? In Chaykowski, R.P., and Verma, A. (Eds.), *Industrial relations in Canadian industry*. Toronto: Dryden.

[4] Craig, A.W.J., and Solomon, N.A. (1996). *The system of industrial relations in Canada*. Toronto: Prentice-Hall Canada.

[5] Forsey, E. (1982). *Trade unions in Canada*. Toronto: University of Toronto Press.

[6] Morton, D., and Copp, T. (1984). *Working people: an illustrated history of the Canadian labour movement*. Ottawa: Deneau Publishers.

[7] Drache, D. (1994). The Canadian working class, 1820–1920. In Bercuson, D.J., and Bright, D. (Eds.), *Canadian labour history: selected readings* (2nd edition). Toronto: Copp Clark Longman.

[8] Russell, B. (1990). *Back to work? Labour, state, and industrial relations in Canada*. Toronto: Nelson.

[9] Lipton, C. (1978). *The trade union movement in Canada, 1827–1959*. Toronto: NC Press.

[10] For example, Williams, J. (1975). *The story of unions in Canada*. Toronto: J.M. Dent and Sons (Canada); Morton and Copp, *op. cit.*

[11] Forsey, *op. cit.*

[12] Heron, C. (1989). *The Canadian labour movement: a short history*. Toronto: James Lorimer.

[13] Logan, H. (1928). *The history of trade-union organization in Canada*. Chicago: University of Chicago Press.

[14] Heron, *op. cit.*

[15] Forsey, *op. cit.*

[16] Heron, *op. cit.*

[17] Forsey *op. cit*; Logan, *op. cit.*

[18] Morton and Copp, *op. cit.*

[19] Heron, *op. cit.*

[20] Heron, *op. cit.*

[21] Drache, *op. cit.*

[22] Heron, *op. cit.*

[23] Forsey, *op. cit.*

[24] Forsey, *op. cit.*

[25] Heron, *op. cit.*

[26] Russell, *op. cit.*

[27] Morton and Copp, *op. cit.*

[28] Drache, *op. cit.*

[29] Lipton, *op. cit.*

[30] Creese, G. (1988). Exclusion or solidarity? Vancouver workers confront the "Oriental problem." In MacDowell, L.S., and Radforth, I.W. (Eds.) (2000), *Canadian working class history* (2nd edition). Toronto: Canadian Scholars' Press.

[31] Lipton, *op. cit.*

[32] Williams, *op. cit.*

[33] Logan, *op. cit.*

[34] McKay, I. (1983). Strikes in the Maritimes, 1901–1914. In Bercuson and Bright, *op. cit.*

[35] Palmer, B.D. (1983). *Working-class experience: the rise and reconstitution of Canadian labour, 1800–1980.* Toronto: Butterworth and Co.

[36] Leier, M. (1999). *Rebel life: the life and times of Robert Gosden, revolutionary, mystic, labour spy.* Vancouver: New Star Books.

[37] Heron, *op. cit.*, p. 52.

[38] Leier, *op. cit.*

[39] Leier, *op. cit.*

[40] Leier, *op. cit.*, p. 84.

[41] Palmer, *op. cit.*

[42] Lipton, *op. cit.*

[43] Palmer, *op. cit.*

[44] Bercuson, D. (1978). Labour's civil war. In Bercuson and Bright, *op. cit.*

[45] Bercuson, *op. cit.*

[46] Palmer, *op. cit.*

[47] Rouillard, J. (1987). Major changes in the Confédération des travailleurs catholiques du Canada. In MacDowell and Radforth, *op. cit.*

[48] Palmer, *op. cit.*

[49] Williams, *op. cit.*

[50] Wejr, P., and Smith, H. (1978). Fighting for labour: four decades of work in British Columbia, 1910–1950. *Sound Heritage 7(4)*, 63–64.

[51] Heron, *op. cit.*

[52] Heron, *op. cit.*

[53] Williams, *op. cit.*

[54] Heron, *op. cit.*

[55] Williams, *op. cit.*

[56] Heron, *op. cit.*

[57] Morton and Copp, *op. cit.*

[58] Roberts, W., and Bullen, J. (1985). A heritage of hope and struggle: workers, unions, and politics in Canada, 1932–1982. In Bercuson and Bright, *op. cit.*

[59] Morton and Copp, *op. cit.*

[60] Heron, *op. cit.*

[61] Morton and Copp, *op. cit.*

[62] Morton and Copp, *op. cit.*, p. 200.

[63] Godard, J. (1990). *Industrial relations, the economy and society.* Toronto, ON: McGraw-Hill Ryerson.

[64] Heron, *op. cit.*

[65] Williams, *op. cit.*

[66] Williams, *op. cit.*

[67] Morton and Copp, *op. cit.*

[68] Bill amending *Labour Relations Act*, Newfoundland House of Assembly, 6 March 1959, quoted in Williams, *op. cit.*

[69] Godard, *op. cit.*

[70] Heron, *op. cit.*

[71] Heron, *op. cit.*

[72] Williams, *op. cit.*

[73] Williams, *op. cit.*, p. 213.

[74] Heron, *op. cit.*

[75] Heron, *op. cit.*, p. 121.

[76] Russell, *op. cit.*

[77] Heron, *op. cit.*

[78] Russell, *op. cit.*

[79] Heron, *op. cit.*

[80] Lipsig-Mummé, C. (2000). Trade union and labour relations systems in comparative perspective. In Gunderson, M., Ponak, A., and Taras, D.G. (Eds.), *Union-management relations in Canada* (4th edition). Toronto: Addison Wesley Longman.

[81] Déom, E., and Boivin, J. (2000). Labour-management relations in Quebec. In Gunderson, Ponak, and Taras, *op. cit.*

[82] Social Development Canada. Minister Fontana announces appointment to lead review of federal labour standards. (2004, December 2). Available at <http://www.sdc.gc.ca/en/cs/comm/hrsd/news/2004/041202.shtml>; Human Resources and Skills Development Canada,

"Discussion Paper on the Review of Labour Standards in the *Canada Labour Code*." (2009, June 1). Available at <http://www.rhdcc-hrsdc.gc.ca/eng/labour/employment_standards/fls/discussion_paper/page01.shtml.>.

[83] Workplace Information Directorate. *Union Membership in Canada—2007*. Available at <http://www.hrsdc.gc.ca/en/lp/wid/union_membership.shtml>.

[84] OpenNet Initiative, Telus blocks consumer access to labour union web site and filters an additional 766 unrelated sites (2005, August 2). Available at <http://www.opennetinitiative.net/bulletins/010/>.

[85] Walmart Canada website. Available at <http://www.wal-martcanada.ca>.

[86] Lipset, S.M., and Meltz, N.M. (2004). *The paradox of American unionism: why Americans like unions more than Canadians do but join much less*. Ithaca, NY: Cornell University Press.

[87] Van Alphen, T. (2007, October 16). CAW shelves right to strike: Magna and auto workers aim to build union-management relationships. *The Star*. Toronto. Available at <http://www.thestar.com/Business/article/267140>.

[88] Chrysler, CAW reach deal to save company $240m a year (2008, April 28). CBC News. Available at <http://www.cbc.ca/money/story/2009/04/24/chrysler-caw-union-concessions.html>

Labour Council Addresses Larger Issues

Almost 20 years ago, the Calgary and District Labour Council (CDLC) changed its focus to helping not only its union members, but also the community they serve.

"We really wanted to add our community's perspective to the labour council and the actions that we do," says Gordon Christie, who was executive secretary/organizer at the CDLC until his retirement in 2008. This entails working closely with local women's groups, environment groups, peace groups, and other community-based and non-governmental organizations.

"We try to represent the best views of all working people," says Christie. While unions

represent workers on work sites and negotiate collective agreements, the council reaches beyond labour negotiations to lobby for human rights and social justice.

The CDLC represents 64 union locals, with approximately 33,000 members. 95 percent of these members are located in the City of Calgary. However, the council's reach extends east and west to the British Columbia and Saskatchewan borders, north to Airdrie and south to High River. These unions and their members cover a full range of employee types and levels, from unskilled to semi-skilled to highly skilled. The number of members is divided equally between the public and private sector and between men and women.

In addition to providing strike support and education for all workers in the community, the CDLC has been involved in a number of activities, including helping to create the Alberta Coalition Against Poverty, which works with Calgary's homeless people, and lobbying for higher minimum wage rates by waging a Living Wage Campaign.

The CDLC is one of 135 labour councils across Canada, all under the umbrella of the Canadian Labour Congress.

"Whether you're in Calgary or Toronto or in rural Nova Scotia or rural Saskatchewan, the struggles of the labour councils and the struggles of our unions and our workers are very similar," says Christie. "What really makes me proud about the labour movement is that we have national, provincial, and local organizations . . . We have the best structure and communications right across Canada."

THE STRUCTURE OF CANADIAN UNIONS

objectives

In this chapter, we discuss the structure of unions in Canada. We begin by examining the function, structure, and role of the local union. Then we will turn our attention to labour councils. Finally, we will discuss the provincial, national, and international organizations of labour. At the end of the chapter, you should be able to:

- describe the formation and operation of a local union
- understand the relationship between a local union and its regional, national, and international union
- outline the function of labour councils
- describe how a labour federation is structured
- identify the role played by provincial, territorial, national, and international labour federations

INTRODUCTION

The labour movement in Canada consists of a large and complex network of direct and indirect relationships. The structure of the Canadian labour movement contains three levels that roughly parallel the three levels of Canadian government. The Canadian Labour Congress (CLC) is the largest national labour federation, and several smaller, Quebec-based national labour federations also represent specific groups within the Canadian labour movement. At the provincial or territorial level, provincial or territorial labour federations act as the coordinating bodies for the labour movement in each area. At the municipal or regional level, labour councils are the coordinating body for joint union activity. And at the workplace level, we find the local union. The local union is the smallest unit of regional, national, and international unions, but it is considered the cornerstone of the union structure, as it is the basis for all other parts of the structure.

Figure 4-1 outlines the relationships between the various union structures in Canada. To facilitate our discussion of this complex structure, we will start our examination of union structures at the local level and then move upward through the larger levels of union structures.

THE LOCAL UNION

The first level of the Canadian labour movement structure is the **local union**, often referred to simply as the "local". The term "local" is used to indicate the fact that most workplace-level unions in Canada are smaller units of a larger union. The local union's name will reflect this relationship with the larger union. For example, the local union representing workers at one Edmonton location of TELUS, the telecommunications company, is Local 208 of the Telecommunications Workers Union.

A local union is created when workers at one or more work sites, often having the same occupation or working at different locations for the same employer or type of employer, come together to form a union. At the point of formation, the workers have the choice of forming an independent union or joining an existing one. Usually, workers choose to join an established union, because of the expertise and resources that an existing union can offer new members who may be relatively inexperienced in such skills as negotiating collective agreements. However, workers do occasionally decide to establish

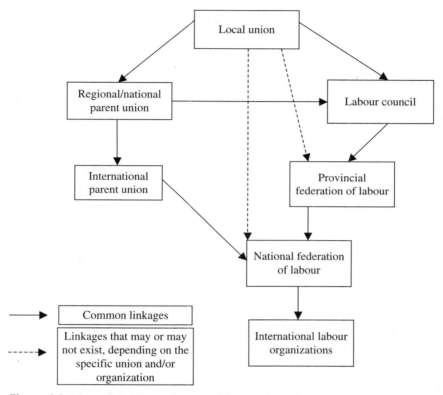

Figure 4-1 *Relationships Between the Parts of the Canadian Labour Movement*

an independent union. One Canadian example of a new independent union was the one formed by workers at a McDonald's restaurant in downtown Montreal. A Quebec labour federation assisted the restaurant workers in their organizing, but the workers chose to create a new union: le Syndicat des travailleuses et travailleurs du McDo-CSN.[1] (The name translates as "McDonald's Workers' Union"; the "CSN" indicates the new union's affiliation with the Confédération des syndicats nationaux, the labour federation that assisted the workers.) The workers' intent in creating this new union was to be independently represented, since they believed that the working conditions in McDonald's restaurants were not identical to those at other eating establishments. (The union was successful in gaining certification at the Montreal location, but soon after the union was certified, the employer closed the business, blaming a rent increase.)[2]

Local unions can vary considerably in size depending on the potential number of union members, the number and proximity of workplaces that could have members of the same local, and the structure of the relevant employment sector. A single local could contain all the workers at a number of different workplaces, or all the workers who perform the same type of work; it could also contain all the workers at a single workplace regardless of their individual occupations. Thus, there is really no such thing as a "typical" local size, because the size of a local depends on specific characteristics of the employer and the employees. Labour relations boards have been known to certify locals that have only a single or a few members, but these are rare exceptions rather than the rule. Larger locals have more bargaining power with the employer or employers than smaller ones, so unions are more likely to expend their resources organizing larger rather than smaller groups of workers.

The principles of democracy and collectivism are the guiding principles of the Canadian labour movement. The application of these principles in union operations is demonstrated by the fact that many of the most important functions of unions take place at the local level. It is, essentially, the members of the locals who decide on the direction the union will take. Thus, the structure of the local union is designed to put the principles of participation and democracy into action.

Structure of the Local Union

The "administrative apparatus" of Canadian unions is "only lightly regulated" by Canadian labour law.[3] Most Canadian labour legislation only requires unions to file their constitutions with the appropriate labour relations board and to make regular financial reports to the membership. Beyond those minimal requirements, the union membership is generally free to structure the union as it sees fit. However, as we will see, the union is also expected to operate in a manner that is free from discrimination and that allows democratic participation by the membership.

At the initial meeting of a new local, and at regular intervals thereafter, the local members elect the members they wish to run the local. This group of elected individuals is known as the **union executive**. Most local unions are governed by an executive consisting of a president, one or more vice-presidents, a secretary, and a treasurer. There may be other positions on the executive depending on the size of the local and the strategic interests of the membership. For example, if a local includes workers from different work sites, there may be an elected position on the local executive for a representative from each site where the local has members. Other unions have executive positions to represent particular constituencies within the membership, such as an executive member representing female or First Nations workers. Some unions have executive positions to represent specific issues such as health and safety or human rights. These types of positions are more common in larger locals, where issues of concern to particular constituents or individual workplaces might not otherwise come to the executive's attention.

Depending on the size of the local, executive positions can be full- or part-time, paid or volunteer positions. Some unions negotiate clauses in their collective agreements to allow paid time off work for those members who are elected to executive positions in the local. Workers who take time away from their jobs to serve on the union executive usually retain the seniority, benefits, and other conditions associated with their jobs. In other words, their status when they return to their job is the same as it would have been if they had not taken any time off, and they must be permitted to return to the same job they had before taking time off for union activities. Most union constitutions also allow executive members to be appointed rather than elected if there are no candidates for an elected position, or if other circumstances preclude holding an election (for example, if an executive member resigns and the vacated position needs to be filled immediately).

There are two other positions in the structure of many local unions: shop stewards and paid staff. **Shop stewards** are union members who investigate individual workers' complaints or grievances and act as the workers' advocate to management. The shop steward is the union's first-line representative—the person whom workers will approach if a situation requiring immediate assistance arises in the workplace. One of the several functions shop stewards serve is to attend disciplinary meetings, where a worker meets with management to discuss his or her behaviour. Shop stewards attend such meetings to ensure that correct disciplinary procedures are followed and also to act as a witness to the events in case there are subsequent disputes over what was discussed or agreed to. Distributing union literature and welcoming new union members are other functions that shop stewards perform in the workplace. Shop stewards may be elected or they may be volunteers.

Larger local unions will often have a paid staff to assist in the administration of the union's operations. Some locals, particularly those that are part of craft unions, will have a **business agent**. This individual is responsible for handling day-to-day union functions and assisting the executive members in their jobs.[4] In some industries and occupations, one business agent may serve more than one local, especially if the union has many small locals in the same geographic area.

In addition to providing support to the union executive members, the business agent usually plays a significant role in important union activities such as contract negotiations and grievance handling. Both of these activities are outlined in greater detail in subsequent chapters, but at this point we will note that the business agent is usually a member of or an advisor to the union negotiating team during collective bargaining. The business agent also may be responsible for presenting grievances to the employer and achieving a resolution of the conflict, or for presenting grievance cases to a third party for resolution.

In many unions, the business agent has a great deal of responsibility and power. The business agent has the advantage of remaining in his or her job on a permanent basis, while union executive members serve for a limited term. This situation means that the business agent usually acquires in-depth knowledge of the union and its operations; executive members usually do not have the time to develop this level of familiarity. Consequently, executive members often rely on the business agent for guidance and direction, rather than the other way around. In some unions, the business agent is not hired by the local union itself, but is appointed by the regional, national, or international union—which means that the business agent may also serve as the messenger who tells the local what direction its larger union wishes it to follow.

Locals also may employ administrative or secretarial support staff. It is interesting to note that these paid staff members may be unionized, but they generally belong to a different union than the one they are employed by.

The members of a local union pay monthly membership dues; these are either calculated as a flat fee or as a percentage of salary or wages. The amount of dues and the method of calculation are outlined in the local's constitution and bylaws. The funds generated by the monthly dues pay for the services and support required to operate the local union: staff salaries, operating costs, and fixed expenses such as office rent or equipment maintenance. Some of the revenue from membership dues may be directed to special causes, such as building funds or cash reserves to be used for strike pay in the event of a strike or lockout. As we will see, a portion of the dues revenue is also given to the larger regional, national, or international union, and some of those funds are directed to the operations of the Canadian Labour Congress if the union is affiliated with that organization.

Functions of the Local Union

The local union carries out several important functions on behalf of its members. As noted, the direction of each of these functions is determined by collective and democratic action, usually through a vote of the membership. Unions usually have regular membership meetings to vote on issues, although most union executives have the power, through the union's constitution, to call for votes to be held independent of regular meetings if an issue warrants immediate attention.

The local union carries out three major functions: dealing with workplace problems or grievances, collective bargaining, and coordinating political or social activity. As we saw in the discussion of the shop steward's role, the local union represents its membership in day-to-day interactions in the workplace, and this extends to representing workers if there are problems or complaints. The union also represents its members in the process of collective bargaining. In this process, which is discussed in more detail in Chapters 7 and 8, the union is responsible for three types of bargaining-related activity: it determines what outcomes the membership wants to achieve from the bargaining process, it prioritizes the desired outcomes and determines bargaining strategy, and it participates in bargaining sessions with the employer. And finally, the local union usually participates in political or social activities outside the workplace. Examples of this sort of activity include making presentations to local government bodies such as city councils, participating in events to support other unions or social organizations that are facing difficulties, and participating in charitable or fundraising activities.

The Canadian Auto Workers Union (CAW) participates in many campaigns on social issues, such as advocating for national child care.

As previously indicated, decisions on how these functions are carried out are made by the membership, usually through votes or through discussion at membership meetings.

In reality, however, two factors determine whether the union's actions are actually those that the majority of the membership desires.

The first factor is the influence of the union's business agent. If the business agent has more experience than the union members or executive in dealing with a particular issue, the agent may advise (or pressure) the membership into following his or her preferred course of action. This situation may be particularly noticeable when the business agent has several years of experience in the job and the union executive has undergone turnover on a regular basis, thus giving the business agent far greater expertise than the elected officials. As well, the business agent is sometimes encouraged by the local's regional or national affiliate union to advise (or pressure) the membership into following the regional or national union's preferred direction.

The second factor affecting whether union activities truly reflect the membership's wishes is the proportion of union members who actually participate in votes or discussions. Historically, there are varied levels of participation in local union activities in Canada. Member participation tends to be high for important events, such as votes to ratify collective agreements after the conclusion of negotiations, but low for regular unexceptional events, such as monthly meetings.[5] The number of members willing to undertake such activities as running for executive positions or serving on committees also varies considerably.[6]

The effects of varying member participation in local unions have been addressed by a number of researchers. Some have argued that low levels of participation in regular union activities are not a problem, because low participation indicates that the membership is satisfied with the executive's work and the direction that the union as a whole is taking. According to this perspective, unions should be concerned about participation levels only if participation is low for important events like contract ratification votes.[7] Others argue that continuously low participation levels are a problem because they cause excessive amounts of work for those who do participate, which can ultimately lead to burnout, stress, and frustration for those individuals.[8] Low levels of general participation can make it difficult for union leaders to determine the membership's true needs or wishes, since the majority of the membership have not taken part in activities like meetings or voting to demonstrate their opinions.

Another problem caused by low membership participation in union activities is suggested by the so-called **iron law of oligarchy**.[9] This "law" states that if the majority of the membership of any organization does not consistently participate in the organization's operations, leadership of the organization eventually becomes concentrated in the hands of an elite who are not easily removed from their positions of power. In the case of a union, the iron law of oligarchy explains the possible effect of actions such as union executive members serving multiple terms. If union members do not regularly volunteer to be part of the executive, the same small group of individuals will continue to form the executive. These individuals' extensive executive experience allows them to acquire even more experience and power, making it difficult for other, non-executive union members to oppose them.

Researchers point out that union participation can take many different forms.[10] Informal participation may simply involve talking about union issues with other union members, while formal participation may entail serving on the union executive. If members participate in both informal and formal ways, then their degree of participation is not accurately reflected in the numbers attending meetings or standing as candidates in union elections. There are varied reasons for participation, and different forms of participation are driven by distinct motivations. Members may participate because they want a voice in the organization, or because they feel obligated to serve the organization that works to represent them—that is, their motivation is similar to the motivations that result in "organizational citizenship" behaviour.[11] Interestingly, union participation does not appear to be related to an employee's level of job satisfaction, but does appear to reduce the likelihood that the employee will leave the organization.[12] The willingness to participate may also be driven by the individual's perception of how successful the union is in serving its members. If that perception is negative—that is, if the union is seen as not adequately serving its members—the individual may participate in a negative way, such as by complaining about the union's activities to co-workers or to the union leadership.[13] It should also be noted that an individual's union participation may not be consistent over time. Participation in union activities at one point may not be a reliable predictor of later union participation; the strongest influence on continued union participation appears to be an individual's attitudinal commitment to the union.[14]

To conclude our discussion of local union functions, we should mention that some research suggests that while Canadians are generally satisfied with the common functions that unions carry out, some feel that the range of union activities could be broadened. A survey of 341 employed Canadians indicated that they are generally satisfied with unions' performance in so-called **business union** activities such as bargaining.[15] However, a significant number of respondents felt that local unions placed a relatively low level of importance on "integrative" activities such as conflict resolution and representing workers to management—activities that they felt should also be considered important union functions. Respondents also thought that unions should put more effort into informing workers about political issues, advocating laws to help working people, and fighting for the interests and values of working Canadians.

Report: Lack of Worksite Inspectors Is Dangerous for Workers

CALGARY—Alberta has less work site health and safety inspectors than many other provinces, even with an increasing number of workers in dangerous industries, according to a new report from the Alberta Federation of Labour.

"Albertans face one of the most dangerous workplaces in the country," said Gil McGowan, president of the federation, which represents more than two dozen Alberta unions.

The federation's report is being released to coincide with the National Day of Mourning, an annual union and community event to remember workers injured or killed on the job.

The report, titled *Danger: Workers at Risk*, says the provincial government employs 1.4 health and safety inspectors per 10,000 workers, while the national average is 2.08.

Only British Columbia and Quebec employ fewer inspectors, says the report, which examines federal census data.

The federation's report says that spending on Alberta's workplace safety programs has not kept pace with inflation, even as Alberta's oil and gas and construction industries have flourished.

Both industries include large numbers of high-risk jobs.

Alberta's rate of workers killed on the job, nine per 100,000, was the second highest among the provinces in 2008—Newfoundland and Labrador was first. The national rate was 7.24.

"If something isn't done, there will be consequences," McGowan said.

Source: Cryderman, Kelly. "Alberta Lags Other Provinces in Funding Work Inspections." *The Calgary Herald*, April 28, 2010, p. B3.

REGIONAL, NATIONAL, AND INTERNATIONAL UNIONS

As noted in the previous section, most, although not all, local unions belong to a larger regional, national, or international union. As we know from the history outlined in Chapter 3, an "international" union in Canada is usually one based in the United States, a "national" union is based in Canada, and a "regional" union is one that, for practical reasons, has a specific attachment to a region. In British Columbia, for example, the Federation of Post-Secondary Educators is a regional union representing instructors at some universities, colleges, and technical institutes in that province only. Because of differences in how post-secondary education is structured and administered across Canadian provinces, these instructors have chosen to belong to a regional union existing only in their province. (In contrast, however, college instructors in some other provinces have decided to join national unions [e.g., the National Union of Public and General Employees or the Canadian Union of Public Employees] because of the increased power associated with membership in a larger union.)

The generic term for regional, national, and international unions is **parent unions**. For the sake of brevity, we will use this term in our subsequent discussion, although we will use the specific terms when appropriate in order to identify differences in how regional, national, and international unions are structured.

In Canada, there are 175 national unions, 39 international unions, and 605 unions that have no national or international affiliation. However, a more meaningful indicator of union affiliations is the numbers of members in each of these types of unions. Approximately 67 percent of union members in Canada belong to a national union, 28 percent to an international union, and only 5 percent to an unaffiliated union.[16]

To give some further perspective on the size of parent unions, Table 4-1 presents membership figures for the largest regional, national, and international unions in Canada.

Structure of Parent Unions

Like local unions, parent unions are governed by an elected executive. The executive of a parent union usually consists of the same main positions as the executive of a local union (e.g., president, vice-president(s), secretary, and treasurer). Parent union executives usually also include representation from constituencies within the union. For example, a regional union executive often has representation from each local in its membership. A national union executive usually has representation from each region where it has members (e.g., by province or by area, such as Western Canada or Atlantic Canada). International unions operating in Canada usually have a designated executive position for a Canadian representative. The individuals in these positions are, depending on the individual union, either elected directly by the entire membership, or elected by delegates who are expected to represent the views of the members at the local level. As at the local level, under certain circumstances executive members can be appointed rather than elected.

TABLE 4-1   Largest Regional, National, and International Unions in Canada

Name of Union	Number of Members in 2007	Affiliation with National or Centralized Labour Federation
Canadian Union of Public Employees (CUPE)	548,880	CLC
National Union of Public and General Employees (NUPGE)	340,000	CLC
United Steel, Paper and Forestry, Rubber, Manufacturing, Energy, Allied Industrial and Service Workers International Union – AFL-CIO/CLC	280,000	AFL-CIO/CLC
National Automobile, Aerospace, Transportation, and General Workers Union of Canada (CAW-Canada)	265,000	CLC
United Food and Commercial Workers International Union (UFCW)	245,330	CtW/CLC
Canadian Teachers' Federation	219,000	n/a
Public Service Alliance of Canada	166,960	CLC
Ontario Teachers' Federation (a component of the Canadian Teachers' Federation)	155,000	CLC
Communication, Energy and Paperworkers Union of Canada	150,100	CLC
Canadian Federation of Nurses	135,000	CLC
Fédération de la santé et des services sociaux	117,130	CSN
Ontario Public Service Employees Union (a component of the National Union of Public and General Employees)	113,500	CLC
Teamsters Canada	108,510	CtW/CLC

TABLE 4-1 Largest Regional, National, and International Unions in Canada (Continued)

Name of Union	Number of Members in 2007	Affiliation with National or Centralized Labour Federation
Service Employees International Union - Canada	86,860	CtW/CLC
Elementary Teachers Federation of Ontario	71,690	CLC
Alberta Union of Provincial Employees	69,000	Independent
Canadian Police Association	66,800	n/a
Laborers' International Union of North America	65,000	CtW
FTQ Construction	61,600	CLC
BC Government and Service Employees' Union (a component of the National Union of Provincial and General Employees)	61,564	CLC

Key to affiliations:
CLC – Canadian Labour Congress
AFL-CIO – American Federation of Labor–Congress of Industrial Organizations
CSN – Confédération des syndicats nationaux
CtW – Change to Win

Source: *Union Membership in Canada–2007*, Strategic Policy, Analysis, and Workplace Information Directorate, Labour Program, Human Resources and Skills Development Canada. Available at <www.hrsdc.gc.ca/en/lp/wid/union_membership.shtml>.

The affairs of the parent union are governed by a democratic decision-making process based on membership participation. However, parent unions do not usually rely on a decision-making mechanism involving every individual member at the local level. The main decision-making mechanism for a parent union is the **convention**, or **congress**—a meeting that is usually held annually. Each local union is entitled to send delegates to the convention; delegates are elected by the local members, appointed by the executive, or chosen by some combination of these two methods.

The number of delegates that each local is allowed to send to the convention is usually based on the size of the local union. One method of allocating the number of delegates allows larger locals to send more delegates than smaller locals. In some parent unions, however, each local is allocated the same number of delegates regardless of the number of members in the local, based on the principle that one member's vote should not carry more weight than another's simply because that member happens to belong to a larger local.

At the convention, delegates usually hear reports on the union's business since the previous convention, such as financial and activity reports. They may also vote on such issues as altering the terms of the parent union's constitution or adjusting the amount of dues that members of local unions pay. Policies of a more general nature may also be brought forward with a request for a formal motion of support from the parent union; for example, a human rights organization may request that the convention pass a motion condemning the actions of a certain government or country. The delegates also decide upon the policies and directions that will guide the parent union in its operations. Some parent unions hold executive elections at their conventions as well.

Decisions and votes at conventions usually occur in general plenary sessions that all delegates attend. However, committees or caucuses of delegates often discuss issues or motions before they are presented to the plenary, and make recommendations on whether the plenary should support a particular motion. As in any large organization, the parent union's convention is characterized by a great deal of political activity, as individuals or delegations lobby others in attempt to sway the direction of votes on a motion. Sometimes a motion is passed or defeated not because that choice represents the preferences of the union members, but because the motion's supporters or opponents have been the most persuasive lobbyists.

Canadian Labour Congress members Bertrand Begin (L) and Allan Pride (R) hang a banner on an Ottawa overpass to promote the CLC's support for public medicare.

Like the local union, the parent union also has a paid staff, but because the parent union is larger and performs more functions than the local union, its staff is larger and fulfills a wider range of functions. Most parent unions have specially trained staff to provide assistance in negotiations with employers or to help organize new locals. Parent unions may also employ economists, lawyers, and research specialists to assist locals or the parent union itself in gathering and analyzing information. National or international unions may also employ, directly or on contract, government lobbyists to present the union's views to government members. And, of course, the parent union will employ administrative staff to oversee day-to-day operations.

Functions of Parent Unions

Parent unions serve a variety of functions designed both to support the locals and to maintain the overall health of the union as a whole. Parent unions help create local unions by providing support, often in the form of a trained organizer who will guide potential union members through the process of gaining legal recognition for the new local. Once a local is established, the parent union supports the local's ongoing activities. This support includes assisting the local union with workplace issues. For example, the parent union can help a local to resolve a conflict with an employer by informing the local of solutions reached by other locals facing the same problem. It is also common for the parent union to offer advice to locals involved in collective bargaining, even to the point of having parent union representatives observe bargaining sessions and suggest strategy to the local union's negotiators. If the parent union includes locals that represent workers in similar occupations, the parent union can help those working in the same occupation achieve comparable gains in collective bargaining or assist them in promoting changes to legislation governing their occupation. The parent union may conduct educational programs for its members. These are delivered by trained union educators and cover issues such as labour law or conflict-resolution techniques. Member education can also be conducted through regular publications or website updates that keep all of the parent union's membership informed on union activities and issues.

The parent union's operations are financed through the union dues paid by individual union members. A percentage of the fees paid to the local union is sent to the parent union to finance its operations. A parent union usually designates a percentage of the fees it receives for a strike fund, which is used to make payments to the union's members during strikes or lockouts. This fund may be channelled directly to local members as soon as a strike or lockout begins if the local does not have its own strike fund, or it may be used as a supplement if the individual local has insufficient funds in its own strike fund.

The parent union may also perform the important function of representing its membership on labour councils, provincial labour federations, or national labour federations. This is a somewhat difficult function to describe in structural terms because a parent union or a local union may belong to these organizations either directly or through another affiliation. For example, if a regional union is also part of a national union, it may belong to a provincial or national labour federation directly or it may be represented in the federation by the national union. Local unions that are not affiliated with a parent union may also be affiliated with these organizations either directly or through an intermediary organization. For example, a local union that belongs to a labour council may be represented in a provincial or national labour federation through the labour council, or it may be directly affiliated on its own. The form of this affiliation depends on the individual union, its own affiliations, and the membership policies of the labour council or labour federation.

Rather than attempting to untangle these potentially complex structural relationships, we will instead focus on explaining the structure and functions of labour councils and labour federations in order to provide a general understanding of how these organizations operate.

LABOUR COUNCILS

A **labour council** is an organization composed of delegates from many different local unions. It is distinct from a labour federation in that it usually represents unions in a region within a province or territory, whereas labour federations in Canada are provincial or national in scope. Table 4-2 provides examples of labour councils in some Canadian provinces.

Structure of Labour Councils

Each local union that is a member of the labour council appoints or elects a delegate to represent the local on the labour council. These delegates then democratically elect officers to form an executive of the labour council. Each officer of the labour council must

TABLE 4-2 Examples of Labour Councils in Canada	
Alberta	Edmonton and District Labour Council
	Medicine Hat and District Labour Council
British Columbia	North Okanagan Labour Council
	Vancouver and District Labour Council
Manitoba	Selkirk and District Labour Council
	Winnipeg Labour Council
New Brunswick	Acadian Peninsula Labour Council
	Restigouche District Labour Council
Newfoundland and Labrador	St. John's and District Labour Council
Nova Scotia	Cape Breton and District Labour Council
	Truro and District Labour Council
Ontario	Guelph and District Labour Council
	Sarnia and District Labour Council
Quebec	Conseil du travail de la Côte-Nord à Sept-Îles
Saskatchewan	Saskatoon and District Labour Council
	Weyburn and District Labour Council

be a member **in good standing** of an affiliated union. To be a member in good standing, a member must be eligible for membership in his or her local union and must comply with the constitution and bylaws of the local union. This provision is in place to ensure that delegates to labour councils, rather than acting on their personal beliefs, act as much as possible in accordance with the wishes of the local union members they represent.

As most labour councils across Canada have limited funds and no full-time staff, unpaid elected officers, together with volunteers from among the delegates and other union members, carry on the labour council's work. This work is financed through dues from local union affiliates, usually calculated on a per capita basis (each union affiliate is charged a membership rate based on how many members the affiliate has).

Affiliation with a labour council is voluntary for a local union, but all local unions are encouraged to join a labour council. The constitution of the Canadian Labour Congress (CLC), the largest national labour federation in Canada, requires that local unions affiliated with the CLC also be affiliated with a labour council in their region to maintain their standing as CLC members.

Functions of Labour Councils

Labour councils represent workers' interests to local government, municipal councils, boards, and commissions. They bring together local unions in a community and help these unions actively participate in their community. Labour councils are also responsible for carrying out the policies of the labour movement at the regional level.

A labour council involves itself in a diverse range of activities. It is often involved in providing strike support for local unions, and it works toward broader social goals such as available and affordable child care, accessible education, and maintenance of health care and social services systems. Labour councils are also involved in regional community campaigns and fundraising for charitable organizations. Those labour councils that are affiliated with the Canadian Labour Congress also take on the task of hosting local CLC education programs.

Labour councils have also sought alliances among other organizations such as women's, anti-poverty, and seniors' groups, churches, and non-affiliated unions to build consensus and support for legislation and other actions to benefit all Canadians. For example, the New Westminster and District Labour Council in British Columbia was strongly involved in the campaign that resulted in the New Westminster City Council adopting a "living wage" policy—the first of its kind in Canada. This policy states that all persons working on the city's premises and properties, even if they are not directly employed by the city, will be paid no less than the hourly wage rate needed to support a family of four with two parents working full-time.[17]

Labour councils are also active in their provincial or territorial federations of labour. They often serve as the mechanism through which information from the provincial or territorial federation is distributed to unions in their region. We will now outline the structure and functions of provincial labour federations.

PROVINCIAL LABOUR FEDERATIONS

Like a labour council, a **provincial labour federation** is an organization composed of unions. However, as the name suggests, the federation comprises unions from an entire province or territory. Local unions without a regional, national, or international affiliation may join a provincial labour federation directly; local unions that are affiliated with parent unions are usually represented in the provincial labour federation by the parent union. Table 4-3 outlines the size of each Canadian provincial labour federation.

TABLE 4-3 Provincial Labour Federations in Canada	
Name	**Number of Members**
Alberta Federation of Labour	137,000
British Columbia Federation of Labour	450,000
Manitoba Federation of Labour	90,000
New Brunswick Federation of Labour	35,000
Newfoundland and Labrador Federation of Labour	50,000
Northwest Territories Federation of Labour (includes Nunavut)	8,500
Nova Scotia Federation of Labour	70,000
Ontario Federation of Labour	700,000
Prince Edward Island Federation of Labour	10,000
Quebec Federation of Labour (Fédération des travailleurs et travailleuses du Québec)	500,000
Saskatchewan Federation of Labour	85,000
Yukon Federation of Labour	4,000

Note: Membership figures as of April 2010.

Structure of Provincial Labour Federations

The structure of provincial labour federations is very similar to the structure of regional, national, and international unions. The members of the federation elect executive officers who are in charge of carrying out the federation's business; this election usually takes place at a convention that is attended by delegates from member unions. At the conventions, policies and action plans are developed and voted on. As well, delegates decide upon the directions and issues that the federation will pursue in the coming year. The labour federation executive also meets with memberships and constituencies as needed to deal with issues of immediate concern.

Participation issues and the effect of the "iron law of oligarchy" are as apparent within provincial labour federations as they are within local or regional unions. Small unions or unions with limited resources may belong to a provincial labour federation, but they may not have sufficient membership or resources to participate fully in the federation's operations. Other unions may put a higher priority on managing their own internal operations and serving their membership's immediate needs than on participating in external organizations. Thus, the direction and control of provincial federations may fall primarily to larger unions or to unions with the time or inclination to devote resources to participation in the federation.

Per capita dues from union members finance the operations of provincial federations of labour. Because of the size of these organizations, as shown in Table 4-3, most employ a number of full-time paid staff, and most executive members take a leave from their regular jobs to devote their full attention to the federation's affairs.

Functions of Provincial Labour Federations

As we have seen, labour legislation in most employment sectors is a provincial responsibility. Therefore, one of the most important roles played by provincial labour federations is dealing with issues affecting the labour legislation within their respective jurisdictions. Provincial labour federations pressure and lobby provincial or regional governments in order to promote their point of view, especially if the government appears likely to change labour legislation in ways that do not favour union interests. The federations also coordinate the activities of their member unions to support federation lobbying efforts.

Provincial federations provide their local unions and affiliated labour councils with a range of services in the fields of communications, education, and research. In the same manner that a regional or national union supports individual locals, the provincial federations support their affiliates by acting as a source of information, a coordinator of joint action, and a provider of resources that may be beyond the reach of individual members.

Provincial labour federations also engage in campaigns around workplace and social issues that affect all workers, unionized or not. For example, the Ontario Federation of Labour has conducted a campaign to bring attention to workplace violence against women workers; the Nova Scotia Federation of Labour sponsors a literacy program; and the British Columbia Federation of Labour is one of the major participants in a campaign to raise the province's minimum wage rate.

NATIONAL AND CENTRALIZED LABOUR FEDERATIONS

The Canadian union movement includes several federations that have affiliates either across the country or within certain geographic areas. Table 4-4 identifies the major national and centralized federations and the size of their respective memberships. We will discuss each of these federations in detail.

TABLE 4-4 National and Centralized Labour Federations in Canada

Name	Number of Members
Canadian Labour Congress	3,000,000
(including the membership of the Fédération des travailleurs et travailleuses du Québec/Quebec Labour Federation)	(500,000)
Centrale des syndicats du Québec	175,000
Confédération des syndicats nationaux	300,000
Centrale des syndicats démocratiques	62,000

Note: Membership figures as of April 2010.

NATIONAL LABOUR FEDERATIONS

Canadian Labour Congress

The **Canadian Labour Congress (CLC)** is the largest central labour body in Canada. It is made up of 60 national and international unions that represent workers such as steelworkers, government workers, autoworkers, postal workers, retail and service sector workers, and resource sector workers. The CLC membership also includes provincial and territorial labour federations, and 137 community labour councils. A number of local unions are directly affiliated to the CLC: that is, they are CLC members on their own, as opposed to being represented in the CLC's membership through membership in another group such as a regional or national union or a labour council. The CLC member organizations are referred to as **affiliates**.

Structure of the Canadian Labour Congress

As Chapter 3 outlined, the CLC's current structure has evolved over several decades through the amalgamation of several earlier national and regional labour federations. Perhaps because of this complex history and the desire to avoid some of the conflict that has doomed earlier national labour federations in Canada, the present-day CLC has a clear set of principles that guide its actions. These principles are outlined in the CLC constitution, which includes a code of union citizenship, a code of ethical organizing, and a code of ethics.[18]

The code of union citizenship acknowledges the different sizes, internal structures, and geographic locations of the CLC affiliates. It also recognizes that each local union, as well as its regional, national, or international union, develops structures and functions that are appropriate for its industry and its collective bargaining situation. The code of union citizenship is presented in Table 4-5. Without unduly restricting the ability of individual unions to adapt to their unique circumstances, it outlines how CLC affiliates should provide service to their members.

The CLC code of ethics is presented in Table 4-6. It outlines the principles that should be followed to ensure a free and democratic union. As well, the CLC constitution has a code of ethical organizing. This code, presented in Table 4-7, outlines the desired relationships between unions that are involved in competitive organizing campaigns or encounter other disputes resulting from jurisdictional conflicts. The CLC encourages

TABLE 4-5 Canadian Labour Congress Code of Union Citizenship

Article 24

Code of union citizenship

The affiliates of the Canadian Labour Congress vary substantially in their size, internal structures and geographic distribution. All unions develop in a way that fits their industries and their collective bargaining situations. Within those differences, all affiliates serve their members and promote union principles and practices according to this constitution.

Affiliates strive to:

1. Fully protect workers' rights and make sure they are applied at work and in the community.

2. Conduct union business and provide services to all members without regard to race, colour, creed, sex, age or national origin in an environment free of harassment.

3. Provide whatever help is needed to ensure members get all the social insurance benefits that may be available for lay-off, unemployment, disability, retirement or any other legitimate cause.

4. Provide all possible help to members who are injured or disabled at work or suffer from industrial disease.

5. Provide the best available facts on wage levels, benefits and contract language and other negotiating services to get the best possible contract.

6. Coordinate bargaining or other activities with other unions where such cooperation will benefit the members of each union.

7. Press for changes in the law to protect and enhance their members' welfare and rights.

8. Educate their members about union principles and practices, the duties of officers and representatives, their union structure, and the important issues in their own union, the Canadian Labour Congress and the labour movement.

9. Ensure that all their members can exercise their union rights.

10. Provide the means for all their members to have an equal opportunity to participate actively and effectively in their own union.

11. Encourage their members to participate actively in local labour councils and federations of labour.

12. Encourage their members to participate fully in the political life of this country.

TABLE 4-6   Canadian Labour Congress Code of Ethics

Article 25

Code of ethics

The overwhelming majority of unions both preach and practise the principles of democracy. Still, too often members forfeit their union citizenship through their own indifference.

The record of union democracy, like the record of our country's democracy, is not perfect. A few constitutions do not adequately set out the elements of democratic practice. A few unions do not practise the principles in their constitutions.

All unions try to get as many of their members as possible to take part in union meetings and affairs. The answer is not so much setting out new principles as using present rights. Just as eternal vigilance is the price of liberty, so is the constant exercise of union citizenship the price of union democracy.

All free and democratic unions abide by these principles:

1. All members have the right to take part fully and freely in their union.

    This includes the right to:

    a. vote regularly in honest elections for their local, national and international officers, either directly or through delegated bodies

    b. stand for and hold office, subject only to fair qualifications uniformly imposed

    c. voice their views about how their union conducts its affairs

    d. attend local membership meetings, which are held regularly with proper notice of time and place.

2. All members use their rights as union citizens. They also loyally support their union. Their right to criticize the policies and personalities of union officers does not include the right to undermine the union as an institution, to advocate dual unionism, to destroy or weaken the union as a collective bargaining agent, or to carry on slander and libel.

3. All members are treated fairly under union rules. Union disciplinary procedures contain all the elements of fair play. No particular formality is required. No lawyers need be used. However, the basic requirements—notice, hearing and judgment based on evidence—are observed. A method of appeal to a higher body exists to ensure that judgment at the local level is impartial.

TABLE 4-6   Canadian Labour Congress Code of Ethics (Continued)

4. Unions hold regular conventions, not more than four years apart. The convention is the supreme governing body of the union.

5. All conventions are open, except for needed closed sessions. Convention proceedings or an accurate summary are published and open to the members.

6. The officials and bodies that govern between conventions are elected. They abide by and enforce the union's constitution and carry out the decisions of the convention.

7. The term of office of all officials is stated in the constitution or is for a reasonable period.

8. To ensure democratic, responsible, and honest administration of their locals and other subordinate bodies, unions have the power to start disciplinary proceedings, including the power to set up trusteeships. Such powers are used rarely and only under the union's constitution. Autonomy is restored promptly.

9. Unions ensure, through appropriate constitutional or administrative measures, that anyone who exercises a corrupt influence or engages in corrupt practices does not hold union office.

10. Unions ensure that no person can hold office or appointed position who has been proven guilty through union procedure or court of law of preying on the labour movement for corrupt purposes.

11. If changes to a constitution or procedures are needed to comply with this code, the union will make these changes as soon as practical.

TABLE 4-7   Canadian Labour Congress Code of Ethical Organizing

Article 27

Code of ethical organizing

One major goal of the labour movement is to extend the benefits of collective bargaining to workers who are not yet members of unions. Public attacks by one affiliate on another result in publicity that gravely injures the labour movement. More serious is the fact that jurisdictional disputes, boycotts, and the resulting bad publicity give rise to restrictive laws.

TABLE 4-7 Canadian Labour Congress Code of Ethical Organizing (Continued)

1. Where two or more affiliates seek to organize the same employees, each affiliate campaigns so as to increase the respect of the workers involved for the union movement. No affiliate attacks the motives or character of any competing affiliate, its officers or locals.

2. Affiliates do not, directly or indirectly, issue any propaganda that:

    a. alleges or implies that another affiliate is guilty of undemocratic practices, corruption, or any other improper conduct;

    b. attacks the principles of international, national, provincial or regional unionism;

    c. attacks the craft or industrial structure of other affiliates; or

    d. criticizes the benefits received from or the dues paid to another affiliate.

3. Affiliates do not organize boycotts against products or services produced under the collective agreement of another affiliate.

4. An affiliate having a complaint about a violation of this code will send it to the ranking official of the other affiliate, requesting that the spirit and intent of this code be observed.

5. If the other affiliate does not comply promptly, the complainant may file a complaint with the Congress. After investigating, the Congress will try to obtain compliance. If that fails, the complaint will go to the executive council. The council will report its decision to the parties and act as it thinks appropriate to enforce compliance.

affiliated unions or organizations to organize new locals primarily, if not exclusively, in the jurisdictions they have historically occupied. The CLC's constitution expresses the belief that the interests of non-unionized workers in a given industry are best served by joining a union that has developed resources and expertise in the same industry. If disputes occur between CLC-affiliated unions wanting to represent the same group of non-unionized workers, the CLC will act as a mediator to clarify the issue of jurisdiction.

The CLC constitution sets out the premise that affiliates should not organize or attempt to represent employees who are already organized and have an established collective bargaining relationship with another affiliate. This constitutional provision is intended to discourage unions from expanding their influence and their numbers by taking over the membership of other unions; this process can consume excessive amounts of both parties' resources and result in long-lasting feelings of bitterness. This provision is also intended to reinforce the principle that unions should concentrate on organizing non-unionized workers as the preferred way to expand their membership.

If an affiliate of the CLC undertakes an action that might be considered a violation of the provision against unionizing workers in an existing union, the affiliate can claim **justification** to the CLC by outlining the reasons for the organizing action that is being contemplated. The provisions of the constitution outline the process of investigation for such a claim, which can result in a "justification hearing" before the executive committee of the CLC. The executive committee has the ability to impose penalties if the affiliate's actions are found to be unjustified. In 2000, a dispute over the issue of unions organizing already unionized workers resulted in the Canadian Auto Workers, one of the largest private sector unions in Canada, receiving "full sanctions" from the CLC. These full sanctions meant that CAW representatives were temporarily removed from all CLC and CLC affiliates' executive bodies, and that CAW members were restricted from participating in CLC activities.[19] More recently, in 2009, the CLC issued similar sanctions against the British Columbia Nurses Union for attempting to organize licensed practical nurses and members of other British Columbia health care unions.[20]

Another provision of the CLC constitution allows some unions to join the CLC directly, instead of through membership in a larger union, a provincial or territorial labour federation, or a labour council. These independent unions come into existence in a number of ways. For example, workers might want to belong to a union but might not want to join the existing union that would usually represent workers in their industry or occupation. Independent unions can also be formed by organizing workers into unions that do not have any regional, national, or international parent unions; an example is the Professional Employees Association, which represents locals of educators, lawyers, librarians, and other types of professionals in British Columbia.

In cases such as these, if the independent union wants to join the CLC, the CLC will directly charter the independent union as an affiliate and provide this directly chartered union with the same type of services that a regional, national, or international union provides to its local union. If the independent affiliate decides to join a parent union, the independent affiliation ends, and the union is then represented within the CLC by its new parent union.

The structure of the CLC is designed to ensure that, as with other democratic union structures, the organization is directed by the wishes of the membership. The CLC national convention, held every third year, is the major mechanism through which this direction is determined. The convention has been described as "the parliament of Canadian labour." Every local union, provincial federation of labour, and labour council is entitled to send at least one delegate to the convention and to submit motions to be voted on by the delegates. Some 2,500 delegates attend the convention, which lasts five days, and devote most of their time to discussing the motions that are presented for consideration. These motions usually cover a broad range of concerns: economic policy, regional economic development, health care, social legislation and equity programs, labour legislation, women's and human rights, technological change, pension issues, environmental concerns, immigration issues, consumer issues, and international issues. The motions are either adopted or rejected through a vote of the delegates, and the results of the motions direct the policies and activities to be followed by the CLC in the next three years. This direction by the vote of the convention delegates enables the CLC to act as the "voice of labour" at the national and international levels.

The delegates to the CLC convention elect four full-time salaried officers: the president, the secretary-treasurer, and two executive vice-presidents.[21] These individuals lead the executive council, which is the governing body of the CLC between conventions. The executive council also includes representatives of CLC-affiliated unions. In order to encourage diversity within the executive council membership, council seats are reserved for representatives of women workers, workers of colour, Aboriginal workers, and LGBT (lesbian, gay, bisexual, and transgender/transsexual) workers. Many CLC executive council members have extensive experience in other labour organizations or federations. Bob White, CLC president from 1992 to 1999, was the national president of the Canadian Auto Workers before becoming CLC president; Ken Georgetti, the current CLC president, was previously the president of the British Columbia Federation of Labour.

Like the structure of other labour organizations in Canada, the CLC structure includes a number of paid staff members. These staff members work at the CLC's central office in Ottawa as well as at a number of regional offices throughout the country. Staff members may be professional employees, such as economists or statisticians; others may be union members who are on paid or unpaid leave from their regular jobs to work with the CLC.

Functions of the Canadian Labour Congress

One of the most important functions of the CLC is to provide services to its affiliates. The CLC assists its affiliates through union education and organization, communications, political education, research and legislation, and representation on international issues. The CLC's services are financed through per capita dues charged to each CLC affiliate. In addition, the CLC maintains staff and organizers in its regional offices throughout Canada to assist existing unions and to assist workers who wish to form new unions. An example of the service and education programs that the CLC provides is the "Labour College," a multi-day workshop that union executives or members can attend to acquire skills such as grievance handling or contract negotiating.

The CLC—with the power of a big fish through the congregation of many little fish—acts as the voice of labour at the national level, and has spearheaded many positive reforms through collective action.

The CLC at the national level acts as the "voice of labour" and frequently speaks for workers as a whole, regardless of whether or not they are members of trade unions. This is particularly true in representations made to governments on issues such as unemployment insurance, health care, workers' compensation, and pension legislation.

CENTRALIZED LABOUR FEDERATIONS

One distinctive feature of the Canadian industrial relations system is the existence not only of a large national labour federation but also of several large centralized labour federations located in Quebec. The complex history of industrial relations in Quebec, outlined in

Chapter 3, explains why there are several centralized labour federations in Quebec rather than a single provincial labour federation, as is the case in most Canadian provinces. The different labour federations in Quebec have developed to represent different sectors of the Quebec union movement and in response to the different forces that have shaped Quebec society. The influences of language, culture, religion, and outside ownership and control, and the desire to retain a distinctive character in the larger Canadian society, have all contributed to the development of centralized labour federations in Quebec. We will describe the three largest federations.

Quebec Federation of Labour

The **Quebec Federation of Labour** is generally referred to by its French acronym, **FTQ** ("Fédération des travailleurs et travailleuses du Québec"). The FTQ is the largest centralized labour federation in Quebec. Its membership includes 40 unions, primarily from the private sector, which collectively have nearly half a million members.

The FTQ is affiliated with the CLC, but, as noted in Chapter 3, its relationship with the CLC is structured somewhat differently than the CLC's relationship with other labour federations. The president of the FTQ is guaranteed a vote on the CLC executive committee, and the FTQ has an assigned seat on the CLC executive council. The FTQ's relationship with the CLC has three distinct features that do not exist in other federations' terms of affiliation with the CLC. First, the FTQ has exclusive jurisdiction in Quebec over some functions, such as education, that the CLC carries out in other regions of Canada. Second, the per capita fees paid by FTQ members to the CLC are adjusted to compensate for the cost of CLC services that FTQ members do not benefit from, such as materials produced only in English. Third, the FTQ has exclusive jurisdiction over the operation of local labour councils in Quebec, which means that the FTQ decides how funds and staffing are allocated to those organizations. The FTQ also has the right to create its own policies on such issues as internal jurisdictional disputes.

Thus, the FTQ functions as an affiliate of the CLC in some respects and as an independent federation in others. This arrangement has been called the "sovereignty-association" agreement.[22] It recognizes not only the FTQ's special role within the CLC as the representative of Quebec labour organizations, but also the need for special membership provisions for the FTQ in light of the so-called plurality[23] of labour federations within Quebec. The FTQ is given more authority over its own operations than other provincial labour federations affiliated with the CLC, on the basis that such authority and the accompanying flexibility is needed to maintain the FTQ's status as Quebec's largest labour federation and the CLC's "voice" in Quebec.

The internal structure of the FTQ is very similar to the structure of the CLC. The congress of the FTQ, held every three years, is the supreme authority of the organization and sets direction and policy based on the votes of the delegates. Each union that is an FTQ member is entitled to send at least one delegate to the congress, and each of the 14 regional councils within the FTQ can send a three-person delegation. The congress also elects a 19-person executive, that, with the FTQ general council, oversees the operations of the organization between congresses. The general council has approximately 150 members representing FTQ-affiliated unions.[24]

Functions of the FTQ

As noted, the FTQ plays a dual role as a regional labour federation and as a CLC-affiliated federation. Thus, it not only provides many of the functions that provincial labour federations provide in other parts of Canada, but also provides services that the CLC provides elsewhere. Its functions include lobbying several levels of government, providing assistance in organizing, providing assistance to member unions in grievances and collective bargaining, and supplying information and resources. As noted above, the FTQ is responsible for educational services for its members, whereas the CLC provides these services for its other regional affiliates.

One initiative of the FTQ and other Quebec-based labour federations that has since been replicated in other parts of Canada is the creation of labour-sponsored investment funds. The FTQ fund, the Solidarity Fund, was established in 1983 and was the first labour-sponsored investment fund in Canada.[25] Investors in the fund receive both provincial and federal tax credits for their contributions, and the fund's proceeds are used to create new job opportunities and to assist companies in preserving existing jobs.

Centrale des syndicats du Québec

The **Centrale des syndicats du Québec (CSQ)** is a "federation of federations." Its membership contains 12 federations that in turn contain more than 250 unions. There are also some unions that are affiliated directly to the CSQ. Nearly two-thirds of the CSQ's members are employed in education, and the majority of CSQ members are public sector employees in Quebec.[26] The CSQ was known as the CEQ (Centrale de l'enseignement du Québec) until 2000, when the name was changed to reflect the broadening of its membership beyond unionized workers in education.

Structure of the CSQ

The CSQ, like the other federations described in this section, is directed by the votes of delegates at the general congress, which occurs every three years. Nearly 1,000 delegates attend each conference. A five-person executive is elected at each congress for a three-year term. An executive council with approximately 300 members oversees the CSQ's operations between general congresses. The CSQ also has an "intersectoral council" consisting of approximately 20 representatives from member federations and unions. The intersectoral council deals with issues such as budgets and integrating new affiliates.

Functions of the CSQ

Because the CSQ's membership base is located in the public sector, negotiation of collective agreements is a major concern. In order to ensure consistency across the different collective agreements in the Quebec public sector, the CSQ has established a number of "negotiation structures" to determine consistent negotiation strategies and to coordinate bargaining among its members. The CSQ has an intersectoral negotiation council, which coordinates the strategy for and content of all negotiations, and a general negotiation council, which defines bargaining objectives and establishes common bargaining demands and settlements.

Other services that the CSQ provides to its members are legal services, support for organizing efforts, insurance plans, union education and training, research, communications, administrative services, and representation in lobbying the Quebec and federal governments.

Confédération des syndicats nationaux

As described in Chapter 2, the **Confédération des syndicats nationaux (CSN,** or Confederation of National Trade Unions) was founded in Quebec in 1921 as the Confédération des travailleurs catholiques du Canada. As the original name suggests, this organization was founded as a federation for Catholic workers; at the time of its name change in 1960, individual members were no longer required to be Catholic and the federation's formal connection with the Catholic Church had ended. During the 1960s and 1970s, the CSN had a reputation as a "radical" federation, prompting several member union groups to leave in order to start their own federations.[27] In the 1980s, new leadership and a recognition that membership was declining led to the federation's gradual change from being "a hotbed of hardline Marxism riven with factional disputes over ideological purity"[28] to being a more "civilized" and less confrontational organization. The CSN membership currently includes nine affiliated union federations.[29]

A recent development in the history of the CSN, and an unusual one for Quebec-based labour federations, is the CSN's affiliation with a union that has members outside of Quebec. In 2000, the CSN became the labour federation affiliated with the Union of Canadian Correctional Officers (UCCO-SAAC), which represents officers at 51 federal penitentiaries and other correctional institutions across Canada. The UCCO explains that its affiliation with the CSN gives it the freedom to create and control a union solely devoted to the concerns of correctional officers.[31]

Structure of the CSN

The CSN membership includes federations of unions in commerce, construction, communications, education, mining, forestry and pulp and paper, the professions, health and social services, and the public service. There are 13 regional councils to represent unions in particular geographic areas. The CSN membership also includes a number of directly affiliated unions that are chartered as members, under a structure similar to the one governing directly affiliated unions in the CLC. The CSN has three offices in Montreal.

The supreme authority in the CSN is the congress, which meets every three years and has approximately 2,000 delegates. The delegates at the congress vote on such matters as budgeting, dues, and action plans. Each member union has the right to present motions for consideration by the congress. Seven committees that meet during the congress also present recommendations. Between congresses, the CSN's direction and day-to-day activities are overseen by the executive committee, which consists of six executive members elected by the congress, and a council representing the member federations and regional councils.

Functions of the CSN

The CSN provides services to its membership similar to those provided by the other federations described in this section. It offers its members, among other services, an information service that produces publications and audio-visual materials, a research service, a library, support services for unions on strike, organizing services for workers who wish to form a union, coordination for collective campaigns, assistance to union members dealing with workers' compensation claims, and legal services for unions involved in arbitrations and bargaining.

Two other major activities of the CSN should be mentioned. One is the CSN's involvement in several labour-management cooperation agreements that have explored alternative forms of workplace relationships between the parties, often as a way to preserve jobs that otherwise might disappear. The other activity is the establishment of a labour-sponsored investment fund, named Fondaction. Like the FTQ's Solidarity Fund, the monies from this capital investment fund operated by the CSN are used to encourage investment in creating new jobs or in maintaining existing ones. Some commentators point to the CSN's creation of this fund as evidence of the federation's ideological evolution, since the CSN leadership at the time the Solidarity Fund was created accused the FTQ of "co-opting the labour movement."[30]

Delegates at the 2010 congress of the International Trade Union Confederation, held in Vancouver, discuss trade union alliances to promote global justice.

INTERNATIONAL LABOUR FEDERATIONS

To this point, we have focused our discussion on the activities of the Canadian union movement within Canadian borders. Several Canadian unions and federations, however, have international affiliations. We will conclude our overview of the Canadian union movement with a look at the activities of Canadian unions outside Canada. International affiliations are becoming more important to many Canadian unions and labour federations because of globalization of businesses and employers, which puts greater pressure on Canadian unions to work in cooperation with other unions throughout the world.

The CLC, the CSN, and the smallest Quebec-based federation, Centrale des syndicates démocratiques (CSD), are affiliated with the **International Trade Union Confederation (ITUC)**, an "international union of unions" that assists union organizations throughout the world. Another Canadian union, the Christian Labour Association of Canada (CLAC), is directly affiliated with the ITUC; the FTQ also has an affiliation with the ITUC through the FTQ's affiliation with the CLC. The ITUC is a worldwide organization representing some 175 million workers in 155 countries and territories.[32] One of its most important functions is delivering labour education programs to assist workers in such regions as Asia, Africa, and Latin America in forming their own unions, developing leadership, and engaging in collective bargaining.

Another important international body is the **International Labour Organization (ILO)**, which is based in Geneva, Switzerland. The ILO is not an international federation in the sense of having formal affiliates in member countries; it is an agency of the United Nations and has been in existence since 1919, when it was created as part of the League of Nations, the precursor to the United Nations. The ILO's main purposes are to formulate and promote international labour standards and to offer technical assistance in labour-related matters to countries around the world.[33] The ILO researches and publishes reports on international labour issues, such as women in the workplace and employment policies. It also collects comparative statistics from around the world on such issues as strike and lockout rates and unionization rates.

The CLC is an affiliate of two other international organizations. One is the **Trades Union Advisory Committee of the Organisation for Economic Co-operation and Development (TUAC-OECD)**. The TUAC acts as an information conduit between its member organizations and the OECD on labour-related issues that come before the OECD partners.[34] The TUAC also holds plenary sessions twice a year to guide the direction of the organization, and has an elected nine-member administrative committee (which currently includes representation from the CLC) and a five-member executive committee. The CSN is also an affiliate of this organization. The other organization is the **Commonwealth Trade Union Group**, which represents unions in the 53 Commonwealth countries. This group has now become a part of the ITUC. The council's membership includes unions representing a total of 30 million members, and its main purposes are to promote international labour standards and to exchange information among its member unions.[35]

SUMMARY

The structure of Canadian unions can be as simple as an independent union representing a single group of workers or as complicated as a union that has regional, national, and even international affiliations. We can see from this overview that the variations in Canadian union structure, although they may seem unnecessarily complex, reflect the variations in occupations, employers, and regions within the Canadian industrial relations system. There is a common theme, however; unions and federations are democratic organizations that are guided by the direction of their members and by structures designed to facilitate the democratic process.

At the individual workplace level, local unions represent workers in collective bargaining and dispute resolution procedures. While there are some independent local unions, most locals belong to a larger parent union, which can be regional, national, or international in scope. Locals have an elected executive directed by votes of the membership and, depending on their size, may also have a business agent and other paid staff.

Most locals belong to a labour council, which is an organization representing unions in a particular geographic area. Labour councils provide networking and information sharing for their members and may also sponsor activities and participate in events within their communities and regions.

Parent unions, like locals, also have an elected executive and paid staff. Their directions are governed by delegate votes at a regular convention. Parent unions provide services to their members such as lobbying, education, and assistance in bargaining.

On a larger geographic level, each province and territory in Canada has a provincial or territorial labour federation. This organization's membership consists of independent locals, parent unions, and labour councils, and these members appoint delegates to a convention that sets the federation's direction by voting on motions. The provincial or territorial federation acts as the "voice of labour" in its area and represents organized labour's concerns to governments and the media. The federation also offers support services to its membership.

Provincial and territorial labour federations in Canada are affiliated with the Canadian Labour Congress (CLC), which is the largest centralized labour federation in the country. The CLC's membership also includes independent unions and locals. Other centralized labour federations include the Quebec Federation of Labour (FTQ), the Confédération des syndicats nationaux (CSN), and the Centrale des syndicats du Québec (CSQ). The CLC and the FTQ have a number of international affiliations that connect them with other labour organizations throughout the world.

KEY TERMS FOR CHAPTER 4

affiliates (p. 142)

business agent (p. 126)

business union (p. 129)

Canadian Labour Congress (CLC) (p. 142)

Centrale des syndicats du Québec (CSQ) (p. 151)

Commonwealth Trade Union Group (p. 155)

Confédération des syndicats nationaux (CSN) (p. 152)

convention/congress (p. 133)

in good standing (p. 137)

International Labour Organization (ILO) (p. 155)

International Trade Union Confederation (ITUC) (p. 155)

iron law of oligarchy (p. 128)

justification (p. 147)

labour council (p. 136)

local union (p. 122)

parent unions (p. 131)

provincial labour federation (p. 139)

Quebec Federation of Labour (FTQ) (p. 150)

shop stewards (p. 125)

Trades Union Advisory Committee of the Organisation for Economic Co-operation and Development (TUAC-OECD) (p. 155)

union executive (p. 124)

DISCUSSION QUESTIONS FOR CHAPTER 4

1. Explain how a local union is formed. What role can a regional, national, or international union play in forming a local union?
2. What distinguishes the structure of a labour council from the structure of a local union?
3. Give some examples of services that a federation of labour might provide for its affiliates.
4. Why is the CLC called the "union of unions"?
5. Discuss the role of democracy in the formation and operation of unions in Canada.
6. What is the role of the CLC in resolving disputes between affiliated members?
7. Explain why there are several centralized labour federations in Quebec.
8. Why are international affiliations becoming more important to Canadian unions?

EXERCISES FOR CHAPTER 4

1. Choose a union that you are familiar with or that you can research. Using Figure 4-1 as a guide, draw a diagram of the relationships that this union has with other organizations within the Canadian union structure. Explain how these relationships have come to exist and outline what the union gains from having these relationships.
2. Choose a labour organization or federation, such as a labour council or provincial or centralized labour federation, in your region of the country. Describe how that organization is structured, identify its membership, and describe how that membership has evolved or developed. Also describe some of the functions that the organization carries out and identify what you think are the most important functions or activities of the organization.

References

[1] Yakabuski, K. (2001, September). Arch enemy. *R.O.B. Magazine*, 34–43.

[2] Yakabuski, *op. cit.*

[3] Lynk, M. (2000). Union democracy and the law in Canada. *Journal of Labor Research*, 21(1), 37–63.

[4] Godard, J. (1994). *Industrial relations, the economy, and society*. Toronto: McGraw-Hill Ryerson.

[5] Godard, *op. cit.*

[6] Kelloway, E.K, Catano, V.M., & Carroll, A.C. (1995) The nature of member participation in local union activities. In Tetrick, L.E., and Barling, J. (Eds.), *Changing employment relations: behavioral and social perspectives*. Washington, DC: American Psychological Association.

[7] Strauss, G. (1991). Union democracy. In Strauss, G., Gallagher, D., and Fiorito, J. (Eds.), *The state of the unions*. Madison, WI: IRA.

[8] Kelloway, K., & Barling, J. (1994). Industrial relations stress and union activism: costs and benefits of participation. In *Proceedings of the 46th Annual Meeting of the Industrial Relations Research Association*. Boston: Industrial Relations Research Association; Winch, G. (1993). The turnover of shop stewards. *Industrial Relations Journal, 14*, 84–86.

[9] Michels, R. (1962). *Political parties*. New York: Collier Books.

[10] McShane, S.L. (1986). The multidimensionality of union participation. *Journal of Occupational Psychology, 59*, 177–187.

[11] Fullagar, C.J.A., Parks, J.M., Clark, P.F., & Gallagher, D.G. (1995). Organizational citizenship and union participation: measuring discretionary membership behaviors. In Tetrick, L.E., and Barling, J. (Eds.), *Changing employment relations: behavioral and social perspectives*. Washington, DC: American Psychological Association.

[12] Iverson, R.D., & Currivan, D.B. (2003). Union participation, job satisfaction, and employee turnover: an event-history analysis of the exit-voice hypothesis. *Industrial Relations, 42(1)*, 101–105.

[13] Shore, L.M., & Newton, L.A. (1995). Union-member relations: loyalty, instrumentality, and alienation. In Tetrick and Barling, *op. cit.*

[14] Fullagar, C.J., Gallagher, D.G., Clark, P.F., & Carroll, A.E. (2004). Union commitment and participation: a 10-year longitudinal study. *Journal of Applied Psychology, 89(4)*, 730–737.

[15] Godard, J. (1997). Beliefs about unions and what they should do: a survey of employed Canadians. *Journal of Labor Research, 18(4)*, 621–639.

[16] *Union Membership in Canada—2007.* Strategic Policy, Analysis, and Workplace Information Directorate, Labour Program, Human Resources and Social Development Canada. Available at <www.hrsdc.gc.ca/eng/lp/wid/union_membership.shtml>.

[17] Fleming, A. (2010, April 28). New West city council adopts living wage bylaw. *New Westminster News Leader.* Available at <www.bclocalnews.com/greater_vancouver/newwestminsternewsleader/news/92348704.html>.

[18] The full version of the constitution is available at <www.canadianlabour.ca/about-clc> (English) or <www.congresdutravail.ca/le-ctc> (French).

[19] Parsons, L. (2001, March 5). Canada: what lies behind the split in the union officialdom? *World Socialist Website,* <www.wsws.org/articles/2001/mar2001/can-m05.shtml>.

[20] BCNU actions constitute a raid. Hospital Employees' Union press release, July 31, 2009. Available at <www.heu.org/MemberNews/2009/07/Newsletter6754/index.cfm?call2=HOMEPAGE&type=3>

[21] Information from the CLC website, <www.canadianlabour.ca> (English), <www.congresdutravail.ca> (French).

[22] Déom, E., & Boivin, J. (2001). Union-management relations in Quebec. In Gunderson, M., Ponak, A., and Taras, D.G. (Eds.), *Union-management relations in Canada* (4th edition). Toronto: Addison Wesley Longman.

[23] Déom & Boivin, *op. cit.*

[24] Information from the FTQ website, <www.ftq.qc.ca>.

[25] Déom & Boivin, *op. cit.*

[26] Information from the CSQ website, <www.csq.qc.net>.

[27] Déom & Boivin, *op. cit.*

[28] Bauch, H. (1999, March 20). Larose tough act to follow: labour scene will not be so colourful. *The Gazette* (Montreal), B1.

[29] Information from the CSN website, <www.csn.qc.ca>.

[30] Bauch, *op. cit.*

[31] Information from the Union of Canadian Correctional Officers/Syndicat des agents correctionnels du Canada–CSN website, <www.ucco-sacc.csn.qc.ca>.

[32] Information from the International Trade Union Confederation website, <www.ituc-csi.org>.

[33] Information from International Labour Organization website, <www.ilo.org>.

[34] Information from the Trades Union Advisory Committee website, <www.tuac.org>.

[35] Information from the Commonwealth Trade Union Group website, <www.ituc-csi.org/commonwealth-trade-union-group.html>.

Union Local Finds Strength in Numbers

SEIU Local 2 is one of the fastest growing unions in Canada, increasing from 3,500 members in 2005, when two unions merged to form SEIU Local 2, to more than 12,000 members in 2010. The Ontario-based local is now involved in organizing campaigns in British Columbia, Alberta, and the Maritimes as well as in its home province. With an organizing staff of 15 people working in the property services industries, such as food services and the janitorial and security sectors, SEIU Local 2 has an organizing department that is now larger than the organizing departments at some national unions.

The reason for this significant growth, says Tom Galivan, the union's organizing director, is SEIU's unique approach to organizing. "SEIU [the Service Employees International Union] puts a substantially larger amount of its collective resources and energy into trying to organize unorganized workers than any other union in North America. That's in large part because we've seen that union density, or the levels of union organization in the sectors where our workers work, ties directly to the working conditions and the types of wages and benefits we can negotiate."

SEIU employs "comprehensive campaigns" in which it attempts to unionize an entire industry sector. "A lot of the workers we represent are in 'precarious work'," explains Galivan. They often work in an industry structured on the competitive bidding model, meaning the work goes to the lowest bidder. Employers try to lower their labour costs, which may violate workers' statutory rights. "For us to be successful," says Galivan, "it's not enough to organize the workers in a single workplace or even a single company. We have to organize entire sectors in order to affect labour standards."

For example, the union plans to organize the workers at every major janitorial company in Ottawa and then establish a multi-employer collective agreement with all those employers.

SEIU uses a number of tools in its organizing campaigns. With "trigger agreements," the union will campaign to win recognition with the understanding that its bargaining process won't take place until it reaches a certain threshold of union density within the sector. "Client leverage campaigns" involve going to the clients of the contractors in its members' industry and communicating the reputational risk of hiring contractors with questionable employment practices.

While these types of campaigns can take longer, the results are bigger. A representation election with workers in one building could take two weeks, while these larger campaigns can take years. "But, when we're finished, every worker in the whole city in that sector is unionized," Galivan points out, adding that the sector-wide approach is reminiscent of the way unions were formed during the labour movement of the 1930s.

THE ORGANIZING CAMPAIGN

objectives

In this chapter, we discuss the reasons why employees decide to unionize and outline how an organizing campaign is conducted. We explain what making and assessing an application for certification entails. At the end of the chapter, you should be able to:

- explain why workers would want a collective bargaining relationship
- describe the steps in an organizing campaign
- understand what is required to apply for certification
- identify what factors must be addressed in a certification application
- identify two special situations involving organizing campaigns and certification applications

INTRODUCTION

Canadian labour legislation in all jurisdictions recognizes the right of most kinds of employees to freely choose to be a member of a trade union and to participate in the union's lawful activities. In this chapter, we will focus on how employees exercise that right.

Many employees are first introduced to the idea of joining a union through an **organizing campaign**, which is the campaign that a union conducts in a workplace to persuade employees to choose the union as their legal representative. The organizing campaign is a very important part of the industrial relations system, because its success or failure ultimately determines whether employees will be represented by a union. Thus, it is important to understand what an organizing campaign is, how it is initiated, and what legislation governs how the campaign is conducted.

We will start by examining reasons why employees might support a union and will then describe how a union organizing campaign is initiated. We will conclude by looking at the means by which unions come to be recognized as the freely chosen workplace representative of the employees.

FACTORS AFFECTING EMPLOYEE SUPPORT FOR A UNION

There are many reasons why employees might want to establish a union in their workplace. A number of studies have attempted to identify these reasons and also to identify the reasons that are most influential in employees' decisions to actively support a union organizing campaign. In other words, what are the factors that ultimately determine whether employees will vote for or against having a union as their representative in the workplace? Identifying these factors is important because the difference between the number of votes for and against a union can be very small, even in a large workplace with many potential voters. Every single vote is important in determining whether an organizing campaign is ultimately successful.

It is important for unions to understand the reasons why workers would support a union, since unions can then address those reasons in their organizing campaigns. If unions know what influences motivate employees to support a union, they can tailor their organizing campaigns to address and build on those influences. Conversely, an employer who wishes to resist a unionization drive would find it useful to understand why workers reject unions. The employer can then, within the guidelines of labour legislation, address those factors in communications with employees. Additionally, an employer who understands why workers are dissatisfied enough to consider joining a union has the opportunity to address the causes of dissatisfaction and to create a workplace where employees feel they are treated fairly.

The research exploring why employees do or do not support unions is wide-ranging. Many different and potentially influential factors have been identified. It is important to note, however, that this research has not always distinguished between the three decision points that employees pass through in the organizing process. Workers first must decide whether a union would be an asset for them in the workplace. Then they must decide whether to invite a union to undertake an organizing campaign among the employees. Finally, each individual worker must decide whether to cast a formal vote in favour of union representation. Different factors may be more or less important in affecting choices at each of these three decision points.[1] Nevertheless, the research studies roughly fall into four categories based on the type of factors that have been examined: personal factors, workplace factors, economic factors, and societal factors. We will discuss each of these in turn.

Personal Factors

Interestingly, an employee's intention to support a union may be influenced by factors that were present long before the union entered the workplace or even before the employee joined the organization. One study showed that individuals whose parents held positive attitudes toward unions or whose parents were active participants in unions tended to have positive attitudes toward unions themselves.[2] This may be because they received positive rather than negative information about unions as they were growing up. Subsequent research has suggested that parents' participation in union activities has a stronger and more direct effect on their children's attitudes toward unions than does the parents' general attitudes toward unions.[3] Socioeconomic status is another influential factor; members of ethnic minorities and low-income or low-status workers, for example, have more positive attitudes toward unions than do higher status workers.[4] It is speculated that these favourable attitudes are a consequence of

Supporters of SEIU Local 2 in Ontario join a demonstration in support of the union's "Justice for Janitors" campaign.

the fact that unions address issues related to race, gender, and other attributes that may result in low social status; unions develop member loyalty by extending their focus beyond wage and benefit issues, which are employers' main methods of developing worker loyalty.

Positive attitudes toward unions, however, whether pre-existing or developed after employment at an organization, do not necessarily translate into active support for unions in the form of a vote in favour of union representation. Several intervening factors may determine whether an employee with a pro-union attitude will actually vote in favour of a union in his or her own workplace. In order to support a union, an employee must feel that he or she lacks any individual ability to influence or change unsatisfactory working conditions, and feel that a union is the mechanism by which that change can be achieved.[5] This perception—that a union is an effective means to achieve what individual employees want but cannot achieve on their own—is called the **instrumentality** of the union.[6] Even employees with pro-union attitudes will not support a union that, in their view, lacks the ability to make the desired changes in the workplace. The concept of instrumentality also implies that employees might not support a union, even one they feel positively toward, if they think that they can make desired changes without the union's assistance.

An important implication of instrumentality, and one that is often very significant in the success or failure of a unionization vote, involves the employee's perception of a particular union. For example, the Teamsters union was historically perceived as being controlled by individuals with ties to organized crime.[7] This perception might lead an employee with generally pro-union attitudes to vote against being represented by the Teamsters. We should also keep in mind that instrumentality can have a positive effect for a union in situations where the union is not actually capable of achieving what the employees desire. As long as the employees perceive that the union can cause the desired change, even if in reality it cannot, instrumentality may still motivate the employees to support the union.

The fit between an individual's self-perception and the image presented by the union, or the individual's perception of unions in general, can also influence whether the person supports unionization. One study examined an organizing campaign in the grocery industry in which the union presented itself as a "business with a product to sell" (the product being job security and better wages and benefits). This approach was successful in gaining the support of those workers who felt that they needed the product and that the union could deliver on its promise. It was largely unsuccessful, however, with workers who felt that the product did not address their own workplace situation, as well as with those who resented the salesperson approach of the union organizers.[8] A study of workers in the high-tech industry suggested that these workers' self-perceived identity led them to reject unionization because they felt that the characteristics of their job (e.g., continual learning, long hours, merit-based promotion) did not fit with what they perceived as the features of a unionized workplace. Many also perceived that unionization could remove some of the job characteristics that they found most appealing (e.g., flexibility in job assignments).[9] However, positive self-identification with the union and with fellow workers (and potential fellow union members) has also been found to increase the likelihood of support for the union during and after certification.[10]

Table 5-1 summarizes the personal factors that may affect union support.

Workplace Factors

Most studies that explore the reasons for unionization acknowledge that dissatisfaction with workplace conditions is the most common reason why employees consider joining a union.

Dissatisfaction with the workplace can be generated from a number of different sources. Compensation levels are an important factor in determining whether dissatisfaction exists or not. Compensation affects dissatisfaction not only in absolute terms (the actual amount of pay and benefits), but also in relative terms (how one's pay and benefits compare with those of other workers in the organization or workers in similar positions in other organizations). Historically, unions have been able to gain higher wages for their members in comparison to non-unionized workers; also, firms with more unionized workers generally pay more in benefits than do firms with fewer unionized workers.[11]

TABLE 5-1 Personal Factors Affecting Union Support

Factor	Effect
Parental attitudes or union activity	If their parents were active in unions or held positive attitudes toward unions, workers may be more likely to support a union.
Socio-economic status	Low socio-economic status, low income, or minority group membership may make workers more likely to support a union.
Instrumentality	If a specific union is perceived as being able to achieve changes that the worker cannot achieve alone, the worker may be more likely to support the union.
Perception and identity	If the image the union presents does not fit workers' self-perception, they may be less likely to support the union.

Dissatisfaction may result if an employee perceives that he or she is being paid significantly less or receiving fewer benefits than other workers, and the prospect of unionization may become more attractive if unionization is seen as a way to remedy the perceived discrepancies.

A similar comparative effect arises with employees in industries that have already been unionized to some degree. One study indicated that the likelihood of unionization in a particular organization rises when the level of unionization in the organization's industry is 35 percent or higher.[12] This effect may occur because workers in non-unionized organizations within an industry perceive unionized workers in the same industry as having better working conditions, and they want to gain the same outcomes for themselves. It has also been pointed out, however, that some non-unionized firms in highly unionized industries adopt the same levels of pay and benefits as those in unionized firms in order to be competitive in the labour market and to remain non-unionized; this is known as the "union threat effect."[13] If the union threat effect comes into play, non-unionized workers will have the same workplace conditions as unionized workers.

These non-unionized workers may be less inclined to support a union because they do not see that joining a union would provide any additional improvements for them.

Dissatisfaction within the workplace can also be generated by management's refusal to correct problems brought to its attention, problems with administration in general, inadequate benefits, lack of opportunity for promotion, perceived unfairness of workplace policies or procedures, and job security concerns.[14] Workers also identify the lack of opportunity for worker participation and cooperation with management in decision-making as a major cause of dissatisfaction in the workplace.[15] However, the factor of instrumentality is again important in determining whether a worker's dissatisfaction will result in his or her actively supporting a union. As noted above, in order to gain the employees' support, the union must be perceived as being able to correct whatever conditions are causing dissatisfaction.

One study suggested that the union-related attitudes of others in the workplace may be another workplace factor that affects whether an individual supports a union. If co-workers feel positively about the presence of a union, an individual is more likely to support a union.[16] A second study showed that a similar effect is apparent if an individual's family members want him or her to support the union.[17] The individual's co-workers and family members are interested in the individual's work-related activities, and thus both can influence the worker's decisions related to the workplace. These two studies demonstrated another interesting result of workplace attitudes.[18] While most of the participants in these studies perceived that their management and supervisors did not want them to vote for the union, the supervisors' and managers' attitudes did not affect whether the individual employees supported the union or not.[19] In fact, if it was perceived that management might actually retaliate against employees if they supported a union (e.g., by demoting or firing union supporters), the subjects were more, not less, likely to support a union.[20]

Another study identified the structure of the workplace itself and the type of work engaged in by the organization as important factors in determining the level of support for a union.[21] This study, which investigated why the level of unionization was relatively low in the American high-tech industry in comparison to other American industries, reported that the high-tech industry was characterized by "rule-bound, rigid and insecure" work climates. These conditions would usually suggest a workplace that would be favourable to unionization, but the study's authors observed that this was not so in the high-tech industry. They suggested that workers were anxious to hold on to their jobs and feared that actively pursuing unionization would threaten what little job security they had. The results of this study suggest that there may be factors or conditions in specific organizations or industries that affect whether employees support unionization.

Table 5-2 summarizes the workplace factors affecting support for a union.

TABLE 5-2 Workplace Factors Affecting Union Support

Factor	Effect
Compensation	Absolute and comparative levels of compensation may increase support for the union if these are perceived as insufficient.
Level of unionization in industry	Support for the union may increase if the rest of the industry is unionized; however, non-unionized firms may match unionized firms' conditions.
Dissatisfaction with management/administration	This dissatisfaction may increase support for the union if the union is perceived as being able to resolve dissatisfaction.
Dissatisfaction with workplace conditions	This dissatisfaction may increase support for the union if the union is perceived as being able to resolve dissatisfaction.
Union attitudes of co-workers and family	If attitudes are positive, workers may be more likely to support the union.
Union attitudes of management	While management attitudes generally have no influence on employees' intentions to support union, if management is perceived as being willing to act against the union, intention to support the union may increase.
Organizational structure	Factors unique to a specific industry or organization may increase or decrease union support.

Economic Factors

Factors beyond the organization and the individual affect whether individuals support unionization of their workplace or not. An American study found that the level of unemployment in the individual's state had an effect on whether an individual would vote for a union or not.[22] As unemployment in a state increased, the likelihood of an individual voting for unionization increased and the overall probability of a union organizing campaign being successful also increased. The amount of change in the unemployment rate in the previous year was also important; the greater the amount of change, the more likely it was that individuals would support a union. These findings indicate that many workers feel that a union shields them from the effects of an unstable labour market by increasing job security. However, we should keep in mind contradictory findings that suggest that the fear of unemployment makes some individuals less likely to unionize.[23]

Another possible economic influence on the decision to unionize is the rate of inflation. Some evidence suggests that if the inflation rate increases, workers are more likely to want to join a union, since they believe that unions will help them to offset the decrease in real wages caused by price inflation.[24] However, analysis of economic data on union membership trends has not always demonstrated that inflation rates affect union membership rates; furthermore, the suggested relationship between these two variables has not been found in some countries outside North America.

A further economic factor is the impact that the presence of a union might have on workers' pay levels—the "union wage premium." A number of studies have examined whether there are differences in pay between employees at unionized organizations and those at non-unionized organizations, and found higher wages for unionized workers in different industries[25] and higher wages for unionized workers even in traditionally low-paying jobs.[26] Unionized organizations also tend to offer higher levels of benefits, and the "union premium" for benefits is often considerably larger than it is for wages.[27] The presence of a union also appears to act as a deterrent to wage reductions,[28] and, as mentioned previously, a significant level of unionization in a particular occupational or demographic group may also have the effect of increasing non-union workers' pay, since non-union employers must compete with unionized workplaces when they attempt to recruit and retain employees.[29] However, as mentioned previously, workers will only be influenced by economic factors to join a union

TABLE 5-3 Economic Factors Affecting Union Support	
Factor	**Effect**
Unemployment rate in region	If the rate increases, the likelihood of a worker joining the union may increase.
	If there is a significant change in the rate, unionization is more likely.
Inflation	Price inflation can increase intent to unionize and the actual rate of unionization.
Union wage premium	Unions can improve wage and benefit levels, but workers must perceive that unions are able to do so.

if they perceive the union as being capable of providing the economic changes they desire.

Table 5-3 summarizes the economic factors affecting support for a union.

Societal Factors

General societal attitudes about unions influence individuals' inclinations to support a union in their own workplace. One study investigated the union-related attitudes of people in two western Canadian cities in 1981 and 1987.[30] The time periods covered by this study included a recession in both cities and a very visible, prolonged, and violent strike in one of the cities. Despite these events, approximately half the respondents in both surveys had generally positive attitudes toward unions. However, more than half of the respondents said that they themselves would not join a union. The researchers attributed these apparently contradictory findings to a variety of possible factors, including that some individuals may extol the positive effects of unions but personally distrust their power; a recession may cause residents with less positive union attitudes to seek opportunities elsewhere; the union-related experiences of an individual's friends and family members may have a negative effect; and individual demographic characteristics such as age and levels of education may discourage union participation.

A similar discrepancy between attitudes and intentions was discovered in a study of 622 American non-union workers.[31] Roughly three-quarters of the respondents thought that unions were effective in improving wages and working conditions, but only one-third stated that they themselves would join a union. The authors of this study suggested that specific beliefs about the effects of a union in one's own workplace are more influential than general beliefs about unions in determining whether an individual will support a union or not. The authors of the study involving western Canadian cities made a similar suggestion, noting that if individuals do not see a benefit for themselves in the presence of a union in their own workplace, they may not wish to join a union, even if they generally hold pro-union attitudes.[32]

Another societal factor affecting the decision to unionize that deserves mention at this point (one that will be discussed in subsequent chapters) is whether the relevant labour legislation facilitates or hinders the certification process. Anti-union legislation could include, for example, legislation requiring a mandatory vote in the workplace on every certification application. A comparative analysis of Canadian and American unionization rates between 1984 and 1998 indicated that a shift toward anti-union legislation in Canada may be one explanation for the decline in Canadian unionization rates during this period; a study of American unionization rates over the same period suggested that there was a decline not only in the number of certification votes, but also in the number of organizing campaigns, due to anti-union attitudes in regulatory agencies and among those appointed by the government to serve on those agencies.[33] Studies of changes in Canadian legislation—across jurisdictions, across time, or both—have consistently shown that the requirement for a mandatory workplace vote reduces the success rate for certification applications, in comparison to success rates when other forms of assessing workplace support are used (e.g., signatures from a majority of workers).[34] This difference in success rates is present even when the effects of external environmental factors (e.g., economic indicators, rates of production, employment growth, and seasonal fluctuations) are controlled, indicating that legislative provisions may be one of the major factors affecting the success of unionization attempts.[35] (Some reasons that might explain this difference will be discussed in subsequent chapters.)

Table 5-4 summarizes the societal factors that may affect support for a union.

TABLE 5-4 Societal Factors Affecting Union Support	
Factor	**Effect**
General attitudes toward unions	These may not affect individual attitudes, even during labour-related events such as strikes and recessions.
	An individual may support the general concept of unions but not be personally willing to join one.
Labour legislation	Anti-union legislation may reduce the likelihood of a successful organizing campaign.

STEPS IN THE ORGANIZING CAMPAIGN

If, for whatever reason, enough employees in a workplace feel that a union is needed to represent their interests, the employees may decide to initiate an organizing campaign. A successful organizing campaign results in a legally recognized level of support for the union that allows it to request recognition as the **bargaining agent** for the employees. Being the "bargaining agent" means that the union is legally recognized as the sole representative of employees in that particular workplace. As bargaining agent, the union acts on behalf of the employees in negotiating conditions and terms of work and in administering the resulting collective agreement.

An organizing campaign can be initiated either by a union or by the employees. If a union becomes aware of a group of dissatisfied employees, it may contact the employees to see if there is already sufficient interest in pursuing unionization or if there is a good chance that the union can persuade the employees to consider unionization. If the employees initiate the campaign, they must decide whether to start their own union or contact an established union with the intention of joining that union. As described in Chapter 4, most employees who initiate an organizing campaign decide to contact an established union because of the organizing experience and campaign resources that the union can offer. Organizing campaigns in the Canadian private sector generally follow the pattern outlined in Figure 5-1. We will now look at this pattern in detail.

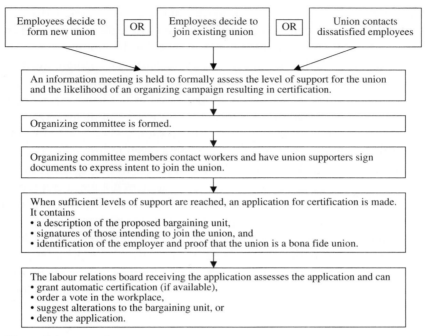

Figure 5-1 *Steps in the Organizing Campaign*

The Information Meeting

The first formal step in the organizing campaign is to plan and hold an information meeting, which takes place after working hours and off company property. This meeting may be preceded by smaller informal gatherings, during which those employees considering unionization attempt to determine whether there are enough co-workers interested in unionization to justify holding a formal meeting. If sufficient interest exists, one of the initiators will usually ask an existing union to send a representative to the first formal meeting (although, as we have noted in previous chapters, some employee groups choose to form an independent union).

The information meeting is held after hours and at a neutral location (off company property) to avoid alerting the employer that there is interest in unionization, and also to avoid any suggestion that the union is interfering with the workplace's normal operations.

At the information meeting, interested employees and a union representative discuss the issues that are generating interest in unionization, and assess the likelihood of an organizing campaign resulting in a majority vote of support for the union.

It is important to note that at this point in the organizing campaign, the identities of the employees interested in unionization are, as much as possible, kept secret from the employer, and also from employees who are perceived as not being sympathetic to the idea of a union. The fact that an information meeting is being held may also be kept secret from these parties. This secrecy serves two purposes. First, it attempts to prevent the employer from finding out that actions are being taken to form a union. As we will see, labour relations law makes it illegal for an employer to fire, demote, or otherwise punish an employee for union-related activity, but that does not mean employers do not attempt to do these things. Second, excluding employees who are perceived to be unsympathetic to the union reduces the possibility that an employee will act as a "mole" and leak the union's or employees' campaign plans to the employer. This exclusion does not eliminate the possibility that an employee initially involved in the information campaign will change his mind and decide to act as an informant for the employer, but the initial exclusion of unsympathetic employees may minimize the amount of information reaching the employer.

The Organizing Committee

If sufficient interest in unionization is apparent at the information meeting, and those present at the meeting perceive that an organizing campaign could be successful (that is, it might result in certification), an organizing committee will be created. The organizing committee usually consists of several employees in the workplace as well as, perhaps, an experienced organizer from the union who can provide assistance. The reason that the organizing committee tends to consist of employee's rather than professional organizers from the union, is that employees are generally considered more credible than "outsiders" in discussions about workplace issues. Also, employees will already be familiar to the potential union members and will have better knowledge of workplace issues because of their first-hand experience.

The members of the organizing committee will contact other employees before or after work, on breaks, or at their homes to sound them out on their union sympathy. Under Canadian labour law, an employer is entitled to forbid individuals who are acting on behalf of the union from soliciting support at the workplace during working hours, for the simple reason that such activity could significantly disrupt the normal operations of the workplace. When the organizing committee members contact other employees, their goal is to obtain a formal indication of support for the union. This is accomplished by having employees sign a membership card or a petition indicating their intent to join the union. In some jurisdictions, employees may also be asked to pay a small sum of money, usually one or two dollars, to materially signify their support for the union. This money is held in trust until the results of the unionization vote are known. If the vote results in support for the union, the union retains the money; if the vote is against

Posters and union publications are often used during an organizing campaign to introduce workers to unions and collective action.

the union, the money is returned to those who paid it. Table 5-5 (later in the chapter) indicates what is considered proof of support in Canadian jurisdictions.

A constant concern throughout the organizing campaign is the possibility of **unfair labour practices**. These will be discussed in more detail in Chapter 6, but essentially, unfair labour practices are any actions by the employer or the union that make potential union members act differently than they would have otherwise. Unfair labour practices are a concern during the organizing campaign because of their potential to influence the vote for or against the union in such a way that the outcome of the vote does not reflect the employees' actual desires. Canadian labour relations law contains guidelines describing what is and what is not an unfair labour practice. As we will see, however, it is sometimes very difficult to determine whether an action is an unfair labour practice or what impact the action had on the employees' attitudes or intentions. Notably, in many Canadian labour relations board decisions, the employer's intention in undertaking the action has been deemed less important than whether employees were intimidated by the action. In other cases, employer actions have been so blatantly intimidating that a labour relations board has certified the union even without sufficient levels of employee support.[36]

FACTORS AFFECTING THE SUCCESS OF AN ORGANIZING CAMPAIGN

A number of studies analyzing how organizing campaigns are conducted have attempted to identify the factors that distinguish successful organizing campaigns from unsuccessful ones ("successful" usually being defined either as obtaining sufficient numbers of expressions of employee support to file an application for certification, or as obtaining sufficient support in a representation vote to achieve certification).

Several studies in the United States have examined union activities during organizing campaigns and their influence on success rates.[37] We should keep in mind that American legislation governing union organizing is somewhat more restrictive than Canadian legislation, and thus similar studies in Canada might produce different results. Nevertheless, the results of these studies provide some indication what a successful organizing campaign might look like. The union strategies that appear to have the strongest influence on success are the so-called rank-and-file strategies involving personal contact with members, such as telephone contacts, house calls, small group meetings, and the presence of a representative organizing committee. Interestingly, less than a third of the unions represented in the data used these strategies in their campaigns. These studies also indicated that a combination of strategies is more likely to result in success than a single strategy, and that demographic or situational factors in individual workplaces can be more influential on success rates than the union's actions (e.g., the higher the percentage of women and/or minorities in the workforce, the higher the probability of success).

Another important factor influencing the outcome of organizing campaigns is the manner in which the campaign is conducted. One previously mentioned study indicated that, to be successful in organizing, unions must identify what is important to the workers they are attempting to represent, and must present their case in a way that shows they are aware of workers' concerns and are willing to address them.[38] In this study, which was based on data from interviews with workers, even workers with pro-union attitudes did not support the union when the union organizers treated the vote like a business deal in which workplace improvements would be exchanged for the payment of union dues, or when the union failed to pay much attention to the workers' specific concerns or their responses to the union's campaign strategy. In the words of one interviewee, "Maybe they [the union] were in it for us, maybe they really cared about us, but I don't think so. All they cared about was that they would be more competitive, because all the other stores were [unionized]."[39]

Thus, not surprisingly, two increasingly important factors in the success of an organizing campaign appear to be the amount of control over the campaign exerted by the employees targeted by the campaign and the amount of participation by those employees in the campaign activities. With greater diversity in the workforce, low rates of unionization in some demographic groups, and changes in the labour market and how work is conducted (all of which will be discussed in Chapter 13), successful organizing campaigns are, more often than not, those that involve the employees themselves, rather than those that are controlled or directed by the union or by the union's organizers. A number of case studies have shown that employee involvement in and control of organizing campaigns results in a better understanding of the industry and the workplace, better mobilization of the workforce, and more extensive internal and external contacts. All of these contribute to the union being able to operate a campaign that addresses the specific needs and concerns of the workers and that is better able to mobilize internal and external support for the unionization effort.[40] Participating in an organizing campaign can also help workers develop leadership and management skills that they otherwise might not have the opportunity to acquire. However, the model of worker-centred organizing represents a significant change from the traditional method of union organizing, and it can be resented by more traditional and bureaucratic union leaders who feel that worker-centred organizing undervalues or misuses their own extensive experience in running organizing campaigns.[41]

Finally, the employer's response to the organizing campaign can be a very strong influence on the campaign's success or failure. As we will see in our discussion of unfair labour practices in Chapter 6, part of the reason for legislation that restricts employer conduct during organizing campaigns is the potential power of the employer's words or actions to influence employee support for unionization. An analysis of American data shows that American employers faced with an organizing campaign commonly undertake five to nine tactics in response, such as hiring a consultant to help them conduct a counter-campaign, holding meetings with supervisors, and making promises of improvement.[42] While we should keep in mind that some of the more common employer tactics in the United States would be prohibited under Canadian legislation (e.g., threatening plant closures or holding "captive audience meetings"), the analysis indicates that using such tactics reduces the success rate of organizing campaigns by an average of 20 percent. A similar analysis using Canadian data indicates that approximately 80 percent of Canadian employers actively oppose organizing campaigns; their most common tactics include hiring lawyers, communicating directly with employees, and limiting communications between the union and the employees.[43] The employer actions with the strongest negative impact on the success of organizing campaigns are training managers to deal with the campaign (which reduces campaign success rates by 15 to 16 percent) and limiting the union's communication with employees (which reduces success rates by as much as 14 percent). Employer actions against the organizing campaign are particularly effective in reducing employee support for unions when they are used between the time when the union has filed its application for recognition and when the formal vote of support takes place.[44]

The Application for Certification

When the organizing committee believes it has sufficient membership support, as defined in their jurisdiction's labour legislation, the union will file an **application for certification** form with the appropriate labour relations board. The application indicates that a group of employees wish to be represented by a particular union in their dealings with the employer.

The application form has three major components:

- an indication of sufficient membership support for the application
- a description of the desired **bargaining unit** (the group of employees that will be represented in collective bargaining with the employer)
- an indication of the employer and the trade union covered by the application

We will discuss each of the components of the certification application in turn.

Migrant Farm Workers Unionize

SURREY.—For the first time, foreign workers imported to pick British Columbia crops have been allowed to join a union.

Migrant workers at Greenway Farms in Surrey have voted to join the United Food and Commercial Workers (UFCW) of Canada. The historic certification was granted with the support of more than 75 per cent of the roughly 40 affected workers. Never before had B.C.'s Labour Relations Board approved a union to represent workers brought to Canada under the federal Seasonal Agricultural Workers Program.

The program matches foreign workers, primarily from the Caribbean and Mexico, with agricultural employers who claim they cannot find Canadian employees. It has been criticized by observers who see it as a way of keeping wages in agriculture low and institutionalizing the exploitation of vulnerable guest workers, historically a group very hard to unionize.

"Right now, we're seeing small changes, nothing major yet," said a worker at Greenway Farms who spoke on condition of anonymity because he fears employer retaliation.

"Now we are hoping we will get our pay on time. We hope now we will finally get clean water. The water now isn't even good enough to take showers. Some of us are getting sick. We've never had decent water," he said, speaking through an interpreter.

The Greenway worker—call him Carlos—has been coming to B.C. to work since 2004. The income from Canadian farm work supports him and his family. He claims to have been unable to find work in his home country.

Asked why he was interested in joining a union, Carlos replied: "The bad treatment by the boss. We have been under a lot of pressure. For example, we don't have adequate housing and the water situation is bad. The water is contaminated and people are getting sick. The boss said he didn't have time to fix it. People were getting sick."

"I always tell the workers, 'Don't let people treat you like you don't count. You may not be Canadian citizens, but you are Canadian workers and you do have rights,'" says Lucy Luna, a UFCW organizer with the Abbotsford Agricultural Workers Alliance Support Centre.

She said workers at Greenway approached the union because of "unbearable" conditions at the Surrey farm. Greenway workers complained of verbal abuse and insults from supervisors, overwork, late paycheques and a general lack of respect.

Source: Sandborn, Tom. "Foreign Farm Workers Unionize: A First in BC." TheTyee.ca, August 21, 2008.

Sufficient Membership Support

The union filing a certification application must be able to show that it has sufficient support from the "employees" of the "employer" to make the application worthwhile. (The terms "employee" and "employer" have specific meanings in the context of labour relations legislation that will be outlined later.) The question of what constitutes sufficient support for certification is one of the more contentious issues that labour relations boards and legislators have to deal with. On the one hand, if not enough employees in a workplace support the union, serious problems may occur with negotiating and administering the collective agreement because the union's position may not truly reflect the feelings of the employees. On the other hand, given that union membership is established as a basic legal right of employees, it might be unfair to turn away a group of employees who want to exercise their right to form a union simply because of the size of the group.

In most Canadian jurisdictions, a certification application must be accompanied by an indication of a sufficient level of support from the employees in the proposed bargaining unit. Table 5-5 shows how different Canadian jurisdictions define a "sufficient" level of membership support.

TABLE 5-5   Required Levels of Support for Certification Applications

	Level of Support Required for Certification Application to be Considered	Level of Support Required for Application for Automatic Certification	Required Proof of Support
Federal	35% of employees in the proposed bargaining unit	Over 50% of employees in the proposed bargaining unit	Signing the membership application and paying at least $5 to the union in the 6 months preceding the certification application
Alberta	40% of employees in the proposed bargaining unit	No automatic certification	Maintaining and/or applying for membership and paying at least $2 on one's own behalf to the union, or signing a petition of support, within 90 days preceding the application

TABLE 5-5 Required Levels of Support for Certification Applications (Continued)

British Columbia	45% of employees in the proposed bargaining unit; a majority if the application is to displace another union	No automatic certification	Signing and dating a membership card or paying dues within 90 days preceding the application
Manitoba	40% of employees in the proposed bargaining unit; 45% if the application is to displace another union	At least 65% of employees in the proposed bargaining unit	Being a union member or joining the union 6 months before the application and maintaining membership prior to the application date
New Brunswick	40% of employees in the proposed bargaining unit	At least 60% of employees in the proposed bargaining unit; may certify without a vote if more than 50% support	Paying at least $1 on one's own behalf to the union
Newfoundland and Labrador	40% of employees in the proposed bargaining unit	No automatic certification; however, the union and the employer may jointly request that a vote not be held	Signing membership application at least 90 days before the application for certification
Nova Scotia	40% of employees in the proposed bargaining unit	No automatic certification; the Labour Relations Board may certify if it believes that a vote does not reflect employees' true wishes and it is satisfied that the application represents at least 40% of employees in the proposed bargaining unit	Joining a union or signing an application for membership, and paying the union at least $2 on one's own behalf, within 3 months before the date of the certification application

TABLE 5-5 Required Levels of Support for Certification Applications (Continued)

Ontario	40% of employees in the proposed bargaining unit who are members of the union on the application date	No automatic certification	Must be union member on the date of certification application
Prince Edward Island	Majority of employees in the proposed bargaining unit	At the discretion of the Labour Relations Board, if majority support is demonstrated	Joining a union or signing a document of support, and paying at least $2 in dues within 3 months before the certification application
Quebec	35% of employees of an employer	More than 50% of employees in the proposed bargaining unit	Signing a dated application for membership and personally paying at least $2 to union within 12 months preceding the application. Support is valid only if the membership application is not revoked during that time
Saskatchewan	45% of employees in the proposed bargaining unit	No automatic certification	Signing a card stating that the employee wishes to be represented by the union

Source: Human Resources and Skills Development Canada, Labour Program, Synoptic Charts on Legislation Pertaining to Certain Major Collective Bargaining Issues: Trade Union Application for Certification: General Private Sector Collective Bargaining Legislation (available at <www.rhdcc-hrsdc.gc.ca/eng/labour/labour_law/ind_rel/tuac.shtml>).

As Table 5-5 shows, all Canadian jurisdictions set a minimum level of support that must be demonstrated for an application for certification to be considered. However, a labour relations board may consider applications with less than the required level of support if the union making the application can show that the employer committed an unfair labour practice that intimidated the employees into not expressing support for the union. In such situations, a labour relations board will attempt to assess the effect of the employer's behaviour and, depending on the result of the assessment, will either allow the application to proceed; permit the union to attempt to collect further indications of support; or deny the application. As previously noted, a labour relations board also has the option of immediately declaring a certification if it believes that the employer's actions have had such an impact that the employees' intentions can no longer be discerned by a vote or by the number of signatures supporting the application. A labour relations board might also take this action if it believes that the employer may not cease its intimidating behaviour before a vote on the application is taken in the workplace.

If the percentage of bargaining unit employees expressing support for the union exceeds the minimum required percentage, the certification process may be faster in some jurisdictions. As Table 5-5 indicates, in some jurisdictions, if the level of support exceeds a specified amount, the union making the application may receive what is called **automatic certification**. Automatic certification means that the union is granted the right to represent the employees without undergoing any further tests of employee support. The reasoning behind this policy is that if a large number of employees support the application, any further polling of employee opinions would be redundant. Further polling would also allow employers more time to intimidate employees and pressure them to vote against their true feelings.

If the level of support for the certification exceeds the stated minimum but does not reach the level needed for automatic certification (in jurisdictions where automatic certification is allowed), the labour relations board will, after assessing the application criteria described below, require an employee vote before granting certification. This process is described in more detail in Chapter 6.

The level of support required for certification applications is a part of labour legislation that tends to fluctuate in accordance with the philosophy of the government in power. A political party with anti-union opinions is likely to raise the necessary level of support, with the justification that there must be support from a clear majority of the bargaining unit members. This point of view contends that it would be unjust for a

A certification vote in the workplace may not be necessary if automatic certification is available.

relatively small group of employees to impose their feelings about unionization on the majority of the workers.

A pro-union political party is likely to lower the required level of support or to create mechanisms—such as automatic certification—that speed up the certification process. The justification for this position is that the employer, who controls how the workplace operates and what the organization does, always holds the balance of power in a workplace. Thus, legislation must give the benefit of the doubt to the workers and assist them in exercising their legal right to form a union. This argument also contends that the opportunity for employers to influence their employees' expression of opinion should be minimized and that procedures like automatic certification are appropriate because they reduce the opportunity for employer interference when a clear majority of workers have already expressed their support for unionization.

One other factor that may affect a labour relations board's assessment of sufficient membership support is the timeliness of the application. As Chapter 6 will show, every Canadian jurisdiction has guidelines restricting when an application for certification can be filed. However, we should also note here that in addition to counting the level of support accompanying an application for certification, a labour relations board also looks at how long it has taken the organizing committee to assemble the expressions of support. If, in the board's opinion, an excessively long period has passed between the start of the organizing campaign and the attainment of the required level of support, the board may be concerned that the expressions of support obtained near the start of the campaign may no longer be valid; that is, given the amount of time that has passed between the expression of support and the filing of the certification application, some employees may have changed their minds about supporting the union or may have even left the organization altogether. As long as there is no evidence that unfair labour practices by the employer unduly extended the organizing campaign, a labour relations board may decide to disallow an application for certification if, in the board's opinion, the campaign was long enough to cause concerns about the timeliness or accuracy of expressions of support. We should also note that, as shown in Table 5-5, some Canadian jurisdictions have time limits regulating the period during which expressions of support must be collected for those expressions of support to be considered valid.

Appropriate Bargaining Unit

Every certification application must contain a description of the bargaining unit that the proposed union is seeking to represent. Generally, this description consists of the titles of the jobs that will or will not be represented by the union. For example, a proposed bargaining unit might be described as "all production, distribution, and support employees of Cardboard Box Manufacturers at the location of 1234 Jones Road, Industrytown, with the exception of supervisors, managers, payroll clerks, and human resources clerks."

The purpose of the bargaining unit description is twofold. First, there is sometimes concern about whether signatures in support of the certification application are valid—that is, whether the signatures are legitimate or whether they are the signatures of employees who are not included in the union. The labour relations board can cross-check the description of the proposed bargaining unit against the organization's list of employees and thus identify the specific employees who are included in the proposed bargaining unit. It can then be determined whether individual signatures should or should not be included in calculating whether the required level of support exists.

Second, a description of the proposed bargaining unit allows a labour relations board to assess whether the proposed unit is appropriate or not. There are several considerations that a board will address in determining whether a bargaining unit is appropriate: size and location of the bargaining unit, managerial and non-managerial employees, and definition of an employee. The principle underlying each of these considerations is **community of interest**: that is, there should be enough relevant characteristics in common among the applicants to make the union a cohesive and representative unit, structured to effectively represent its members in interactions with the employer. We will now outline each of these considerations.

Size and Location   The determination of an appropriate bargaining unit is an important issue for both the union and the employer. The union would like to represent as many workers as possible. This is desirable for the union not only because it will gain more revenue from **union dues**—the membership fees paid to the union by its members—but also because representing more workers gives the union more power in dealing with the employer.

However, there are practical difficulties associated with administering a bargaining unit that is too large or too widely dispersed. Communicating with or getting agreement among a very large membership can be challenging. Also, members located in several different places or performing very different jobs may have issues particular to their job or location that are overshadowed by more common issues within a large bargaining unit. Thus, the union may not be able to represent its members competently if the bargaining unit is too large or too diverse.

A labour relations board must also consider the effect of the bargaining unit's size and location on the relationship with the employer. One of the goals that a labour relations board tries to achieve in establishing an appropriate bargaining unit is a relative balance of bargaining power between the employer and the union. A bargaining unit so large that it gives the union far more bargaining power than the employer might be as inappropriate as a bargaining unit so small that the union would have very little bargaining power against the employer.

Managerial and Non-Managerial Employees   Another consideration in determining an appropriate bargaining unit is the question of who is eligible to be represented by the union. In other words, who is eligible to be in the bargaining unit? A general policy in labour legislation is that bargaining units should not include both managerial and non-managerial employees. This policy exists for several reasons. First, since managers are the workplace representatives of the owners of the company and the employer is entitled to rely on the loyalty of its representatives, management employees should not cause the employer concern by favouring other interests within the organization, such as the union or the employees. Second, a conflict of interest might exist if a manager with the power to discipline another employee was in the same bargaining unit as that employee. A general principle of union democracy is that all members are equal; a situation where one union member could discipline another would violate that principle. Third, as we know, a trade union by definition is legally entitled to be established and administered without employer interference. Placing managers in the same bargaining unit as non-managers would violate this principle, because the manager, as the employer's representative in the workplace, could influence issues such as union bargaining proposals to favour the employer's interests. And fourth, managers often have access to confidential material, such as budgets and personnel records. Hence, excluding them from a bargaining unit that represents non-managerial employees would protect the employer's interests (by not making this material available to bargaining unit members) and would also preserve the equality principle of union democracy.

While there are clearly several very good reasons to exclude managers from the same bargaining unit as non-managers, to do so is not always easy in practice, as it is sometimes very difficult to determine who is a manager and who is not. The job title alone may not be sufficient. Consider, for example, a situation at a restaurant where someone fills a position with the title of "shift manager." This person may be in charge of operations during a particular period and may have managerial authority while the shift is in progress, but this same person, during the "managerial" shift, may fill in for regular workers who are absent, or assist those workers who need help in their non-management tasks. This same person may also be scheduled to work as a regular employee at other times during the working week. Is this person a manager, and should he or she be excluded from the bargaining unit?

The question of who is or is not a manager has become even more difficult to answer in light of workplace trends such as downsizing, flattened organizational hierarchies, teamwork, and flexible organizational structures. All of these trends have blurred the traditional boundaries between managerial and non-managerial work. Thus, it is no longer appropriate to exclude a position from a bargaining unit simply because the position is titled "manager." A labour relations board will usually look beyond the job title and consider the following criteria in determining whether a position should be included in the bargaining unit:

1. Does the job description of the position give the person in the position the authority to hire, fire, and discipline other persons in the organization?

2. Does the job description of the position indicate that the position is responsible for production or operations?

3. In the organizational structure, do other positions report to this position? Does this position involve direct supervision of the work performed in other positions?

4. Is the person in this position the immediate authority if a crisis or emergency occurs?

5. Does the person in this position have access to confidential information such as employee records or budgets?

6. If the position includes both managerial and non-managerial work, what is the division of working time between these two sets of duties?

If the answer to any of the first five questions is "yes", a labour relations board will likely exclude the position from the bargaining unit, regardless of the formal title of the position. A labour relations board may go beyond the written job description and examine evidence of actual workplace practices if there appears to be a significant discrepancy between the job description and the actual operations of the organization. In assessing the answer to the sixth question about the proportion of time spent on managerial and non-managerial duties, a labour relations board will likely exclude a position from the bargaining unit if the majority of the employee's time is spent performing managerial duties, regardless of the formal job title the employee holds.

Some Canadian jurisdictions have attempted to deal with the issue of managerial exclusion from bargaining units by permitting managers to unionize in different bargaining units from those they supervise. This provision recognizes the right of workers to unionize, but also maintains the separation between manager and employees that is considered fundamental to the democratic operation of a union.

Another consideration in this regard is whether to include employees in the bargaining unit whose work shares some of the characteristics (but not all) of managerial positions. These employees are usually referred to as **exempt employees**. Exempt employees usually perform work involving administrative support to top managers. In such a position, the employees may have access to confidential information such as employee records or employers' plans for collective bargaining. Although these employees do not possess other powers that managers traditionally have, such as authority over hiring, they are usually excluded from the bargaining unit because their access to confidential information could benefit the union or harm other bargaining unit members.

Defining an "Employee"

Another consideration in determining who should be included in the bargaining unit is deciding who is an employee. This may seem like a fairly straightforward question, but because of changing employment relationships, it is actually quite complex. New forms of employment such as contract work, temporary work, limited-term contracts, and job sharing make the employment relationship much more variable than in the past.

The labour codes in all Canadian jurisdictions clearly state that one must be an employee in order to be included in a bargaining unit. The definition of "employee" is included in each jurisdiction's labour code as well as in the relevant act governing employment standards, but generally these definitions recognize an "employee" as someone who works on a regular basis for an employer in a dependent relationship. In other words, the worker depends on the employer for the majority or all of his or her work, and the employer compensates the worker for performing the work. An employee is also someone who performs his or her work under the direction and control of the employer. The employer determines what the work will be and how it will be conducted, assigns the work to the employee, and determines when the work is completed and what level of performance or quality is needed for successful completion.

These criteria for defining an "employee" are broad enough to include most full-time and part-time employees and shift workers. However, it is questionable whether employees in <u>less permanent forms of work</u>, including some kinds of part-time work or some forms of contract work, would be defined as employees if these criteria were used. This issue of definitions is of particular concern to unions, since the size of the bargaining unit may be eroded if employers replace full-time permanent workers with temporary, part-time, or contract workers. Another concern is the possibility that the employer might eliminate positions entirely and instead have the work performed by workers employed by another (non-union) company, in the employment arrangement known as **outsourcing**.

In situations where it is unclear whether a worker is an "employee," the position of labour relations boards has generally been that if a worker has an ongoing dependent relationship with the organization, the worker should be considered an employee and included in the bargaining unit, regardless of their job title or their type of contractual relationship with the organization. For example, if an employee is a limited-term contract employee whose only contract is with the employer (i.e., the employee does not perform contract work for any other employer), then he or she would likely be considered an employee. Likewise, if a worker is hired on a less-than-permanent basis but performs the same work as bargaining unit members, the worker might be considered part of the bargaining unit. Temporary workers who are rehired on successive contracts to perform the same work and essentially work as permanent workers–but who are not recognized as such because they are formally employed on a temporary basis—would likely also be considered part of the bargaining unit.

Labour relations boards and legislators are strict about enforcing the definition of "employee" in order to prevent employers from escaping their responsibilities under the collective agreement by decreasing the size of the bargaining unit. A smaller bargaining unit means a less powerful union, and thus employers who would prefer to deal with a less powerful union might be tempted to hire workers who do not meet the definition of an employee and thus would not be included in the bargaining unit. Often, too, there is a considerable cost incentive for employers to replace permanent full-time unionized employees with temporary, part-time, or contract employees, since these types of employees usually receive lower rates of pay and fewer benefits. Because of these factors, a labour relations board will generally insist that an employer demonstrate that the removal of work or workers from the jurisdiction of the bargaining unit was done for legitimate business reasons and was not motivated solely by a desire to weaken the union. "Legitimate business reasons" are usually ascertained by determining whether the employer would have undertaken the action regardless of whether the union was present or not. (This issue of employer motivation for actions will also be discussed in the sections on unfair labour practices and successorship in chapters 6 and 12.)

In concluding our discussion of issues related to the appropriate bargaining unit, we will note that a labour relations board will not reject an application for certification simply because the application contains a bargaining unit description that the board considers inappropriate. If such an application is received, the board will usually contact the union making the application and suggest alterations to the proposed bargaining unit that in the board's opinion would make the unit appropriate. The union then has the choice of proceeding with the application as it stands and taking the chance that it may be rejected because of the concerns over the proposed bargaining unit, or resubmitting the application with the suggested alterations.

Defining an "Employer"

The application for certification requires the applicant to indicate which employer the application is intended to address. Not every Canadian labour law provides a definition of "employer." The laws that do (federal, British Columbia, Alberta, Saskatchewan, New Brunswick, Prince Edward Island, Newfoundland and Labrador,

Quebec, and Nova Scotia) generally state that an employer is someone who employs at least one employee (at least three in Saskatchewan), and/or who uses the services of at least one dependent contractor. This lack of precision in definition has led to some practical difficulties that become apparent when one considers the many different forms of ownership that exist (e.g., sole proprietorship, partnership, franchise, branch office, subcontracting, one company owning another differently named company).

Generally, it is expected that the certification application will name the business entity that is the actual employer. Thus, a certification application may contain employer definitions such as "Company [name] doing business as [another company name]" or "[Corporation] franchise located at [franchise location]." If a certification application covers more than one geographical location of the same employer—for example, multiple locations of a chain store or restaurant—the certification application will specify which locations will be included in the proposed bargaining unit.

In situations where the structure or operations of a business make it difficult to determine the actual employer, a labour relations board will consider several criteria in identifying the employer. One question a labour relations board may ask is where the authority for hiring lies. The part of the business that actually hires employees or carries out other human resource management functions (e.g., keeping employee records) may be identified as the employer. A second question a board may ask is what part of the business is accountable for establishing and monitoring work conditions. This question can be particularly relevant in situations such as a franchise arrangement, where one part of the business may have to follow directions established by a central authority, such as a franchisor. If such directions are absolute and the business has little or no flexibility in applying them, the franchisor rather than the operator of the franchise may be considered the actual employer. A third question a board may ask is who exercises control over day-to-day work and production. Does one part of the business completely control another part, or does each part have individual autonomy and judgement in overseeing everyday functions? The answers to these questions assist a labour relations board in determining who the actual employer is.

In some organizational structures, an owner or corporation conducts business through multiple corporate entities that share resources such as workers, supplies, or work sites. In situations involving such a complex structure, a labour relations board has the option of declaring all of the entities to be a **single employer** or **common employer**,

Franchise operations are often difficult to unionize. This McDonald's restaurant outside Montreal closed down during a certification campaign because the owners alleged the restaurant was losing money.

as long as all the entities are under the same control and direction. For example, if one individual operates several franchises of the same restaurant in different geographic locations, a labour relations board could declare that, despite the geographic dispersion, the restaurants are a single operation and thus workers at all the restaurants should be included in the same bargaining unit. Giving labour relations boards the power to make this declaration discourages employers from avoiding unionization by creating non-union subsidiary companies and shifting operations into those companies and away from unionized operations.

Defining a "Trade Union"

The final component in a certification application is an indication that the application comes from a bona fide trade union. Most labour codes state that a bona fide trade union is a union that was established free of employer interference and is run on democratic principles (i.e., every member is entitled to a vote and has an equal voice in running the union's business).

As previously mentioned, most certification applications come from established unions that are seeking to organize new locals. However, there is nothing to stop a group of workers from starting their own union, provided they can show that the employer did not assist them or force them to do so and that there is no employer interference in the ongoing operation of the union. If a certification application is submitted by a new union, a labour relations board will examine such documents as the new union's constitution and meeting minutes to ensure that there was and is no employer interference in the union's formation and operations. A labour relations board will also usually ensure that the union's constitution indicates that the union operates on democratic and non-discriminatory principles.

ORGANIZING IN THE CONSTRUCTION INDUSTRY AND VOLUNTARY RECOGNITION

Before closing our discussion of organizing campaigns and certification applications, we will describe two situations that do not completely fit the process of organizing and applying for certification described above. The first situation involves organizing in the construction industry, which does not follow the same model as organizing in other Canadian industries. In the second situation, the employer voluntarily agrees to recognize the union as the employees' bargaining agent.

Before addressing these special situations, however, we will briefly discuss how labour legislation deals with the possibility that an employer, rather than the employees, might initiate an organizing campaign. Most Canadian labour legislation does not recognize as a union any organization or association of employees that is dominated or influenced by an employer. The common name for unions created or dominated by an employer is a **company union**. Historically, when employers have created or dominated unions, the result—known as a **sweetheart agreement**—is a union-management agreement that unduly favours management and/or does not consider the needs and wants of the employees. A company union is usually powerless or unwilling to negotiate a collective agreement that is not a sweetheart agreement because, in effect, the union is controlled by the employer. Thus, the employer would insist that the union agree to contract clauses that favour the employer (e.g., clauses that give the employer unilateral power to set and change wage rates). Another problem with company unions is that normal union-management processes such as addressing employee grievances become essentially meaningless if the union cannot independently represent the employees' interests or concerns.

Because of the disadvantages of company unions, it is almost unknown for an employer to initiate an organizing campaign successfully. The employer's initiation of the campaign, even if it is done with the worthy intention of giving employees a formal voice in the workplace, could lead to an employer-dominated union. This would likely be the case if the union was financially dependent on the employer, since the employer could withdraw financial support if there was a disagreement with the union and thus leave the union unable to function. While a labour relations board would not reject outright an application for certification that was generated by an employer-initiated organizing campaign or that came from an employer-dominated union, it would certainly examine

the application with much more care and precision than it would an application resulting from an employee-initiated organizing campaign or from a union free of employer
domination.

The Construction Industry

Canadian labour legislation recognizes that conditions for organizing bargaining units
in the construction industry are somewhat different than in other Canadian industries
because of the mobility of workers and employment. Most Canadian labour laws thus
have a separate section dealing with the construction industry. In effect, each project
or work site is considered to be a workplace, and a separate certification must be
obtained for each project and for each unionized trade working on the project.
Timeliness is clearly an important consideration of certification for construction work
sites because of the time schedules associated with completing the project in an efficient manner. It would be pointless to issue a certification order after the project had
been completed.

Thus, most Canadian labour law permits the unions that represent workers on construction projects to dispense with the responsibility of conducting an organizing campaign and filing an application for certification. Instead, the process of obtaining
unionized workers is initiated by the employer. A construction employer who bids on
and secures a contract stipulating the use of unionized workers will contact the appropriate union and request that the union provide the appropriate unionized employees
for the project. If, for example, a contractor secures a contract that requires the project
to be completed with the use of unionized carpenters, the contractor will contact the carpenters' union and request that the union supply the required number of carpenters.
This form of employer involvement in certification is accepted by labour relations boards
because the union providing the workers is an independent union and not one created
by the employer.

Voluntary Recognition

In some situations, a union may be able to satisfy an employer that it has organized
employees in a unit appropriate for collective bargaining without going through the
formality of making an application for certification to a labour relations board. If the

employer accepts the union's proposed bargaining unit, most Canadian labour law permits the employer to recognize the union's right to act as the exclusive bargaining agent for those employees without official recognition from a labour relations board. This acceptance by the employer is called **voluntary recognition**. If voluntary recognition occurs, the appropriate provisions of the relevant labour legislation will govern the employer-union collective bargaining relationship.

Under voluntary recognition, the employer accepts the union as the employees' bargaining agent without any representation vote or other formalization of the union's existence. Labour law in several provinces allows a labour relations board to grant certification if a voluntary recognition agreement has been in effect for several years. Table 5-6 identifies the jurisdictions in Canada that have provisions for voluntary recognition.

TABLE 5-6 Voluntary Recognition

	Voluntary Recognition Available
Federal	Yes
Alberta	Yes
British Columbia	Yes
Manitoba	Not specified
New Brunswick	Yes
Newfoundland and Labrador	Not specified
Nova Scotia	Yes
Ontario	Yes
Prince Edward Island	Not specified
Quebec	Immediate certification is available if employees and the employer agree on the composition of bargaining unit
Saskatchewan	Not specified

SUMMARY

The organizing campaign is important to understand because it is the start of the process through which a union enters a workplace. There are numerous reasons why employees may decide to join a union. The most common are dissatisfaction with workplace conditions or dissatisfaction with management. Personal, economic, and societal factors may also affect whether or not employees decide to support a union in their workplace.

If there is sufficient interest among workers to justify pursuing the idea of unionization, an organizing campaign can be initiated. The purpose of the organizing campaign is to generate sufficient support to make an application for certification to a labour relations board. The labour relations board assesses several components of the application, including whether there is sufficient support for unionization, whether the composition of the proposed bargaining unit is appropriate, whether the members of the proposed bargaining unit meet the definition of "employee," and whether the proposed union meets the definition of a legitimate trade union. The labour relations board will also determine if there was employer or union activity that might have persuaded employees to act against their true wishes.

If a labour relations board is satisfied that the application for certification meets the required standards and that the indications of support have not been unduly influenced, the board will then proceed with the process of certification. This process is described in detail in Chapter 6.

KEY TERMS FOR CHAPTER 5

application for certification (p. 181)
automatic certification (p. 185)
bargaining agent (p. 174)
bargaining unit (p. 181)
community of interest (p. 187)
company union (p. 195)
exempt employees (p. 190)
instrumentality (p. 166)

organizing campaign (p. 164)

outsourcing (p. 191)

single employer/common employer (p. 193)

sweetheart agreement (p. 195)

unfair labour practices (p. 177)

union dues (p. 188)

voluntary recognition (p. 197)

DISCUSSION QUESTIONS FOR CHAPTER 5

1. Why would an employee's family background influence whether an employee would want a union in his or her workplace?

2. What factors in the workplace are likely to cause the kind of dissatisfaction that would lead to unionization?

3. Outline the steps in an organizing campaign.

4. Explain why most provincial labour codes require a minimum level of support among workers for a certification application to be filed.

5. A small group of clerical workers who are employed in the administrative office of a large manufacturing plant want to form a union. Identify and discuss the considerations that would be raised in deciding whether this group is an appropriate bargaining unit.

6. What are the factors to consider in determining who is an employee? What factors should be considered in deciding who is a manager?

7. If workers at a franchise operation want to unionize, who would be named as the employer and why?

CASE 5-1

DRIVERS UNION AND *DAILY NEWS*

(Based on *Teamsters and Leader Post*, 2007)

The union is applying to represent a bargaining unit of drivers who deliver bundles of newspapers and advertising materials. The employer opposes the application because it believes that the drivers are independent contractors, and thus they are not eligible to be part of a bargaining unit because they are not employees. The labour relations board has been asked to determine if the proposed bargaining unit is appropriate.

Case Facts

The union has applied to represent a group of 39 individuals who work as drivers. These individuals are responsible for picking up bundles of newspapers and advertising packets and delivering the bundles to drop sites, where they are then sorted for individual distribution. Some of the bundles are delivered daily, but other bundles are distributed three days a week or six days a week, depending on the materials' publication schedule. Deliveries may also be required on short notice Monday through Saturday if there is a shortage of materials at a distribution site. Most of the deliveries are within the boundaries of the city served by the *Daily News*, but there are some deliveries that go to rural areas outside the city. The work schedule for each individual driver depends on which materials they have signed contracts to deliver. There are 64 "distribution runs" in total, and each driver services between one and five runs.

The person who manages the distribution process, Jim Farnsworth, is an employee of the *Daily News*. He negotiates a contract with each individual driver. The contract outlines the delivery requirements of the "distribution runs" the driver is assigned to, and also sets out the obligations of each party. The rate that the driver is paid for the runs is based on the *Daily News*' calculation of the daily cost of the run. Farnsworth testified to the board that there is no shortage of persons who want to do this work, and that while payment rates can be negotiated, new contracts or open contracts are often taken by current drivers. Therefore, many times the rate that the *Daily News* offers to the driver is accepted without negotiation. The contracts are not automatically renewed, and can be terminated on 14 days' notice from either party.

The union told the board that the application for certification was intended to include drivers who subcontracted their work, since the union knew of at least one contract-holder who had employees doing the actual deliveries for him.

Farnsworth told the board that the drivers' pay is set for the term of the contract and does not vary even if there are changes in external variables such as fuel costs. He described a recent situation where one of the newspapers included in the bundles switched its distribution to another carrier. That reduced the amount of work required in some of the contracts, but the rate paid to the drivers did not change.

The contracts that the drivers sign are for the most part standardized. Any differences reflect such factors as the driver negotiating a specific payment rate; the way in which the driver is paid; whether the driver will use subcontractors to do the contracted work; whether the driver is part- or full-time, and who will carry out the work if the driver is not full-time; and whether the driver will use particular "methods to achieve efficiency". The standardized parts of the contracts describe the driver as an independent contractor, and by signing the contract the driver agrees to be acknowledged as having that status. The drivers agree to deliver the bundles on the day of publication; to provide a vehicle and a spare vehicle if needed; to cover all costs of vehicle operation and maintenance; and to carry at least $2 million liability insurance. They also agree to have a replacement driver available if needed. The drivers are allowed to purchase fuel at the cardlock stations used by the *Daily News* if they arrange to do so, but they are not required to purchase fuel by this method.

The drivers are paid each month, upon submission of an invoice to the *Daily News*. Most of the drivers have GST numbers and collect GST on their payments. Most are classified as "self-employed" for tax purposes, and claim expenses and income from their *Daily News* work as part of their self-employment. Some of the drivers who use subcontractors pay the subcontractors as employees; they make the required deductions from their payments to the subcontractors and issue annual T4 slips to them. The *Daily News* does not make any deductions from the payments to the drivers except as required by the workers compensation board. The *Daily News* does not provide any benefits to the drivers or conduct performance evaluations on them. The only equipment provided by the *Daily News* to the drivers is plastic bags to cover the bundles in bad weather.

The drivers are allowed to enter into contracts with other businesses to provide delivery services, but the *Daily News* contract states that they are to "give priority" to their obligations to the *Daily News*. The drivers are free to use any kind of equipment in carrying out their contracted duties, and to carry out the work however they choose. Complaints about deliveries are relayed by the *Daily News* to the driver involved. The costs of any damage caused by the driver are charged back to the driver.

The Union's Position

The union told the board that although the drivers are identified as "self-employed" and "independent contractors," the work that they did was similar to that of workers identified by "employees" in several previous cases brought to the board. The union argued that previous cases had made a distinction between "economic dependency" and "statutory purpose" in defining who was or was not an employee. In this situation, the union argued, the key question should be "statutory purpose," or whether the persons performing the service had a relationship with the contractor that could be the subject of collective bargaining. The union argued that the answer to this question depended on the extent to which the contracted relationship allowed the employee to manage the market for their labour in a way that benefited them.

The union suggested that once the drivers committed to making deliveries at a set pay rate on a route that was designated by the *Daily News*, they no longer functioned on an independent basis and had very limited autonomy to decide how to use the resources that were allocated to them.

The Employer's Position

The employer argued that the drivers were independent contractors and not employees. In the employer's opinion, the drivers' status and work conditions matched many of the criteria for defining an independent contractor that had been established in previous cases decided by the board. These included:

- The right to use substitute workers

- Ownership of materials

- The ability to sell one's services to the market generally

- The freedom to reject job opportunities and to work where and how one wished

- Evidence of variation in fees paid for services rendered

CASE 5-2

SENIOR SERVICES INC. AND HOUSING EMPLOYEES UNION

(Based on *Insite Housing and BC Government and Service Employees' Union*, 2008)

In this case, the union wants to have a bargaining unit certified at one of the employer's places of business. The employer opposes the application on the grounds that an appropriate bargaining unit would include all of its locations in the province. The labour relations board has been asked to determine the composition of the appropriate bargaining unit.

Case Facts

The union and the employer told the board that they agree on the following facts:

- The employer has been in business for five years; it provides care and services to seniors who cannot live independently. The employer delivers its services of supportive and assisted living through different types of partnerships with health authorities, private operators, non-profit groups, and the provincial government's social housing program. The employer operates in 10 communities throughout the province. In six of these partnerships, the employer provides operations management services; in seven others, it acts as a mentor to help other organizations develop their own programs and services. The site covered by the application for certification is a site where the employer provides operations management services, which usually includes personal care services, hospitality services, and social/recreational activities.

- There are seven different job classifications for employees. There are 174 employees in total. 11 work at the organization's head office, and six are managers at different sites throughout the province. A geographical all-employee unit would include approximately 157 employees. The union's application for certification covers 19 employees at a single site.

- At some sites, usually those with more than 20 living units, there is a coordinator who is a licensed practical nurse. At smaller sites, there is a leader who is a certified residential care aide.

- All sites have assisted living workers, who have residential care aide certificates, and cooks. Some but not all sites have a chef, who must have a Red Seal Executive Chef credential. Some but not all sites have a recreation coordinator. All sites have multi-service workers, who provide kitchen help, housekeeping services, and laundry services. The union is applying to certify a unit that includes the classifications of assisted living worker, chef, cook, cook/multi-service worker, multi-service worker, and recreation coordinator.

- All classifications have standardized job descriptions, and wages and benefits are standardized throughout the province. The employer's human resources operations are also standardized, including training, although there is individual on-the-job orientation.

- Depending on the form of partnership, some of the employer's operations fall under specific laws or regulations, but generally the programs are delivered in a standard format regardless of location. The employer also has a trademarked philosophy, and requires all employees to wear standardized uniforms with labels identifying themselves as members of the company.

- There is a Community Manager at each site, who participates in hiring and firing decisions, along with being responsible for staff scheduling (including vacations, overtime, and leaves of absence), staff direction, and relations with clients and residents. The Community Manager makes recommendations for wage increases but does not have final approval. Work schedules are subject to final approval by the employer's head office, which also must approve any deviations from standardized policy.

- The employer has one overall budget covering all of its sites.

- As of the date the union's application for certification was filed, there had been no interchange of employees between the site covered by the application and the employer's other places of business. After the application was filed, one employee from another site applied through the employer's internal posting process and was hired at the site that the union wants to certify. Employees are eligible to bid on vacancies at other sites, and if an employee changes their place of employment, they take with them all of their earned service and benefit entitlements. Some of the sites share "pools" of on-call employees, but the site that is the subject of the application for certification has its own "pool".

- The site that is the subject of the application for certification is more than 200 kilo-metres (a four-hour drive) away from the employer's next closest site of operations.

The Employer's Position

The employer argued that the structure of the employer's organization should be given particular importance in determining an appropriate bargaining unit, and that the union should not expect the employer to alter its business arrangements or operations to accommodate the union's desired bargaining unit. It argued that the board should also be concerned with designing a bargaining unit that is conducive to successful collective bargaining.

The employer stated that all employees have the same skills, which are acquired prior to hiring; that hiring practices and job descriptions are standardized; and that the overall working environment of the sites is standardized. The employer agreed that there is some variation in operations between sites but argued that such variations are usually due to variations in the number of living units at the site, not due to variations in the types of work performed. The employer further suggested that the ability of employees at one site to apply for jobs at another site showed the degree of stan-dardization of jobs and duties across the entire organization.

The employer stated that its operations are highly centralized and are treated as one integrated whole, including day-to-day hands-on management. The sites are not treated as separate profit centres, and certifying one location would require the employer to change many of its business operations, as certain expenses (e.g., those associated with collective bargaining) would have to be charged to that location alone. Certification of only one site would also cause problems in such situations as transfer-ring seniority if employees moved, and potentially cause differences in other areas such as scheduling and disciplinary practices.

The employer agreed that the sites at which it operates are geographically distrib-uted throughout the province, but stated that the community of interest among the employees is shared throughout the entire organization.

The Union's Position

The union argued that despite the centralization of the employer's operations, there is a lack of employee integration between the individual sites. It also argued that the sites are located in distinctly different geographical areas.

CASE 5-3

WATERSIDE CASINOS AND GENERAL EMPLOYEES UNION

(Based on *Lake City Casinos Ltd. and BCGEU*, 2001)

In this case, the union is applying to be certified as the representative of a bargaining unit composed of surveillance operators at a casino. The employer is arguing that these positions involve confidential information and thus the individuals who fill them do not meet the definition of "employee" and should be excluded from unionization.

Case Facts

The company operating Waterside Casinos runs four casinos at different locations throughout the province. The General Employees Union has applied to the labour relations board to be certified to represent the surveillance operators at two of these locations. The union already has bargaining units at all four casinos. The union is applying for a separate bargaining unit for the surveillance employees but has asked the board, as an alternative, to amend the existing certifications to include these employees.

In order to understand the surveillance operators' work and the current situation of unionization in casinos, the board called for evidence in three different areas. Each area will be described in turn.

The Job of Surveillance Operator

The board member hearing the case was not able to discuss some of the testimony publicly, since it would have compromised the integrity of the security systems of the casinos.

However, what was revealed was that surveillance operators report to a shift manager who then reports to the casino general manager, the person ultimately accountable for casino operations. The operators monitor all gaming and money-handling functions and observe and report on all activities of employees and customers on the gaming floor. They ensure that procedures adhere to those established by the provincial gambling regulatory authority and also to the employer's own policies and procedures. They also analyze gaming activity for criminal, suspicious, unusual, or undesirable play.

To perform these functions, the operators monitor a video camera system that covers the inside and outside of the casinos. Each camera has a separate video feed that is attached to a continuously running videotape machine; the tapes in the video recorders are changed regularly. Additionally, operators can choose to watch a certain activity on dedicated monitors. There are no cameras in washrooms, break rooms, or administrative offices. The gaming floor employees do not know how many cameras there are or where they are directed, or whether there are any blind spots in the cameras' coverage. There are also two radio frequencies that broadcast in the casino. One is used by slot attendants and the cash cage, and the other by security and surveillance.

The casino's rules require that monitoring take place when there are "hopper fills" (refilling the coin bins inside slot machines) or during the "drop" when the machine pays out winnings. Apart from situations such as these and others where monitoring is required, the surveillance operators use their own discretion in determining what will be monitored. There may be specific requests from management to monitor certain activities. The choice of what to monitor will depend on how busy the casino is, what areas are busy, and whether there is suspicious activity or activity that might contravene casino policies.

If an impropriety on the gaming floor is noted, the surveillance operators are required to report it to the surveillance supervisor. Depending on the impropriety, the operators may also have to complete a written report, record information on a log sheet, or fill out an occurrence report. They may also be required to complete a table tracking sheet, which records cards and bets on table games; a table win/loss sheet; or other reports on dealer performance. Any of these reports can be used by gaming floor supervisors in reviewing the performance of gaming floor employees. Comments may also be noted in employees' personal records, which in turn can be used in performance evaluations.

Surveillance operators can independently choose to monitor certain employees or any suspicious activity. They can also independently decide to investigate any suspicious activity by reviewing the videotapes from the cameras monitoring the gaming floor. As a result, they may be required to testify in criminal proceedings or other hearings resulting from actions taken against gaming floor employees alleged to have participated in inappropriate conduct.

The employer encourages the surveillance operators not to interact with other employees. While there is some socialization between surveillance operators and gaming floor employees, it is very limited. The surveillance operators are physically isolated from the other casino employees while doing their jobs.

Once an employee has worked as a surveillance operator, the employee is not permitted to work anywhere else in the casino because of his or her knowledge of surveillance and the possibility that he or she could collude with other employees or patrons in breaching the system.

Union Structure

The union has over 500 bargaining units, including several that represent workers in hotels, casinos, and credit unions. Local units usually meet two or three times annually, although occasionally there may be meetings of locals involved in specific components or industries. Each local has its own chair and executive, which are elected by the membership. The chair is elected by employees within the casino, and if the surveillance workers were certified as a bargaining unit, they would have the right to attend local meetings and vote in union elections.

Most locals have social functions that are open to all members. There may also be area social functions for all of the units and locals within a geographical area, in addition to individual bargaining unit functions.

Grievances filed by employees are managed by local shop stewards and the union's business representative. An area grievance appeal committee, which includes two elected members, deals with disputes related to the disposition of grievances. If disputes are not resolved, they can be appealed to a provincial appeals committee.

Each union member is required to abide by the union's constitution and bylaws and to uphold a "pledge of obligation" to the union. The union has the authority to discipline its members for violations in these areas. The union has only rarely had to do this, mostly when union members have crossed union picket lines during legal strikes. The union also expects that members will not divulge information to the employer that has been discussed at union meetings. Union members may be expected to testify against other bargaining unit members if they have witnessed certain events or may be competing for a job transfer or promotion; the union regards this as a regular part of the grievance process.

The union has had limited experience in representing two bargaining units with a single employer. The examples cited at the hearing involved a unit of supervisory employees and a unit of non-managerial employees.

Casino Industry

Six companies operate casinos in the province; five of these companies have certified bargaining units at their casinos. At the time of the hearing, there were 18 casinos in the province, of which eight had certified bargaining units. Three different unions have certifications at casinos in the province. The drive to unionize employees in casinos did not commence in earnest until the late 1990s because, at that time, there was an expansion of the casino industry with the introduction of slot machines. The four casinos operated by the employer in this case were all certified through automatic certification.

The Union's Position

The union argues that although the surveillance operators are responsible for monitoring the performance of other staff, their job is similar to that of casino security staff, who are already included in the existing bargaining units in the casinos. It also argues that there are already employees in other bargaining units who investigate and report on infractions of behaviour by other union members and that the union is able to manage any conflicts that arise as a result of such situations.

The union also argues that the pattern of unionization in the casino industry indicates that this is a "difficult to organize" sector of the labour market, and thus the board should be more lenient than it would be otherwise to acknowledge the problems that unions face in certifying these types of workers.

The Employer's Argument

The employer argues that the surveillance operators have access to information about the employer that other employees do not. Consequently, to put them in a bargaining unit would create a conflict of interest and destroy the "arm's-length" relationship that is expected to exist between the union and management. Thus, the employer believes that the surveillance operators do not meet the definition of "employee" in the relevant labour relations legislation.

References

[1] Barling, J., Fullagar, C., & Kelloway, E.K. (1992). *The union and its members: a psychological approach*. Oxford, UK: Oxford University Press.

[2] Barling, J., Kelloway, E.K., & Bremermann, E.H. (1991). Preemployment predictors of union attitudes: the role of family socialization and work beliefs. *Journal of Applied Psychology*, 76(5), 725–731.

[3] Hester, K., & Fuller, J.B. (2001). Building union commitment: the impact of parental attitudes and participation. *Labor Studies Journal, 26*(2), 17–31.

[4] Cornfield, D.B. & Kim, H. (1994). Socioeconomic status and unionization attitudes in the United States. *Social Forces*, 73(2), 521–532.

[5] Brett, J.M. (1980). Why employees want unions. *Organizational Dynamics*, Spring 1980, 47–59.

[6] Youngblood, S.A., DeNisi, A.S., Molleston, J.L., & Mobley, W.H. (1984). The impact of work environment, instrumentality beliefs, perceived labour union image, and subjective norms on union voting intentions. *Academy of Management Journal*, 27(3), 576–590.

[7] Cooke, W.N. (1983). Determinants of the outcomes of union certification elections. *Industrial and Labor Relations Review*, 36(3), 402–414.

[8] Markowitz, L. (1995). Union presentation of self and worker participation in organizing campaigns. *Sociological Perspectives, 38*(3), 437–453.

[9] Milton, L.P. (2003). An identity perspective on the propensity of high-tech talent to unionize. *Journal of Labor Research*, 24(1), 31–54.

[10] Cregan, C., Bartram, T., & Stanton, P. (2009). Union organizing as a mobilizing strategy: the impact of social identity and transformational leadership on the collectivism of union members. *British Journal of Industrial Relations, 47*(4), 701–722.

[11] Premack, S.L., & Hunter, J.E. (1988). Individual unionization decisions. *Psychological Bulletin, 103*(2), 223–234; Long. R.L. & Shields, J.L. (2009). Do unions affect pay methods of Canadian firms? A longitudinal study. *Relations Industrielles/Industrial Relations, 64*(3), 442–465.

[12] Cooke, *op. cit.*

[13] Cooke, *op. cit.*

[14] Premack & Hunter, *op. cit.*; Brett, *op. cit.*; Buttigieg, D.M., Deery, S.J., & Iverson, R.D. (2007). An event history analysis of union joining and leaving. *Journal of Applied Psychology*, *92(3)*, 829–839.

[15] Freeman, R.B., & Rogers, J. (1999). *What workers want*. Ithaca, NY: ILR Press/Cornell University Press.

[16] Deshpande, S.P. (1995). Factors influencing employee association members' votes for unionization. *The Journal of Psychology*, *129(6)*, 621–628.

[17] Montgomery, B.R. (1989). The influence of attitudes and normative pressures on voting decisions in a union certification election. *Industrial and Labor Relations Review*, *42(4)*, 262–279.

[18] Deshpande, S., & Fiorito, J. (1989). Specific and general beliefs in union voting models. *Academy of Management Journal*, *32(4)*, 883–897; Montgomery, *op. cit.*

[19] Montgomery, *op. cit.*

[20] Deshpande & Fiorito, *op. cit.*

[21] Robinson, J.G., & McIlwee, J.S. (1989). Obstacles to unionization in high-tech industries. *Work and Occupations*, *16(2)*, 115–136.

[22] Cooke, *op. cit.*

[23] Robinson & McIlwee, *op. cit.*

[24] Chaison, G.N., & Rose, J.B. (1991). The macrodeterminants of union growth and decline. In Strauss, G., Gallagher, D.G., & Fiorito, J. (Eds.), *The state of the unions*. Madison, WI: Industrial Relations Research Association.

[25] Bratsberg, B., & Ragan, J.F. (2002). Changes in the union wage premium by industry. *Industrial and Labor Relations Review*, *56(1)*, 65–84.

[26] Cleveland, G., Gunderson, M., & Hyatt, D. (2003). Union effects in low-wage services: evidence from Canadian childcare. *Industrial and Labor Relations Review*, *56(2)*, 295–306.

[27] Jackson, A. (2003). *'In solidarity': the union advantage*. Ottawa: Canadian Labour Congress, Research Paper No. 27.

[28] Christofides, L.N., & Stengos, T. (2003). Wage rigidity in Canadian collective agreements. *Industrial and Labor Relations Review, 56(3)*, 429–449.

[29] Jackson, *op. cit.*

[30] Lowe, G.S., & Krahn, H. (1989). Recent trends in public support for unions in Canada. *Journal of Labor Research, 10(4)*, 391–410.

[31] Deshpande & Fiorito, *op. cit.*

[32] Lowe & Krahn, *op. cit.*

[33] Riddell, C., & Riddell, W.C. (2001). *Changing patterns of unionization: the North American experience, 1984–1998*. Vancouver, BC: University of British Columbia, Department of Economics, Discussion Paper No. 01-23; Tope, D. & Jacobs, D. (2009). The politics of union decline: the contingent determinants of union recognition elections and victories. *American Sociological Review, 74(5)*, 842–864.

[34] Riddell, C. (2004). Union certification success under voting versus card-check procedures: evidence from British Columbia, 1978–1998. *Industrial and Labor Relations Review, 57(4)*, 493–517; Johnson, S. (2002). Card check or mandatory representation vote? How the type of union recognition procedure affects union certification success. *The Economic Journal, 112*(April), 344–361.

[35] Bartkiw, T. (2005). Labour law and union certification success rates in Ontario. In Devine, S., & Grenier, J-N. (Eds.), *Reformulating industrial relations in liberal market economies: selected papers from the XLIth Annual Canadian Industrial Relations Association Conference*. Concord, ON: Captus Press; Bartkiw, T. (2008). Manufacturing descent? Labour law and union organizing in the Province of Ontario. *Canadian Public Policy, 34(1)*, 111–131.

[36] For example, *United Steelworkers of America and Radio Shack* [1980], 1 CLRBR 281 (OLRBR).

[37] Bronfenbrenner, K. (1997). The role of union strategies in NLRB certification elections. *Industrial and Labor Relations Review, 50(2)*, 195–213; Bronfenbrenner, K., & Hickey, R. (2004). Changing to organize: a national assessment of union strategies. In Milkman, R., & Voss, K. (Eds.), *Rebuilding labor: organizing and organizers in the new union movement*. Ithaca, NY: Cornell University Press.

[38] Markowitz, *op. cit.*

[39] Markowitz, *op. cit.*, p. 449.

[40] Milkman, R., & Wong, K. (2001). Organizing immigrant workers: case studies from Southern California. In Turner, L., Katz, H.C., & Hurd, R.W. (Eds.), *Rekindling the movement: labor's quest for relevance in the 21st century*. Ithaca, NY: Cornell University Press; Clawson, D. (2003). *The next upsurge: labor and the new social movements*. Ithaca, NY: Cornell University Press.

[41] Sharpe, T. (2004). Union democracy and successful campaigns: the dynamics of staff authority and worker participation in an organizing union. In Milkman & Voss, *op. cit.*

[42] Bronfenbrenner & Hickey, *op. cit.*

[43] Bentham, K.J. (2002). Employer resistance to union certification: a study of eight Canadian jurisdictions. *Relations Industrielles/Industrial Relations, 57(1)*, 159–187.

[44] Slinn, S. (2008). Captive audience meetings and forced listening: lessons for Canada from the American experience. *Relations Industrielles/Industrial Relations, 63(4)*, 694–718.

Certification Applications Keep BC Labour Relations Board Busy

The first thing the British Columbia Labour Relations Board does when it receives a union's application for certification is record the time it was filed. "Every certification application that gets processed has a vote, and the vote has to happen within 10 days of the application," says Registrar Allison Matacheskie. So, the certification process has to get underway immediately.

The application goes to the Board's Case Administrator for review, Matacheskie explains. The Case Administrator ensures the employer is accurately described, confirms that the proposed bargaining unit information is accurate, and investigates whether the workplace is already certified for worker representation by a different union.

The Board ensures that the application meets three essential criteria: the union must be a trade union; it must be an appropriate bargaining unit; and it must have no less than 45 percent support of the employees in the proposed bargaining unit. In order to

determine whether an application meets the criteria, a hearing will take place before a Vice Chair approximately seven or eight days after the application is filed. The employer receives notice of the application and date of the hearing.

After sending notice of the hearing, the Case Administrator sends the application to an Industrial Relations Officer (IRO) of the Employment Standards Branch of the Ministry of Labour. The IRO confirms the number of employees at the workplace and ensures the membership cards the union included with its application meet all the regulated requirements, such as having been signed within 90 days of the application. The IRO also prepares a voter's list and schedules a tentative time, date, and location for the vote, to be confirmed at the hearing.

The Board devotes three days a week to hearings for certifications, decertifications, expansions of the bargaining unit, or raids of certified bargaining units by different trade unions. "Sometimes nobody shows up if they know it's all in order and the employer has no objections," says Matacheskie. "Sometimes [an objection] is for minor things like the timing of the vote." A Special Investigating Officer (SIO) will help the parties work out these differences during the hearing.

"Sometimes it's a more complicated or controversial objection," Matacheskie continues. For example, the employer may claim the unit is not an appropriate bargaining unit. If agreement cannot be reached with the help of the SIO, a separate adjudication hearing will be scheduled for a later date. The vote will proceed as scheduled within the required 10 days. However, the ballots cast at the vote will be sealed until after adjudication of the objection. The Vice Chair determines after the adjudication hearing whether the ballots are ultimately counted, or whether the objection is upheld and the application dismissed.

The result of all votes must be 50 percent plus one in favour of unionization for the union to be certified by the Board.

ESTABLISHING UNION RECOGNITION

objectives

In this chapter, we discuss in more detail how a labour relations board deals with an application for certification. We also explore some of the problems that arise when there are special circumstances surrounding the application, and we discuss the issue of unfair labour practices. At the end of this chapter, you should be able to:

- explain how an application for certification is handled by a labour relations board
- understand the effect of certification
- explain some of the special circumstances that may arise in a certification application
- define and give examples of an unfair labour practice

INTRODUCTION

In Chapter 5, we outlined the process of organizing in the workplace and described how an application for certification is submitted to a labour relations board. In this chapter, we will describe in more detail how a labour relations board assesses an application for certification and how a vote on the application is conducted in the workplace. We will then discuss some of the special circumstances that can surround a certification application, such as time limits on when applications can be made, and applications to represent workers who are already certified. We will then define unfair labour practices, outline the legislation that governs them, and explain how unfair labour practices can affect the certification process.

ASSESSING THE CERTIFICATION APPLICATION

The Workplace Notice

When an application for certification is received by a labour relations board, in most Canadian jurisdictions the labour relations board must officially inform the employer and the employees that it has received a certification application. The board sends an official notice by registered mail (to ensure a record of receipt) to the employer, along with a similar notice to the employees. The employer must post the notice to the employees in the workplace. The notice will name the union that is applying for certification, describe the union's proposed bargaining unit, indicate that interested parties can make submissions about the application, and specify where such submissions should be directed. The reason for requiring this posting is to ensure that all employees are aware that the application for certification has been made, and to give employees the opportunity to make written submissions supporting or opposing the application to the relevant labour relations board. Any submissions made to the board will be taken into consideration when the board assesses the application. (In some provinces, the notice posted by the employer also includes a **terminal date**, which is the date by which submissions must be received in order for the board to consider them along with the application.)

Determining Employee Support

After determining the appropriate bargaining unit (which is not always identical to the unit the union has applied to represent, as described in Chapter 5), a labour relations board will assess the level of employee support for the application. This process usually requires that the employer provide the board with a list of employees, which the board then compares with the union's list of signatures supporting the application and the list of positions included in the proposed bargaining unit. A labour relations board's intent in making this comparison is to verify that the certification application is supported by the required number of workers in the proposed bargaining unit.

The process of assessing levels of employee support becomes complicated if there has been a delay between the collection of signatures and the submission of the certification application. During that delay, employees may have left the organization or moved to different positions within the organization. The board must be able to verify that the employees who have indicated their support of the application are currently employed by the organization in positions that are part of the proposed bargaining unit. There may also be confusion over the readability of signatures or whether a signature was actually written by the person whose name appears as a union supporter. If these types of questions arise, the board may require additional documentation such as copies of driver's licences or other identification to support the validity of the signatures.

The Representation Vote

As outlined in Chapter 5, the level of support for a certification application must be deemed sufficient for the application to proceed, as determined by the level of support described in the relevant labour legislation. If the level of support is above the required minimum and automatic certification is not an option, a labour relations board will usually set a date for a **representation vote**. This is a vote held to determine whether employees wish to be represented by a union. Table 6-1 outlines the levels of support that must be present among workers in the proposed bargaining unit for a representation vote to take place.

Labour relations boards generally attempt to minimize the time between when a certification application is filed and when a representation vote is held, because of the

TABLE 6-1   Canadian Legislation Governing Representation Votes

	Required Level of Support for Representation Vote to Occur	Required Level of Support for Representation Vote to Succeed
Federal	Between 35% and 50% of employees in the proposed bargaining unit	Majority of votes in favour; at least 35% of eligible employees must vote for the result to be valid
Alberta	At least 40% of employees in the proposed bargaining unit	Majority of votes in favour
British Columbia	More than 45% of employees in the proposed bargaining unit; a majority if the application is to displace another union	Majority of votes in favour; the board may order another vote if fewer than 55% of employees in the unit cast ballots
Manitoba	Between 40% and 65% of employees in the proposed bargaining unit; a minimum of 45% if the vote is to displace another union	Majority of votes in favour
New Brunswick	Between 40% and 60% of employees in the proposed bargaining unit. The board may certify if support is more than 50%, and must certify if support is more than 60%.	More than 50% support from those eligible to vote (excludes those employees absent from work during voting hours who do not vote)
Newfoundland and Labrador	At least 40% of employees in proposed bargaining unit	If at least 70% of eligible employees have voted, a majority of votes in favour; if less than 70% of eligible employees have voted, the support of the majority of those included in the bargaining unit
Nova Scotia	40% of employees in the proposed bargaining unit	Majority of votes in favour

TABLE 6-1 Canadian Legislation Governing Representation Votes (Continued)		
	Required Level of Support for Representation Vote to Occur	**Required Level of Support for Representation Vote to Succeed**
Ontario	40% of employees in the proposed bargaining unit	Majority of votes in favour
Prince Edward Island	At the discretion of the board (no percentage specified)	Majority of votes in favour
Quebec	Between 35% and 50% of employees in the proposed bargaining unit	Absolute majority of employees in the proposed bargaining unit
Saskatchewan	45% of employees in the proposed bargaining unit	Majority of voters in the proposed bargaining unit; a majority of those entitled to vote must cast ballots for the results to be deemed valid

Source: Human Resources and Skills Development Canada, Labour Program, Synoptic Charts on Legislation Pertaining to Certain Major Collective Bargaining Issues: Trade Union Application for Certification: General Private Sector Collective Bargaining Legislation (available at <www.hrsdc.gc.ca/eng/labour/labour_law/ind_rel/tuac.shtml>).

possibility that activities in the workplace in the time between those events may unduly influence the employees' voting intentions. Both unions and employers may take advantage of any excessive delays before the vote to attempt to persuade potential voters to support or oppose the union. In some jurisdictions, a representation vote can be conducted even if all the issues related to the certification have not been completely resolved. This reduces the time before the vote is held, which reduces the opportunities for the employer and the union to influence employees. In some jurisdictions, specified time limits also regulate how much time can elapse between the filing of a certification application and the holding of a representation vote.

The representation vote itself is a vote by secret ballot conducted at the workplace by a labour relations board. In most provinces, only those employees included in the

Home Care Workers Fired After Joining Union

DUNCAN—More than 200 workers at Sunridge Place care home in Duncan were handed their walking papers this week, just days after they voted 72 per cent in favour of joining the Hospital Employees Union.

HEU spokesperson Margi Blamey said yesterday the union plans to file an unfair labour practices complaint against Sunridge's owner, alleging that the "mass firing" was a deliberate attempt to keep the care home from being unionized.

"We've had this happen before, but this one is really suspicious with regard to the speed at which it happened after the vote," Ms. Blamey said.

"We now consider these workers to be union members and it's really important that we stand by them."

Sunridge owner Norman Jones did not return calls yesterday. However he said in a memo to union officials that the facility's operating contract with Duncan Care Campus Ltd. will be terminated effective March 31, resulting in "the termination of all employees within the union bargain unit."

Mr. Jones told staff Tuesday a new contractor will be recruited and said existing employees will be encouraged to reapply for their positions.

Completed in June 2008, the privately owned Sunridge Place facility was built to replace Cowichan Lodge, a government-run care home that served the Cowichan Valley for close to 80 years.

Despite a strong community effort to save Cowichan Lodge, the last patients were moved to Sunridge Place about a year ago.

Dozens of former HEU staff from Cowichan Lodge found jobs at Sunridge Place, making the new facility attractive to union organizers. The HEU held a certification vote late last week and released the results on Saturday.

"Every time a contract flips, workers lose their jobs, they lose their union and their collective agreement as well," Ms. Blamey said.

Source: Clarke, Brennan, "Home care workers fired after joining union," *The Globe and Mail*, December 3, 2009, p. S3.

proposed bargaining unit are eligible to vote. (See Table 6-1 for the provisions in specific jurisdictions determining who is considered eligible to participate in representation votes.) The question on the ballot, requiring a simple yes/no answer, asks the voters if they want the union to become their exclusive bargaining agent. For the representation vote to be successful—that is, for the union to be recognized as the employees' bargaining agent—in most jurisdictions a majority—defined as 50 percent + 1 of voters—must vote in favour of union representation. For example, if there are 100 voters participating in the election, at least 51 must vote "yes" for the representation vote to be successful.

If a representation vote is successful and no other extraordinary circumstances arise (such as evidence of undue influence on the employees), a labour relations board will then issue a **certification order**. This document legally creates the bargaining relationship between the union and the employer, makes the union the exclusive bargaining agent for the employees in the bargaining unit, and compels the parties to commence bargaining for a collective agreement. Certification also compels the parties to bargain in good faith, which essentially means that the parties are expected to bargain honestly and with the intent of completing a collective agreement. (This concept will be discussed in more detail in Chapter 7.) The certification order applies to all employees in the bargaining unit,

"You're lucky with your timing ... we're holding off our strike until we settle a moot point with the Labour Relations committee."

including employees hired into jobs in the bargaining unit after the certification order takes effect.

It should be noted that certification applications can be withdrawn before the certification process is complete. Withdrawals are made for a variety of reasons. A labour relations board and a union may disagree over the structure of an appropriate bargaining unit, and a labour relations board may impose a different definition of the bargaining unit than that proposed by the union. If the union feels that it has little chance of winning a representation vote in the bargaining unit defined by the labour relations board, it may decide that its resources could be used more productively elsewhere, and withdraw its application. Another problem could be an unusually large number of questionable signatures supporting the certification application. Rather than having the application rejected outright, the union may choose to withdraw the application, re-examine its procedures for collecting signatures, and resubmit another application with more reliable indications of support. Table 6-2 outlines the most recent information on certification rates in various Canadian jurisdictions, including the number of unsuccessful or withdrawn applications.

If a representation vote fails, the labour legislation in most Canadian jurisdictions imposes a period after the failed vote during which other certification applications

TABLE 6-2 Certification Rates

	Number of Certification Applications	Certification Granted	Certification Refused or Application Dismissed	Application Withdrawn	Total Resolved[i]
Alberta (2008-2009)	153	92	23 (lost vote) 22 (other reasons)	16	153
British Columbia (2009)	187	88	37	58	183
Manitoba (2008-2009)	52 (38 new, 14 carried over)	36	5	6	47
New Brunswick (2008-2009)	32	14	2	4	20
Newfoundland and Labrador (2008-2009)	16	12	n/a	n/a	n/a
Ontario (2008-2009)	742	396	136	214	746
Saskatchewan (200-2009)	301	165	68	43	276

[i] Numbers for "total resolved" do not equal the number of certification applications if there are applications that have not been resolved at the end of the reporting period, or if applications received in the previous reporting period were resolved in the current reporting period.

Note: Recent data were not available for Prince Edward Island and Nova Scotia. The most recent Quebec data do not distinguish between certification applications and other matters under the jurisdiction of the *Labour Act*.

Source: Labour relations board annual reports for the dates cited.

are banned. The rationale for this restriction is that the certification process is often time-consuming and divisive, and even though organizing activities are usually conducted outside the workplace and outside working hours, there are powerful issues involved in the individual decision to unionize, and the outcomes may spill over to affect productivity in the workplace and relationships between workers. If restrictions on the timing of certification applications were not in effect, workplaces could be seriously disrupted by a never-ending series of organizing campaigns. Thus, some Canadian labour codes set limits, known as **time bars**, that restrict the time within which such organizing efforts can take place.

Table 6-3 outlines the time bars that apply after a previous certification attempt has failed. This particular type of time bar is known as an **application bar**, since it imposes a mandatory waiting period after an unsuccessful certification attempt before another certification application can be made. As Table 6-3 shows, some jurisdictions also impose application bars if a previous certification application is still under review or is the subject of court proceedings.

TABLE 6-3	Time Bars to Certification Applications after a Previous Failed Application		
	Previous Unsuccessful Application for Certification	**Previous Certification Being Reviewed by Court**	**Previous Certification Revoked or Cancelled**
Federal	No specifications	No specifications	No specifications
Alberta	No specifications	10 months from the date of final disposition	No specifications
British Columbia	Bar imposed at the board's discretion; if imposed, 90-day minimum	No specifications	10 months; shorter at the board's discretion
Manitoba	No specifications	12 months after the date of the conclusion of court proceedings	No specifications
New Brunswick	Board may prescribe a waiting period	No specifications	No specifications
Newfoundland and Labrador	No specification	No specifications	No specifications

TABLE 6-3 Time Bars to Certification Applications after a Previous Failed Application (Continued)

	Previous Unsuccessful Application for Certification	Previous Certification Being Reviewed by Court	Previous Certification Revoked or Cancelled
Nova Scotia	At the board's discretion	No specifications	No specifications
Ontario	12 months, if the application is withdrawn or if the board dismisses the application after the representation vote fails	No specifications	No specifications
Prince Edward Island	Board may prescribe a waiting period	No specifications	No specifications
Quebec	No specifications	No specifications	No specifications
Saskatchewan	6 months; less at the board's discretion	12 months from the termination of court proceedings	No specifications

In most Canadian jurisdictions, a union cannot withdraw a certification application for non-technical reasons as a way of avoiding the application bar. This condition exists so that unions are not tempted to salvage an unsuccessful organizing campaign by terminating one certification application and immediately reapplying to represent the same group of workers. However, in most jurisdictions, a labour relations board is able to waive the application bar if the union made some inadvertent error in its application, such as miscalculating the size of the bargaining unit.

The Hearing

At any point during the assessment of the certification application, a labour relations board has the option of holding a hearing to collect more evidence relating to the application. This option is usually exercised if there are disputes over the content of the application or its surrounding circumstances. For example, if an application is made for a very small bargaining unit within a very large company, the labour relations board may hold a hearing to investigate why the union is applying for this particular bargaining unit and to determine the appropriateness of the proposed bargaining unit. A hearing can also be justified if there are allegations of unfair labour practices. A labour relations board may want to collect detailed information on the substance of the complaint and the effect of the alleged practices before issuing its decision and remedy. (See the discussion of unfair labour practices later in this chapter for more details on this issue.) If there is a dispute between the union and employer over the composition of the proposed bargaining unit, the labour relations board may want to investigate both parties' reasons for their positions.

A hearing is conducted in a similar manner to a court session. Labour relations board members assigned to the case will listen to submissions from parties such as the union, the employer, and the employees. Each party will present their evidence and will be questioned by the board members. The parties who testify in front of the board members may also be cross-examined by the other parties. When the hearing is over, the board members will consider the evidence and render a decision.

A labour relations board has several options after completing a hearing. If, for example, the board feels that a proposed bargaining unit is inappropriate, it can reject the application, giving written reasons for its decisions, or it can alter the bargaining unit composition to one it considers appropriate. If the board feels that actions taken on behalf of the union or employer have unduly influenced the employees' decision whether to support the union, it may order a representation vote or reject the certification application entirely. The board can impose these remedies even if the level of support is such that a vote would not usually be required or the certification application would usually be considered. The board may also order a new representation vote if there are circumstances that call the results of an earlier vote into question. These circumstances could include evidence of tampering with sealed ballots, or of individuals voting who should have been excluded from the process. The board can impose remedies such as requiring the employer to post notices or send letters apologizing for its actions. And, as mentioned in Chapter 5, the boards in most jurisdictions have the option of declaring a certification even when the required minimum level of support is not present. This option may be exercised when there is evidence that employer or union actions so intimidated the employees that the results of a vote would not indicate the employees' true wishes.

To this point, and in the previous chapter, we have described the certification process that would take place in a workplace where the employees are not already represented by a union and where no unusual events during the certification process have taken place. We will now turn to describing how labour legislation and labour relations boards deal with special circumstances that may occur during the certification process.

SPECIAL CIRCUMSTANCES DURING CERTIFICATION

Certification for a Previously Unionized Workplace

A certification is, in a sense, timeless. It remains in effect for as long as the parties involved wish it to and as long as the parties themselves do not change. Sometimes, however, a certification is sought for employees who are covered by an existing certification order and have a union in place as their exclusive bargaining agent. A union attempting to certify workers represented by another union is attempting what is known as a **raid**.

Some unions do not conduct raids on principle. These unions feel that if workers have freely chosen to be represented by a particular union, that choice should be respected; also, unions should not deliberately attempt to weaken other unions by taking away their membership. As we learned in Chapter 4, some Canadian labour federations—the Canadian Labour Congress, for example—expect their member unions not to undertake raids. This expectation is based on the belief that while raids may increase the membership of individual unions, they damage the strength of the labour movement as a whole by causing dissent among unions and reducing the ability of smaller unions to effectively represent their membership. This position encompasses the view that union membership should be increased by recruiting unorganized workers rather than by persuading already unionized workers to switch their allegiances.

There are unions, however, that conduct raids regularly. Some unions raid because they feel they could do a better job of representing the workers in question than the currently certified union. Others prefer to recruit unionized workers because these workers already have union experience, and thus the organizing campaign does not have to be as aggressive or as extensive as it might have to be for workers with no union experience; consequently, less cost and effort is involved in the organizing attempt. Raids are also undertaken by unions that see their traditional membership base eroding and want to bring in more members in order to survive. Some public sector unions and unions in the manufacturing and processing sectors of the economy have raided quite vigorously to replace decreasing membership caused by cutbacks in public sector and primary sector employment. More recently, some unions have capitalized on employers' decisions to subcontract work formerly performed by unionized workers; they have arranged deals with the subcontracting firms to be the workers' new representative—a form of raiding that has been strongly criticized because these deals often mean reduced wage rates and poorer protection for the workers.[1]

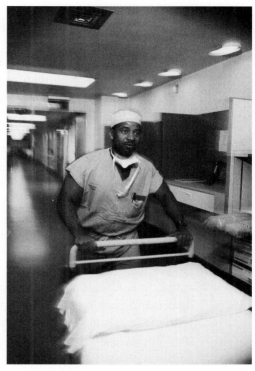

Unionized hospital workers were recruited by the Canadian Auto Workers, but charges of raiding caused a rift between the CAW and the Canadian Labour Congress.

The ability of unions to conduct raids is facilitated by the fact that no Canadian labour legislation explicitly forbids raiding; such a restriction, after all, would interfere with the right of employees to freely choose their workplace representative. There is also no legal requirement for workers to be represented by a union directly associated with their type of employment, which means that unions that choose to conduct raids do not have to confine themselves to industries or occupations similar to those already represented. This leads to situations such as the Canadian Auto Workers representing hospital workers, and the Communication, Energy and Paperworkers Union representing food production workers.

Raids can also occur in situations where employees feel dissatisfied with the representation provided by their current union. If employees do not feel that their union is accurately or competently representing their interests, they may contact a union or unions that they think would be more appropriate representatives and encourage those unions to commence an organizing campaign. Thus a raid may begin on the initiative of either the employees or a union.

As previously noted, organizing campaigns, whether directed at unionized or non-unionized workers, can disrupt the workplace. For this reason, labour codes impose time bars that restrict when a raid can take place. Generally, labour codes ban organizing for a certain time after a certification order has been granted for a previously non-unionized workplace. The purpose of this restriction is to give newly certified unions a chance to represent their members without the threat of a larger or more experienced union poised for a takeover. This protection is particularly important for new unions, which may be run by individuals with little experience in such matters as contract negotiation. The restriction on organizing of newly certified bargaining units allows the new union executives and members to gain the skills needed to run the union effectively, without having to immediately fend off an organizing campaign by another union.

Another time bar that exists in most jurisdictions involves the appropriate time to submit a certification application to represent workers already covered by a collective agreement. Such certification applications can be made only at certain times during the term of the existing collective agreement. The terms of these **open periods** vary by jurisdiction; Table 6-4 describes the conditions in each Canadian jurisdiction. Generally, a certification application can be made only at specified times during the term of a multi-year agreement or within a certain period toward the end of the term of a single-year agreement. The intent of these restrictions is to ensure stability in the collective bargaining process, so that union and management representatives do not have to deal with a raiding attempt while trying to negotiate a new collective agreement. These terms are also intended to allow the negotiated agreement to run its course without the interference or distraction caused by a competing union's attempt to organize the workers.

We should note that there are usually no legal restrictions on the number of unions that can simultaneously attempt to organize the same existing bargaining unit. Although there is usually only one union conducting a raid, it has happened in Canadian jurisdictions that more than one union has attempted to conduct a raid on the same group of workers at the same time.

A certification application covering a currently unionized workplace is assessed by a labour relations board using the same criteria that would be used to assess any other

TABLE 6-4 Time Bars to Certification Applications for Already Certified Bargaining Units

	No Collective Agreement and No Union Certified	No Collective Agreement and Union Certified	Collective Agreement (CA) in Force and Union Certified
Federal	At any time	12 months from the date of certification	CA < 3 years: after the beginning of the last three months CA > 3 years: during the 34th, 35th, and 36th months of the agreement, and during the last 3 months of each subsequent year of the contract
Alberta	At any time	10 months from the date of certification	CA < 2 years: within 2 months of the end of the CA term CA > 2 years: in the 11th and 12th month of the second year of the contract term, in the last 2 months in any subsequent year of the term, or in the 2 months preceding the end of the term or any subsequent year of the term
British Columbia	At any time	6 months from the date of certification, or earlier with the board's consent	7th and 8th month in each year of the CA term; if an application is made, no further applications are allowed within 22 months

TABLE 6-4 Time Bars to Certification Applications for Already Certified Bargaining Units (Continued)

	No Collective Agreement and No Union Certified	No Collective Agreement and Union Certified	Collective Agreement (CA) in Force and Union Certified
Manitoba	At any time	12 months from the date of certification, or 12 months after the conclusion of any court proceedings related to certification	CA < 18 months: during the first 6 months of the agreement, or 3 months immediately before the last 3 months of term
			CA > 18 months: 3 months before the anniversary date, or 3 months immediately before the last 3 months of the term
New Brunswick	At any time	12 months from the date of certification	CA < 3 years: beginning of the last 2 months of the term
			CA > 3 years: during the 35th and 36th months of the agreement and during last 2 months of each subsequent year of the term
Newfoundland and Labrador	At any time	12 months from the date of certification	CA < 2 years: within the last 2 months of term
			CA > 2 years: during the 23rd and 24th months of the agreement and during the last 2 months of each subsequent year of the term
Nova Scotia	At any time	12 months from the date of certification	CA < 3 years: after the beginning of the last 3 months of the term

TABLE 6-4 Time Bars to Certification Applications for Already Certified Bargaining Units (Continued)

	No Collective Agreement and No Union Certified	No Collective Agreement and Union Certified	Collective Agreement (CA) in Force and Union Certified
Ontario	At any time	12 months from the date of certification	CA > 3 years: during the 34th, 35th, and 36th months of agreement and during the last 3 months of each subsequent year of the term CA < 3 years: after the beginning of the last 3 months of the term CA > 3 years: during 35th and 36th month of term and during the last 3 months of each subsequent year of the term
Prince Edward Island	At any time	10 months from the date of certification; earlier with the board's consent	CA < 2 years: after the beginning of the last 2 months of the term CA > 2 years: during the 23rd and 24th months of the term and during the last 2 months of each subsequent year of the term
Quebec	At any time	12 months from the date of certification or 9 months from the date of expiration of the previous agreement	CA < 3 years: from 90 to 60 days before the expiration of the CA CA > 3 years: from 180 to 150 days before the expiration of the CA

TABLE 6-4 Time Bars to Certification Applications for Already Certified Bargaining Units (Continued)

	No Collective Agreement and No Union Certified	No Collective Agreement and Union Certified	Collective Agreement (CA) in Force and Union Certified
Saskatchewan	At any time	Between 30 and 60 days before the anniversary date of certification	Between 30 and 60 days before the anniversary of the effective date of the agreement

type of certification application. However, it is more likely that a representation vote will be ordered in such a situation, to ensure that the employees truly wish to change their representation to the new union. If the representation vote is successful or if a certification order is issued without a vote, a new certification order is issued to replace the previous certification. If the representation vote fails or if the certification application is rejected for other reasons, the time bars on subsequent applications are the same as those that would apply if the workers were previously non-unionized.

Certification if the Parties Change

A certification order, as noted, names the two parties (employer and union) that are covered by the order. However, sometimes there are changes involving the parties named. A union or an employer may merge with another union or employer, cease to exist, or otherwise be altered. If any of these events occur, then a form of re-certification may be required.

For example, if the union changes its status by merging with other unions, the usual procedure is for the merged union to apply for certification under its new name to represent the same bargaining unit. If a labour relations board feels it is appropriate, a representation vote may be conducted to confirm that all the members of the former union or unions wish to be represented by the merged union. This procedure is not required, however, and generally the board can alter the certification without a vote being held. If the union ceases to exist and the workers do not wish to be represented by another union, the usual procedure would be for the workers to file a request for decertification, which, when granted, cancels the existing certification and makes the workplace non-unionized. (See the section on decertification in Chapter 12 for a more detailed discussion of this process.)

Changes on the employer's side are slightly more complex. If the employer goes out of business, the certification is considered to have lapsed, as one of the parties named in the certification order no longer exists and the workers are no longer employees of the named employer. The union or the employer can apply for decertification if they wish to have a legally binding declaration that the union-employer relationship has ended. If, however, the employer merges with another business or expands its operations, there is a question as to whether the existing certification order should automatically include the new employees whose positions were not part of the bargaining unit before the expansion or merger. The labour relations board will have to decide whether to expand the existing certification order or to require a new certification application before the new workers can be unionized. This circumstance is called "successorship" and is discussed more fully in Chapter 12.

Certification Applications during a Strike or Lockout

Another special circumstance that may arise in the certification process is the submission of a certification application while there is a strike or lockout in progress at the place of employment addressed by the application. In several Canadian jurisdictions, there are time bars restricting when or if applications can be made under these circumstances.

In some Canadian jurisdictions, an application for certification cannot be made if an illegal strike has taken place in support of the certification attempt. This provision, where it exists, embodies the philosophy that certification, not striking, is the process through which employees should attempt to promote change in the workplace. As we know from Chapter 3, one reason that legislation was created to formalize the certification process was to make certification a viable alternative to striking as a way for dissatisfied employees to express their concerns. The legislation in some jurisdictions makes it clear that if employees choose to engage in an illegal strike related to certification, their application for certification will not be accepted.

In some Canadian jurisdictions, a certification application cannot take place during a legal strike or lockout. Such an application would usually come from another union that is attempting to represent the workers who are on strike or locked out. An application during this time might be perceived as undue interference with the collective bargaining process or as an attempt by one union to exploit the weak status of another union. A strike or lockout is usually an emotionally charged event for employees and management alike, and if not all employees agree with the rationale for a strike or lockout, some of them may be particularly vulnerable to the suggestion of different union representation. For these reasons, some jurisdictions restrict certification applications during a legal strike or lockout. Table 6-5 outlines the restrictions that exist in Canadian jurisdictions regarding certification applications during strikes or lockouts.

TABLE 6-5 Time Bars Relating to Certification Application during Strike or Lockout Activity

Legal or Illegal Strike or Lockout in Progress

Federal	Application only with the board's consent	New Brunswick	Application only 6 months after the start of a legal strike or lockout, or 7 months after a conciliation report was issued or the Minister of Labour indicates that a conciliation board will not be appointed
		Newfoundland and Labrador	No specifications
Alberta	Application only during a legal strike or lockout with the board's consent	Nova Scotia	No specifications
British Columbia	Application only with the board's consent	Ontario	Application only 6 months after the start of a legal strike or lockout, or 7 months after a conciliation report was issued

TABLE 6-5	Time Bars Relating to Certification Application during Strike or Lockout Activity (Continued)		
Legal or Illegal Strike or Lockout in Progress			
			or the Minister of Labour indicates that a conciliation board will not be appointed
		Prince Edward Island	With the board's consent, only during a legal strike or lockout
Manitoba	Application only 6 months after the start of any strike or lockout, and only with consent of the board	Quebec	No applications during a legal strike or lockout
		Saskatchewan	No specifications

A final special circumstance that may arise during the certification process is the occurrence of unfair labour practices, as noted in Chapter 5. We will discuss this circumstance in a separate section because of the large impact that an unfair labour practice can have on both the progress and the outcome of a certification attempt.

UNFAIR LABOUR PRACTICES

Definition and Legislative Philosophy

In the context of certification, an **unfair labour practice** is an action undertaken by an employer or, less commonly, a union that has the effect of unduly influencing the "private decisions" made by the employee in the certification process.[2]

Legislation dealing with unfair labour practices must incorporate several different considerations. One consideration is the inherent imbalance of power in the structure of most workplaces. The employer has extensive power over an employee's working life, from determining what tasks the organization will carry out and which employees will do which parts of the tasks, to the extent of deciding whether the employee has a job at all. Therefore, it is important to have legal restraints to prevent the employer from abusing this power during the certification process. As we have seen, the employee has the legal right to join a union without retaliation or interference from the employer.

The employer's legal rights must also be considered. Like any other Canadian, the employer has the right to free speech. As a result, a complete ban on employer-employee contact during the certification process is neither feasible nor fair. The fear that an employer might unduly influence employees during an organizing campaign should not result in extreme restrictions such as forbidding the employer to say anything at all about the organizing campaign or to speak to employees while the campaign is going on. It would be nearly impossible for an organization to operate normally if the employer were banned from having any contact or communication with employees.

Bill Nicholson, leader of the Victoria Hunger Strike of 1933, lost his pension due to union activity. Today's labour codes prohibit such unfair labour practices.

Thus, there are some challenging practical issues associated with balancing employer and employee rights in the workplace during an organizing campaign. It may, for example, be hard to establish whether an employer's actions during an organizing campaign are a legitimate part of running the business, or are intended to intimidate employees into not supporting a union. If an employer says, "I do not support a union in this workplace," is that a justifiable expression of opinion or an implied threat? Another issue is the impossibility of ensuring that employers or unions do not engage in activity that could be labelled as unfair labour practices. A labour relations board representative cannot be continuously present in the workplace to monitor employer and employee behaviour and assess the impact of that behaviour. And even if a complaint about an unfair labour practice is upheld (i.e., if a labour relations board rules that the disputed behaviour is indeed an unfair labour practice), the effects of the behaviour can still influence the outcome of an organizing campaign, even after the behaviour has ceased.

Although unfair labour practices can occur at any point in the employer-employee relationship, they tend to occur more often during the certification process than at any other time. This is because employees are vulnerable prior to certification, since they are not yet protected by a collective agreement. After certification is granted and a collective agreement is signed, employees are protected by the terms of the agreement that govern such procedures as promotions, discipline, and dismissal. Before certification takes place, however, employers who wish to discourage unionization may exploit the absence of a collective agreement by demoting, disciplining, or firing employees who are known union supporters. Such actions could intimidate other employees, who might fear that the same thing could happen to them. In a study of 429 Canadian employers who had had organizing campaigns in their workplaces, 12 percent of the respondents admitted to having undertaken at least one action during the campaign that would be considered an unfair labour practice (and comparisons to other data indicated that the respondents appeared to be understating the extent of these activities). By far, the most common forms of these actions were downsizing, laying off, or dismissing employees.[3]

Although unions can also be charged with committing unfair labour practices during certification, it is more common for complaints to be brought against employers. This is because the union has much less power than the employer does to intimidate employees. (It could be argued that the union is much more likely to exert undue influence in its attempt to persuade employees to support certification by promising rewards like better wages and working conditions if the employees join the union.) Unlike the employer, the union does not have the ability to fire or discipline employees for noncompliance with its suggestions; thus, a union's coercion of employees is much less frequent and less compelling than an employer's coercion. Employer complaints about unions' unfair labour practices during certification attempts usually focus on union organizing activity that has taken place during prohibited times (working hours) or in prohibited locations (the employer's premises).

Legislation

In an attempt to balance the rights of employers and employees in the workplace and to restrict the occurrence of unfair labour practices, most labour codes in Canada contain a set of guidelines for employer and union behaviour. We will now look at the general terms of these guidelines.

The first guideline, as discussed in Chapter 5, states that an employer cannot participate in or interfere with the formation, selection, or administration of a trade union. An employer also cannot participate in the representation of employees by a trade union or contribute financial or other support to a trade union. This guideline implies that a manager cannot oppose an organizing campaign (opposition could be interpreted as interference), but also cannot support an organizing campaign (support could be interpreted as participation). This guideline addresses the concern that employer participation in the union or in union activities might compromise the independence of the union's role as representative of the employees, as outlined in Chapter 5.

The second guideline governing employer/union behaviour in most Canadian labour codes is that an employer is free to express views for or against the union so long as the employer does not use coercion, intimidation, threats, promises, or undue influence to pressure employees into acting against their personal beliefs. This language might appear to be very restrictive, but in reality it is often very difficult to apply. Comments that appear to be innocuous in one set of circumstances can seem threatening in a different set of circumstances. An employer's comment such as "I don't like the idea of a union" would seem quite harmless in a casual conversation with a first-level supervisor, but would have a completely different impact in a formal meeting called by the management that employees were compelled to attend. Additionally, comments that one individual perceives as intimidation can be perceived as meaningless by another individual. An employer might say to one employee, "I personally would not vote for a union," and that employee would interpret the comment as the employer's personal opinion and as having nothing to do with the employee's own intentions. Another employee hearing the same comment might interpret it as an implicit threat that there would be negative consequences for anyone who did not agree with the employer's views and voted for the union. Thus, the context and perception of the expressed views, as well as the content of the views themselves, need to be considered when determining what constitutes an unfair labour practice.

The wording of this guideline in Canadian labour law attempts to capture the range of possible behaviour or statements that could be considered unfair labour practices. At the same time, the wording is also broad enough to not explicitly exclude any behaviour that could be an unfair labour practice.

The language in Canadian labour law does not forbid the employer from carrying out actions such as employee discipline and termination of employment in the course of operating the business; however, if such actions take place during a certification attempt, the employer may need to prove that they were justified or necessary. If a complaint of an unfair labour practice is filed, a labour relations board will examine both the motive behind the alleged unfair labour practice and the effect of the alleged practice. For example, if an employee active in an organizing campaign is demoted to a lower-paying position during the campaign, the labour relations board would look at a number of different types of evidence. The board would likely examine the employee's previous work record to see whether the employee was the subject of previous disciplinary action and, if so, whether the disciplinary action followed established procedures, such as progressive discipline. This evidence would indicate whether the employee's performance problems existed before the organizing campaign or whether they had mysteriously emerged as soon as the employee had become active in the union. The board would also investigate whether demotion was a justifiable response to the employee's most recent actions and whether the demotion would have occurred regardless of whether the organizing campaign was in progress or not.

A labour relations board's concern in such a case is whether the employer's action resulted from an **anti-union animus**—that is, whether the employer's opposition to the union manifested itself in actions that harmed employees who were active in the union. In some Canadian jurisdictions, anti-union animus, even if it exists in combination with other reasons for employee discipline, is in itself sufficient to support a declaration of an unfair labour practice; that is, even if an employee's performance record justifies discipline, the employer might still be judged to have committed an unfair labour practice if the employee was disciplined because of an anti-union animus.

Note that a **reverse onus** applies in most Canadian jurisdictions when complaints of unfair labour practices are assessed. This means that the employer is the party that must prove that its actions were not motivated by anti-union animus. In discipline cases not adjudicated by labour relations boards—that is, in discipline cases adjudicated in civil court—the onus would be on the employee to prove that the employer's actions were not justified.

We should also note that an employer might be found to have committed an unfair labour practice if the employer's action had the effect of influencing employees' behaviour, even if that was not the employer's intent. For example, in distributing a handout containing information about union-related problems in other organizations, the employer may merely intend to ensure that the employees are making an informed decision when they participate in a representation vote. However, employees could perceive this action as an implied threat that similar problems will occur in this organization if the employees choose to unionize. Thus, employers need to be aware of both the content and the potential effect of their actions, since actions may be perceived differently than they are intended.

Dealing with an Unfair Labour Practice Complaint

If an employer, a union, or an employee believes that an unfair labour practice has occurred, they can file a complaint with the appropriate labour relations board. The standard of proof that is used to determine the outcome of a complaint in all cases before a labour relations board is the **balance of probabilities**. This standard is somewhat less rigorous than the "beyond a reasonable doubt" standard used in criminal court, but it still requires sufficient evidence to support the probability that the disputed action was justified. For example, if an employee who was active in an organizing campaign was fired, the employer would have to meet the "balance of probabilities" standard by showing such evidence as a poor work record and prior sufficient warnings of poor performance. The warnings would have had to be given before the certification application to show that they were related to the employee's performance rather than his or her involvement in the organizing campaign. To reinforce the relationship of the warnings to the employee's performance, rather than to his or her union activity, the employer might need to show additional evidence. This could include evidence that the employee was offered assistance in dealing with the performance problem, such as additional training, and that the employee was given sufficient time to correct the problem.

An Example of an Unfair Labour Practice Complaint

In order to understand how difficult it can be to regulate unfair labour practices, we will give an example of an unfair labour practice complaint related to an employer's actions during a certification attempt. We will briefly describe the case (*American Airlines Inc. v. Brotherhood of Railway, Airline and Steamship Clerks, Freight Handlers, Express and Station*

Employees [1981] 3 CLRBR 90 at 91-109)[4] and then examine the labour relations board's decision in the case.

A company operated a reservations call centre where employees worked both staggered and rotating shifts. Because of the complicated work scheduling, the employees each had a mailbox that they were expected to check before starting a shift so that they would be up to date on work-related information. All kinds of non-company materials (e.g., notices for blood donor clinics, party invitations) were regularly left in these mailboxes. On at least two occasions during an organizing campaign, employees were forbidden to place union information in the mailboxes. The reasons given for this restriction were that, according to the company's written policies, the distribution of literature on company premises required company approval, and using company time for "purposes not directly related to company business" was prohibited.

After the organizing campaign started, the company's regional vice-president visited the centre and held what the company called "rap sessions." These were meetings that all employees were compelled to attend. During these sessions, management staff introduced themselves, talked about the company's business plans, and answered the employees' questions. The management staff made no specific statements about unionization, but if employees asked about the organizing campaign, they were told that they (the employees) had a choice whether or not to join a union.

The regional vice-president of the company claimed the employees were confused about the impact a union would have, and sent all employees a letter that discussed the certification drive. The letter indicated that other companies in the same industry had reduced their workforce after their workplaces were unionized. The letter also stated, "We firmly believe the interest of both agent and clerical personnel and the company is best served by your remaining non-union." It went on to describe how the presence of a union would change seniority practices, reduce take-home pay because of union fees and dues, and possibly cause a strike if collective bargaining broke down. The letter concluded: "I hope you will think very seriously before you take any action that will make your job a Union job."

When an unfair labour practice complaint was brought to the labour relations board, it was apparent that the company and union disagreed on the intent and impact of the letter to the employees. The company's position was that the letter did not contain any direct threats or instructions not to join the union and that it was only a statement of the company's opinion. The union argued that the information presented in the letter was both coercive and threatening, since the wording of the letter implied that the negative consequences of unionization that occurred in other organizations would also occur in this organization if a union were formed.

After considering the arguments of both sides, the labour relations board ruled that the employer's right to manage efficiently included the right to communicate with employees, but that the employer must be sure that such communications were restricted to business considerations. The board noted that even statements that are not explicit threats can effectively be threats; that is, a statement clearly outlining the employer's position on an issue can intimidate employees who privately or publicly disagree with the employer. On those grounds, the labour relations board found that the letter constituted an unfair labour practice.

On the matter of union literature in the mailboxes, the labour relations board, again acknowledging the company's right to manage its business, recognized that the company had a written policy defining what material was acceptable for mailbox distribution. However, the board noted that the policy outlining appropriate mailbox materials had been in effect for several years and that the company had not enforced the policy when other non-company communications were regularly placed in the mailboxes. The board said that the company had not demonstrated that the presence of the union material in the mailboxes caused any disruption in operations. The labour relations board thus found that the ban on distribution of union material was an attempt to intimidate employees and constituted interference with the employees' right to representation by a union.

This example demonstrates that labour relations boards are very sensitive to the power imbalance between the employer and employees and to the great opportunity for the employer, even unintentionally, to intimidate employees. In this example, the company held meetings and distributed materials to inform employees about its position on unionization. While the company may not have intended these actions to be intimidating, the labour relations board found that they were, since employees could have interpreted the information as threats about what would happen if the employees unionized. The limiting of access to the mailboxes also seemed to indicate that the company was interfering with the employees' right to organize. Even if the company had previously intended to enforce the regulations against non-company materials in the mailboxes, the fact that the company chose to enforce the policy after the organizing campaign had started made the enforcement appear to be an anti-union tactic. And, although the labour relations board did not specifically address the company's "rap sessions" in its ruling, these sessions could also have been interpreted as intimidation, since the employees' attendance was compulsory rather than optional.

Remedies for Unfair Labour Practices

A labour relations board that upholds a complaint of an unfair labour practice can take several courses of action. It will usually choose a remedy that will attempt to **make whole** the situation, meaning that the remedy will attempt to put the parties to the complaint in the same situation they were in before the unfair labour practice occurred. Examples of make-whole remedies include reimbursing a union for the cost of extra organizing expenses incurred in combatting an employer's anti-union activity, or reinstating employees who were disciplined because of anti-union animus. "Make whole" remedies can also attempt to reverse any damage that an unfair labour practice has caused an organizing campaign. These kinds of remedies include allowing union organizers into the workplace, allowing employees or unions to post information on company bulletin boards, or allowing the union to hold information meetings in the workplace during working hours.

However, it can be difficult to make whole the situation caused by an unfair labour practice for the simple reason that the unfair labour practice may already have had the effect of intimidating employees; any subsequent action may be ineffective in counteracting that intimidation. Because of this difficulty, labour relations boards have "wide powers to issue remedial orders" that are appropriate to the particular situation and the behaviour that is in dispute.[5] If the organizing campaign is still in progress when the board issues its ruling, the board can also issue a "cease and desist" order to direct that the unfair labour practice stop.

In most Canadian jurisdictions, labour relations boards can order that employees be compensated for any financial losses they sustained as a result of the employer's actions, such as lost earnings resulting from a demotion or dismissal. If there is concern that an unfair labour practice may not stop after an order is made, most Canadian

McDonald's employees Tessa Lowinger (R), aged 16, and Jennifer Wiebe (L), aged 17, smile as they leave the British Columbia Labour Relations Board offices. They participated in the first unionization of a McDonald's restaurant in North America.

labour codes allow a labour relations board to file an order in provincial or federal court, which gives the order the same power as a judgement from that court. Violation of a court order can result in a finding of contempt of court and the imposition of associated penalties, which could include financial penalties or even jail time.

In extreme cases, employer or union actions may have so intimidated the employees that even pro-union employees would be afraid to vote in favour of certification or, alternatively, anti-union employees would be afraid to not vote for certification. In this situation, a labour relations board may order a new representation vote, the results of which will override the results of any previous votes. Although this remedy may not completely solve the situation, since employees may still be intimidated during a new vote, it at least serves the important purpose of giving employees the chance to vote after having had the employer's or union's previous behaviour condemned. The labour relations board may, in some Canadian jurisdictions, even impose a certification order without the required percentage of support from employees, or without a clear majority in a new or existing representation vote.

What was the remedy in our case that demonstrated unfair labour practices? In that case, the labour relations board's remedy was to direct the regional vice-president to write a letter to all employees, on company letterhead, indicating that the earlier letter had been found to be an unfair labour practice. The regional vice-president was also directed to include with the letter a copy of the reasons for the labour relations board's decision. The company was also directed to allow distribution of union literature in the mailboxes as long as employees distributed the literature on their own time.

To conclude our discussion of unfair labour practices, we will note that although unfair labour practices often occur during the certification process, they are by no means restricted to the certification process. They can also occur after the issuance of the certification order and during the collective bargaining process. We will discuss unfair labour practices in those contexts in chapters 7 and 8.

SUMMARY

The certification process is the process through which unions are formally recognized as employee representatives in the workplace. After an application for certification is filed, a labour relations board will assess the application and determine whether to issue a certification order. The labour relations board has the ability to grant certification if there are exceptional circumstances surrounding the application, even if some of the conditions for certification are not met. Alternatively, the board can deny certification under special circumstances even if all of the conditions for certification are met. A certification order establishes the union as the employees' representative in the workplace and compels the union and the employer to commence bargaining in good faith to reach a collective agreement.

Certification can take place under a variety of different circumstances, and legislation governing certification acknowledges this by restricting when certification applications can be filed. The purpose of these restrictions is to reduce the possibility of workplace disruption from continuous certification campaigns. These restrictions also place some limits on when raids can occur. Raids—a controversial issue in the union movement— are attempts by one union to organize a group of workers who are already unionized.

Labour law has provisions that regulate employer and union behaviour during the organizing process that leads to a certification application. The issue of unfair labour practices is particularly important during the certification process. An unfair labour practice is behaviour by either the union or the employer that unduly influences the employees' actions with respect to the union. Regulating workplace behaviour is difficult because the rights of employers and employees must both be balanced and protected. However, actions and statements can have a significant impact on the certification process, and thus labour relations boards are given a wide range of powers to counteract the negative effects of unfair labour practices.

KEY TERMS FOR CHAPTER 6

anti-union animus (p. 239)
application bar (p. 223)
balance of probabilities (p. 240)

certification order (p. 221)

make whole (p. 243)

open periods (p. 228)

raid (p. 226)

representation vote (p. 217)

reverse onus (p. 239)

terminal date (p. 216)

time bars (p. 223)

unfair labour practice (p. 219)

DISCUSSION QUESTIONS FOR CHAPTER 6

1. Under what circumstances might a representation vote not be required for certification?

2. How does labour legislation balance the employee's right to join a union with the employer's right to free speech during an organizing campaign?

3. Why does most Canadian labour law restrict the times when certification applications can be filed?

4. A maintenance and cleaning company employs many immigrants who are not fluent in English. After a certification application has been filed, the company manager calls each employee in for an individual meeting, with a translator present, to explain the implications of unionization. Would this be considered an unfair labour practice? Why or why not?

5. Why are some unions philosophically opposed to raiding?

6. Explain the difference between "balance of probabilities" and "beyond a reasonable doubt," and outline how these concepts are relevant to the issue of unfair labour practices.

7. What would be the advantages and disadvantages of being represented by a union whose primary membership was in an industry or occupation different than yours?

8. Why is it important to give labour relations boards a wide range of options in issuing remedies for unfair labour practices?

CASE 6-1

SHOPSTORE AND GROCERY WORKERS' UNION

(Based on *Better Buy and UFCW*, 2007)

In this case, the union has applied to certify all workers at a grocery store except for office staff. A representation vote has been taken, and the ballots have been sealed and not counted. The union is alleging that the employer coerced and intimidated employees prior to the vote, and is asking the labour relations board to order an automatic certification.

Case Facts

Shopstore is a warehouse-style grocery store. It has been owned and operated by Charles Chitty for more than 30 years. The warehouse supervisor, Jerry Drost, has worked at the store for more than 25 years.

Last summer, the Grocery Workers' Union started an organizing campaign at Shopstore. Jennifer Cole, a shelf stocker, had a meeting at her home with the union organizer and some of her coworkers. Around the same time, a salesperson told Chitty that the organizing campaign had begun.

Chitty called a workplace meeting with the managers, office staff, sales staff, and a representative of the workers on each shift. There are different accounts of what was said at the meeting, but Bill Monk, the store manager, and Chitty both told the board that Chitty explained that he was not happy with the organizing campaign, wanted to be kept up to date on how it was going, and asked those present to "get more information" and "mind their p's and q's." Drost, who was at the meeting, told the board that Chitty did not instruct anyone to get more information and did not express how he (Chitty) felt about the campaign.

Some time after the meeting, Drost approached Cole while she was at work. Cole told the board that Drost said he knew she had had the union meeting at her house, and that if the union came in, employees would have to work part-time or be laid off. She responded "Whatever happens, happens," and Drost left. Drost told the board that he had approached Cole, but that she said to him that she could do what she wanted on her own time, and walked away.

Later that day, Monk called Cole into his office. He told the board that he had wanted to talk to Cole about the campaign because he had been contacted by some employees who were concerned that their home phone numbers (some unlisted) had been given to the union, and others who felt they had been misled into signing union cards. There were different accounts of the content of their conversation, but both Monk and Cole agreed that Monk indicated that Chitty was not happy.

The next day, a warehouse employee acting as temporary warehouse supervisor told Cole that if she was found talking to any staff member, it would be assumed that she was talking about the union, and she would be "written up." This employee told Cole that Drost had asked him to convey this message. Drost told the board that this was true, and that he had asked the employee to do this because he thought Cole would "take it better" from the employee rather than from him. After the conversation, Cole went to Monk, who said he would talk to Drost, but also told her that if she was talking for more than a few minutes it would be perceived as talking about "things other than work."

During the same period of time, Drost also had several conversations with Ted Jaffee, a truck driver for the store. Jaffee told the board that Drost said if the union were certified, Chitty would shut down the warehouse and use a different distributor to stock his store. Drost also told Jaffee that the company would end its practice of putting unsold fresh deli sandwiches in the employee lunchroom for the employees to have if they wanted them. Drost told the board that these conversations were initiated by Jaffee, not by him, and that anything he said was in response to Jaffee's questions, such as "What do you think is the worst thing that could happen if the union gets in?"

Another warehouse employee, Arnold Powell, told the board that Drost approached him during work on two separate occasions. He said that the first time Drost asked him if he (Powell) knew about the union. He said that the second time Drost stated there was a chance of layoffs or part-time work if the union got in. This scared Powell because he was in the process of buying a house. He told the board he later told Drost privately that he was afraid that his job was "on the line" and that Drost should watch what he (Drost) said because it was being taken seriously. Drost told the board that Powell had asked him if he (Powell) would be laid off, since this is what a union representative had told him. Drost also indicated that Powell had said, since Drost had treated him right, he would be voting against the union.

Cole and Powell both told the board that many employees were concerned about being laid off or having their hours reduced. Drost told the board he did not tell anyone they would be laid off or converted to part-time status. Cole noted that talk about lay-offs decreased while Drost was on vacation and increased when he returned.

At the end of the summer, Chitty distributed a pamphlet to the employees. In the text of the pamphlet, he denied that certification would have any effect on him personally or the business. He also mentioned that in 2002 the business had experienced an economic downturn but no one had been laid off then. He stated that it was the workers' choice if they wanted to join a union, but that he would prefer to deal with the employees directly because "a union can create an 'us vs. them' relationship [and] I believe that is bad for business."

A week later, Chitty distributed another pamphlet to the employees. In it he stated, "I strongly believe that as a non-union Company we can have a more positive, productive relationship with employees," but that "at the end of the day each of you will vote in a way that is best for yourself. I accept that and will accept whatever decision you make." He then re-emphasized that he preferred to deal with employees directly.

The final testimony to the board came from Allan Hardy, the union organizer. He told the board that the campaign began slowly in the middle of the summer, and that the "active solicitation" of employees started toward the end of the summer. Hardy said he approached all the employees, and that there was a "clear turn" in the campaign a few days after the meeting at Cole's house. He said he managed to "pull things back around" and gain some support after that, but there was a severe drop in support after Drost returned from holiday. Employees cancelled appointments they had made to meet with Hardy, and some employees who had told him to call them back now refused to speak to him. Nevertheless, Hardy said, he went ahead and filed the application for certification because there was a sufficient number of signatures for the labour relations board to consider the application.

The Union's Position

The union argued that automatic certification should be granted because Drost's conduct turned the certification campaign into a campaign about whether the employees could keep their jobs. The union stated that while Drost is not the owner or the employer, he is a manager and so his actions are those of the employer. The union also argued that Chitty must have known about Drost's conduct because Chitty was a very hands-on manager and since some of his statements in the pamphlet reflected what Drost was allegedly saying in the workplace, Chitty must have known what Drost was doing.

The union conceded that the statements in Chitty's pamphlet were not unlawful, but argued that discussing layoffs or shutting down the business is a very serious offence during an organizing campaign.

The union also pointed out that Cole was threatened with being "written up" without the employer investigating what she was saying to other employees, and that it did not threaten to discipline other employees who talked to Cole during working hours. The union argued that this is evidence of anti-union animus.

The union suggested that an automatic certification would not only compensate for the employer's actions during the organizing campaign, but would also serve as a deterrent to similar actions by other employers in the future.

The Employer's Position

The employer argued that the union's evidence is only based on rumours and hearsay, and that the employer has made no threats to the employees. The employer stated that the board should not rely on hearsay evidence for a decision this serious, and that an automatic certification is not warranted.

The employer stated that Cole was only advised about the laws governing certification campaigns when she was told not to campaign during working hours. The employer also argued that it is not illegal for a company owner to express his views on unionization, and that Chitty's statements were not intimidating or coercive. Also, any fears the employees had about statements they heard from Drost should have been addressed by the statements in Chitty's pamphlets.

The employer argued that Drost is not a manager because he does not have the authority to hire or fire. He discusses employee issues with Chitty, but Chitty makes the decisions.

The employer also argued that Drost made many of his statements about the effects of unionization only in response to questions from employees, and was only expressing his personal opinion. The employer also questioned how much effect Drost's statements actually had, since he was away on vacation during part of the organizing campaign, and since the union organizer was still able to obtain enough signatures to submit an application for certification. The employer also pointed out that employees had complained about the union obtaining their home phone numbers, and about being misled into signing union cards, so the employees also had concerns about how the organizing campaign was being run.

The employer stated that during the hearing Chitty had never been asked directly about his knowledge of what Drost was doing in the workplace, so the board should not infer anything about whether Chitty approved of, or was directing, Drost's actions.

CASE 6-2

LONGLIFE HEALTH MANAGEMENT AND CARE WORKERS' UNION

(Based on *Pro Vita Care Management and H.E.U.*, 2008)

In this case, an employer has fired an employee during an organizing campaign. The employer argues that the employee had a record of performance problems. The union argues that the employee was dismissed because of his participation in the organizing campaign, and because of the employer's anti-union animus. The union also argues that, during the organizing campaign, the employer made anti-union statements to employees that were coercive and intimidating. The union is asking the Labour Relations Board to reinstate the employee and to order the employer to cease and desist its contraventions of the labour relations legislation.

Case Facts

Longlife Health Management is a company that is contracted to provide health care aides to work at a senior citizens' facility. The facility includes a residential lodge and a hospital, and the health care aides work in both parts of the facility. In the previous year, the Care Workers Union attempted to certify the health care aides, but the union was not able to get enough support to file an application for certification. Then, in the current year, a different union began an organizing campaign for the same group of workers, and the Care Workers Union responded by starting another organizing campaign of its own.

Upon learning of the organizing campaigns, the employer sent a memorandum to all of the employees at the facility. The memorandum started by stating that the employer preferred to deal directly with the employees and not with a union. The memorandum then stated that "having a union also adds extra administrative costs to our business.... and forces us to spend more money on lawyers and consultants—we would rather put that money into wages and benefits." The memorandum then went on to describe events at another facility run by a different company, where, according to the employer, the company "lost the contract to do the work after the facility owner refused to alter its contract ... to compensate for small wage increases [it] had agreed to with the union. ... That is not job security."

On March 19, just over a week after the memorandum was circulated, the employer terminated the employment of Guillermo Gardel, one of the health care aides. The employer stated that Gardel was fired for failing to follow proper lifting procedures and for lying when questioned about his actions.

Because many of the residents of the facility are ill or frail, the facility has a written policy outlining how residents are to be lifted and moved. Instructions for residents requiring special procedures are also listed on a written document kept at the resident's bedside. If lifting a resident involves using mechanical assistance, such as a sling, two persons must be present throughout the entire procedure.

Last year, a health care aide used a sling by herself to move a resident, and the resident slipped out of the sling and suffered a broken leg. The aide was not disciplined, but was transferred out of the facility, and the employer had to pay a considerable amount for physiotherapy for the resident. The aide told the employer that she should not be disciplined because it was common practice for the aides to use mechanical assistance by themselves to move residents. As a result of this incident, the employer required all health care aides to attend a training session on lifting practice, and to sign a document acknowledging that they had received and understood the training and would follow the practices described in the training.

On March 19, Sandra Koster, the facility's assistant care manager, told Joan Havers, the employer's district manager, that she had seen Guillermo Gardel bringing a resident back to her room at the same time that the lift mechanism required to transport that resident was sitting in the hallway outside the room. Koster also told Havers that later that same day she went into the resident's room and found her roommate sitting in a wheelchair, although the same lift mechanism was required to move that resident and the mechanism was still in the hallway.

After Koster's visit to the room, she told Havers, she and Gardel then attended a routine meeting at the nurses' station near the room. After the meeting, Koster saw Gardel enter the room and partially close the door. After a few minutes had passed, Koster went into the room and saw that one of the residents was now in bed. Koster asked Gardel if he had moved the resident without the mechanical lift or without the assistance of another aide. He responded, "I used lift, same thing." Koster then returned to the nurses' station and contacted Havers.

Havers, who was at the facility, then spoke with Gardel. Gardel said that he had moved the first resident without the mechanical lift, but that he moved the other resident into her bed with the mechanical lift and with the assistance of another aide.

Havers contacted the other aide, who said that he had not assisted Gardel in moving the resident. Havers then returned to speak with Gardel. Gardel told the board that Havers said she did not want to be lied to and that he had endangered the safety of a resident, and ordered him to leave the facility.

Havers told the board that prior to initially speaking with Gardel she had reviewed his disciplinary file, which listed two previous incidents: two verbal warnings for "resident-related issues" and a two-day suspension for being absent without leave. Havers also told the board that before speaking to the other aide, she contacted Longlife's president and obtained his approval to terminate Gardel's employment.

The president of Longlife told the board that he and Havers spoke several times by phone on March 19 and the day after. He could not remember in which conversation Havers told him about Gardel's union activities. Havers told the board that she thought it was during their first conversation, but she was not sure. Both the president and Havers stated that they were unaware that any employees were routinely disregarding the facility's policies for moving residents.

Two other health care aides and a registered nurse testified before the board. All three stated that while it was important for safety reasons to follow instructions for lifting or moving residents, it was common for aides to perform lifts or moves without mechanical assistance. The nurse clarified that the two warnings in Gardel's disciplinary file involved a bathing incident with a resident and a feeding incident with another resident. The nurse knew this because Gardel had told him at the time of the incidents that he (Gardel) was "in trouble."

Gardel told the board that he had distributed and collected signature cards during the organizing campaign, and had returned the signed cards to the union. He admitted that he had lied about how he moved the resident, but said he did so because he was nervous. He said that, in the two previous incidents on his disciplinary file, he had "discussed" the incidents with the care aide manager, but said he did not know that he was in trouble, and that he was not told that he was receiving a verbal warning.

Gardel said that while he had signed the attendance sheet at the training session, and had also signed the document acknowledging that he had received the training, he had actually missed most of the session because he missed his regular bus to work. He told the board that he was not present during the part of the training session that stressed the importance of lifting properly. He agreed that the employees had been paid to attend the session and that he had been paid for full attendance at the session. He did, however, add that he was aware of and understood the employer's policies regarding lifting and moving residents.

Gardel also told the board that after the incident that resulted in a resident break-ing a leg, a vice-president of Longlife spoke to the employees and emphasized the importance of using a mechanical lift when this was required. According to Gardel, the Longlife vice-president also stressed the necessity of having two aides perform a lift. However, Gardel stated that he did not agree that two aides were needed for a lift, and that he did not agree with a number of the employer's other policies regarding lifts.

The board was told that after the incident that injured a resident, the care aide man-ager had placed a memo to all staff at the nursing station, reminding staff that two per-sons were required for a lift, and that information regarding lifts could also be found in the information at the resident's bedside. Gardel told the board that he does not read the bedside information except when the resident is admitted. He also said he did not see the memo because he does not always review the information at the nurses' station at the start of every shift. Gardel stated that in the situation for which he was dismissed, he felt it was safe to lift the resident on his own and without a mechanical lift as he weighs 90 pounds more than she does.

Several weeks after Gardel was fired, two other aides were disciplined for violating the employer's lifting policies by moving a resident without a mechanical lift. Both aides received a verbal warning but no other punishment.

The Employer's Position

The employer argues that it is not illegal to want to operate in a non-union environment, and it is not illegal to communicate that wish to employees. The employer believes that it is free to communicate that wish as long as the communication is not coercive or intimidating.

The employer states that it did not threaten to reduce wages if the employees joined a union, and that its statements about the events at another company should be read "in context." The employer points out that another paragraph in its memorandum says that the employer is not afraid of dealing with unions.

The employer says that it had cause to fire Gardel because he violated an impor-tant workplace policy, and the consequences of his actions could have been severe. The employer points out that Gardel lied about the incident in question and that he also had previous disciplinary offenses on his record.

In response to the testimony of other employees that the policies on safe lifting and movement of residents were often ignored, the employer states that while it is possible that these employees witnessed violations of the policy, none of them reported those violations. Gardel's conduct was the only violation of the policy that management was made aware of. The employer argues that Gardel's punishment was more severe than that given to the two aides several weeks later because Gardel had a previous disciplinary history and also lied to the employer about his conduct.

The employer states that it only became aware of Gardel's involvement in the organizing campaign on the day that he was fired, and that his involvement was not a factor in the decision to terminate his employment.

The Union's Position

The union states that the employer's memorandum to the employees was not only intimidating but was intended to be intimidating. The union also points out that many of the employees are recent immigrants from countries where joining a union may lead to "serious reprisals," and therefore are more likely to be intimidated.

The union argues that Gardel's termination was at least in part motivated by anti-union animus because the employer has publicly stated that it is opposed to unionization. The union points out that Gardel was terminated on the same day that the employer became aware of his involvement in the organizing campaign.

The union also notes that Koster, the assistant care manager who reported Gardel's conduct, was not called to testify before the board, and that "adverse influence" should be drawn from this fact. The union states that the assistant care manager's testimony would be crucial in explaining why Gardel was being watched so closely on the day the employer discovered his involvement in the organizing campaign.

The union argues that Havers, the Longlife manager who fired Gardel, did not make notes of the telephone conversations and meetings leading to the termination. The union also argues that Havers could not have accomplished all the activities she claims to have completed during the day that Gardel was fired, and that this is evidence that the reasons for Gardel's termination were not those stated by the employer.

The union states that the verbal warnings that Gardel received prior to the incident that resulted in his firing were "informal discipline," and the employer violated its own policy of progressive discipline by firing Gardel. The union states that it is common practice in residential facilities for care aides to lift and move residents without the use of mechanical aids, and that the employer's own employees routinely violate the employer's policies on lifting and moving residents.

References

[1] Cohen, M. (2004, April 29). IWA health care deals betray women workers. TheTyee.ca. Available at <www.thetyee.ca/Views/2004/04/29/IWA_Health_Care_Deals_Betray_Women_Workers>.

[2] Carrothers, A.W.R., Palmer, E.E., & Rayner, W.B. (1986). *Collective bargaining law in Canada* (2nd edition). Toronto: Butterworths.

[3] Bentham, K. (2002). Employer resistance to union certification: a study of eight Canadian jurisdictions. *Relations Industrielles/Industrial Relations, 57(1)*, 159–187.

[4] As described in Carrothers, Palmer, & Rayner, *op. cit.*

[5] Carrothers, Palmer, & Rayner, *op. cit.*

A Mutually Beneficial Approach

Mount Allison University and the Mount Allison Staff Association signed a three-year collective agreement in June 2010, after six days of collective bargaining and well before the June 30 expiration of their previous agreement. Both sides to the negotiations credit the approach they took—interest-based negotiations (IBN)—for their collective bargaining success.

The Mount Allison Staff Association represents approximately 130 employees in secretarial, clerical, and technical jobs. The university administration and the staff association have used an interest-based negotiations approach to collective bargaining to successfully negotiate their last three collective agreements, says Ron Sutherland, Director of Human Resources at Mount Allison.

"Interest-based negotiation, or mutual gains bargaining, is an approach that focuses on process and encourages creativity, information sharing, and participation," Sutherland explains.

In preparation for collective bargaining, both negotiating teams attended a joint training session where they also prepared a joint opening statement. "The other preparation for the parties would be to canvass their various constituents to see what issues have been causing them problems, but not what they want in terms of solutions," explains Sutherland. Both parties came to the table with a list of issues to talk about and the underlying interests associated with those issues, not with positions.

The staff association set up a bargaining committee six months before the expiration of the contract, notes President Bill Evans. The committee solicited input from members and then spent a few dozen hours in research and meetings to prepare. "It's not a great deal of time compared to what other unions do," says Evans.

The university's labour-management committee, which meets monthly and includes representatives from both the union and employer, has made collective bargaining easier, Evans says. "If there are any issues, we talk about them before they become problems," without going to a formal grievance. In fact, there has not been a single grievance with the staff association since the university and the union started using interest-based negotiations. "You walk in [to collective bargaining], and there are no surprises," Evans adds.

The more traditional positional approach to bargaining normally involves much more preparation, says Sutherland. "You have to decide which articles [of the collective agreement] you want to open and the positions you want to formulate, oftentimes right down to the specific language of proposals." This preparation includes meetings with stakeholders, researching collective agreements at other universities, collecting information on salaries and benefits for equivalent positions, and also trying to anticipate what the other party is going to bring to the table.

"You basically have to have your proposals package in place by that first day, whereas, with IBN, both parties go in with a list of issues that they had identified for discussion," says Sutherland. Interests, possible options, solutions, and ultimately final language are then discussed and worked out during collective bargaining.

DEFINING AND COMMENCING COLLECTIVE BARGAINING

objectives

One of the biggest tasks for unions and employers is negotiating a collective agreement. In this chapter, we will describe the effects of certification on the union-management relationship and the process of preparation for collective bargaining. We will examine the various structures within which collective bargaining can take place, and describe how the participants begin the bargaining process. By the end of this chapter, you should be able to:

- describe how certification changes the relationship between employees and employers
- identify exemptions to the effects of certification
- name the participants on the union and management bargaining teams
- understand how the bargaining structure is determined
- describe the process by which bargaining teams arrive at their list of desired outcomes
- identify practices that are considered bargaining in good faith

INTRODUCTION

In chapters 5 and 6, we described the process of certification through which a union becomes recognized as the legal representative of the employees in a workplace. One of the results of certification is that the union and the employer are compelled to commence collective bargaining: a process that will eventually produce a collective agreement that determines workplace rules and policies. In this chapter, we will start by describing how certification changes the relationship between the workers and the employer. We will then outline how both unions and employers prepare for collective bargaining. In Chapter 8, we will continue our discussion of collective bargaining by describing what actually happens in the bargaining process itself.

THE EFFECTS OF CERTIFICATION

When a certification order is issued, a number of changes occur in the relationship between employers and employees. One of the most immediate changes is the application of various sections of the labour code to ensure that the union has sufficient resources to represent all members of the bargaining unit effectively. These applications are usually reflected in contractual terms between the union and the employer, and are referred to as **union security** clauses. One typical clause requires that all union members pay union dues. Dues are usually calculated either as a standard flat fee or as a percentage of the employee's monthly or annual pay. The percentage-based calculation is more common in Canada because it bases an employee's dues on what the employee actually earns, whereas a flat fee has more of a financial impact on lower paid employees.

All labour codes in Canada provide for the **dues check-off** as a form of union security. The dues check-off provision allows the union member to direct the employer to deduct union dues from his or her paycheque and to forward the deducted amount directly to the union. This provision exists so that the union does not have to go to the trouble of gathering money directly from every member after each paycheque is issued. It also ensures that the union receives its membership dues regularly and promptly.

There are, however, some generally permitted exceptions to the dues check-off provision. If employees object to belonging to a union for reasons associated with their religious affiliation, four provincial labour codes (those of British Columbia, Saskatchewan,

Manitoba, and Ontario) and the *Canada Labour Code* permit a **religious exemption**. Employees can request that the amount they would have paid in union dues be directed to a registered charity mutually agreed upon by the employee and the union. In order to receive a religious exemption, employees must show that their religious beliefs conflict with the general idea of union membership. Employees cannot receive a religious exemption because they object to the particular union in their workplace or to specific actions undertaken by that union. Employees who receive a religious exemption are generally not eligible to participate in votes conducted by the union, although they are covered by the terms of the collective agreement.

Another union security provision is known as the **Rand formula**, whose origins were discussed in Chapter 3. The principle behind the Rand formula is that while not all employees may wish to be members of the union, all employees in a unionized workplace benefit from the contract terms the union negotiates; therefore, all employees, whether union members or not, should financially support the work of the union. The Rand formula is often used to supplement or replace the religious exemption, especially in those provinces where the provincial labour code has no provision for a religious exemption. Unlike the religious exemption, however, the Rand formula makes the payment of union dues compulsory while allowing employees to opt out of actually joining the union.

After a certification order is issued, many unionized workplaces follow the **closed shop** or **union shop** model of employment. Under this union security provision, implemented through terms in the collective agreement, new employees, as a condition of employment, must agree to join the union and pay union dues. The closed shop or union shop provision ensures that the employer will not be able to reduce the union's membership and influence by hiring individuals into the bargaining unit who will not join the union.

A variation on the closed shop model occurs in the skilled trades and construction sectors. Here, prospective workers must already be union members before they are eligible for employment. The reasoning behind this requirement is that since workers in these occupations regularly move from employer to employer as jobs or projects are completed, allowing the union to control the supply of qualified labour protects union security by restricting or eliminating non-union members' access to job openings.

In these types of occupations, the matching of employees with employers occurs in a format known as the **hiring hall**. Employers wanting to hire tradespeople contact the appropriate union, which then posts the job opening at the hiring hall. The "hall" is a permanent posting site at the union offices or a union-run website; members can visit these sites to obtain information on available opportunities. Alternatively, a "hall" can be a scheduled meeting attended by all qualified members seeking employment. During this meeting, the union posts hiring requests and attempts to match up potential employees and employers. Another hiring hall format is one in which the union maintains lists of qualified union members and will assign members, usually on the basis of seniority or specialized experience, to an employer who submits a hiring request. All of these hiring hall formats maintain union security in occupations where employment relationships are flexible and change frequently.

Another union security provision resulting from the contractual linking of union membership to employment compels an employer to discharge an individual from employment if he or she has been expelled from union membership. This provision strengthens union security by reinforcing the expectation that all workers in the bargaining unit will be union members in good standing, or will pay union dues as a condition of employment. Expelling a member from a union is an extreme action that unions rarely undertake because of the impact that expulsion could have on the member's future employment. Expelled union members will generally not be hired at any other unionized workplace, and thus, in a highly unionized industry or occupation, an expelled member would have difficulty finding work. Unions usually expel members only as a last resort when other disciplinary measures have failed. Most union constitutions permit either the union executive or the membership (via a vote) to expel a member for such reasons as non-payment of dues or doing the work of another union member who is on strike or locked out. A number of cases before provincial labour relations boards[1] have established that if the union requests that an employer dismiss an employee because he or she has been expelled from the union, the employer is compelled to do so.

Table 7-1 outlines the most common union security provisions.

Finally, as we saw in previous chapters, one of the underlying principles of Canadian labour relations law is that once a certification order is issued, both the union and the employer are compelled to commence collective bargaining. At this point, neither party can refuse to acknowledge the other's role as a bargaining representative, or refuse to participate in collective bargaining. It is also important to remember that as soon as a certification order is in place, individual employees become bargaining unit members and can no longer bargain individually with the employer to establish workplace conditions.

TABLE 7-1 Union Security Provisions	
Dues check-off	The employer deducts union dues for each employee and forwards money to the union.
Rand formula	Employees in the bargaining unit pay union dues but choose whether or not to be union members.
Closed shop/Union shop	Employees must agree to join the union as a condition of employment.
Hiring hall	The union supplies unionized employees to the employer.
Union provisions to expel members	The employer may be compelled to dismiss an employee if the union expels the employee from union membership.

Conversely, after union certification, the employer can no longer bargain individually with employees. An employer who attempts to bargain directly with individual employees, rather than with the union acting on behalf of the employees, may be breaching the expectation that the parties bargain in good faith. (This expectation will be discussed in detail later in this chapter.)

To introduce the topic of how collective bargaining commences, we will first outline the framework within which collective bargaining takes place.

THE FRAMEWORK FOR COLLECTIVE BARGAINING

The Structure of Collective Bargaining

The word "structure" as applied to collective bargaining refers to the number of unions, employers, workplaces, or industries represented in a particular collective bargaining situation. Depending on the type of bargaining unit established by the certification order or by provisions in the relevant legislation, the structure of collective bargaining can be simple or complex. The degree of complexity depends on how many workplaces or business establishments, bargaining units or unions, and employers will be involved in bargaining.

The simplest and most common bargaining structure is "single unit-single employer," where one union negotiates with a single employer that operates a single location. However, more complex structures are also possible. Individual bargaining units can negotiate with a single employer who operates multiple locations; multiple units can negotiate with a single employer; and multiple units can negotiate with multiple employers. Table 7-2 outlines the different types of bargaining structures and gives examples of industries where each type of structure can be found.

TABLE 7-2 Bargaining Structures

Single Location

Single Union-Single Employer	Multiple Union-Single Employer
This is the most common bargaining structure in Canada. Individual unions bargain with employers operating at a single location.	This is usually found only where multiple unions represent different groups of workers in a single workplace. This model is not common in Canada.

Multiple Locations

Single Union-Single Employer	Multiple Union-Single Employer
One collective agreement is negotiated and applies to all the employer's establishments where the union is certified. This model is used in many parts of the Canadian public sector.	Different unions representing different workers negotiate with one employer for contracts covering all locations. This model is used in the Canadian railway industry.

Multiple Employers

Single Union-Multiple Locations	Multiple Union-Multiple Locations
Different employers operating in different locations negotiate as a group with a single union. This model may require the labour relations board to accredit employers to bargain as an employers' council. This model is used in several parts of the Canadian forest industry.	This highly centralized bargaining model is used mainly where there are multiple unions and employers within a single industry that operates in multiple locations. This model is relatively rare in Canada.

The bargaining structure in a particular collective bargaining situation is usually determined by the certification order, which names the employer(s) and union(s) that will bargain with each other. The relevant labour legislation may also contain guidelines to determine the bargaining structure, especially in the Canadian public sector. Legislation covering public sector bargaining outlines which part of government is considered the employer or the bargaining agent that will act on behalf of the employer in negotiations.

Autoworkers' unions were famous for their use of whipsawing as a bargaining tactic.

While most Canadian bargaining structures, as noted, involve a single employer and a single union, it is possible for groups of employers or groups of unions to bargain as a single entity. This situation most commonly arises when multiple employers in a single industry feel that their interests would be better served if they bargained as a group rather than individually. This structure helps employers in a single industry avoid the bargaining phenomenon of **pattern bargaining** or **whipsawing**, where an agreement reached by one union with one employer is used to pressure other employers in the same industry or that deal with the same union into agreeing to similar terms. In the past, whipsawing was very prevalent as a bargaining tactic in the American auto industry. The United Auto Workers union in the United States made no secret of its strategy of selecting a "target settlement" with one of the Big Three automobile assembly companies (Ford, General Motors, and Chrysler) and then bargaining for the same settlement with the other companies.[2] Since the early 1980s, the effectiveness of whipsawing as a bargaining tactic in the auto industry and associated industries has declined, mostly because of changes in different companies' ability to pay the requested wages.[3] In recent Canadian auto industry negotiations, pattern bargaining was used by both the union and the employers to ensure consistency in the cost-containment terms of the resulting collective agreements. However, it has also been suggested that pattern bargaining, and the resulting labour costs, was one of the major causes of the North American auto industry's financial troubles during the economic crisis of late 2008 and early 2009, and that the subsequent industry restructuring may put an end to pattern bargaining in that industry.[4]

When a number of unions represent different employees of a single employer, the unions may decide to bargain as a group. The unions may feel that they will thereby be able to exert more pressure on the employer. Unions that bargain as a group can exert greater pressure on the employer because of the increased impact of any job action they might take, such as a strike. Union members generally respect any job action taken by another union: for example, by refusing to cross the striking union's picket lines. Thus, in a multiple union–single employer relationship, it would be possible for employees belonging to one union to go on strike and shut down the entire operations of the employer.

The potential threat of a complete workplace shutdown as a result of the job action of relatively few employees would give unions a great deal of power over the employer during bargaining. In fact, labour relations boards are often reluctant to certify small bargaining units within large workplaces because of the power imbalance this bargaining structure might cause. However, labour relations boards recognize that a multiple union-single employer bargaining structure has the advantage of efficiency. This is because issues common to all the unions can be addressed in one set of negotiations, rather than in separate negotiations with each separate union.

Most Canadian labour codes specify that employers wishing to bargain as a group must apply to a labour relations board for certification as an **employers' council**. The process whereby this group of employers is recognized as a single unit for the purposes of bargaining is known as **accreditation**. Unlike unions applying for certification, employers applying for accreditation are not required to conduct a representation vote; the support of potential members is assumed on the basis of their participation in the application. However, members of an employers' council who decide that they no longer wish to bargain as a group and prefer to return to individual bargaining must apply to the labour relations board to have the accreditation cancelled before they can bargain individually.

Unions that bargain together as a group form an entity called a **bargaining council**; no formal recognition from a labour relations board is usually necessary for unions to adopt this bargaining structure.

The Participants in Collective Bargaining

Most collective bargaining is conducted by two teams of negotiators, with one team representing the union and one team representing the employer. The size and composition of the teams are determined to a large extent by the size of the organizations, the number of issues to be resolved, and the resources each organization can draw upon to support the work of its team. However, there are particular individuals who are generally always included on each team. We will describe the composition of each team in turn.

The Union Team

The union negotiating team commonly includes a member or members of the union executive. These individuals are on the bargaining team because they have extensive knowledge of the union's operations and of the issues of concern to the union membership. Ordinary, or "rank and file," members of the union are also commonly included on the negotiating team. It is important for these individuals to be on the team because, as employees, they usually have a realistic perspective on how proposed contract terms will affect the day-to-day operations of the workplace. Having these individuals on the negotiating team also gives the team greater credibility with the

Maria Fitzpatrick of the Public Service Alliance of Canada attends a union meeting at the National Gallery of Canada to explain the collective bargaining process.

union membership, since their presence means the union executives are less likely to be accused of dominating the bargaining process and addressing their own concerns instead of those of the union membership. Rank-and-file members of the union negotiating team are usually elected by the union membership.

If the bargaining unit is a local of a larger union, a regional or national representative of the larger union may be present during negotiations, either as a formal member of the union negotiation team or as an observer/advisor. This sort of representation is considered important for two reasons. First, the regional or national representative may be a very experienced negotiator and thus will be able to give strategic assistance to the local bargaining team; this is particularly valuable if the local members are inexperienced bargainers. Second, the regional or national representative will be aware of terms negotiated in other collective agreements involving the same union, and will seek to ensure that the local team does not agree to terms inferior to those negotiated by other locals, which could set a dangerous precedent for future negotiations.

In large sets of negotiations involving national unions and/or large employers, the union negotiating team may include professional negotiators. These individuals are either union employees or persons hired on contract by the union to assist in developing bargaining strategies and tactics. Union negotiating teams may also include experts such as union researchers and economists. These individuals provide general information, such as trends in employment or inflation rates, to support the union's proposals. They also may provide analyses of proposals from both teams, such as calculating the impact that different wage proposals would have on employees' take-home pay or earning potential.

The Management Team

The management negotiating team represents the employer, and usually includes executives who deal with the union on a regular basis (e.g., the human resources director). These individuals are considered to have enough knowledge of the workplace conditions and requirements to bargain a collective agreement appropriate for the organization and its employees. Because these individuals are usually the ones who handle day-to-day problems arising from the terms of an existing collective agreement, they are also the ones most likely to have information about which terms of the existing collective agreement need to be altered or updated. The negotiating team may also include a financial officer, who will offer advice on the financial impacts of proposed settlements. This individual is aware of the resources the employer has to offer in bargaining and, ultimately, what the employer is prepared to pay in total wage and salary costs. It is important for the employer's negotiating team to have this knowledge so that the team does not make financial offers that the employer cannot fulfill.

If the employer is a sub-unit of a larger organization (e.g., an individual store in a chain or franchise operation, or an organization owned by a larger organization), the management negotiating team may also include representatives from the parent organization.

These individuals play a role on the management negotiating team similar to the role that representatives from the regional or national union play on the union negotiating team. They provide negotiating expertise and try to ensure consistency across the collective agreements covering different parts of the parent organization's operations. Like the union negotiating team, the management negotiating team may also include professional negotiators, researchers, and/or other professionals who will supply negotiating assistance and information.

In negotiations involving a bargaining council or an employers' council, the negotiating team usually includes at least one representative from each of the unions or employers participating in the council. Although the specific concerns of the individual unions or employers are usually incorporated into the council's overall bargaining strategy, it is still important that the council participants be represented in negotiations. This is so that each participant's representative can inform the rest of the council how bargaining proposals would affect the representative's own workplace or membership. If the council has this information during negotiations, it can avoid the problem of the council agreeing to contract terms that are not appropriate for some or all of the participants.

Table 7-3 provides a summary of the participants on each negotiating team.

TABLE 7-3 Members of the Negotiating Teams

Union	Management
Union executive members	Human resources director
Rank and file union members	Financial officer
Regional/national union representatives[i]	Parent organization representatives[ii]
Council member representatives[iii]	Council member representatives[iii]
Professional negotiators[iv]	Professional negotiators[iv]
Researchers[iv]	Researchers[iv]

[i] May or may not be included depending on the union structure.
[ii] May or may not be included depending on the employer's organizational structure.
[iii] May or may not be included depending on the bargaining structure.
[iv] May or may not be included depending on the team's or organization's resources.

What Can the Parties Bargain For?

Generally, the areas that collective bargaining will address are determined by the parties themselves. The issues most commonly addressed are wages, benefits, working hours, procedures for hiring and promotions, and working conditions. Table 7-4 outlines the issues that are commonly addressed in Canadian collective agreements. Theoretically, no issues are off limits in collective bargaining; we should not however, that many collective agreements contain a so-called **management rights clause**. This clause states that management has the right to establish procedures or policies governing any issue not directly addressed in the collective agreement. Thus, while any issue is theoretically available for bargaining, if a collective agreement contains a management rights clause, the collective agreement will not be the absolute authority on how the workplace is to be operated.

Certain guidelines in provincial and federal labour relations legislation frame the terms that the parties can agree to in collective bargaining. Collective agreements in most jurisdictions, for example, must have a minimum term of one year. This stipulation is in place so that employers and unions do not have to commence bargaining for a new agreement immediately after concluding the previous agreement. Bargaining another contract immediately after concluding the previous one would be very time-consuming for both employers and unions. Collective agreements also cannot contain terms that are inferior to the minimum conditions specified in the relevant employment standards act. For example, a collective agreement could not specify a wage rate lower than the applicable minimum wage, or grant fewer holidays than the amounts specified in employment standards legislation. This restriction exists because employment standards legislation is applicable to all workplaces in a jurisdiction, whether unionized or non-unionized.

As outlined in Chapter 1, collective agreements cannot contain any terms that discriminate against particular groups in the workplace. The definition of "discrimination" in this context is found in the provisions of the applicable provincial or federal human rights act and includes both intentional and systemic discrimination. An example of discrimination in a collective agreement would be a clause giving white people priority in promotions. This would be an illegal contract clause because all Canadian human rights acts prohibit discrimination on the basis of race or ethnic origin.

Collective agreements are generally required to contain a grievance procedure so that disputes over interpretation or application of the agreement can be resolved once the agreement is in force in the workplace. Most Canadian labour relations legislation

TABLE 7-4 Some Common Issues Addressed in Canadian Collective Agreements

	Number of Collective Agreements Containing Language Addressing this Issue	Percentage of Collective Agreements Containing Language Addressing this Issue
Union membership as a condition of employment (closed shop or union shop)	280	44.2
Rand formula	592	93.4
Leave for union business (negotiations)	259	40.9
Leave for union business (grievances)	360	56.8
Leave for elected union office	441	69.6
Restrictions on contracting out	391	61.7
Harassment procedure	268	42.3
Reassignment procedure	281	44.3
Technological change	363	57.3
Grievance procedure	244	38.5
Normal number of work hours per week (white collar)	287	45.3
Normal number of work hours per week (blue collar)	372	58.7
Layoffs by seniority	461	72.7

Note: Other common provisions that appear in various forms include overtime provisions, vacation allocations, wage premiums for non-standard work tasks or hours, paid leave, and employer contributions to benefits.

Source: Workplace Information Directorate, Labour Program, Human Resources and Skills Development Canada, 2005. Data taken from 634 collective agreements covering workplaces of 500 or more employees (total number of employees covered = 2,186,476).

includes a grievance procedure that is considered applicable to any workplace without a grievance procedure in its collective agreement. The grievance procedure outlined in provincial labour legislation is similar to that included in most collective agreements. While it is most uncommon for a grievance procedure to *not* be included in a collective agreement, the legislative provision is in place to ensure that there are grievance procedures available in all unionized workplaces. This provision can also serve as a model for dispute resolution procedures in non-unionized workplaces. We will discuss the grievance procedure in greater detail in Chapter 11.

PREPARING TO COMMENCE BARGAINING

Once the bargaining structure has been determined and the bargaining teams have been formed, the teams commence the process of preparing for collective bargaining. Through this process, both teams jointly determine how bargaining will proceed, and each team individually determines what outcomes it wants to achieve through bargaining. We will now describe how these two sets of decisions unfold.

Timelines for Bargaining

As we know, once a certification order is in place, the parties named in the order are compelled to begin bargaining. However, especially in situations where the certification order applies to a previously non-unionized group of workers, one or both parties can be reluctant to start bargaining. Sometimes employers resent the union's formalized presence or are bitter about events during the certification process, and these feelings are manifested as an unwillingness to bargain. On the union side, the union members may be worn out from the effort of the certification campaign and may not feel ready to embark on another major process; there also may be concerns about the newly unionized workers having enough expertise to bargain effectively.

To ensure that the collective bargaining process actually begins, most Canadian labour codes specify times by which collective bargaining must commence. There are also timelines to encourage the parties to begin the process of bargaining when an existing collective agreement is about to end. In both situations, the bargaining process is initiated by one party issuing a **notice to bargain** to the other party. Most Canadian labour codes specify a deadline after the issuance of the notice, and bargaining is expected to begin by that deadline. If bargaining does not begin, the party that issued the notice can file a complaint of an unfair labour practice with the labour relations board. The other party may have reasons for not commencing bargaining that it considers valid—for example, the absence of a key member of the bargaining team. In such cases, the other party is not compelled to file an unfair labour practice complaint if it agrees that the reasons for the delay are valid and if the parties can mutually agree on an acceptable time to start bargaining. However, a party that is reluctant to bargain at all might manufacture numerous excuses to avoid starting bargaining; if the other party recognizes this pattern of behaviour, it can use an unfair labour practice complaint as a means to force the other party to the bargaining table.

At this point, we should mention briefly that if the union does not submit a notice to bargain to the employer or does not respond to an employer's notice to bargain within the specified time, it may be considered to have abandoned its bargaining rights. If a labour relations board determines that a union has indeed abandoned its bargaining rights, it may issue a decertification. We will discuss the issue of abandoned bargaining rights in more detail in Chapter 12.

Table 7-5 summarizes the timelines in each Canadian jurisdiction for commencing bargaining. Note that most of these legislative provisions permit the parties to set their own deadlines within the existing collective agreement for the commencement of collective bargaining toward a new agreement.

Setting Bargaining Priorities

One of the first actions that a well-prepared negotiating team will undertake is to decide what its priorities will be in bargaining. More specifically, the team will attempt to answer two questions: what outcomes does the team want to achieve, and which of these outcomes are the most or least important to achieve? Identifying and prioritizing outcomes is essential if the team is to bargain effectively. A comprehensive list of bargaining priorities ensures that all team members are directing their efforts in negotiation toward reaching agreed-upon outcomes. A prioritized list also allows a team to act strategically in assessing offers from the other team. The order of items on the list helps the team determine which of their bargaining goals they are prepared to concede and which they should maintain in response to the other side's proposals.

TABLE 7-5 Timelines for Commencing Collective Bargaining

	First Agreement	Prior to Expiry of Existing Agreement	Timeline for Commencing Bargaining
Federal	Upon notice issued by either party	Notice within 4 months preceding the date of expiry if no other agreement exists between the parties	Within 20 days of notice being given unless parties agree otherwise
Alberta	Upon notice issued by either party	No less than 60 days and no more than 120 days preceding the date of expiry if no other agreement exists between the parties	Within 30 days after notice is given unless parties agree otherwise; proposals must be exchanged within 15 days of the first meeting unless parties agree otherwise
British Columbia	Upon notice issued by either party	Any time within 4 months preceding the date of expiry; if notice is not given at least 90 days prior to the date of expiry, the parties are deemed to have given notice 90 days prior to expiry	Within 10 days after the date of the notice
Manitoba	Upon notice issued by either party	No more than 90 days and no less than 30 days preceding the date of expiry if no other agreement exists between the parties	Within 10 clear days after the date of the notice or such further time as the parties may agree upon
New Brunswick	Upon notice issued by either party	Between the 90th and the 30th day preceding the date of expiry if no other agreement exists between the parties	Within 20 days after notice has been given or such further time as the parties may agree upon

TABLE 7-5 Timelines for Commencing Collective Bargaining (Continued)

	First Agreement	Prior to Expiry of Existing Agreement	Timeline for Commencing Bargaining
Newfoundland and Labrador	Upon notice issued by either party	No more than 60 days and no less than 30 days before the expiration or termination of the agreement, or within a period outlined in the collective agreement	Within 20 days after notice has been given or such further time as the parties agree upon
Nova Scotia	Upon notice issued by either party	Within 2 months preceding the expiry of the agreement	Within 20 days after notice has been given or such further time as the parties agree upon
Ontario	The trade union must give notice to commence bargaining	Within 90 days before the expiry of the agreement or according to provisions in the collective agreement	Within 15 days after notice has been given or such further time as the parties agree upon
Prince Edward Island	Upon notice issued by either party	Within the time prescribed by the collective agreement or, if not specified, at least 2 months before the expiry date	Within 20 days after notice has been given or within such further time as the parties agree upon
Quebec	Either party must issue 8 days' written notice to the other of the time and place its representatives will be ready to meet	Notice may be given by either party within 90 days preceding expiration unless another time is provided in the collective agreement; if no notice is issued, the parties will be expected to begin bargaining by the date of expiration of the collective agreement	After a notice of meeting has been received, negotiations must begin and be carried out diligently and in good faith

	First Agreement	Prior to Expiry of Existing Agreement	Timeline for Commencing Bargaining
TABLE 7-5 Timelines for Commencing Collective Bargaining (Continued)			
Saskatchewan	None specified	Either party may give notice to bargain no less than 30 days and no more than 60 days preceding expiration of agreement	Where notice is given, parties must immediately bargain collectively in good faith

Agreeing on a set of goals and priorities can be a very challenging process for a negotiating team. For the union team, the challenge is to balance the different needs and wants of what is usually a diverse group of employees. Some employees may identify a pay increase as their desired outcome of bargaining; others may want changes in benefit packages or work schedules. Still other employees may have encountered ongoing problems in the workplace that they want resolved by new language in the collective agreement. Employees will expect all of these concerns to be addressed in bargaining, but this can be problematic if the union team considers other issues to have higher importance, or if the team believes there is little realistic chance of obtaining the members' desired outcomes.

Job security has emerged as a union bargaining priority in many recent labour disputes, as employers seek to take work out of the bargaining unit and assign it to less expensive workers.

For the management team, the challenge may be to balance the desires of various stakeholders inside and outside the organization. Some stakeholders may identify cost containment or cost reduction as a priority; others may want increases in pay so that the company can retain a skilled workforce; and others may want to invest in training programs to increase productivity. Some stakeholders may want to improve workplace efficiency through the enforcement of standardized rules and regulations, while others may favour flexible rules that allow the organization to adapt quickly to changing conditions. Like the union team, the management team may consider some desired outcomes more achievable than others, or it may disagree with individual stakeholders about the relative importance of some issues.

How, then, do the negotiating teams identify and prioritize these competing demands? The process of identifying and prioritizing goals is accomplished through several means:

- *The union may conduct a survey of its membership to discover their concerns and their bargaining priorities.* This can be done by distributing a questionnaire and analyzing the results, or by holding votes at membership meetings. Since the union members must ultimately approve the negotiated agreement, it is important for the bargaining team to know what the membership wants so that the eventual agreement will not be rejected.

  Some research shows that union leaders believe bargaining effectiveness is one of the key determinants of how union members rate union effectiveness.[5] Therefore, incorporating the membership's wishes into bargaining priorities is a way for union leaders to demonstrate their effectiveness to the membership. (However, other research indicates that bargaining effectiveness is not as important a determinant of union effectiveness for union members as union leaders think it is. Members may place a higher priority on effectiveness criteria such as quality of leadership, opportunity to participate in union activities, the degree of formalization and centralization in the union structure, and the willingness of the union to undertake innovative activities.[6])

- *The negotiating teams may look at what was and was not accomplished in any previous negotiations.* This review provides two important kinds of information: how likely it is that current bargaining issues can be resolved satisfactorily, based on past experience, and whether goals that were not previously achieved are still important. For example, if in the past the union was reluctant to agree to work arrangements that could reduce work for union members, the management bargaining team will wonder whether it is worth the effort to introduce proposals similar to those the union previously rejected. If, however, management believes that these types of work arrangements are important to enable the organization to adapt to changing market conditions, it may reintroduce the proposals regardless of the previous rejection.

- *The negotiating teams may examine collective agreements in other locals of the union and/or in similar industries to see what has been agreed to elsewhere.* This source of information is particularly important if the union is a local of a larger union or if the organization has a "parent" organization, since neither team will want to unknowingly agree to contract terms inferior to what has been achieved elsewhere in the union or organization. This information can be the basis of pattern bargaining or whipsawing, as previously discussed.

- *The negotiating teams will examine the record of grievances filed since the last collective agreement went into effect.* If disputes have consistently arisen as a consequence of the application of a particular part of the agreement, that part of the agreement may need to be clarified or re-examined to determine whether it is accomplishing what it was intended to accomplish. The outcome of grievances, particularly resolutions where the complaint was found to be valid, may also indicate to either the union or the management team how likely it is that certain bargaining objectives will be achieved. For example, if a grievance resulted in the ruling that management must consult with the union before substantially changing work schedules, the management negotiating team will probably not give a high priority in bargaining to any proposal suggesting that management should have the sole right to determine working hours. The management negotiating team would foresee that the union negotiating team would likely cite the result of the grievance to argue that management should not have that right.

- *The negotiating teams will look at factors outside the organization (e.g., inflation rates, labour market demographics, and economic indicators) or other information to identify future trends that may affect the outcomes of bargaining.* A predicted increase in the inflation rate, for example, may affect whether the union bargaining team requests higher wages, since the employer's ability to pay may be reduced by increased costs. External factors also might come into play, for example, if the union considers whether it should bargain for a pay increase for workers with a particular skill. If labour market information indicates that there will soon be an oversupply of workers with this skill, it would be difficult for the union to successfully bargain for a pay increase, because in the future the employer will not have to pay higher wages to attract and retain those particular workers.

In the following news story, a union discusses an issue that was previously raised and rejected in bargaining, and presents it as a possible bargaining item in the next negotiations for a collective agreement.

Police Chief Opposes Bid for Paid Workouts

WINNIPEG—Giving police officers paid time for physical fitness is not an option, Winnipeg Police Service Chief Keith McCaskill said Wednesday, after the police union called on the city to consider the idea.

Earlier this week, Winnipeg Police Association president Mike Sutherland said the city should pay officers to work out for 20 or 30 minutes each shift, with officers matching that with their own time.

Sutherland said offenders are bulking up in prison and combating police with mixed martial arts moves.

"It really would take a lot of resources off the street," McCaskill said.

He said more than 1,000 officers successfully completed mandatory physical fitness tests last year, out of about 1,400. Officers receive 20 hours of time off annually if they pass the test, which is also required for pay increases and promotion.

McCaskill said scheduling one hour of fitness time for each officer would reduce the number of officers available to answer the calls, taking away from three to six general patrol units. "It's a lot of units off the air."

McCaskill said paid time for exercise could be addressed during collective bargaining for the next union contract, which begins later this year.

"Our main job as police officers is to be able to provide the services as necessary to the citizens we serve," he said. "And I think that means (getting) officers out on the street as much as they possibly can to be able to answer those calls."

Nine gyms in Winnipeg police stations are outfitted with union-bought equipment and free space from the city.

Officers, who work 10-hour shifts, plus overtime, voluntarily pay about $70 annually to use the gym facilities.

Sutherland said the issue of paid time for fitness was dropped during the last round of collective bargaining.

He's especially concerned for aging members of the force who may sustain back damage from carrying equipment.

"Law enforcement has evolved, technologies have evolved, our offender population has evolved, we need to evolve with it," he said. Sutherland said the issue is "particularly acute" because officers have a heavy workload and encounter a high level of violence.

"It's not that we're not asking the taxpayer to foot the whole bill, just meet us halfway," he said.

Sutherland said there has been an explosion in interest in mixed martial arts fighting by offenders.

"We have well-known gang members who are training at martial arts gyms throughout the city on an almost daily basis," he said.

Officers have been angrily confronted in gyms, he said, so having a separate workout space is key for their safety.

McCaskill acknowledged that officers are dealing with more violent offenders and weapons like firearms on the street. The force is trying to protect officers with initiatives such as the recently launched Tactical Support Team, and plans to bring in a police helicopter, he said.

He said the force encourages its members to stay in shape and has a fitness co-ordinator.

"I think most officers realize they have to be physically fit."

Source: Giroday, Gabrielle,. "Police Chief Opposes Bid for Paid Workouts." *Winnipeg Free Press*, January 14, 2010, p. B2.

A negotiating team's perception of what goals are realistic can also be influenced by the demographics of the team itself. This is particularly true with respect to the union negotiating team. While the priorities of the team representing the union theoretically represent the concerns of all members of the bargaining unit, the team's priorities may instead end up reflecting the priorities of the team members themselves. Some research has indicated that union members who are more dissatisfied with their job conditions than their co-workers tend to turn to union activism as a way to improve those conditions.[7] Since members who are active in the union are likely to be interested in participating in an important activity such as collective bargaining, the issues that personally motivated them to become active in the union may thus assume greater importance in the prioritizing of bargaining demands.

Another study addressing how unions determine their bargaining priorities examined how the Canadian labour movement deals with issues of sexual orientation.[8] The results of this study indicated that issues of concern to minority groups in unions are usually only considered "important" once the minority group members form a significant part of the union membership, or once they succeed in promoting their concerns within the union. If neither of these conditions is present, the concerns of demographic or numerical minorities within the union membership are not likely to be given priority in bargaining demands, even if the issue is significant to that group or affects union members who are not part of the minority group. For example, extending spousal benefits to individuals who are not married could affect heterosexual couples who are in a common-law relationship as well as same-sex couples. But if the issue of extended spousal benefits is being proposed as a bargaining concern by only a small number of minority group members, the bargaining team may consider the issue relatively unimportant and give it a low priority.

The results of another study indicate that decision-making in local unions tends to be governed by explicit rules and policies, and while this formalization does not appear to inhibit a local union's ability to innovate, members unfamiliar with the formal regulations may be unable to participate effectively and make their particular issues visible.[9] Thus, newcomers to the union or members who do not regularly participate in union activities may not be able to influence the setting of bargaining priorities, since they do not know how to follow the formal procedures that help determine those priorities, such as the procedure for proposing motions at a membership meeting.

When union negotiating teams prioritize desired bargaining outcomes, however, they must remember that the collective agreement they negotiate will eventually have to be ratified by the entire membership. Therefore, they must be careful to ensure that the prioritized list of bargaining demands reflects, as much as possible, the will of the membership and not their own personal preferences. If the eventual collective agreement does not at least appear to reflect the priorities of the membership, the membership may reject the agreement and send the bargaining team back to negotiate a more acceptable contract.

The process of identifying and prioritizing bargaining goals for the management negotiating team is somewhat more efficient and less formal than for the union team. This is because the management team is not usually formally accountable to its constituents, since, for example, it probably would not face a ratification vote on the negotiated contract. In creating its own set of bargaining goals and priorities, however, the management team will usually gather information on desired outcomes from the groups or individuals it represents, and will examine previous bargaining experiences or completed agreements in other organizations. Management may also acquire advance information on the union's bargaining intentions through discussions with supervisors and other non-union staff who interact with union members, and thereby be able to prioritize its bargaining demands accordingly.

There is one other source of information that both the union and management teams will draw on prior to bargaining. Court decisions and legislative changes may point to parts of the collective agreement that need re-examination. For example, if new employment legislation changes the way certain benefits are provided or funded, or changes the eligibility requirements for certain benefits, the collective agreement language governing the administration of those benefits may have to be rewritten to reflect the new regulations.

Preparing for the Start of Bargaining

After bargaining issues have been identified and prioritized, both negotiating teams will develop a "laundry list" of proposals, usually ranked from the most to the least important and/or achievable. Each team will give a list of its proposals to the other team when negotiations actually start, but the exchanged versions do not indicate the priority of each individual item. In fact, the lists that are exchanged may include items that are considered to be low priority or unachievable.

While it may seem counterproductive to present proposals that the team does not seriously intend to pursue, there are two strategic reasons for using this tactic. First, the tactic is useful because it allows the team to assure the individuals or groups it represents that "their" items were introduced in bargaining, even if these items were subsequently dropped from negotiations or were not resolved. This tactic is particularly important to union negotiators who have been chosen by a vote of the membership; to ensure they continue to have the membership's support, the elected negotiators will want to be perceived as being responsive to members' concerns. The union negotiators can tell union members that the members' concerns were presented in bargaining but were not pursued when it became obvious that the management team would not agree to the proposals. The negotiators can also justify their lack of action on particular items on the grounds that their energy was better expended on bargaining for items that were seen as more achievable.

Second, the tactic of presenting a complete list of proposals, including unimportant items, allows the team to hide the true priority of individual items on the list and thus achieve its desired outcomes more easily. For example, the union might readily agree to a proposal that it considers minor but that, unknown to the union, management considers important; thus, one of the management team's desired bargaining outcomes would be achieved with minimal effort on the management team's part. If the union was aware that the issue was a high priority for management, it might not immediately agree to the item; instead, the union might offer to exchange the union's agreement on that item for management's agreement on an item of equal importance to the union.

The length of the list of proposals can also play a strategic role. A very lengthy list that shows the range of issues that one side is (theoretically) prepared to address may intimidate the other team. The grim prospect of interminable negotiations may encourage the other team to reduce the number of its demands or to rethink its priorities so that bargaining does not drag on for an excessively long time.

Bargaining in Good Faith

When commencing collective bargaining, the parties must be aware of the legal requirement that they **bargain in good faith**. A complaint about bargaining in bad faith can be made at any point in the collective bargaining process; however, we will discuss the issue before outlining the actual bargaining process, because the first significant place where bargaining in bad faith can occur is before the bargaining process even begins. Specifically, if one party refuses to start negotiations or to meet at all, that party can be charged with bargaining in bad faith. The expectation that the parties will bargain in good faith underlies the entire bargaining process. This expectation should govern the parties in their preparations for bargaining, compelling them, for example, to ensure that they are making honest bargaining proposals.

Bargaining in good faith has two components. First, the parties are expected to enter into honest bargaining. In practice, this means that the parties must not, for example, make offers that they are not prepared to commit to, or withhold information that might affect how the other party responds to a proposal. Second, the parties are expected to bargain with the intent of reaching a collective agreement. This does not mean that one party must agree to every proposal from the other party, or that there cannot be delays or breaks in the bargaining process. What it does mean is that the parties are expected to actively work toward achieving an agreement and should not jeopardize the process by, for example, making outlandish proposals that no reasonable negotiator would agree to, or skipping scheduled negotiating meetings without good reason.

If one party believes that the other party is not bargaining in good faith, it can file a complaint of an unfair labour practice with a labour relations board. In seeking to determine whether bargaining in bad faith has taken place, the board will generally use both objective and subjective criteria. Objective criteria include the definitions and language in the relevant labour legislation that address what behaviours constitute bargaining in bad faith. An example of such behaviour would be one party's refusal to commence bargaining after the deadline for starting has passed if the other party has not consented to an alternative date for bargaining to begin. Subjective criteria involve ethical or moral issues. These criteria would be used to judge, for example, whether one party was justified in withholding confidential financial records from the other party.

Bargaining in good faith involves a commitment on both sides to an open and honest appraisal of the facts, with the intent of finalizing a contract that is agreeable to all.

In most Canadian jurisdictions, through legislation and case law, the following actions have been identified as bargaining in bad faith:

- outright refusal to bargain.

- **surface bargaining** (i.e., participating in negotiations but having no intent of concluding a collective agreement).

- presenting an initial offer, possibly based on an employer survey of union members, as a final offer—without any justification or rationale—and refusing to negotiate further. This "take it or leave it" approach is known as **Boulwarism**, named for a vice-president of General Electric in the United States in the 1950s who used this bargaining tactic.

- firing or disciplining union members or negotiators for reasons unrelated to their performance at work, or for no reason, during the negotiation process.

- the employer bargaining directly with employees rather than with the union (e.g., surveying bargaining unit members directly to identify their preferences and desired outcomes, or presenting proposals to the membership rather than to the union bargaining team).

- refusing to provide the rationale for a bargaining position.

- attempting to reopen the negotiation of terms that have already been settled (except if there has been some change in the workplace or external environment that requires the terms to be revisited).

It should be noted that the expectation that the parties will bargain in good faith does not require them to actually reach a collective agreement. What is important is that the parties should be committed to concluding a collective agreement and should actively work toward that goal; failure to reach an agreement is not in and of itself evidence of bargaining in bad faith. As well, the expectation that the parties will bargain in good faith does not mean that parties should "give in" or accept unsatisfactory terms for an item that is a bargaining priority just to conclude a collective agreement.

Most Canadian labour codes contain the provision that once collective bargaining begins, the workplace terms and conditions in place at the start of bargaining are under a **freeze**, or are "frozen," until a collective agreement is concluded. This means that the employer cannot unilaterally change contractual terms such as wage rates during the bargaining process. This provision applies even when a previous collective agreement has expired. The terms and conditions of the expired collective agreement are considered to be in effect as long as collective bargaining toward a new collective agreement is taking place. The terms and conditions cannot be changed until the new collective agreement is accepted or ratified by both parties and formally comes into effect.

A labour relations board faces a particular challenge in resolving complaints related to bargaining in bad faith. For example, it is often difficult to distinguish between a hardline bargaining stance and surface bargaining. If one party consistently rejects the proposals of the other party, it may be because that party genuinely believes that the proposals are unreasonable. Alternatively, the party could be attempting to prolong the bargaining process to make it so unpleasant and difficult that the other party, in order to end the process, will eventually agree to proposals it ordinarily would have rejected. The labour relations board must sort through evidence from both parties—evidence that can be quite contradictory—to determine what has actually happened or what has actually motivated the parties' actions.

Since the principles of collective bargaining suggest that the parties should, as much as possible, negotiate freely without the interference of third parties, it is often difficult for a labour relations board to prescribe an appropriate remedy when allegations of bargaining in bad faith have been made. The board does not want to actively manage the negotiations between the parties, since this would contradict the principle of allowing the parties to negotiate freely. However, if bargaining in bad faith has occurred, the labour relations board is charged with the responsibility of repairing the damaged relationship between the parties, and that repair can sometimes only be achieved by the board's directing or suggesting how the parties should act when negotiating.

If a labour relations board determines that a party to negotiations has not bargained in good faith, the usual remedy is for the board to state clearly what behaviour is and is not "bargaining in good faith." This declaration is intended to give the parties behavioural guidelines to follow in their subsequent bargaining sessions. These guidelines may be suggested to the parties even if the board does not uphold the complaint of bargaining in bad faith, since the board may feel that such guidance may avert future complaints or questionable behaviour. If necessary, or possible, the board will repair whatever substantive damage was caused by the illegal behaviour; for example, it can restore wages to pre-negotiation levels if a freeze was broken, or require that an unjustly fired union member be rehired.

A labour relations board must also come up with a remedy when a complaint of bargaining in bad faith is made while parties are negotiating their first collective agreement. Most Canadian labour legislation permits a labour relations board to impose a collective agreement if the parties are not able to settle a collective agreement themselves. As we will see in the discussion of third-party involvement in negotiations in Chapter 10, such a solution is not ideal, since it takes the responsibility for creating the agreement away from the parties that will administer the agreement in the workplace. If there are subsequent problems in applying or carrying out the imposed agreement, the parties may blame the problems on the third party that created the agreement, rather than taking a more proactive approach to resolving the disputes.

However, there are good reasons to allow a labour relations board to impose a first collective agreement. The imposition of an agreement will end the bargaining disputes between the parties, which is sometimes the only solution, particularly if the parties are inexperienced negotiators who lack the skills to resolve disputes on their own. The parties may still have disagreements, but at least there will be a collective agreement in place so that the workplace can continue to function. A labour relations board may also impose a collective agreement in order to control an employer who is resisting a union's presence by being stubborn in contract negotiations. If a reluctant employer refuses to meet with a union or refuses to consider the union's proposals, imposing a collective agreement will bypass that resistance and ensure that a collective agreement is achieved. An employer that does not like the terms of an imposed agreement may be more motivated to participate seriously in future negotiations so that subsequent contract terms will be more to its liking.

SUMMARY

When certification is granted, the parties are in a legal position to begin bargaining for a collective agreement. Union security provisions ensure that the union is able to effectively represent its members in bargaining. These provisions can include mandatory dues deductions, religious exemptions, the Rand formula, the closed shop (which requires union membership as a condition of employment), and the hiring hall, which gives the union some control over work assignments.

Several variables underpinning the bargaining process are established before the bargaining actually begins. The bargaining structure determines who will participate in bargaining; there can be different combinations of unions, employers, and workplaces, although the most common structure in Canada involves a single union and a single employer. The composition of union and management bargaining teams is also important in determining how the bargaining process unfolds. Each team has representatives who provide various kinds of expertise and guidance during bargaining.

The union and management negotiating teams prepare for bargaining by identifying and prioritizing their own desired bargaining outcomes. The bargaining teams collect various kinds of information to determine bargaining priorities. They will, for example, conduct surveys of union members, review events in previous rounds of bargaining, review disputes resulting from the application of the existing collective agreement, and examine external information such as inflation rates and labour market statistics. The union bargaining team must balance its own perceptions of reasonable outcomes against what the membership hopes to achieve through bargaining. The union bargaining team must, however, remember that the membership will eventually have to ratify any collective agreement achieved through bargaining. The management team is not as formally accountable to those it represents, but it will still have to satisfy the demands of various internal and external stakeholders.

Before the parties commence collective bargaining, they must be aware of the legal provisions that ensure that bargaining actually begins and that the parties bargain in good faith. Most Canadian labour codes set deadlines by which collective bargaining must begin; the deadline is usually based on the date that one party issued a formal notice to bargain to the other party. Bargaining in good faith requires that the parties bargain honestly and with the intent of concluding a collective agreement. Bargaining in bad faith is sometimes why the parties cannot settle a first collective agreement. In this situation, most Canadian jurisdictions permit the labour relations board to impose a collective agreement.

In Chapter 8, we will continue our discussion of collective bargaining by describing what actually happens in during negotiations.

KEY TERMS FOR CHAPTER 7

accreditation (p. 266)
bargaining council (p. 266)
bargain in good faith (p. 282)
Boulwarism (p. 284)
closed shop (p. 261)
dues check-off (p. 260)
employers' council (p. 266)
freeze (p. 284)

hiring hall (p. 261)

management rights clause (p. 270)

notice to bargain (p. 272)

pattern bargaining (p. 265)

Rand formula (p. 261)

religious exemption (p. 261)

surface bargaining (p. 284)

union shop (p. 261)

union security (p. 260)

whipsawing (p. 265)

DISCUSSION QUESTIONS FOR CHAPTER 7

1. Most Canadian labour codes require that a collective agreement be a minimum of one year in length. Why do you think this provision exists?

2. Despite the fact that collective bargaining is one of the most important activities in labour relations, labour relations legislation concentrates mostly on establishing the conditions under which bargaining will proceed. Why do you think the legislation says relatively little about the bargaining process itself?

3. Identify the members of the union's and the employer's bargaining teams, and discuss the reasons for each member's participation.

4. Why do labour codes generally require that wages and working conditions remain frozen during collective bargaining?

5. An employer presents an initial offer to a union and then makes minimal changes in response to the union's concerns. Is this bargaining in good faith? Why or why not?

6. Why is the issue of bargaining in good faith particularly important in negotiations for a first collective agreement?

7. What is the reason for giving labour relations boards the power to impose a first collective agreement?

8. If a first collective agreement is imposed, what effects might this event have on future negotiations for collective agreements?

CASE 7-1

SPEEDY TRANSIT AND BUS DRIVERS UNION

(Based on *Amalgamated Transit Union and Firstbus*, 2007)

In this case, the union and the employer are bargaining for a collective agreement. The union has filed a complaint with the labour relations board alleging that the employer did not bargain in good faith, because it unilaterally raised the wages for probationary employees. The union is also alleging that the employer interfered with the union's operations and intimidated employees through comments that were made to employees about wage rates and the union's motives in bargaining.

Case Facts

Speedy Transit provides transportation services for disabled people, under the terms of a service contract it has negotiated with the city government. The city pays Speedy a lump sum for providing this service, and Speedy has the discretion to decide how these funds are allocated. The only stipulation for Speedy's spending is that the service must be financially self-sufficient. The bargaining unit represented by the union includes all 44 bus and van drivers that Speedy employs. The drivers are responsible for driving the vehicles and escorting the passengers. The drivers are allowed to choose the schedules and routes that they want to work; casual employees are brought in to cover any unclaimed work. Probationary employees are part of the bargaining unit.

The current collective agreement is for a three-year term, and it expires next year. A third party had to be brought in to help the parties negotiate, and the union served strike notice on the employer just prior to the agreement being reached. As part of this negotiation, the employer told the union that there was a lump sum for wage increases, and the union had to choose whether it wanted this sum applied to wages or to paying for the benefits it was requesting. The union chose to have the sum applied to wages. The union also asked the employer for an increase to the wages of the probationary employees. The employer did not want to increase these, but the two sides compromised on a reduction to the length of the probationary period (from one year to six months) and the same percentage increase to the wages for probationary drivers as was being given to the permanent drivers. The wage differences between the classifications range from approximately $4 to $7.

As the collective agreement was being put into effect, the province's minimum wage law changed, with the result that the probationary drivers' wage rate was now lower than the provincial standard. Both parties agreed that the probationary wage rate would be raised to the minimum wage rate, which meant a 40-cent increase from the negotiated rate. This agreement was not formalized and was not added to the collective agreement, as neither party felt this was necessary.

At the start of this year, the employer decided it wanted to increase wage rates for both categories of drivers. It felt that it was having trouble attracting new drivers because of the wage rates, and had experienced some difficulties in replacing unavailable drivers. The employer was also worried about burnout among the drivers who were working overtime shifts. There were fines in the contract with the city that would be imposed if the employer did not meet its obligations. There was also additional contract work (e.g. driving fans to sports events) that the employer could not take on because it did not have enough staff. Harold Francis, the service supervisor, mentioned the staffing issues in some informal conversations with George Gilmore, the union president, but the employer and the union never had a formal meeting about these issues.

In spring, the senior management team at Speedy decided to increase the wage rates for probationary drivers by $2.25 an hour. Jim Olsen, the Speedy contract manager, told the board that he felt there was too much of a gap between the probationary wage rates and the regular wage rates, and that overtime was not an issue except that it was affecting the health of the regular drivers. He said that the company's main concern was to provide the customer service it promised.

Before the wage increase was implemented, Gilmore received a phone call from Erin Irving, Speedy's human resource director, who told him about the proposed increase and said that the reason for the increase was to attract new drivers and give existing drivers more time off. Gilmore responded that the wage increase should only be $2 an hour, and that any change would have to be ratified by the union executive and then by the membership. Irving then sent Gilmore an e-mail with an attached letter of understanding to be signed by the union. The increase outlined in the letter was the $2.25 rate proposed by the employer.

The union executive decided to recommend that the union membership accept the increase, and the issue of the increase was added to the agenda of the next membership meeting. At that meeting, the executive told the membership that the executive members were in favour of the company's proposal to increase probationary drivers' hourly wages by $2.25. The discussion at the meeting focused on how regular drivers were working hard and using up their paid sick leave, and why the employer wanted to give more money to new employees instead of increasing the amount of paid sick leave. Only one probationary driver, Steve Chandler, was present at the meeting; he told the board that he sensed the proposal would have been more popular if it had offered wage increases to everyone. The vote, by secret ballot, was seven votes in favour of the proposed increase and 14 against.

After the meeting, Gilmore sent an e-mail to Irving informing her that the union membership voted to reject the letter of understanding. Irving responded that she did not understand why the union would reject a proposal for higher wages and questioned the "true, underlying reasons" for the rejection. Gilmore answered that the members were "sick and tired" of being treated the way they were and that "people have been busting their tails, coming to work sick and you won't help them." He added, "By labour standards, you will have to bring your rate up to minimum wage. [The union] believes that minimum wage is not fair, but our members have spoken." Irving replied that it was the employer who had proposed in collective bargaining to increase the probationary wage rates, and "the union was not receptive."

Gilmore told the board that since the increase had not been ratified by the union membership, he assumed that was the end of the matter, and interpreted Irving's e-mail to mean that there would be no change to any wage rate in the collective agreement.

Not long after the union meeting, Francis told Chandler—who at that time was the only probationary employee—that his wage rate would be going up to $11 per hour. This change did occur, and the employer did not tell the union about the change. Lana McCoy, one of the union's vice-presidents, found out about the change, and "had a disagreement" with Chandler about it. McCoy told Gilmore about the change, and Gilmore filed a grievance.

The Union's Position

Gilmore and two other union officials explained to the board that the union was in favour of higher wages for probationary employees, and had tried to obtain this through collective bargaining. During bargaining, they said, the employer was satis-fied with the gap between probationary and regular wages and was aware that the probationary wages were going to be below minimum wage. They said they could not explain why the union members rejected the proposed probationary wage increase, but that the union members had the right to accept or reject such propos-als, and the members made their choice, which was then communicated to the employer.

The union officials thought that it was wrong for the employer to ignore the union members' choice and to unilaterally impose a wage increase instead of negotiating with the union. They also thought that after the rejection of the probationary wage increase, the employer should have agreed with the union's suggestion of negotiating a change to all wage rates, starting with the rates paid to the employees who had been there the longest and working their way down from there. The union believed that the employer's decision to increase wages after the union's rejection of its proposal constituted bar-gaining in bad faith, and that Irving's questioning the union's motives for its decision was an unfair labour practice.

The union officials argued that the employer's actions undermined the union in the eyes of its members, and made it appear as though the employer could do whatever it wanted, even when the union objected. The union officials stated that the members feel they are not appreciated and are not treated fairly by the employer, which, in the offi-cials' opinion, will make future collective bargaining even more difficult. They also stat-ed that the members are well aware that the employer has "one pot of money" and that giving more to some means giving less to others, which is divisive and discriminatory. They argued that this would not be a problem if the employer had followed the collec-tive agreement as written.

Chandler told the board that he agreed with the argument that the change by the employer undermined the union's authority and that, while he liked the wage increase, he thought the employer should have respected the union's vote on the matter.

The union requested that the board make the probationary wage rate increase retroactive to the start of the current collective agreement, or, alternately, that the increase be retroactive to the date of the proposed letter of agreement. The union also requested that the board award all employees a $2/hour wage increase, because the hiring of new employees has led to a decrease in overtime for the regular employees. However, the union also proposed that it would consider and review a "rectification plan" from the employer if the employer was prepared to address the wage issues. The union also asked that the employer be ordered to refrain from further violations of the relevant labour relations act, and to pay the union's legal costs.

The Employer's Position

Francis and Olsen told the board that Speedy could not understand why the union rejected the offer of a wage increase. They thought that perhaps the regular drivers did not want more probationary drivers because that would mean less work for the regular drivers, but there was no evidence presented to support this. Olsen said that, in his opinion, the major problem was the gap between the probationary wages and the regular wages, and that he did not see a problem with raising the probationary wage rates but not the regular wage rates.

The board was told that the employer did not inform the union about the increase in probationary wage rates because Chandler was the only employee affected. There was no explanation of why Chandler was not given retroactive pay dating from the time of the employer's original proposal to the union.

Francis and Olsen explained that the employer's actions were not intended to undermine the union or to discriminate among the members. The employer was concerned with being able to quickly recruit more drivers and to meet its service expectations. The employer felt that it was not getting cooperation from the union and that it had met its duty to bargain by giving the union the initial proposal. Olsen admitted that an exchange of e-mails was not his understanding of how negotiations should be conducted. However, after the exchange of e-mails between Irving and Gilmore, the union did not contact the employer to pursue further bargaining, nor did the union discuss the wage increase with the employer once the union became aware of the change. The employer said it "did not try to hide anything" about the change because it paid union dues on the increased wages.

The board was told that, after the probationary wage increase, Speedy was able to hire nine probationary drivers, and that, as a result, the employer felt there was an improvement in its service. Thus, the employer argued, while the decision may have been "the wrong thing," the employer did it for the "right reasons."

The employer argued that the union is the one discriminating against the probationary employees and that the union members were being "selfish" in rejecting the proposed wage increase. The employer pointed out that it is given a fixed sum of money under its contract, and that if it is unable to meet its service requirements under that contract, it will have to pay financial penalties and there will be even less money available for wages. The employer suggested that a raise for everyone could result in layoffs.

In response to the union's requests for remedies, the employer stated that there was no point in the board ordering a "rectification plan" since the union would not accept anything other than an increase in wages for all employees. The employer also stated that it should not have to pay the union's legal costs because the union made the choice to hire a lawyer.

CASE *7-2*

UNION OF RETAIL WORKERS AND BEAUTIFUL SPRINGS

(Based on *Temple Gardens Mineral Spa and Joint Board R.W.D.S.U.*, 2002)

In this case, the parties are bargaining for a first collective agreement. News stories in the local paper have indicated that the employer plans to expand its operations, although these plans have not been mentioned during negotiations. The union has filed a complaint of bargaining in bad faith with the labour relations board on the basis that if the employer does have plans for expansion, this is a material fact that could affect the negotiations and the employer should have disclosed this to the union during bargaining. The union is also complaining that the employer has refused to provide it with information on individual employees, such as dates of hire and current wage rates, which the union needs to prepare its bargaining positions. The labour relations board has held a hearing to investigate both complaints.

Case Facts

The Union of Retail Workers represents a unit of employees at Beautiful Springs, a spa facility built around natural hot springs. The union was granted certification last fall. The spa is marketed both as recreation for local residents and as a destination for tourists.

The union representative, Neil Ishikawa, told the board that the parties had commenced bargaining for a first collective agreement in the spring. On April 17, the union wrote to the employer and requested a list of employee names, addresses, dates of hiring, current wage rates, and amounts of wage increases during the past year. Ishikawa said that the union needed this information for several reasons: it needed the dates of hiring because both parties had agreed to base seniority on these dates, and the union needed to be able to verify the dates in case of disagreement; it needed the employees' addresses so that it could communicate directly with its members; and it needed the wage information in order to prepare its bargaining positions for monetary items.

On April 29, the employer provided some, but not all, of the requested information. The employer provided addresses and dates of hiring for employees working in food services but not for employees in other areas. The employer did not provide any wage-increase information.

On May 6, the parties met for a bargaining session. At this meeting, the union specifically asked if the employer "was considering any plans" that could affect collective bargaining. The union was interested in this issue because the employer had proposed that it be given the ability to create new departments and had expressed concern about a union proposal that dealt with the creation of new job classifications. According to Ishikawa, Elizabeth Valmont, the spa's chief executive officer and head of the employer's bargaining team, said that even if there were plans she would not tell the union because she was afraid of what the union would do with the information. Ishikawa said he informed her that refusing to disclose this information would be an unfair labour practice.

The next bargaining session was scheduled for June 1. On May 28, the local newspaper ran a special advertising feature entitled "Beautiful Springs Developing Expansion Plans." The article described several plans for redevelopment in the local area and indicated that in mid-June the spa management was planning to approach city council for approval of the expansion plans. At the June 1 meeting, Ishikawa showed Valmont the article and asked again for disclosure of plans that could affect the negotiations. Valmont replied "tersely" that because of the newspaper story the plans were now disclosed. Ishikawa asked for more specific information, such as the numbers of employees in the expanded facility, their job classifications, and any new areas of operation that would be included in the expansion. Valmont refused to provide this information.

The same day, the union wrote to the employer again to request the missing employee information. Valmont replied to Ishikawa that afternoon with a fax that read, in part, "Based on your volume of letters of complaints/threats, I assume that you are using a well-known 'anti-management tactic.' I was warned about this, but expected as much from you. Your complaints are not substantiated and lack substance, so appear to be an attempt to bury me in paperwork. I promise I'm trying to do my best. (Sometimes my job gets in the way. Ha. Ha.)"

On June 2, Ishikawa wrote to Valmont to verify that on May 6 the union had asked about the plans for the expansion at the spa and that it had asked again at the bargaining session of June 1 after the May 28 news article appeared. Ishikawa's letter stated that the employer's refusal to discuss the plans was an unfair labour practice. Ishikawa told the board that he had received no response to this letter.

On June 6, Valmont held a meeting with employees to discuss the expansion plans. Mary Charleson, who had worked at the spa as head lifeguard for more than three years, attended the meeting and described it to the board. She said that attendance had not been mandatory and that approximately 50 employees were present. At the meeting, according to Charleson, Valmont described the expansion plans and told the employees that they were the first to hear about them. The plans included a 70- to 100-room expansion of the adjoining hotel and expansion of the existing swimming pool; the addition of a smaller second pool, a doctor's office, and a theatre; an expanded fitness centre; a renovation of the original hot springs facility; and parking for 600 vehicles. There were also plans by a separate company to open a casino adjacent to Beautiful Springs, and Valmont estimated that if this occurred, the additional tourist traffic would generate a 70 to 90 percent occupancy rate at the hotel. Construction on the expansion was expected to start the next year, with an opening two years after that, and both the construction activities and the expansion would create "a significant number of new jobs." Valmont showed the employees a set of professional sketches of the planned expansion and told them that the spa would be going to city council with the plans and would appreciate the employees' support. Under questioning by the board, Valmont admitted having asked an employee at the meeting who was taking notes whether the employee was taking notes for the union.

On June 12, Ishikawa attended a city council meeting at which Valmont and others made a presentation about how the planned casino would affect Beautiful Springs' operations. The presentation included some information about anticipated increases in employee numbers during and after construction of the expansion.

On June 22, the parties met in another bargaining session. At this session, the employer presented what it called a "comprehensive contract" offer and asked that it be presented to the employees. The union indicated that it would study the proposal and respond when it was ready.

On July 31, Ishikawa received a letter from Valmont that had also been distributed to all employees. The letter stated that the casino project had received municipal approval at the previous night's council meeting and that it would now be referred to the provincial government for the next level of approval. Valmont's letter also stated the following:

"As I'm sure you are aware, our current confrontational relationship with the union only hampers our ability to expand. I am sure you are also aware that the union's "strike vote," its five unfair labour practices [complaints] filed with the labour relations board, unresolved dispute over the facility manager position, the unconcluded out-come of an arbitration, and, most important, your refusal to present the "compre-hensive contract" to the employees for ratification is not creating an environment conducive for either financiers or investors interested in our expansion proposal. At this time, I can only urge you to set your personal animosities toward me aside, and work cooperatively to bring closure to this year-long dispute as quickly as possible by giving our employees an opportunity to vote on our "comprehensive contract" offer. It is time for both of us to do what is in the best interest of both our company and its employees."

Attached to the letter was the regional "Vision Document," a glossy brochure intended for public distribution. It outlined eight proposed projects, one of which was a 50- to 70-room expansion of Beautiful Springs, costing $8 million. The text of the doc-ument estimated that the expansion would create 45 new permanent jobs worth approximately $850,000 annually.

In addition, much evidence was introduced at the hearing "with respect to rather unbecoming behaviour and snide remarks by the representatives of both parties."

The Union's Position

The union argued that the employer clearly had plans for expansion, despite what the employer had indicated in bargaining, and that the union had not been aware of these plans until the May 28 newspaper article. The union also argued that the plans were clearly beyond the preliminary stages and that the employer should have fully disclosed the plans during bargaining so that the changes caused by the expansion could be addressed in the collective agreement. The union characterized the employer's reasons for not disclosing the information as "specious" and alleged that these reasons were further discredited by the fact that the employer told the employees about the plans a few days after refusing to tell the union.

The union also argued that the employer was bargaining in bad faith by not pro-viding all of the employee information the union had requested. The union stated that it needed this information in order to prepare accurate bargaining proposals and to be able to communicate with and represent its members.

The union alleged that both these disputes were caused by Valmont not wanting to be open and honest in bargaining and that, while she claims she wants to be open and honest with the employees, she does not respect the union as the employees' representative or respect the bargaining process.

The Employer's Position

The employer argued that the expansion plans were contingent on the approval of the casino and that the failure of a previous expansion proposal indicated that there was no guarantee that the expansion would happen. The employer also stated that because of the long timeline of construction and completion, the expansion—should it go ahead—would not affect conditions during the life of the collective agreement. The only issue that could affect bargaining in the future was a potential increase in the number of employees.

The employer stated that, in previous labour relations board cases involving disclosure during bargaining, the employers' plans were much more concrete and well developed than the spa's plans currently were. The employer also said that, according to legal advice it had received, the plans did not have to be disclosed in bargaining because they were preliminary and would not affect bargaining.

The employer also indicated that the information about the expansion had been withheld during bargaining because of a dispute between two groups over who would operate the new casino. The employer did not want the information to influence the outcome of the dispute. The employer had not favoured either group in the conflict, but had been mostly concerned that if the expansion were to go ahead, the casino had to be located next door to the spa facilities instead of elsewhere in the city.

The employer addressed the issue of the June 6 employee meeting by saying that the meeting had been intended to encourage employees to attend the June 12 council meeting and express their support for the casino; it had also been scheduled as a celebration of the spa's fourth anniversary. The employer stated that all of the expansion ideas presented at the meeting were only possibilities.

The employer also stated that it did not trust Ishikawa, alleging that Ishikawa had been aware of the expansion plans well before the May 28 newspaper article because there had been much discussion in the city's business community about both the spa's desire to expand and the application for a new casino. (Ishikawa firmly denied this in his testimony to the board and was adamant that the newspaper article was the first he had heard of the expansion.)

In addressing the complaint about the missing employee information, Valmont told the board that the employer's accounting department had been overwhelmed with work and had had difficulty compiling the requested information, that she had been suspicious of the request because she believed the union was trying to overload her with work, and that she feared the union would use the wage information to create conflict among employees by disclosing who had received what increases.

References

[1] E.g., *British Columbia Hydro and Power Authority and Office and Technical Employees Union Local 378 and Tottle* (BCLRB No. 9/78).

[2] Budd, J.W. (1992). The determinants and extent of UAW pattern bargaining. *Industrial & Labor Relations Review, 45(3),* 523–540.

[3] Budd, *op. cit.*

[4] Van Alphen, T. (2005, September 27). GM, union closer, but issues linger: CAW leader says 'show stoppers' are in way of deal—auto giant agrees to pattern pact, cost cuts in dispute. *Toronto Star,* p. C01; Sova, G. (2009, May 5). Is pattern bargaining dead? CAW meets Chrysler. *Canadian HR Reporter,* <http://chrrlabour.wordpress.com/2009/05/04/is-pattern-bargaining-dead/>.

[5] Fiorito, J., & Stepina, L.P. (1997). Visions of success: national leaders' views on union effectiveness. *Labor Studies Journal, 22(1),* 3–20.

[6] Hammer, T.H., & Wazeter, D.L. (1993). Dimensions of local union effectiveness. *Industrial & Labor Relations Review, 46(2),* 302–320; Mellor, S., & Mathieu, J.E. (1999). A discriminant validity study of aggregate-level constructs and measures of local union formalization, centralization and innovation. *Journal of Psychology, 133(6),* 669–684.

[7] McShane, S.L. (1986). The multidimensionality of union participation. *Journal of Occupational Psychology, 59(2),* 177–187.

[8] Hunt, G. (1997). Sexual orientation and the Canadian labour movement. *Relations Industrielles, 52(4),* 787–809.

[9] Mellor & Mathieu, *op. cit.*

Ontario Colleges Avoid Instructors' Strike

The end of 2009 and the start of 2010 were tense times for Ontario's 200,000 full-time college students. Collective bargaining negotiations between the council representing the province's 24 community colleges and the union representing 9,000 faculty members broke down after six months of negotiations. The Ontario Public Services Employees Union (OPSEU) had accused the College Appointments and Compensation Council of refusing to negotiate in good faith, and had threatened strike action that would have affected classes across the province.

A key issue for the faculty members was improving the quality of education by implementing the recommendations of an independent task force that examined workloads, academic freedom, and quality of education following a three-week faculty strike in 2006. Both sides had agreed to the task

force recommendations; however, the union claimed management reneged on that agreement in negotiations. The colleges represented by the Council claimed the union's demands weren't in line with the report's recommendations. The Council also indicated the union's settlement position would add $218 million in annual costs.

The community college faculty members voted in favour of a strike in January. The parties met on several days following the strike vote, but were not able to resolve the major issues. The colleges tabled a final offer, which the union rejected.

"The offer from the employer is not acceptable," said Ted Montgomery, chair of the OPSEU negotiating team, in a press release. "However, we are emphatic that a settlement can be reached at the negotiating table without any work stoppage." He urged the colleges to submit all outstanding issues to binding arbitration if a settlement could not be reached.

The colleges didn't return to the bargaining table but asked the union to hold a vote on their final offer. In late February, the faculty voted 51.45 percent in favour of the final offer. "We are pleased that faculty saw this offer as fair and reasonable and one that they could accept," said Dr. Rachael Donovan, chair of the colleges' bargaining team, in a press release. "We will now have a collective agreement in place and we have avoided a strike."

The approved offer provided workload and salary improvements for faculty members , including a 5.9 percent salary increase. The workload improvements included giving faculty members more control over how workload is assigned.

Fear was a motivating factor for the acceptance of the colleges' offer, Montgomery said in a press release. "We did not want a labour disruption, and had planned to avoid one, but the employer took a stance with our members that it was either accept the offer or be forced out on strike ... The vote is not an endorsement of the imposed terms and conditions or the employer's last offer."

Sources: The College Appointments and Compensation Council, www.theCouncil.on.ca; Ontario Public Service Employees Union, www.opseu.org.

THE COLLECTIVE BARGAINING PROCESS

objectives

After the union and management bargaining teams have determined their respective goals and priorities, they are ready to negotiate and make every reasonable effort to conclude a collective agreement. This chapter outlines the negotiation stages and negotiation subprocesses, along with the strategies and tactics that each side uses to reach a collective agreement. We will also look at two alternatives to the traditional process of negotiation. At the end of this chapter, you should be able to:

- define the stages that negotiations go through
- describe the subprocesses that occur within negotiation stages
- understand how each side in negotiations acquires bargaining power
- outline an alternative model for union-management negotiations

INTRODUCTION

In Chapter 7, we described how unions and employers prepare for collective bargaining. As we noted in that chapter, union-management negotiations are regulated by legislation outlining how often negotiations must occur and requiring certain terms to be included in the resulting collective agreement. Beyond the legislative framework, though, the "how" of negotiations is not easily captured. Union-management negotiations usually proceed through specific stages:

- the pre-negotiation stage
- the stage of establishing the negotiating range
- the stage of narrowing the negotiating range
- the crisis stage
- the ratification stage

After briefly outlining the basic process of negotiation, we will describe each of these stages in turn, and outline the subprocesses that may occur in each stage.

HOW DO NEGOTIATIONS WORK?

As described in Chapter 7, the negotiation process begins when one side issues a formal notice to bargain to the other side. Legislation in most Canadian jurisdictions specifies a deadline by which negotiations must begin after the notice to bargain has been issued. The parties must then agree on when to have their first joint bargaining meeting.

At the initial meeting, each party introduces the members of its negotiating team. The teams exchange written proposals and demands, and decide when the next joint meeting will be. After the initial meeting adjourns, each negotiating team holds its own private meetings to discuss the other team's proposals and demands and to formulate a response.

At the second and subsequent joint meetings, each team makes counter-proposals and uses a variety of strategies and tactics to uncover the other team's real goals and priorities. These meetings continue until an agreement is reached or an impasse is declared.

When an agreement is reached, each team must go to its constituency or stakeholders and obtain their approval before the agreement can become official. If an impasse is declared (i.e., the parties do not believe they can settle on a mutually acceptable agreement), the parties may elect to take a short break from negotiating or to ask for the intervention of a third party to help them overcome the impasse. The union may choose to undertake a strike, or the employer may choose to undertake a lockout. The intent of each of these actions is to make the parties return to the bargaining table so that they can reach an agreement.

STAGES OF UNION-MANAGEMENT NEGOTIATIONS

Although the process described in the previous section sounds relatively straightforward, it can unfold over varied periods of time and with varying degrees of cooperation or hostile conflict. Despite this variability, however, studies of union-management negotiations have noted the remarkable similarity in the stages of negotiations in most circumstances, despite the fact that every set of negotiations occurs in a different setting and involves distinct issues.[1] The process of union-management negotiations commences with the pre-negotiation stage, discussed in Chapter 7, in which each party prepares its priorities for negotiations. The actual negotiations proceed through three specific stages: the stage of establishing the negotiating range, the stage of narrowing the bargaining range, and the crisis stage preceding the decision to settle or to invoke economic sanctions such as a strike or lockout.[2] It is not always possible to define clearly when one stage has ended and another has begun; however, for the parties to reach an agreement, it is important that the negotiations progress through each of these three stages. Aborting or short-circuiting any stage in the negotiation process can cause the process to end abruptly or to fail to produce an agreement. To elaborate on these stages further, we will outline the events that occur in each of them.

Pre-negotiation Stage

In this stage, each side determines its priorities, goals, and ultimate proposals for the upcoming negotiations. As discussed in Chapter 7, the parties accomplish this by collecting information from a variety of sources and developing a laundry list of proposals. Some proposals are considered essential, while others—once negotiations have begun—may be traded or "dropped off the table" in exchange for agreement on more important proposals. Still other proposals may be included to introduce the other side to issues that may become important in future bargaining. A long and inclusive list of proposals disguises real priorities and enhances each side's relationship with its own constituents by demonstrating to them that their negotiating team has heard and responded to their concerns.

It is common for the two sides to agree to meet jointly during the pre-negotiation stage to sound each other out informally on negotiating protocol and procedures. The purpose of these pre-negotiation informal meetings is to ensure that the negotiations themselves do not get bogged down in procedural wrangling. It is also a more efficient use of the parties' time to agree on procedural and protocol issues before negotiations begin, so that the time scheduled for negotiations can actually be spent in bargaining.

Establishing the Negotiating Range

This stage of bargaining typically begins at the first formal bargaining session, where all the representatives of both parties are present. In this stage, both parties introduce their bargaining team members and present their proposals. Usually, the chief negotiator for each side orally presents the rationale for each proposal to the other side. These oral presentations are vigorous, spirited, and sometimes aggressive, because the negotiator is expressing the views of that side's members or constituencies. While the presentations are often characterized by emotional and even extreme rhetoric, the chief negotiators actually have a respectful and professional relationship with one another. The two negotiators may know each other from other negotiations and may perhaps have represented their respective parties in earlier negotiations within the same organization. Experienced negotiators know that bargaining will not proceed smoothly if the negotiators alienate each other at the first meeting. They also realize that a forceful presentation is expected of a chief negotiator, and thus they will not be personally offended by aggressive statements.

These oral presentations serve several purposes. One is to establish the bargaining range by identifying the issues of importance to each side and stating what each side initially intends to achieve on these issues. The chief negotiator will typically outline the issue and attach an offer to the issue; for example, in presenting the issue of salaries, the chief negotiator will indicate the desired salary range. (Keep in mind that these are initial offers, and, at this point, the union or the employer will likely not fully reveal what they are actually willing to settle for.) Another purpose of these presentations is to demonstrate the degree of commitment each side has to its own positions. A spirited presentation indicates that the union or the employer is serious about its proposals and is willing to work to achieve the desired outcomes. Finally, these presentations provide an opportunity for each side to explain the reasoning behind its proposals and positions and thereby influence the perceptions and expectations of the other side. Giving some background on why a proposal is reasonable is a way to persuade the other side that the proposal should be adopted. This background also gives the other side some basis for developing counter-proposals, because if counter-proposals are to be successful, they must address the reasoning used to support the original proposal.

Narrowing the Bargaining Range

The activities in the stage when the bargaining range is narrowed are perhaps best illustrated by the **zone of agreement** model.[3] Figure 8-1 gives an example of how the zone of agreement dictates each side's decisions in narrowing the bargaining range and, ultimately, whether the parties reach an agreement.

As Figure 8-1 demonstrates, each team enters negotiations (if it is well prepared) with an initial offer and a **bottom line** position for each proposed item. The initial offer is the first proposal given to the other side and is usually the team's most optimistic outcome for that item. Some initial offers may seem outlandish, but because there is always

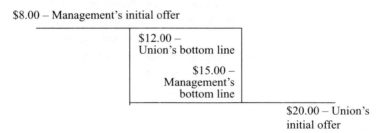

Figure 8-1 *The Zone of Agreement*

Source: Adapted from Walton, R.E. & McKersie, R.B. (1963). *A behavioral theory of labor negotiations: an analysis of a social interaction system.* (New York: McGraw-Hill).

a chance that the other side will accept the initial proposal, it is common for an initial offer to represent the team's "dream" outcome for that item. In contrast, the bottom line position is the absolute minimum or maximum that the team would be willing to accept as a settlement for that item.

Figure 8-1 uses the issue of wages to demonstrate how the zone of agreement affects bargaining behaviour. The initial offers of the two sides are far apart, which usually inspires the negotiators to consider offers that are more realistic and therefore possibly mutually acceptable. During the stage of narrowing the bargaining range, both sides start to retreat from their original positions in an attempt to find a point where a mutually satisfactory resolution can be reached. As Figure 8-1 shows, for an agreement to be reached, the wage rate must not exceed the employer's maximum or drop below the union's minimum; if it does, it will not be accepted, since the bargaining teams have not been authorized by their constituencies to settle for any wage rate outside their previously agreed limits. It is also apparent that for a settlement to be reached there must be some overlap between both sides' positions. If there is no zone of agreement, either there will be no settlement, or each team must adjust its bottom line, based on its perception of what the other side would be willing to agree to, in order to achieve an agreement.

The timing of counter-proposals and **concessions** (i.e., deciding to agree to the other side's proposal or to change one's own position) is crucial during the narrowing stage of bargaining. It is first important for both sides to exhaust their arguments for their own positions. It is only when those discussions are thoroughly concluded that any movement from a position becomes timely. Each side will likely want to meet privately to make sure each team member supports a change in position or a counter-proposal before it is presented to the other side. The back-and-forth discussion, combined with the time each team spends in private meetings, means that narrowing the bargaining range is often the longest of all the bargaining stages. This process of extensive debate, exchange of counter-proposals, concessions, and agreement on mutually acceptable positions continues, often issue by issue, until the crisis stage is reached.

The Crisis Stage

During the **crisis** stage of negotiations, one or both sides must decide whether to settle or whether to use economic sanctions such as a strike or lockout to pressure the other

Foes in a Numbers Game

MONTREAL—In contract negotiations, zero, two, two and two doesn't mean zero, two, two and two.

It turns out the percentage wage increases that Mayor Gerald Tremblay's administration offered all of the city's municipal unions for 2007 through 2010 are adjustable, if other contract clauses concerning such things as overtime, vacation or sick days are tweaked to pay for bigger raises.

It's one of the nuances in the verbal gymnastics that have characterized the latest—and unfinished—round of contract negotiations between the city and its 10 unions, as well as the six unions of the Société de transport de Montreal since late 2006.

The city argues that it's financially hamstrung because of decrepit infrastructure and a built-in deficit caused by decades of dependence on a regressive property tax and a lack of new sources of revenue from the province.

Current salaries are in line with the market, said Jean-Yves Hinse, the city's director of professional relations. On top of salaries, the city pays overtime, unused sick days and about 60 per cent of an employee's top salary at retirement, he said.

"How much is job security worth?" he asked.

The unions contend that wage increases in the past two contracts have resulted in an erosion of employees' standard of living and of the city's ability to woo top candidates from the private sector.

"If (the city) really had financial difficulty, then how can it allow itself to have more elected officials in Montreal than in Toronto (and) how can it allow itself to have more managers in Montreal than in New York?" Michel Parent, president of the blue-collar union, Local 301 of the Canadian Union of Public Employees, told the RDI television network last month.

"So it's an internal management problem (in Montreal), and that's what has to change."

"Collective bargaining is really a game of political pressure on economic issues," said Patrice Jalette, who teaches in the department of industrial relations at the Université de Montreal.

He calls the war of figures between the city and unions a "coercive comparison." It's a way of forcing the other side to be reasonable. "All these comparisons aim to tell the other side, 'Look, if you make a concession on this, it won't be dishonourable because we're behind, for example, or ahead of somewhere else.'" The Montreal Police Brotherhood, for instance, argues the city's salary proposal of a wage freeze for 2007 and annual increases of two per cent in 2008, 2009 and 2010 would make Montreal officers, who are currently among the top 10 highest-paid police departments in Quebec, drop to between 20th and 24th place.

Montreal Firefighters' Association president Perry Bisson said that a Montreal firefighter's job is more demanding in a city the size of Montreal than other municipalities in Quebec. Montreal firefighters are also handling more than twice as many calls as before now that they're trained as first responders, he added. They provide urgent medical treatment before an ambulance arrives.

The blue-collar union called for a two-per-cent pay hike for 2007 and 2008, and 2.5 per cent for 2009, 2010, 2011 and 2012, with a provision for a bigger increase in the final two years if inflation is higher.

The city says the unions' wage demands would equal a hike of about 10 per cent over four years, while the city's proposal would be 6.2 per cent over the same period. The unions are asking for more than the city is capable of paying, Hinse said.

Source: Gyulai, Linda (2010, April 17). "Foes in a numbers game: city and municipal union negotiators throw figures back and forth in attempt to show they have reason on their side", *The Gazette*, [Montreal], p. A4.

side into agreeing to its demands. The decision to settle or to invoke economic sanctions can be triggered by disputes over a single issue or disputes over a "package" deal involving several interrelated items.

By the time this stage of negotiations is reached, each side has argued extensively and tensions have increased. Hard and difficult decisions must now be made. Experienced negotiators view the noticeable rise in the tension level as confirmation that they have narrowed the bargaining range and are entering the crisis stage.

The process of invoking a strike or lockout is discussed in detail in Chapter 9. The purpose of one side undertaking such action as a negotiating tactic is to place a heavy financial burden on the other side so that the other side will eventually "give in" to bargaining demands. The use of these tactics can shorten or extend the crisis stage, depending on the strength of the parties' resolve to resist pressure and the amount of resources they have to support their operations during a strike or lockout. However, once the desired concession occurs, both sides will settle on the terms and conditions of a collective agreement, and recommend acceptance of the tentative agreement to their members or shareholders.

Canadian Auto Workers (CAW) members (from left) Pat Cushing, Rod McGill, and Ken Ravenberg listen to an update on negotiations between the CAW and Chrsyler Canada.

Ratification

Once mutually acceptable contract terms are agreed upon, both sides face the necessity of **ratification**. During ratification, the negotiating teams return to the constituencies they represent and present the negotiated contract terms for the constituencies' approval. Management negotiators have diverse stakeholders, such as the employer's finance, marketing, and production departments, and must satisfy the concerns of each in the ratification stage. The constituencies represented by the management negotiating team will want to be sure that the negotiated terms do not make the organization less efficient or less productive. The union faces similar challenges in presenting the negotiated terms to the union members. The union negotiators will want to have satisfied the legitimate and specific needs of the members, and they must assure members that the negotiated contract terms address these needs.

The actual process of ratification is under the control and direction of each side. Generally, the union will conduct a vote among its membership on whether to accept the negotiated agreement, and management will contact all relevant stakeholders to ensure that the terms of the negotiated agreement are acceptable. The bargaining structure is a major influence on how the ratification process is conducted. For example, if a number of employers have bargained as a single group, the ratification process would involve ensuring that the contract terms are accepted by all the employers represented in the negotiations. Similarly, if a number of unions representing different employees of a single employer have negotiated together, the ratification vote would include bargaining unit members from each of the unions. If one side rejects the negotiated agreement, the parties will have to return to the bargaining table and attempt to fashion an agreement that is acceptable to all constituencies. Once the ratification from each side has been completed, representatives from each side officially sign the collective agreement to bring it into legal effect.

Table 8-1 presents a summary of the bargaining stages. Having outlined these stages, we will now discuss the subprocesses within each stage that influence how teams behave during that stage. We noted earlier that it is not always possible to determine when one bargaining stage concludes and another begins; likewise, within each stage, it is not always easy to identify which subprocesses are present. The subprocesses can occur independently of each other or simultaneously; in addition, not every subprocess is present in every bargaining situation.

NEGOTIATION STAGES AND NEGOTIATION SUBPROCESSES

We have seen that union–management negotiations progress through a series of distinct stages. However, within each stage, we can also identify subprocesses that influence the parties' behaviour in that stage. Richard Walton and Robert McKersie[4] present a theoretical framework that is useful in helping us understand participants' behaviour during

TABLE 8-1 The Stages of Bargaining	
Pre-negotiation	Parties determine and prioritize bargaining issues and determine desired outcomes
	Informal meetings are held to determine bargaining procedure and protocol
Establishing bargaining range	Parties meet and exchange initial offers
	Parties adjust expectations based on the other side's offers
Narrowing the bargaining range	Parties discuss offers and develop and exchange counter-proposals
Crisis	Parties disagree over items
	One side may decide to start strike or lockout to pressure the other side into agreeing to its terms
	One side must agree to other side's proposal for the crisis stage to be resolved, after which parties settle an agreement
Ratification	Parties take the agreement to their constituencies for approval

the negotiation process. Within this framework, four sets of activities are identified as negotiation subprocesses. After first exploring how these stages and subprocesses ebb and flow, merge and mesh, throughout the negotiation process, we will discuss each subprocess in detail.

The Subprocesses within Each Bargaining Stage

In the pre-negotiation stage, several subprocesses can be identified. The first is intra-organizational bargaining. In this subprocess, each side's negotiators seek to achieve consensus within their own bargaining team and within the organization their team represents. As we have seen, bargaining teams must first decide which of the various and often conflicting demands will be addressed in bargaining, and then assign the priority each demand should receive. This process often causes conflict within the bargaining team and the organization. Intra-organizational bargaining is the subprocess through which the bargaining team achieves its own consensus on bargaining priorities and obtains the support of the organization for the decisions it has made.

In their separate pre-negotiation meetings, each side also engages in the **attitudinal structuring** subprocess. This subprocess has to do with the formation of each side's attitude toward the other side and toward the relationship between the bargaining teams. Attitudinal structuring can result in positive attitudes among a team's members if the team perceives that the other side will be relatively receptive to its proposals and that bargaining will be relatively speedy and cooperative. On the other hand, attitudinal structuring can result in negative attitudes if a team perceives that the other team will be hostile and is likely to cause conflict in bargaining. Whether attitudinal structuring results in positive or negative attitudes depends on such factors as each team's knowledge of or experience with members of the other team; each team's perception of how difficult it will be to negotiate certain issues; and any previous bargaining history shared by the two sides. The subprocess of attitudinal structuring also includes adjusting perceptions that have already been formed. For example, if one team member shares with his or her team previously unknown information about members of the other team, that information can alter the attitudes of all team members. The subprocess of attitudinal structuring affects the degree of trust each side feels toward the other side as well as the basic relationship between the teams; thus, its results can have a significant impact on the subsequent success of the bargaining process.

In the pre-negotiation stage, both sides also determine which items in their proposals are potentially suitable for the **integrative bargaining** subprocess. In integrative bargaining, the two sides try to resolve issues by identifying common interests and thereby influencing the joint gain, or "win-win," available to each side. In other words, during the integrative bargaining subprocess, the parties focus on what they have in common, rather than on where they differ, and try to develop solutions that benefit both sides, rather than having one party "win" and the other party "lose." Bargaining teams may attempt to identify items that would be appropriate for integrative bargaining, or they may look at items and try to find potential solutions that would result in gains for both sides. Making these identifications before the negotiations begin helps the parties go into bargaining with a cooperative rather than a conflictual attitude; this also gives the parties a proactive, problem-solving perspective on the entire bargaining process.

Finally, each side will identify bargaining items that are suitable for **distributive bargaining**. In the distributive bargaining subprocess, the two sides compete with one another over the division of limited resources. In this subprocess, when one side wins, the other side loses. When one negotiating team feels that it cannot compromise its desired outcomes for certain bargaining items, distributive bargaining may be the only way in which differences over desired outcomes can be resolved.

Different subprocesses become apparent during different stages of negotiations. The intra-organizational and attitudinal structuring subprocesses are most obvious during the negotiation stages of establishing and narrowing the bargaining range. The presentation and discussion of bargaining proposals during these stages affect each side's perceptions of, attitudes toward, and expectations of the other side. The integrative and distributive bargaining subprocesses, however, are more obvious during the narrowing of the bargaining range than during the establishment of the bargaining range, since narrowing the bargaining range involves determining which issues can be settled integratively and which must be settled distributively.

In the crisis stage, the distributive bargaining subprocess becomes more apparent as the parties move toward settlement of a collective agreement. The ratification stage is the closure stage for both sides, since this stage allows each side's members and constituents to have a say or vote on the resulting collective agreement.

Having identified the subprocesses and where they might occur during bargaining, we will now examine them in more detail, highlighting the strategies and tactics used while each subprocess is occurring.

The Intra-organizational Bargaining Subprocess

The intra-organizational bargaining subprocess involves the internal relationships that exist within each organization and bargaining team. It is thus distinct from the other three subprocesses, which involve external relationships between the union and management during negotiations.

The intra-organizational bargaining subprocess is the process through which each bargaining team and the organization it represents reach internal agreement on bargaining priorities and strategies.[5] This process takes place prior to and sometimes during bargaining, although well-prepared bargaining teams attempt to reach internal agreement before the start of negotiations with the other side.

During the intra-organizational bargaining subprocess, two main types of internal conflict appear: role conflict and factional conflict. Role conflict occurs because there are conflicting expectations of each side's chief negotiator. There is an expectation that the negotiator will use all available strategies and tactics to secure the team's bargaining priorities, but there is also the expectation that the negotiator will respond to the other side's negotiator in a manner that does not jeopardize their professional relationship and hence the bargaining process itself. Thus, each side's negotiator has an internal leadership role within the organization he or she represents, as well as an external relationship role within the context of the negotiations. There may be conflict between these two roles because the behaviour and attitudes demanded by each of them may not be easy to reconcile. For example, if the chief negotiator acts respectfully toward the other side's chief negotiator when presenting important proposals, the members of his or her bargaining team may be upset if they feel that the chief negotiator should be aggressive and forceful in this situation.

The second kind of conflict, factional conflict, develops within an organization when different groups have conflicting demands. As we have seen, different constituencies within the union or the organization may have different ideas about which issues should receive priority in bargaining. The result of these differences in ideas is disagreement over bargaining goals and priorities.

Negotiators can use a variety of strategies and tactics to manage role and factional conflict during intra-organizational bargaining.[6] Table 8-2 outlines these strategies and tactics. Although the intra-organizational bargaining subprocess: primarily occurs during the pre-negotiation stage, role or factional conflict can arise at any time during the bargaining process, and the strategies and tactics outlined in Table 8-2 can be used during or after the pre-negotiation stage. These strategies and tactics are designed to facilitate the desired outcome of the intra-organizational bargaining subprocess: that is, to bring the expectations of the organization's members into alignment with the achievements of their negotiators.

The Attitudinal Structuring Subprocess

One of the defining characteristics of the union-management negotiation process is the long-term relationship between the two parties. This relationship exists before the bargaining process, and it continues to exist after negotiations conclude, because the parties

TABLE 8-2 Strategies and Tactics for Resolving Role and Factional Conflict in the Intra-organizational Bargaining Subprocess

Avoiding incompatible expectations

- keeping the expectations of the organization's members vague and conservative

- focusing the members on specific bargaining or process objectives

- limiting the direct participation of members in union-management negotiations

Revising expectations

- ensuring that the organization's members are informed of the other side's counter-arguments

- using the negotiator's personal leadership power and prestige to generate support for bargaining strategies or priorities

- considering the impact of taking a strike or lockout vote

Rationalizing the result

- maintaining a laundry list of goals or priorities as camouflage for true intentions

- utilizing mediators, fact finders, or conciliators to save face by shifting accountability for decisions to a third party

- providing substitutes for any unmet expectations, goals, or priorities

Obscuring the result

- limiting participation in decision-making to key members of the organization

- controlling communications during the final stage of negotiations

- emphasizing the importance of gains in negotiations and downplaying the impact of perceived losses

not only participate in collective bargaining, but also interact daily in the workplace and engage in other processes together, such as grievance resolution. Therefore, the quality of existing union-management relationships affects how each side approaches the negotiation process, as well as how the resulting collective agreement is administered. The attitudinal structuring subprocess is one part of the larger process that establishes the relationship patterns that define and shape each side's negotiation behaviour.

Prior to the start of negotiations, the relationship between the parties includes the following characteristics: [7]

- each side's motivation to be competitive or cooperative with the other side

- each side's attitudes and beliefs about the legitimacy of the other side's organization and leadership

- the level of trust each side has in the other side

- each side's feelings of friendliness or hostility toward the other side

Ideally, union-management negotiations should be conducted in an atmosphere of trust, respect, and openness, and this positive atmosphere should be maintained during the administration of the resulting collective agreement. The attitudinal structuring subprocess can assist in creating this atmosphere by confirming, or if necessary changing, each side's beliefs and perceptions of the other side.

The Integrative Bargaining Subprocess

In integrative bargaining, a gain for one side is also a gain for the other side, and the resolution of goals, priorities, and demands results in a joint advantage for both sides. The integrative bargaining subprocess is different from the distributive bargaining subprocess in that the former deals with mutual problems, while the latter deals with more contentious issues.[8] Table 8-3 outlines other major differences between these two subprocesses.

When problems are being negotiated, the use of the integrative bargaining subprocess potentially permits both sides to win, since both sides want to find solutions to the problems. Integrative bargaining is often one of the elements of a "fostering strategy"[9] that is used to develop cooperation between the parties and that ultimately may create a better overall relationship and facilitate other parts of the bargaining process.

Because integrative bargaining creates a cooperative atmosphere by emphasizing the parties' shared interest in reaching a resolution to problems, problems that can be solved through integrative bargaining are often addressed before distributive issues are negotiated.

TABLE 8-3   Differences Between the Distributive and Integrative Bargaining Subprocesses

	Distributive Bargaining	Integrative Bargaining
Type of item being negotiated	Issue	Problem
Focus of each side's strategy	Maximizing own gains	Mutual interests between the two sides
Use of information during bargaining	Selective disclosure of information, designed to maintain the side's power	Openly sharing information to motivate joint resolution of the problem
Spokesperson	Single spokesperson for each side controls disclosure and disguises the bottom line	Groups or committees have informal, exploratory discussions
Trust	Distrust between the parties because of adversarial positions	Higher level of trust because of shared interest in resolution and greater disclosure of information

This is done in the hope that a cooperative atmosphere will carry over into the discussion of more contentious issues.

However, despite its cooperative nature, the integrative bargaining subprocess can cause difficulties in union-management negotiations.[10] This is because in order for each side to realize its gain, the two sides must jointly decide how to divide the overall gain equitably. In this way, integrative bargaining becomes "distributive" in nature. The negotiating teams must address issues such as equity in sorting out how gains are to be shared, and they may have different ideas about what is an "equitable" division. Thus, the success of an integrative bargaining subprocess can be blocked if either side is unable or unwilling to agree to distributive solutions.

Table 8-4 outlines the strategies and tactics that are used to resolve disputes during integrative bargaining.[11] The success of the integrative bargaining subprocess often depends

TABLE 8-4 Strategies and Tactics for Resolving Disputes in the Integrative Bargaining Subprocess

Identifying the problem

- convening frequent negotiation sessions at the request of either side

- developing items that have the potential for joint problem-solving, rather than presenting items in a format that requires resolution by individual teams in isolation

- formulating negotiation items as specific problems rather than as general, undefined concerns

Searching for alternative solutions

- giving advance notice of negotiation times

- holding informal and exploratory discussions prior to exchanging formal proposals or formally bargaining

- addressing easily resolved items first, to create a pattern of early success

Systematically comparing alternatives

- accurate reporting of each side's preferences

- combining or dividing proposals to make patterns of agreement or disagreement more apparent

- considering remedial actions as part of solutions in order to improve the relationship between the parties as well as solve the problem

on how well each side's chief negotiator handles the different but potentially simultaneous requirements of integrative bargaining and distributive bargaining.

The Distributive Bargaining Subprocess

The most highly visible negotiation subprocess and the one most often associated with union-management negotiations is the distributive bargaining subprocess. In distributive bargaining, both sides are involved in a fundamental conflict over the allocation of a fixed and limited amount of resources.[12] As a result, distributive bargaining is essentially adversarial in nature, since each side is committed to achieving maximum gain for itself. One of the parties may use distributive bargaining as part of a "forcing strategy" to achieve a desired change.[13] Distributive bargaining strategies are commonly used when wage and benefit issues are being negotiated. Unions are usually concerned with maximizing wages and benefits for their members, and management is usually concerned with minimizing costs. These are opposing goals, and therefore, a gain for one party means a loss for the other.

During the distributive bargaining subprocess, each side strives to collect and exchange whatever information might persuade the other side to agree to its demands. Each side will seek to collect and distribute this information in a manner that benefits its own interests without unduly empowering the other side. A variety of strategies and tactics can be used in doing this; some of these are presented in Table 8-5.[14]

The goals, priorities, and demands that are addressed through the distributive bargaining subprocess are usually central issues in most labour-management negotiations and in the ongoing relationship between the parties. Ultimately, the determination of these distributive issues—that is, who ends up winning—involves the use of bargaining power. We will now discuss the role of power in determining the outcomes of the bargaining process as a whole.

THE ROLE OF BARGAINING POWER IN UNION-MANAGEMENT NEGOTIATIONS

Distributive bargaining implicitly involves the use, implied use, or potential use of power.[15] The classic definition of **bargaining power**, in the context of the union-management negotiation process, is the actual or perceived ability of one side to secure the other side's agreement to its terms.[16] The amount of bargaining power that each side holds in negotiations cannot be precisely measured, and the amount will vary depending on a number of factors—some of which may be unique to the particular set of issues being negotiated or to the specific teams or individuals involved in the negotiations.

Environmental, socio-demographic, and organizational factors, for example, can affect the amount of bargaining power held by both sides.[17] Environmental factors affecting

TABLE 8-5 Strategies and Tactics for Collecting and Controlling Information during the Distributive Bargaining Subprocess

Discovering the other side's bottom line

- observing non-verbal behavioural cues, such as facial expressions, to discern the other side's true intentions
- using probing and clarifying questions to elicit reactions to proposals
- using open-ended questions to determine the other side's interests

Disguising your own side's bottom line

- having a single spokesperson in order to present a unified front and to control the amount and type of information that is revealed
- submitting a laundry list of proposals or demands to obscure actual priorities
- safeguarding all written material

Persuading or pressuring the other side to move its bottom line

- making public pleas for support
- negotiating for long periods of time to exhaust the other side
- discussing cost implications

Emphasizing your commitment to a position

- repeating your demands
- invoking the reputation of your side to reinforce the legitimacy of your position
- raising the expectations of your side's membership to create support for your position

Blocking the other side's commitment to a position

- limiting opportunities for commitment to a position
- minimizing opportunities for the other side to repeat its position
- ignoring any commitments

the amount of power held by each side include public opinion, legislation, and the economy. These can either decrease or increase each side's bargaining power, depending on whether these factors support or undermine a side's position or demands. For example, the public perception that a union is being greedy in its bargaining demands reduces the union's bargaining power, because this perception gives the employer a reason to disagree with the union's proposals. The socio-demographic factors affecting bargaining power include the diversity of bargaining priorities among negotiators and their constituencies. When negotiators and their constituencies have the same bargaining priorities, their unity can increase the negotiators' bargaining power, particularly if the other side is aware of this unity and feels there is less unity on its own side. The organizational factors affecting bargaining power include the intra-organizational dynamics of both the union and management. Because unions and management interact daily in the workplace, each bargaining team is usually well aware of the internal disputes or conflicts within the other team or the workplace and can exploit these problems to gain power in negotiations.

Garbage is piled up by a receptacle in downtown Toronto during the 2009 city workers' strike.

Other factors affecting bargaining power can be more specifically associated with either the employer's or the union's characteristics or situation.[18] Factors affecting the employer's bargaining power may include the size of its inventory, the structure of its operations, its competitiveness, whether the business is seasonal, whether the business can operate during a strike, and the business's labour costs. For example, a large amount of inventory would increase the employer's bargaining power, because having materials in stock would allow a company to continue production during a strike or lockout.

Factors affecting the union's bargaining power may include the strength of the union's commitment to specific issues, the union's access to funds for supporting strike activity, and the timing and effectiveness of a possible strike. For example, having access to extra funds to support locked-out union members would increase the union's bargaining power, since the funds would enable the union to resist the threat of a lockout by the employer as a bargaining tactic.

Despite the role that bargaining power plays in determining bargaining outcomes, union-management negotiations involve much more than a clash of differing amounts of bargaining power. Integrative bargaining, as we have seen, is an important part of the negotiation process, and because it emphasizes mutually developed and mutually beneficial solutions to problems, it does not require one side or the other to exercise its bargaining power to achieve desired outcomes. However, as mentioned above, distributive bargaining requires the use of bargaining power to achieve outcomes, and distributive bargaining is the more common and more visible form of bargaining in most negotiations.

Although distributive bargaining is the subprocess most commonly used to achieve the eventual outcome of a completed collective agreement, it can have damaging long-term effects on the relationship between the parties because of its competitive nature. In distributive bargaining, one side ends up failing to achieve its desired outcome; the resulting resentment may spill over into the parties' relationship long after negotiations have concluded. Thus, while distributive bargaining is commonly used, it is not the most positive—nor always the most effective—means of resolving bargaining disputes.

Because of the potentially harmful effects of distributive bargaining, a number of authors and researchers have proposed alternative models of negotiation that focus on building productive long-term relationships between unions and management, as well as on achieving the short-term goal of settling a collective agreement. We will examine two of these models as a way of understanding other forms that union-management negotiations can take.

TWO ALTERNATIVE MODELS OF UNION-MANAGEMENT NEGOTIATIONS

In examining how the distributive and integrative bargaining subprocesses affect the parties' behaviour in negotiations, it becomes clear that the strategies and tactics used in these subprocesses are not always conducive to building a positive relationship between the parties. This shortcoming is significant because it may eventually lead to disharmony in the workplace. The negotiation process is essentially a way to introduce change to the workplace through revisions to the collective agreement. Most attempts to introduce change generate conflict—not only in the short term around specific proposals, but also potentially, in the long term as the workplace evolves. Conflict generated in negotiations can spill over into the workplace and generate further conflict there.

Ideally, the goal of maintaining a positive relationship between the parties should be emphasized through the negotiation process. But a number of historical, institutional, and economic realities work against the achievement of this goal. Union-management relationships are usually adversarial in nature because of the inherently different interests of the parties. As discussed in previous chapters, unions are concerned with protecting or improving their members' working conditions, while management is concerned with operating the workplace in an economically efficient manner. There is also a general acceptance of conflict as a way to obtain desired outcomes. This acceptance exists not only in the context of negotiations but also in society at large. In fact, a lack of conflict during negotiations may be perceived by either team, or by their constituencies, as an indication that bargaining is not being pursued seriously or with adequate commitment.

These realities must be acknowledged in the union-management negotiation process, which is generally emotional and hard fought, and characterized by distrust between the parties. However, negotiations often address mutual problems that could be resolved in a "win-win" or cooperative manner, without adversarial interactions. We will examine two alternative models of bargaining that attempt to emphasize cooperation, rather than confrontation, between the parties.

The "Cost of Disputes" Model

The "cost of disputes" model of union-management negotiations focuses on the interactions among the bargaining power, the interests, and the rights of each side, and how these interactions affect the costs associated with negotiating disputes.[19] **Interests** are the needs, wants, fears, concerns, desires, or other motivators that underlie a **position**, or the preferred outcome, of one side in negotiations. **Rights** are formal powers that are granted to the two sides in a number of ways. Rights may be defined in the legislation governing collective bargaining, in any existing collective agreement, in other legislation (e.g., employment standards acts), or in **arbitral jurisprudence**, which is the body of decisions on legal cases dealing with the interpretation and/or application of collective agreement language.

The "cost of disputes" model outlines how interests, rights, and power interrelate during the bargaining process. The parties' differing interests are reconciled within the context of each side's rights and bargaining power; for example, the party with more rights may be able to dominate the process and choice of outcome, even within a supposedly collaborative framework. The determination of each side's rights also takes place within the context of each side's bargaining power; the authority associated with one party's rights may be overshadowed by the bargaining power of a stronger party. As well, at any given stage in union-management negotiations, the context of negotiations may shift to interests, rights, or bargaining power, depending on the issues being discussed and the power of each party to promote its interests or positions.

The "cost of disputes" model proposes that to assess how the interrelationship among rights, interests, and power has influenced the outcome of a bargaining dispute, we should assess the costs incurred by the parties involved in the bargaining process. There are four criteria to consider in determining the amount of these costs: transaction costs, satisfaction with the outcome, the effect on relationships, and whether there has been a recurrence of a problem.

Transaction costs associated with negotiations include expenditures of time, money, resources, and emotional energy; they also include the value of opportunities lost because of disagreement. In the specific context of union-management negotiations, transaction costs could include the costs of striking, locking out, or attempting to operate during a strike.

The second criterion in evaluating the cost of bargaining—the level of satisfaction with the result of bargaining—addresses how well the ultimate resolution fulfills each side's underlying interests. An unsatisfactory resolution will incur costs later on because it will be an inefficient resolution to disputed issues and will also cause frustration to the parties.

The third criterion for evaluating bargaining costs—the long-term effect of bargaining on the union-management relationship—examines outcomes similar to those that the attitudinal structuring subprocess has on the union-management relationship: in other words, how the relationship between the parties has changed as a result of their interactions with and perceptions of each other. A contentious relationship will be costly because it will lead to disputes between the parties, and disputes are sometimes based more on the parties' dislike of each other than on any substantive problem.

The last criterion for determining costs—recurrence—examines whether the negotiations produced an agreement that resolved the issues between the parties, or whether the problems recurred after ratification and during the administration of the new collective agreement. Recurring issues will be costly because of the expenses associated with each subsequent resolution.

An assessment of a bargaining process using these four criteria will result in an estimate of the overall costs incurred by the two parties in bargaining the disputes between them.[20] The "cost of disputes" model suggests that, in general, the cost of disputing will be less when interests are reconciled within the context of rights and bargaining power.[21] In other words, the overall financial impact of disputes can be reduced if, in bargaining, the parties focus on shared interests rather than on issues that can only be resolved if they exercise their rights or bargaining power. Because interests involve common problems and mutually acceptable solutions, it will be ultimately less costly to deal with interest-based issues since better-quality solutions will be produced.

This model does not suggest that negotiations should ignore distributive issues or should persist in using collaborative bargaining techniques when it is apparent that no solution can be generated. The exercise of rights and bargaining power can sometimes bring about resolutions to disputes when other forms of negotiations cannot. But, ideally, a focus on interests in bargaining, rather than on rights or power, results in lower transaction costs, greater satisfaction with the resulting agreement, less strain on the ongoing relationship between the parties, and a lower recurrence of disputes.

The Mutual Gains Model of Bargaining

Over the last few decades, both unions and employers have been actively searching for alternative models of negotiation—or solutions to bargaining issues—that would incorporate changing economic realities. While union-management negotiations are traditionally adversarial, many leaders on both sides are interested in collaborative arrangements that respect differences but search for common ground and win-win resolutions.[22]

A model of negotiations that is widely used to change both the focus of bargaining and its adversarial approach is the one proposed by Roger E. Fisher and William L. Ury.[23] Their model is referred to by several different names: principled negotiations, negotiation on the merits, mutual gains, or interest-based negotiations. In the context of union-management negotiations, it is most often called "mutual gains bargaining." The process of bargaining outlined by this model is similar to the distributive bargaining subprocess described earlier in this chapter.

The mutual gains model of bargaining is founded on four principles that define a straightforward method of negotiations. These principles, with their corresponding actions, are as follows:

1. People: Separate the people from the problem.

2. Interests: Focus on interests, not positions.

3. Options: Generate a variety of possibilities before deciding what to do.

4. Criteria: Insist that the result of negotiations be based or evaluated on some objective standard.

There have been a number of attempts to change the adversarial model of union-management negotiations to a mutual gains model of bargaining.[24] Improving the collective bargaining relationship and the resulting collective agreement requires joint union-management training.[25] Joint union-management training has produced positive effects. Some participants say that their training in mutual gains bargaining has helped them to listen better, has helped them to avoid unproductive arguments, and has strengthened their trust in the other side by allowing them to gain a perspective on the other side's interests and positions.[26]

However, the results of various studies have indicated that there is, at best, an imperfect fit between mutual gains bargaining techniques in general and the specific demands of union-management

The traditionally adversarial relationship between employer and employee is not the only model for collective bargaining. The mutual gains model focuses on cooperation and collaboration.

negotiations.[27] Often there is an inherent power imbalance between the parties, as well as different perspectives on what constitutes an acceptable solution to an issue. These conditions can make it difficult to use the mutual gains model of bargaining, since the model emphasizes equality and commonality between the parties. Mutual gains bargaining in union-management negotiations is more feasible with increased trust between the union and management sides, reshaping the roles and responsibilities of individuals on both negotiation teams, and reducing the power imbalance between the sides.

It has also been noted that adversarial conflicts in bargaining can be caused by the traditional bargaining model's division of issues into integrative bargaining and distributive bargaining. Three different approaches have been proposed to resolve the adversarial conflicts caused by the differences between the distributive bargaining and integrative bargaining subprocesses.[28] First, each side should strive to establish a minimum degree of trust in and level of communication with the other side. Second, each side should determine a minimum level of acceptance of the other side. Third, both sides should recognize the common dependency they share. These suggestions are intended to help the parties maintain a positive relationship, regardless of whether integrative or distributive bargaining is taking place.

The studies that have investigated the effect of mutual gains bargaining conclude that this bargaining method can lead to more positive attitudes generated by attitudinal structuring. As well, it can result in more innovative solutions being generated or accepted during the integrative bargaining subprocess. However, a major transformation of the traditional structures of both unions and management will be required for a wider acceptance of mutual gains bargaining. Improved methods of implementation and practical suggestions for action are also needed to complement the mostly theoretical discussions of mutual gains bargaining. Without these changes, it will be difficult to institutionalize mutual gains bargaining techniques, even in circumstances where using these techniques would be potentially beneficial to both sides.

SUMMARY

In this chapter, we have attempted to describe what actually goes on in collective bargaining by outlining the basic process of bargaining and then identifying the subprocesses that take place during the various bargaining stages. Most negotiations begin with a pre-negotiation stage, during which the parties prepare their bargaining priorities.

During the first few formal meetings of the negotiating teams, the parties enter the stage of establishing the bargaining range; here the parties determine the range of acceptable outcomes for each item presented at the bargaining table. The parties then narrow the bargaining range by exchanging proposals and counter-proposals on each item. Agreement on an item can only be reached if there is a zone of agreement or a set of possible solutions that would be acceptable to both sides. During the crisis stage, each party must decide whether to settle or whether to exert pressure on the other party to accept its demands. Finally, when a settlement is reached, the parties enter the ratification stage, where the negotiated agreement is presented to stakeholders for acceptance or rejection.

Within each of the bargaining stages, various subprocesses can be observed. In the pre-negotiation stage, intra-organizational bargaining shapes the parties' bargaining priorities and attitudinal structuring influences both the parties' attitude toward each other and their mutual relationship. During this stage, the parties may also identify which bargaining items are suitable for integrative and distributive bargaining. Intra-organizational bargaining and attitudinal subprocesses are also evident in the stages of establishing and narrowing the bargaining range, during which the parties exchange information and modify their expectations on the basis of solutions suggested by the other side. In the crisis stage, distributive bargaining ideally results in a satisfactory agreement and movement into the ratification stage.

The role of bargaining power is also important in determining bargaining outcomes. The amount of power that each party has and is able to use in negotiations can vary depending on a number of factors. Environmental conditions, socio-demographic factors, organizational factors, and the different kinds of resources available to both unions and management can affect how much power each party has and how much effect that power has on the outcome of negotiations.

Finally, because there are deficiencies in the way that collective bargaining is usually conducted, alternative models of bargaining have been suggested that encourage more positive relationships between the parties and better-quality solutions. The "cost of disputes" model identifies the effect on negotiations of interactions between bargaining power, interests, and rights. This model encourages negotiators to look at various financial and non-monetary costs incurred in bargaining and afterwards, and suggests that a focus on interests in bargaining will reduce those costs. The mutual gains model of bargaining uses four principles and suggestions for action to encourage negotiations focused on producing results that are satisfactory for both parties.

Our discussion of bargaining continues in Chapter 9, where we will describe strikes and lockouts in the context of the bargaining process.

KEY TERMS FOR CHAPTER 8

arbitral jurisprudence (p. 324)
attitudinal structuring (p. 313)
bargaining power (p. 320)
bottom line (p. 307)
concessions (p. 308)
crisis (p. 308)
distributive bargaining (p. 314)
integrative bargaining (p. 313)
interests (p. 324)
intra-organizational bargaining (p. 312)
position (p. 324)
ratification (p. 310)
rights (p. 324)
zone of agreement (p. 307)

DISCUSSION QUESTIONS FOR CHAPTER 8

1. Outline the stages of union-management negotiations.
2. What are the four subprocesses identified by Walton and McKersie?
3. Explain the link between bargaining stages and bargaining subprocesses.
4. Why is the zone of agreement important in negotiations?
5. The bargaining power of both sides is affected by a number of factors. Identify the factors that affect management's and the union's bargaining power.
6. Mutual gains bargaining is based on four principles. Identify these principles and explain what difference they make in the way a negotiation process is conducted.
7. What criteria can be used to assess the cost of disputes in negotiations?

CASE *8-1*

SPECIALTY WORKERS UNION AND WINNING CASINO

(Based on *UFCW and Gateway Casinos*, 2007)

In this case, the union and the employer are engaged in collective bargaining. The bargaining process has encountered many problems along the way. The parties had previously filed unfair labour practice complaints against each other, which resulted in the board ordering that bargaining recommence with a new chief spokesperson for each side; that each party provide complete sets of proposals; that the parties use a predetermined protocol for their communications with each other; and that the parties set dates for bargaining. Under these new conditions, all but a few outstanding issues had been resolved. Against the union's wishes, the employer asked the board to order that the union's members vote on the employer's most recent offers on these issues. The board ordered the vote, and the members rejected the employer's offers, which included a two-tier wage system.

The union alleges that the employer is failing to bargain in good faith, for several reasons:

- The employer is intimidating union members through surveillance in the workplace.

- The employer is interfering with the union's ability to represent its members by refusing to provide the union with office space and by restricting what union representatives can do in the workplace.

- The employer wants to reintroduce into bargaining the two-tier wage system that was rejected by the union membership.

The union is asking the board to order the employer to remove the two-tier wage proposal from the bargaining table, and to order the employer to refrain from the practices that allegedly interfere with the union's ability to represent its membership.

Case Facts

The workplace in this situation is a casino. The casino employees have been unionized for the past decade. Initially they were represented by a small independent union, but three years ago that union merged with the larger Specialty Workers Union, and the certification order was amended to reflect this change.

The first collective agreement in this workplace stated that the employer would provide the union with a furnished private office in the casino. Since the change of representation, however, the employer has tried to close this office, because it claims it needs the space for management offices, and because the new union has more resources than the former union; therefore, the employer claimed that the union does not require a subsidized office. The union took this dispute to arbitration, and the arbitrator ruled that the employer must maintain a union office in the casino until the end of the collective agreement (which has now expired).

The employer has offered to provide "suitable space" for union activities on an *ad hoc* basis and on 24 hours' notice. The employer has suggested an alternative space in the workplace, and the union has agreed to consider an office space adjacent to the lunchroom (the union office was formerly located immediately adjacent to the casino floor). However, when the parties could not reach an agreement on the wage issue, the employer withdrew its proposals around the office issue.

At the end of last year, the employer announced a policy that union staff representatives (who are employees of the union, not employees of the casino) were not allowed in the employee lunchroom to conduct union business, except to post notices. On at least one occasion a union staff representative was escorted out of the lunchroom by management staff. The employer says that employees have expressed the wish not to be bothered by union representatives while they are on their breaks.

When the employees were represented by the previous union, the union staff representatives were also casino employees, and so were frequently on the casino floor. Approximately two years after the union merger, the employer barred union staff representatives from being on the casino floor unless they follow a designated route to the union office or they are escorted by a management representative. The employer has also used the casino's surveillance equipment to track the movement of union staff representatives. The employer claims this is necessary because on several occasions union staff representatives have been observed, or have been suspected of, entering parts of the casino that are off limits to non-employees. The employer also states that these policies are necessary because of the regulations the casino is licensed under, which restrict who has access to certain parts of the casino's operations, and because security is important in a workplace where large amounts of cash are being handled. The employer also has an internal policy banning "idle conversations" among staff who are serving the public.

The board viewed two security videos of union staff representatives that were taken approximately two months before the current collective bargaining commenced. The first video was about four minutes long and tracked the staff representative as she entered the casino, spoke briefly with three employees in different locations, and took notes during one of the conversations. No customers were in sight during any of the conversations. The second video was less than a minute and a half long. It tracked another staff representative as he walked through the gaming tables in the casino and had two brief conversations with dealers at different tables. No customers were playing at either table.

The issue of wages has been contentious during the bargaining process. The casino's original wage structure allowed employees to earn annual wage increases, to accumulate hours of service and receive wage increases when "target" amounts of hours were reached, and to earn increases by acquiring additional skills (e.g., dealers learning to deal additional games). This led to what was called the "diagonal" wage structure. This was a difficult wage structure to re-negotiate because, with all the different classifications and rates, it was not easy to calculate the impact of a percentage increase in wages (the traditional form of quantifying wage increases during bargaining). There was also the added complication of calculating the impact of employee movement, such as employees being promoted to higher-paying classifications, or new employees joining the organization at lower rates of pay than longer-serving employees. Nevertheless, the employer's early proposals in the bargaining process were based on the "diagonal" structure, and the union responded on the same basis for the first 14 months of bargaining.

At the start of this year, the employer tabled a proposal to eliminate the "diagonal" wage structure for new employees. Under this proposal, current employees would continue to be paid under the "diagonal" structure, but new employees would be paid under a structure that did not include pay increases based on hours. The employer also proposed "equity adjustments" that would increase the pay rates in several job classifications that were considered underpaid compared to the rates in the current labour market.

The union rejected this proposal on the basis that the wages for new employees were too low, and that a two-tier wage structure would create divisions in the workplace. It also said that the proposal was made too late in the bargaining process, and that if the employer began bargaining on the basis of the "diagonal" grid, then it should continue doing so.

The Union's Position

The union argues that the employer is bargaining in bad faith and attempting to undermine its ability to represent its members. It argues that the employer's unwillingness to provide a union office, the employer's rules regarding union staff representatives' activity in the workplace, and the problems in the collective bargaining process are all part of a general strategy to minimize and neutralize the union's presence. The union believes that this strategy is motivated by the employer's desire to not have a union in the workplace at all, or to make the union members so disaffected that they decide to decertify the union.

The union states that there are no regulations in the licensing of the casino, either by gaming authorities or by liquor control authorities, specifically addressing what union representatives are permitted to do in the workplace. The union also says that it has never been provided with any policy manual that contains restrictions on "idle conversations" in the workplace.

The union argues that the two-tier wage proposal, if allowed, will make it difficult for the union to organize other employers in the gaming industry, as it creates a group of "second class citizens" within the workplace and does not make the union look credible. The union suggests that such a change in bargaining position should only be allowed if the employer is in serious financial trouble that would make it impossible to continue negotiating as before. The union states that while the proposal is not illegal, allowing it to be reintroduced at this point would destroy the framework of collective bargaining that has already been established.

The Employer's Position

With respect to the issue of office space for the union, the employer states that the previous arrangement was designed to assist a small union with limited resources. Since the new union is a large international union with considerable financial and staff resources, the employer believes it should not have to continue subsidizing the union's operations.

The employer states that the restrictions on union staff member activity are necessary to comply with internal and external policies related to workplace security. In the case of the video surveillance of the two union staff representatives, the employer argues that these individuals were "wandering" around the gaming floor and distracting employees by engaging in conversations during working hours.

The employer argues that the two-tier wage proposal is not intended to destroy collective bargaining, but is instead intended to help achieve a collective agreement. The employer characterizes the proposal as not being fundamentally new, but instead as an alternate version of the original proposal, recognizing the need for cost containment, which the employer expressed at the start of collective bargaining. The employer argues that the board should not consider whether the two-tier system would affect the union's ability to organize other workplaces, since boards usually do not intervene in collective bargaining or organizing efforts.

CASE 8-2

WRIGHT COLLEGE AND WRIGHT COLLEGE FACULTY UNION

(Based on *St. Thomas More College* and *St. Thomas More College Faculty Union*, 2008)

In this case, the union and the employer are engaged in collective bargaining and have reached a tentative agreement. However, the union has elected a new executive, and some members of the new executive are not happy with the terms of the agreement. The union held a ratification meeting at which some of the new executive members expressed their dissatisfaction, and the union members voted to reject the tentative agreement. The employer asked the union to redo the ratification vote, and the union refused. The employer is alleging that the union has bargained in bad faith by negotiating a collective agreement and then not recommending it to the union membership.

Case Facts

The Wright College faculty union represents approximately 70 faculty members and librarians, including permanent and sessional employees. The last collective agreement ran for three years and expired three years ago. The negotiations for the new collective agreement began 18 months ago.

The union executive committee consists of four active members who are elected by the membership. After the elections, those four members decide who will fill the roles of president, vice-president/secretary, and treasurer. Under the union's constitution, the executive committee is responsible for negotiating collective agreements and dealing with any other aspect of the relationship between the college and the union. The executive's actions are guided by motions passed at the union's membership meetings.

The union's constitution states that collective bargaining will be carried out by a two- or three-member negotiating committee, whose members may be from the executive or from the general membership. The negotiating committee is expected to consult with the membership when setting its bargaining priorities, and to keep the membership informed on bargaining progress through newsletters. The negotiating committee is also expected to meet regularly with the executive committee "for advice and direction."

When the most recent set of negotiations began, the union appointed a bargaining committee, but the committee's membership changed over time. When bargaining ended, the committee had two members: Dr. Milton, the union president who had been on the committee for the entire bargaining process; and Dr. Hines, a member of past negotiating committees who replaced another committee member for the last few months of the current negotiations. Dr. Hines was also elected to the union executive after negotiations had ended. The college's bargaining committee had the same members throughout the negotiation process: the college's human resource manager, Mary Owen; the college's dean; and the college's director of administration.

Dr. Hines told the board that the union negotiating committee was mandated to make any decisions that were necessary to reach a collective agreement, although the union executive set the agenda for negotiations. The union executive and the union negotiating committee were in close contact throughout the negotiating process. Dr. Hines explained that the union's membership includes members with different employment situations and different concerns, and that the union's members were not unanimous on what they wanted to achieve, to the point where there was dissent and division among several groups of members. Because of this, the executive committee helped the negotiating committee to conduct surveys of the membership to find the union members' views on certain issues; the executive committee also made recommendations to the negotiating committee on what positions to take on certain issues or which issues should be traded off or given priority in bargaining. But, Dr. Hines pointed out, there were some issues where the different positions of the union's members could not be reconciled, and the executive committee gave the negotiating committee the authority to pursue whichever settlement would ultimately result in a collective agreement.

A tentative collective agreement was reached approximately nine months ago. Both parties knew that the agreement would have to be ratified by both sides before it became effective, and all the negotiators verbally agreed that they would recommend ratification. Both sides agreed on some editorial changes to a draft of the agreement before it was accepted by all of the negotiators. At this point, Dr. Hines was the only member of the union negotiating committee, as Dr. Milton had taken a job elsewhere. Dr. Hines, Owen, and the director of administration shook hands and reiterated that they would all recommend ratification. All parties understood that the union would circulate the tentative agreement to the union membership, and give the membership two weeks' notice of a membership meeting at which the union would conduct a ratification vote.

Three days before the parties shook hands on the agreement, the union's executive committee changed as a result of the union's annual executive elections. The new president, Dr. Lemar, had been on the previous executive committee. The three other committee members were new to the executive.

Prior to circulating the tentative agreement to the union membership, Dr. Hines met with the new executive committee. He explained the compromises that the union had made in negotiations, and emphasized that he thought the agreement was the best one the union could get. However, after reviewing the agreement, the new executive committee felt it did not agree with some of the terms that had been negotiated.

A week after meeting with Dr. Hines, the executive committee sent a letter to the employer stating that it did not feel it could circulate the agreement to its members or recommend ratification. The letter stated that the committee did not agree with the settlements on items involving seniority, pay rates for one classification of sessional faculty, conflicts of interest, and two other issues. The letter stated that the executive was willing to bring the agreement to the membership if the settlements on those items could be changed. Dr. Hines told the board that this letter was signed by the new executive, rather than the negotiating committee, because he did not think it was appropriate for the negotiating committee to send such a letter. He felt that the negotiating committee had agreed to terms on all the items mentioned in the letter, and that the issues in question were not new issues but ongoing issues that had always been problematic for the union. He added, though, that in the past the union had raised matters that could become problems with the collective agreement, and that the union and the employer had always dealt with these questions through collegial discussion. Dr. Hines thought this letter had been sent in that same spirit.

Three days later, the employer responded in writing to the union, stating that it was not prepared to re-negotiate issues that had been discussed and agreed to in good faith.

At the start of the following month, the new executive committee e-mailed a letter to its members, which was sent along with a copy of the tentative agreement. Both documents were also posted on the union's website. The document showing the new collective agreement included the relevant language from the previous collective agreement. The letter thanked the negotiating committee for its hard work, described the proposed changes to the collective agreement, and encouraged the members to attend the ratification meeting. However, the letter also contained a lengthy section in which the new executive explained that there were parts of the new collective agreement that it did not agree with, and stated that these were "some of the main changes in the proposed agreement" and "some possible concerns for our members."

Dr. Hines told the board that he did not think the letter to the union membership had to recommend ratification of the tentative agreement; he said it only raised issues that had been long-standing concerns for some of the union's members, and that the letter was intended to let those members know that the executive was aware of those concerns. One of the new executive members told the board that the letter was designed to make the union members read the new agreement and to encourage them to think seriously about it. Under questioning, she agreed that the letter did not contain any mention of a recommendation to ratify.

At the ratification meeting, one new executive member acted as a neutral chairperson. Dr. Hines spoke to the members present, explained the reasoning leading to the terms in the tentative agreement, and recommended ratification of the agreement. He explained that tradeoffs had been made during bargaining and that the negotiating committee had acted on the advice and recommendations of the previous executive committee. He also told the members that the agreement was the best that could be achieved at this time and that the agreement contained mechanisms to encourage future change.

The other two members of the new executive committee spoke against the tentative agreement, saying that they were concerned about the language around seniority and job security. However, both emphasized that they were speaking as individuals and not as executive members. Other members pointed out that the change in language around job security had the effect of extending job security to one group of members while taking it away from another group. Other members mentioned that enrolment numbers at Wright College were dropping and that the tradeoffs around job security did not, in their opinion, address this situation. The ratification vote was conducted by secret ballot, and a majority of the membership voted against ratification.

The union informed the employer in a letter that the members had not ratified the tentative agreement and asked for the negotiators to reconvene. Two weeks later, the employer responded in writing, stating that it felt the union had committed an unfair labour practice by not presenting the agreement to its membership as a negotiated agreement, reflecting the compromises that are required to reach such an agreement. The employer requested that the union hold another ratification vote. The union refused and asked the employer again to reconvene the negotiations. The employer rejected this request and filed the unfair labour practice complaint with the board.

The Union's Position

The union argues that the failure to ratify the agreement did not cause any sort of crisis, and that the duty to bargain in good faith does not include the duty to ratify the agreement. The union points out that the bargaining committee had a mandate to bargain on behalf of the union's members, and that the evidence showed the committee considered the various demands of its members and tried to balance those in the bargaining process.

The union states that the letter sent to the membership was its attempt to improve the chances of ratification, and that when the employer refused to negotiate on the items mentioned in the letter, the union accepted this and went ahead with the ratification vote.

The union agrees that the letter to the membership did not recommend ratification of the agreement, but argues that this is not required by law, and that the negotiating committee honoured its commitment when Dr. Hines recommended ratification to the executive and to the membership. The union states that the discussion at the ratification meeting shows that some issues had become more important than when they were bargained and that was the reason the ratification vote failed.

The Employer's Position

The employer argues that the current situation is a crisis because of the failure to ratify the agreement. The employer states that the union failed in its duty to bargain by not recommending the agreement for ratification to its members, and by not giving the negotiating committee a sufficient or proper mandate.

The employer argues that part of the duty to bargain in good faith is the duty to use reasonable efforts to conclude a collective agreement, and that includes recommending ratification of a tentative agreement. The employer believes that the union did not fairly present the agreement as the product of collective bargaining, and that the executive committee used disparaging language in expressing its concerns about the agreement. The employer states that if there are troublesome areas in a proposed collective agreement, the only way to get an agreement is if the union leadership supports the negotiators.

The employer also argues that the union should have given the negotiating committee enough authority to reach an agreement that had a reasonable chance of success. If the membership did not ratify the agreement, then the executive committee did not give the negotiating committee the mandate to reach settlements that would be acceptable to the membership. The executive committee also sought to re-negotiate items that the negotiating committee had already settled, which, in the employer's view, is further evidence that the executive committee did not sufficiently empower the negotiating committee.

The employer believes that the change in the union executive should not be allowed to affect bargaining, and that new members should not be allowed to back out of agreements made by the previous executive.

The employer does not believe that further bargaining can take place, since the union now knows what contract terms are acceptable to the employer. The employer is asking the board to impose the tentative agreement, because a further re-vote would not be fair as long as the union executive is opposed to the agreement. Alternatively, the employer is asking the board to order a re-vote with conditions that minimize the executive's opposition.

COLLECTIVE BARGAINING SIMULATION EXERCISE

Newtown School Dispute

Introduction

In this bargaining simulation, you will play a member of either a school board's or a teacher association's bargaining team. You, the other members of your team, and the members of the other team are negotiators representing specific constituencies. You will deal with a complex mix of bargaining issues, and you will be subjected to a variety of pressures during the negotiations.

Advance Preparation

Before the bargaining session, you should read two sets of information:

- the "Background Information" presented below. This is information that both teams have.

- the "Team Information" (either Board of Education or Teacher Association) for your team in the negotiations. This information will be provided by your instructor. You should not permit any members of the other side's bargaining team to have access to this information.

Based on this information, you and your team will prepare a written proposal to present to the other side at the start of negotiations. This proposal should outline your opening position on each of the bargaining issues. Your team should also be prepared with alternate positions and a bottom line for each bargaining issue. This information will guide your strategies in the actual bargaining.

Bargaining Procedure

Your instructor will announce the team assignments and time schedules for bargaining; he or she will also designate locations for negotiations and private team meetings.

Your instructor will expect each set of negotiators to record agreements on each item, and to provide a document containing the final agreement on each item at the conclusion of the bargaining period. This document must be signed by all participants. If the agreement is incomplete, each party's final bargaining positions on those items still in dispute should be recorded.

Teams may negotiate as a group or through spokespersons. Who makes the first offer, how the time for negotiations is used, how time is used for private meetings, and other rules for conducting bargaining are all controlled by the teams themselves.

When the bargaining process has been completed, the instructor will provide a summary of the final settlement(s) to all the participants.

Background Information

It is now September 10, the opening day of the school year in Newtown. The contract between Newtown School District and the Newtown Teacher Association expired on June 30. Since then, the Board of Education and representatives of the Teacher Association have met on several occasions in an attempt to finalize the contract, but these attempts have not been successful.

Prior to June 30 and during the summer months, there was increasing talk among the membership of the Teacher Association of the possibility of calling a strike if the contract was not finalized by the start of the school year. However, the executive of the Teacher Association agreed that, for the benefit of the community, the teachers would resume normal operations on opening day throughout the system, without a contract, on a day-to-day basis. This was in response to parent pressure to resume normal operations. Parents have been placing pressure on both teachers and the board to keep schools operating, but they have twice defeated referenda on increased taxes to cover budgetary increases over and above those of the previous year. Owing to decreased enrolments, fixed income from local taxes and from provincial and federal grants, and increased costs, maintaining of the school budget at a level consistent with the previous year would produce a budget shortfall. The board believes that allocations for budget items would begin to be exhausted in April of the coming school year. Therefore, the board feels that if the system is to function effectively within its budgetary constraints to the end of the current fiscal year (June 30), programs and personnel must be cut and teachers' productivity (workload) must be increased. In this regard, the school district must provide 190 instructional days, as mandated by provincial law.

The Board of Education is caught between the Teacher Association and community pressure groups. The board believes that it must satisfy the pressure groups and at the same time keep the teachers on the job with a contract that is acceptable to the bargaining unit's membership. The board is concerned that if it fails to respond appropriately to community pressures for cost reductions, the board members may be removed. The board's primary objective, therefore, is to cut costs while retaining as many programs as possible. It hopes to accomplish this through cutbacks in the number of teaching personnel and increases in teacher workload. The board also wishes to eliminate certain existing agreements in order to increase productivity. To achieve this objective, the board wants to negotiate a three-year contract that will stabilize the situation by creating orderly and predictable budgetary needs that will be seen to be less excessive by various community groups. The Teacher Association, on the other hand, wants a one-year contract in order to maintain flexibility.

The Teacher Association also feels caught between community pressure groups, who hope that a strike can be averted, and the board's apparent unwillingness to fight for increased budgetary allocations to run the system. The teachers feel that the board has not confronted the community over its unwillingness to accept increased taxation in order to pay for education, and that its response to this community unwillingness is simply to pass the burden along to teachers.

Newtown is a relatively settled and stable upper-middle-income community with a strong interest in quality education. However, as mentioned, the residents are reluctant to increase the community's already burdensome tax rate. The Newtown School District consists of 12 schools: nine elementary schools (kindergarten–Grade 8) and three senior high schools. The student population is 12,000, divided into 8,000 elementary and 4,000 high school students. The bargaining unit represents 95 percent of all teachers and consists of 250 elementary teachers in all categories and 125 high school teachers in all categories.

Both sides wish to conclude an agreement to avert a strike. However, the Teacher Association's bargaining team is adamantly committed to improving the conditions of its membership, and the board is just as committed to keeping its costs as low as possible. Nevertheless, each side feels it has some room to move on certain issues.

Newtown School District Teachers' Salary Schedule

		Last Year's Number of		Current Year's Number of	
S*	Amount	Teachers	Cost	Teachers	Cost
0	36,000	20	720,000	0	0
1	40,500	20	810,000	20	810,000
2	42,000	28	1,176,000	20	840,000
3	45,000	31	1,395,000	26	1,170,000
4	48,000	30	1,440,000	28	1,344,000
5	52,500	23	1,207,500	26	1,365,000
6	55,500	24	1,332,000	23	1,276,500
7	58,500	15	877,500	22	1,287,000
8	63,000	16	1,008,000	15	945,000
9	66,000	13	858,000	16	1,056,000
10	69,000	180	12,420,000	179	12,351,000
TOTALS		400	23,244,000	375	22,444,500

(*S = steps on salary scale; 0 = entry level.)

Current School Year, July 1–June 30: Projected Budget

1. INCOME

1.1 Local tax (same rate as last year, $14.58 per $1,000 $36,453,000
of property value. No significant increase in property
values expected.)

1.2 Provincial funding (formula per pupil will remain   14,750,640
the same. Legislature may possibly raise formula
next year.)

1.3 Federal funding   2,250,000

TOTAL INCOME $53,453,640

Note: this is a decrease of $1,141,551 (−2.13%) from the previous year's income.

2.   **EXPENDITURES**

2.1 Administration

2.1.1	Professional salaries	$3,412,500	
2.1.2	Clerical/secretarial salaries	843,750	
2.1.3	Other	750,000	
Subtotal			5,006,250

2.2 Instruction

2.2.1	Teachers[i]		
	Salaries	$ 22,450,500	
	Other benefits	4,260,000	
2.2.2	Aides	3,562,800	
2.2.3	Materials/supplies[ii]	2,831,250	
Subtotal			33,104,550

2.3 Plant operation/maintenance

2.3.1	Salaries	3,798,750	
2.3.2	Utilities[iii]	2,925,000	
2.3.3	Other[iv]	776,250	
Subtotal			7,500,000

2.4 Fixed charges

2.4.1	Retirement[v]	$3,529,350	
2.4.2	Other[vi]	1,277,100	
Subtotal			4,806,450

[i] Twenty-five teachers did not return to the system owing to retirement or other reasons.

[ii] Costs of materials and supplies will be up 12 percent over last year based on currently known price increases.

[iii] Cost of utilities is expected to increase by more than 20 percent over the current year's costs.

[iv] Cost projections indicate a 15 percent increase in this category.

[v] The cost of teacher retirements is up by 5 percent owing to increases in the cost of benefits mandated by the provincial legislature.

[vi] Other fixed charges have increased 32 percent for this current year.

2.5	Debt servicing[vii]		3,078,000
2.6	Transportation		
	2.6.1 Salaries	$ 1,200,000	
	2.6.2 Other[viii]	1,185,000	
Subtotal			2,385,000
TOTAL EXPENDITURES		$55,880,250	
BUDGET SURPLUS (SHORTFALL)		(2,426,610)	

Total number of pupils: 12,000

Total number of teachers: 375

Per pupil expenditure: $4,657

[vii] The cost of debt servicing has increased 14 percent owing to changes in interest rates.

[viii] Transportation costs have increased 31 percent owing to increases in operating and maintenance costs.

Last School Year, July 1–June 30: Audited Budget ───────────────

1. INCOME

1.1	Local tax ($14.58 per $1,000 of property value)	$36,612,000
1.2	Provincial funding (based on an equalization formula, improved during the last sitting of the legislature. Yielded $1,229,22 per pupil in administration last year)	15,734,127
1.3	Federal funding	2,247,732
TOTAL INCOME		$54,593,859

2.   EXPENDITURES

2.1 Administration

2.1.1	Professional salaries	$3,411,744
2.1.2	Clerical/secretarial salaries	843,201
2.1.3	Other	783,387

Subtotal $5,038,332

2.2 Instruction

2.2.1	Teachers	
	Salaries	$23,244,000

Other benefits   4,183,929

2.2.2	Aides	3,549,825
2.2.3	Materials/supplies	2,527,899

Subtotal $33,505,653

2.3 Plant operation/maintenance

2.3.1	Salaries	$3,798,750
2.3.2	Utilities	2,436,804
2.3.3	Other	675,594

Subtotal $6,911,148

2.4 Fixed charges

2.4.1	Retirement	$3,361,284
2.4.2	Other	974,319

Subtotal $4,335,603

2.5 Debt servicing		$2,700,780	
2.6 Transportation			
	2.6.1 Salaries	$1,199,094	
	2.6.2 Other	904,581	
Subtotal			$ 2,103,675
TOTAL EXPENDITURES			$54,595,191
BUDGET SURPLUS (SHORTFALL)			($1,332)

Total number of pupils: 12,800

Total number of teachers: 400

Per pupil expenditure: $4,265.25

Source: Lewicki, Roy (2003). *Negotiations: Readings, Exercises and Cases.* Fourth Edition. New York: McGraw-Hill. Material originally developed by Frank W. Masters.

References

[1] Downie, B.M. (1990). The negotiation process. In, J.A. Willes (ed.), *Labour relations in Canada: readings and cases.* Scarborough, ON: Prentice-Hall.

[2] Downie, *op. cit.*

[3] Walton, R.E., & McKersie, R.B. (1963). *A behavioral theory of labor negotiations: an analysis of a social interaction system.* New York: McGraw-Hill.

[4] Walton & McKersie, *op. cit.*

[5] Peach, D.A., & Bergman, P. (1991). *The practice of labour relations* (3rd edition). Toronto: McGraw-Hill Ryerson.

[6] Education Relations Commission of Ontario (1983). *The bargaining process and mediation.* Toronto: Education Relations Commission of Ontario.

[7] Walton and McKersie, *op. cit.*

[8] Walton and McKersie, *op. cit.*

[9] Walton, R.E., Cutcher-Gershenfeld, J.E., and McKersie, R.B. (1994). *Strategic negotiations: a theory of change in labor-management relations.* Boston: Harvard Business School Press.

[10] Katz, H.C., and Kochan, T.A. (1992). *An introduction to collective bargaining and industrial relations.* New York: McGraw-Hill.

[11] Education Relations Commission of Ontario, *op. cit.*

[12] Peach and Bergman, *op. cit.*

[13] Walton, Cutcher-Gershenfeld, and McKersie, *op. cit.*

[14] Education Relations Commission of Ontario, *op. cit.*

[15] Peach and Bergman, *op. cit.*

[16] Chamberlain, N.W., and Kuhn, J.M. (1986). *Collective bargaining* (3rd edition). New York: McGraw-Hill.

[17] Chaykowski, R.P. (2001). Collective bargaining: structure, process and innovation. In M. Gunderson, A. Ponak, and D. Taras (Eds.), *Union-management relations in Canada* (4th edition). Don Mills, ON: Addison-Wesley.

[18] Craig, A.W.J., and Solomon, N.A. (1993). *The system of industrial relations in Canada* (4th edition). Scarborough, ON: Prentice-Hall.

[19] Ury, W.L., Brett, J.M., and Goldberg, S.B. (1988). *Getting disputes resolved: designing systems to cut the cost of conflict.* San Francisco: Jossey-Bass.

[20] Ury, Brett, and Goldberg, *op. cit.*

[21] Ury, Brett, and Goldberg, *op. cit.*

[22] Fisher, R.E., and Ury, W.L. (1991). *Getting to yes: negotiating agreement without giving in* (2nd edition). Boston: Houghton-Mifflin.

[23] Fisher and Ury, *op. cit.*

[24] Susskind, L.E. and Landry, E.M. (1991, January). Implementing a mutual gains approach to collective bargaining. *Negotiation Journal*, 5–10.

[25] Hunter, L.W., and McKersie, R.B. (1992, October). Can 'mutual gains' training change labor-management relationships? *Negotiation Journal*, 319–330.

[26] Walton and McKersie, *op. cit.*

[27] Heckscher, C., and Hall, L. (1994, July). Mutual gains and beyond: two levels of intervention. *Negotiation Journal*, 235–248.

[28] Hunter and McKersie, *op. cit.*

CHAPTER NINE

Engineers Strike at CN

Locomotive engineers at Montreal-based Canadian National Railway (CN) went on strike in November 2009. 14 months of bargaining failed to produce a collective agreement between CN and the Teamsters Canada Rail Conference (TCRC), which represents approximately 1,700 locomotive engineers across Canada. The union's contract expired on December 31, 2008, and the parties had been negotiating with the assistance of federal mediators for several months.

With no agreement in sight, CN gave the union notice of its plan to increase wage rates by 1.5 percent and increase the mileage caps for the locomotive engineers by 500 miles. "CN regrettably reached an impasse with the TCRC after bargaining in good faith with the union for more than a year, and has decided to invoke these contractual changes to move the company forward," the company stated in a press release.

The union claimed the mileage caps would force some engineers to work seven days a week and cause layoffs of conductors, trainmen, and yardmen. Within days, it sent CN a 72-hour strike notice. The strike began on November 28.

CN claimed it had urged the TCRC to resume negotiations rather than strike, and if a settlement was not possible, to submit the issues in dispute to binding arbitration. Meanwhile, the union claimed it offered to withdraw or suspend the strike notice if CN would withdraw its notice to change the collective agreement and get back to the bargaining table.

"It's obvious to us that CN is counting on the federal government intervention to settle the issues rather [than] exploring solutions to a negotiated agreement," TCRC President Daniel Shewchuk said in a press release. The union also planned to file a complaint of bargaining in bad faith against CN.

During the strike, which lasted just a few days, CN implemented a labour contingency plan, in which management personnel worked as locomotive engineers to ensure continued service. There was concern that a service disruption could affect the Canadian economy, since CN trains transport a significant amount of goods—grains, lumber, metal, and minerals—across Canada and into the United States. In order to end the strike, the company offered to agree to binding arbitration on wage and benefit issues, and to roll back the monthly cap for engineers on the condition that the TCRC withdraw its work-rule demands.

With back-to-work legislation introduced but not yet debated in the House of Commons, the strike ended on December 2. Both parties returned to the bargaining table, and the unsolved wage and benefit issues were submitted to binding arbitration.

Sources: Canadian National Railway news releases, October 23, 2009; November 23, 2009; November 25, 2009; November 27, 2009; December 1, 2009; December 2, 2009 December 13, 2009, <http://www.cn.ca/en/media-news-releases.htm>.

Teamsters Canada Rail Conference news releases, October 6, 2009; November 23, 2009; November 25, 2009; November 27, 2009; November 28, 2009; November 29, 2009; December 1, 2009, <http://www.teamstersrail.ca/TCRC_News_Archives.htm>.

Canadian Press, "CN Rail strike settled as two sides reach agreement," December 2, 2009.

Frank Peebles, "Engineers hope strike drives settlement," The Ottawa Citizen, November 29, 2009.

STRIKES AND LOCKOUTS

objectives

In this chapter, we will discuss how strikes and lockouts take place, why and when they are used in the collective bargaining process, and how legislation controls their use. By the end of this chapter, you should be able to:

- define a strike and a lockout
- explain why a strike or lockout would be used as a bargaining tactic
- outline the legislative guidelines for the use of a strike or lockout in bargaining
- describe an essential service
- outline legislative guidelines on picketing
- explain the idea of replacement workers and describe when and how they might be used in strikes
- assess the impact of strikes in Canada

INTRODUCTION

The strike and the lockout are the two most public events in the entire industrial relations process. Because strikes and lockouts are visible actions—deliberately so, since one of their purposes is to draw public attention to a bargaining dispute—they are often perceived as being regular, inevitable events. In fact, when viewed in the context of the amount of collective agreements annually negotiated in Canada, strikes and lockouts are unusual events. Approximately 90 percent of collective agreements are settled without a strike or lockout taking place.[1]

However, even though strikes and lockouts are relatively uncommon, they can have widespread impacts and long-lasting effects. Therefore, it is important to understand what strikes and lockouts are and how they are conducted. We will begin our discussion by explaining what strikes and lockouts are, and describing why and when they are used as part of the bargaining process. We will then outline the restrictions and conditions that labour legislation places on activities related to strikes and lockouts, such as picketing and using replacement workers. We will conclude by describing how a strike or lockout ends and by analyzing the overall impact of strikes and lockouts in Canada.

DEFINING STRIKES AND LOCKOUTS

A **strike** occurs when union members in a bargaining unit withdraw their labour—that is, they refuse to perform part or all of their regular duties or refuse to come to work. A **lockout** occurs when the employer closes all or part of the workplace so that the workers cannot enter the premises and perform their jobs. The terms **industrial action** and **industrial conflict** are also used to describe either strikes or lockouts.

As we know from previous chapters, strikes were often used in the early days of Canadian unionism to pressure an employer into recognizing a union as the representative of employees in a workplace. A strike undertaken for this purpose is known as a **recognition strike**. The need for recognition strikes disappeared when Canadian labour legislation formalized the process of certification and gave employers the legal responsibility to accept their employees' chosen workplace representative.

While recognition strikes are no longer necessary (and in fact are banned in every Canadian jurisdiction), there are still legal restrictions on the use of strikes or lockouts in every Canadian jurisdiction. A legal strike or lockout can only take place while collective bargaining is in progress. It is important to note that negotiation sessions do not actually have to be taking place; in fact, most strikes or lockouts occur as a consequence of the parties being reluctant to continue bargaining sessions that are perceived as unproductive. However, for a strike or lockout to be legal, the parties must be in the process of bargaining and a collective agreement must not have been settled. Additionally, in most Canadian jurisdictions, the employer is prohibited from dismissing striking employees while a strike is taking place, and striking employees are entitled to return to their jobs after the strike is over.

It is also important to note that work does not have to stop completely for a legal strike to occur. Several provincial labour codes and the *Canada Labour Code* state that a work "slowdown" can be considered a strike. A number of activities fall into the category of "slowdown," including union-imposed overtime bans and **rotating strikes**, where workers at one location of a business stop their work but workers at other locations continue working. **Work-to-rule campaigns**, where union members interpret the terms of the collective agreement very narrowly and follow them very closely in order to slow down production, have also been determined to constitute strike action.[2]

WHY STRIKES OR LOCKOUTS HAPPEN

The basic purpose of a strike or lockout is to inflict "economic pain" on the other side in a bargaining situation in order to force acceptance of bargaining demands. If a strike takes place, the employer is hurt financially by losing revenue as a consequence of being unable to produce or sell products or services. The striking union members are also hurt financially, since they do not receive their regular pay. Similarly, if a lockout takes place, the union members are not paid because they are not able to go to work, and the employer loses money because production is halted. While both parties suffer economic pain during a strike or lockout, the goal of the party undertaking the action is to make the other party suffer more and thus be motivated to accept the first party's bargaining demands. Thus, the successful party in a strike or lockout (i.e., the party that achieves the outcome it desires) is, in many cases, the party with enough resources or determination to withstand the economic pain inflicted by the action. A strike or lockout is not always won by the party with the more reasonable, ethical, or equitable proposals; in fact, it is more often won by the party with more resources, regardless of the merits of that party's positions.

Financial Pinch Felt by Strikers

WINDSOR—Sympathetic words from strikers greeted Windsorites driving their garbage-laden cars through city worker picket lines at the just-opened public waste depot off Central Avenue.

"We completely understand—people need to get rid of their garbage," said Al Wheatley, a striking member of CUPE Local 82 who works in Windsor's forestry division.

The Ministry of the Environment relented on an earlier order that now allows private sector drop-offs to continue serving residents, but the city was ordered to reopen its waste transfer station to offer free drop-offs. The order also calls on the city to open a second site within a week.

"The residents have been pawns in this thing for too long," Wheatley said of the six-week-old strike.

With private security officers looking on, and under the watchful eye of Windsor cops regularly passing by, a group of strikers on North Service Road delayed arriving vehicles only long enough to pass on leaflets. They asked the motorists to contact the mayor and councillors and urge them to agree to binding arbitration to end the strike.

"We've had a great response—we've got to win back the trust of the public," said Wheatley.

While some recent strike tactics, like picketing the mayor's home, may have backfired, Wheatley and fellow pickets on the line said they just want to get back to their jobs.

Several motorists arriving at the public drop-off and asked for comment expressed support for the strikers but added they had no choice when it came to the task at hand.

"If you smell that garbage in the back, you'll know why I'm here," said Joe Johnson, pointing to a pickup load of trash from his home and some neighbours.

He described as "brutal" some of the alleys around his Walkerville home.

"These guys are making their point, but I've got to get rid of my garbage," said Colin, who would only give his first name. He blamed stubbornness by both sides for the strike with no end in sight.

"They've got to keep talking," said another elderly gentleman, who wouldn't give his name but added his son is one of those on strike.

The leaders of Windsor's two striking CUPE locals have returned home from Toronto after securing emergency funding to assist members suffering financial hardship because of the work stoppage.

"I am extremely pleased with the generosity shown—I'm ecstatic," said Jean Fox, president of Local 543, which represents about 1,400 inside workers.

Delegates at a CUPE Ontario division convention were asked to vote on a motion for additional financial assistance for the Windsor strikers' compassionate fund.

Fox wouldn't say how many idled city workers are receiving benefits on top of their $200 weekly strike pay, but she said a growing number of families are suffering after six weeks off the job. She said Local 543 is predominantly female, with "a lot of single mothers and members whose spouses are in the auto sector."

Source: Schmidt, Doug. "'We've got to win back the trust of the public': Financial pinch felt by strikers." *The Windsor Star*, May 29, 2009, p. A3.

Several factors affect a union's or employer's decision to commence a strike or lockout. Much research has been conducted to identify these factors and to determine when they may or may not be important in the strike or lockout decision. A thoroughly comprehensive review of this research is beyond the scope of this discussion, but we will briefly examine some of the major determinants of strikes and lockouts that have been identified.

Motivations for Striking or Locking Out

One way to understand why a strike or lockout occurs is to look at the motivations of the parties undertaking the action. We already know that the party instigating a strike or lockout intends to inflict economic suffering on the other party. However, some research suggests more complex motivations, which can be classified into two categories: "strikes as mistakes" and "strikes as collective voice."[3]

The strikes-as-mistakes perspective suggests that strikes or lockouts occur as a result of mistaken perceptions developed during bargaining. One party may misunderstand the position of the other party and thus erroneously believe there is no common ground for settlement. This party then undertakes a strike or lockout to force an agreement. In this scenario, the strike or lockout is a mistake because the parties actually could have agreed on the issues without the pressure of industrial action to motivate them into settling.

Why do parties develop inaccurate perceptions of each other's positions? The strikes-as-mistakes perspective proposes several reasons why inaccurate perceptions develop. They may result from a lack of experience on the part of the bargainers, limited disclosures of information during bargaining, the complexity of the issues being negotiated, miscalculations of the other side's position, or changes in the parties' expectations during bargaining.[4]

If the parties are not experienced bargainers, they may not know how to obtain or interpret information during bargaining. Less experienced bargainers may also misinterpret how much the other party is willing to concede or compromise on specific bargaining items. Misunderstandings may also occur if complex issues such as downsizing or new job classifications are being bargained and one or both of the parties do not fully understand the issue or the related proposals. In other situations, one party may choose to withhold information that could affect the other side's perceptions. For example, if management negotiators are proposing a wage freeze, in order to strengthen the credibility of their position they might withhold from the union negotiators the fact that the company made a large profit in the last financial quarter. And finally, as outlined in previous chapters, the parties' expectations may change during bargaining because of input from their constituencies or changes in the external environment, such as new legislation. All of these errors in perception can cause a strike or lockout when there is no actual reason for one.

The strikes-as-mistakes perspective acknowledges that there are financial burdens on both sides during a strike or lockout. Striking or locking out is often not the ideal choice of action to support a bargaining demand, particularly when the financial burdens caused by such action might result in the resources of one or both parties becoming seriously depleted.

The second perspective, "strikes as collective voice," suggests that strikes and lockouts are likely to occur because there is always an element of mistrust in the union-management relationship. Unions and management represent different interests and have different philosophies on how the workplace should be governed. Thus, according to this perspective, the two parties have fundamental reasons to distrust each other, even if a particular relationship is relatively cordial. What, then, determines whether this basic distrust will be manifested in a strike or lockout?

According to the strikes-as-collective-voice perspective, the likelihood of a strike or lockout occurring depends on several factors.[5] The first is the amount of worker discontent. Obviously, dissatisfied workers are more likely to strike than relatively satisfied workers. The second factor is the extent of management's willingness or ability to address discontent, since reducing discontent or dissatisfaction will also likely reduce the possibility of a strike. The third factor is the existence or non-existence of other means to express discontent. Formal or informal means of employee-management communication, such as a grievance procedure or "open door" management policies, may provide alternative ways for workers to express unhappiness. The ability of union leaders to mobilize discontent is the fourth factor. Union leaders must be able to persuade their members that a strike is a reasonable and productive expression of discontent if union members are going to commit themselves to that means of expression. The fifth and final factor is the social legitimacy of strikes. If society in general does not see strikes as legitimate, a strike will not gain public support and thus may not be successful in pressuring management to accept union demands.

The strikes-as-collective-voice perspective suggests that although strikes and lockouts are usually a means of inflicting economic pain, they may also be used for non-economic purposes, such as expressing worker discontent. Non-economic motivations for strikes and lockouts sometimes dominate over economic motivations, causing a strike or lockout even if the parties recognize that such action is not economically rational or viable. The opportunity for a party to have a "voice" to express its concerns visibly and to release tension or high emotions that have built up during the bargaining process may be considered more valuable than the economic impact of the action.

Both the strikes-as-mistakes and the strikes-as-collective-voice perspectives suggest that strikes may be caused at least in part by factors relating to employees' attitudes toward the employer. One problem with assessing whether this is true is the difficulty in accurately measuring the attitudes and their actual impact. However, some research has attempted to link strike propensity (the willingness to engage in a strike in support of union goals) with the quality of the worker-employer relationship and other workplace factors. The results of one study addressing this linkage indicated that employees who had a generally positive perception of the worker-employer relationship in their workplace were less willing to support a strike; however, attitudes related to economic factors (such as perceived pay inequities and the perceived availability of employment alternatives) had a stronger effect on strike propensity.[6]

Bargaining Structure

The size of the bargaining unit has been identified as another factor that affects the incidence of strikes. In the United States, larger bargaining units have been found to be more likely to go on strike than smaller bargaining units.[7] This finding is attributed in part to the perception that larger bargaining units will have a greater economic impact on the employer by striking than smaller bargaining units will, simply because more workers are involved in a larger bargaining unit and thus more labour is withdrawn with greater impact.

Ascertaining whether this tendency also exists in Canada is somewhat difficult, since national strike statistics in the past have been consistently collected only for bargaining units of more than 500 members. This cut-off point excludes data from smaller bargaining units, and thus a comparison of strike rates in different-sized bargaining units would be somewhat skewed. However, a study conducted in Ontario, using nine years of data from all public and private sector certifications in the province, found that strikes were most frequent in bargaining units of 150 to 300 members, least common in units with less than 21 members, but almost even in frequency in units of 50 to 149 members and units of 300 to 499 members.[8] Another analysis using strike data from Ontario also found that smaller bargaining units were less likely to go on strike than larger bargaining units, but discovered that strikes involving smaller bargaining units tended to be longer than strikes involving larger bargaining units.[9] These findings indicate, at least, that very small bargaining units in Canada are less likely to strike but that the tendency to strike varies among larger-sized units. We should also keep in mind that workers' ability to strike may be more restricted in the Canadian public sector than in the private sector, so the lack of a strike may not always indicate an unwillingness to strike. There may instead be legislative barriers that prevent a strike from happening or that discourage strike propensity.

Individual Factors

Another important factor in whether a strike occurs is how willing the union members are to undertake strike action, since they will individually bear a large part of the economic pain inflicted by a strike. One study involving a survey of 44 workers in a single bargaining unit indicated that higher loyalty to the union results in a higher propensity to support strike action.[10] Another study of workers in a variety of bargaining units, industries, and occupations suggested that the combination of a high level of solidarity among workers and a high level of commitment to the union, not union commitment alone, increased the likelihood of strike action occurring.[11]

It is not illogical to deduce that employees who are loyal to the union will be more likely than less loyal union members to support actions proposed by the union. Furthermore, as we will see, it is the union members, not only the union executive, who give the mandate for strike action, and thus the support of the union members is essential for a strike to take place.

Another individual factor that may be relevant in determining whether a strike or lockout occurs is the history and quality of the relationship between the parties. If the parties have a history of using strikes or lockouts against each other in past bargaining disputes, this may affect their willingness to engage in future strikes. If the parties have experienced strikes or lockouts in the past and thus are knowledgeable about how these actions are conducted, they may feel differently about using these actions than parties that are unfamiliar with the strategic use of strikes or lockouts. In addition, if the parties had a hostile relationship before the start of bargaining, or if their relationship became contentious as bargaining progressed, they might be more willing to consider more confrontational bargaining tactics. Some research has also indicated that hostile union-employer relationships prior to or during strike activity can have other effects in the workplace, such as increases in the number of defective products generated during those times.[12]

Economic Conditions

The general economic conditions in which the bargaining takes place also have an effect on whether a strike or lockout occurs. Such factors as unemployment rates, the financial position of the employer, the general profit picture in the industry, and the current stage in the employer's "business cycle" all affect strike or lockout propensity.[13]

High unemployment rates may reduce union members' willingness to strike if the members perceive that other work opportunities are not readily available; this factor is particularly important if union members perceive that a strike will be lengthy rather than brief.

The financial position of the employer or the industry affects the union's perceptions of the employer's ability to pay. Such perceptions are then balanced against the perceived likelihood of obtaining desired financial goals through strike action. A union may want a large wage increase, but if the employer is perceived as being unable to afford that increase and a strike is not perceived as a means of changing that situation, it is unlikely that a strike will be perceived as the most effective action to gain a wage increase. A strike in such a situation may even have a negative economic impact on individual union members, if the gains from a negotiated wage increase do not equal or exceed the amount of wages the members lost during the strike.

The stage of the employer's business cycle is also influential because strikes will not have a particularly large financial impact on the employer during slow times in the employer's business. For example, a strike by employees of a ski resort would not have much impact during the summer, when the resort might be closed or might be operating on a very limited basis. However, a strike by the same employees would have a very large impact in January or February when the resort is operating in peak season. An employer, particularly one in a seasonal business, cannot afford a long closure during the time when most of its revenue is generated. When planning strike action, unions might also take into consideration any major events the employer is planning. For example, hotel employees could threaten to go on strike when a large convention is scheduled for the hotel facility. The employer would not want to lose the revenue (or suffer the damage to its reputation) that a cancellation would likely cause, and thus the employer might be more willing than at other times to accede to the union's bargaining demands.

Legislative Restrictions

As we will see in the next section, federal and some provincial labour laws require that several conditions be met for a legal strike or lockout to take place. While these laws have a direct bearing on whether a legal strike or lockout is possible, they do not always completely discourage a strike or lockout from happening without those requirements. Most Canadian labour codes ban strikes during the term of a collective agreement, but Canada has a long history of these types of strikes. These strikes may occur spontaneously as an expression of union members' dissatisfaction, or they may be planned and facilitated by union leaders, despite the fact that they are technically illegal.

Additionally, in many jurisdictions in Canada, the ability of public sector workers to strike is severely restricted or banned outright. Nevertheless, public sector strikes usually represent between 20 and 30 percent of annual strike activity in Canada.[14] It has been argued that the restrictions on striking in the public sector are themselves a major cause of public sector strikes.[15] It has been proposed that "no-strike laws" restrict the ability of public sector union negotiators to press their demands to the limit; this is because the government's negotiators know that the union cannot threaten to strike if the union negotiators' demands are not met. No-strike laws can also cause dangerously high levels of conflict to build up between the parties, since a legal strike cannot be used as a means of expressing discontent or resolving bargaining disputes.[16]

Bargaining Process Factors

Strikes and lockouts are sometimes used to provide a break from bargaining and an emotional release for the bargainers and the parties they represent. If tensions are running high at the bargaining table, a strike or lockout may be perceived as a way to give the parties time away from bargaining and to return with new energy and ideas. Moreover, the union members represented in bargaining will have an opportunity to express their feelings through picketing and other forms of public action. While it is highly unlikely that a potentially costly or lengthy strike or lockout would occur for the sole reason of releasing emotional tension, a beneficial side effect of a strike or lockout may be that the bargainers will return to the negotiating table in a better frame of mind.

Another factor related to bargaining that may affect strike propensity is the impact of the issues raised during bargaining. If a new issue is brought to the bargaining table, or if issues that have been presented as straightforward turn out to be more complex than they initially appeared, a bargaining team may consider taking strike or lockout action in support of its position, even if such action was not initially planned or was not historically part of the bargaining strategy. For example, in a past set of negotiations, the union local representing the customer sales and service agents at Air Canada undertook a three-week strike over the issues of job security and part-time work. This was the first strike in the union local's history, and it occurred in resistance to the employer's bargaining demands for more part-time jobs and increased workforce flexibility—demands that the employer had not presented in previous negotiations but which it claimed it now needed to operate in a newly deregulated industry.[17]

We should also remember that a party can be pressured into accepting the other party's demands without a strike or lockout actually occurring. The mere threat of strike or lockout action may be enough to gain bargaining concessions, especially if one party knows that the other party does not have the resources to endure even a minor work stoppage. One party can therefore use the possibility of a strike or a lockout as a bargaining tactic to make gains in bargaining without a strike or lockout actually taking place.

Table 9-1 summarizes the factors affecting the likelihood of a strike or lockout taking place. We will now go on to discuss how a strike or lockout actually occurs.

HOW DOES A STRIKE OR LOCKOUT BEGIN?

Provincial and federal labour laws in Canada specify several preconditions that must be in place for a strike or lockout to occur. Table 9-2 outlines preconditions in the specific federal and provincial jurisdictions. Several general preconditions, however, are fairly consistent across jurisdictions, and we will now turn our attention to these.

TABLE 9-1 Factors Affecting the Likelihood of a Strike or Lockout

Motivations for striking or locking out	- strikes as mistakes
	- strikes as collective voice
Bargaining structure	- size of the bargaining unit
Individual factors	- willingness of union members to support or authorize a strike
	- worker solidarity
	- history or quality of the previous relationship between the parties
Economic conditions	- unemployment rate
	- employer's business cycle
	- employer's financial position
Legislative restrictions	- conditions that must be met for a strike or lockout to be legal
	- ability to strike, especially in the public sector
Bargaining process factors	- level of tension at the bargaining table
	- strike or lockout as a break from bargaining
	- strike or lockout as a form of emotional release
	- issues raised in bargaining
	- effectiveness of threat of strike or lockout, not actual event

The first general precondition is that a legal strike or lockout can only occur while collective bargaining is taking place and when an existing collective agreement has expired. Occasionally, a strike will take place during the term of the collective agreement, usually in reaction to a controversial workplace event or series of events. This type of illegal strike is called a **wildcat strike**. In a wildcat strike, employees will usually walk off the job or not show up for work, even if directed to do otherwise by their union executive. When a wildcat

TABLE 9-2 Preconditions for a Legal Strike or Lockout

	Strike Vote	Third-Party Intervention Prior to Strike or Lockout	Notice
Federal	Compulsory vote by secret ballot; results valid for 60 days or a period agreed to in writing. Results are determined by a majority of those in the bargaining unit who vote. No vote is required if a legal lockout has occurred.	Notification of failure to settle a dispute must be issued before a strike or lockout permitted, unless the minister responsible for labour has already assisted the parties.	At least 72 hours' notice to the other party, with a copy to the minister of labour. Notice is not required if legal strike/lockout by the other party has already occurred.
Alberta	Compulsory supervised secret-ballot vote; results are valid for 120 days. Results determined by the majority of those in the bargaining unit who vote.	No strike or lockout can be declared unless a mediator has been formally appointed.	At least 72 hours' notice to the other party, with a similar notice to the appointed mediator.
British Columbia	Compulsory secret-ballot vote unless lock-out has lasted more than 72 hours. Results valid for three months or an agreed-upon period. Results determined by the majority of those in the bargaining unit who vote.	Not required	At least 72 hours' notice to the other party, unless the parties agree otherwise, and the same notice to the labour relations board. The board may order a longer notice period for the protection of property or persons.

TABLE 9-2 Preconditions for a Legal Strike or Lockout (Continued)

	Strike Vote	Third-Party Intervention Prior to Strike or Lockout	Notice
Manitoba	Compulsory secret-ballot vote. Results are determined by the majority of those in the bargaining unit who vote.	Not required	Not required
New Brunswick	Compulsory secret-ballot vote; results are valid for one year. Results are determined by the majority of employees in the bargaining unit who vote.	No strike or lockout may be declared unless one party has requested the appointment of a conciliator.	24 hours' notice to the other party.
Newfoundland and Labrador	Compulsory secret-ballot vote. Results are determined by the majority of those in bargaining unit who vote.	No strike or lockout may be declared unless a party has requested a conciliation board.	Not required.
Nova Scotia	Compulsory secret-ballot vote. Results determined by the majority of those in the bargaining unit who vote.	No strike or lockout may be declared unless a conciliation board has been appointed and the minister of labour has received 48-hour strike/lockout notice.	48 hours' notice to minister of labour.
Ontario	Compulsory secret-ballot vote taken no earlier than 30 days before the collective agreement expires or, if no agreement, from the date of	No strike or lockout may be declared unless a mediator or conciliator was appointed.	Not required.

TABLE 9-2 Preconditions for a Legal Strike or Lockout (Continued)

	Strike Vote	Third-Party Intervention Prior to Strike or Lockout	Notice
	the conciliator's appointment. Results are determined by the majority of employees in the bargaining unit who vote.		
Prince Edward Island	Compulsory secret-ballot vote. Results determined by the majority of employees in bargaining unit who vote.	No strike or lockout may be declared unless a mediator, conciliator, or conciliation board has been appointed.	Not required.
Quebec	Compulsory secret-ballot vote. Results determined by the majority of union members in the bargaining unit who vote.	Not required.	Not required for the private sector; public sector unions must give the employer and minister of labour at least 7 working days' notice.
Saskatchewan	Compulsory secret-ballot vote unless unit is one or two employees. The labour relations board may supervise the vote upon application by the union or affected employees for supervision. Results are determined by the majority of unit members who vote.	Not required, although the minister of labour must be informed of the beginning of a strike or lockout.	At least 48 hours' notice to the other party and to the minister of labour.

Source: Human Resources and Skills Development Canada. "Synoptic Charts on Legislation Pertaining to Certain Major Collective Bargaining Issues." (available at <www.hrsdc.gc.ca/eng/labour/labour_law/ind_rel/votes.shtml> and <www.hrsdc.gc.ca/eng/labour/labour_law/ind_rel/int.shtml>).

strike occurs, the employer usually applies to a labour relations board for a declaration that the strike is illegal and an order for the strikers to return to work. The employer usually obtains the declaration within a few hours so that the impact of the strike can be minimized and so that the workers return to work as soon as possible.

The second precondition for a legal strike is that it must be authorized by a vote of the bargaining unit. This precondition is in place to ensure that strike action truly reflects the will of the union membership and is not just an idea of the union executive or bargaining team. The vote authorizing strike action, known as the **strike vote**, is conducted by secret ballot. The vote consists of a simple yes/no response to the question of whether the voter supports the union's undertaking strike action.

In most provinces, a majority (usually defined as 50 percent plus 1) of votes in favour of a strike is required for a **strike mandate**: that is, for the union to be authorized to begin a legal strike. As shown in Table 9-2, most jurisdictions simply require majority support among bargaining unit members who participate in the strike vote. The reasoning for using the simple majority of voters as the determinant of strike support is that since unions are democratic organizations, every member of the bargaining unit has the opportunity to participate in the strike vote, but if individuals choose not to use that opportunity, that choice should not affect the outcome of the votes from those who did participate.

A vote in support of a strike does not guarantee that a strike will occur immediately or even that it will occur at all. Often, a vote to strike is used to support the union's bargaining demands, since it shows the employer that the bargaining unit members are prepared to withdraw their labour to achieve their demands. It is not uncommon that the bargaining following a successful strike vote results in a collective agreement without a strike

Alexandra Jurisic of Calgary Separate Local 55, Alberta Teachers' Association, sits beside strike vote ballots, 92 percent of which were in favour of a strike.

ever happening. However, in some jurisdictions, there is a time limit on the validity of a strike vote. If this time limit passes and the union still wishes to have a valid strike mandate, the union must conduct another strike vote and again receive the required level of support.

The third precondition for a legal strike or lockout in several (but not all) Canadian jurisdictions is that there must be third-party intervention before the strike or lockout. Depending on the jurisdiction, this intervention can take the form of a conciliator who reports on the bargaining situation to the relevant minister of labour, or a mediator who actually participates in the bargaining process to help the parties reach an agreement. Third-party intervention will be discussed in more detail in Chapter 10, but we will briefly comment at this point on its role in the strike/lockout process.

The philosophy behind requiring third-party intervention in collective bargaining is that since a strike or lockout has a potentially widespread damaging effect, the parties should explore every possible opportunity for resolution before a strike or lockout occurs. The role of the third party is to assist in identifying such opportunities and to help bring the parties to an agreement. The participation of a neutral third party may help the parties to recognize common ground on contentious issues and to shift their focus away from perceived differences and conflicts that obscure potential mutually acceptable solutions. However, others believe that if the parties are committed strongly enough to their bargaining positions to be considering a strike or lockout, it is unlikely that a third party will be able to overcome such major differences, and the intervention of the third party will be resented and ineffectual.[18] Third-party intervention, furthermore, can have the opposite effect than intended if the parties are forced to sit through a process they are not committed to and did not request; in such situations, their differences and resentments may be heightened rather than reduced.

The fourth precondition for a legal strike or lockout in several jurisdictions is that the party initiating a strike or lockout must give notice to the other party of when the strike or lockout will begin. There may be arrangements that must be made in the workplace to accommodate the effects of a strike or lockout, since there will be limited or blocked access to the workplace during the strike or lockout. For example, the employer may have cash, business documents, or other valuables in the workplace that need to be secured or moved to a more accessible location. In some workplaces,

Some occupations, such as police officer, are often deemed essential services. This designation restricts or forbids work stoppages, as a stoppage would compromise public health and safety.

there are perishable goods that must be removed and stored elsewhere. As well, employees may have personal belongings that they would like to remove from the workplace. A strike or lockout notice gives time for all these activities to occur.

Most jurisdictions in Canada also have legislation that restricts or forbids workers in certain occupations from striking. These occupations are referred to as **essential services**. The criteria used to designate these occupations vary, and the occupations are not always specifically named in the labour legislation. However, the general principle defining this group of occupations is that workers are considered to be providing an essential service if their absence from the workplace would cause a threat to public safety or health. Therefore, occupations such as police officer, correctional officer, medical doctor, and firefighter are usually considered essential services. An example of legislation defining essential services is section 41(5) of the *Labour Act* of Prince Edward Island, which states: "No member of a police department nor any person being a full-time employee of any fire department... nor any persons employed as security police officers by the University of Prince Edward Island, nor any employee of a nursing home or community care facility nor non-instructional personnel as defined in the *School Act* has the right to strike, or to engage in any stoppage of work."

When a breakdown or dispute in collective bargaining involves an occupation designated as an essential service, the relevant collective agreement or labour legislation usually provides for resolution through some form of third-party intervention rather than by a strike or lockout. Similarly, in any public sector bargaining situation where strikes are restricted or not permitted, disputes are resolved through some form of third-party intervention. However, if a legal or illegal public sector strike occurs, governments can use **back-to-work legislation**, a dispute-resolution method that is not available to employers in the private sector. Provincial or federal legislatures can pass a law ordering the strike to end and the public sector workers to return to work, usually with a provision that some form of third-party intervention be employed to resolve the disputes that caused the strike. Governments and private sector employers can also use the courts to order an end to a strike that is deemed illegal.

According to a study covering the years 1965 to 1993, Canadian federal and provincial governments used back-to-work legislation 62 times during that period as a method of resolving public sector strikes.[19] This figure indicates that Canadian governments are not reluctant to use back-to-work legislation as a method of resolving bargaining disputes. However, passing such legislation can be a tricky political matter for governments. While the passage of such legislation has the immediate desired effect of ending the strike, this method of dispute resolution can make the government appear heavy-handed, especially if public support is on the side of the strikers. Even strikes that are clearly illegal, such as strikes by workers in essential services, may draw support from other unions in the form of similarly illegal "sympathy strikes" and also from the general public.[20] Government use of back-to-work legislation can also cause long-term problems in the bargaining relationship between the government and its employees, as the employees may resent the government's exercising this exceptional power rather than constructively addressing the disputes that caused the strike.

In several Canadian jurisdictions, workers in some parts of the public sector, such as health care, must provide a designated minimum level of service during a strike in order for the strike to be designated as legal. The numbers and types of employees that must be working to maintain this level of service are determined either by legislation, by negotiation, or by third-party intervention, depending on the jurisdiction or on what the parties themselves can agree to.

Now that we have outlined the conditions that must be met for a legal strike or lockout to take place, we will turn to describing what actually happens during a strike or lockout.

WHAT HAPPENS WHEN A STRIKE OR LOCKOUT TAKES PLACE

During a strike or lockout, as previously described, the workplace is usually inaccessible, the workers do not perform their regular jobs, and the employer is generally unable to continue with its regular business activities. It is not illegal for workers on strike to seek employment elsewhere, and many do so in order to supplement **strike pay**, which is payment issued by the union to its striking members to partially compensate for the loss of regular employment income.

Collective bargaining may or may not resume while a strike or lockout is in progress. Once the strike or lockout starts to have a noticeable economic impact, one or both of the affected parties may be sufficiently motivated to return to the bargaining table. On the other hand, one party may refuse to return to the bargaining table simply because of the pressure of a strike or lockout, and may instead demand that the strike or lockout end before they will participate in bargaining again.

Two major factors affect how a strike or lockout proceeds once it begins: picketing and the use of replacement workers. We will discuss each of these factors in turn.

Picketing

Picketing is probably the most visible indication of a strike or lockout. Picketing union members walk around the perimeter of the employer's premises on a **picket line**, usually wearing or carrying signs to indicate that a strike or lockout is in progress. Picketers may hand out information pamphlets to passers-by, or engage interested members of the public in discussions about their dispute with the employer.

Picketing serves two major functions. First, it attempts to help the strikers gain the support of the public by physically demonstrating the workers' lack of access to their workplace and publicizing their dispute with the employer. Second, it discourages individuals from attempting to enter the premises. Although the workplace is closed to the union members, management employees may be expected to attend work regardless of the strike or lockout. In addition, suppliers may bring materials to the workplace, and workers who maintain the premises may be expected to provide their usual services. Customers, clients, or service users may also attempt to continue business transactions with the employer. The presence of a picket line is intended to hamper physical access to the entrances and thus discourage these parties from entering the premises.

While picketing itself is a fairly straightforward activity, attempting to regulate it can be quite complex. As discussed in Chapter 1, the Supreme Court of Canada has dealt with cases challenging whether the right to picket is addressed by the provisions in the *Charter of Rights and Freedoms* guaranteeing freedom of association and freedom of expression. The Supreme Court's rulings indicate that the definition of "picketing" and any associated restrictions on picketing activity must be carefully applied so as not to restrict the picketers' freedom of expression. However, the Supreme Court has determined that picketing is not an inherent right under the Charter provisions, and thus reasonable limitations can be placed on picketing activity.[21]

Another consideration in regulating picketing is the need to balance the rights of the various parties involved or affected. A labour relations board must ensure that striking or locked-out workers have the opportunity to promote their cause through picketing; at the same time, other individuals, such as non-union staff or suppliers, should not be unduly constrained from conducting their regular business. Because of the many factors that are specific to each strike or lockout, and the different parties involved or affected in each individual case, labour relations board or court rulings in most picketing cases are fairly situation-specific. However, a few general guidelines can be presented.

Shared Premises

If the employer shares premises with businesses or organizations that are not directly involved with the strike or lockout, the picketers must not interfere with the legitimate business activities of these tenants. For example, the picketers should not picket in front of a doorway that is the primary business entrance for other tenants, and they should picket only the employer's premises in an industrial park and not the common gateway shared by all tenants. A labour relations board may restrict picketing to specific times of day or limit the number of picketers in order to reduce the amount of disruption that a picket line may cause to other tenants' activities.

Secondary Picketing

To interfere with the employer's business, picketers often appear at the "non-struck" premises of suppliers that are doing business with the employer, or other locations of the same business, or other businesses operated by the employer where workers are not on strike. This type of picketing is called **secondary picketing**. The main purpose of secondary picketing is to restrict or curtail the possibility of the employer using a different location to carry out work that would usually be conducted at the struck or locked-out location. Secondary picketing is also intended to hamper the employer's ability to generate revenue by making it difficult for the employer to conduct its usual business with suppliers or in other locations.

Secondary picketing of the employer's other business locations is usually permitted without much dispute. However, for secondary picketing of the employer's suppliers or other business associates to be considered legal, the union usually must prove that the supplier or other business associate is doing business only or primarily with the "struck" employer. Irregular or infrequent transactions (such as a pickup or drop-off once a day) are rarely sufficient to justify legal secondary picketing. Some form of dependency or ongoing regular business relationship with the struck employer must usually be shown for legal secondary picketing to be permitted at the locations of businesses not operated by the employer.

Compliance with the Law

The picketers, their supporters, the employer, and anyone else involved in the strike or lockout must conduct themselves according to the law. Destruction of property, physical violence, and/or intimidation of individuals entering or leaving the employer's premises are not legal, just as they would not be legal in any other setting. If such events occur, the individuals involved could face charges under civil or criminal law, as well as penalties from a labour relations board. However, it is often difficult to determine when picket line behaviour becomes unacceptable, since what is intimidating to one person may not be to another. Representatives of the struck employer, or inconvenienced customers, may complain about behaviour that in other contexts might be considered simply forceful or rude. In such situations, it may be up to the authorities present at the event (if there are any), such as police officers, to determine whether the behaviour should cease and to take appropriate action. Alternatively, a labour relations board may have to assess the evidence of the participants in or witnesses to the event and decide whether permanent intervention is warranted (such as a "cease and desist" order to stop the behaviour from happening again).

Adherence to the Facts

Picket signs and information leaflets distributed by picketers must contain factual statements and must not be libellous. **Libel** is broadly defined as a statement of something untrue that would damage an individual's reputation. For example, it would probably be considered libellous to say that the employer is a liar or is corrupt; if such a statement is made, the employer could sue the union for compensation to repair its damaged reputation or to make up for lost business. To avoid such legal entanglements, picket signs usually contain the simple statement "On Strike" and the name of the union or unions involved. Information leaflets generally describe the bargaining situation as factually as possible: for example, "On [date] the union proposed a wage of $15. On [date] the employer responded by offering a wage of $10. The union considers this offer unacceptable and is now on strike." Information leaflets may contain a request for public support and, possibly, the employer's contact information so that members of the public can contact the employer directly and encourage the employer to address the union's concerns.

Although, as we have mentioned, the purpose of a picket line is to discourage individuals from entering the employer's premises, some union members choose to cross their own union's picket line or the picket line of another striking union. Generally, they do this because they do not agree with the rationale behind the strike. However, most unions consider it a serious offence for a unionized worker to cross a picket line, particularly a picket line maintained by his or her own union. The slang term for a person who crosses a picket line is a **scab**; this term is also used to refer to replacement workers, who will be discussed in the next section. Although replacement workers are usually not union members, they usually must cross picket lines to enter the employer's premises.

Unions consider it a serious offence for a unionized worker to cross a union's picket line, or for a unionized worker to perform work that would ordinarily be done by another worker who is on strike or locked out. Both these actions have the effect of undermining the unity of the striking workers, and a unified front for unions is important in maintaining a strong position at the bargaining table and in gaining public support for the striking or locked-out workers. The action of crossing a picket line could result in the offending individual being penalized by his or her own union; in extreme cases, the individual could be expelled from the union, which, as discussed in Chapter 7, would severely hamper his or her ability to find work at other unionized workplaces.

Two other forms of pressure that can be brought to bear on the employer during a strike are the **boycott** and the **hot declaration**. If a union is on strike and the employer is still able to produce and sell goods, whether directly to the consumer or through secondary sources such as distributors, the union will often contact other unions or labour federations to request a boycott declaration. This declaration encourages other union members not to purchase the employer's products while the strike or lockout is in progress. The intent of the boycott is to further reduce whatever revenue the employer is able to generate during the strike or lockout.

A hot declaration is somewhat more direct in its impact than a boycott. If a union or labour federation issues a hot declaration for a struck company's goods or services, other union members may have the right to refuse to handle those goods or services in the course of their work. For example, if a company whose workers are on strike or locked out attempts to place an advertisement in a newspaper that has unionized production staff, a hot declaration might mean that the production staff will refuse to accept the advertisement, refuse to create the advertisement's layout, or refuse to print the section of the paper with the advertisement in it. The right of union members to honour a hot declaration is usually outlined in a provision in the collective agreement.

The success of a boycott depends on the union's ability to make other union members and the public aware of the strike or lockout and the request not to buy the employer's products. Members of other unions must also be informed about what the employer's products are—a tricky undertaking if the employer sells its goods or services under a variety of brand names. And, of course, the boycott will only be successful if union members or the public actually refuse to purchase the boycotted products. Most labour federations strongly encourage their members to honour boycotts as a means of building unity within the entire labour movement. The websites of most large unions and labour federations list boycotts that are currently in effect.

Usually, a boycott ends when the strike or lockout ends. If an employer has a history of poor labour relations, however, an ongoing boycott may be imposed to discourage individuals from seeking work there. Two examples of ongoing boycotts are the Canadian Association of University Teachers' and the American Association of University Professors' "censure lists." The employers on these lists are universities or colleges that, in the associations' opinion, have violated principles of academic freedom. While members of unions belonging to these associations are not formally forbidden from taking employment with an employer on these lists, they are encouraged to educate themselves on the employer's past actions before they do so. In the words of the American Association of University Professors, "The association leaves it to the discretion of the individual, possessed of the facts, to make the proper decision."[22]

Replacement Workers

As we have seen, the intent of a strike is, through a variety of tactics, to interfere with the employer's ability to continue business. These tactics can include work stoppages or absence from the workplace by the workers that carry out the business's operations.

Thus, one of the more controversial areas in Canadian labour law is whether the employer should be permitted to use or hire **replacement workers**: workers who carry out tasks usually performed by workers who are currently on strike.

The theoretical argument in favour of permitting replacement workers is that the employer's business should not be affected by the decision of the workers to withdraw their labour, and that a prolonged shutdown or reduction in production could cause the business lasting harm. It is also

Striking workers prevent a bus carrying replacement workers from entering Lakeside Packers in Brooks, Alberta, in October 2005.

argued that if workers are not banned from earning money through other sources of employment while on strike, it is unfair to ban the employer from earning money from its business operations while a strike is taking place.

The theoretical argument against permitting replacement workers is that giving the employer the ability to use replacement workers creates a severe imbalance in bargaining power. A withdrawal of labour will have virtually no economic impact on the employer if the employer can easily replace the striking workers and continue operating as usual. Thus, the argument proceeds, the balance of power in bargaining is clearly weighted in the employer's favour if replacement workers are permitted. The ability to replace striking workers removes any economic incentive for the employer to agree to the union's demands. There is also a great potential for conflict and violence on the picket line if replacement workers are regularly confronting picketing union members when entering or leaving the employer's premises. It has also been suggested that, with technological advances in the workplace such as email and Internet access, it is much easier for employers to use replacement workers if the workers do not need to be physically present at the workplace, and thus the need to regulate the use of replacement workers is even greater than before.[23]

Both of these philosophical positions are apparent in the different ways that the use of replacement workers is addressed in labour legislation across Canada. As we can see from Table 9-3, restrictions on the use of replacement workers range from being non-existent in some jurisdictions to being very strict in others. British Columbia and Quebec have the strongest restrictions on the use of replacement workers. Legislation in both of these jurisdictions defines "replacement workers" as not only those brought in to perform work once a strike or lockout begins, but also as any workers hired after collective bargaining begins. This type of legislation attempts to prevent the employer from avoiding the effects of absent workers during a strike or lockout by hiring extra employees prior to a strike or lockout. These extra employees could replace unionized workers who would not be present in the workplace once a strike or lockout started.

The *Canada Labour Code* also restricts the employer's ability to "stack" the workplace with additional workers prior to a strike or lockout. However, the federal code stipulates that workers brought in after collective bargaining begins are only considered replacement workers if they are hired or assigned to do the work of striking or locked-out employees. Manitoba legislation does not allow employers to hire, or threaten to hire, permanent replacement workers before or during a strike or lockout. British Columbia and Ontario forbid the use of **professional strikebreakers**: individuals whose sole source of employment is replacing workers on strike. Usually, these individuals can be supplied through an employment agency that specializes in providing such workers to employers undergoing a strike or lockout. Some of these agencies specialize in providing workers with skills in particular occupations or industries, so the employer can resume production with minimal disruption or lost time for training.

However, most jurisdictions in Canada do not explicitly forbid managers from doing the work of union members during a strike or lockout. As we know, managers are usually excluded from union membership and are usually employed in the workplace on an ongoing basis. Thus, managers who continue to work during a strike or lockout are not generally considered to be replacement workers, even if they do tasks that would usually be done by union members. Some jurisdictions specify that managers can only legally work in a

	TABLE 9-3 Regulations on the Use of Replacement Workers during a Strike or Lockout		
	Who Can Work During a Strike or Lockout	**Other Conditions**	**Returning to Work After a Strike or Lockout**
Federal	Employers or their agents are prohibited from using "for the demonstrated purpose of undermining a trade union's representational capacity, rather than the pursuit of legitimate bargaining objectives" the services of persons not in the bargaining unit on the date notice to bargain was given, and hired or assigned after that date to perform duties of striking or locked-out employees.	Certain activities must be maintained to the extent necessary to prevent an immediate and serious danger to public health or safety. No later than 15 days after the notice to bargain is given, either party may give notice to the other specifying activities that in its opinion must be continued to ensure public health or safety, and the approximate number of employees required to continue those activities. If the parties cannot agree on the designation of activities or number of employees, the board may make a ruling. The board may issue orders to ensure maintenance of activities.	Employees in the bargaining unit who were on strike or locked out have the right to be reinstated in preference to any persons not in the bargaining unit on the date notice to bargain was given and hired or assigned after that date to perform duties of striking or locked-out employees.
Alberta	No specific prohibitions.	No specific prohibitions.	When a strike or lockout ends through a settlement or the cancellation of bargaining rights, or two years after the strike or lockout began, any employee whose employment relationship has not been legally terminated can

TABLE 9-3 Regulations on the Use of Replacement Workers during a Strike or Lockout (Continued)

	Who Can Work During a Strike or Lockout	Other Conditions	Returning to Work After a Strike or Lockout
			apply in writing to return to work, in preference to any employee hired as a replacement worker.
British Columbia	Employers are prohibited from using the paid or unpaid service of anyone transferred, hired, or engaged after notice to bargain was issued; anyone who ordinarily works at another of the employer's operations; or anyone employed, engaged, or supplied to the employer by another person. These individuals cannot be used to perform the work of striking or locked-out workers, or the work ordinarily done by personnel permitted to perform replacement work (i.e., managers or members of the bargaining unit who consent to do such work). An employer must not require anyone at a struck or locked out location to perform any work of a striking or locked-out employee without that person's consent. An employer cannot threaten,	The board chair or either party in bargaining may request an investigation into whether a dispute poses a significant threat to public health, safety, or welfare, or to the provision of educational programs as defined by the *School Act*. The minister, upon receiving the board's report, may direct the board to designate an essential service in the case of a danger of this nature that is immediate and serious.	No specifications.

	Who Can Work During a Strike or Lockout	Other Conditions	Returning to Work After a Strike or Lockout
	refuse to employ, discriminate against, intimidate, coerce, or penalize any worker who refuses to perform any or all of the work of a striking or locked-out employee.		
Manitoba	Prior to or during a work stoppage, employers or their agents cannot hire, offer to hire, or threaten to hire replacement workers for the purpose of performing the work normally performed by employees in the bargaining unit, for any period of time longer than the duration of the work stoppage.	Employers cannot take action against an employee who refuses to perform the work of a striking or locked-out worker Employers cannot take action against an employee covered by a collective agreement who refuses to do work that would directly facilitate the business of another employer whose employees within Canada are on strike or locked out.	The employer must reinstate employees returning from a strike or lockout in the jobs they held prior to the work stoppage. An employer may refuse to reinstate an employee if the employee has engaged in conduct related to the strike or lockout that resulted in a criminal conviction and that would be considered just cause for dismissal.
New Brunswick	No specific prohibitions.	No specifications.	No specifications.
Newfoundland and Labrador	No specific prohibitions.	No specifications.	No specifications.
Nova Scotia	No specific prohibitions.	Employers are prohibited from refusing to employ or discriminating against anyone who has participated in a legal strike. Employers are prohibited from penalizing an	No specifications.

TABLE 9-3 Regulations on the Use of Replacement Workers during a Strike or Lockout (Continued)

TABLE 9-3 Regulations on the Use of Replacement Workers during a Strike or Lockout (Continued)

	Who Can Work During a Strike or Lockout	Other Conditions	Returning to Work After a Strike or Lockout
		employee who refuses to perform the work of another employee participating in a legal strike.	
Ontario	No specific prohibitions.	Employers are not permitted to employ professional strike-breakers, and no one is permitted to act as one.	Within six months of the start of a legal strike, an employee can apply to the employer to return to work. The employer is then obliged to reinstate the employee unless the work formerly done by the employee no longer exists.
Prince Edward Island	No specific prohibitions, although the employment of replacement workers is considered temporary and is terminated at the end of a strike or lockout.	No specifications.	When a legal strike or lockout ends, affected employees are to be reinstated unless operations have been discontinued or suspended or if a decline in the employer's business as a result of the work stoppage has caused work to be eliminated. If operations resume, or if eliminated work is resumed, the striking or locked-out employees must be reinstated first.
Quebec	Employers are prohibited from using replacement employees, defined as:	Employers are prohibited from using the services of striking or locked-out employees in any of their other establishments.	At the end of a strike or lockout, any affected employee is entitled to return to his/her employment in priority over any

	Who Can Work During a Strike or Lockout	**Other Conditions**	**Returning to Work After a Strike or Lockout**
	- those hired between the start of negotiations and the end of a strike/lockout - employees of other employers or sub-contractors - members of the bargaining unit involved, unless the work is a designated essential service - persons employed in the employer's other establishments - managers employed by the employer in other establishments - employees who do not belong to the bargaining unit on strike or locked out	The government, on the recommendation of the minister, may require essential services to be maintained. This order may be issued any time prior to the filing of a completed collective agreement.	other person, unless the employer can produce a "good and sufficient reason" for not recalling the employee.
Saskatchewan	No specific prohibitions.	No specifications.	At the conclusion of a strike or lockout, if the parties have not reached an agreement on reinstatement, the employer must reinstate employees to their original positions. An employee who is not reinstated due to lack of work is entitled to layoff notice or pay in lieu of notice. Striking or locked-out employees are entitled to displace any persons hired to perform their work during a work stoppage.

TABLE 9-3 Regulations on the Use of Replacement Workers during a Strike or Lockout (Continued)

struck or locked-out location if they were managers at that location prior to the commencement of the strike or lockout. This provision prevents employers from stacking the workplace with managers in the event of a strike or lockout; the intent of this is the same as the restrictions on the hiring non-managerial employees prior to a strike or lockout.

We should note that in the jurisdictions that restrict the use of replacement workers, there are provisions for the maintenance of essential services, as mentioned above. Replacement workers might be needed to keep essential services functioning during a strike or lockout. Thus, the legislation in these jurisdictions usually makes some distinction between work that takes place during a strike or lockout to generate revenue for the employer and work that contributes to maintaining essential services.

Jurisdictions that allow the use of replacement workers during a strike or lockout generally specify in their legislation what will happen to replacement workers when the strike or lockout ends. Without such legislation, it would be unclear whether the replacement worker or the worker on strike has the right to the job when regular work resumes. Most jurisdictions indicate that the worker on strike must be given priority over a replacement worker for the job when the strike ends, or that the striking worker must be reinstated in his or her previous position after the strike or lockout ends. Alberta and Ontario both allow striking workers to apply to the employer for reinstatement and to return to work after a strike has continued for a certain length of time. These provisions are intended to allow workers who so choose to resume their regular jobs and not suffer the financial consequences of a lengthy strike. We should, however, note that unions on strike do not encourage their members to exercise this option. The return of union members to their jobs while the strike is still in progress would considerably weaken the united support behind the strike, and increase the employer's ability to withstand the impact of the union's strike action.

Having outlined some of the events and conditions that happen while a strike or lockout is in progress, we will now describe why and how a strike or lockout ends.

ENDING A STRIKE OR LOCKOUT

A strike or lockout ends in one of two ways: (1) the bargaining parties reach a collective agreement, or (2) one party chooses to cease its actions and, usually, return to bargaining. The length of time it takes to reach either of these forms of resolution depends on a number of factors, the most important being the ability of the parties involved to endure the economic impact of a strike or lockout.

As mentioned, unions are usually able to replace at least some of their members' lost wages with strike pay during a strike or lockout. The funding for strike pay comes from the union's own financial resources. Many unions have funds banked specifically for this purpose, set aside from the regular revenues generated by union dues. The union's ability to provide strike pay is clearly an important determinant of how long a strike lasts. If the strike is longer than the union has budgeted for, union members may be dissatisfied with reduced or non-existent strike pay. If the union is a local of a larger national or international union, the parent union may provide additional funds for strike pay, allowing the union to prolong the strike action beyond what it could afford on its own. However, strike pay is rarely at the same levels as the pay that workers regularly earn, and poorer unions may not be able to offer any strike pay at all. Therefore, the individual financial situations of the members and the amount of financial support the union is able to offer can strongly influence a strike's duration.

If the local unemployment rate is low and union members are easily able to find alternative work during a strike, the strike may be longer than it would otherwise be. The loss of income for individual members might not be as dramatic as it would be with a shorter strike, since striking union members can make money working at other jobs while the strike is in progress. However, the relevance of this factor is somewhat dependent on the individual union members and the type of alternative work available. If, for example, union members are older clerical workers and the only type of short-term employment available involves hard physical labour, the availability of alternative employment is not as relevant, as the striking workers may not want to, or cannot, take the jobs that are available.

The employer's ability to endure the economic pain of a strike or lockout is also affected by a variety of factors. The employer, like the union, may have funding set aside to offset the impact of a shutdown, perhaps in a contingency fund established for exactly this purpose. The employer may also have sufficient inventory on hand or enough alternative sources of income to allow it to continue production or operations. And though a business may suffer loss of income from reduced sales during a shutdown, it also saves money by not having to pay many of its normal operating expenses, including wages and benefits, which are a significant portion of most employers' budgets. And, like the local union, if the employer is a branch or subsidiary of a larger company, there may be funds available from the parent organization to offset losses from a work shutdown. The employer's ability to hire replacement workers also affects its ability to withstand a strike. A study of Canadian strike data from 1966 to 1985 indicated that strikes were significantly longer in jurisdictions that banned the use of replacement workers. This finding suggests that an employer that can use replacement workers has a much greater ability to compel the union to settle a collective agreement quickly.[24]

Public attention to the strike may also influence its length. An American study identified the amount of media attention a strike receives as another factor affecting the length of a strike.[25] Although this study analyzed only 90 American strikes, each involving more than 10,000 workers, the results indicated that pre-strike media attention significantly increased strike duration. The author of the study speculates that such attention causes the negotiators to increase their commitment to their publicized bargaining positions and thus become less willing to make compromises. The parties can also use media attention to increase their own power in bargaining and to generate public sympathy for their cause; such efforts can be expected to intensify conflict at the bargaining table. The results of a recent Canadian study examining the effects of public support for strikes indicates that strikes may not do much to generate general public support for the union; support for striking workers tends to be stronger among those who already have positive attitudes toward unions. However, even those who have more negative attitudes toward unions may be willing to support the strike if they believe that the employer is making unfair contract offers to the strikers.[26]

When a strike or lockout ends because the negotiating teams have settled on a collective agreement, the union members must vote on whether to accept the terms of the proposed collective agreement. This vote is known as a **ratification vote**, as described in Chapter 8. If the majority of bargaining unit members vote to accept the terms that have been negotiated, the terms are incorporated into a collective agreement that is signed by union and management representatives. Once the collective agreement has been signed, the strike formally ends.

The union and the employer will usually also agree on conditions governing the employees' return to work. For example, it is common to set a deadline by which employees must report to work, allowing employees who have undertaken other commitments during the strike (such as jobs elsewhere) to finish those commitments. Other issues that might need to be negotiated at the end of a strike include how to deal with disputes related to incidents on the picket line (e.g., how or whether the employer will discipline employees involved in unlawful or disruptive activities).

If the ratification vote fails, the negotiated terms of the agreement are reopened at the bargaining table, and the union negotiating team must continue negotiating for an agreement more acceptable to the union membership. As Chapter 8 describes, members of the management negotiating team will also ensure that the terms of the agreement are acceptable to the stakeholders they represent; if the stakeholders are not satisfied with the agreed-upon terms, the team will have to return to the table and reopen negotiations.

We should note, however, that the effects of a strike or lockout may last far beyond its formal ending. Since strikes and lockouts are clearly hostile events that generate strong emotional reactions, the resentments and conflicts fuelled by a strike or lockout may, directly or indirectly, cause further conflict after the parties return to work. The attitudes toward the "other side" created by a strike or lockout, particularly a lengthy one, may influence how union members and management treat each other on a daily basis in the workplace. Residual hostility between union and management can also have a negative effect on future interactions, such as grievance resolution or bargaining for subsequent collective agreements. There may even be reduced levels of commitment to the union from the union's own members, if the members are upset about the strike itself or about the outcome, which may have a negative effect on future support for the union or participation in union activities.[26]

Having outlined the process of strikes and lockouts, we will now attempt to put those processes in context by discussing some data that attempt to measure the impact of strikes in Canada.

PUTTING CANADA'S STRIKE RECORD IN CONTEXT

To attempt to understand the impact that strikes have in Canada, we will examine two kinds of data relating to Canadian strike activity. The first is data that relate to Canada's strike record over several decades. The second is data that compare Canada's strike record to that of other industrialized countries.

Measuring the impact of strikes is a challenging task because of the many different measures that can be used, and the difficulty of accurately capturing some data. Counting the frequency or duration of strikes is relatively straightforward, since it is easy to maintain actual records of strikes and their length. However, these measures in isolation do not always fully reflect a strike's impact. The average length of strikes in a certain period may be skewed upward by a few very long strikes, and a simple count of how many strikes occur during a given period will not reflect such important information as the number of workers involved and the length of time they were affected. Other potential measures, such as financial impact, are also difficult to estimate accurately. Determining the value of lost sales or production during a strike or lockout is not easy because it is not always apparent what sales or production levels would have been if the strike or lockout had not occurred. It is also difficult to assign a dollar value to potentially affected intangibles such as customer goodwill and relationships with suppliers.

The measure of strike and lockout activity that has been used most often in Canadian strike records is **lost person-days**: that is, the number of days of labour that were lost in a year because of industrial disputes. Lost person-days in a given year are calculated by multiplying the number of disputes by the total duration of the disputes (in days) and by the total number of workers who were involved in all the strikes or lockouts. In order to put the number of lost person-days into context, it is useful to compare the number of lost person-days to the total number of person-days worked during the same period. Table 9-4 presents this data for the past few decades in Canada.

In assessing the data in Table 9-4, we must keep several historical facts in mind. Unionization levels in Canada have increased steadily since strike and lockout data have been collected, so increases in strike and lockout levels will in part reflect the increase in the number of unionized workers. The size of the Canadian workforce has also increased, so the greater number of workers involved in industrial disputes may in part reflect this growth in the workforce. However, there are increasingly more unionized Canadian workers in the public sector than in the private sector, and as we know there may be bans or restrictions on strike activity in the public sector; therefore, the amount of strike activity may be contained or reduced by these restrictions.

Furthermore, some of the figures relating to lost person-days in Table 9-4 have been inflated because of unusually long disputes or short disputes involving unusually large numbers of workers. For example, in 1976, there was a one-day, Canada-wide strike (the "Day of Protest") against the federal government's wage and price controls. In 1981, there was a lengthy strike involving Canada Post, a large national employer. Clearly, these strikes contributed significantly to the amount of strike activity in those

TABLE 9-4 Work Stoppages in Canada, 1976-2009

Year	Total Stoppages during Year[i]	Number of Workers Involved (in thousands)	Lost (in thousands) Person-Days	% of Estimated Working Time[ii]
1976	1,040	1,584	11,544	.53
1977	806	217	3,320	.15
1978	1,057	400	7,357	.32
1979	1,049	462	7,819	.33
1980	1,028	439	9,129	.37
1981	1,049	341	8,850	.35
1982	679	464	5,702	.23
1983	645	329	4,440	.18
1984	716	186	3,883	.15
1985	829	162	3,125	.12
1986	748	484	7,151	.27
1987	668	581	3,810	.14
1988	548	206	4,901	.17
1989	627	444	3,701	.13
1990	579	270	5,079	.17
1991	463	253	2,516	.09
1992	404	149	2,110	.07
1993	381	101	1,516	.05
1994	374	80	1,606	.06

TABLE 9-4   Work Stoppages in Canada, 1976-2009 (Continued)

Year	Total Stoppages during Year[i]	Number of Workers Involved (in thousands)	Lost (in thousands) Person-Days	% of Estimated Working Time[ii]
1995	328	149	1,583	.05
1996	330	281	3,351	.11
1997	284	257	3,610	.12
1998	381	244	2,443	.08
1999	413	158	2,445	.08
2000	379	144	1,657	.05
2001	381	221	2,199	.07
2002	294	168	3,033	.09
2003	266	80	1,736	.05
2004	297	259	3,185	.09
2005	157	67	2,178	.01
2006	151	42	792	.02
2007	206	65	1,770	.05
2008	188	41	875	.02
2009	157	67	2,178	.01

[i] Includes work stoppages in progress at the start of the year and strikes that began during the year.

[ii] Lost person-days divided by the estimated total person-days worked during the year.

Source: Human Resources and Skills Development Canada, Labour Program, Strategic Policy, Analysis and Workplace Information Directorate (available at <www.hrsdc.gc.ca>); Statistics Canada, "Fact Sheet on Unionization," *Perspectives on Labour and Income*, August 2005.

two years, but the overall figure of lost person-days probably does not reflect the impact of the average strike or lockout during those periods. We should also note that analyses of data from individual strikes indicate that the average length of strikes in Canada has increased notably from 1990 onward, to more than 40 working days. Canadian strikes also tend to occur during renegotiations of existing contracts, not negotiations of first collective agreements, and tend to be settled more quickly if the strike involves more than 50 workers.[27]

"Gosh, everyone seems to be out celebrating Labour Day..."

Despite these considerations, we can see that strikes and lockouts in Canada have hardly ever represented a significant loss of working time. The rate in any single year has never exceeded six-tenths of one percent.

Given this information, however, it is also worth remembering that Canada has traditionally been considered more strike-prone than other industrialized nations.[28] To see whether this reputation is justified, we can compare recent industrial dispute rates in Canada with those in other North American countries and other industrialized nations. Table 9-5 shows some comparative data, but before assessing these, we should be aware that, as the table footnotes indicate, different countries have different criteria for defining strikes and collecting strike data. Many countries rely on voluntary, rather than mandatory, reporting of industrial disputes to a national or local government agency.[29] Also, some countries include in their count of lost person-days workers who are not themselves on strike but who cannot work because, for example, the supplier of their raw materials is involved in a work stoppage. This makes it difficult to meaningfully compare the impact of work stoppages in different countries. We should also keep in mind that the labour legislation governing strikes may differ from jurisdiction to jurisdiction, so that the conditions under which strikes can occur may also not be comparable.

TABLE 9-5 Canadian Work Stoppage Activity in Comparison with Other Countries

	Canada[i]	United States[ii]	Japan[iii]	United Kingdom[iv]	Spain	Denmark	Australia[v]	Mexico[vi]
1998								
Number of strikes and lockouts	379	34	145	166	632	1,258	520	33
Workers involved (thousands)	244.4	386.6	26.3	92.7	680.6	502.3	348.4	10.8
Workdays not worked (thousands)	2,441	5,115.7	101.5	282.4	1,280.9	3,173.0	526.3	89.4
1999								
Number of strikes and lockouts	413	17	154	205	749	1,079	731	32
Workers involved (thousands)	159.6	72.6	25.7	140.9	1,132.7	75.2	461.1	50.2
Workdays not worked (thousands)	2,440.6	1,995.8	87.1	241.8	1,504.6	91.8	650.6	65.7
2000								
Number of strikes and lockouts	378	39	118	226	750	1,081	700	26
Workers involved (thousands)	142.6	393.7	15.3	183.2	2,067.3	75.7	325.4	60.0
Workdays not worked (thousands)	1,1644.1	2,419.4	35.1	498.8	3,616.9	124.8	469.1	847.2
2001								
Number of strikes and lockouts	381	29	90	207	737	832	675	35
Workers involved (thousands)	221.3	99.1	12.2	179.9	1,244.6	49.5	225.7	23.2
Workdays not worked (thousands)	2,202.5	1,151.3	29.1	525.1	1,923.8	56	393.1	246.2
2002								
Number of strikes and lockouts	294	19	74	162	688	1,349	767	45

TABLE 9-5 Canadian Work Stoppage Activity in Comparison with Other Countries (Continued)

	Canada[i]	United States[ii]	Japan[iii]	United Kingdom[iv]	Spain	Denmark	Australia[v]	Mexico[vi]
Workers involved (thousands)	165.6	45.9	7.0	942.9	4,534.3	110.9	159.7	22.6
Workdays not worked (thousands)	2,985.9	659.6	12.3	1,323.3	4,945.1	193.6	259.0	371.3
2003								
Number of strikes and lockouts	266	14	47	138	678	681	643	44
Workers involved (thousands)	78.8	129.2	4.5	150.6	729.0	44.4	275.6	11.8
Workdays not worked (thousands)	17,303.4	4,077.4	6.7	499.1	792.1	55.1	439.4	107.6
2004								
Number of strikes and lockouts	297	17	51	135	708	804	692	38
Workers involved (thousands)	259.2	173.3	7.0	292.7	555.9	75.7	194.0	24.6
Workdays not worked (thousands)	3185.2	1,017.2	9.8	904.9	4,472.6	76.4	379.8	178.8
2005								
Number of strikes and lockouts	260	22	50	116	685	534	472	50
Workers involved (thousands)	199.0	99.7	4.1	92.6	404.8	32.8	241.0	12.2
Workdays not worked (thousands)	4,147.6	1,348.0	5.6	223.8	951.5	51.1	228.3	222.4
2006								
Number of strikes and lockouts	151	23	46	158	783	476	202	55
Workers involved (thousands)	42.3	76.6	5.8	713.3	499.6	79.1	122.7	59.8

TABLE 9-5 Canadian Work Stoppage Activity in Comparison with Other Countries (Continued)

	Canada[i]	United States[ii]	Japan[iii]	United Kingdom[iv]	Spain	Denmark	Australia[v]	Mexico[vi]
Workdays not worked (thousands)	7,929.2	2,687.5	7.9	754.5	927.7	85.9	132.6	661.4
2007								
Number of strikes and lockouts	206	23	54	152	752	862	135	28
Workers involved (thousands)	65.5	192.9	20.8	744.8	497.0	61.1	36.0	10.6
Workdays not worked (thousands)	1,770.7	1,264.8	33.2	1,041.1	1,187.6	91.7	49.7	200.9
2008								
Number of strikes and lockouts	187	16	52	144	811	335	177	21
Workers involved (thousands)	41.3	82.7	8.3	511.2	543.0	91.4	172.9	13.2
Workdays not worked (thousands)	875.6	1,954.1	11.2	758.9	1,510.2	1869.1	196.5	286.4
2009								
Number of strikes and lockouts	155	5	n/a	n/a	1,001	207	236	19
Workers involved (thousands)	67.1	12.5	n/a	n/a	653.5	12.7	89.3	24.5
Workdays not worked (thousands)	2,170.3	124.1	n/a	n/a	1,290.9	15.0	132.7	274.1

n/a = data not available

[i] Only includes work stoppages involving more than 10 lost workdays and lasting more than half a day.
[ii] Excludes work stoppages involving fewer than 1,000 workers and lasting less than a full day or shift.
[iii] Excludes work stoppages lasting less than half a day.
[iv] Includes work stoppages lasting less than one day and including fewer than 10 workers only if more than 100 were workdays not worked.
[v] Excludes work stoppages involving fewer than 10 workdays.
[vi] Strikes only. Excludes enterprises covered by local jurisdiction. Only union members are included in "workers involved."
Source: International Labour Organization (ILO Department of Statistics, http://laborsta.ilo.org/)

We can see that even with these problems in making direct comparisons, Canada does not seem to have an excessively high number of strikes or lockouts in comparison to other countries. It does, however, tend to have a comparatively high rate of workdays not worked because of strikes or lockouts, even though the numbers of workers involved are not large in comparison to other countries. As previously noted, while Canada has fewer strikes or lockouts than other industrialized nations, Canadian strikes or lockouts tend to be longer than those in other countries, which accounts for the relatively high number of lost workdays.

SUMMARY

The strike or lockout is used by one party as a tactic in bargaining to pressure the other party into conceding to its bargaining demands. This is achieved through closing down the employer's operations or withdrawing the labour of union members so that revenue cannot be generated or wages cannot be earned. A strike or lockout is intended to cause enough economic pain to the other party to convince it that settling a collective agreement is preferable to bearing the cost of a continued workplace shutdown.

Labour legislation establishes several preconditions that must be met for a strike or lockout to be legal. A legal strike or lockout can occur only once a collective agreement has expired and bargaining is in progress. A strike vote must be taken among union members to ensure that there is majority support for strike action. In some Canadian jurisdictions, the party intending to commence a strike or lockout must give notice to the other party. As well, in some Canadian jurisdictions, a third party must be brought in to assist the parties in reaching an agreement before a strike or lockout can commence.

Once a strike or lockout occurs, legislation that governs the ability of the union to picket and of the employer to use replacement workers comes into effect. Picketers must not interfere with the activities of other tenants that share premises with the employer, and they can only engage in picketing at other, non-struck locations under certain circumstances. Picketers and other individuals involved in a strike or lockout must not commit illegal acts on the picket lines. The legislation governing the use of replacement workers varies across Canada; replacement workers are permitted in some jurisdictions but not in others, and the definition of who qualifies as a replacement worker also varies.

The length of a strike or lockout is dependent on the ability of the parties to withstand the economic pain inflicted. This ability may be affected by a number of specific and general factors, such as the financial resources available to the parties and the unemployment rate in the area where the strike or lockout occurs. A strike or lockout usually concludes when the parties return to bargaining or when a collective agreement is reached.

Finally, data on Canadian work stoppages indicate that strikes and lockouts in Canada cause a relatively small amount of lost work time each year, in comparison to the total amount of days worked. In comparison to other industrialized countries, Canada does not have excessive rates of strikes and lockouts, but strikes and lockouts tend to be longer than in other countries.

KEY TERMS FOR CHAPTER 9

back-to-work legislation (p. 370)
boycott (p. 375
essential services (p. 370)
hot declaration (p. 375)
industrial action (p. 354)
industrial conflict (p. 354)
libel (p. 374)
lockout (p. 354)
lost person-days (p. 388)
picket line (p. 372)
professional strikebreakers (p. 378)
ratification vote (p. 386)
recognition strike (p. 354)
replacement workers (p. 377)
rotating strikes (p. 355)
scab (p. 375)
secondary picketing (p. 373)
strike (p. 354)
strike mandate (p. 368)

strike pay (p. 372)
strike vote (p. 368)
wildcat strike (p. 364)
work-to-rule campaigns (p. 355)

DISCUSSION QUESTIONS FOR CHAPTER 9

1. Why would a union choose to engage in a work-to-rule campaign or a rotating strike rather than a full-scale strike?
2. Identify some of the individual and situational factors that might determine whether a strike or lockout happens or not.
3. Different provinces have different rules on whose votes will count when a strike vote is taken. What effects might these differences have on the outcome of a strike vote?
4. Explain why a union would take a strike vote when it had no immediate intention of actually going on strike.
5. Why might advance notice be required before a strike or lockout begins?
6. Labour codes have general rules that regulate picketing. Explain why labour boards often have to make situation-specific rulings on picketing activity.
7. Outline the arguments for and against the use of replacement workers.
8. Does Canada deserve its reputation as a strike-prone country? Discuss.

CASE *9-1*

PAVEMORE ROAD SERVICES AND PUBLIC EMPLOYEES UNION

(Based on *Mainroad and BCGEU*, 2007)

In this case, a union wants to picket work sites where work is being done by a company that has a contract with the employer. The employer has applied to the board for a declaration that the planned picketing is illegal.

Case Facts

Pavemore is a company that provides road maintenance services. It has a contract with the local government to provide routine maintenance to roads in the area, and to provide planned non-routine services throughout the year. At the start of each fiscal year, the company provides the government with a plan for routine and non-routine maintenance throughout the coming year; the government then approves and finances the plan. However, the plan can be modified as needed during the year. The plan also includes the schedule and specifications for carrying out the routine and non-routine maintenance, along with performance time frames for completion of the work.

The union that represents Pavemore's workers is currently on strike. The board has previously declared some roads that Pavemore maintains to be essential services. Under the essential services order, some bargaining unit members have been scheduled to carry out maintenance work on the roads, or they can be called in to work if management staff cannot perform the maintenance tasks. The essential service order specifies that maintenance levels and work hours will be approximately half of what is provided during regular operations.

Prior to the strike, Pavemore had contracted with another company, Happy Trails, to provide paving services on some of the roads it normally maintains. The union and Pavemore had encountered some previous disputes involving the use of subcontractors during job action, so they had agreed that Pavemore would inform the union when it planned to use subcontractors, and the union would inform Pavemore when it planned to picket sites where the subcontractor's employees were working. These notices have been exchanged, and Pavemore is now challenging the union's intent to picket Happy Trails' operations.

The work that Happy Trails has been subcontracted to provide is work that bargaining unit members do not usually perform. It involves patching stretches of road that are longer than those usually patched by bargaining unit members. The bargaining unit members would not usually be working on the roads at the same time as Happy Trails employees would be, because that would cause too much congestion on the roads. If Happy Trails employees were working on a road, the Pavemore employees would be scheduled to do maintenance work elsewhere in the area.

Pavemore's annual service plan, as filed at the start of the fiscal year, does not have any work scheduled on the roads for the time when Happy Trails employees will be working there. It is possible that some routine maintenance work might take place on the roads during that time, but that work is a very small percentage of the work performed in the entire service area during the year.

The annual service plan contains a specification for regular patrolling of all the roads in the service area. Thus, Pavemore may carry out service patrols while the Happy Trails employees are at work.

Pavemore maintains two marshalling yards in the service area, where equipment is kept and where employees report at the start of their shift to receive their work directions. Usually an employee spends around five minutes at the marshalling yard and then is on the roads in the service area for the rest of their shift. The marshalling yards have been designated as essential services facilities under the essential services order.

The Employer's Position

The employer argues that the sites where the Happy Trails employees are working are not sites or places of work for Pavemore employees. It asks that the board restrict picketing to the marshalling yards.

The employer argues that the possibility that bargaining unit members might drive on a road or might do work at a location does not make that location a place where the union can picket. It also argues that any work that Pavemore employees might do at a site where Happy Trails employees might also work is not a substantial or significant part of Pavemore's work. The employer admits that routine maintenance work might occur where the Happy Trails employees are working, but it also says that maintenance work might never be done at that location depending on the circumstances.

The employer also points out that the sites where the union is planning to picket are public highways.

The Union's Position

The union argues that every road in the service area is a place where bargaining unit members perform work, and that if work is being performed in a location under an essential services order, the location is clearly a place where bargaining unit members work. The union points out that the employer did not ask for an exemption under the essential services order to exclude the roads where the Happy Trails employees are working.

The union admits that its members may only do a small amount of work at the places where the Happy Trails employees are working. However, it also argues that the work at these sites is an integral part of the employer's operations because the employer is a road maintenance contractor with performance responsibilities under its service plan.

The union states that its pickets will be at the side of the road with signs and that it has no intention of impeding or obstructing traffic. It points out that the roadside is a public space, and that it is also an appropriate site for picketing because it is where the public sees its members working throughout the year.

CASE *9-2*

CIVIC LIBRARY BOARD AND LIBRARY WORKERS UNION

(Based on *Greater Victoria Public Library Board and CUPE*, 2008)

In this case, the union has been carrying out job action (as part of a legal strike) for a year. The union is asking the board to declare that the employer has committed an unfair labour practice by threatening to discipline employees for participating in a "food for fines" campaign that the union has initiated as part of its job action. The employer is asking the board to order the union to cease its campaign and to reimburse the employer for its financial losses as a result of the campaign.

Case Facts

The library operates a central library and eight branch libraries. Each branch has a "branch clerk" who is the circulation supervisor. The "branch clerk" is part of the bargaining unit, and there is no other regular management presence in the branches. The branch clerks meet every two months to discuss policy and operational issues. Holly Powell, the circulation supervisor at the central branch, chairs the branch clerks' meetings and is responsible for communicating policy to staff and for implementing policy. The library has a written circulation manual that includes policy.

The union and the employer started bargaining for a new collective agreement two years ago. The union served strike notice a year ago and has been engaged in job action since then. The union members have not completely withdrawn their labour, but have instead undertaken such tactics as selective closures, stopping some library programs, and closing public Internet access.

The library fines customers who return items late or who do not return them at all. Customers are encouraged to pay fines less than $10, but there are no penalties if they do not. If a customer's total fines are more than $10, their borrowing privileges may be suspended until they pay the amount owing over $10. The library's written policy allows staff to waive fines in certain circumstances such as illness, bad weather, accident, or family bereavement. The reasons on this list are not the only reasons for which exemptions can be granted, and fines may also be waived on approval of the senior clerk or the librarian.

The board encourages the public to use the library and to expand that use wherever possible, and this policy has led to fines being waived in the past. Powell told the board that two years ago the provincial government launched a program to increase library membership and use among middle school and high school students, and as part of that program librarians went to schools and helped students fill out applications for library cards. However, when Powell processed the applications, she found that many of the applicants had outstanding fines on old accounts. She thought it would be appropriate to waive the fines, but because the amounts involved totalled hundreds of dollars, she asked Dan Foley, the library's director, to approve a waiver of the fines, which he did.

Powell also told the board that if a customer owed more than $10 in fines and could not pay the full amount immediately, she would arrange a payment schedule and place a note on the customer's file saying that as long as payments were being made regularly the customer could continue borrowing items from the library.

While the union and the employer were still in bargaining, the union announced that its members would no longer collect any fines, including fines for lost materials and the administrative costs that were assessed when an overdue fine was referred to a collection agency. Customers who wanted to pay fines were referred to management staff.

Two months ago, the union issued a press release and posted notices in the branches and on its website saying that union members would forgive any fines over $10 if customers brought an item for the local food bank. In past years, the library had collected items for the food bank at the end of the year, but had not waived fines in exchange for donations.

Foley saw the press release and sent an e-mail to Patrick O'Leary, the union president, advising him that the union and its members did not have the authority to waive fines, and that members doing so would be subject to discipline. Foley told the board that he was concerned about customers being confused if the "food for fines" campaign ended, and that the annual donations to the food bank would decline as a result. Therefore, Foley said, the library management decided to "adopt the initiative as its own." Management posted a notice in branches that announced that fines over $10 would be reduced to "under $10" if a donation was made to the food bank, and that "management staff assume all responsibility for waiving of fines." The notice also gave the contact information for the library's public services manager. That same day, the public services manager sent an e-mail to all staff asking them to refer all fine payments or questions directly to her, and reiterating that "management staff will continue to assume all responsibility for waiving of fines for the duration of the strike actions."

The union invited the local media to the start of the "food for fines" campaign. At this event Foley saw O'Leary and a bargaining unit member waive fines. He met with them the next day and informed them that only management had the authority to waive fines during the strike. However, neither was disciplined.

During the following month, management did not monitor how or when fines were being waived. Foley told the board that there was no management presence outside the central library to keep such records, and that, at the same time, the library's manager of information technology had retired, and no one else knew how to run the computer reports that monitored fine activity.

At the start of the next month, the union posted notices in the branches stating that fines would be waived to zero for any customer bringing in a food bank donation. Ten days after the notices were posted, Foley wrote to O'Leary saying that the union and its members were being put "on notice" that they did not have the authority to waive fines, and that if any union member waived fines, the library would take immediate steps to discipline them. On the same day, Foley sent an email to all staff members stating that express consent of a managerial employee was needed to waive fines, and that disciplinary action would be taken if any union members waived fines without this consent.

By this time, the library had hired a new manager of information technology, and Foley asked him to run a report to determine to what extent fines were being waived. The resulting report showed that over $37,000 in fines had been waived in the previous 18 days, and that fines were being waived at all library branches. However, it was not possible to determine from the report who had waived the fines.

Foley decided to schedule "exploratory meetings" with each of the branch clerks. Powell was the first to be scheduled for one of these meetings. Foley told the board that this was because she was on site at the branch where he worked—the central library—and because the central library was the largest branch and the location where the largest amount of fines had been waived.

Powell told the board that she was aware of management's position on the fine waiver issue, but said that she interpreted management's communications as resentment against the union's "food for fines" initiative. She also said she did not think that the communications changed the policy that was described in the circulation manual, although she did admit that management had the right to determine when fines should be waived, and that management had stated during the previous months that only management had the right to waive fines.

Powell also told the board that the union informed its members that they could not be disciplined for waiving fines because this was action by the union, not by individual members.

Powell and Foley met two weeks after the union issued its most recent notice. Foley told Powell that she was directed not to waive any fines and that she was to supervise her work area in such a way that her subordinates would not waive any fines. Later that same day, Foley and Powell met again. Foley again told Powell not to waive any fines, and warned that she would be disciplined if she continued to do so. Powell's staff continued to waive fines that day, and later that same day Foley gave Powell a written warning that she and her staff were not to waive fines and that any further contravention would result in a suspension.

On the same day, Foley met with three other branch clerks, and similar warnings were issued in those meetings.

The day after Foley and Powell's meetings, the union wrote to Foley requesting that the employer immediately cease threatening its members for engaging in legitimate strike action. The employer did not do so; that same day, it suspended Powell for one day because fines continued to be waived at the central library and because she "refused to answer legitimate workplace questions." The "question" to Powell was whether she was waiving fines herself.

As a result of Powell's suspension, there was a full-scale walkout by union members, and Foley's scheduled meetings with the other branch clerks were cancelled. When Powell returned to work after her suspension, Foley met with her because fines continued to be waived at the central library. In that meeting, Powell acknowledged that she was waiving fines and was doing so on the instructions of the union. Foley suspended her for two days after this meeting, and the union filed its unfair labour practice complaint.

The Union's Position

The union states that its members, in waiving fines, are exercising their lawful right to refuse to work, and that their actions fall within the legal definition of a strike. The union argues that the employer's actions are motivated at least in part by anti-union animus, and that Powell was being singled out because she was one of two union members to sign a group grievance involving pay equity. This grievance has not yet been resolved.

The union points out that of the three branch clerks that met with Foley on the same day that Foley met with Powell, one is a shop steward and one is a member of the union's bargaining committee. The union states that these employees being "singled out" for meetings with Foley is further evidence of the employer's anti-union animus.

The Employer's Position

The employer states that management had the right to set workplace policy before the job action began, and continued to have that right during the job action. The employer states that it issued clear directions to its employees regarding the waiver of fines, which it was entitled to do.

The employer agrees that a strike includes the right to refuse work or to refuse to continue to work, but argues that legitimate strike action does not include "affirmative steps" such as those that had to be taken to waive fines. The employer points out that for a library worker to waive a customer's fines, it is necessary to get access to the customer's records, to select "waive fine" as the desired activity, and to confirm that action before it is carried out. This is the only way to delete amounts owing from a customer file, and once this action has been completed, the library has no way to recover the debt previously recorded.

The employer argues that it used progressive discipline, starting with a written notice and then proceeding to a verbal warning, a written warning, and then suspension. The employer argues that it had just cause to use this procedure.

The employer denies that it has anti-union animus and says that all branch clerks were scheduled to be interviewed. The employer claims that it was logistics such as geographic proximity and the amount of fines waived that determined the order of interviews with the branch clerks. It states that the only reason that all branch clerks were not interviewed was because of the full-scale walkout.

References

[1] Yates, C.A.B. (2009). In defence of the right to strike. *University of New Brunswick Law Journal*. Available at <http://findarticles.com/p/articles/mi_7000/is_59/ai_n35619196/>.

[2] Snyder, R. (1995). *The Annotated Canada Labour Code*. Scarborough, ON: Carswell.

[3] Godard, J. (1994). *Industrial Relations, the Economy and Society*. Toronto: McGraw-Hill Ryerson.

[4] Godard, *op. cit.*

[5] Godard, *op. cit.*

[6] Martin, J.E., & Sinclair, R.R. (2001). A multiple motive perspective on strike propensities. *Journal of Organizational Behavior, 22*(4), 387–407.

[7] Card, D. (1990). Strikes and bargaining: a survey of the recent empirical literature. *American Economic Review, Papers and Proceedings*, May 1990, 410–415.

[8] Hebdon, R., Hyatt, D., & Mazerolle, M. (1999). Implications of small bargaining units and enterprise unions on bargaining disputes. *Relations Industrielles/Industrial Relations, 54*(3), 503–525.

[9] Campolieti, M., Hebdon, R., & Hyatt, D. (2005). Strike incidence and strike duration: some new evidence from Ontario. *Industrial and Labor Relations Review, 58*(4), 610–630.

[10] Barling, J., Fullagar, C., Kelloway, E.K., & McElvie, L. (1992). Union loyalty and strike propensity. *Journal of Social Psychology, 132*(5), 581–590.

[11] Dixon, M., Roscigno, V.J., & Hodson, R. (2004). Unions, solidarity and striking. *Social Forces, 83*(1), 3–33.

[12] Krueger, A.B., & Mas, A. (2004). Strikes, scabs and tread separations: labor strife and the production of defective Bridgestone/Firestone tires. *Journal of Political Economy, 112*(2), 253–289.

[13] Gunderson, M., Hebdon, R., Hyatt, D., & Ponak, A. (2005). Strikes and dispute resolution. In Gunderson, M., Ponak, A., & Taras, D.G. (Eds.), *Union-Management Relations in Canada* (5th edition). Toronto: Pearson Education.

[14] Gunderson, et al., *op. cit.*

[15] Hebdon, R. (1998). Behavioural determinants of public sector illegal strikes: cases from Canada and the U.S. *Relations Industrielles/Industrial Relations, 53*(4), 667–689.

[16] Barnetson, B. (2010). Alberta's 2002 teacher strike: the political economy of labor relations in education. *Education Policy Analysis Archives, 18*(3), 1–23.

[17]Shalla, V. (2003). Part-time shift: the struggle over the casualization of airline customer sales and service agent work. *Canadian Review of Sociology & Anthropology, 40*(1), 93–110.

[18]Godard, *op. cit.*

[19] Ponak, A., & Thompson, M. (1995). Public sector collective bargaining. In Gunderson, M., & Ponak, A. (Eds.), *Union-Management Relations in Canada* (3rd edition). Toronto: Addison Wesley Longman.

[20]Camfield, D. (2009). Sympathy for the teacher: labour law and transgressive workers' collective action in British Columbia, 2005. *Capital & Class, 99*(3), 81–107; Kelloway, E.K., Francis, L., Catano, V.M., & Dupré, K.E. (2008). Third-party support for strike action. *Journal of Applied Psychology, 93*(4), 806–817.

[21] Jackson, R. (2000). Collective bargaining legislation in Canada. In Gunderson, Ponak, & Taras, *op. cit*; Dessler, G., Cole, N., & Sutherland, V.L. (1999). *Human Resources Management in Canada* (7th Canadian edition). Scarborough, ON: Prentice-Hall.

[22] "List of Censured Administrations" (2010). American Association of University Professors. Available at <www.aaup.org/AAUP/about/censuredadmins/>.

[23] Canwest News Service (2010, April 19). Revamp anti-replacement-worker legislation, Quebec unions urge. Available at <www.canada.com/Revamp+anti+replacement+worker+legislation+Quebec+unions+urge/2962474/story.html>.

[24]Budd, J.W. (1996). Canadian strike replacement legislation and collective bargaining: lessons for the United States. *Industrial Relations: A Journal of Economy and Society, 35*(2), 245–260.

[25] Flynn, F.J. (2000). No news is good news: the relationship between media attention and strike duration. *Industrial Relations: A Journal of Economy and Society, 39*(1), 139–160.

[26] Chaulk, K., & Brown, T.C. (2008). An assessment of worker reaction to their union and employer post-strike. *Relations Industrielles/Industrial Relations, 63*(2), 223–245.

[27]Briskin, L. (2007). From person-days lost to labour militancy: a new look at the Canadian work stoppage data. *Relations Industrielles/Industrial Relations, 62*(1), 31–65.

[28] Gunderson, et al., *op. cit.*

[29]Akyeampong, E. (2001, September). Time lost to industrial disputes. *Canadian Economic Observer* (Statistics Canada Catalogue No. 11-010-XPB), 3.1–3.4.

Helping Parties Find Their Own Solutions

In Quebec's private sector, third-party intervention is not tied to the right to strike or lockout. Unions or employers can request the help of a ministry of labour mediator at any time. As well, parties can proceed to strike or lockout without intervention, although this is extremely rare.

The amount of mediation Quebec's ministry of labour does has decreased significantly in recent years. "We had only one case of second level mediation last year," says Suzanne Thérien, assistant deputy minister, workplace relations, at the Ministère du Travail du Québec. The ministry's work is now more focused on "preventive mediation," which takes place outside collective bargaining and deals with repairing damaged relations between the union and management, settling grievances, or simply improving communication.

The decrease in the need for third-party intervention during the collective bargaining process, Thérien says, is due to the increasing lengths of collective agreements (they are now often for five years, instead of the three years seen in the past); the weaker economy; and, for many, better working relations between the parties.

"They are coming less often, but when they do come it's longer because they haven't settled a lot of the small problems," Thérien adds. Mediation can take 1.5 days or 20 days, depending on the specific situation. "We stay with

[the parties] until the end, until they get to their settlement. Our main goal is to have a settlement and at the same time encourage them to have better relations between themselves, to help them get healthy habits in negotiations."

The ministry's intervention process for the public sector, in negotiations involving health care workers, civil servants, or educators, has changed quite significantly in recent years. While in the past, the ministry acted as a conciliator early in the negotiating process, it now provides mediation similar to that provided to the private sector.

"Both parties want to have a settlement," says Thérien. "In a few cases, it was really helpful, even when linked to the right to strike."

Thérien believes this approach is more effective than conciliation. The parties ask for help at the end of the process or when there is no prospect of a settlement. "We cannot impose anything, and we don't need to do so," she says. "We respect both parties [union and employer] and their ideas. We also assure confidentiality of the information the parties give us."

"At some point, the parties lose confidence in their ability to settle their disagreement," she adds. "We never lose confidence in their creativity and ability to [achieve a settlement]."

THIRD-PARTY INTERVENTION DURING NEGOTIATIONS

objectives

Collective bargaining is usually an adversarial process. Strikes and lockouts happen because the parties are unable to reach an agreement. When it appears that a strike or lockout may occur, certain individuals enter the process to prevent the strike or lockout or to help the parties resolve their underlying disputes. These neutral third parties—mediators, conciliators, arbitrators, and other forms of intervenors—assist the union and management in finding a solution to the immediate dispute. At the same time, they encourage the parties to create harmonious relations in the future. By the end of this chapter, you should be able to:

- explain why a third party would be used to help negotiators reach a collective agreement
- understand the difference between conciliation, mediation, and arbitration
- outline the conciliation process
- define interest arbitration and understand how it is used
- explain the role of mediators
- discuss industrial inquiry commissions
- understand the purpose of a disputes inquiry board

INTRODUCTION

As we saw in Chapter 9, strikes and lockouts have the potential to be damaging and lengthy. Because of this possibility, labour legislation in most Canadian jurisdictions provides for various forms of third-party intervention in collective bargaining. The intent of bringing a third party into the bargaining process when disputes occur is to help the parties resolve their differences without using a strike or lockout as a bargaining tactic.

Ideally, a third party is perceived as neutral by both negotiating teams, so he, she, or they can provide suggestions to one side in bargaining without being perceived as promoting the interests of the other side. Since the third party has not been involved in the bargaining process from the beginning, it is possible that they can identify solutions or outcomes that the parties may have missed because of their focus on their own bargaining positions. As we will see, third parties are also occasionally introduced to the bargaining process by the government; in such cases, the government uses the third party as a direct or indirect messenger to convey its interest in seeing a speedy resolution to the disagreement.

The main types of third-party intervention used in Canadian jurisdictions are conciliation, mediation, and arbitration. Depending on the circumstances of the bargaining situation and the relevant legislation, the use of these types of third-party intervention may be voluntary or mandatory. There are also less common forms of third-party intervention: mediation-arbitration, industrial inquiry commissions, and disputes inquiry boards. We will describe each of these types of third-party intervention and explain when and how they are used.

CONCILIATION

In all Canadian jurisdictions except British Columbia and Alberta, **conciliation** is the first possible step in attempting to resolve an impasse in negotiations. The conciliator's role is to assess the positions of the parties and the reasons for their inability to reach agreement. The conciliator will then submit a report of his or her findings to the minister of labour, the parties, or both. Table 10-1 outlines the legislation providing for the use of conciliation.

TABLE 10-1 Conciliation Legislation in Canada

	Type	Appointed By	Are Recommendations Binding?
Federal	Conciliation officer	Minister of labour on own initiative	No
	Conciliation commissioner/ Conciliation board	Minister of labour on own initiative	No
Manitoba	Conciliation officer	Either party, or minister of labour on own initiative	No
New Brunswick	Conciliation officer	Either party, or minister of labour on own initiative	No
	Conciliation board	Either party, or minister of labour on own initiative	No
Newfoundland and Labrador	Conciliator	Either party, or minister of labour on own initiative	No
	Conciliation board	Either party, or minister of labour on own initiative	No
Nova Scotia	Conciliator	Either party, or minister of labour on own initiative	No
	Conciliation board	Either party; a board must be appointed if both parties request it after a conciliation report has been submitted	No
Ontario	Conciliator	Either party; the minister of labour must appoint a conciliator when requested by either party after notice to bargain is given, or may do so if no notice has been issued	No

	Type	Appointed By	Are Recommendations Binding?
TABLE 10-1 Conciliation Legislation in Canada (Continued)			
	Conciliation board	At discretion of minister of labour, if conciliator is unsuccessful	No
Prince Edward Island	Conciliator	Either party, or minister of labour on own initiative	No
Quebec	Conciliator	The minister of labour must appoint a conciliator at the request of either party, or may do so on own initiative	No
Saskatchewan	Conciliation board	Either party, or minister of labour on own initiative	No

Source: Human Resources and Skills Development Canada, Labour Program, Summaries of General Private Sector Collective Bargaining Legislation (available at <www.rhdcc-hrsdc.gc.ca/eng/labour/labour_law/ind_rel/int.shtml>).

The conciliator does not participate in bargaining sessions or impose an agreement on the parties. Because of this, conciliation is preferred as the initial form of third-party intervention, since it allows the bargaining parties to retain a greater amount of control over the bargaining process and outcomes.

In some jurisdictions, conciliation is required as a precondition to a legal strike or lockout; that is, the conciliator's report must be completed and submitted before a strike or lockout can occur. However, even in jurisdictions where conciliation is voluntary, the parties can undertake conciliation on their own initiative to see if their differences can be resolved by this means. The parties may prefer to take this voluntary step before using (or being forced to use) other forms of third-party intervention that give the parties less control over bargaining outcomes.

The conciliator can be a conciliation officer (a single individual) or, in the federal jurisdiction, a conciliation commission. Saskatchewan provides for the appointment of a three-member conciliation board rather than an individual officer. A conciliation officer or conciliation commissioner is usually a government employee, appointed at the request of the parties or on the initiative of the minister of labour. Conciliation officers usually have experience in collective bargaining or in dispute resolution, which helps them to assess a specific collective bargaining situation and evaluate the issues causing conflict between the parties.

The actual process of conciliation begins with the conciliation officer meeting with the parties and investigating the issues in dispute. The officer will take note of the bargaining items that have already been settled, look at the issues still being negotiated, and see what the parties' current positions are on unresolved items. The officer will also ascertain what factors, in his or her opinion, are preventing the parties from reaching an agreement. These factors could include the quality of the parties' bargaining relationship, the amount of difference between the parties' offers on bargaining items, or the parties' willingness to make concessions. If conciliation was not undertaken voluntarily by the parties, all of this information will then be compiled in a report and submitted to the minister of labour. If conciliation was voluntarily undertaken by the parties and was not ordered by the minister of labour, the report of the conciliation board or officer will be given directly to the parties themselves.

A minister of labour may use conciliation not only as a means of assisting the parties to reach an agreement, but also to create pressure from the public to encourage the parties to resolve the dispute. If the conciliation order is made public or becomes the subject of media attention, the parties may settle their dispute because of the threat of embarrassment or damage to their public image. When an order for conciliation is made with the intent of creating this kind of pressure, the minister will likely specify that the recommendations of the conciliation officer will be made public. This directive lets the parties know that the details of their dispute will be publicized if they are not able to come to an agreement prior to the submission of the conciliation officer's report. If the parties do not reach an agreement and the conciliation officer's recommendations are made public, the parties may experience negative public reaction that could have long-term effects. The parties may agree to accept the conciliation officer's recommendations, even if they do not completely agree with them, in order to preserve their reputations.

In several Canadian jurisdictions, if the report of the conciliation officer fails to resolve the dispute by bringing the parties to an agreement, legislation provides for a further step in the conciliation process. The minister of labour can then appoint a tripartite conciliation board. This board is made up of an individual appointed by the employer, an individual appointed by the union, and a neutral third party, hence the name "tripartite" (which means "three parties" or "three interests"). The neutral third party can be appointed either jointly by the union and employer representatives or by an external authority such as the minister of labour.

The conciliation board carries out the same basic process of investigation and reporting as the conciliation officer or commission, with one major difference in the method of collecting information on the dispute. The conciliation board will hold a formal hearing, at which both parties will present their respective positions on the bargaining issues in dispute. Shortly thereafter, the conciliation board will make recommendations to the minister of labour. If the parties agree in advance, the recommendations of the conciliation board can be **binding**—that is, the parties will accept the board's recommendations as the resolution to their dispute.

The conciliation process is used in federal disputes, as well as in many provincial and municipal or regional public service disputes, because these disputes often involve essential services. The use of conciliation can delay a strike or lockout or, if the conciliation is binding, can avoid a strike or lockout entirely, which is an important consideration in negotiations involving essential services. For example, conciliation was used in a past negotiating dispute between the federal government and 8,500 technical workers in the public sector.[1] Bargaining broke down over the issue of wages when the Treasury Board, which negotiated on behalf of the federal government, offered a pay increase of two to two and a half percent per year over three years, and the union requested a pay increase of five percent a year over the same period. A conciliation board was appointed to investigate the dispute and recommended a settlement of three and a half percent in the first year, four percent in the second, and four percent in the third. This recommendation was sufficiently satisfactory to bring the parties back to the bargaining table and to temporarily prevent a full-scale strike.

As this example demonstrates, conciliation can help the parties settle their bargaining disputes by recommending potential solutions the parties may have overlooked. As we know from our discussion of bargaining in Chapter 8, parties are sometimes so committed to a particular desired outcome that they overlook other solutions that could actually satisfy the concerns of both sides. Conciliation is one way to make the parties aware of solutions that they might not recognize on their own. It can also be used as a means to help the parties overcome differences, whether large or small, between their positions. One past example of this function of conciliation occurred when a conciliator was appointed to investigate a bargaining dispute between NAV Canada, the company that provides air traffic control services at Canadian airports, and the union representing the workers who install and repair electronic systems at those airports.[2] The union wanted a 60 percent increase in wages over three years, basing its demands on what its members could earn in the private sector or in similar jobs in other industrialized countries. The leader of the union negotiating team acknowledged that the employer's

Miners from Thompson, Manitoba burn a conciliation board report in 1964 before calling a strike.

negotiators "almost died" when they were presented with the wage demand. In a situation like this, a conciliator could investigate whether the evidence supporting the demand was valid, and consider whether the employer would be able to meet such a demand. Presenting such information to the negotiators on both sides might cause them to consider whether the demand should be seriously entertained, and move them toward a mutually acceptable solution.

Despite its extensive use in the public sector, however, the conciliation process rarely resolves disputes. The two parties may perceive conciliation only as a first step that they are forced to take before they can use more intensive means to pressure for acceptance of their demands, such as a strike or lockout, or before they can use other forms of third-party involvement in bargaining. These attitudes may lead the parties to not give their full support to the conciliation process. Additionally, because conciliation usually happens relatively early in the bargaining process, the parties are seldom prepared to compromise at this early stage.

One study of bargaining-related legislation governing the Canadian private sector investigated whether the use of conciliation reduced the likelihood of strikes or the cost of strikes, which was calculated by estimating the amount of wages lost during the strike and the costs incurred by employers.[3] This study looked at data on strike activity and wage settlements in Canada between 1967 and 1993. The analysis of the data indicated that the use of conciliation did not significantly reduce strike activity, either in reducing the number or the length of strikes. More detailed analysis of the data suggested that the two-stage conciliation process (a conciliation officer and then a conciliation board) was somewhat more effective in reducing strike activity when a two-week "cooling-off" period was part of the conciliation process. (This cooling-off period took place between the date that the final conciliation report was submitted and the date that a legal strike could begin; legislation incorporating this requirement existed in some Canadian jurisdictions during the period for which data were collected.) With respect to conciliation's impact on the cost of strikes, the study indicated that, because of conciliation's general ineffectiveness in reducing strike activity, conciliation was not significantly effective in reducing the cost of strikes. During the period studied, it was estimated that strikes cost each striking worker approximately $100 per day and employers approximately $900 per day.

Table 10-2 summarizes the features of conciliation. If conciliation is unsuccessful, the next kind of third-party intervention that may be used is mediation. However, particularly in the public sector, interest arbitration may directly follow a failed conciliation attempt. We will first turn our attention to mediation.

TABLE 10-2 Features of Conciliation

Conducted by	– Conciliation officer
	– Conciliation board (second step, some jurisdictions)
When it is used	– When it is ordered by the minister of labour
	– When it is voluntarily chosen by parties (where this option is available)
	– Prior to the start of a legal strike or lockout (in some jurisdictions)
What happens	– Officer is appointed
	– Officer meets with the parties and investigates disputed issues
	– Officer writes a report with recommendations
	– Report is submitted to the minister of labour or to parties (or to both)
	– Minister may publicize the report's recommendations

TABLE 10-2 Features of Conciliation (Continued)

- Recommendations are not binding unless parties agree to this in advance

- In some jurisdictions, a legal strike or lockout cannot begin until officer has submitted the conciliation report to the minister of labour

- In some jurisdictions, if the report does not resolve the dispute, the minister of labour appoints a conciliation board

- Conciliation board holds a hearing and submits a report and recommendations to minister of labour

MEDIATION

When union and management negotiators are unable to resolve their differences during collective bargaining, they may apply for the assistance of a mediator. **Mediation** is a more intensive form of third-party intervention than conciliation because the mediator, unlike a conciliator, usually participates in the actual bargaining process, meeting jointly and separately with the parties during bargaining sessions.

Table 10-3 outlines the legislation in each Canadian jurisdiction governing the use of mediation. In most Canadian jurisdictions, a mediator is appointed at the request of one or both parties, or at the initiative of the minister of labour. In addition, in all jurisdictions except Prince Edward Island, the mediator's recommendations are not binding; in Prince Edward Island, the mediator's recommendations can be binding if both parties in the negotiations agree to this condition prior to the start of mediation.

Generally, either the labour relations board or the ministry of labour is responsible for appointing mediators. However, the person appointed as a mediator does not need to be an employee of the labour relations board or the government. Those appointed as mediators often have experience as labour or management negotiators, or they are lawyers, university professors, or other suitable individuals who have earned the parties' trust and confidence. The cost of using a government-appointed mediator is usually paid by the government agency that makes the appointment.

TABLE 10-3 Mediation Legislation

	Type	When Appointed	Are Recommendations Binding?
Federal	Mediator	At the request of either party, or at the discretion of the minister of labour	No
Alberta	Mediator	The minister of labour may require mediation; otherwise, at the discretion of the Director of Mediation Services upon request of either party	No, but one party accepting the mediator's recommendations may request that the other party vote on accepting
British Columbia	Mediation officer	At the discretion of the Labour Relations Board's mediation division, upon request of either party	No
	Special mediator	At the discretion of the minister of labour	No
Manitoba	Mediator	At the request of either or both parties, or on the initiative of the minister of labour	No
New Brunswick	Mediator	At the request of either party, or on the initiative of the minister of labour	No
Newfoundland and Labrador	Mediator	At the request of either party; the Minister of Labour may also appoint a mediator when a request for a conciliation board is received, or on his/her own initiative	No

TABLE 10-3 Mediation Legislation (Continued)

	Type	When Appointed	Are Recommendations Binding?
Nova Scotia	Mediator	At the discretion of the minister of labour	No
Ontario	Mediator	At the request of both parties; either party may apply for mediation after conciliation has concluded	No
Prince Edward Island	Mediator	At the request of either party, or at the discretion of the minister of labour; if conciliation is unsuccessful, the minister may appoint a conciliation board or a mediator	Yes, if parties agree
Quebec	Special mediator	The minister of labour may appoint a special mediator at any time	No
Saskatchewan	Special mediator	At the request of either party or at the discretion of the minister of labour; the minister may establish a conciliation board and/or appoint a special mediator	No

Source: Human Resources and Skills Development Canada, Labour Program, Summaries of General Private Sector Collective Bargaining Legislation (available at <www.rhdcc-hrsdc.gc.ca/eng/labour/labour_law/ind_rel/int.shtml>).

When a mediator becomes involved in negotiations, he or she investigates the dispute using slightly more proactive methods than a conciliator. The mediator will attend bargaining sessions and observe the negotiating teams in action to see if there are factors in the negotiation process, such as the parties' attitudes or behaviour toward each other, which could be blocking a potential settlement. The mediator will also listen to each party's position to determine where differences on bargaining items exist. He or she will then suggest to the parties, either privately or jointly, possible resolutions for the issues under dispute. Since the suggestions are not binding, the parties are under no obligation to accept them.

At the conclusion of the mediation process, at the request of either party, the mediator will provide a report that may include recommended terms of settlement. These recommendations are often persuasive and of real use in helping the parties reach a collective agreement. The mediator's recommendations tend to be more persuasive than the conciliator's because the mediator has been more closely involved in the bargaining process. The mediator's recommendations are generally more realistic or practical than the conciliator's, since he or she has a greater familiarity with the parties and the issues. Similarly, the parties may treat the mediator's recommendations more seriously than the conciliator's because of the parties' close contact with the mediator during the bargaining process.

The end to the lengthy Vancouver public transit bus drivers' strike in 2001 is a good example of how a mediator's recommendations can be used to create pressure for a settlement, even though these recommendations are not binding. Two months into the strike, when negotiations were clearly becoming unproductive, the British Columbia minister of labour appointed a mediator to assist in finding a resolution to the dispute. The mediator investigated the dispute and offered a proposal for settlement to the parties; the parties then shared the proposal with the constituencies they represented.[4] The mediator's report also noted that there was an important public interest issue involved in settling the strike; 37 percent of the transit company's customers did not have access to a car, and thus, the longer the strike went on, the more these individuals would be inconvenienced.

The bus drivers' union, a local of the Canadian Auto Workers, conducted a membership vote to assess the level of support for the mediator's proposed settlement. The union membership voted overwhelmingly in favour of accepting the terms of the proposal, and the union negotiating team subsequently indicated that it was willing to settle for the contract terms recommended by the mediator. The employer, however, rejected the mediator's recommendations, claiming that implementing the recommendations would be too expensive. This decision was highly unpopular with the bus-riding public, many of whom were encountering significant difficulties because of the lack of public transit. At the same time that the employer announced its decision to reject the mediator's recommendations, the Vancouver media carried numerous stories about senior citizens who could not go shopping or visit doctors, and individuals who had lost their jobs because they did not have reliable transportation. The employer's decision to reject the mediator's recommendations became even more unpopular when the transit shutdown lasted another two months. The strike ended only after the provincial government imposed back-to-work legislation. The legislation contained contract terms substantially similar to those recommended by the mediator.[5]

As we know from Chapter 9, in some Canadian jurisdictions (Alberta and Prince Edward Island), a mediator or conciliator must be appointed prior to the start of a legal strike or lockout. In other jurisdictions (New Brunswick, Newfoundland, and Nova Scotia), a conciliator or conciliation board must be appointed before a legal strike or lockout can happen. Although mediators or conciliators are not required to complete their work before a strike or lockout begins, the usual practice is that they will "book out" of the negotiations before the strike or lockout occurs. **Booking out** means that the mediator stops trying to help the parties overcome their differences and formally leaves the proceedings. This occurs either at the request of the parties or on the initiative of the mediator, either because the mediator is unable to help the parties resolve their disputes or because the parties have no common ground on which to reach an agreement.

Table 10-4 outlines the basic features of mediation. To conclude our discussion of mediation, we will briefly describe two specific forms of mediation that occur in some Canadian jurisdictions: special mediation and fact finding.

Other Forms of Mediation
Special Mediation

British Columbia, Saskatchewan, and Quebec have a provision in their labour relations legislation for the minister of labour to appoint a **special mediator** at any time during collective bargaining. A similar provision exists in Nova Scotia, although the process is

TABLE 10-4 Features of Mediation

Conducted by	– Mediator
When it is used	– When ordered by the minister of labour
	– When requested by either party or both parties
	– Before the start of a legal strike or lockout (in some jurisdictions)
What happens	– Mediator is appointed
	– Mediator observes bargaining sessions
	– Mediator meets with parties (individually or at the same time) and investigates disputed issues
	– Mediator proposes solutions
	– Recommendations are not binding; in some jurisdictions they can be if parties agree to this in advance, or if mediation has been privately requested with this condition agreed to
	– Mediator usually books out before a strike or lockout starts

called "preventive mediation" in that jurisdiction. Alberta also permits "informal mediation" after the notice to bargain has been issued. The special mediator often has expanded protection, privileges, and powers under the legislation that allows him or her to be appointed, and the special mediator is usually directed to keep the minister informed on the progress of mediation. One of the distinctions between special mediation and the usual forms of mediation is that much of the special mediator's authority is determined by the terms of each individual appointment. However, the main distinction between special mediation and the usual forms of mediation is that a special mediator can usually be appointed at any time during the bargaining process, not only after a dispute or disagreement has arisen. Therefore, a minister of labour may choose to appoint a special mediator to participate in a bargaining process from the very beginning if, in the minister's opinion, the bargaining is likely to be difficult, or if the minister believes that a strike or lockout would have an unusually negative impact.

In special mediation, the mediator may be requested to submit a report to the minister of labour, to the parties involved, or to both. If the minister so chooses, this report can be considered to have the same status as a report from a conciliation officer and be treated accordingly.

Fact Finding

In British Columbia, the associate chair of the mediation division of the Labour Relations Board can appoint a **fact finder** to meet with parties engaged in bargaining. The fact finder is responsible for inquiring into the issues between the parties and submitting a report on these issues to the associate chair. The fact finder's report describes the issues that the parties have already agreed upon, as well as the issues still in dispute. The fact finder's report may also include "any findings in respect of a matter considered relevant to settling a collective agreement between the parties."[6] Upon receipt of the fact finder's report, the associate chair provides the parties with a copy and may also make the report public. Thus, the fact finder, although technically a mediator, serves a function similar to that of a conciliator.

Having outlined the first two forms of third-party intervention, we will now turn to describing the third form—interest arbitration.

INTEREST ARBITRATION

Interest arbitration is considered the most intensive and invasive form of third-party intervention in the bargaining process. This is because in interest arbitration the arbitrator establishes some or all of the terms of the collective agreement between the parties. If the parties are unable to agree on mutually acceptable solutions to bargaining disputes, the arbitrator will create a solution that then becomes part or all of the collective agreement.

Interest arbitration is distinct from grievance arbitration, which will be discussed in Chapter 11. In grievance arbitration, a third party determines the application or interpretation of the terms and conditions of the collective agreement. In other words, interest arbitration takes place while the collective agreement is being negotiated, and grievance arbitration is used to settle disputes that arise once the collective agreement is in place. Table 10-5 summarizes the Canadian legislation governing interest arbitration.

TABLE 10-5 Interest Arbitration Legislation

	Type	When Arbitration is Used	Are Recommendations Binding?
Federal	Arbitration	When both parties agree	Yes
Alberta	Arbitration board	When both parties agree	Yes
New Brunswick	Arbitration	When both parties agree	Yes, when parties file a signed agreement to this effect with minister of labour
Ontario	Arbitration	When both parties agree; arbitration can be by individual or board	Yes
Quebec	Arbitration	Ordered by minister of labour, after application from both parties	Yes
Saskatchewan	Labour relations board (acting as arbitrator)	When both parties agree	Yes

Source: Human Resources and Skills Development Canada, Labour Program, Summaries of General Private Sector Collective Bargaining Legislation (available at <www.rhdcc-hrsdc.gc.ca/eng/labour/labour_law/ind_rel/int.shtml>).

As the table shows, not all Canadian jurisdictions have formal provisions for interest arbitration to resolve disputes during bargaining, although all Canadian jurisdictions specify procedures for the use of grievance arbitration after the collective agreement is in effect. However, in jurisdictions with no legislation to govern it, interest arbitration can still be used during collective bargaining if both parties agree and can settle on a mutually satisfactory arbitrator or arbitration board. And, as noted in Chapter 7, in most Canadian jurisdictions, an arbitrator can be appointed to create a collective agreement in first-contract situations where the union is newly certified and the parties have been unable to settle on a first collective agreement. This use of interest arbitration is intended to motivate employers and newly certified unions to commence negotiations and reach a mutually satisfactory first collective agreement by themselves, rather than have a third party impose a possibly unsatisfactory collective agreement on them.

An important feature of interest arbitration as a method of dispute resolution is that, unlike the conciliator's or mediator's decision, the arbitrator's decision is binding. In other words, the arbitrator's decision settles the disputes, and the parties cannot appeal the arbitrator's decision. (There are some rare and exceptional circumstances under which interest arbitration and grievance arbitration decisions can be appealed; these are described in Chapter 11.)

In jurisdictions where legislation provides for the use of interest arbitration, the arbitration process commences when one or both of the parties request that the minister of labour appoint an arbitrator. The minister of labour then appoints either an individual or a tripartite panel to act as an interest arbitrator or interest arbitration panel. Arbitrators or members of an arbitration panel usually have experience similar to those of mediators, either as negotiators or as labour lawyers. An exception to this process occurs in Saskatchewan, where members of the Labour Relations Board serve as arbitrators.

Once an interest arbitrator or arbitration panel has been appointed, a formal hearing is held. The purpose of the hearing is to give the arbitrator or the arbitration panel the opportunity to investigate the parties' positions and gather information on the dispute. The hearing is conducted very much like a court session. The arbitrator or the panel will call witnesses for each side, who will present oral and documentary evidence (such as written bargaining proposals) to persuade the arbitrator of the correctness of their position. The arbitrator or the panel will ask questions of the witnesses to clarify the presentations and the evidence. Once the hearing is completed, the arbitrator or panel will then consider the evidence and create a binding decision.

In some Canadian jurisdictions, legislation provides criteria that guide interest arbitrators in their decision-making. However, in the majority of Canadian jurisdictions, where criteria are not mandated, interest arbitrators traditionally use a form of arbitration known as **final offer selection**. If the parties agree, the arbitrator is free to create contract terms based on his or her own judgement rather than on the final offers submitted by the parties; however, final offer selection is the more common form of interest arbitration in Canadian jurisdictions. There are two types of final offer selection used by Canadian interest arbitrators: total-package final offer selection and item-by-item final offer selection. We will briefly outline the features of each of these types of selection.

Total-Package Final Offer Selection

When **total-package final offer selection** is used to determine arbitration outcomes, each party presents the interest arbitrator with a package of offers covering all the outstanding issues. The package includes the party's desired solutions to the issues and suggested wording for the parts of the collective agreement addressing each issue. During the hearing, each party will present evidence to convince the arbitrator of the superiority of its package. The interest arbitrator then selects one party's total package, and that package forms part or all of the terms of the collective agreement. If the parties have previously been able to agree on resolutions for some issues, those agreements will remain, and the total-package selection will create terms and conditions only for the unresolved issues. If the parties have not agreed on any issues, the total package will create all the terms and conditions of the collective agreement. The suggestions and wording in the package that is not selected will not be incorporated into the collective agreement.

To illustrate how total-package final offer selection works, here is a simple fictional example involving two disputed issues. (In real-life arbitrations, an arbitrator may have to deal with many difficult issues and examine extensive and complex evidence supporting the validity of each party's position on each issue.) In this example, negotiations have broken down, and the parties have been asked to submit proposals on two issues: wages and the number of hours in a working week. The union has proposed a wage of $20 an hour and a working week of 37 hours. The employer has proposed a wage of $15 an hour and a working week of 40 hours. Under total-package final offer selection, the arbitrator's decision will be either $20 a week and a 37-hour week, or $15 an hour and a 40-hour week.

The advantage of using total-package final offer selection to resolve bargaining disputes is that it encourages the parties to submit realistic suggestions, since they know that if the arbitrator finds these suggestions more acceptable than the other party's, their suggestions will end up being part of the collective agreement. However, the parties will not, or should not, suggest contract terms that they would not be willing to work with, since the arbitrator will not alter the terms of the package that is selected. The disadvantage of using total-package final offer selection is that it establishes a win-lose scenario. The party whose package is not chosen by the arbitrator will end up having its suggestions completely excluded from most or all of the collective agreement. This party will likely be irritated and resentful, and since this "losing" party has not had any direct input into the agreement, that party may not be fully committed to making the collective agreement work.

Total-package final offer selection was used in the arbitration that settled the high-profile Nova Scotia nurses' strike in the summer of 2001.[7] Among other issues, the nurses' union and the government disagreed on the wage increases and how these would be paid. The union wanted an 18 percent increase compounded over three years; the government offered 12.87 percent compounded over three years, in addition to a $3,000 lump-sum payment. The actual difference in payment between the two final offers was only $121 per worker over the life of the contract, but the nurses' union argued that its proposal was superior because it would be more effective in attracting nurses to the province and reducing the province's nursing shortage. The arbitrator, Susan Ashley, agreed with this reasoning and selected the nurses' proposal, but she also outlined in her report what she perceived as the deficiencies in the total-package solution in this case. She noted, among other things, that the employer would possibly attempt to compensate for the nurses' higher wage costs by giving nursing duties to lower-paid health-care staff. Ashley commented, "The [final offer arbitration] process has not operated to bring the parties closer together. The unions would never have accepted the employer's final offer if it had been presented in free collective bargaining."[8]

Item-by-Item Final Offer Selection

As the name suggests, when **item-by-item final offer selection** is used to determine interest arbitration outcomes, the interest arbitrator can select specific items from either side's proposals, rather than choosing only one side's complete proposal. In item-by-item final offer selection, each party submits its package of proposals and the arbitrator selects from either package a proposal for each outstanding item. Therefore, the resulting collective agreement could contain all, some, or none of the proposals made by a particular party. As with total-package final offer arbitration, the parties' offers should be realistic to improve their chance of being incorporated into the collective agreement.

The combination of items selected by the arbitrator forms some or all of the terms of the collective agreement, Whether the arbitrator's decision forms some or all of the agreement depends, as noted before, on whether the parties have previously reached agreement on other items and any previously terms the parties had previously agreed upon will be incorporated into the collective agreement along with the arbitrator's choices.

Our fictional example from the previous section can also illustrate the process of item-by-item final offer selection. The union's proposal was a wage of $20 an hour and a working week of 37 hours, while the employer's proposal was $15 an hour and a 40-hour working week. If item-by-item final offer selection is used, the arbitrator has several potential choices:

- $20 an hour and a 37-hour week

- $15 an hour and a 40-hour week

- $20 an hour and a 40-hour week

- $15 an hour and a 37-hour week

The advantage of using item-by-item final offer selection to resolve bargaining disputes is that the arbitrator can incorporate items from both parties' proposals. This lessens the possibility that one side or the other will have its suggestions ignored and thereby become resentful. The collective agreement will, ideally, include terms proposed by both parties, and thus both parties will be committed to supporting the agreement and making it work. The disadvantage of using item-by-item final offer selection is that the resulting collective agreement does not integrate both sides' suggestions in a way that could satisfy both parties; instead, it is simply an arbitrary collection of choices between the positions of both parties. Thus, neither party is likely to be completely satisfied with the agreement.

In several Canadian jurisdictions, interest arbitration is used as a compulsory method of solving bargaining disputes. If the parties cannot agree on a solution to a bargaining issue, they must use interest arbitration rather than undertake other actions such as strikes or lockouts. Interest arbitration is also used as a "last resort" form of third-party intervention in bargaining when neither conciliation nor mediation has been successful. Both these situations may result in the regular use of interest arbitration to settle bargaining disputes, especially if the parties have historically had very different interests that are not easily reconciled. This is often the case in the public sector. The employer in the public sector (the government) has a limited ability to pay large wage increases because it can gain revenues only through changes in taxation, and taxpayers usually resent increases in taxes. However, public sector unions want their members to have reasonable wage parity with the private sector, and thus expect their members' wages to increase to keep pace with private sector wages.

The regular use of interest arbitration to resolve bargaining disputes, despite the disadvantages mentioned above, does result in a completed collective agreement and ensures some degree of workplace stability for the term of that agreement. However, two significant problems have been identified with the use of interest arbitration (or of binding conciliation, which produces similar results) on a continuing basis as a means of resolving bargaining disputes. The first problem is that the availability of compulsory or binding processes may reduce the parties' desire to resolve outstanding issues on their own. The parties may not be seriously committed to bargaining because they know that if they reach an impasse, a third party will resolve the impasse for them. This phenomenon is called the **chilling effect**. The second problem is that the parties can become addicted to the habitual use of compulsory conciliation or interest arbitration and may lose the ability to resolve disputes on their own. If the responsibility for resolving disputes is consistently taken away from the parties and given to a third party, the parties will not develop effective conflict-resolution skills of their own and over time will become progressively less skilled at bargaining successfully. This phenomenon is called the **narcotic effect**.[9]

One Canadian study attempted to determine if the narcotic effect actually existed. The author of the study examined the use of interest arbitration in one public sector setting: 35 years' worth of contract settlements involving British Columbia teachers.[10] During this period, one province-wide teachers' union negotiated on an individual local level with district school boards. This study looked at the factors that had influenced the parties in these negotiations to pursue a bargaining dispute to the point of arbitration. The factors included whether the most recent set of negotiations had been settled through interest arbitration and the number of times each set of parties (the teachers' union and each district school board in the province) had used interest arbitration over the entire length of the bargaining relationship. The study also analyzed whether the overall level of interest arbitration use in the province as a whole had affected whether the individual school boards and the teachers' union had used interest arbitration.

The results of the analysis indicated general support for the existence of the narcotic effect. When interest arbitration was used in one set of negotiations, there was a greater possibility that the next set of negotiations would end through the use of interest arbitration. Also, the more times an individual set of parties used interest arbitration, the more likely it was to use interest arbitration in subsequent negotiations. The author of the study suggests that these findings support the existence of the narcotic effect, since they appear to indicate that the parties increasingly rely on interest arbitration to reduce the perceived uncertainty of reaching settlements through negotiations. However, the analysis included one contradictory finding: following periods of increasing rates of interest arbitration use across the entire province, there was a slight decrease in the likelihood of interest arbitration being used in an individual set of negotiations. This finding contradicts the existence of the narcotic effect, since it seems to indicate that having previous general examples of successfully concluded arbitrations does not always predispose individual parties to use arbitration themselves.

Table 10-6 summarizes the general features of arbitration. Before concluding our discussion of arbitration, we will discuss one other form of arbitration that is available in some Canadian jurisdictions.

TABLE 10-6 Features of Interest Arbitration	
Conducted by	– Arbitrator or arbitration board
	– Labour relations board (in Saskatchewan)
When it is used	– By request of parties to the labour relations board
	– May be voluntarily chosen by parties if they can mutually agree on acceptable arbitrator
What happens	– Arbitrator or board is appointed
	– Arbitrator or board holds hearing
	– Each party presents proposals and evidence supporting the validity of the proposals
	– Arbitrator considers the proposals and evidence and then creates an award
	– Award can be based on the total-package final offer selection, item-by-item final offer selection, or arbitrator's own solution
	– Award is binding and forms part or all of the collective agreement

Walmart, Union Divide Spoils in St.-Hyacinthe

MONTREAL—St. Hyacinthe now boasts the only unionized Walmart store in North America with a contract after a Quebec arbitrator imposed one yesterday.

Both Walmart Canada Corp. and the United Food and Commercial Workers union are claiming victory after reading Alain Corriveau's 46-page ruling.

"It's a significant decision because it is virtually a status-quo contract," Walmart spokesman Andrew Pelletier said yesterday.

Despite a provision that gives current employees an immediate 30-cent-an-hour raise and another 30-cent hike next April, Pelletier noted Corriveau linked his decision to an "offset" for union dues since there wasn't a wage increase in the provisional two-year pact.

Walmart had argued its salaries were in line with those paid to fellow discount retailer Zellers workers while the union wanted comparisons with Maxi & Co. supermarket employees.

Corriveau said Walmart wages were comparable and sometimes better than those of Zellers, a Hudson's Bay Co. unit.

Louis Bolduc, Quebec director of the UFCW, said his 180 Local 501 members in St. Hyacinthe are happy to "finally have a contract after four years."

Their store was certified in January 2005 and binding arbitration began in 2006.

Bolduc said the union won certain benefits, such as health and safety advantages, as well as year-end bonuses.

It was Corriveau who imposed a collective agreement last summer on Walmart for nine employees at the store's Tire & Lube garage in Gatineau, calling for 33-per-cent wage hikes for entry-level auto workers.

Walmart subsequently closed that garage and another unionized store in Jonquiere before contracts were negotiated, blaming union demands for making those operations unprofitable.

Source: King, Mike. (2009, April 9). Walmart, union divide spoils in St. Hyacinthe. *The Gazette* [Montreal], p. B1.

Mediation/Arbitration

In some Canadian jurisdictions, there is a provision for parties involved in bargaining to use another form of interest arbitration. This form of arbitration is called **mediation-arbitration**, or med-arb. Med-arb has occasionally been used to resolve bargaining disputes in the Canadian public sector. In this form of third-party intervention, the third party initially enters the bargaining process in the role of a mediator, and attempts to resolve the bargaining disputes in the same fashion that a "regular" mediator would. However, if the issues in dispute cannot be resolved through mediation, then the third party changes its role to become an arbitrator and, in that capacity, chooses the terms and conditions of the collective agreement.

Med-arb is an attractive form of third-party intervention because it guarantees that a solution to bargaining disputes will be reached. Furthermore, with med-arb, the parties can avoid some of the time delays that may occur if mediation is unsuccessful and arbitration is implemented only after that point. Because the mediator and the arbitrator are the same person or persons, there is a minimal turnaround time between the two steps. Also, less time is needed for the further collection of evidence and subsequent decision-making that arbitration requires, as the mediator is already familiar with the situation. Using the same individual or panel as both mediator and arbitrator may also promote better solutions in arbitration, since the individual or panel is more closely acquainted with the parties and the situations in dispute.

However, notwithstanding these advantages, med-arb is not widely used as a form of third-party intervention, because the parties may not respond as cooperatively to the third party acting as mediator when they know that if the third party later becomes an arbitrator, he or she will ultimately determine the content of the collective agreement.[11] Thus, the mediation part of med-arb tends to be ineffectual, and med-arb essentially functions as an extra-lengthy form of arbitration. Additionally, an arbitrator who enters into a dispute as an arbitrator may be more objective about the bargaining situation than an arbitrator who has previously served as a mediator in the same dispute. Even if the mediator-arbitrator does his or her best to be neutral in the arbitration phase of the process, the parties may distrust the final result if they suspect that the arbitrator's objectivity has been clouded by his or her experience as a mediator with the parties.

Having outlined the three main kinds of third-party intervention in bargaining disputes, we will now discuss in greater detail the conditions under which the parties in negotiations may choose to use one or the other of these forms of intervention.

USING CONCILIATION, MEDIATION, OR ARBITRATION

We have presented the three main types of third-party intervention in the order of conciliation, mediation, and arbitration for two reasons. First, this order arranges the forms of third-party intervention from the one that is least intrusive on the bargaining process (i.e., conciliation, where the third party observes or investigates and makes recommendations) to the one that is most intrusive (i.e., arbitration, where the third party actually formulates part or all of the collective agreement). Second, as we have seen, several jurisdictions in Canada require third-party intervention to proceed in this order. Initially, the parties must submit to conciliation if they are unable to reach an agreement; if that effort fails, mediation takes place; and if mediation does not succeed, then arbitration is used to resolve disputes. The structure of this process clearly encourages the parties to resolve their disputes themselves. They know that if they do not do so, they may end up with the terms of the collective agreement imposed on them, having lost the freedom to fashion their own terms.

However, in some Canadian jurisdictions, the parties have a greater degree of freedom to choose the form of third-party intervention they see as appropriate to their own situation. In this section, we will briefly discuss the requirements or options for choosing third-party intervention in Canadian bargaining disputes. Because the public and private sectors differ in the kinds of third-party intervention they use, our discussion will focus on the two sectors separately.

Third-Party Intervention in Private Sector Bargaining Disputes

Management and unions operating in the private sector in Canada generally prefer the mediation process to either conciliation or arbitration. As we know, conciliation is not always effective in resolving private sector bargaining disputes, and arbitration reduces the bargainers' control over the final outcome. As a result, conciliation and arbitration are seldom used in private sector disputes, except where required by legislation. Mediation is preferred because it gives the parties some practical assistance in solving their disagreements while allowing them to retain control over the contents of the eventual collective agreement.

We should note that bargainers involved in private sector negotiations can either use a mediator supplied by the labour relations board or ministry of labour, or can privately choose their own mediator. A privately chosen mediator can have any combination of skills and experience, as long as both parties agree on the choice. In some private sector bargaining scenarios, the parties agree in advance on the mediator who will be brought into the process if a dispute arises. The parties may even agree to include in their collective agreement the names of potential mediators who will be called upon to resolve disputes during the term of the collective agreement or during negotiations for a subsequent agreement. If a privately chosen mediator is used, the parties usually share the cost of the mediator's services equally.

Third-Party Intervention in Public Sector Bargaining Disputes

As we have seen, because of the potential impact of work stoppages in the public sector, most Canadian jurisdictions require that public sector bargaining disputes be resolved through some form of third-party intervention. These requirements are in place to avoid the use of strikes or lockouts in the bargaining process. Such job actions are particularly damaging or dangerous if they result in an essential service becoming unavailable.

Canadian jurisdictions have different requirements about which form of third-party intervention will be used at which point in the public sector bargaining process. In some jurisdictions, because of the potential negative impact of a protracted dispute or the lack of a completed collective agreement, the parties are required to proceed immediately to arbitration if a dispute arises. In other jurisdictions, the parties follow the progression of interventions previously described, using arbitration only if conciliation and mediation have been unsuccessful in resolving disputes.

Some jurisdictions in Canada do not require binding conciliation or arbitration for some types of public or para-public sector workers if other forms of third-party intervention do not succeed in resolving bargaining disputes. The philosophy underlying these regulations is that employers and unions, even those in the public sector, should be free to agree—or not to agree—to use arbitration to resolve their disputes, and that they should not have arbitration forced upon them if they do not see that process as appropriate for their situation. If these public or para-public sector employers and unions choose to use arbitration to settle bargaining disputes, they are free to fashion their own decision criteria for the arbitrator to follow, including whether the arbitrator will use total-package or item-by-item final offer selection.

We will now conclude our discussion of third-party intervention in bargaining by describing other, less common forms of intervention that are available in some Canadian jurisdictions.

OTHER FORMS OF INTERVENTION IN THE BARGAINING PROCESS

Up to this point, we have reviewed methods of resolving bargaining disputes that involve a third party. There are, however, three methods of resolving bargaining disputes that do not always actively involve a third party in the bargaining process: final offer votes, industrial inquiry commissions, and disputes inquiry boards. We will outline each of these methods in turn.

Final Offer Votes

Most Canadian labour relations legislation provides for a **final offer vote** to be taken during a strike or lockout. The minister of labour is permitted to order that the bargaining unit members, or the employers in an employers' organization, be given an opportunity to accept or reject the last offer made by the other party. A secret-ballot vote is conducted to determine whether the party's constituents accept or reject the other party's position on all matters that remain in dispute between the parties. The voters are presented with the terms of the other party's final offer and asked whether they would accept or reject the offer. If the majority of the employees in the bargaining unit, or the majority of the employers in the employers' organization, accept the last offer received, then the parties must conclude a collective agreement incorporating the terms of that final offer. Some jurisdictions specify that only one final offer vote can be conducted in each dispute.

The purpose of making a final offer vote available is twofold. First, a final offer vote determines whether a party's offer is actually acceptable to the constituents represented by the other party's negotiating team, even if the offer has been rejected by the negotiating team itself. In essence, a final offer vote circumvents the possibility that the negotiating team, either intentionally or unintentionally, is not fully communicating the other party's offer to its constituents. Second, a final offer vote provides another opportunity for bargaining disputes to be resolved before a strike or lockout takes place, or before a third party is brought into the process.

Industrial Inquiry Commission

All Canadian jurisdictions except New Brunswick, Quebec, Alberta, and Saskatchewan provide for the appointment of an **industrial inquiry commission** to investigate a bargaining dispute. In most jurisdictions, the minister of labour appoints the commission on his or her own initiative, but in some jurisdictions, the negotiating parties also have the opportunity to request that an industrial inquiry commission be appointed. While the appointment of an industrial inquiry commission is a relatively rare event, it is still important to understand what the commission is and under what circumstances it might be used.

After 20 months of unsuccessful bargaining between Medicine Hat Catholic teachers and their school board, Mike Cardinal, Alberta's Minister of Human Resources and Employment, established a disputes inquiry board.

When an industrial inquiry commission is created, the minister of labour provides it with a statement of the matters in dispute that are to be investigated. The commission then commences its investigation of the identified matters. If the parties do not settle the matters in dispute within a short time (usually 14 days) after the commission's appointment, the commission must report the results of its investigation, along with recommendations for resolving the dispute, to the minister of labour. Thus, the appointment of an industrial inquiry commission is a clear sign to the parties that the minister of labour will be informed of the dispute and will possibly get involved in its resolution if they do not quickly act to resolve the dispute on their own. The terms of appointment for most industrial inquiry commissions also provide another method of dispute resolution. The parties will be bound by the recommendations contained in the commission's report, if they agree in writing to this condition before the commission begins its work.

It is important to note that while industrial inquiry commissions are usually appointed in relation to a bargaining dispute, a strike, or a lockout, most legislation permits commissions to be appointed for any situation that the minister of labour or the parties consider appropriate. An industrial inquiry commission can be empowered to promote conditions favourable to the settlement of disputes as well as to do whatever is necessary to maintain or secure labour relations stability. For example, in British Columbia, an industrial inquiry commission can be appointed if a dispute in an industry is likely to arise; there is no need to wait until a dispute actually exists.

Disputes Inquiry Board

In Alberta and Ontario, the minister of labour can establish a **disputes inquiry board**. A disputes inquiry board is usually composed of three individuals who are charged with the responsibility of gathering evidence about a dispute that has led to a strike or lockout or a breakdown in bargaining. Like industrial inquiry commissions, disputes inquiry boards are appointed on a relatively infrequent basis.

The board usually carries out its mandate by holding a formal hearing at which the employer and the union each present oral and written evidence. At the conclusion of the hearing, the board presents recommendations for the resolution of all outstanding issues in dispute to the minister of labour. In Ontario, the minister of labour is then free to act on the recommendations as she or he sees fit. In Alberta, if the recommendations of the disputes inquiry board are not accepted by the representatives of one side in the bargaining dispute, that side's members are given the opportunity to vote on whether to accept or reject the recommendations. In other words, the recommendations are subjected to a process very similar to that of a final offer vote. If a majority of those voting agree to accept the recommendations of the disputes inquiry board, the recommendations are then considered binding and are incorporated into the terms of the collective agreement.

The purpose of a disputes inquiry board is similar to that of an industrial inquiry commission. However, the major difference between the two is that a disputes inquiry board is specifically charged with investigating disputes that have led to a strike or lockout or to difficulties in concluding bargaining, while an industrial inquiry commission can be appointed at any time to investigate any issue the minister or the parties feel is appropriate. In addition, the recommendations of a disputes inquiry board have more formal weight than the recommendations of an industrial inquiry commission. The recommendations of a disputes inquiry board may result in a vote to accept or reject the recommendations, or to informal action on the recommendations by the minister of labour. The recommendations of an industrial inquiry commission may also be acted upon by the minister of labour, but the power of an industrial inquiry commission to resolve disputes is more dependent on the power of persuasion.

SUMMARY

Third-party intervention in collective bargaining is available in a variety of forms in Canada, and it is voluntary or mandatory depending on the type of negotiations. Mandatory third-party intervention is more common in the public sector as a means of delaying or replacing a strike or lockout. Third-party intervention is intended to introduce a party into the bargaining process who either helps the parties reach agreement on their own or who recommends or imposes solutions to bargaining disputes.

The most common forms of third-party intervention are conciliation, mediation, and arbitration. Conciliation is a form of investigation in which an individual or board investigates bargaining disputes and makes recommendations for solutions to the parties or to the minister of labour. In mediation, the mediator actually becomes involved in the negotiations and encourages or assists the parties to find their own solutions to disputes. In arbitration, the arbitrator creates a solution that becomes part of the collective agreement; he or she does this either by fashioning a solution or by choosing final offers made by the parties. In some jurisdictions, parties can choose the form of third-party intervention they prefer; in others, they are required to try each form in turn as long as the disputes remain unsettled.

In some Canadian jurisdictions, other forms of intervention are available, such as mediation-arbitration, special mediation, fact finding, industrial inquiry commissions, final offer votes, and disputes inquiry boards. All of these are intended to assist the negotiating parties in resolving bargaining disputes and completing a collective agreement or, if the parties are unable to overcome their differences, to ensure that a solution is put into place and a collective agreement is reached.

KEY TERMS FOR CHAPTER 10

binding (p. 414)
booking out (p. 421)
chilling effect (p. 429)
conciliation (p. 410)
disputes inquiry board (p. 437)
fact finder (p. 423)
final offer selection (p. 425)
final offer vote (p. 435)
industrial inquiry commission (p. 436)
interest arbitration (p. 423)
item-by-item final offer selection (p. 427)
mediation (p. 417)
mediation-arbitration (p. 431)
narcotic effect (p. 429)
special mediator (p. 421)
total-package final offer selection (p. 426)

DISCUSSION QUESTIONS FOR CHAPTER 10

1. Explain the rationale for using the conciliation process.
2. What is interest arbitration and when might it be used?
3. Explain how interest arbitration differs from grievance arbitration.
4. Outline how the mediation process works.
5. Distinguish between a mediator and a fact finder.
6. When would a final offer vote be ordered?

7. Explain the advantages and disadvantages of using total-package final offer selection and item-by-item final offer selection.

8. When do parties have the option of choosing conciliation, mediation, or arbitration?

9. Why would either an industrial inquiry commission or a disputes inquiry board be established? When might one be used in preference to the other?

CASE *10-1*

AIRPORT AUTHORITY AND AIR TRAFFIC CONTROLLERS UNION

(Based on *NAV Canada and CAW-Canada*, 2003)

In this case, the parties had been bargaining for a collective agreement for nearly three years and had several major outstanding issues. The parties disagreed on the interpretation of the legislation that determines whether a strike or a lockout is permitted. The employer asked the labour relations board to refer the outstanding contract issues to binding arbitration so that the collective agreement could be settled, as provided for in the relevant labour legislation. The union argued that such a referral would be premature as long as a legal strike or a lockout could be used by one of the parties to support its bargaining demands, and that it had not yet been proven that a strike or lockout was forbidden under the provisions of the legislation. The labour relations board scheduled a hearing to address the questions of whether the outstanding contractual issues should be referred to arbitration.

Case Facts

The bargaining relationship between the employer and its workers had existed for six years. A first collective agreement was negotiated a year after the union was certified, but despite its acceptance by management and the union's executive board, the union membership refused to ratify it. Collective bargaining then resumed, and a lack of progress led to the appointment of a federal conciliation commissioner a year later. The commissioner's report was released after six months of investigation, but both parties disagreed with different recommendations in the report and were reluctant to accept it as the framework for a new collective agreement. However, the parties then became aware that the federal government was prepared to legislate a collective agreement if they could not agree on one themselves, and thus they returned to bargaining with greater motivation to finish.

A collective agreement was concluded and ratified four months after the commissioner's report was released, and its term ran for two years. Since the agreement took effect, two significant changes occurred in the parties' relationship. The workers, while remaining in the same bargaining unit, affiliated themselves as a local of a larger national union, and the employer was no longer part of the federal government but had become a private sector organization. However, the relationship between the parties remained regulated by the same federal legislation.

The parties were in the process of negotiating the collective agreement that would replace the existing one. Bargaining sessions began three months before the collective agreement expired, and the parties had met for 40 to 45 days since then. The union initially presented 600 contract demands, but this number had been reduced to about 225. Some items had been settled, but many were still outstanding, including wage increases.

The parties last had a formal bargaining session four months before. They had an informal meeting two months later, at which the union offered an unspecified "creative proposal" to settle the impasses that existed. The union's chief negotiator said, however, that he needed to consult with the bargaining unit on certain aspects of the proposal. However, the employer's request for referral to arbitration was filed just after the informal meeting, so no further negotiations or meetings occurred.

A further complication in the situation was the provisions of the legislation governing the relationship between the two parties. Both the workers (air traffic controllers) and the employer (airport ownership/management) offered services that would have a significant impact on the public if they were withdrawn or reduced. Because of this, the relevant legislation established that if a strike or lockout occurred, the parties would have to continue to supply their services or operate their services at a level that would "prevent an immediate and serious danger to the safety or health of the public." The parties were also permitted, 15 days after the notice to bargain had been issued, to mutually agree on a list of services or operations that they considered essential in the event of a labour disruption, along with an estimate of the number of employees involved. This list was filed with the labour relations board and was expected to be followed if a labour disruption occurred.

The labour relations legislation also gives the labour relations board the power to make its own essential service designations in the industries it regulates if it believes a strike or lockout could endanger public safety. It can designate which supplies, operations, or services it considers necessary, designate the manner in which the union or employer will carry out those functions, and impose any other measure it deems necessary. However, the legislation also gives the labour relations board the right to make the determination that the level of activity needed to maintain operations is such that any strike or lockout activity would pose a threat to public safety. In such a case, the board is able to refer any outstanding bargaining issues to binding arbitration so that a settlement will be reached without labour disruption.

In an earlier case involving the same parties, the board was asked to outline the general principles that it would use to determine essential services, as this would then indicate whether the board would permit a strike or a lockout in this particular situation. The board had indicated that it could not make a determination without a detailed safety study that would identify precisely what services could be withdrawn without immediate or serious danger. The board had commissioned this study, which was expected to be available in approximately six months. As a result of previous decisions, a small number of the bargaining unit members had the right to strike.

The employer's chief negotiator, Jerome Ferrier, told the board that he had been involved in negotiations between the parties since the bargaining for the first collective agreement. He described the progress in this round of bargaining as "painfully slow" and attributed this to the workers' new union affiliation. He characterized the union's bargaining strategy, which it had used in negotiations with other employers, as completing all the steps that were required to be in a position to strike and then being prepared to strike if a collective agreement was not concluded. When asked to describe the impact of a strike or lockout, he stated that the employees who had the right to strike represented only about 10 percent of the total bargaining unit membership of 2,300, and that those who had the right to strike in general are not licensed air traffic controllers. He also stated that he did not think a lockout by the employer would be an effective bargaining strategy.

Under questioning, Ferrier stated that the relationship between the union and the employer had generally shown improvement over the previous few months, with the exception of the incomplete negotiations. There was general progress in how disputes were being resolved, and fewer grievances were going to arbitration. He attributed this to the involvement of the union with which the workers were now affiliated.

Henry Gordon, the union's chief negotiator, told the board that the air traffic controllers represented by his union were highly professional employees who had expected their situation to be very different when their employer changed from being part of the government to being a private corporation. Gordon said that the employees had expected that, as private sector employees, they would have improved collective bargaining rights and "the right to withdraw [their] services." He alleged that "many promises were made either directly or indirectly to the members" when the privatization occurred, creating "great expectations" on the part of the members. He also stated that the members were "an extremely professional group, who study absolutely everything. For me they're the best I've ever worked with, they read everything, they analyze everything, they want to debate everything. That kind of tells you that they're confident in themselves and the professional services they provide."

Gordon stated that the ability to strike was extremely important to the air traffic controllers, since they needed to be sure they could get the best collective agreement possible. When asked his opinion on the effect of a strike or lockout on the bargaining process, he stated that he did not feel that the right to strike as currently established was extensive enough to be effective, but that a lockout would be very effective.

Gordon agreed with Ferrier that the bargaining process had been difficult, and also confirmed that both parties were dissatisfied with having had the resolution to the previous set of negotiations "forced upon them" by the threat of a legislated settlement. He also agreed that the general industrial relations climate between the two parties was improving.

The Employer's Position

The employer argued that binding arbitration of the outstanding issues was needed to achieve "stability and harmony" in the relationship between the parties.

The Union's Position

The union stated that it was willing to agree to send the outstanding monetary issues to arbitration if the parties could agree on the outstanding non-monetary issues by themselves.

The union was also willing to wait for the outcome of the safety study and the board's final definition of the union's right to strike before taking any action.

References

[1] Mofina, R., & May, R. (2001, August 25). PS workers, government closer to settlement: conciliation report viewed as a basis for renewed negotiations. *The Ottawa Citizen*, p. A3.

[2] Guy, D. (2001, July 7). Conciliator to resolve NAV Canada dispute: workers demand 60% wage increase. *The Ottawa Citizen*, p. A7.

[3] Cramton, P., & Gunderson, M. (1999). The effect of collective bargaining legislation on strikes and wages. *Review of Economics and Statistics, 81*(3), 475–490.

[4] Bohn, G. (2001, June 16). Mediator's report fails to solve transit strike: union urges acceptance, but company says: 'We don't have the funds.' *The Vancouver Sun*, p. A1.

[5] McInnes, C., & Nuttall-Smith, C. (2001, August 2). Three days of free rides when buses return on Tuesday: Back-to-work bill sends part-time issue to committee. *The Vancouver Sun*, p. A1.

[6] British Columbia Labour Relations Board. *Guide to the Labour Relations Code, Province of British Columbia, Chapter 8*. Available at <www.lrb.bc.ca/codeguide/chapter8.htm>

[7] Flinn, B. (2001, August 14). Unions win some, lose some: arbitrator picks nurses' proposal over government's, but other health workers disappointed. *The Daily News* (Halifax), p. 4.

[8] Quoted in Flinn, *op. cit.*

[9] Godard, J. (1994). *Industrial relations, the economy and society*. Toronto: McGraw-Hill Ryerson.

[10] Currie, J. (1989). Who uses interest arbitration? The case of British Columbia's teachers, 1947–1981. *Industrial and Labour Relations Review, 42*(3), 363–379.

[11] Craig, A.W., & Solomon, N. (1996). *The system of industrial relations in Canada* (5th edition). Scarborough, ON: Prentice-Hall.

Standing Up for Workers' Rights

Over the past 25 years, Danny Cavanagh has held almost every position in his local union, including president, secretary, chief steward, and shop steward. He is currently president of the Canadian Union of Public Employees provincial division in Nova Scotia (CUPE NS), but he spent years holding many positions at CUPE Local 734, which represents about 40 municipal outside workers in the town of Truro.

Cavanagh has done all this on a volunteer basis, in addition to his own job as a municipal worker. Currently, he is on leave to fill the now full-time position as the president of CUPE NS, which has 17,000 members in the public sector.

"I got involved in the union to make sure there's somebody there to stand up for employees' rights," Cavanagh says. When he was a shop steward, this often meant taking individual employees' complaints to management and, if necessary, filing a grievance against the employer.

These complaints frequently concerned the fair treatment of employees. Cavanagh recounts one instance when a driver smashed into two or three other cars. The employer was going to suspend the driver, arguing that drivers were supposed to care for and have control of their vehicles at all times. As shop steward, Cavanagh pointed out that the crash had been an accident, and that someone in management had recently had an accident as well and had not been suspended for it. "We told them we would file a grievance and take the issue to human rights if the suspension was upheld, since they were treating different levels of employees differently," Cavanagh explains.

One of the most important things to consider when dealing with these complaints is the language and wording of the collective agreement, Cavanagh stresses. "A shop steward needs to have a good understanding of the collective agreement, government legislation, and basic labour law." He or she must figure out what has been violated in the collective agreement and how legislation applies, and then combine this information to form an argument.

The goal is to avoid the grievance arbitration process if at all possible, as it can be costly and litigious. Often the arbitration hearing takes place before an arbitrator and is between lawyers representing the two parties, rather than between the employer and employee themselves. "This is not what it was meant to be," says Cavanagh. "The grievance system was supposed to be a system where employees could have a reasonable way to resolve disputes."

THE GRIEVANCE ARBITRATION PROCESS

objectives

Once collective bargaining has concluded, a collective agreement is settled and put into effect. While the collective agreement is in effect, there may be disputes about the interpretation or application of its terms. These disputes are resolved through a process known as grievance arbitration. By the end of this chapter, you should be able to:

- discuss and give examples of different types of grievances
- describe the grievance procedure
- define the duty of fair representation
- distinguish between different standards of proof in arbitration
- describe the purpose and role of an arbitrator
- explain alternatives to the arbitration process

INTRODUCTION

After studying the process of negotiation that leads to a collective agreement, we know that the document resulting from those negotiations contains terms and conditions that govern the operations of the workplace. However, we also know that the parties represented in negotiations have different concerns that may or may not be addressed either in bargaining or in the final version of the collective agreement. We also know that the collective agreement may not completely represent the desired outcomes of one or both of the parties, but may instead be an acceptable settlement that both parties feel they can live with. In addition, it is possible that conditions in the workplace or the external environment will change during the time the collective agreement is in effect, which can make applying the collective agreement difficult if the changes affect conditions the agreement was intended to address. Given all these possibilities, even the best-intentioned and most-skilled negotiators find it difficult to create a collective agreement that will suit the workplace perfectly for the agreement's full duration.

How, then, are disputes over the collective agreement resolved while the collective agreement is in effect? As we know from Chapter 9, strikes and lockouts are prohibited during the term of the collective agreement. If a strike or a lockout were used as a means of settling a dispute every time there were problems in applying the collective agreement, these actions would not only be illegal but would also be very disruptive to the efficient functioning of the organization. Thus, it is obvious that there needs to be another way to settle disagreements about the interpretation, application, or administration of the collective agreement's terms. Disagreements of this kind are known as **grievances**, and Canadian labour legislation provides for a process called **grievance arbitration** to settle them.

It is important to understand the grievance arbitration system because this system is one of the major mechanisms that facilitate the development of the relationship—whether positive or negative—between the union and the employer. Since grievances arise from the application of the collective agreement to the day-to-day events in the workplace, dealing with grievances requires the union and the employer to interact on a regular basis. If the parties are able to work together constructively and productively, and both parties feel satisfied with the outcomes of the grievance procedure, that positive relationship can affect how the parties interact in other ways, including during collective bargaining. A positive relationship developed through interactions over grievances can lead to more positive interactions in bargaining, and thus to a more satisfactory collective agreement.

On the other hand, if the union and the employer experience conflict in dealing with grievances and as a result come to distrust or dislike each other, that negative relationship can make other forms of interaction more adversarial and less productive.

Grievance arbitration is also referred to as **rights arbitration** to distinguish it from interest arbitration. As we discussed in Chapter 10, interest arbitration determines the terms and conditions of the collective agreement itself. In contrast, rights arbitration is concerned with the rights of the employer, the individual, and the union that arise from the interpretation, application, or administration of the collective agreement. These rights include the right of the employee to be treated fairly by the employer, the right of the employer to exercise control over its operations, and the right of the union to act as the representative of the employees. Frequently, the central issue in resolving grievances is determining which of these rights is most important in specific workplace situations.

As noted in Chapter 7, Canadian legislation establishes that each collective agreement must outline a grievance resolution procedure; moreover, Canadian labour law in every jurisdiction contains a grievance procedure that is considered to apply if a collective agreement does not include its own procedure. Thus, there is a grievance procedure present in every unionized workplace, either explicitly in the collective agreement or implicitly in the labour legislation governing the workplace. We should also note that grievance resolution procedures are not limited to unionized workplaces. Although non-unionized workplaces do not have collective agreements containing grievance procedures, many have disciplinary or "fair treatment" procedures in place to deal with disagreements between workers and managers or the employer.[1] These procedures are very similar in intent and structure to the grievance procedures found in unionized workplaces. In addition, the *Canada Labour Code* and the Nova Scotia and Quebec labour codes permit non-unionized workers to file appeals similar to grievances in cases of dismissal and discipline.[2] Therefore, although this chapter will describe grievance procedures that deal with disagreements related to collective agreements, the general process that we will outline is also present in many non-unionized workplaces.

Since a collective agreement is a legal contract, disagreements over its interpretation, application, or administration are legal disputes over rights, and these disputes can be resolved by the adjudicative process of grievance arbitration. Grievances are initially addressed within the workplace, and it is only when a resolution cannot be reached there that grievances are taken to grievance arbitration. We will first examine the grievance process within the workplace, which involves the union, the employee, and the employer. We will then describe the grievance arbitration process, which involves a third party as a decision-maker. Lastly, we will discuss some alternatives to the traditional grievance arbitration process.

THE GRIEVANCE IN THE WORKPLACE

In order for a grievance to be addressed through arbitration, it must first be determined whether grounds for a grievance actually exist. What one person perceives as a misinterpretation or misapplication of the collective agreement may be different from what another person perceives. Therefore, we will start our discussion of the grievance arbitration procedure by outlining what constitutes a grievance. We will then describe how the procedure unfolds once it has been established that grounds for a grievance exist.

Definition of a Grievance

The term "grievance" is used to describe an alleged violation of one or more of the terms of the collective agreement. Not every complaint arising in an employment relationship meets the test of being a grievance. From a union's perspective, a grievance occurs when the employer violates the collective agreement by either taking or failing to take a specific action.[3] For example, there would be grounds for a grievance if the collective agreement states that work schedules must be posted two weeks in advance of the scheduled shifts, but the employer posts the schedule only one week in advance; the late posting would violate the terms of the collective agreement. Employers and employees should be aware that when they act or fail to act, and such action or non-action violates the collective agreement, a grievance may arise; in other words, any violation of the collective agreement has the potential to generate a grievance.

Under most grievance procedures, both the union and the employer can file grievances against the other party. However, it is far more common for the union to file grievances against the employer, for the simple reason that the employer is responsible for controlling the day-to-day operations in the workplace. Thus, the employer has the greater amount of responsibility for carrying out the terms of the collective agreement as they relate to the workplace's functioning, and so there is more opportunity for the employer to be perceived as violating the collective agreement. Most grievances filed by employers against unions are the result of union actions arising from work stoppages during the term of a collective agreement.

We should also note that in some provincial labour codes, specific definitions make distinctions between different kinds of disagreements in the workplace. The Quebec *Labour Code* specifies that a "grievance" is any disagreement respecting the interpretation or application of a collective agreement and that a "dispute" is a disagreement respecting the negotiation or renewal of a collective agreement. The Alberta *Labour Relations Code's* definition of "dispute" is similar to that in the Quebec legislation. The New Brunswick *Industrial Relations Act*, the British Columbia *Labour Relations Code*, the Newfoundland and Labrador *Labour Relations Act*, and the Nova Scotia *Trade Union Act* all define a "dispute" as relating "to any manner or thing affecting or relating to terms or conditions of employment of work done or to be done," but none of these laws defines "grievance." For a disagreement to be handled under a grievance procedure it must meet the definition of a grievance or a dispute that can be settled in this manner, as specified in the relevant labour legislation. Therefore, to accommodate the variations in terminology among the different Canadian labour laws, we will use the term "disagreement" to describe the differences between employers, employees, and unions that may lead to grievances.

Types of Grievances

While each individual grievance relates to the specific terms and conditions of a particular collective agreement, there are four general types of workplace grievances. We will outline each of these types.

Individual Grievance—If an action taken or not taken by the employer specifically affects an individual employee, the resulting grievance is called an **individual grievance**. Discipline is a common cause of individual grievances. An example of an individual grievance involving discipline is a situation where an employer suspends an employee the first time that the employee is late for work. If the collective agreement states that suspension can be used as a form of discipline only after other disciplinary actions such as warning letters have been used, the suspended employee could file an individual grievance. The news story on page 459 of this chapter discusses an example of an individual grievance.

Group Grievance—If the action of the employer affects a number of employees in the same manner, then a **group grievance** may be filed. For example, suppose an employer has decided that it must undertake layoffs, and tells all the employees in a particular department that they will be laid off. If the collective agreement states that any layoffs must be conducted on a company-wide basis and must be allocated on the basis of employee seniority, then the employer's action has apparently violated this part of the collective agreement. The employees who have received the layoff notices could file a group grievance.

Continuing Grievance—Grievances can also be recurring; they may not involve a single incident but instead involve an ongoing practice. Grievances of this kind are called **continuing grievances**. An example of a continuing grievance would be one involving the employer's refusal to consider seniority in scheduling shifts within a particular division of the company. If the union or an employee disagrees with the employer's interpretation of the contract terms defining how seniority is to be used in determining shift assignments, a continuing grievance could be filed.

Policy Grievance—The union files a **policy grievance** on behalf of all employees, alleging that an employer's action or lack of action is a violation of the collective agreement that affects all employees. A policy grievance could occur over an issue such as the employer's interpretation of contract provisions for payment of holiday pay, since under employment standards law all employees are entitled to holiday pay. Thus, all employees of the organization would be affected by the employer's interpretation of holiday pay provisions. A policy grievance can be filed regardless of whether the contract interpretation or application has actually affected all employees; the feature that distinguishes policy grievances from continuing grievances or group grievances is the potential of the issue in dispute to affect all employees. If the issue could potentially affect all employees, the grievance is a policy grievance.

An example of a policy grievance occurred in Ottawa when the Canadian Union of Public Employees filed several grievances against the Ottawa Public Library.[4] The library had a policy of not filtering or restricting Internet access on the computer terminals available for public use. The union filed a policy grievance alleging that library employees were being forced to see sexually explicit material when Internet users left the terminals logged on to pornographic websites, and that this created a "hostile work environment" for all employees.

We should also note that grievances can be classified according to which part of the collective agreement was allegedly violated; for example, there are job classification grievances, work-scheduling grievances, compensation grievances, and discharge and discipline grievances, to name a few. As we can see, these groups of grievances are defined by the contract term involved in the disagreement, not by the number of employees affected or by the manner in which the contract was allegedly violated.

Having established what a grievance consists of and what types of grievances might occur in a workplace, we will now discuss the importance of timing in filing a grievance.

Timeliness of a Grievance

A grievance commences when the affected individual or group knows, or ought to reasonably know, that an action (or lack of action) violates the collective agreement. It is impossible for a union to constantly police the application, administration, and interpretation of the collective agreement in every part of a workplace. Therefore, employees are expected to notify the union immediately when they believe that the collective agreement has been violated. It is also important to note that a violation of the collective agreement can be said to have occurred if an individual or group "ought to reasonably know" that an action contravenes the collective agreement. This expectation implies that the employer, the union, and the employees should all be familiar with the contractual terms of the collective agreement and should all be aware of what actions, or lack of actions, might be considered grounds for a grievance. It also implies that any parties affected by an alleged violation of the collective agreement have a responsibility to make their concerns known as soon as possible.

If the party filing a grievance fails to complain when an alleged grievance first occurs, two problems can arise. First, the employer may dismiss the grievance on the basis that the practice has been ongoing and no previous complaint has been filed. The employer may state that even if the practice is clearly in contravention of the collective agreement, the employees have in effect accepted it and have no grounds to complain. This principle is sometimes referred to as the principle of **past practice**. The principle of past practice does not mean that employees have no right to complain about an alleged violation of the collective agreement if they have not done so previously when the same violation occurred, but instead means that their ability to make an effective complaint (and to receive a remedy) is reduced. When a complaint is not made in a timely manner, the union retains the right to proceed with the grievance procedure even if the employer dismisses the grievance, but the union's chances of success in an arbitration may be reduced.

The second problem associated with a failure to file a timely grievance is that even if the grievance proceeds, the lack of timeliness can affect the eventual remedy granted. For example, an arbitrator might make a monetary award to restore payments that employees lost because of the employer's misinterpretation of the collective agreement. However, if the affected employees did not complain as soon as the first miscalculated payment was made, and the employer continued making incorrect payments, the monetary award to the employees might reflect only those payments lost after the grievance was filed, not all of the incorrect payments.

We will now look at how the grievance procedure is initiated in the workplace.

The Steps in the Grievance Procedure

As previously noted, Canadian labour legislation does not enforce any specific process for handling grievances between the union and the employer. Rather, the legislation leaves it to the individual union and employer to develop their own internal process, although the legislation provides a standard procedure that is considered to apply if the parties have neglected to include a grievance procedure in their collective agreement. Table 11-1 presents an example of a standardized grievance procedure outlined in labour law.

TABLE 11-1   An Example of a Legislated Grievance Procedure

Provision for final settlement
78(1) Every collective agreement shall contain a provision for final settlement without stoppage of work, by arbitration or otherwise, of all differences between the parties thereto, or persons bound by the agreement or on whose behalf it was entered into, concerning its meaning, application, or alleged violation.

Deemed arbitration procedures
78(2) Where a collective agreement does not contain a provision as required under subsection (1), it shall be deemed to contain the following provisions, which shall be numbered or lettered as may be required in the collective agreement:

(a)   Where a violation of this agreement is alleged, or a difference arises between the parties to this agreement relating to the discipline or dismissal of an employee, or to the meaning, interpretation,

TABLE 11-1   An Example of a Legislated Grievance Procedure (Continued)

application or operation of this agreement (including a difference as to whether or not a matter is arbitrable), either party, without stoppage of work and after exhausting any grievance procedure established by this agreement, may notify the other party in writing of its desire to submit the alleged violation or difference to arbitration; and thereafter the parties shall, subject to clause (b), agree on an arbitrator to hear and determine the matter and issue a decision, which decision is final and binding on the parties and any person affected thereby.

(b)   Where the parties agree that an arbitration board rather than an arbitrator should determine a matter, the parties shall appoint an arbitration board to hear and determine the matter and issue a decision, which decision is final and binding on the parties and any person affected thereby.

(c)   The provisions of *The Labour Relations Act* respecting the appointment, powers, duties and decisions of arbitrators and arbitration boards apply hereto.

Source: Manitoba *Labour Relations Act* R.S.M. 1987 c. L10.

Having a grievance procedure available to resolve disagreements is very important to ensure that the collective agreement is correctly and effectively applied in the workplace. Therefore, the grievance procedure is usually negotiated into the collective agreement, and the process of negotiating this procedure is an opportunity for the employer and union to develop their own dispute resolution process. While unions and employers naturally make an effort to shape the grievance procedure to suit their own organizations and workplaces, grievance procedures in general share a number of characteristics. We will now outline these common features. Table 11-2 summarizes the steps in the grievance process before arbitration.

Filing the Grievance: Step One

The first step of the grievance process is the filing of a complaint about a violation of the collective agreement. As outlined, an individual, a group of employees, or the union on behalf of all employees can file a complaint. The person or party initiating the grievance is referred to as the **grievor**. The grievance itself is usually submitted, orally or in writing, either to the immediate supervisor of the area where the violation is alleged to have

[handwritten margin note: Describing tenants as "Step 0" asked in the question]

Step	Who Is Involved	Process
Step 1	Individual employee with or without a shop steward or grievance committee member	Normally an oral presentation by the employee to the immediate supervisor with or without representation by the union
	Foreperson, section head, supervisor, or other employer representative	Immediate supervisor has time limits (usually 14 days) within which to resolve or reject the grievance
Step 2	Grievance committee member(s) or shop steward	Grievance is presented in written format to the next level of management
	Union business agent may accompany committee or steward	If not resolved, the grievance advances to the next step within the time limits (usually 14 days)
	Department head, superintendent, or intermediate management	Time limits may be extended or waived (in writing) by mutual agreement. If the grievance is not advanced within time limits, or time limits are not jointly waived, grievance can be deemed to have been abandoned
Step 3	Local union executive member, usually with a business agent	Senior levels of the union and employer discuss grievance
	Senior management with a human resource/industrial relations officer	Usually all outstanding grievances are discussed as part of regularly scheduled labour-management meetings
		If the grievance is not resolved, the union may refer it to arbitration within the time limits (usually 14 days)

TABLE 11-2   Steps in the Grievance Procedure

occurred or to the human resources department. Most grievances are filed in response to specific actions, such as decisions or orders, by supervisors.[5]

In some workplaces, the first step of the grievance procedure, in practice, actually contains two parts. In the first part, the grievance is brought to the attention of the employer through an oral complaint, and there is an initial attempt to resolve the grievance through informal discussion between the parties. Several studies of grievance arbitration processes have indicated that a significant percentage of grievances are settled through informal discussion before more formal steps in the grievance procedure are taken.[6] If the grievance is not successfully resolved through this relatively informal method, it may proceed to the second part, in which a written complaint is submitted.

At the first step in the grievance procedure, the parties involved are usually the individual employee, with or without a shop steward to assist him or her, and the employee's immediate supervisor. Although the collective agreement does not always require that a shop steward be involved in this part of the grievance procedure, some employees choose to have a shop steward assist them from the first step to ensure that the grievance procedure is correctly followed. Similarly, although the human resources department of the organization is not usually formally involved at this stage of the grievance procedure, the supervisor may consult this department for advice or direction in dealing with the grievance.

A Halifax longshoreman meets with his union representative. Every grievance procedure includes a face-to-face meeting like this.

In some workplaces, a grievance committee member may fill the role of a shop steward in assisting the employee. Grievance committee members are elected by union members, usually on a departmental or occupational basis to ensure representation of the diversity among employees. Shop stewards and/or grievance committee members may also be useful participants at an early stage of the grievance procedure because of their expertise in assessing the validity of a grievance (thus, they may be able to estimate how much effort should be given to resolving it). Shop stewards and grievance commit-tee members may also be able to promote an informal resolution, so that the grievance does not unnecessarily proceed to more formalized steps in the grievance procedure.[7]

An issue that often arises along with the filing of a grievance is whether the employ-ee should continue working under the disputed conditions or should withhold his or her labour until the grievance is resolved. The general principle governing this situation is "grieve, then work"—that is, in most situations, the employee is expected to continue his or her regular work. If the grievance is upheld, usually any material harm the employee suffered as a result of the collective agreement's violation, such as lost wages or working time, will be reversed or compensated as part of the grievance resolution. The only generally recognized exceptions to the "grieve, then work" rule are situations where the alleged violation of the collective agreement puts the employee in a physical-ly dangerous situation. For example, if the collective agreement sets out safety rules for performing particular tasks, and a supervisor orders the employee to ignore those rules, the employee is generally entitled to refuse to perform the dangerous work and may also file a grievance.

For the individual worker, step one is the most important in the grievance pro-cedure. It is the only step in which the individual, with or without the steward or grievance committee member, has control over the grievance and its outcome. Occasionally, an employee may bring a complaint to the union's attention that the union feels is not substantial enough to warrant filing a grievance. In this situation, the grievance will not likely proceed beyond the first step in the grievance procedure. If the employee feels that the union has unjustly refused to consider his or her com-plaint, the employee has the option of filing a complaint against the union for not ful-filling its duty of fair representation. This type of complaint will be discussed later in the chapter.

To conclude our discussion of the first step in the grievance procedure, we will note that most grievance procedures include time limits governing how long each step in the procedure must take. Each step has its own time limit, which usually ranges from 10 to 14 days. If the matter is not resolved during the stated time limit, the grievance auto-matically proceeds to the next step. The purpose of these time limits is to ensure that when grievances are filed, they are promptly addressed and not ignored in the hope that the grievors will abandon their complaints. However, time limits can be waived by mutual consent. For example, if a particular employee is needed to provide evidence relating to another employee's grievance, and this employee is on vacation, the employer and the union or employee could agree to waive the time limit for that stage of the grievance procedure until the needed employee is available. We should note, though, that failure to obtain an agreement to waive a time limit can result in a grievance being deemed abandoned and not being pursued any further.

Teacher Wins Battle to Hang Union Sign Outside Classroom

VANCOUVER—A teacher who hung a small sign outside her classroom identifying herself as a "staff representative" for her union—and filed a grievance after the principal ordered it down—has won a decision in a lengthy battle over freedom of expression.

Arbitrator John Steeves sided with Brenda Head and the Abbotsford and District Teachers' Association, saying removal of the sign, one of many hanging on the school's walls, could not be justified and left the erroneous impression that the staff rep and her union were not a part of the school.

The thin plastic sign, 45 mm by 200 mm, was an "expression about pride and support for the union and it reflected the status of the [teacher] as a union representative who participates in the dialogue of the workplace, in the context of the collective agreement and legislation. This is a form of political democracy and it requires a high level of protection," Steeves wrote in his decision.

The case began when Head was settling into a new classroom at the Abbotsford Traditional middle school.

According to evidence at a two-day hearing in December, she hung the sign outside her door so that teachers, especially new ones, could find her and because she was proud to have been elected as a union representative.

It was one of several signs on the school's walls, including others identifying the general office and the learning assistance centre as well as student photographs, sports awards and a display about Harry Potter and the 2010 Olympics.

When district officials found out about the sign, they contacted principal Daljeet Rama and advised her she had the authority to decide what signage is permitted and that the union has a bulletin board for posting information. Eventually, Rama ordered the sign down and the union filed a grievance.

District principal George Keys sent an e-mail to all principals, advising them about the grievance and urging them to remove "staff representative" signs posted in any place other than the union bulletin board. Some followed his directions, and some did not.

The school district and the B.C. Public School Employers' Association acknowledged that teachers have freedom-of-expression protections, but argued they do not have the right to use the walls outside a classroom "as a forum for promulgating their message," the ruling noted.

Steeves accepted that principals have the right to make policy about signs in schools, and said there are undoubtedly signs about union affairs that would not be appropriate in school hallways. But this particular sign, unobtrusive and inoffensive, was not one of them, he concluded.

Hugh Finlayson, chief executive officer of the employers' association, said the dispute was a local one and not likely to have implications for other districts.

But Irene Lanzinger, president of the B.C. Teachers' Federation, said the decision was "a great victory" and another freedom-of-speech win for teachers.

Source: Steffenhagen, Janet. (2010, March 18). "Teacher Wins Battle to Hang Union Sign Outside Classroom; Principal Had Ordered Abbotsford Instructor to Take It Down". *The Vancouver Sun.* p. A8.

Formal Complaint and Investigation: Step Two

If a grievance is not satisfactorily resolved by the individual employee and the employer within the time limit established for step one of the grievance procedure, the grievance will proceed to the next step: the written complaint. As noted, in some organizations, steps one and two are combined.

The individual grievor (or group of grievors) is not extensively involved at step two, even though he or she may have initiated the grievance. This is because the union, on behalf of its members, is the party that signed the collective agreement, and is therefore also the party that would allege a violation of the collective agreement.

In most cases, the grievance is formally put into writing at step two of the grievance procedure. Most unions have a grievance form that the grievor fills out with the assistance of the shop steward or grievance committee member. This form usually contains the following information:

- the name of the grievor

- the date, time, and specifics of the alleged violation

- the provisions of the collective agreement that are affected

- the identification of witnesses (if any) to the violation

- the immediate supervisor involved

- the requested remedy for the damage caused by the alleged violation

The grievance form is signed by the grievor and the shop steward or grievance committee member, as well as by the immediate supervisor, whose signature indicates that he or she is aware that the grievance has been filed. The grievance form is then given to the employer. The union and grievor each retain a copy.

After the formal written grievance has been submitted, the union and employer each commence their own investigation of the facts surrounding the grievance. This investigation usually entails interviewing the grievor, interviewing the manager or employer representative alleged to be responsible for the violation of the collective agreement, interviewing any witnesses, and collecting any physical evidence (such as payroll records or work schedules) that may support or disprove the allegations. Once the investigations are complete, the shop steward or the grievance committee will meet with management.

Typically, middle-level managers such as senior supervisors represent management at this meeting; the union's business agent may also attend.

Since the union and the employer have independently investigated the allegations, both sides come to the meeting prepared to argue their position. Each side presents its evidence and position, and the parties attempt to determine whether a mutually satisfactory resolution is possible. A resolution at this stage of the grievance procedure is desirable because it allows both management and grievance committee members to retain control of the issue and its solution; it also reduces the likelihood of interference from higher levels of the union or management. If, however, the grievance is not resolved at this step within the specified time limit, the grievance will advance to step three.

The Final Attempt Before Arbitration: Step Three

At the third step of the grievance procedure, the union business agent, along with a representative of the local union, meets with senior management representatives. In most organizations, these parties meet regularly to discuss larger matters requiring input from both sides. Grievances that have proceeded to step three are usually considered important enough to be discussed at these high-level meetings. As in the first two steps of the grievance procedure, both sides present their evidence related to the grievance, along with information on what happened in the first two steps of the procedure. After discussing the evidence, the parties attempt to reach a mutually satisfactory solution.

The third step of the grievance procedure is the last opportunity for the union and management to resolve the issue between them and to control the outcome of the grievance without input from a third party. The amount of control that the parties perceive they have over the grievance procedure affects their level of satisfaction with the results; the more control the parties perceive they have over the procedure, the more satisfied they will likely be with the outcome.[8] Failure to reach a satisfactory settlement at this step leads to the option of undertaking an arbitration to resolve the grievance. As mentioned previously, the union may have to decide whether the grievance justifies proceeding to arbitration. However, if the union chooses not to proceed to arbitration and decides to abandon the grievance, it may be subject to a complaint from one or more of its members that it has abandoned its duty of fair representation. Before describing the process of grievance arbitration, we will discuss the issue of fair representation.

Duty of Fair Representation

The union, as the exclusive bargaining agent for the employees, is obligated by Canadian labour legislation to fairly represent its members. The **duty of fair representation** means that a union (as well as an employers' association) must not act toward its members in a manner that is arbitrary, discriminatory, or in bad faith.

When deciding whether or how to settle a grievance, to withdraw a grievance, or to proceed to arbitration with a grievance, the union must make its decision in a manner that does not contradict its duty of fair representation. To fulfill the obligation that its conduct not be arbitrary, the union must fully investigate the grievance and make a reasonable determination based on a consideration of all the facts. Arbitrary conduct by a union has been described as conduct that is superficial, capricious, indifferent, or reckless with regard to the members' interests.[9] For example, a union would be acting arbitrarily if it assembled evidence that clearly indicated a violation of the collective agreement and then refused to pursue the grievance for the reason that the grievance was unjustified.

For a union to fulfill its obligation to fairly represent its membership without discrimination, it must not be influenced in its handling of the grievance by factors such as the grievor's race, religion, gender, or age. As noted in previous chapters, the various forms of "discrimination" are defined in the relevant human rights legislation. A union would be discriminatory if, for example, it refused to pursue a grievance only because the grievor was female or of Asian descent.

Finally, a union acts in bad faith if its decision respecting the grievance is influenced by dishonesty, personal hostility, or revenge. It can be difficult to determine whether a union has acted in bad faith in situations where there is a history between the union and the grievor that might have influenced the union's decision. For example, if a grievor has filed several grievances on the same issue that were not upheld by the employer, the union might refuse to pursue any further similar grievances on the grounds that the grievance would probably not be successful. The grievor, however, may believe that the union, in its refusal, is seeking to discourage a "troublemaker" and has ignored an injustice that the grievor genuinely believes he or she has suffered.

Sometimes, the duty of fair representation may appear to be in conflict with the union's willingness or ability to pursue a grievance to the point of arbitration. As we will see later in this chapter, grievance arbitration can be very expensive and time-consuming for all of the parties involved. In deciding whether to take a grievance to arbitration, unions sometimes weigh the likelihood of winning the grievance against the cost of the grievance arbitration. In other words, does the financial investment in the case justify the potential value of the outcome? "Value" could be determined either by the potential financial award the arbitrator could give to the winning party or by the usefulness of the precedent the arbitrator's decision could establish. While an arbitration award might not completely reimburse the parties' cost of going to arbitration, the union might still decide to proceed to arbitration because the arbitrator's decision could establish an important precedent affecting future workplace policies or practices.

In other situations, there may be sufficient evidence to support the union's position on the grievance, but the union may feel that the chances of winning are not good enough to warrant the cost of pursuing the grievance. The union might also feel that any precedent set by an arbitrator's decision would not be significant enough to justify the cost of arbitration. However, the grievor may disagree with the union's assessment of these possible outcomes, and interpret the abandonment of the grievance as the union's failure to fulfill its duty of fair representation.

If a union member decides to file a complaint against a union for failing to fairly represent him or her, the procedure usually commences with the member completing a standardized form and submitting it to a labour relations board. The board will then decide whether to accept or reject the member's complaint. If the union has an internal appeal process to deal with member complaints about the union's decisions or actions, the labour relations board usually expects the union member to first take his or her complaint through that internal process. Usually, a labour relations board will only consider a union member's complaint about the union's decisions or actions if the complaint has already been appealed through the union's own processes. If the board accepts the union member's complaint, it will commence an investigation and, if warranted, hold a hearing to determine whether the complaint is justified.

It is important to note that even if the labour relations board accepts a complaint regarding a union's duty of fair representation, the board will not investigate the actual grievance. In other words, the labour relations board is not concerned with whether the grievance itself was justified; rather, the board will attempt to determine whether the union acted in a manner that was arbitrary or discriminatory or in bad faith in representing the union member, both in the grievance procedure and in the union's decision on whether to pursue the grievance.

If the labour relations board finds that the complaint is justified and that the union did not fairly represent the member, it can choose from a number of potential remedies. If the union member has suffered in some way because of the union's lack of representation, the board may attempt to remedy the damage. For example, a union member might file a grievance if she or he was demoted to a position that paid less than her or his original job. If the union refused to pursue the grievance, the board could order the union to compensate the member for the difference between the salary in the original position and the salary in the position that the member was demoted to, for as long as the member is in the lower-paying job.

If the failure to fairly represent the member involved a decision not to take a grievance to arbitration, a common remedy is for the board to rule that the union must continue to represent the member in the grievance and that the grievance must proceed to arbitration. We will now describe how the process of grievance arbitration works.

Shiv Chopra leaves a hearing in Ottawa after filing a grievance alleging management was pressuring him and other Health Canada scientists to approve questionable drugs.

THE GRIEVANCE ARBITRATION PROCESS

Preparing for a Grievance Arbitration

If a grievance is not settled by the end of step three of the grievance procedure, it may proceed to arbitration. Grievance arbitration, as the final step in the grievance procedure, is designed to bring a final and conclusive resolution to the disagreement. Arbitration is also the only step in the entire grievance procedure where both the union and the employer can have a decision imposed on them by a neutral third party.

Appointment of an Arbitrator

All Canadian jurisdictions leave the initial selection of a single **arbitrator** or an arbitration panel to the mutual agreement of the parties. This agreement is usually reached during the collective bargaining process. The parties will have to live with any decision imposed on them by an arbitrator; therefore, it is important that they agree on the person or persons who will make the final and binding decisions on grievances that may arise during the term of the collective agreement. Because of the importance of mutual agreement in this context, grievance arbitration is sometimes referred to as **consensual adjudication** to distinguish it from other types of adjudication imposed by legislation. Accordingly, grievance arbitrators are also referred to as "adjudicators."

A collective agreement may contain a list of names of individuals who are acceptable to the parties as arbitrators during the term of the agreement. The parties usually rotate through the names on the list to determine which individual will arbitrate a particular grievance. Individuals named in collective agreements as potential arbitrators generally have a background in industrial relations or law. They usually have experience as advocates for either a union or an employer in grievance arbitrations, but most also have some experience as a neutral third-party decision-maker.

If the parties are unable to agree on a mutually acceptable arbitrator or list of arbitrators, all jurisdictions make some provision for the appointment of an arbitrator, usually by the labour relations board on the request of the parties. Labour relations boards usually maintain a list of active arbitrators and either name one who is acceptable to both parties or select an arbitrator on the basis of a simple rotation through the list.

The parties may choose to appoint a tripartite arbitration board rather than an individual arbitrator to arbitrate the grievance. The composition of a board for grievance arbitration is similar to that used in interest arbitration; each party chooses one member, and then both parties mutually choose a third member who will act as chair of the board. An alternative way to appoint a tripartite board is for each party to select one member and then for those two members to select the third member. Some unions and employers prefer a tripartite board over an individual arbitrator because of how the board members are appointed. Since each party is allowed to choose one member of the board, they may feel that at least one board member is "on their side." There may be a perception that a single arbitrator, although theoretically neutral, will not thoroughly consider all aspects of each party's case, whereas the union or employer appointees to a tripartite board can advocate for having "their" side's evidence taken into account. Also, members of a board who are familiar with an industry or occupation can provide information that would result in a more informed decision than that of a single arbitrator without similar experience to draw on.[10] However, because of the extra costs involved in using three arbitrators instead of one, and the extra time it takes for three individuals to arrive at a decision, it is not common to see tripartite boards in grievance arbitrations.

The role of the arbitrator in the grievance arbitration process is to investigate the grievance and to render a decision. The primary method of investigating the grievance is through a hearing, which the arbitrator presides over much like a judge in a court case. As in interest arbitration, which was discussed in Chapter 10, the decision of an arbitrator in a grievance procedure is binding. There are, however, limited circumstances under which an arbitrator's award can be appealed. These circumstances will be outlined later in the chapter.

Arranging an Arbitration Hearing

Once the parties have agreed on an arbitrator, they notify the arbitrator in writing of the appointment. The letter of appointment typically indicates how long the parties anticipate the hearing will take and whether the parties have a preferred location for the hearing. Most arbitration hearings are held near the location of the employer in a neutral facility, such as a hotel meeting room. It is important to the smooth functioning of the arbitration that the location be perceived as neutral; there could be concerns about undue influence on the arbitrator if, for example, the employer allocated a meeting room at the workplace at no cost for the arbitrator's use.

At this stage in the process, the arbitrator also responds to requests from either party to issue subpoenas to ensure that the appropriate witnesses and documentation are available for the hearing. A **subpoena** is a legal order that compels a witness to attend and testify at a hearing. The employer or the union may want particular individuals to testify at the hearing, or want certain pieces of evidence to be presented for the arbitrator's information. If so, they will ask the arbitrator to inform the desired individuals—or those in possession of the evidence—of the date and location of the hearing. The arbitrator will then issue subpoenas to request that those individuals be present at the hearing with any relevant evidence.

Costs of an Arbitration Hearing

An arbitration hearing involves many expenses, including the rental of the space where the hearing is held, the arbitrator's fees and expenses, the cost of recording and transcribing the proceedings, and any legal assistance the parties decide to retain. The union and employer each pay their own costs for the hearing. These costs include legal fees if a lawyer is retained, lost time and wages for the participants (such as the grievor and union or management representatives), and one-half of the arbitrator's costs. The arbitrator's costs include a fee for conducting the hearing, a writing fee for time spent considering and rendering an award, and travel and per diem expenses. The average cost per side for a one-day hearing has been estimated at $15,000.[11]

Having discussed the preparation for the arbitration hearing, we will now outline what happens at the hearing itself.

The Arbitration Hearing

Preliminary Issues

At the start of the hearing, the arbitrator confirms that both parties agree that he or she has jurisdiction under the collective agreement to hear the issue in dispute and to determine an award. This confirmation is necessary to establish that both parties accept the arbitrator's jurisdiction and authority. The question of the arbitrator's jurisdiction is crucial, for under Canadian labour law the arbitrator is empowered to rule only on whether an interpretation, application, or administration of the collective agreement is correct; the arbitrator is not empowered to change the terms of the collective agreement. To ensure the success of the arbitration, it is important that the question of jurisdiction be resolved at the outset of the hearing, so that one or both of the parties do not later attempt to overturn the arbitrator's decision on the grounds that he or she exceeded his or her jurisdiction.

At this stage of the hearing, any objections concerning the timeliness of the grievance, or whether the issue in question constitutes a grievance, are also raised before the arbitrator. This is also the stage of the hearing where any other procedural objections are presented to the arbitrator. When an objection is raised, the party making the objection usually asks the arbitrator to adjourn the hearing until the objection can be resolved. The arbitrator then has the choice of acceding to this request and adjourning the hearing, ruling against the objection and proceeding with the hearing, or reserving judgement on the objection and proceeding with the hearing. Usually, the arbitrator will choose one of the latter two actions. This is because considerable time, effort, and cost have already been expended to prepare for the hearing, and it may be very difficult or expensive for the parties to reconvene at a later date. Thus, it makes more sense for the arbitrator to deal with the objection in a way that will allow the hearing to proceed as scheduled.

When dealing with any of these preliminary objections, arbitrators refer to the relevant labour legislation; this legislation gives them the authority to provide a final and conclusive settlement of the disagreement. Arbitrators appointed under a collective agreement are granted a wide range of powers under Canadian labour legislation. These include, for example, the ability to hear a grievance even if the time limits were exceeded in the previous steps in the grievance procedure: a situation that theoretically should disqualify the grievance from proceeding any further. The arbitrator is allowed to **relieve** against breaches of time limits or other procedural requirements in the collective agreement, and to hear the grievance regardless of these breaches, if he or she believes that there are just and reasonable grounds for doing so.[12]

Procedural Onus

Also determined at the start of the hearing is which party bears the **procedural onus**: that is, which party bears the responsibility for proving their case in the proceedings, rather than simply responding to allegations. As in all proceedings of this type, "he who alleges must go first and prove." Since it is usually the union that files a grievance, it is usually the union that proceeds first in the hearing and that bears the onus of proving its allegation of a violation of the collective agreement. The major exception to this rule is a grievance arbitration that involves the discipline or discharge of an employee. In arbitrations involving these issues, the onus is on the employer to prove that the discipline or discharge was justifiable. The onus is reversed in these types of cases because it is the employer who is best able to explain the reasoning behind the decision to discipline or discharge the employee.[13] It would be difficult for the discharged or disciplined employee to explain the employer's reasons for taking the action, or to produce evidence that is generally only held by the employer, such as personnel records.

Standard of Proof

The final procedural issue that is dealt with before the hearing commences is the establishment of a **standard of proof** to determine whether a party has sufficiently proved its case. The standard of proof used in arbitrations is the **balance of probabilities**, which is the standard used in most civil proceedings. In an arbitration hearing, the party alleging a violation must prove "on balance" that its version of the facts or events is true. The arbitrator may not be satisfied that either party's case is completely accurate or reasonable, but the "balance of probabilities" standard requires the arbitrator to accept the case that is more likely to be true, even if the case is not complete in and of itself. The "balance of probabilities" standard is more liberal than the standard of **beyond a reasonable doubt** used in criminal proceedings, which requires the party making the allegation to present enough evidence to remove any doubt about the justification of the allegation.

However, certain employment offences that lead to discipline or dismissal, such as theft of company property, theft of company time, or other forms of dishonesty, demand a standard of proof higher than the "balance of probabilities" standard and yet not as high as the criminal standard of "beyond a reasonable doubt". The concern here is whether someone who is alleged to have committed such a serious offence should be reinstated or compensated simply because one party's weak case is comparatively better than the other party's weak case. Thus, in arbitrations involving serious employment offences, most arbitrators use the standard of proof of **clear and cogent evidence**. This standard of proof requires that there be sufficient relevant evidence to convince the arbitrator that the grievance is or is not justified.

Winnipeg Police Chief Jack Ewatski testifies at an arbitration hearing. Six officers filed a grievance after being placed on leave over allegations that they failed to warn a murder victim about the threat to his life.

Order of Proceeding

Once any preliminary issues are resolved, the actual hearing of the grievance begins. The party proceeding first makes an opening statement. This statement is designed to tell the arbitrator about the issue in dispute and the elements of the alleged violation of the collective agreement. The statement will also include a summary of the evidence that the party will present, and a summary of case law (decisions in previous similar arbitration cases) that the party will rely upon to support its position. The other party then has an opportunity to make a similar opening statement to the arbitrator. After both opening statements have been made, the party proceeding first calls its witnesses. Witnesses participating in an arbitration hearing may include the actual grievor, other employees affected by the alleged violation of the collective agreement, supervisors or managers involved in the alleged violation, and any workers or managers who observed events related to the alleged violation.

The party calling a witness to the stand has the first opportunity to ask questions of the witness. This process, called **direct examination**, is intended to allow the party to present its case through the witness's statements. When direct examination has concluded, the witness is then cross-examined by the other party. The intent of **cross-examination** is to clarify statements that the witness made in direct examination and, through questioning, to reveal inconsistencies or flaws in the witness's statements or to provide evidence that strengthens the other party's position. When cross-examination has concluded, the party that originally called the witness then has a limited right of re-examination. During **re-examination**, the party is allowed to ask its witness further questions to clarify any point raised during cross-examination or any information not addressed during direct examination.

This procedure of direct examination, cross-examination, and re-examination is repeated for each witness. In addition to the parties' examinations of the witnesses, the arbitrator may also ask questions of the witnesses. During examinations, the witnesses may be asked to present physical evidence such as letters, memos, or personnel records. If such evidence is presented, copies are given to the arbitrator and to the other party. The arbitrator is entitled to rule on the admissibility of evidence or on any other procedural issue that may arise while the hearing is being conducted.

Once all the evidence has been presented and all the witnesses have testified, the first party makes a closing argument. This argument follows the elements of the opening statement. It states the issues from the perspective of the first party, summarizes how the evidence of its witnesses relates to the alleged violation of the collective agreement, and, if necessary, quotes other arbitration cases in support of its perspective. The second party then makes its closing argument. The first party has a limited right of reply to make a brief response to the second party's closing argument. The arbitrator then formally adjourns the hearing.

Creating the Arbitration Award

After the hearing is adjourned, the arbitrator retires to write the arbitration award. Some collective agreements prescribe time limits within which the arbitration award must be written after the hearing ends. The award will usually contain the following elements:

- a summary of the evidence presented by each party

- the arbitrator's assessment of the evidence (which party's case is more convincing and why)

- the arbitrator's verdict on the grievance, along with an explanation of the reasoning leading to the verdict

- the arbitrator's prescribed remedy if the grievance is found to be justified

- any direction for the implementation of the remedy (e.g., a deadline by which the remedy must be carried out)

When the arbitration award is completed, it is sent to the union and the employer. The receipt of the award by the union and the employer formally concludes the grievance arbitration process.

Arbitration awards are designed to be final and binding on the union, its members, and the employer. It is possible to appeal an arbitration award, but if an appeal is permitted, it is heard in civil court. Canadian labour legislation restricts the use of this process so as to reinforce the provision that the arbitration award is the final resolution of the grievance. Most jurisdictions make limited provisions for a judicial appeal based on a matter of general law. Appeals may be permitted if one or both of the parties can show that any of the following conditions existed:

- The arbitrator was biased in some fashion (e.g., the arbitrator's conduct or ruling was unduly influenced by some connection with one of the parties).

- The arbitrator did not follow correct procedure in conducting the hearing (e.g., the arbitrator did not allow a witness to testify or refused to let a witness present his or her evidence).

- The arbitrator ruled on matters outside his or her jurisdiction or on matters not related to the issue he or she was asked to arbitrate.

- The arbitrator fundamentally misunderstood or misinterpreted the collective agreement language involved in the grievance.

We should emphasize that a successful appeal of an arbitrator's award is very rare. Most experienced arbitrators are careful not to put themselves in any situation that might be subsequently interpreted as grounds for an appeal of their award. For example, experienced arbitrators will excuse themselves from an arbitration where their neutrality might be questioned (e.g., where there is a professional or personal relationship between the arbitrator and one of the witnesses). If the parties disagree with the arbitrator's award, that in and of itself is not grounds for appeal, as the parties enter into arbitration knowing that the arbitrator's award is binding. By agreeing to the arbitration process, the parties are implicitly expressing trust in the arbitrator's skills and decision-making ability; notwithstanding that trust, there is always the possibility that the arbitrator's decision may contradict one or both parties' expectations. This is simply one of the inherent risks of engaging in the arbitration process. The potential for disappointment is countered by the fact that at least the arbitration ends in a resolution of the grievance, which the parties have been unable to achieve by themselves.

When parties disagree with the arbitrator's award, they will sometimes attempt to appeal the award by alleging that the arbitrator committed one of the errors noted above and claiming that this error led to an incorrect ruling. For example, one party might claim that the arbitrator did not allow a witness to finish giving his or her evidence at the hearing, and that if the arbitrator had heard all the evidence, his or her perspective on the case would have been different and the award would consequently have been different. However, for an appeal of this sort to be successful, the party making the allegation must produce fairly substantial and convincing evidence both of the alleged error and of the alleged error's effect on the arbitrator's award.

Since the arbitrator's award is binding, the parties are expected to abide by the terms of the award and to carry out any ordered actions, such as making a payment or reinstating a dismissed or demoted employee. If a party does not comply with the terms or direction of an arbitration award, the award may be filed in the relevant provincial court registry and enforced as if it were a decision of that court.

Having concluded our outline of how the traditional grievance arbitration process operates, we will now turn our attention to some alternatives to this process. We will first identify some problems that can occur when the traditional grievance arbitration process is used, and will then show how alternative forms of arbitration may help avoid those problems.

PROBLEMS WITH THE TRADITIONAL GRIEVANCE ARBITRATION PROCESS

The purpose of the grievance arbitration process is to provide a method of resolving grievances that arise under the terms of the collective agreement without having the parties resort to work stoppages to force a resolution. As mentioned earlier, this process is presumed to be fast, cost-effective, and informal. In reality, the grievance arbitration process can be slow, costly, formal, and legalistic.[14]

Speed of the Process

The intent of the grievance arbitration process is to resolve workplace issues in a timely manner. In reality, grievances filed in Canadian jurisdictions can take up to one year to be resolved, from the time a grievance is first filed until an arbitration award is finally issued.[15] A number of factors affect the length of the arbitration process.

In all Canadian jurisdictions, a few well-known and busy arbitrators conduct the majority of arbitration cases. Once an arbitrator has been appointed, it is often difficult to find hearing dates that are convenient for all the participants—the arbitrator, legal counsel for the parties, representatives of the parties, and all the individual witnesses. When the parties finally agree on acceptable dates and the hearing begins, complex issues can be raised that may require scheduling additional hearing days. Finally, the arbitrator must spend considerable time writing the arbitration award or decision if he or she is to produce a high-quality document.

The amount of delay at different stages of the arbitration process is related to different factors that may or may not be relevant in individual cases.[16] If the grievance involves highly complex and legalistic issues, there can be a considerable length of time between when the initial grievance is filed and when it is finally referred to arbitration. Selecting an arbitrator may also be a lengthy process when legal counsel are involved in the selection decision and when an arbitration board, rather than a single arbitrator, must be chosen. The time to write a decision may also be extended if an arbitration board must collectively reach a verdict or if the case is complex.

Formality and Legality of the Process

The grievance arbitration process was initially designed to be an informal proceeding conducted by the union and the employer representatives. Since the union and the employer negotiated the terms and conditions of the collective agreement, it was assumed that these parties, or their representatives, would be comfortable enforcing the administration of the agreement they jointly negotiated.

In reality, the grievance procedure is usually an adversarial process, because unions and employers have different and conflicting interests in the workplace. The adversarial nature of the process commonly results in both parties retaining legal counsel to advise them prior to the arbitration hearing and/or to represent them during the hearing. The involvement of lawyers, coupled with the fact that most arbitrators are also lawyers, introduces a level of formality and legalism into the arbitration process that was not intended in the initial design.

On the one hand, formalizing the arbitration process to the degree that arbitration hearings resemble court proceedings gives some degree of consistency and rigour to the process. The relatively standardized hearing procedure ensures that all parties in the case receive a fair hearing. On the other hand, this degree of formalization may negatively affect the quality of the process and outcome by unduly intimidating witnesses who are not comfortable testifying in a court-like atmosphere. It may also bring further conflict into the process in the form of arguments over procedure.

It is questionable whether the involvement of legal counsel in arbitration makes a difference to whether a party is effectively represented in the proceedings. One study addressing this question examined the outcome of 272 Canadian arbitration and labour relations board cases involving disciplinary issues. The study attempted to determine whether the involvement of lawyers as advocates made a difference in the direction of the decision.[17] The results of the study indicated that legal representation for employees makes it more likely that employees will win the arbitration, whereas there is no such advantage to legal representation for employers. However, if both sides use lawyers to represent them in the proceedings, neither side increases its chances of obtaining its desired outcome.

Another consideration in the formality and legalism of the traditional arbitration process is the nature of the arbitration award itself. The arbitration award is often lengthy and written with a view to furthering labour relations policy. Consequently, the award is legalistic in form and results in one party winning and the other party losing. Arbitration decisions in this form can have a negative impact on the labour-management relationship, since the parties may not understand the discussion in the decision or agree with the legalistic reasoning that led to the award.

Cost-Effectiveness of the Process

Another result of the involvement of lawyers in the arbitration process is an increase in the cost of the process. As noted earlier, each party is responsible for its own legal fees as well as for one-half of the arbitrator's fees and one-half of other expenses associated with conducting a hearing. These other expenses can include the cost of a neutral hearing room (usually in a hotel), travel expenses for the arbitrator, and other miscellaneous costs. Less direct costs associated with the arbitration process include production and labour lost while the parties are preparing for and attending the arbitration hearing. As well, hidden or indirect costs are generated by the impact of an adversarial adjudication process on the parties' relationship and the workplace.

The cumulative impact of these costs can discourage parties from pursuing valid grievances that could be resolved through arbitration. As mentioned earlier, unions and employers both have to decide whether the potential value of an arbitration award is worth the cost of participating in arbitration. Furthermore, because of the impact of costs associated with arbitration, one party might use the grievance process as a way to damage the other party, not as a way to resolve significant issues related to the collective agreement. If one party knows that dealing with a grievance will negatively affect the other party financially, that party may be tempted to file as many grievances as possible, regardless of their merit, simply to drain the other party's finances or resources. The grievance procedure is sometimes misused when one party has much greater resources than the other party. The richer party may be tempted to engage in behaviour that clearly violates the collective agreement in order to provoke the other party into filing a grievance and then having to bear the costs associated with pursuing that grievance.

Despite these problems with the grievance arbitration process, the process continues to play a major role in the Canadian labour relations system. However, some jurisdictions are attempting to develop alternative processes that complement or replace the traditional grievance arbitration process. These alternative processes can be either imposed by legislation or mutually agreed to by the parties in their negotiations. We will now examine a few of these alternatives.

ALTERNATIVES TO THE TRADITIONAL GRIEVANCE ARBITRATION PROCESS

Expedited Arbitration

Expedited arbitration is designed to be faster, less expensive, less formal, and less legalistic than the traditional arbitration process. Table 11-3 describes how expedited arbitration

TABLE 11-3 Expedited Arbitration					
	Preconditions	**How the Process Is Started**	**Settlement Officer**	**Hearing Timelines**	**Decision Timelines**
Alberta	Not specified	Not specified	Not specified	Not specified	In any arbitration, if one of the parties complains that an award has not been rendered within a reasonable time, the board may issue a directive to ensure an award

TABLE 11-3 Expedited Arbitration (Continued)					
	Preconditions	How the Process Is Started	Settlement Officer	Hearing Timelines	Decision Timelines
					is rendered or may appoint a new arbitrator or arbitration board
British Columbia	The matter must not have already been referred to arbitration and must not exceed any time limits in the collective agreement for referral to arbitration	One of the parties submits a request to director of the Collective Agreement Arbitration Bureau	Single arbitrator appointed by the director of the Collective Agreement Arbitration Bureau	Not specified, but if the settlement officer attempts mediation and fails, expedited arbitration must proceed as soon as the officer reports to the director	Within 21 days after the conclusion of the hearing
Manitoba	Not specified	Not specified	Not specified	Not specified	In all arbitrations, a single arbitrator must issue a decision within 30 days of the hearing conclusion and an arbitration board must issue a decision within 60 days of the hearing conclusion

TABLE 11-3   Expedited Arbitration (Continued)

	Preconditions	How the Process Is Started	Settlement Officer	Hearing Timelines	Decision Timelines
Ontario	Not stated	If there is a failure to appoint an arbitrator under a collective agreement, the minister may appoint one on the request of either party. The minister may also, on the request of either party, appoint a settlement officer to effect a settlement before an arbitrator begins to hear the matter; however, no appointment will be made if the other party objects	Single arbitrator, board, or settlement officer; arbitrator or arbitration board appointed through terms in the collective agreement or by the minister; settlement officer appointed by the minister	None specified, other than that the settlement officer must endeavour to effect a settlement before the start of any hearing by the arbitrator or arbitration board	Arbitrator must give a decision within 30 days after hearings conclude; the arbitration board must give a decision within 60 days after hearings conclude. These times may be extended with the consent of the parties or at the discretion of the arbitrator or arbitration board, as long as reasons are stated. The arbitrator or arbitration board may give oral decisions (in which case, they must be given promptly after hearings are concluded) and shall give written

TABLE 11-3 Expedited Arbitration (Continued)

	Preconditions	How the Process Is Started	Settlement Officer	Hearing Timelines	Decision Timelines
					decisions promptly or written decisions with reasons within a reasonable time period, on the request of either party
Saskatchewan	The matter must not have been already referred to arbitration and must not exceed any time limits in the collective agreement for arbitration	Both parties apply to the minister of labour	Single arbitrator appointed by the minister of labour. If one party requests and the other agrees, a grievance mediator may be appointed prior to a hearing to assist parties in reaching a resolution	Date for hearing must be set within 28 days of date of application to the minister of labour	Decision must be issued within 21 days after the conclusion of the hearing

works in the Canadian jurisdictions where it is available. Expedited arbitration processes created by legislation are known as statutory expedited arbitration processes. In jurisdictions where expedited arbitration is not provided by legislation, the parties to a grievance can use expedited arbitration to resolve the grievance if they both accept its use. Expedited arbitration processes that are voluntarily adopted by the parties are known as consensual expedited arbitration processes.

In most Canadian jurisdictions, either the union or the employer can refer a grievance to expedited arbitration. If the parties have mutually agreed to establish an expedited arbitration process, the process usually includes a clear definition of which types of grievances will be handled in this manner. Some expedited arbitration processes are only used to resolve minor discipline grievances, such as those involving a penalty of 30 days' suspension or less, or a maximum amount of lost pay. Others are used to resolve all discipline grievances, including discharge grievances, but not to resolve policy grievances or grievances involving interpretation of the collective agreement.

A distinctive characteristic of expedited arbitration is its reliance on specified timelines for holding the arbitration hearing and issuing the arbitration award. These timelines work because most expedited arbitration processes involve a roster system for appointing arbitrators. In statutory processes, the arbitrators on the roster report their availability weekly or monthly to an administrator, who then assigns the arbitrators as needed, knowing the length of time the arbitrators are available and the timelines within which the cases must be resolved. In consensual processes, if an arbitrator on the roster is not available to conduct the hearing within the specified time, he or she is passed over in favour of the next available arbitrator.

Arbitration awards issued in expedited arbitrations are usually not considered to be precedent-setting. This means that the parties will not quote the award to support their arguments in other grievances or otherwise attempt to use the award to set a precedent for future grievances. In many expedited arbitration procedures, the parties do not quote other arbitration awards in their presentation or argument. As a result, awards in expedited arbitrations are shorter, more fact-based, and less legalistic than traditional arbitration awards.

Finally, in most expedited arbitrations, the parties are encouraged to represent themselves before the arbitrator, without the assistance of legal counsel. By presenting their own case, the parties reduce the costs of the arbitration.

In summary, both statutory and consensual expedited arbitration processes reduce the cost of participating in an arbitration, lessen the time within which the grievance must be heard and a decision must be given to the parties, and provide awards that are shorter, are less legalistic, and which do not set a precedent. Any solution to the problem of the time involved in arbitrations must address factors such as the presence of legal counsel, the method of selecting an arbitrator, and the arbitrator's workload, and must focus on the impact that these factors have on the different stages of the arbitration process.[18] We can see that the intent of the expedited arbitration process is to minimize the delays associated with these factors throughout the arbitration process, and for this reason the expedited process has several advantages over the traditional arbitration system. However, as noted, expedited arbitration is sometimes considered appropriate only for smaller or less complicated grievances, and thus traditional grievance arbitration is still used to resolve more complex or lengthy grievances.

Grievance Mediation

Another alternative to the traditional grievance arbitration process is **grievance mediation**. Table 11-4 describes the provisions for grievance mediation in the Canadian jurisdictions that allow it.

In grievance mediation, the mediator is often an industrial relations officer or settlement officer employed by a labour relations board. These highly trained individuals meet with the parties within five or 10 days of their appointment to inquire into the grievance and assist the parties in settling their differences.

Grievance mediation is timely, cost-efficient, informal, and non-adversarial. A further advantage of grievance mediation, as noted in the wording of the Nova Scotia legislation, is its ability to assist the parties in developing effective long-term labour-management relations by emphasizing mutual problem solving. It may seem that mediation is not totally suitable as a mechanism to resolve disputes over contractual rights, since mediation does not determine whose rights take precedence. However, as one researcher states, "The focus of mediation is reaching a mutually acceptable agreement, rather than winning a rights dispute."[19] Clearly, then, for grievance mediation to be successful in resolving grievances, the employer and the union must be willing to work actively toward a mutually beneficial solution and not be primarily concerned with which party is declared a winner and which party becomes a loser.

TABLE 11-4 Grievance Mediation

	How Mediator Is Appointed	Time Frame	Mediator's Mandate	Person or Body to Whom Mediator Reports
British Columbia	On request of one of the parties, the director of the Collective Agreement Arbitration Bureau appoints a settlement officer. The officer may be appointed before the expedited arbitration hearing takes place	Must commence proceedings within 5 days of officer's appointment	Inquire into differences between parties; assist in settling differences; report to the director on results of the inquiry and success of the settlement effort	Director of the Collective Agreement Arbitration Bureau
Manitoba	On request of both parties, the minister of labour appoints a grievance mediator. If the collective agreement names a grievance mediator, the minister of labour may pay one-third of the cost of the mediator's expenses. Grievance mediator may be appointed before the arbitration hearing takes place	Must commence proceedings within 7 days of appointment or as the minister of labour specifies	Inquire into the grievance; assist in settling the grievance; report to the minister of labour and labour board on the result of the inquiry and success of the effort	Minister of labour and Manitoba Labour Board

TABLE 11-4 Grievance Mediation (Continued)			
	How Mediator Is Appointed	**Time Frame**	**Mediator's Mandate**	**Person or Body to Whom Mediator Reports**
New Brunswick	Appointed by the minister of labour at the request of either party. Grievance mediator may be appointed before the arbitration hearing takes place	Must commence proceedings within 10 days after mediator's appointment or as the minister of labour specifies	Inquire into differences; assist the parties in settling differences; report to the minister of labour on the results of the inquiry and success of the effort	Minister of labour
Nova Scotia	The minister of labour may appoint a mediation officer at any time to bring about settlement of an industrial dispute or to prevent an industrial dispute	Not specified	Investigate causes of the dispute; attempt to bring about a settlement or prevent a dispute; assist in the development of effective labour-management relations; make a report to minister of labour	Minister of labour

TABLE 11-4 Grievance Mediation (Continued)

	How Mediator Is Appointed	Time Frame	Mediator's Mandate	Person or Body to Whom Mediator Reports
Ontario	The minister of labour may appoint a settlement officer prior to an arbitration hearing. An arbitrator may also act as a mediator at any stage in the pro- ceedings with both parties' approval	Not specified	To effect a settlement between the parties	Minister of labour
Saskatchewan	Joint request by parties. Grievance mediation may occur prior to a hearing in expedited arbitration	Must begin proceedings within 10 days of being appointed	Assist parties to settle the grievance by mediation; if unsuccessful, assist parties to agree on material facts, after which parties may take the matter to grievance arbitration	Minister of labour

As in other forms of mediation, the grievance mediator assists the parties in reaching their own mutually satisfactory solution to the grievance. Most jurisdictions permitting grievance mediation also establish the rule that information disclosed to a mediator is considered confidential and cannot be disclosed in any subsequent arbitration hearing (i.e., if the grievance is not resolved through mediation and proceeds to a formal arbitration).[20] This rule is intended to encourage the parties to share information freely with the mediator, without fearing that such information could be used to their disadvantage in any subsequent proceedings. Because the mediator does not act as an arbitrator and thus does not make a formal decision on the grievance, grievance mediation does not require a written award.

Different mediators bring different philosophical approaches to grievance mediation.[21] One approach, referred to as the **settlement orientation**, is often found in situations where grievance mediation is imposed by legislation. In these situations, where mediation is not voluntary, there is increased pressure on the parties to agree on a resolution, and thus many parties feel unsatisfied with the resulting agreement. However, the advantage of the settlement orientation is that the parties are persuaded or influenced to reach a resolution without having to resort to the arbitration process.

Another approach to grievance mediation is referred to as the **transformative orientation**. This approach focuses on teaching the parties to resolve their own disagreements and to understand each other's point of view, information, and interests. It enhances communication between the parties, assists in fostering their ongoing relationship, and results in higher satisfaction with the mediated result. However, the transformative orientation often results in a more time-consuming process than does the settlement orientation.

Mediation-Arbitration

Another alternative to the traditional grievance arbitration process is a combination of the mediation and arbitration processes known as **mediation-arbitration** or med-arb. Med-arb was described in Chapter 10 as a method for resolving disputes during collective bargaining, but it can also be used for resolving disputes related to the application or interpretation of the collective agreement. Table 11-5 describes the provisions for med-arb in the Canadian jurisdictions that allow it.

Med-arb processes in most jurisdictions use arbitrators skilled in dispute resolution techniques. The med-arb process used in grievance resolution is very similar to the med-arb

	Preconditions	How Process Is Started	Timelines for Proceedings	Mediator's Mandate	Timeline for Arbitration Decision
TABLE 11-5	Mediation-Arbitration				
Federal	Not specified	Not specified	Not specified	Arbitrator may assist in resolving differences; issues not settled in mediation may continue without prejudice to arbitration	Not specified
British Columbia	The parties must agree on the nature of any issues in dispute	Both parties agree to refer issues to mediation-arbitration; parties may choose their own single mediator-arbitrator or may ask the director of the Collective Agreement Arbitration Bureau for an appointment if unable to agree	Proceedings must begin within 28 days of the mediator-arbitrator's appointment	Mediator-arbitrator assists parties to settle the grievance by mediation; if mediation is unsuccessful, the mediator-arbitrator must assist parties to reach an agreement on material	Within 21 days of the completion of proceedings

TABLE 11-5   Mediation-Arbitration (Continued)

	Preconditions	How Process Is Started	Timelines for Proceedings	Mediator's Mandate	Timeline for Arbitration Decision
				facts in dispute and then determine the outcome by arbitration	
Ontario	The parties must agree on the nature of any issues in dispute. An arbitrator may mediate at any stage with the consent of both parties	The parties may choose their own single mediator-arbitrator or may ask the minister of labour for an appointment if unable to agree	Within 30 days of the mediator-arbitrator's appointment	Mediator-arbitrator assists parties to settle grievance by mediation; if unsuccessful, the mediator-arbitrator must assist parties to reach an agreement on material facts in dispute and then determine the outcome by arbitration	Within 5 days of the completion of proceedings

process used in resolving collective bargaining disputes. The third party first acts as mediator and, in an informal setting, attempts to assist the parties in resolving their differences. As with other expedited arbitration processes, there are specific time frames (usually less than 30 days) within which all parties must meet and attempt to resolve the grievance. If the third party is successful in helping the parties reach settlement on some but not all of the grievance's issues, the third party then arbitrates the outstanding issues and writes an arbitration award.

Med-arb attempts to combine the advantages of the grievance mediation and the grievance arbitration systems. Its first part is an informal process that facilitates the relationship between the parties and helps them develop problem-solving skills through the use of mediation. If mediation is not successful in resolving all the disputed issues, the parties have a timely and cost-effective method of reaching a final and binding resolution through arbitration.

SUMMARY

Because it is not possible to create a collective agreement that will apply perfectly to all parts of a workplace over the agreement's entire term, it is necessary to have a process by which disagreements over the application, interpretation, or administration of the collective agreement can be resolved. The grievance arbitration process fills this role. Grievance arbitration is also known as rights arbitration and consensual adjudication.

There are four generally recognized types of grievances. An individual grievance is a single employee's complaint about an employer action that allegedly violates the collective agreement. If the employer's alleged violation affects several employees, then any resulting grievance is referred to as a group grievance. A continuing grievance involves a series of ongoing actions that allegedly violate the collective agreement. And, finally, a policy grievance is filed by the union on behalf of all employees and usually concerns the employer's interpretation or application of the collective agreement.

The grievance procedure has several steps. The usual first step is an informal meeting between the complainant and his or her immediate supervisor. If the disagreement cannot be resolved at this point, the grievance is usually recorded in writing and brought to the attention of union and management representatives. These parties then meet and attempt to reach a mutually satisfactory solution to the disagreement. If they are unsuccessful, the disagreement is generally brought to higher authorities within the union and management in a final attempt to resolve the disagreement internally.

If the parties cannot agree on a solution to the grievance on their own, a third party—the grievance arbitrator—becomes involved in the process. In most situations, the arbitrator holds a hearing to investigate the evidence for and against each party's position and then issues a decision that is binding on both parties. However, the effectiveness of the traditional grievance arbitration process can be hampered by factors such as the potentially long time to reach a resolution, high costs, and excessive formality.

Several alternative forms of grievance arbitration are characterized by faster, less legalistic processes and by solutions that attempt to build positive long-term relationships between the parties. Expedited arbitration deals only with particular types of grievances and has predetermined timelines to ensure a solution is reached within a certain period. Grievance mediation attempts to resolve grievances by informally assisting the parties to reach their own solution. Mediation-arbitration is a two-step process in which a third party first acts as a mediator and then, if necessary, acts as an arbitrator to resolve any disputes that have not been settled through mediation.

KEY TERMS FOR CHAPTER 11

arbitrator (p. 465)
balance of probabilities (p. 469)
beyond a reasonable doubt (p. 469)
clear and cogent evidence (p. 469)
consensual adjudication (p. 465)
continuing grievances (p. 452)
cross-examination (p. 470)
direct examination (p. 470)
duty of fair representation (p. 462)
expedited arbitration (p. 476)
grievances (p. 448)
grievance arbitration (p. 448)
grievance mediation (p. 481)
grievor (p. 455)

group grievance (p. 452)
individual grievance (p. 451)
mediation-arbitration (p. 485)
past practice (p. 453)
policy grievance (p. 452)
procedural onus (p. 468)
re-examination (p. 470)
relieve (p. 468)
rights arbitration (p. 449)
settlement orientation (p. 485)
standard of proof (p. 469)
subpoena (p. 466)
transformative orientation (p. 485)

DISCUSSION QUESTIONS FOR CHAPTER 11

1. Define and give examples of the different types of grievances.

2. Outline and explain the steps in a typical grievance procedure.

3. Why would the employer or the union raise preliminary objections at an arbitration hearing?

4. What does it mean to have the "procedural onus" in an arbitration case?

5. What are the different "standards of proof" used in arbitration, and when would each apply?

6. Describe how an arbitration hearing is conducted.

7. Explain the disadvantages of the traditional grievance arbitration process.

8. What is meant by "expedited arbitration"?

9. Discuss the advantages and disadvantages of grievance mediation.

10. What is "med-arb"?

TAMMY QUINTON, PROVINCIAL CAREWORKERS UNION, AND RESTFUL CARE HOME

(Based on *Parker and SEIU Local 183*, 2003)

In this case, Tammy Quinton is alleging that her union breached its duty of fair representation by withdrawing a grievance against her dismissal. She is alleging that this decision on the part of the union was arbitrary and discriminatory, and she is asking the labour relations board to order the union to proceed with the grievance.

Case Facts

All three parties have agreed on the basic facts of the case.

Quinton, a registered practical nurse, worked at Restful Care Home, where the employees were members of a local of the Provincial Careworkers Union. On February 15, Quinton was the nurse in charge of the night shift. On that night, as part of her regular duties, she examined one of the residents. This patient, who had Alzheimer's disease and was unaware of her surroundings, had a mole on her back with long hairs growing from it. When Quinton examined this patient, she noticed that someone had braided the hairs. The home's rules required Quinton to report events such as this, but while planning to do so, she tied a green ribbon to the braid as "a little fun" to amuse the health care aide who she thought would be examining the patient later. Quinton forgot to report the event and did not remove the braid and ribbon, which were discovered on the next shift by another employee, who also happened to be the shop steward.

The shop steward reported the event to the home's management. Quinton was allowed to work her next scheduled shift but was then suspended indefinitely pending an investigation. On February 20, management phoned Quinton to discuss the incident. Quinton stated that she was responsible for tying the ribbon to the hair, and took responsibility for not reporting the event as required. She also apologized for her conduct.

On February 21, Quinton was called to a meeting with management. A union representative was present at this meeting. Quinton was told that the issue would go to the vice-president of human resources of the company that owned Restful Care Home. The next day, Quinton's employment was terminated on the grounds that she had failed to report the braided hair and that, by her own admission, she had tied the ribbon on the hair. The company stated that these actions, in its view, constituted patient abuse.

On February 23, Quinton filed a grievance challenging her dismissal. On March 8, the union and the company met to discuss the grievance. On March 13, the union called Quinton to advise her that the employer had offered a proposal to settle the grievance. The College of Nurses had not yet been advised of the incident, and the company proposed that if Quinton were to resign her employment, the College would not be notified. Moreover, if Quinton were to resign, the health care aide involved in the incident, who had also been terminated, would get her job back. The union advised Quinton that if the case went to arbitration, the company might be sued by the patient's family and the College would automatically be notified.

On March 14, Quinton received a letter from the College notifying her that it had received a complaint from the company about the incident. The letter was dated March 8. Quinton then contacted the union and said she felt that the company was, in essence, bargaining in bad faith and that she wished to take the case to arbitration.

On March 15, a union representative, Lisa Iwaki, sent a letter to the employer stating that it wished to "proceed with the above-noted grievance." The collective agreement states that if the parties are unable to resolve a grievance regarding termination of employment within five days of the termination, the matter may be pursued to arbitration.

On March 21, a different union representative, Ken Dumont, wrote to Quinton to state the union was withdrawing her grievance. Dumont stated in the letter that, after reviewing the circumstances involved and the nature of the incident, "I don't believe the union would be able to successfully argue your case before an arbitrator." On April 10, Quinton, following the union's internal process, appealed this decision in writing to the president of the local. The union did not respond.

In September and October, the College of Nurses conducted its review of Quinton's conduct. On October 15, it wrote a non-disciplinary caution letter to Quinton. Quinton sent a copy of this letter to Dumont on November 23 and requested that, in view of this decision, the union attempt to get her job back. Dumont wrote to the company and asked it to reconsider its decision to terminate Quinton, but the company refused. The union advised Quinton that it had no further options. Quinton filed her complaint against the union with the labour relations board the following February.

The board noted that Dumont and Iwaki are no longer employed with the union.

The Union's Position

The union argues that Quinton had waited too long to file her complaint with the labour relations board and therefore her complaint should be dismissed for delay. The union also argues that, in addition to the reasons it had previously given for withdrawing the grievance, it feels that patient abuse was a sensitive issue and that its relationship with the employer would have been damaged if Quinton's case proceeded to arbitration. The union also states that Quinton's response to the charges against her was unacceptable because, as part of her response, she relied on the fact that the patient was unaware of what had happened.

The Complainant's Position

The complainant states that her delay in filing the application was partially due to the actions of the union, including its failure to respond to her appeal of the decision to not proceed to arbitration. She also alleges that the union rejected pursuing her grievance in favour of pursuing a grievance involving another employee and a separate incident. In the complainant's view, this employee's behaviour had been much worse than hers, and she alleges that the decision to proceed with this grievance but not hers constituted discrimination on the part of the union.

CASE *11-2*

CARLOS MUNIZ, PAUL IRVING, AND TRADES WORKERS UNION

(Based on *Ali and UA*, 2007)

In this case, Muniz and Irving, who are trades apprentices, were terminated from their jobs because the employer alleged they were inattentive and disruptive during a mandatory safety training session. Muniz and Irving have complained to the board that the union failed to fulfill its duty of fair representation by not pursuing their grievance after the termination. They are asking the board to order the union to proceed with the grievance.

Case Facts

Muniz and Irving are members of the Trades Workers Union. At the time the dispute arose, they were working as apprentices at an oil production facility. Because of the nature of the work at the facility, all trades workers are required to attend a harness safety training session, and the employer has a "zero tolerance" policy for inattention at these sessions (i.e., anyone refusing to listen or participate will be fired).

Muniz and Irving attended the training session about one week after they were hired, along with 10 other employees. Muniz and Irving told the board that when they arrived at the session, they sat at the back of the training room, where a radio was turned on and tuned to a hockey game. When the instructor started, he asked them to turn the radio off, and Irving complied. Muniz and Irving say that they sat and listened attentively to the safety presentation and were not disruptive in any way.

In the employer's version of events, Irving refused to turn off the radio the first time he was asked, and neither Muniz nor Irving paid attention during the presentation or participated in group activities. Both were also disruptive during the class. The class instructor asked three management staff to come to the safety meeting; these managers asked Muniz and Irving to come with them to the facility's main office, after which both were fired. Muniz and Irving told the board that this came as a complete surprise to them.

As the safety meeting was held during the night shift, Muniz and Irving had to wait until the next morning to contact the union's business agent. They met individually with the agent for about half an hour. Both gave him the same version of what had happened and informed him that they wanted their jobs back. Both also informed the agent that there were approximately a dozen individuals present at the training session.

In both meetings, the business agent took notes and told them that a grievance would be filed but that it would take some time. Irving also had a brief meeting with the business agent a week later, during which he provided the name of a witness to the incidents that allegedly were the basis for the firing.

Over the next two months, both Muniz and Irving made several attempts to contact the business agent to find out what was happening with their grievance. On the occasions where they were able to speak to the business agent, he told them that "these things take time" and that he was still investigating. At the end of the second month, Muniz and Irving each received a letter from the business agent stating that the union would not be proceeding with the grievance because he was unable to substantiate their version of events.

The business agent told the board that he first contacted the shop steward, who told him that he (the shop steward) had tried to get Muniz and Irving rehired but that he was told both individuals had previously received verbal warnings for "not listening" and that their supervisor refused to rehire them. The business agent then contacted the human resources manager at the facility. The human resources manager told the board that he and the business agent had "three or four" conversations about the terminations. In the first conversation, he was asked to reinstate Muniz and Irving, but refused on the basis that the company took safety concerns very seriously. In the other conversations, he and the business agent discussed extending the time for filing the grievance, the acknowledgement that a grievance had been filed, and statements that the course instructor and her supervisor had given to the human resources manager. At some point (neither party could recall the exact date) the human resources manager allowed the business agent to review the statements from the instructor and her supervisor.

The human resources manager told the board that a formal grievance was filed a week after the incidents. Both Muniz and Irving told the board that they never received copies of the grievance.

The business agent told the board that he talked to Muniz four or five times over the two months after the incident, including two meetings in person, and that he also met Irving in person four times over the same period. He could not recall exactly how many times he was in contact with Irving during this period. Muniz told the board that he gave the business agent a written statement immediately after their initial meeting. The business agent told the board that he had never seen this statement before.

The business agent also stated that he did not contact the witness named by Irving because of "past involvement and knowledge" about this individual.

After receiving the letters from the union, both Muniz and Irving were very upset. Muniz phoned the business agent and demanded that the union pursue the grievance, and the business agent refused. Irving was away on another job when he received the letter, so his mother attempted to reach the business agent, leaving several messages that were not returned. The business agent stated that he did not recall receiving these messages.

The Complainants' Position

Muniz and Irving allege that the union has failed in its duty of fair representation by refusing to pursue their grievance. They allege that the decision to abandon the grievance was arbitrary and was not based on a thorough investigation of the situation.

The Union's Position

The union argues that, as Muniz and Irving's version of events could not be substantiated, it was justified in deciding to withdraw the grievance.

EXERCISE

The "Wally Worker" Grievance Arbitration Simulation

(Reproduced with the permission of the Canadian Labour Congress)

In this exercise, you and your classmates will participate in a simulation of a grievance arbitration hearing. Each simulation will have eight participants:

- the arbitrator
- Wally Worker, the grievor
- Bobby Boss, Wally's supervisor
- Tanker Treadmill, the union business agent
- John Demanding, the company personnel manager
- Sidney Steward, the shop steward
- the union's lawyer
- the company's lawyer

The arbitrator will preside over an arbitration hearing, after which the arbitrator will make his or her decision and report his or her award to the participants.

Your instructor will give you the information you need to prepare for the simulation as well as the times and locations for the hearings.

References

[1] Dessler, G., Cole, N.D., & Sutherland, V.L. (1999). *Human resources management in Canada* (7th Canadian edition). Scarborough, ON: Prentice-Hall.

[2] Craig, A.W.J., & Solomon, N.A. (1996). *The system of industrial relations in Canada* (5th edition). Scarborough, ON: Prentice-Hall.

[3] Trower, C. (1974). *Arbitration at a glance.* Labour Research Institute, 9–14.

[4] Gray, K. (2003, January 25). City library becoming a 'porn palace.' *The Ottawa Citizen*, p. D1.

[5] Bemmels, B. (1994). The determinants of grievance initiation. *Industrial & Labor Relations Review, 47*(2), 285–302.

[6] Thornicroft, K.W. (2000). The grievance arbitration process: theory and practice. In Gunderson, M., Ponak, A., & Taras, D.G. (Eds.), *Union-management relations in Canada* (4th edition). Toronto: Addison Wesley Longman.

[7] Bemmels, B., & Lau, D. (2001). Local union leaders' satisfaction with grievance procedures. *Journal of Labor Research, 22*(3), 653–668; Bemmels, B. (1995). Shop stewards' satisfaction with grievance procedures. *Industrial Relations, 34*(4), 578–592.

[8] Bemmels & Lau, *op. cit.*

[9] B.C. Labour Relations Board, Practice Guideline No. ADJ-3, 3–6.

[10] Craig & Solomon, *op. cit.*

[11] Elliott, D.C., & Goss, J.H. (1994). *Grievance mediation: why and how it works*. Toronto: Canada Law Book.

[12] See, for example, British Columbia *Labour Relations Code*, section 89.

[13] Thornicroft, *op. cit.*

[14] Elliott & Goss, *op. cit.*, 7–14.

[15] Olson, C., & Ponak, A. (1990). Time delays in grievance arbitration in Alberta. Presented at 8th Annual Arbitration Conference, Calgary, AB; Weatherill, J.F.W. (1980). *The grievance arbitration process: problems and perspectives*. Edmonton, AB: Alberta Labour Preventive Mediation Services.

[16] Ponak, A., & Zerbe, W. (1996). Using event history analysis to model delay in grievance arbitration. *Industrial & Labor Relations Review, 50*(1), 105–122.

[17] Harcourt, M. (2000). How attorney representation and adjudication affect Canadian arbitration and labour relations board decisions. *Journal of Labor Research, 21*(1), 149–159.

[18] Ponak & Zerbe, *op. cit.*

[19] Thornicroft, *op. cit.*, 377.

[20] Thornicroft, *op. cit.*

[21] Beattie, S. (1997). *Grievance mediation*. Vancouver, BC: British Columbia Continuing Legal Education Labour Arbitration, 5–6.

HandyDART Employer Changes Routes

In 2009, drivers and office workers for Vancouver's HandyDART bus service, which provides transportation for passengers with physical and cognitive disabilities, underwent a significant workplace change that resulted in a new employer and a two-month-long strike.

Following a public consultation process, TransLink, Vancouver's transit provider, contracted out the HandyDART service to MVT Canadian Bus, a subsidiary of U.S.-based MV Transportation Inc. "The decision stemmed out of dissatisfaction of users with an inefficient system," explains Peter Hill, manager of Access Transit at TransLink. For 30 years, the HandyDART service operated under seven different contracts in eight areas in Greater Vancouver. Under the restructuring, the service was amalgamated into one small and two large areas. TransLink sent out a request for proposals and MVT won in all three areas.

"The paramount issue for us was that a U.S. company came in," says Tim Johnston, president of Amalgamated Transit Union Local 1724, which represents the HandyDART workers. "Previously, the HandyDART services were all run locally through local societies."

Under the previous model, three unions—the BC Government Employees Union, the Canadian Auto Workers, and the Amalgamated Transit Union (ATU)—represented the HandyDART workers under the various contracts. With the change in employer, the union members voted on which union would represent them, and the ATU, which represented 160 employees in Vancouver at the time, won the majority vote.

MVT took control of the HandyDART service on January 1, 2009, with the mandate to keep as many existing employees as possible, to meld five collective agreements into one, and to make the system more efficient.

Collective bargaining failed to reach an agreement, and HandyDART's 500 employees went on strike in October, providing transportation only for essential services such as dialysis and cancer treatments. Many issues were outstanding when talks broke down, says John Siragusa, vice-president of Operations at MV Transportation Inc. "When the union gave their 72-hour strike notice, there were 71 open articles in collective bargaining including all of the economic issues such as wages, benefits, and pension."

"We basically had a strike vote of 97 percent," says Johnston at ATU. Although there were a significant number of issues on the table, the biggest issue was pensions, he adds. The employees wanted to participate in the BC Pension Plan, while the company backed an RRSP retirement savings program.

Mediation began in December with the BC Labour Relations Board, resulting in an agreement that 57 percent of the union members still voted down. The dispute then went to binding arbitration, resulting in a collective agreement that runs from January 13, 2010, to December 31, 2013. Still, a number of issues, including benefits, continued to be sent to arbitration.

CHANGES TO THE UNION OR THE EMPLOYER

objectives

In this chapter, we will discuss how labour legislation accommodates changes that occur in the union or the company while a certification or collective agreement is in effect. By the end of this chapter, you should be able to:

- define successorship and understand what criteria are used to assess whether successorship has occurred or not
- describe the process of decertification
- understand what happens to certifications and collective agreements when unions or companies merge
- explain some of the ways that technological change and restructuring affect union-employer relationships

INTRODUCTION

In previous chapters we have described the process of certification, through which a union becomes the legal workplace representative of a group of employees, and the process of collective bargaining, through which a collective agreement is reached. The outputs of both of these processes—certifications and collective agreements—have time elements. A certification is considered to be in effect indefinitely, while a collective agreement lasts for a predetermined period, after which a new collective agreement is negotiated.

The fact that both these documents have a life over time—whether for a fixed or an indefinite period—presents a problem, since both reflect the status of the union and the employer only at the time when these documents were completed. What happens if something changes after a certification begins or a collective agreement goes into effect? What if the workplace conditions change, or there is a change in the status of the parties named in the certification or collective agreement?

This chapter will address how labour legislation deals with changes that occur in the parties or the workplace conditions during the life of a collective agreement or a certification. We will start by discussing the issue of successorship, and move on to explain what happens when the union or the employer experiences a merger or some other kind of change. Our discussion will conclude with an overview of how changes in the actual work itself, such as technological change, are accommodated.

SUCCESSORSHIP

The term **successorship**, as used in labour legislation, relates to the status of a certification after some material change in a business or employer occurs, when a certification order was in place before the change. If a labour relations board determines that the past and present forms of the business are sufficiently similar, then successorship is declared to exist. The employer is then bound by the terms of any certification or collective agreement—or other formal relationships with a union—that existed in the earlier form of the business.

The question of successorship can arise in a number of different situations: a change in location, such as when an employer moves the place of business or when a business expands to new locations or closes existing locations; when the business itself is sold or transferred to a new owner; when the purpose of the business changes or broadens (e.g., the business moves into new types of services or products not necessarily related to the original business); or when the employer transfers work to other locations or to other workers or organizations through subcontracting.

In situations like these, it is sometimes unclear whether the existing certification and collective agreement should continue to apply. The terms of both documents may refer to an entity that no longer exists, if the business has changed its name or location, or they may refer to a workplace that is substantially different, if the types or numbers of workers have changed because of changes in the purpose or type of business. As we know, a certification order is very specific in naming the parties to the certification and the locations and positions that the certification covers; we also know that certifications and collective agreements are legally binding documents. Any change to the parties may or may not make a certification or collective agreement invalid. Whether the certification or collective agreement is still valid after a change in the workplace is a fairly significant question for the business and for the employees, because the presence or absence of a collective agreement and union representation has major implications for how the workplace functions.

If a change to the employer or business occurs, one of the parties to the certification or the collective agreement can apply to a labour relations board to determine whether a declaration of successorship should be issued. If a declaration of successorship is issued, it has the effect of applying the existing certification or collective agreement to the new form of the business. Thus, a declaration of successorship ensures that the new employer is bound by the same obligations to bargain and to recognize the union as the previous employer. It is important to note that Canadian labour legislation clearly states that the new employer is automatically bound by the certification or collective agreement covering the previous employer, unless the change in the business entailed exceptional circumstances. The language in the New Brunswick *Industrial Relations Act* (Section 60(2)) is a good example of the wording that most Canadian labour codes contain to make this relationship explicit:

> Where an employer who is bound by or is a party to a
> collective agreement with a trade union or council of
> trade unions sells his business, the person to whom the
> business has been sold is, until the Board otherwise
> declares, bound by the collective agreement as if he
> had been a party thereto.

Scott Hand (left), chairman and CEO of Inco Ltd., and Derek Pannell, CEO of Falconbridge Ltd., shake hands after announcing Inco's friendly takeover of Falconbridge in 2005. Successorship is not an issue in every change to a business, but when it is, it can be challenging to resolve.

When the change in the business involves an expansion, a spinoff of part of the business, or a merger, a declaration of successorship serves to clarify the extent of the employer's new obligations, especially if different unions or collective agreements are involved. A declaration of successorship clarifies which employees are in the new bargaining unit, which union is the new bargaining agent for the employees, and which collective agreement is now in force.

We should note that a declaration of successorship can also apply to situations where the employer is involved in some union-related process that has not yet been completed. These processes could include a certification campaign, a notice to commence collective bargaining, an application for decertification, or a case involving the employer that is before a labour relations board. According to Canadian labour laws, if the employer sells or changes the business while any of these processes are unfolding and not yet complete, the altered employer is still considered the employer and is bound by the obligations of these processes, unless a labour relations board declares otherwise. The purpose of this legislation is to discourage employers from attempting to avoid dealing with a union by selling or changing the business during processes that might alter the union-employer relationship. Without such legislation, an employer could, for example, avoid entering into collective bargaining by changing the form or ownership of the business and then claiming that a notice to commence bargaining was not valid because the notice was issued to a form of the business that no longer existed.

Determining whether successorship exists can be quite complicated. Labour relations boards recognize that changes in a business can occur for legitimate business reasons—that is, the changes would have taken place regardless of whether the certification existed. Labour relations boards also recognize that changes in a business may be as simple as a name change or as complex as a total reorganization, and that change in one area of a business may not represent the strategic direction of the organization as a whole. Thus, a change in how a business operates may not be intentionally undertaken to disrupt the union-employer relationship. It is even possible that the employer has not considered how changes in the business may affect the ability of the union to represent its membership.

However, labour relations boards must balance these realities against the possibility that an employer has undertaken change for no other reason than to weaken the power of the union or to avoid the obligations associated with unionization. For example, if a business is unionized and then expands its operations to multiple locations that are not unionized, the employer would gain a distinct advantage in collective bargaining. The workers at the unionized location would be disadvantaged in bargaining because they would be representing the interests of only a small part of the employer's total workforce. Also, the employer could easily transfer business to non-unionized locations during bargaining disputes, thus lessening the impact of a strike or lockout. These advantages might entice an employer to expand locations simply to weaken the union. Alternatively, an employer could sell or transfer the ownership of the business but retain control over its operations, and then claim that a certification should no longer apply because the business was not the same business that existed at the time the certification was issued. The employer could then continue to run the business, which would not have changed at all except for the legal ownership, without having to deal with the presence of a union.

Because of these possibilities, when labour relations boards assess whether successorship exists, they look for evidence that employer actions are not motivated by anti-union animus. As previous chapters have noted, while employees may be enthusiastic about joining a union, employers are not always as enthusiastic about having a union in their workplace. Employers may see the presence of a union as a threat to their ability to operate the organization efficiently or effectively, or they may fear that a union will inflate labour costs to the extent that the business will no longer be profitable. Some employers are opposed to unions on general principle because they perceive that unions interfere with management's right to control the workplace.

We have previously discussed employers' anti-union attitudes in the context of the certification process, but it is important to know that these anti-union attitudes do not always disappear after certification. If the employer feels that its concerns were not fairly or completely addressed during the certification process, its anti-union attitudes may become even more intense after a certification declaration. Therefore, labour legislation usually contains language to deal with employer actions that may be motivated by a desire to evade responsibilities after certification. Such language includes, for example, timelines outlining when collective bargaining must commence, and provisions for grievance procedures to resolve disagreements over the application of the collective agreement. The sections of labour law dealing with successorship are also part of the legislation intended to ensure that employers, as well as unions and employees, fulfill the obligations that certification and collective agreements place upon them.

Because the circumstances of successorship may vary considerably from case to case, depending on the structure of the business and the events that have occurred, there are no hard and fast rules that determine when successorship has occurred and when it has not. The legislation summarized in Table 12-1 gives some guidance, but it is only a starting point, as it only deals with successorships involving changes to a business. As we know, successorship issues can also arise when a union merges or changes (these issues will be discussed separately later in the chapter). Since employers who are vehemently opposed to unionization can be quite creative in their attempts to avoid dealing with a union, labour relations boards regularly find themselves having to evaluate and pass judgement on new situations. Thus, many of the criteria used to determine whether successorship has occurred have developed through case law (decisions on previous cases that interpret and apply the wording of the law). Judgements from previous cases may or may not be relevant to a current case, depending on the amount of similarity between the cases.

If there is any general guideline underlying decisions on successorship cases, it is whether there is any evidence of **continuity** or **control** between the previous and the present form of the business. "Continuity" refers to any form of connection between the two forms of the business. Continuity could be indicated by evidence as substantial as financial records showing that two supposedly separate businesses are actually incorporated as a single entity, or as minor as a new business honouring coupons or discounts issued by the previous form of the business. The amount of evidence of continuity that is required to prove successorship is dependent on the facts of the individual situation; however, some evidence of continuity, no matter how small, would usually be expected to form at least the basis of an argument that successorship exists.

TABLE 12-1 Legislation Governing Successorship		
	Who Can Apply for Declaration of Successorship	**Situations that May Be Considered Successorship[i]**	**Actions Labour Relations Board Can Take if Successorship Exists**
Federal	Any employer or trade union affected	Sale, transfer, lease, or other disposition of a business; sale, transfer, lease, or other disposition of a provincial business so that it falls under federal regulation, or an employer under federal regulation	Determine an appropriate bargaining unit; determine any questions arising
Alberta	Any employer, trade union, or person affected	Sale, transfer, lease, merger, or other disposition of a business, an undertaking, or part of it, so that control, management, or supervision of business passes to the purchaser, lessee, transferee, or person acquiring it	Make any inquiries and direct the taking of any votes considered necessary; decide any questions arising; declare which union shall be the bargaining agent; amend certification(s); cancel or amend the collective agreement(s) in force; determine whether results of ongoing proceedings are binding
British Columbia	Any person	Sale, lease, transfer, or other disposition of a business or part of it	Determine what rights, privileges, or duties have been acquired or retained; make enquiries or direct votes as necessary or advisable; determine appropriate bargaining unit; determine bargaining agent; amend certification(s); modify collective agreement(s) to define seniority rights; give direction

TABLE 12-1 Legislation Governing Successorship (Continued)

	Who Can Apply for Declaration of Successorship	Situations that May Be Considered Successorship[i]	Actions Labour Relations Board Can Take if Successorship Exists
Manitoba	Any bargaining agent affected, or by labour relations board's own motion	Where an employer sells the employer's business to another person, or where two or more businesses are amalgamated or merged	Determine appropriate bargaining unit; determine bargaining agent and order a vote if necessary or advisable; amend certification(s); amend collective agreement(s); give any further direction; declare timelines for applicability of any determination or declaration
New Brunswick	Any person, trade union, or council of trade unions concerned	Sale of a business or part thereof to a person, including leases, transfers, and any other manner of disposition	Determine bargaining unit; amend certification(s); declare which collective agreement shall continue in force
Newfoundland and Labrador	An employer, purchaser, lessee, transferee, person otherwise acquiring the business, bargaining agent, trade union, or council of trade unions	Sale, lease, transfer, or other disposition of business, its operations, or a part of either of them, or agreement to sell, lease, transfer, or otherwise dispose of business, its operations, or a part of either of them	Amend or rescind existing collective agreement(s); revoke or amend certification(s); modify or restrict the operation of any notice; determine the appropriate bargaining unit; designate employees to be covered by continuing collective agreements; define the rights of employees covered by the collective agreement; declare which trade union will be the bargaining agent; interpret any collective agreement provision

TABLE 12-1 Legislation Governing Successorship (Continued)			
	Who Can Apply for Declaration of Successorship	**Situations that May Be Considered Successorship[i]**	**Actions Labour Relations Board Can Take if Successorship Exists**
Nova Scotia	Any employer, purchaser, lessee, transferee, bargaining agent, or trade union	Sale, lease, transfer of business, it operations, or any part of either, or agreement to sell, lease, or transfer a business, its operations, or any part of either. Successorship legislation may also apply if the board determines that the employer has contracted out work to avoid obligations under *Trade Union Act*	Modify or rescind any collective agreement(s); amend or revoke any certification(s); modify any notice or entitlement to give notice; determine appropriate bargaining unit; determine coverage of collective agreements if more than one is to remain in force; declare bargaining agent; interpret any provision of any collective agreement
Ontario	Any person, trade union, or council of trade unions concerned	Sale of business to a person, including lease, transfer, and any other manner of disposition of a business	Determine appropriate bargaining unit; amend certification(s); declare bargaining agent
Prince Edward Island	Any employer, purchaser, lessee, transferee, bargaining agent, or trade union	When an employer sells, transfers, or leases or has agreed to sell, lease, or transfer a business, its operations, or any part of them	Amend or rescind the existing collective agreement(s); revoke or amend certification(s); modify or restrict the operation of any notice; determine the appropriate bargaining unit; designate employees to be covered by continuing collective agreements; define the rights of employees covered by the collective agreement; declare which trade union will be the bargaining agent; interpret any collective agreement provision

	Who Can Apply for Declaration of Successorship	Situations that May Be Considered Successorship[i]	Actions Labour Relations Board Can Take if Successorship Exists
TABLE 12-1 Legislation Governing Successorship (Continued)			
Quebec	Not specified	Alienation or operation by another in whole or in part of an undertaking, including judicial sale	Labour commissioner can rule on any matter arising, can determine applicability of legislation, can issue any order deemed necessary, and can settle any difficulty arising out of application of legislation
Saskatchewan	Any employer, employee, or trade union directly affected	Sale, lease, transfer, or other disposition of a business or part thereof	Determine whether disposition relates to a business or part of it; determine appropriate bargaining unit; determine what trade union represents the majority of employees in new unit; direct a representation vote; amend the description of the unit in collective agreement; give any direction the board considers necessary

[i] All of the legislation summarized in this table states or implies that at least some of the employees in the affected business must be represented by a certified bargaining agent, or be in the process of applying for certification, in order for successorship to be declared.

The question of control is usually considered in determining successorship if it appears that an employer has established a new business entity mainly for the purposes of avoiding the obligations that come with certification. "Control" refers to how much direction the management or owners of the previous business give to the new business. For example, the owner of a unionized business might set up a separate non-unionized business and hire a separate management staff, but still give direction and orders to those managers and that business. A labour relations board might find that there was successorship in this situation because the owner of the first business retained control over the operations of the second business.

We should note that it is not necessary to prove both continuity and control for a declaration of successorship to be issued. The issue of continuity is more important in situations involving a sale, lease, or transfer of a business; the issue of control is more important when a new business is established or part of an existing business's operations is assigned to another employer or another business entity.

There are other criteria that labour relations boards will often consider when determining if successorship should be declared.[1] We will briefly describe each of these.

Direct Contact   Successorship may be declared if there has been direct contact between the owner or manager of the previous form of the business and the owner or manager of the new form of the business. Sometimes direct contact is very easy to prove because the previous owner or manager and the new one are the same person. In situations where these individuals are not the same person, determining whether direct contact existed would include such considerations as

- whether the individuals previously knew each other;

- whether they had any previous business relationships, or any current relationships involving other businesses; or

- whether any of the individuals had previously been an employee of any of the other individuals.

Transfer of Assets   A labour relations board would also consider whether there has been any transfer of assets between the two forms of the business. If a new business uses assets previously owned by the former business, the board will usually consider this as evidence of continuity. The board might also be concerned with the price associated with a transfer of assets, and would likely be suspicious if the selling price of the assets is considerably lower than what the assets would usually be expected to sell for. The reason that a labour relations board would be suspicious about such a transaction is that an employer trying to avoid dealing with a union might sell assets to an associate at an artificially low price. The employer might then attempt to have the certification cancelled on the grounds that the business has ceased to exist and, if successful, would then repurchase the assets at the same low price and resume operations as a non-unionized company. The board would also examine the disposition of goodwill and other intangible assets in determining whether a transfer of assets took place.

Identification   If there was a transfer of a logo, trademark, or some other distinctive identification from the previous business to the new business, this action would likely be considered evidence of continuity. A logo or trademark is generally the legal possession of a business and thus its transfer could be considered a transfer of assets. Moreover, a logo or trademark is a strong public indicator of a business's identity, and a transfer of such identification to another business would give a public impression of continuity.

Transfer of Customer Lists   A present business having the same customer base as the former business is not, in and of itself, an indication that successorship exists. However, the transfer of customer lists from one business to another would indicate continuity, since most businesses that maintain such lists rarely share them with other companies, particularly those in the same industry or serving the same consumer market.

Transfer of Accounts Receivable, Existing Contracts, and/or Inventory
Accounts receivable and inventory are both assets that generate revenue for the company. Contracts are assets that will produce future revenue, so they are not likely to be transferred from one business to another except under exceptional circumstances.

Pledges by the Successor to Maintain the Good Name of the Predecessor, or Pledges by the Predecessor Not to Compete with the Successor   If these sorts of promises exist between the owners or managers of the old and new businesses, they are evidence of continuity because they determine the terms under which the business transition will occur.

Whether the Same Employees Perform the Same Work   If the new business uses the same employees carrying out the same tasks that they did in the old business, this could indicate continuity between the two businesses. Another staff-related criterion for determining successorship is the key person doctrine, discussed below.

Whether There Was a Hiatus in Business Between the Two Companies   This criterion may or may not assist in determining whether successorship exists. Business owners quite commonly close one business and, after a period of time, open another business without ever having intended to avoid the obligations associated with certification or a collective agreement. However, an employer who wants to avoid those obligations may try to disguise their intent by closing the unionized business, waiting for a while, and then opening a non-unionized business, claiming that there is no continuity because the second business did not immediately replace the first business. An employer might also use a hiatus in business to attempt to avoid certain obligations; for example, a collective agreement might expire during a hiatus. (This would not, however, relieve the employer of the responsibility to participate in collective bargaining for a new collective agreement.)

Whether the Customers of the Predecessor Business Are Now Serviced by the Successor Business   This criterion is distinct from the criterion involving customer lists. It looks at whether a new business is serving the same geographic or demographic market or, in some other way, serves the same customer base as the previous business. This in and of itself is not an indication that successorship should be declared, but it could be significant in combination with other criteria.

Another criterion that is used in some successorship cases is the **key person doctrine**. Successorship may exist if the successor business employs individuals from the previous business whose knowledge or skills were essential for the operation of the business. For example, if the previous business used a specialized piece of equipment and only a few employees knew how to operate and service that equipment, successorship might exist if those individuals performed the same work with the equipment at the new business. The key person doctrine can also apply to individuals with specialized contacts or customer lists, such as salespeople whose rosters of customers and contacts cannot easily be duplicated.

In addition to evidence of continuity, as mentioned, a labour relations board also looks at the actions that caused the transformation of the business, and tries to determine whether these actions were motivated by legitimate business reasons or by anti-union animus. In successorship cases, as in complaints alleging unfair labour practices by the employer, the onus is on the employer to prove that there were legitimate business reasons for its actions. In the words of the Ontario Labour Relations Board, "the applicant has the onus to prove that the sale of a business took place. However, when the union is the applicant, the employer has an obligation to present all of the relevant facts of which it has knowledge."[2]

If a labour relations board decides that sufficient evidence exists to establish continuity or control within the two forms of the business, or that changes in the business were motivated by the intent to avoid the obligations associated with certification or by anti-union animus, a declaration of successorship is issued. As Table 12-1 indicates, there are a variety of other actions that a labour relations board can take to clarify the successorship, including altering the scope of certifications or the application of collective agreements, or redefining the bargaining unit to reflect the new form of the business. In most provinces, a labour relations board also has the ability to order representation votes if the new bargaining unit includes employees from two or more unions and there is a question of which union should represent the employees in the newly defined bargaining unit.

If the successorship situation involves a unionized business expanding to non-unionized locations or the creation of a completely separate business entity owned by the employer, the board may issue a **common employer declaration** in addition to a declaration of successorship. A common employer declaration states that all the employer's businesses are considered to be a single business for the purposes of certification and the collective agreement. A labour relations board usually issues this declaration where the board has determined that the employer attempted to avoid obligations by moving some or all of the unionized parts of the business to a non-unionized business or to a non-unionized part of the business.

If the application for a declaration of successorship is denied, the original certification order continues to exist without any changes. However, in cases where the business has changed substantially, a labour relations board's failure to declare successorship may substantially impair the union's ability to function effectively as the workers' representative. This is especially true if the union represents workers in what is now a small part of an expanded business, or if the certification now applies to a business that has effectively ceased to function, such as a location that has closed or downsized. In such cases, the union members may choose to apply for decertification. (We will discuss decertification in the next section of this chapter.) On the other hand, if the change in the business involves expansion or the creation of new business entities, workers at the new non-unionized business or at the new parts of the unionized business may apply for a separate certification as a new bargaining unit if successorship is not declared.

DECERTIFICATION

During the term of a collective agreement or a certification, union members may decide that they no longer wish to have the certified union as their representative in the workplace. This situation can occur because the members are dissatisfied with the performance of their particular union in representing their concerns, or because they no longer wish to have any union represent them. In order for any change to be made to the designated bargaining agent, the existing certification must be cancelled. The process used to cancel the certification is called **decertification**.

The process of decertification is an important part of labour relations legislation because it provides a way for union members to hold their unions accountable for performance. Having decertification available as an option allows employees to remove "weak, indifferent, or ineffective unions"[3] or union representation of any type if they feel that union representation no longer serves their interests in the workplace. If workers are to have the unrestricted ability to choose how they want to be represented in the workplace, providing them with a method of leaving a union is as important as providing them with a method of joining a union.

Table 12-2 outlines the specific provisions for decertification in each Canadian jurisdiction. We can see from this table that, as with certification, specific timelines restrict when applications for decertification can be made. The timelines serve two main purposes. First, they give newly certified unions a chance to establish themselves as credible worker representatives. As discussed in Chapter 5, new unions often have difficulty in obtaining certification, and members or executives of a newly certified union may be relatively inexperienced in union administration or participation. The timelines restricting when decertification applications can be made are intended to give new unions and new union members a reasonable chance to establish themselves in the workplace and gain some experience in union operations. The second purpose of these timelines is to minimize the possibility that decertification applications will be made during times when feelings about the union might be particularly heated, such as during collective agreement negotiations. Banning applications entirely during these times would be an unfair restriction on the employees' right to freely choose their representation in the workplace. Nevertheless, the legislation recognizes that employees can be dissatisfied with their union's performance under certain circumstances but generally satisfied with its performance otherwise. Negotiations, for example, can cause heightened conflict and strong emotions because of the significance of the matters being bargained; at these critical times, employees might be tempted to apply for decertification, even though they would not have considered doing so in less extreme situations. It is also important to note that several jurisdictions completely ban decertification applications during strikes or lockouts.

As Table 12-2 indicates, some jurisdictions in Canada allow employers, as well as employees or unions, to make applications for decertification. This provision may seem somewhat contrary to one of the primary purposes of certification, which is to allow the "true wishes" of the employees to be expressed without interference from the employer. To some degree, allowing employers to apply for decertification gives them another way to resist unionization. When employers object to having to deal with the presence of a union or to abide by the conditions of a collective agreement, they might be tempted to apply for decertification. This phenomenon has been observed in the United States, where the number of employer applications for decertification has increased along with the use of other employer anti-union tactics such as shutdowns, relocations, and the hiring of non-union employees.[4] In Canada, it is much less common for employers to successfully use decertification as a tactic to avoid union influence.

Prior to describing how the process of decertification actually works, we will point out two other features of the relevant Canadian legislation. The first is that most jurisdictions have some provision that permits a labour relations board, on its own initiative, to declare a decertification if there is evidence that fraud took place during the certification process. Fraud of this kind most often involves falsified evidence on the application for certification, such as forged signatures. Usually, such evidence is uncovered relatively soon after the original certification is issued, but most legislation places no time restriction on when a decertification can be declared owing to fraud. In a case in British Columbia, a decertification was declared four years after the original certification was issued when evidence was produced to show that four signatures on the initial certification application were false.[5]

The second notable feature in most Canadian labour codes is a provision that permits an employer to make an application for decertification, or a labour relations board to issue a decertification on its own initiative, if there is an **abandonment of bargaining rights** by the union. As we know, a certification order places an obligation on the union, as well as on the employer, to commence collective bargaining. If a union has not issued a notice to bargain to the employer or has not commenced bargaining, it may be

TABLE 12-2 Decertification Legislation

	Timelines	Criteria	Other Conditions
Federal	If a collective agreement exists, the timelines are the same as for certification; if no collective agreement exists, applications can be made 12 months after the date of certification; no application can be made during a strike or lockout.	A majority of employees in the unit must support the application. A vote may be held if the board deems it appropriate. If no collective agreement exists, the board must be satisfied that reasonable effort was made to obtain one.	If certification was obtained by fraud, an application can be made at any time by a concerned employee, employer, or union.
Alberta	If no collective agreement is in force, application may be made at any time by the union. Employees may apply under the same timelines as for certification. An employer may only apply when it has not bargained collectively for at least 3 years after the date of certification, if no collective agreement has been reached, or it is 3 years after the end of the first collective agreement. Former employers may also apply. An application cannot be made during a strike or lockout without the board's consent.	At least 40 percent of employees in the unit must indicate in writing their support for the application. A representation vote will be conducted and results must indicate that a majority of employees voted in support of decertification. If a former employer applies, they must show there have been no employees in the unit for at least 3 years or that the bargaining agent has abandoned its bargaining rights.	The board may decertify if it is satisfied that the bargaining rights of the union should be revoked. The board may at any time give notice of intent to decertify and may do so if it receives no objection within 60 days of notice. A union cannot negotiate with the employer or apply for certification for the same or substantially the same bargaining unit until 6 months after the date of decertification. If an application for decertification is withdrawn or abandoned, no similar or substantially similar application can be made for 90 days without board consent.

TABLE 12-2 Decertification Legislation (Continued)			
	Timelines	**Criteria**	**Other Conditions**
British Columbia	There may be no applications during the 10 months after certification, during the 10 months following a refusal to decertify because of interference or unfair labour practices, and during a period (minimum 90 days) prescribed by the board following a refusal to decertify if a majority of votes are in favour of the union.	At least 45 percent of employees in the unit must sign an application to cancel the certification. The vote must be held within 10 days after the application or a longer period as ordered by the board if conducted by mail. The board may order another vote if participation by eligible employees is less than 55 percent. The board may refuse to cancel certification, regardless of vote results, if employees are affected by an order pertaining to a prohibited act or if employer interference is likely to make a vote not reflect the true wishes of the employees.	The board may cancel certification if it is satisfied the union has ceased to be a union or that the employer has ceased to employ the employees in the unit, or if it is satisfied that the trade union has abandoned its bargaining rights. If decertification is granted, the same union cannot apply to represent the same bargaining until 10 months after the date of decertification.
Manitoba	The same timelines apply as for certification. An application may be made at any time with the consent of the board.	An employee may apply if he or she claims to represent a majority of the members of the bargaining unit. If the board is satisfied that fewer than 50 percent of employees in a unit support the application, it shall dismiss the application. The board conducts a vote if support is greater than 50 percent. A majority of employees in the unit who participate in the vote must support the decertification.	If certification was obtained by fraud, an employee, employer, or union may apply. The board may dispense with a vote if the union does not oppose the application and the board is satisfied that more than 50 percent of the bargaining unit members support the application. The board may dismiss an application, even with sufficient support, if it believes employer failure to bargain in good faith resulted in the bargaining process being frustrated.

TABLE 12-2 Decertification Legislation (Continued)			
	Timelines	**Criteria**	**Other Conditions**
New Brunswick	The timelines are the same as for certification. The board may allow earlier applications in certain circumstances. If a certification is in effect and no collective agreement has been reached, an application may be made only after one year from the date of certification. An application is subject to delays related to conciliation, mediation, strike, or lockout. Decertification may take place at any time when there have been no employees in the bargaining unit for 2 years or where certification was obtained fraudulently.	At least 40 percent of employees must support the application. A representation vote is taken. At least 50 percent of all those eligible to vote must support decertification. Employees absent from work during voting hours and who do not cast their ballots are not counted as eligible. Decertification may take place without a vote if there is failure to give notice to bargain, to commence bargaining, or to seek to bargain within the specified time limits.	The board may refuse to accept new applications from an unsuccessful applicant for a period not exceeding 10 months. An application may be made by any employee, another trade union, or the employer if the board is satisfied that there is a question over whether a majority of employees support an application.
Newfoundland and Labrador	Application may be made 12 months after certification, 6 months after an application for decertification was dismissed, 12 months after the union gave notice to bargain, or earlier at the board's discretion.	Application must be supported by at least 40 percent of employees in a bargaining unit. The board will take a vote that must be taken no later than fiveworking days after receipt of the application. A majority of the unit must vote in favour, or 70 percent of the unit must vote and a majority of those must vote in favour. The board is bound by the outcome of a vote unless it determines the results have been influenced by intimidation, threat, or coercion.	Following investigation and a hearing if necessary, the board may revoke certification, on application or on its own initiative, if it determines that a bargaining agent no longer represents the majority of employees in a bargaining unit.

TABLE 12-2 Decertification Legislation (Continued)

	Timelines	Criteria	Other Conditions
Nova Scotia	If no agreement is in force, application can be made at least 12 months after certification; if an agreement is in force, the timelines are the same as for certification.	A significant number of members of the union must indicate that the union is not fulfilling its responsibilities or that it no longer represents a majority of employees in the unit. The board may order the taking of a vote and may revoke or confirm the certification in accordance with the result.	None specified.
Ontario[i]	The same timelines as for certification. Upon application by the employer or any employees in the bargaining unit, decertification may take place with or without a vote if there is failure to give notice to bargain, to commence bargaining, or to seek to bargain within the timelines prescribed in legislation. Employees may apply for decertification one year after the date of certification if no collective agreement has been reached. If the board has ordered the settlement of a first collective agreement by arbitration, no application can be considered until after the agreement is settled.	Applications must include a list of the names of employees in the bargaining unit who express a desire not to be represented by the union, along with evidence of those wishes. If no less than 40 percent of employees in the bargaining unit express such wishes, the board must order a secret-ballot vote within 5 working days of the application's filing. More than 50 percent of ballots must be in opposition to the union for decertification to occur.	The board may bar a new application by any employee affected by an unsuccessful application for no longer than one year. The board may not consider any challenge to the information supporting the application. An application may be dismissed if the employer or its representative engaged in threats, coercion, or intimidation.

TABLE 12-2	Decertification Legislation (Continued)		
	Timelines	**Criteria**	**Other Conditions**
Prince Edward Island	The timelines are the same as for certification. An employer, the trade union, or any employee in the bargaining unit may make an application.	If the majority of the employees desire decertification, the board will decertify the union.	The board will take a decertification vote whenever it deems necessary.
Quebec	The timelines are the same as for certification.	A labour commissioner may cancel the certification if the association has ceased to exist or if it no longer comprises an absolute majority of employees in the unit.	An association may be dissolved if it is proven that the association is dominated or financed by the employer or its representative. The association has the opportunity to be heard and to attempt to prove that it is blameless.
Saskatchewan	If an agreement exists, applications can be made no less than 30 days or more than 60 days before the anniversary of the effective date. If no agreement exists, applications can be made no less than 30 days or more than 60 days before the anniversary date of the certification order.	If the board finds that the union or an employee has committed an unfair labour practice or other illegal act and there is no evidence of majority support for an application that otherwise would have been obtained, it must order a representation vote.	If the board is satisfied that a certification order was obtained by fraud, it may rescind the order.

[i] Ontario's legislation also requires employers with a certified bargaining unit in their workplace to post information on decertification and distribute this information to bargaining unit members annually.

considered to have abandoned its bargaining rights. Thus, it is no longer fulfilling its obligation to represent the employees as their bargaining agent and may consequently be decertified.

However, we should also note that it is fairly unusual for a decertification to be granted on the basis of abandonment of bargaining rights. There may be circumstances to explain a union's failure to issue a notice to bargain after a certification is granted; for example, union members might be unwilling or unable to participate on the bargaining team, even if the union itself intends to bargain. As one decision in an abandonment case stated, "A certification order is ... proof that employees have chosen to bargain collectively through the union designated in the order. The onus of proving that this right has been lost through abandonment ... is on the party alleging it, and is a heavy one.... A clear repudiation of bargaining rights [is] needed to support a finding of abandonment."[6] Labour relations boards have even refused to declare an abandonment of bargaining rights in situations where an employer has terminated its employees and closed its place of business and the union no longer has a group of employees to represent. The usual reason for such decisions is that the union has expressed an intention to continue representing the employees if the employer resumes operations at some point in the future.[7]

The actual process of decertification is similar in structure to the process of certification. An application for decertification must be made to a labour relations board, showing a sufficient level of support for the decertification among the bargaining unit members. In most Canadian jurisdictions, the level of support required for a decertification application is identical to the level of support required for a certification application. A labour relations board will also usually conduct the same verification of signatures and employment status that it would conduct in assessing an application for certification. This task is somewhat easier in an application for decertification because the composition of the bargaining unit has already been established. Thus, in a decertification application, the question of whether an individual signing the application is in the bargaining unit is much more straightforward to answer than it might be in a certification application, where the membership of the bargaining unit may not yet be definitively determined.

Many jurisdictions in Canada require a vote to be taken among the members of the bargaining unit after the application for decertification has been received. The purpose of this vote is to determine the actual level of support in the workplace for the decertification attempt. As we know, in certification applications a vote may or may not be required, depending on the circumstances of the application and the level of support for the application. However, a vote on a decertification application is mandatory in most Canadian jurisdictions to ensure that the majority of employees truly support the cancellation of the certification and that the decertification application is not simply the work of a dissatisfied minority.

The decertification vote is a secret-ballot vote conducted in the workplace by the labour relations board. As in a certification vote, the ballot in a decertification vote contains a simple yes/no question asking if the voter wishes the union to continue as the bargaining agent for the employees in the bargaining unit. Under most Canadian labour relations laws, for decertification to occur, a majority (50 percent plus 1 of eligible voters, or as defined in the relevant labour relations legislation) must indicate that they do not want to be represented by the union. In some jurisdictions, a minimum number of eligible voters must participate in the vote for the results to be considered valid. If the labour relations board is satisfied that the results of the vote represent the true wishes of the majority of bargaining unit members, the board will then issue an order of decertification. After this order, the union ceases to legally represent the employees in the workplace, and any current collective agreement is no longer in force.

When an application for decertification has been submitted by an employer, most labour relations boards will scrutinize the application quite carefully to ensure that the application is not motivated by anti-union animus. Successful applications for decertification made by employers are likely to involve situations where the employer has ceased to do business, and the decertification is simply part of the task of concluding the employer's existing contractual relationships.

Another circumstance in which a decertification application might be submitted to a labour relations board is when a raid is taking place. **Raiding** was described in Chapter 6 as an attempt by one union to certify a group of workers already represented by another union. When a raiding attempt takes place, a decertification application may be filed for the current union prior to or at the same time as when the raiding union makes an application for certification. As also noted in Chapter 6, there are time bars in place to restrict when applications for certification can be made for a group of workers already in a certified bargaining unit. Table 6-3 outlines these time bars.

In a raiding situation, if the decertification vote rejects the representation of the previous union, the previous union is decertified and a new certification order is issued, with the newly certified union identified as the legal representative of the employees in the bargaining unit.

Another situation where decertification—and even successorship—issues might become relevant is when there are changes in the union itself, rather than changes in the employer or in the union's status as employee representative. We will now turn our attention to a description of what happens in this situation.

Regina Starbucks Workers' Union Situation Left in Limbo

REGINA—It could take months, maybe years, before employees at Canada's last unionized company-owned Starbucks store get to vote on whether to sever their union ties.

Last year workers at seven Vancouver Starbucks locations voted to cut their ties with the Canadian Auto Workers union, leaving the Regina location as the only unionized shop in Canada.

The Regina employees were certified as members of the Retail, Wholesale and Department Store Union (RWDSU) in January 2006. However, in November 2006, one of the workers applied to rescind the certification order on the grounds that a union was not necessary because the employees had good benefits, working conditions and competitive wages.

The Saskatchewan Labour Relations Board (LRB), in a decision written by former board chairman James Siebel, has ordered a vote on the decertification. However, that vote is currently in limbo, pending the negotiations of a first contract and the disposition of a court challenge relating to the government's firing of Siebel and two former vice-chairs, and the matter of board jurisdiction to render decisions.

"We get this decision out of the blue. I didn't even know (Siebel) was writing. I had no idea that this was coming down the pike," said union spokesman Mark Hollyoak.

"Our position is that (Siebel) doesn't even have the jurisdiction to make this decision. We don't even know yet whether we are going to challenge this decision because of all the crap that is going on."

At the time the decertification application was filed, the union and company were in negotiations for a first contract. Two years later a first contract has still not been reached. The LRB has ordered a secret ballot vote on the decertification to be held at least 180 days after the implementation of the terms of a first collective agreement.

The delays in the case were caused in part by a number of developments at the LRB. The decertification application was the subject of a hearing at the board, but there was also a union application alleging the employer committed an unfair labour practice. Subsequently, the LRB found the employer guilty of the unfair labour practice and issued a cease and desist order.

To complicate matters, Siebel, who heard the decertification application, had his appointment terminated in March prior to rendering a decision in the case. However, Siebel and former vice-chair Angela Zborosky subsequently agreed to complete the cases they were involved with when their appointments were terminated.

In his decision on the decertification application, Siebel wrote: "(As a board) we must balance the democratic right of employees to choose to be represented by a trade union pursuant to (the *Trade Union Act*), against the need to ensure that the employer has not used coercive power to improperly influence the outcome of that choice." The board concluded the employer's actions had no significant influence on the employees' decision to support the decertification application or on their ability to make an informed, uncompromised decision on a decertification vote.

Seibel's decision, however, ordered that the vote be delayed until after a first contract was in place, on the grounds that the employees have not had the opportunity to experience working with a collective agreement and union representation under a contract.

Hollyoak noted that the worker who filed the decertification application and half of the original 22 employees in the bargaining unit are no longer working at the Starbucks outlet.

"If this decision stands, then that gives the employer incentive to come to the table and reach a negotiated deal, and if [we don't settle] we will be off to first-contract arbitration and get a deal," he said. "If it stands, then 180 days down the road there will be a vote. I don't know exactly where the shop is at the moment, but I bet you we could win a vote right now."

Source: Kyle, Anne. (2008, November 17). Regina Starbucks workers' union situation left in limbo. *Leader-Post*, [Regina], p. A4.

UNION MERGERS

The merging of existing unions is a relatively recent trend in Canadian industrial relations. This action has become more common for a number of reasons. A merger can help ensure the continued viability of unions, particularly smaller unions. As we know, the more members a union has, the more impact it can have in the workplace and the more "economic pain" it can inflict on the employer during bargaining disputes. Smaller unions may have particular difficulty dealing with the employer if they do not represent enough workers in a business or industry to be able to exert a significant influence on the employer; merging with a larger union is one way to counteract this problem.

Larger unions, too, may find a benefit in mergers. If they see that their historical membership base is diminishing (e.g., if there is downsizing or workplace closures in the relevant industry), they may feel that a merger with other unions offers a way to maintain their existence. An example

The Canadian Congress of Labour was formed by a merger of two earlier union federations, and it later merged with the Trade and Labour Congress to form the CLC. However, mergers of individual unions can be considerably more complex.

of this kind of merger is the International Wood and Allied Workers of America joining the United Steelworkers of America. Through a merger, a union can also enjoy the benefits of increased size without having to expend the effort and resources to recruit unorganized workers. In this situation, mergers usually take place among unions that have a common interest, either through representing the same kind of workers at different employers or through representing workers in related industries. An example of this kind of merger occurred in the Canadian newspaper industry when several bargaining units of workers formerly represented by The Newspaper Guild joined the Communications, Energy and Paperworkers Union (CEP). The CEP was itself the product of a merger of unions representing electrical, chemical, and pulp and paper industry workers. Its merger with The Newspaper Guild was based on the recognition that newspapers are one of the primary consumers of a major forestry product (newsprint) and thus there would likely be common concerns among workers in these different industries. Some research has suggested that mergers of unions across different jurisdictions do not always provide improvements in financial effectiveness or greater success in organizing campaigns or collective bargaining[8]; however, such mergers may be the only perceived means of continued survival for unions whose membership base or major industry is declining.

After the merger of Air Canada and the former Canadian Airlines, union merger issues took many years to settle.

Union mergers are also a response to the general trend in business toward larger organizations. Globalization and increased ease of communication, among other factors, have encouraged businesses to grow through mergers or acquisitions. In order to match the bargaining power of these larger businesses, unions themselves may also need to be larger, and mergers are one way to accomplish this. Larger unions have greater power than smaller ones because of their strength in numbers and also because of the increased financial resources that a larger membership provides.

Finally, union mergers may also be forced by business mergers. If workers at two different companies are represented by different unions and those companies merge, the unions are usually also forced to merge, unless there is some exceptional reason for maintaining two separate bargaining units with separate union representation within the new company. These types of union mergers raise complicated issues, such as how to determine criteria for seniority among the newly merged workforce and how to combine two different organizational cultures. The complexity that can occur in such mergers is demonstrated by the fact that union merger issues involving Air Canada and the former Canadian Airlines were still being settled several years after the two companies merged.[9] Table 12-3 summarizes the legislation in Canada that regulates union mergers and changes.

As we can see, this legislation is quite similar to successorship legislation, with the major difference being, of course, that it is the union that is changing rather than the employer. The legislation governing these changes is intended to ensure, as is legislation governing successorship, that there is continuity in representation for the union members after the change takes place.

Union mergers have different effects on existing certifications, depending on the reason for the merger. If one union merges with another or if locals merge within a single union, the affected locals usually apply to a labour relations board for a change in the existing certification order to reflect the status of the newly merged union. These types of changes do not usually require a labour relations board to conduct a vote among the affected employees, although in most Canadian jurisdictions a labour relations board would be able to order such a vote if it was considered necessary.

If a business merger results in two unions now representing the employees of a single company, the employees are usually asked to vote on which union they wish to represent them; the result of this vote would determine which collective agreement would be in effect. The vote itself is a secret ballot similar to a representation vote, and a majority of employees in the new bargaining unit must vote in favour of a union for it to be certified as the representative of the new company's employees. If a sufficient level of support for one union is indicated by the vote, the certification of that union is changed to reflect its representation of the new bargaining unit. The collective agreement negotiated by that union is considered to regulate the newly formed workplace until it expires and a new collective agreement is negotiated. The certification of the other union is cancelled, and the collective agreement it negotiated is no longer in effect.

TABLE 12-3 Legislation Governing Changes in Certified Unions	
	Situations Where Legislation Applies	**Effect of Change**
Federal	Merger or amalgamation of trade unions or transfer of jurisdiction among trade unions. Successor union must be certified as a bargaining agent.	Successor union is deemed to have acquired the rights, privileges, and duties of its predecessor; the board may resolve any question arising and may order a representation vote if necessary.
Alberta	Merger or amalgamation of trade unions or transfer of jurisdiction. Successor union must be a bargaining agent for a unit of employees of an employer.	On application by the union or any person concerned or through a hearing, the board may declare that a successor union has acquired its predecessor's rights, privileges, and duties; the board may examine evidence or order a representation vote.
British Columbia	Merger or amalgamation of trade unions or transfer of jurisdiction. Successor union must be certified or voluntarily recognized as a bargaining agent.	On application by the union or through a hearing, the board may either declare that successor union has acquired its predecessor's rights, privileges, and duties, or dismiss the application; board may also order representation vote or examine evidence.
Manitoba	Merger, amalgamation, or transfer of jurisdiction. Successor union must be a bargaining agent.	Board may declare that a successor has or has not acquired the rights, privileges, and obligations of its predecessor or may dismiss application.
New Brunswick	Merger, amalgamation, or transfer of jurisdiction between unions or councils of trade unions. Successor union or council must be the certified bargaining agent of a unit of employees of an employer.	On application of any person or trade union concerned or in a board hearing, the board may declare that a successor has or has not acquired the rights, privileges, and duties of its predecessor; the board may also examine evidence, order evidence to be produced, or conduct representation vote.

TABLE 12-3 Legislation Governing Changes in Certified Unions (Continued)

	Situations Where Legislation Applies	Effect of Change
Newfoundland and Labrador	Merger, amalgamation, or transfer of jurisdiction between trade union(s) or councils of trade union(s). Successor union or council must be bargaining agent of a unit of employees of an employer.	On application of person, trade union, or council of trade unions affected, board may declare that a successor has or has not acquired the rights, privileges, and duties of its predecessor; the board may also examine evidence or order votes as necessary. If the union changes its name, the board will order the certification order to be amended.
Nova Scotia	Merger, amalgamation, or transfer of jurisdiction. Successor union must be a bargaining agent of a unit of employees of an employer.	On application of any person or trade union affected, the board may declare that a successor has acquired the rights, privileges, and duties of its predecessor; the board may examine evidence or order a representation vote.
Ontario	Merger, amalgamation, or transfer of jurisdiction. Successor union must be a bargaining agent of a unit of employees of an employer.	On application of any person or trade union concerned, the board may declare that a successor has or has not acquired the rights, privileges, and obligations of its predecessor or may dismiss application; the board may examine evidence or order a representation vote.
Prince Edward Island	Merger or amalgamation of trade union or transfer of jurisdiction. Successor union must be certified as a bargaining agent of a unit of employees of an employer.	On application of any person or union affected or in a board hearing, the board may declare that a successor has or has not acquired the rights, privileges, and duties of its predecessor; the board may examine evidence, order evidence to be produced, or order a representation vote.

TABLE 12-3   Legislation Governing Changes in Certified Unions (Continued)

	Situations Where Legislation Applies	Effect of Change
Quebec	No specifications.	No specifications.
Saskatchewan	Merger, amalgamation, or affiliation of one trade union with another.	All existing orders, assignments, and proceedings relating to the predecessor apply to the successor; board-ordered collective agreements or proceedings are not voided, terminated, abrogated, or curtailed by reason of a name change; by amalgamation, merger, or affiliation of union or part of a union; or by transfer or assignment by one union of its rights to another union.

TECHNOLOGICAL CHANGE

Change during the lifetime of a collective agreement may come about because of changes in the workplace itself. Work restructuring can occur when **technological change** alters the content of jobs or how work is conducted. Although technological change is usually described in terms of computerization or mechanization, it encompasses any change in the tools used to perform a job that leads to a change in the way the job itself is done. For example, many jobs in banking have been affected by technological change. The introduction of automatic teller machines (ATMs) has allowed bank customers to perform many functions, such as cash withdrawals and bill payments, that were formerly handled by bank employees. While technological change does not always cause a substantive change in working conditions, in the composition of the bargaining unit, or in the structure of the employer, it may create new situations that the existing collective agreement does not adequately address.

When technological change occurs, its effects may be addressed through collective bargaining if the timing in the bargaining cycle allows the issue to be dealt with relatively quickly—for example, if an existing collective agreement is close to its expiry date. However, if a collective agreement is in place and will be for some time, an alternative way to address the effects of technological change may need to be found—especially since technological change can occur at a rapid pace.

Two methods are available under Canadian labour legislation to address workplace changes caused by technological change. First, the legislation in some jurisdictions contains language dealing

Technological change, such as this Air Canada self-service check-in kiosk, may alter the content of jobs or how employees conduct their work.

specifically with how the impact of technological change is to be handled. Second, some legislation permits collective agreements to contain a **reopener clause**. A reopener clause in a collective agreement allows the union and employer to renegotiate terms of the collective agreement while it is still in effect, rather than observe the legislated timelines for renegotiating the entire agreement. Table 12-4 outlines the availability of these two methods in different Canadian jurisdictions.

With respect to the first method, in five Canadian jurisdictions (federal, British Columbia, Manitoba, New Brunswick, and Saskatchewan), labour legislation requires employers to give notice of intended technological changes. As Table 12-4 shows, this notice usually must specify the intended date for the change's implementation, identify which employees will be affected, and describe what the effect of the change will be. After this notice has been issued, the parties will either reopen collective bargaining to alter the collective agreement or will develop a mutually acceptable plan to facilitate the implementation of the proposed change. While these requirements do not protect unionized employees against substantive changes in working conditions caused by

TABLE 12-4 Provisions for Technological Change and Reopener Clauses

	Definition of Technological Change	Provisions for Technological Change	Provisions for Reopener Clauses
Federal	The introduction by an employer into his or her work, undertaking, or business of equipment or material of a different nature or kind than that previously utilized by the employer in the operation of the work, undertaking, or business; and a change in the manner in which the employer carries on the work, undertaking, or business that is directly related to the introduction of that equipment or material.	Employer must give at least 120 days' written notice of proposed change to bargaining agent; notice must state the nature of the change, the proposed date of the change, the approximate number and type of employees affected, and the effect that the change is likely to have. The bargaining agent may apply to the board for an order permitting the bargaining agent to serve a notice to commence collective bargaining to revise or replace terms of the existing collective agreement. The change may not take place until the board rejects the bargaining agent's request or the collective agreement has been revised.	The parties can agree to revise any provision of a collective agreement other than the term of the agreement itself.
Alberta	None specified.	None specified.	None specified.
British Columbia	None specified, but legislation provides for adjustment if an employer introduces or intends to introduce a measure, policy, practice, or change that affects the terms, conditions, or security of the employment of a significant number of employees to whom a collective agreement applies.	Employer must give 60 days' notice to the relevant trade union before date on which measure, policy, practice, or change is to be effected; after notice is given, the employer and union must meet to develop an adjustment plan, which is then enforceable as if it were part of the collective agreement.	None specified.

TABLE 12-4 Provisions for Technological Change and Reopener Clauses (Continued)

	Definition of Technological Change	Provisions for Technological Change	Provisions for Reopener Clauses
Manitoba	A change that is likely to affect the terms and conditions, or the security, of employment of a significant number of employees in the unit, or to alter significantly the basis upon which the collective agreement was negotiated.	Employer must give bargaining agent at least 90 days' notice in writing of the nature of the change, the date on which the change is proposed to take effect, the approximate number of employees affected, and the effect that the change is likely to have. Bargaining agent may then give notice to negotiate a new collective agreement or to negotiate revisions to the present agreement. Arbitration may be used to settle questions over the change or its effects.	Parties can agree to amend a provision of the collective agreement during the term of that agreement.
New Brunswick	None stated in legislation, but every collective agreement must contain a definition of technological change.	None stated in legislation, but every collective agreement must contain terms requiring the employer to give reasonable advance notice of technological change to the bargaining agent and specifying the content of such notice.	If the parties consent, any provision of a collective agreement can be revised at any time except for provisions relating to the term of the agreement.
Newfoundland and Labrador	None specified.	None specified.	None specified.
Nova Scotia	None specified.	None specified.	Collective agreements may provide for the revision of any part of the collective agreement during the term of that agreement, with the exception of parts relating to the term itself.
Ontario	None specified.	None specified.	If the parties mutually agree, they may revise any part of a collective agreement at any time other than the term of the agreement itself.

TABLE 12-4   Provisions for Technological Change and Reopener Clauses (Continued)

	Definition of Technological Change	Provisions for Technological Change	Provisions for Reopener Clauses
Prince Edward Island	None specified.	None specified.	The parties may by mutual consent revise any provisions of a collective agreement, but the term of agreement must not be less than one year.
Quebec	None specified.	None specified.	None specified.
Saskatchewan	The introduction by an employer into the employer's work, undertaking, or business of equipment or material of a different nature or kind than previously utilized by the employer in the operation of the work, undertaking, or business and a change in the manner in which the employer carries on the work, undertaking, or business that is directly related to the introduction of that equipment or material; or the removal or relocation outside of the appropriate unit by an employer of any part of the employer's work, undertaking, or business.	The employer must give the bargaining agent and minister of labour at least 90 days' written notice of the change, specifying the nature of the change, the proposed date of the change, the number and type of employees affected, the effect that the change may have, and any other information requested by the minister. Within 30 days of receipt of the notice, the bargaining unit may serve notice to the employer to commence bargaining for the development of a workplace adjustment plan. A conciliator may be appointed to assist in the process at the request of either party. The change may not be implemented until a plan has been developed or the minister has been informed that the parties have bargained but failed to develop a plan. On application by an employer, the board may make an order relieving the employer from complying with this section if the board is satisfied that the technological change must be implemented promptly to prevent permanent damage to the employer's operations.	None specified.

technological change, they do at least provide for advance notice of such change, so that employers and unions can make adjustments and perhaps attempt to mutually agree on how the change will be carried out.

Of course, in dealing with technological change, the parties to a collective agreement can always negotiate appropriate language in the collective agreement itself—language that recognizes the possibility of such change occurring and creates conditions whereby such changes can be addressed during the term of the collective agreement. A 1987 study examined the language dealing with technological change in a selection of Canadian collective agreements covering more than 500 workers.[10] This study found that slightly over half of the agreements had some technological change provision, although most required only advance notice of such change. Less than half of the agreements addressed change-related issues such as retraining, employment security, relocation, joint consultation, and layoff notices. A more recent survey indicated that retraining, or training in the new technology, has become a more common provision in those collective agreements dealing with technological change, but that the proportion of agreements without technological change provisions is now approximately 40 percent.[11] Other studies have indicated that even where such provisions exist in collective agreements, labour relations boards have been reluctant to enforce them, and even when applied, these provisions appear to provide little real protection for workers in the change process, which employers continue to control.[12]

The second method of dealing with technological change, or indeed with any change that may arise during the term of the collective agreement, is for the parties to make use of the reopener clause included in the agreement itself. As Table 12-4 shows, this provision is available in several Canadian jurisdictions. A reopener clause in a collective agreement allows the parties, by mutual consent, to revise any part of the collective agreement during its term without having to renegotiate the entire collective agreement. Thus, if technological change occurs, the parties can immediately negotiate new collective agreement terms to address the change; they do not have to postpone dealing with the change until negotiations for a completely new collective agreement can begin. We should note that some Canadian jurisdictions specify that the term of the collective agreement itself cannot be revised while the agreement is in effect. This provision exists to prevent the parties from avoiding negotiations for a new collective agreement by simply extending the term of the existing agreement.

WORKPLACE RESTRUCTURING

Changing economic conditions have led to another type of change during the life of the collective agreement: **workplace restructuring**. This rather wide-ranging term encompasses such events as downsizing in the workforce; work being partially or completely shifted to other locations, companies, or countries; and increased industry competitiveness leading to changes in working conditions or redesigned work.

Most collective agreements have language in place to deal with such events as layoffs or termination. This language usually outlines the procedure for making such changes and the criteria to be used in determining which employees will be affected. The collective agreement generally specifies, for example, how much notice must be given to employees who will be laid off or terminated; whether financial compensation above the legal minimum will be provided for laid-off or terminated employees; whether the employer will provide employees with services such as retraining or assistance in finding new employment; and how factors such as seniority, experience, and current employment status will be applied in identifying candidates for layoff or termination.

However, a larger issue that to date has not been widely addressed by Canadian labour relations boards involves the role a union can or should play in any decision-making process leading to restructuring, and the union's part in managing the layoffs or terminations that may result. On the one hand, most collective agreements in Canada explicitly or implicitly give management the ultimate right to manage the workplace, including the right to make decisions about areas not addressed in the collective agreement.[13] The principle expressed in these collective agreements is known as the doctrine of **management rights** (also called **residual rights**). According to the doctrine of management rights, management has the unchallenged right to decide on whatever workplace changes it deems appropriate—unless the collective agreement specifically states that the union must be consulted or must share in such decisions. Applying this doctrine to workplace restructuring would mean that management has the right to make its own decisions on when restructuring is necessary, how it will be carried out, and what the results will be, as long as the collective agreement does not address these questions.

On the other hand, collective agreements also implicitly contain a competing principle, usually called the doctrine of **implied obligations**. This principle suggests that when a union is certified as the bargaining agent for employees and engages in collective bargaining with the employer, a relationship is established within which the union and the employer share the responsibility for the regulation and administration of the workplace.[14] According to this principle, once such a relationship is established, it is unreasonable to set arbitrary limits that allow some aspects of the workplace to be jointly governed by the union and the employer but allow other aspects of the workplace to be left solely under the employer's control. Thus, this principle implies that if restructuring occurs, the union, as the designated representative of employees in the workplace, should be involved in planning workplace restructuring because of the large impact restructuring could have on the employees the union represents. The union may have information or expertise that could result in a more effective restructuring process, and its involvement might facilitate employee acceptance of a change that might otherwise be perceived as a unilateral or insensitive management action.

If restructuring issues are present when collective bargaining commences, they can be addressed in negotiations. Workplace restructuring could also be addressed, if both parties agree, by using reopener clauses in the collective agreement to negotiate language dealing with restructuring issues. But in the absence of either of these conditions, it is unclear whether an employer is obligated to involve a union in planning or carrying out workplace restructuring. To date, only a few cases before Canadian labour relations boards have attempted to define whether unions have a right to participate in restructuring and, if so, what part unions should play in that process.

In one case, an employer had established a process to solicit employee input on proposed workplace changes; the employer believed this workplace restructuring was necessary because imminent technological and funding changes were about to significantly affect how the employer conducted its business.[15] The union contended before the labour relations board that it had been excluded from participating in the planning and implementation of the process to solicit employee input, and the board agreed that this exclusion had undermined the union's position as bargaining representative for the employees. In another case, an employee who had been demoted from his first-level managerial position claimed that his removal was due to anti-union animus. However, the employer claimed that the demotion was justified because of workplace restructuring and that the management rights clause in the collective agreement gave the company the unilateral right to make such changes.[16] The arbitrator hearing this case ruled that the restructuring undertaken by the employer had created the necessity for changes in the management structure of the organization, but that there was insufficient evidence to find that the change in this particular employee's work was due to anti-union animus. However, the arbitrator also found that the restructuring had the effect of shifting job duties formerly performed by bargaining unit members to non-union positions in the organization, and that this change violated the collective agreement.

While these cases are far from definitive, simply because to date there are so few of them, they do suggest some concerns that need to be addressed when workplace restructuring is undertaken. While it is not clear whether the employer is legally compelled to include the union in planning or carrying out restructuring efforts, the employer must be careful to ensure that restructuring does not undermine or bypass the union's legal role as representative of the bargaining unit membership. As we know, once a certification is in place, the employer is prohibited from bargaining directly with employees, and employer actions such as requesting employee input on organizational structure or operations could be interpreted as bypassing the union on potential bargaining issues. As we also know, employers must be careful that their actions are not perceived as being motivated by anti-union animus, and if restructuring involves changes to job descriptions or workplace structure, employers must ensure that there are legitimate business reasons for those changes. Employers and unions should also ensure that changes do not contravene any terms of the applicable collective agreement. Language that defines the ability of non-union personnel to carry out work usually done by bargaining unit members or that determines the role of seniority or relevant experience in reassigning workers to new positions may suggest some guidelines for how restructuring can be designed or implemented.

In studies of restructuring efforts in Canadian workplaces that have involved union participation, researchers have attempted to identify factors that affect whether unions can or cannot effectively participate in restructuring. One study contrasted the restructuring processes at four different steelmaking sites where all of the workers were represented by different locals of the same union.[17] There was particular value in studying these processes, as the union took similar approaches to restructuring issues at all four workplaces. Thus, any differences in the success of the union's participation in restructuring would be more directly attributable to factors specific to the individual union local and/or the workplace, since the actions of the union as a whole were consistent regardless of the workplace setting.

The results of this study indicated that two of the union locals were successful in participating in restructuring and in obtaining their desired outcomes and two were not.

The following four factors were identified as contributing to whether the union local was successful in its participation in restructuring:

- the local's ability to access and transmit internal and external information among its membership

- the local's ability to convey the union's vision to the membership and mobilize the membership in support of that vision

- the local's ability to participate in decision-making at multiple rather than single points in the restructuring process

- the local's ability to cooperate with management while retaining its independence as the workers' representative

These findings suggest that strong internal and external relationships established prior to restructuring may strengthen a union's ability to represent its membership effectively in a restructuring process. In other words, a union's ongoing activities in representing its membership serve to support its effectiveness if or when restructuring occurs; unions are less effective in dealing with restructuring when they do not already have internal and external resources to draw on.

Another study examined how a union's response to workplace restructuring affects different types of employees.[18] This study is valuable in that it recognizes that union membership is not homogeneous; rather, it is made up of workers with different personal attributes and different statuses and responsibilities within the workplace. This diversity means that the same restructuring plan may affect different union members in different ways. The study focused on the Ontario supermarket industry at a time when the number of competitors was increasing and there was downward pressure on wages because of the entrance of several large non-union employers into the market. There was a general desire on the part of management for greater flexibility in the workforce.

The unions in this industry chose to respond to the employers' requests for restructuring by negotiating new collective agreements with two-tier wage systems (different pay rates for current employees and those hired later on), buyouts for existing employees, and wage cuts. The results of the study indicate that this method of dealing with employer restructuring affected the workforce in several ways. The employers, for example, increased the numbers of new part-time employees, who under the new collective agreement occupied the lowest-paid job classification. There was also increased management pressure on part-time workers to work full-time hours even though these workers were still classified and paid as part-time workers. Also, the newly negotiated terms of the collective agreement had much more impact on female than on male workers, since female workers dominated the occupational categories that were most severely affected by the restructuring.

The results of this study suggest that unions involved in restructuring efforts must be conscious of the overall effect of restructuring proposals and should attempt to ensure that the interests of all members are equally represented and defended. In the restructuring process examined in this study, the employers' argument in support of restructuring was that the existing collective agreement, if continued, would lead to job loss. The employers argued that the cost of wages (and the consequent cost of goods) would make the companies incapable of competing in a price-sensitive market. A union faced with this argument has to make a difficult choice: should it protect the status of some existing jobs and lose others, or should it retain the majority of jobs but with a general reduction in working standards? (This assumes, of course, that the union accepts the employer's reasoning and/or is unable to suggest an alternative solution that the employer would accept.) However, the union's duty of fair representation would suggest that in restructuring, as in other situations, the union should be motivated to ensure that any change does not unduly harm one group of bargaining unit members while protecting or benefiting other groups.

More recently, another study examined the different restructuring experiences of two union locals at two Canadian workplaces operated by the same multinational corporation and following the same organizational model of restructuring.[19] In one workplace, the union local was challenged by major divisions within the union membership, which had resulted from different changes to different parts of the plant as part of restructuring. In this workplace, the union ended up making concessions to management demands for further workplace flexibility, to ensure the plant's continued survival and to attempt to develop more unity within the union itself. In the other workplace, there was much less dissent within the union, and the union was able to participate in restructuring with the employer (e.g., jointly developing a plan for worker retraining) without feeling that it was compromising its' members interests or its ability to resist change it perceived as being detrimental to workers. The results of this study suggest, in keeping with the results of the earlier studies, that unions' communications with their members are key to creating internal unity and also to understanding the reasoning behind changes that might have different effects on different workplace groups. The results of this study also indicate that unions facing workplace restructuring within the same corporate structure are well advised to familiarize themselves with the employer's management style and corporate programs, and to share this information with other locals of the same employer in order to develop a unified response to those programs.

SUMMARY

Because workplace conditions change over time, both certifications and collective agreements must have some flexibility to allow the parties to adapt to these changes. In this chapter, we have outlined some of the mechanisms that facilitate this flexibility. Successorship legislation ensures that certifications and collective agreements remain in effect if there are changes in the employer's business; it also serves as an attempt to discourage employers from avoiding interaction with the union by moving or changing their businesses. Decertification allows employees to remove union representation or to change union representation if they feel that the current union is not doing an adequate job of protecting their interests. Technological change, addressed either in legislation or in collective agreements, can affect job content and organizational structure; legislation and collective agreements can ensure that unions have the opportunity to be involved in how technological change is planned or implemented. Reopener clauses in collective agreements permit the renegotiation of agreements so that the parties can deal with technological change or other kinds of change within the life of a contract. And finally, unions have a role to play in representing the interests of the workers when workplace restructuring takes place, although, to date, unions have played this role in relatively few situations in Canada.

KEY TERMS FOR CHAPTER 12

abandonment of bargaining rights (p. 516)
common employer declaration (p. 514)
continuity (p. 506)
control (p. 506)
decertification (p. 515)

implied obligations (p. 536)
key person doctrine (p. 513)
management rights (p. 536)
raiding (p. 523)
reopener clause (p. 531)
residual rights (p. 536)
successorship (p. 502)
technological change (p. 530)
workplace restructuring (p. 536)

DISCUSSION QUESTIONS FOR CHAPTER 12

1. Why might employers be tempted to use expansion or relocation as a tactic to avoid the effects of unionization?

2. Name and describe some of the criteria that labour relations boards might use in determining whether successorship should apply or not.

3. Why is it important to have both certification and decertification processes available to workers?

4. Why might an employer apply for decertification?

5. Explain why it is difficult for collective agreements to include exact language dealing with technological change.

6. What sorts of issues do you think would be important for a union to negotiate in managing technological change?

7. Outline the reasons for and against union participation in the planning of workplace restructuring.

8. What factors might affect whether a union is successful in achieving its desired outcomes in workplace restructuring?

EMPLOYEES OF TREEBRANCH FORESTRY, TIMBER WORKERS UNION, AND TREEBRANCH FORESTRY

(Based on *Foothills Forest Products*, 2007)

In this case, a group of employees have applied to decertify the bargaining unit that they belong to. They want the certification order cancelled because, in their view, the union has failed to represent them adequately. The union argues that it has been unable to carry out many of the regular functions of a bargaining agent because it was involved in an extended dispute over whether it still had bargaining rights. A decertification vote has already been held, and the ballots have been sealed. The union is asking the board to dismiss the decertification application.

Case Facts

The union has been certified for the past 20 years as the bargaining agent for the employees. The company runs a sawmill. The last collective agreement expired four years ago. The union issued a notice to bargain four months before the expiration date. The day after the union issued the notice to bargain, the company that owned the mill at that time announced that it intended to close the mill four months later. Collective bargaining never occurred, and the mill closed as scheduled.

Six weeks after the mill closed, the company announced that it intended to sell the mill to new owners. The current owners, Treebranch, concluded the deal to purchase the mill six months later. The day after the sale was concluded, the union asked Treebranch to contact it regarding the recall of employees and other transitional issues.

Treebranch management told the union that Treebranch did not consider itself a successor employer, and as such did not recognize the union's certification and did not consider the collective agreement to be binding. The union then filed a grievance alleging that Treebranch had not respected the terms of the collective agreement which outlined a recall procedure, when Treebranch recalled laid-off employees before the mill reopening a few weeks later. Treebranch management did not respond to the grievance, so the union went to the board and requested a declaration of successorship.

The board took 22 months to investigate the union's request, including holding a hearing, and to issue its order. It declared Treebranch as the successor employer to the mill's original owner and stated that the terms of the expired collective agreement were in effect until a new collective agreement was negotiated. During those 22 months, the union did not maintain contact with the bargaining unit members. The union told the board that it had no means of maintaining contact because of the employer's lack of cooperation and because it had to spend most of its resources on the successorship application.

At the hearing involving the successorship application, a group of the mill employees, led by spokesperson Bill Hardy, testified that they opposed the application. They stated that even if the board declared a successorship, there should be a "confirmation vote" among the employees. The board rejected this request.

When the declaration of successorship was issued, the union immediately contacted Treebranch's management to begin re-establishing the bargaining relationship. The union wanted to appoint shop stewards and members for union-management committees. This meeting was scheduled for a date three weeks later. The union also attempted to contact the members of the bargaining unit, but found that many of the mailing addresses it had on file were out of date. Thus, it placed a notice in the local newspaper advertising a union meeting on the day before the meeting with management.

Before these meetings happened, the union filed another grievance alleging a number of violations of the collective agreement dating from the time the mill was sold.

The union meeting took place as advertised. The next day, Hardy and several other employees circulated a petition supporting the decertification of the union. They achieved the minimum 40 percent support that same day and filed an application for decertification the next day. The board official assigned to the application recommended a decertification vote be held. This occurred four months ago, and the ballots have remained sealed.

The Union's Position

The union states that it had no choice but to file the application for successorship, which ended up consuming so much of its time. It states that because the employer was uncooperative, including denying the union's status and refusing it access to the mill property, it had no way to stay in touch with its members in the bargaining unit. In the union's view, during the time that passed between the sale of the mill and the issuing of the board's decision on the successorship issue, it lost contact with most of its membership through no fault of its own.

The union believes that it should be given an opportunity to carry out its mandate as the certified bargaining agent, and be allowed to pursue its grievances and re-establish itself in the workplace.

CASE *12-2*

PUBLIC WORKERS UNION AND FIRST NATIONS FAMILY CENTRE

(Based on *AFS Aboriginal Family Service Centre Inc. and CUPE Local 4279*, 2001)

In this case, the union represents the staff at an agency that delivers a variety of programs to the local First Nations community. Most of the programs are delivered through contracts with various levels and agencies of government. One of the agency's program contracts has not been renewed, and the funding for the program has been awarded to another agency. The union has filed an application for a declaration of successorship, stating that since the program itself has not substantially changed, the union should be recognized as the bargaining agent for the staff of the agency now delivering the program.

Case Facts

The Provincial Friendship Centre had a contract with Health Canada, a division of the federal government, to provide a childhood education program to First Nations children in its area. The contract was for a three-year term, running from July 1996 to March 1999. When the contract expired in March, it was not renewed and the staff associated with the program were laid off in April. The contract was offered to other providers via a tendering process, and the First Nations Family Centre was the successful bidder. The First Nations Family Centre began offering the program in September 1999.

Bonnie Patrick worked at the Provincial Friendship Centre during the time the centre had the contract with Health Canada. She worked as a child care worker and as the executive director of the program and was employed as a child care worker at the time the program ended. She told the board that the program was designed to start First Nations children in the formal education process through the use of Aboriginal cultural resources. Health Canada provided the funding for the program, and the centre administered the funding and kept financial records. Together, the two agencies hired and fired program staff. The program also had a volunteer parent advisory committee. There were six paid staff associated with the program: the director, a child care worker, a nutrition worker, two teachers, and a bus driver. The program budget also had an allocation for training the parents of the children enrolled in the program.

Patrick described the work of the program staff as including child care, daily instructional activities, cooking daily snacks for the children, and cleaning the facilities where the program was held, which were rooms in a local school building. The program also included parent social activities and designated "cultural days."

Patrick told the board that providers of programs such as this one have some flexibility in designing the program content, subject to Health Canada guidelines. Delivery of the program was overseen by a Health Canada consultant, Marnie Salmon, who had a role in hiring and firing staff and who also acted as a liaison with the parent advisory committee. Another childhood education program, which operated under the same Health Canada guidelines and was funded by Health Canada, was offered in another part of the city by the Community Co-Operative, which also leased space in a school building for the program.

Patrick said that the program staff first discussed unionization after the centre's annual meeting in the fall of 1998. She also said that around that time she had told Salmon of the staff's desire to unionize. Patrick said that the centre was aware of the organizing campaign prior to the application for certification being filed, which took place in April 1999.

Patrick told the board that in December 1998 Salmon called a meeting that included herself, the program director, and three members of the parent advisory committee. The purpose of the meeting was to discuss the renewal of the funding for the program. Salmon described how the renewal application package should be completed, advised the others at the meeting that the program was "not in danger," and described the renewal as "routine." However, Patrick said, she learned in March 1999 that the funding would not be renewed and that the program would close at the end of the month. She said that the program's employees met with Salmon, who assured them that they would not lose their jobs and that the only change would be in the agency delivering the program. Salmon also said that the current funding would be extended until June. In fact, Patrick said, the program funding ended at the end of March, and on April 9, the centre laid off all the program employees, including Patrick. The layoff notices gave no reason for the layoffs.

On June 17, according to Patrick, Health Canada held a meeting for any agencies interested in bidding for the program contract. Applications were distributed, along with an explanation of how the contract would be awarded. The contract was eventually awarded to the First Nations Family Centre. Patrick said that she was not contacted by Health Canada or the Family Centre with respect to employment in the program.

Emmett Logan is the union staff representative assigned to the bargaining unit at the Provincial Friendship Centre. He told the board that he was given a letter dated April 9, 1999, signed by the provincial Health Canada program manager and addressed to the Friendship Centre executive director. The letter stated that the program contract was not being renewed because of concerns about poor financial accountability, high staff turnover, and lack of support to the parent advisory committee. The letter also stated that the Friendship Centre had not demonstrated the ability to effectively and efficiently manage and deliver the program, and that Health Canada had hoped to extend the agreement until the end of June, which was the end of the school term. However, the letter continued, on March 30 Health Canada had requested a meeting with the Friendship Centre to discuss the possibility of renewal and the centre had declined such a meeting. The centre had instead requested a written list of reasons for non-renewal and asked that the non-renewal be reconsidered. The letter concluded, "Please note that the decision remains as stated and no further review will be conducted ... and further, after recent events, we no longer have confidence that this program can operate appropriately … and there will not be an extension."

Logan told the board that he interpreted the reference to "recent events" as meaning the application for certification. The board was also told that on March 31 Health Canada terminated the contract for the Community Co-Operative childhood education program, although no reason was given.

Elsa Quennell is the executive director of the First Nations Family Centre. The centre is a non-profit corporation established in 1996 and operated by a community-based board of directors. Like the Friendship Centre, it works in association with various government agencies to deliver a variety of programs to its community.

Quennell stated that the Family Centre received a letter dated January 13, 1999, that invited it to an informational meeting on January 21. The meeting was announced as a solicitation for delivery of a childhood education program previously offered by the Friendship Centre. The letter indicated that the program's current funding would end on March 31. Quennell told the board that she believed that a similar letter went to five other organizations. On January 27, the Family Centre submitted a proposal to Health Canada indicating its interest in delivering the program. On February 12, Health Canada notified the Family Centre by letter that it would be awarded funding for the program effective April 1. The draft contract for the program was sent to the Family Centre for signing on March 26.

Quennell said that the Family Centre placed a newspaper advertisement for seven program staff. She confirmed to the board that the Family Centre ran the program from the same school building that the Friendship Centre had used, but it had negotiated a different lease for the space with the same landlord (the regional school board). The Family Centre also used a different name for the program than the Friendship Centre had used.

On June 2, Quennell said, the Family Centre and six other agencies received a notice from Health Canada about an information meeting to be held on June 17. The purpose of the meeting was to discuss finding a new provider for another childhood education program to be offered in the area. Unlike the notice in January, this notice did not identify the former provider of the program, but the application form carried the name that the Friendship Centre had used for its childhood education program. The application stated that the program would be offered starting August 15. On June 27, the Family Centre submitted a proposal for the program to Health Canada and explained in its proposal how it would integrate this program into the childhood education program it was already offering. On August 5, 1999, Health Canada awarded the program to the Family Centre and, rather than create a separate second contract, amended the contract for the existing program by doubling the amount of funding.

Because of the increased funding and increased program capacity, Quennell told the board, the Family Centre decided to create four additional staff positions and add to the hours of an existing part-time clerical position. The Family Centre again advertised for staff in the local newspaper. It received at least one application, for a teaching position, from a former employee of the Friendship Centre program. The Family Centre also decided that it would need more space to offer the program; however, because of the short notice it had received from Health Canada, it arranged with the school board to take over the space in the school building that was used by the Community Co-Operative program. The Family Centre now maintains its administrative offices, a kitchen, and parent training facilities at this school, and delivers the two childhood education programs in the space at the other school formerly used by the Friendship Centre.

Quennell was asked to explain the differences between the Friendship Centre program and the Family Centre program. She said that the Friendship Centre program had more of a spiritual and language component, while the Family Centre program emphasized culture and training. She also stated that the Family Centre has not had any contact with the Friendship Centre about the program. At the time the hearing was held, the Family Centre had issued layoff notices to its childhood education program staff, pending Health Canada's decision on the renewal of funding for the two programs.

Tina Tremblay, the provincial Health Canada program manager, told the board that the childhood education program is a national program, with 16 such programs offered throughout the province. The Friendship Centre was one of the first organizations to deliver the program when it was first offered.

Tremblay told the board that in December 1998 the Friendship Centre was invited to a meeting with Health Canada to discuss the funding-renewal process for the program. She said that the Friendship Centre submitted a renewal proposal, which, along with the other proposals, was reviewed by a panel of program consultants and experts in early childhood learning. The panel decided not to renew the Friendship Centre's contract. Because Health Canada's fiscal year end did not coincide with the end of the school year, Tremblay said, Health Canada was prepared to extend the Friendship Centre's funding until June 30 to minimize the disruption to the students. However, she added, the Friendship Centre opted not to meet to discuss the extension.

Tremblay described to the board the concerns that Health Canada had about the Friendship Centre's delivery of the program, as outlined in her April 9 letter. She insisted that Health Canada had had no knowledge of the union organizing campaign when it was considering the renewal of the Friendship Centre's contract, and that it had not learned about the campaign until some time between March 26 and April 9. She said that the reference to "recent events" in her letter was to the "disturbing recriminations" that the Friendship Centre staff, the centre's management, and the parents involved in the program were levelling against each other. These "recriminations" included allegations of intimidation, stalking, and tire slashing, and they were so stressful that Marnie Salmon, the program consultant, had to take time off. Tremblay said that, after Salmon's departure, she assumed personal responsibility for the program.

Tremblay told the board that the Friendship Centre director at the time the program ended cancelled the lease of the school premises where the program had operated and transferred control of the program's assets to Health Canada. These actions were in keeping with the terms of the program contract.

Under questioning, Tremblay revealed that the second childhood education program, operated by the Community Co-Operative, had actually been subcontracted by that organization to another agency. It was suggested to Tremblay that the Community Co-Operative's program contract was not renewed because the employees of that agency were unionized. Tremblay denied this suggestion. It was then suggested to Tremblay that a program contract awarded to an agency in another community had not been renewed because there was an organizing drive in progress to unionize that agency's employees. Tremblay denied any knowledge of this situation.

The Employer's Position

The employer argues that there is no evidence of a sale, transfer, or disposition of a business in whole or in part, which must be proven for successorship to occur. The employer also states that a contract to deliver a program is not a business as defined in the labour relations legislation and that once a program contract expires, the agency delivering the program loses its rights to control or deliver the program. The employer points out that the Family Centre had no contact with the Friendship Centre about the program, had delivered the program under a different name than the Friendship Centre had, and did not acquire any of the assets that the Friendship Centre had used for the program when it had the contract.

The employer also argues that the Family Centre is operating at least some of the functions associated with the program, such as administration, from facilities that the Friendship Centre did not use, and that no one who was employed by the Friendship Centre program is working at the Family Centre program. There was also a hiatus of several months between the end of the Friendship Centre contract and the start of the Family Centre contract.

The Union's Position

The union argues that there are several connections between the Friendship Centre program and the Family Centre program. The Family Centre received several assets from the Friendship Centre, including the program guidelines and the equipment in the school space where the program had been delivered. The program name used by the Friendship Centre appeared in the Health Canada application for funding that the Family Centre submitted, and the program is being delivered in the same place.

The union also argues that there is evidence that every time there was an attempt to unionize staff associated with this particular program, Health Canada failed to renew the program contract. The union points out that the Friendship Centre staff were assured in December 1998, prior to their unionization campaign, that the funding renewal was "routine," but the funding was not renewed after the bargaining unit was certified. The union states that this is evidence of suspicious motives on Health Canada's part.

The union states that if successorship is not declared in this case, unions will have a very difficult time organizing employees of agencies delivering contract programming.

References

[1] These criteria were originally established in *Expert Floors* (British Columbia Labour Relations Board, Case No. B279/93) and were restated in *Cineplex Odeon & Bollywood Cinemas* (British Columbia Labour Relations Board, Case No. B490/00).

[2] Ontario Labour Relations Board (2000). *A guide to the Labour Relations Act, 1995, and other statutes administered by the Ontario Labour Relations Board*. Toronto: Ontario Labour Relations Board.

[3] Craig, A.W.J., & Solomon, N. (1996). *The system of industrial relations in Canada* (4th edition). Scarborough, ON: Prentice-Hall, 149.

[4] Godard, J. (1996). *Industrial relations: the economy and society*. Toronto: McGraw-Hill Ryerson.

[5] *Certain employees of R.C. Purdy Chocolates Ltd. and Communications, Energy and Paperworkers Union of Canada, Local 2000*. British Columbia Labour Relations Board, Case No. B376/2001; decision issued October 15, 2001.

[6] *Federated Co-operative Ltd.*, *Saskatoon, and R.W.D.S.U., Locals 539 & 540*. Saskatchewan Labour Relations Board, file no. 256–88; decision issued July 14, 1989.

[7] For example, *R.P. Scherer Canada Inc. and CAW-Canada and Local 195*. Ontario Labour Relations Board, Case No. 3825–97–R; decision issued September 17, 1998.

[8] Moody, K. (2009). The direction of union mergers in the United States: the rise of conglomerate unionism. *British Journal of Industrial Relations*, 47(4), 676–700.

[9] Air Canada, pilots OK with mediator, *The Province* (Vancouver). (2005, September 25). p. A44.

[10] Peirce, J. (1987). Collective bargaining over technological change in Canada: a quantitative and historical analysis. Ottawa, ON: Economic Council of Canada, Discussion Paper No. 338.

[11] *Provisions in Collective Agreements*. Workplace Information Directorate, Labour Program, Human Resources and Skills Development Canada. (2005).

[12] Peirce, *op. cit.*; Giles, A., & Starkman, A. (1995). The collective agreement. In Gunderson, M., & Ponak, A. (Eds.), *Union-management relations in Canada* (3rd edition). Toronto: Addison Wesley Longman.

[13] Giles, A., & Starkman, A. (2000). The collective agreement. In Gunderson, M., Ponak, A., & Taras, D.G. (Eds.), *Union-management relations in Canada* (4th edition). Toronto: Addison Wesley Longman.

[14] Godard, *op. cit.*

[15] *Canadian Union of Public Employees, Broadcast Division, and Canadian Broadcasting Corporation.* Canada Labour Relations Board, file no. 745–4575, decision no. 1102; decision issued December 23, 1994.

[16] *United Food and Commercial Workers International Union, Local 175,* v. *Canadian Waste Services Inc.* Ontario Labour Arbitration, Case Nos. A/Y001600, A/Y001601, A/Y001602; decision issued October 28, 2000.

[17] Frost, A.C. (2000). Explaining variation in workplace restructuring: the role of local union capabilities. *Industrial & Labor Relations Review, 53*(4), 559–578.

[18] Kainer, J. (1998). Gender, corporate restructuring, and concession bargaining in Ontario's retail food sector. *Relations Industrielles/Industrial Relations, 53*(1), 183–205.

[19] Grenier, J-N. (2006). Local unions and the restructuring of work within the multinational company: internal solidarity and local context. *Labor Studies Journal, 31*(3), 65–84.

Providing the Youth Perspective

Five years ago, at age 19, Carly Sonier started working at Post Foods Canada Corp. in Niagara Falls, Ontario, where most of her co-workers were 30 years her senior, and the vast majority of them were men. "I'm the only woman on my floor, and the guys that work there are all in their 50s," she confirms. Still, this didn't discourage her from getting involved.

At the encouragement of her father, who also works at Post Foods, Sonier went to a meeting of her union, Canadian Auto Workers (CAW) Local 1101. Within months Sonier was elected shop steward and sent to Port Elgin for training. "I didn't even know what it meant to be a shop steward," she says. However, during her first year, she filed and won two grievances, so she must have been doing something right.

This led to involvement in the organizing campaign at the Niagara Falls casino, where she met other young union members. It was refreshing to meet and discuss issues with others like her. "At the time I was being laid off a lot, while they [her co-workers] hadn't faced layoffs because they'd been working there for 30 years. We're facing totally different issues."

The CAW youth network provided support she found lacking at her workplace. She's since tried to create a youth committee at her local, but with so few young workers there, has not been successful.

"Youth need to know the issues," she continues. "Someone has to step up to the plate when these people retire." In addition, she feels someone needs to be there to speak out on issues particularly important to youth, such as keeping their job during the economic downturn. "We're losing youth from the network every day," she says. While making cereal at Post Foods is not like working in the auto industry, Sonier and other more recent hires have faced regular temporary layoffs when the work slows down.

While pensions are important for all workers, things like health and safety may be of more concern for young workers. "When you get a job at 16 or 17 years old, you're going to do anything the boss tells you to. You don't know your rights," Sonier says, adding that young workers need to be informed of their rights and know that they can say no and not be fired when asked to do something that they feel isn't safe.

After five years as shop steward, Sonier, now 24, was recently elected as a member-at-large on her union executive committee, after pointing out that she was the only woman and the only person under 40 who regularly attended meetings, Thus, she said, she was the best person to represent these interests on the executive. No doubt she'll keep things in perspective.

FUTURE ISSUES FOR WORKERS, WORK ARRANGEMENTS, ORGANIZATONS, AND THE INDUSTRIAL RELATIONS SYSTEM

objectives

In the last few decades, there have been significant changes in the Canadian workplace. The demographics of the workforce have altered, and work arrangements, workplace practices, and organizational structures have also evolved. These changes have posed considerable challenges for unions, forcing them to redefine their relevance in this new reality. In this chapter, we will describe some of the ways in which Canadian unions are adapting to the changing workplace. We will also discuss some of the environmental factors that may affect Canadian industrial relations in the future. By the end of this chapter, you should be able to:

- describe the demographic changes occurring in the Canadian workplace
- identify some of the union strategies that address demographic change
- understand the different forms of work arrangements
- explain how unions have responded to new work arrangements and workplace practices
- discuss new forms of organizational structure and unions' response to them
- identify factors that may influence Canadian industrial relations in the future

INTRODUCTION

As we have seen in previous chapters, the period of the greatest growth in Canadian union membership occurred in the mid-1960s, mostly as a result of organizing in the public sector. Since then, the Canadian workplace and workforce have both changed significantly. Employment in traditionally strong areas of the workforce, such as the public sector and primary industries, has stabilized or shrunk, and employment has grown in the private sector and in service industries. New types of workers and new forms of work arrangements have also emerged.

These changes have posed challenges to the survival and vitality of Canadian unions. Many unions were originally structured to function as employee representatives in industries or occupations with a relatively stable workforce and traditional hierarchical relationships between workers and management. Unions are now having to adapt to new realities of work and prove their relevance to a new generation of workers in a variety of workplaces.

Both unions and employers must also consider factors that will affect the Canadian industrial relations system in the future. Declining union membership in the United States has raised the question of whether a similar trend will occur in Canada. The Canadian union movement has a stable, but not expanding, membership and is not immediately threatened by the same decline that has occurred in the United States. However, other factors, such as legislative changes and new organizing strategies, will perhaps determine whether Canadian union membership stays the same, grows, or follows the same path of decline as American union membership.

In this chapter, we will describe some of the issues that unions face in adapting to a changing workforce, a changing work environment, and changing types of work. We will outline the challenges related to these changes and then describe specific initiatives that Canadian unions are undertaking to address these challenges. We will conclude the chapter by discussing what the future may hold for industrial relations in Canada.

CHANGES IN WORKFORCE DEMOGRAPHICS

The composition of the Canadian workforce is changing in many ways. There is a wider age range among workers than in the past, since more young people are entering the workforce and older workers are not retiring as early as in previous decades. There are more women in the workforce, owing to fewer barriers to women working outside the home and the need for a family to have two incomes if a certain standard of living is to be maintained. And there is also more ethnic and racial diversity in the workforce because of changing trends in Canadian immigration and stronger legislative prohibitions against discrimination in hiring. Each of these trends poses a different challenge to unions.

Young Workers

Approximately two and a half million Canadians aged 15–24 hold some sort of paid job.[1] In this age group, 47 percent of workers hold part-time jobs, with the majority of these part-time workers reporting they work part-time because they are also going to school. Part-time employment (fewer than 30 hours per week) is more prevalent among this age group than among any other age group in the Canadian workforce.[2]

Opinions vary on whether the dominance of part-time work among young workers should be a concern. Some researchers argue that the high incidence of part-time jobs among workers in this age group is not a problem, since part-time work is the only option available to many of these workers because of school commitments[3]; in other words, part-time work is not something these workers undertake only because they are unable to find full-time employment. Others, however, contend that we gain a more accurate picture of younger workers' employment by examining the broader category of **non-standard work**, which includes—in addition to part-time work—temporary work, multiple job-holding, and self-employment.[4] The majority of workers aged 15–24 fall into this broader category of employment, and the predominance of this kind of work among young people may be a concern because of the non-permanence and insecurity of these kinds of employment relationships.

These conflicting perspectives on youth employment, although differing in their analysis, both acknowledge that younger workers' jobs are concentrated in the more unstable segments of the labour market. In the past, this concentration was not seen as a concern, because it was assumed that younger workers would gain their initial work experience in the unstable, lower-paying parts of the labour market and then move into more permanent and stable employment with higher pay. However, it appears that younger workers are not, as expected, finding permanent and better-paying work as they gain experience. Young workers continue to be concentrated in lower-paying occupations such as retail sales, hospitality and food services, and clerical jobs.[5] This is partly because employment in these segments of the labour market has grown, while employment in more stable segments, such as primary industries, has declined,[6] but also because part-time work is more common in these segments.

Among young workers, 13.5 percent between the ages of 15 and 24 belong to a union—a significantly lower percentage than for any other age group in the Canadian workforce. In contrast, 29.4 percent of workers aged 25–44 are union members; 37.7 percent of workers aged 45–54 are union members; and 34.6 percent of workers aged 55 and older are unionized.[7] Several characteristics of younger workers' employment make union organizing among this age group particularly challenging. Historically, the types of work and work arrangements most prevalent among young workers have not been conducive to success in organizing. There is a high turnover rate in the occupations and sectors where young workers are more likely to be employed. This means that workers who promote unionization may suddenly leave the workplace to pursue other opportunities, and once they are no longer present, support for a union among the remaining workers may quickly dissipate.

Furthermore, workers in these occupations and sectors tend to be more vulnerable to employer retaliation against organizing attempts. Because the skill level in many jobs in the service and retail sectors is relatively low, workers can easily be replaced; the knowledge that they are easily replaceable can increase workers' fear of employer retaliation against pro-union employees. If employers can change workers with little disruption to the workplace or to productivity, they may be tempted to resist unionization by firing or reassigning union supporters—even though such actions are illegal.

Moreover, employers in the industries employing non-standard workers traditionally display higher resistance to unionization than employers in industries where more stable employment relationships are the norm. Employers in retail and service industries generally operate with small profit margins in highly price-sensitive markets. They may therefore resist unionization more strongly because of their perception that union demands for higher wages would lead to reduced profits.

Organizing campaigns targeting young workers must also confront the reality that young workers are often unfamiliar with unions or have an unfavourable perception of them. A survey of young workers conducted by the Australian Council of Trade Unions indicated that young people are generally not aware of unions, that the information they do have tends to be negative, and that they do not see unions as being useful in helping them enter or stay in the workforce.[8] The results of this survey also showed that, while young workers felt that unions protected workers in general from exploitation, they themselves did not see any personal value in union membership. The attitudes of parents toward unions have also been shown to influence their children's attitudes significantly; if parents express negative attitudes toward unions, it is likely that their children will express similar attitudes.[9] Other research has suggested that negative images of unions in popular culture—for example, movies showing union corruption or connections between unions and organized crime—may also support young people's negative attitudes toward unions.[10] Research investigating Canadian youths' attitudes toward unions indicates that youths' attitudes toward unions are more strongly influenced by family and peers than by adults' attitudes. However, Canadian youths appear to have a stronger preference for unionization than adults, in part because of their exposure to workplace practices that are perceived to be unfair (e.g., lack of standardized pay policies).[11] Labour market experiences also seem to influence youth's attitudes, with periods of unemployment, frequent job changes, or "involuntary part-time employment" increasing the willingness to join a union.[12]

But the problems associated with unionizing young workers cannot always be attributed to the actions or opinions of workers or their employers. There can also be opposition within the union movement to organizing the industries or sectors where young workers are usually employed. Some unions oppose the organization of part-time and temporary workers because of the perceived threat that these forms of work pose to the job security of the full-time workers who dominate union membership. Unions supporting this position argue that organizing part-time and temporary workers (and thus giving them the same protection under the collective agreement as full-time workers) encourages employers to create part-time or temporary jobs rather than full-time permanent jobs. Thus, the argument proceeds, unionizing part-time and temporary workers indirectly promotes work arrangements that counteract unions' goals of improving employment security and working conditions. Unions may also be reluctant to organize workers in less stable parts of the labour market because of the cost of potentially challenging and lengthy organizing campaigns. They may not anticipate a sufficient financial benefit from entering sectors of the labour market that are historically difficult to organize— particularly if there is a perception that an organizing campaign has a low chance of success—and they may prefer to concentrate their efforts and resources in areas where organizing campaigns are more likely to succeed.

Labour Movement Rallies Youths: Young Delegates Urged to Defend Workers' Rights

WINNIPEG—Leaving the province to young workers who haven't a clue about the labour movement is risky business, said young delegates at the 50th annual Manitoba Federation of Labour convention.

Young workers don't know where their rights came from, and see things like holiday time and sick pay as automatic entitlements rather than something they'll have to fight to keep, said the MFL's youth achievement award winner.

"I remind them that the employer doesn't give them these out of the kindness of their heart," said Brian Spencler, who was honoured by the 500 members at the Winnipeg Convention Centre.

With a wife and three children, the 31-year-old union steward at the Victoria General Hospital is still considered a "youth" by the greying labour movement. Of the 500 MFL delegates at the convention, most are over 45. About two dozen are under 35.

Spencler said he didn't know the difference between an "issue" and a "grievance" when he first became involved seven years ago. Spencler got active after he became a victim of the "frozen food fiasco," when the provincial government got rid of hospital kitchens for a centralized food service. The move disrupted people's lives, killed jobs, cost taxpayers more, and reduced the quality of patients' food, Spencler said.

He got another job at the hospital and was mentored by an older union member. Now he does the same with newer employees, or at least pointing out what they have to lose.

"Usually a little light will go on," said Spencler. He took part in a lunch-hour MFL youth forum looking for strategies to get more young people involved in the labour movement. The young father and others at the forum said children aren't learning enough about the work world from a worker's perspective at school or in the home.

Diane Beresford of the Manitoba Teachers Society said that there is an emphasis on entrepreneurship and how the stock market works, but teaching about the 1919 Winnipeg General Strike—an epic event in Canada's labour history—has been optional. One of the resolutions the MFL will vote on this weekend calls for the province to include teaching about the Winnipeg General Strike in the Manitoba school curriculum.

Source: Sanders, Carol. (2006, November 3). Labour Movement Rallies Youths. *Winnipeg Free Press*. p. A6.

Female Workers

The current size of the Canadian workforce is nearly 17 million workers; over eight million of those workers are female.[13] The number of Canadian women in the workforce has increased steadily over the past few decades, rising from 37.1 percent of the total workforce in 1976 to approximately 48 percent in 2010.[14] The majority of Canadian women who work outside the home work in full-time jobs, although the proportion of part-time to full-time workers is higher for women than for men.[15] The number of women in managerial and professional jobs is steadily increasing, but the majority of women still work in occupations that are traditionally regarded as female, such as clerical and administrative jobs, nursing and health care occupations, sales and service work, and teaching.[16]

As the number of women in the Canadian workforce has risen, so has the number of Canadian women who belong to unions. This number has risen to a point where both the percentage (women as a percentage of total union membership) and density (female union members as a percentage of all working women) are comparable to those of male workers. This increase has been attributed both to the larger

Captain Rosella Bjornson (L, with First Officer Lee O'Riley) was the first female pilot for a commercial airline in North America. More women are working in non-traditional occupations, which could lead to greater union involvement for women.

numbers of women in the workforce and to the unionization of the Canadian public sector, which has a large number of female workers. Also, more recently, the union density rate for male workers has declined as a result of job losses affecting unionized male workers more than unionized female workers.[17] In 2009, the most recent year for which data are available, union density for female workers was 30.8 percent, while union density for male workers was 28.2 percent.[18] It should be noted, however, that density patterns change somewhat when union membership totals are subdivided into public and private sector segments. Approximately 76 percent of female workers in the public sector are unionized, while only 14 percent of women working in the private sector are union members.[19]

However, the relatively comparable levels of unionization of female and male workers are not an indication that unions have been targeting female workers as a source of membership. A study analyzed union organizing attempts in Ontario from 1985 to 1999 to determine whether the gender of workers made a difference in the success of an organizing campaign (i.e., whether gender had a bearing on whether certification was achieved).[20] Female-dominated workplaces (defined either as workplaces with a simple majority of female workers or as workplaces where more than 60 percent of the workforce was female) were much more likely to vote in favour of certification than male-dominated workplaces, but 62 percent of the organizing attempts counted in the study were conducted in male-dominated workplaces (36 percent were conducted in workplaces with no female employees at all). Only 38 percent took place in female-dominated workplaces, where women constituted between 51 percent and 80 percent of the workforce.

Another study, which surveyed the union organizers involved in 1,281 organizing campaigns in Ontario between 1996 and 1998, examined the characteristics of organizing campaigns in male- and female-dominated workplaces.[21] It found that workers in female-dominated workplaces, especially small workplaces (less than 50 employees) were more likely to initiate contact with the union themselves, rather than have their workplace targeted by the union for organizing. Also, employers responded to organizing campaigns with fewer anti-union tactics in female-dominated workplaces; yet even when the number of anti-union tactics was the same in organizing campaigns in male- and female-dominated workplaces, there was a higher success rate for organizing campaigns in female-dominated workplaces.

The results of these analyses suggest that while female workers may be more likely than male workers to support unionization, and that female-dominated workplaces may be easier to unionize because of less employer resistance and more employee initiative, unions may not always recognize these tendencies when they seek to identify workplaces suitable for organizing campaigns; in fact, unions would apparently sooner organize a male-dominated workplace than a female-dominated workplace. The author of these studies attributes this oversight to unions' "internal inertia"; that is, unions have focused more on consolidation than on expansion, and current union members may fear that there will be a reduction in existing services if resources are diverted into organizing or addressing diverse groups of non-unionized workers.[22]

Unions' ability to represent their female members effectively has also been hampered by the frequent inability or unwillingness of female workers to participate in union activities. Because many female workers have commitments outside of work, such as family, they tend to have less time than male workers for activities such as union participation. Studies examining gender differences in union participation have indicated that while men and women may not differ significantly in their attitudes of commitment to their union, men are more likely to actually participate in union activities (e.g., they are more likely to serve as elected officers and attend membership meetings).[23] A gender imbalance in union participation, even when men and women are equally represented in a union's membership, may mean that issues of concern to female union members, such as wage disparities between female- and male-dominated occupations, are not adequately addressed. If there are not enough women actively involved in the union to advocate for these issues, the importance of the issues may not be recognized (this point was made in our discussion in chapters 7 and 8 about how issues for collective bargaining are identified and prioritized). It has also been argued that gender imbalances in union participation may result in some "traditional" union goals being mistakenly conceptualized as gender-neutral if there are not enough "non-traditional" participants to point out instances when traditional goals do not serve diverse populations. Such misconceptions about the neutrality or universality of some issues may lead to women's issues being marginalized as "special interest" issues and consequently not being given a high priority.[24]

One further challenge that unions face in organizing and representing women is that women enter and leave the labour force or change their employment status more often than men do. This is primarily due to women having the primary responsibility for child care and domestic duties in most Canadian households. Women leave the workforce to care for children more often than men do (although 96 percent of Canadian women who leave a paid job for maternity leave intend to return to work within 18 months of childbirth).[25] Furthermore, more women than men engage in temporary work, part-time work, self-employment, or multiple jobs as ways of balancing family responsibilities with work commitments, and more Canadian women than men are involved in non-standard work arrangements.[26] It may be more difficult for unions to organize women workers, or to represent them effectively, when women's patterns of participation in the workforce are not consistent and linear over time.

Older Workers

In past decades, over 90 percent of Canadian men and over 70 percent of Canadian women held paid employment outside the home by the time they reached the age of 25.[27] However, it is surprising to see how many older workers continue to participate in the labour force beyond the standard ages for retirement. In 2009, the **participation rate** (the percentage of individuals in a given demographic group who hold paid employment outside the home) for men aged 55–59 was 76.4 percent; for men aged 60–64, the rate was 57.4 percent; and for men aged 65 and older, the rate was 14.5 percent. For women, the participation rates for the same age groups were 67.1 percent, 43.8 percent, and 6.7 percent respectively.[28]

These numbers indicate that there are fewer older female workers than older male workers, echoing the gender-based patterns found in younger age groups. But we should also be aware that the participation rate for older female workers has been increasing while the participation rate for older male workers has been decreasing. The largest increases in labour force participation for older female workers have occurred in the 50–54 and 55–59 age groups.[29]

Several different reasons have been cited for the changes in participation rates among older Canadian workers. The median age of retirement for both men and women has declined since the 1970s, partly owing to changes in pension administration that allowed individuals to begin drawing federal pensions at younger ages. In addition, many organizations started using early retirement as a means of downsizing their workforces, and past recessions have caused general reductions in employment opportunities, which affected older workers as much as younger ones.[30]

However, there are also trends that have encouraged older workers to stay in the workforce. As a result of Canada's system of social security programs, many jobs offer subsidized benefits—medical and dental care plans, for example—that would be very expensive for a worker to pay for on their own. Older workers may be tempted to stay in the workforce longer to take advantage of employer support for these benefits. Researchers have also speculated that women just entering the older age groups will stay in the workforce longer than their predecessors because they have a greater commitment and attachment to work outside the home.[31] Older workers are also staying in the workforce in part-time work and in self-employment; the percentage of older workers in these types of work rises steadily as the age of the workers increases. It has been suggested that workers choose these forms of employment as a means of delaying retirement—that is, as an alternative to simply leaving the workforce when full-time work is no longer appealing or feasible.[32] The elimination of mandatory requirement at age 65 in most Canadian jurisdictions has also made it possible for workers to continue working as long as they are capable of doing so.[33]

Just as we saw in the data presented in the discussion of younger workers, the unionization rate for older workers aged 55 and up (34.4 percent in 2009)[34] is comparable to the overall average rate of unionization in the Canadian workforce. Therefore,

Canadian unions have apparently not felt the need to increase unionization among older workers. It is also possible that unions prefer to direct their organizing efforts toward workers who have most of their working lives (and potential union membership) before them, rather than trying to attract workers who are closer to departing from the workforce and thus leaving the union. However, if older workers are a minority within a union, they may have difficulty promoting their issues, just as any other minority group would. Older workers may have trouble demonstrating the benefits of "their" issues to younger workers. For example, in Canada, workers between the ages of 45 and 54 are the ones most likely to contribute to registered retirement savings plans (RRSPs).[35] RRSPs can be opened as soon as a worker enters the workforce, and many financial planners recommend that workers start RRSPs as soon as possible so that they can build up enough funds to support a decent lifestyle after retirement. Thus, RRSPs can benefit younger workers as much as they do older workers and may even benefit younger workers more, since younger workers have a longer earning period during which to make RRSP contributions. However, older workers who want their union to negotiate for contract terms such as employer contributions to RRSPs may have trouble achieving this goal if younger workers dominate the union. Younger union members may not see the value in bargaining for employer-supported retirement benefits, since retirement security is not as immediately important to the younger worker.

Ethnic and Racial Diversity in the Workforce

Another major change in the Canadian workforce has been an increase in the number of workers belonging to visible minority groups. The Canadian census defines visible minorities as Chinese, South Asian, Black, Filipino, Latin American, Southeast Asian, Arab, West Asian, Korean, and Japanese, and also includes categories for visible minorities not included in these categories and for those who belong to multiple visible minority groups.[36] Data from the 2006 Canadian census indicate that about 16 percent of the Canadian population can be classified as belonging to one of these categories.[37] According to the 2006 census data, 67.3 percent of the visible minority population in Canada participates in the labour force. This rate is almost the same as the 66.8 percent total participation rate for all Canadians. (The participation rate measures the number of Canadians 15 years and older who are part of the labour force, and also includes individuals who are unemployed or not working for other reasons but are available to work.) The occupational patterns for visible minority men and women are very similar to those of non-minority men and women, with women most often employed in administrative, clerical, sales, or service work and men in managerial, technical, or professional work. [38]

It is interesting to note, however, that more visible minority than non-minority women work in jobs involving manual labour, and that more visible minority than non-minority men work in sales and service jobs.[39] Employment data also show that adults who belong to a visible minority are more likely to have university degrees than adults who do not belong to a visible minority, but tend to have fewer years of work experience. Also, visible minority members with university degrees "are not as likely as others with the same level of education to be employed in the higher-paying professional or managerial occupations."[40] This mismatch between education level and occupational level is referred to as **underemployment**. Similar patterns are also found in comparisons between visible minority workers born and educated in Canada and other Canadians.[41]

The increase in ethnic and racial diversity in the Canadian workforce can be attributed to several interrelated causes. One is higher rates of immigration to Canada, especially among members of visible minorities. Since the mid-1980s, immigration has been the largest source of growth in the Canadian population.[42] The patterns of immigration to Canada have also changed. The number of immigrants from Western Europe, the United Kingdom, and the United States, formerly the major sources of immigration to Canada, has dropped since the late 1960s. The majority of immigrants to Canada now come from Asia, the Middle East, Eastern Europe, and Central and South America.[43] Obviously, many of these immigrants belong to the visible minority groups identified in the Canadian census.

Another reason for increased workforce diversity in Canada is legislation such as federal and provincial employment equity laws. Most of these laws identify demographic groups that have historically been under-represented in employment in relation to their proportion in the population as a whole. The federal *Employment Equity Act* identifies four of these groups: women, visible minorities, Aboriginal/First Nations people, and people with disabilities. Employment equity law encourages organizations to develop plans to increase representation of these groups in the workforce to match the group's representation in the population or relevant workforce. For example, if women make up 40 percent of the labour force in a particular region, employers should strive to have a workforce that is 40 percent female. There are many debates over whether these laws are effective or whether they cause **reverse discrimination**, where individuals not belonging to designated groups are unjustly excluded from hiring or promotion opportunities. Assessing these arguments is beyond the scope of this discussion, but we will simply note that the presence of employment equity laws may encourage employers to consider members of visible minorities for employment opportunities in situations where these individuals might otherwise be ignored.

Statistics Canada currently does not collect data on union membership or density among workers who belong to visible minorities, so it is difficult to estimate how extensive union membership is among visible minorities. A study by the Canadian Labour Congress estimated that in 1999, 22.1 percent of visible minority workers were covered by a collective agreement; the rate for all other workers was 32 percent.[44] A later study incorporating data from 1996 to 2001 indicated that 21.3 percent of visible minority workers were covered by a collective agreement, with the coverage rate at 21.2 percent for male visible minority workers and 21.4 percent for female visible minority workers; the percentage of visible minority members among all union members was estimated at 6.9 percent.[45] It is not unreasonable to assume that problems of racial and ethnic inclusion in unions would be similar to the previously identified problems regarding the inclusion of working women. Members of racial or ethnic minorities may not be willing or able to be active participants in union governance, or they may be actively discouraged from doing so. Exclusion may result from intentional discrimination (e.g., individuals may not be informed of meeting times and places) or from less explicit forms of discrimination (e.g., individuals may lack the linguistic or cultural skills to fully participate in union activities, and the union does not make adjustments to its activities for them). Either form of discrimination can lead unions to neglect the concerns of visible minorities. We should also note that members of visible minorities in Canada are more likely than non-minority workers to be employed in occupations that have traditionally been difficult to organize, for the reasons discussed earlier.

An additional concern in unionizing members of visible minorities is that immigrants may come from cultures or countries where unions are perceived as corrupt or as an unwarranted challenge to management's right to manage. In some countries or cultures, moreover, union members are the target of violence because of unions' social activism or opposition to the government. Individuals with these sorts of attitudes or experiences may not wish to support unions in Canada, even though the union experience in this country is considerably different.

UNION STRATEGIES FOR DEALING WITH THE CHANGING WORKFORCE

It is generally acknowledged that if unions are to survive and provide effective representation for their membership, some of the characteristics of traditional unionism, including those based on the assumption that workers are "masculine, white, heterosexual, [and] full-time," need to change.[46] As one writer notes, "As [unions'] traditional manufacturing base wanes, they are being forced to look elsewhere for membership."[47] To achieve this membership expansion, unions need to recognize the characteristics of diverse sectors of the labour market and develop strategies to address these characteristics or to promote the value of unions in addressing the problems experienced by workers in those sectors.

Some Canadian researchers have attempted to determine whether unions are actually attempting to attract a wider range of potential members, and if so, whether those unions undertaking such attempts are attaining their desired outcomes. The results of these studies are mixed. On the positive side, most national unions in Canada now have policy statements on issues like workplace equality, affirmative action, harassment, and violence.[48] In addition, many collective agreements, particularly in the public sector, have specific language addressing issues related to workplace equality.[49] The fact that these statements exist shows, at least at a strategic level, that these issues are acknowledged as being important to a diverse workforce and are worthy of attention. However, policy statements at the national level do not always translate into action at the local level. There appears to be "entrenched resistance" at some local levels, either to adopting these policies or to taking such actions as creating bargaining initiatives that address the concerns of diverse segments of the union membership.[50] This resistance is attributed to a lack of support from elected union officials, to the influence of individuals with attitudes or values that contradict the policies, to insufficient resources to support every single issue that is presented, and to inadequate education on the issues and on the reasoning behind them.

Some unions have gone beyond simply formulating policy statements and have undertaken more substantive actions to address increased workforce diversity and to make unions more relevant to diverse groups of workers. For example, the Canadian Union of Public Employees (CUPE) has created two "diversity vice-president" positions on its national executive. One of these vice-presidents represents First Nations workers and the other represents workers from ethnic or racial minorities. The existence of these positions ensures the formal presence on the national union executive of members of demographic groups that otherwise might not be represented. CUPE has also attempted to increase the visibility of traditionally marginalized groups of union members, for example by sponsoring national conferences for lesbian, gay, bisexual, transgender, and transsexual (LGBTT) union members, and creating national action committees to work on issues relevant to LGBTT members, women members, workers with disabilities, and young members.

In an effort to gain future potential union supporters, some Canadian unions are targeting their activities toward recruiting and educating young workers.

Union activities targeting young workers are also becoming more common. Some researchers have suggested that the lack of interest in unionization among younger workers may not be a problem. Issues traditionally addressed by unionization, such as long-term employment and economic security, are more important to older workers than to high school students who are only working part time. Unionization likely becomes more important to young workers only as they move into more substantive and permanent employment.[51] However, some Canadian unions have taken the position that young workers can benefit from union membership even when they are starting their careers in non-permanent positions. Also, young workers are the potential union supporters of the future, so there may be long-term benefits from early recruitment or education of young workers.

The Canadian Labour Congress has attempted to reach young workers by creating a national working committee for young workers (under age 30) and adding a "young" section to its website.[52] The Confédération des syndicats nationaux has embarked on a similar venture by creating a youth committee and having a separate section for this committee on its website.[53] Most provincial federations and large national or regional units also have a committee or group dedicated to young workers and have resources available on the Internet for these workers. Using the Internet as an information and organizing strategy is particularly appropriate for young workers because it recognizes the importance of the Internet as a source of information for young people (as opposed to older people who may be less comfortable using computers). Unions wanting to reach young workers are also disseminating information through websites and through social media such as Facebook and YouTube, rather than through more traditional means of contact, such as telephone calls, printed literature, or workplace visits. Internet and social media contact also allow young workers to investigate unionization without the fear of employer discovery and possible retaliation.

Other unions have initiated education programs for young people as a means of reaching potential young union members. Local 401 of the United Food and Commercial Workers in Alberta offers a "Young Workers in Action" course to its members, which teaches young workers about labour history and develops skills for young union members to be activists in their workplaces.[54] The British Columbia Federation of Labour offers a workshop for young workers on "Labour Education," which informs young workers, unionized and non-unionized, about their rights under employment standards law. The Federation also offers a similar workshop for high school students on health and safety issues in the workplace.[55]

As most of these initiatives are relatively recent, their long-term success remains to be determined. They do, however, follow the direction taken by the successful organizing strategies identified in the previously cited study of union organizing in Ontario.[56] This study indicated that at least some unions were recognizing the changes in the labour market by concentrating their organizing efforts on growing rather than declining employment sectors. In the 1980s, approximately 17 percent of certification applications in Ontario were for private sector employers, but by the mid-1990s, this figure had risen to 48 percent, indicating that unions were acknowledging increased employment activity in this sector and adjusting their organizing efforts accordingly.

Internal problems in union administration can sometimes inhibit organizing activity, however. Declining union membership results in reduced revenues from membership dues, and that reduced revenue has, in some cases, led to union staff cutbacks and difficulties with burnout among remaining staff.[57] Such a situation may then result in fewer union resources to support organizing, potentially leading to a downward spiral, as reduced organizing results in fewer new members and even less financial support for further organizing efforts.

It should be noted that the most successful organizing campaigns do not rely only on the participation of paid union staff. One of the most effective organizing tactics is the technique of **salting**—using workers already employed in the potential bargaining unit as the "inside" primary organizers, rather than having a paid union staffer direct the organizing campaign externally. Salting is especially effective in workplaces with diverse groups of workers because inside organizers will, or should be, aware of the particular issues and problems facing different types of workers. The union and the organizers can then conduct an organizing campaign that addresses concerns specific to the workplace and the workers. Moreover, the message of unionization may have more impact coming from a co-worker than from an external and possibly less credible source. The salting technique has been used in organizing campaigns for taxi drivers[58] and fast food workers.[59]

Having described the changes in the composition of the Canadian workforce and their implications for unions, we will now turn our attention to changes in the workplace itself, beginning with changes in work arrangements.

CHANGING WORK ARRANGEMENTS AND PRACTICES

Unionism first evolved, as outlined in Chapter 2, according to an "industrial" model, which means that unions were developed in workplaces where workers attended work regularly and worked shifts determined by the employer. Partly because of advances in technology that allow more flexibility in how work is carried out, and partly through the recognition that not all workers work efficiently or productively in rigidly structured settings, many workplaces have moved away from the industrial model and are exploring alternative ways of structuring work. Many organizations are also exploring new ways to manage, motivate, and retain their employees. While these new work arrangements and policies may offer advantages to workers and employers, they have also posed challenges for unions, which now have to develop new ways to organize and represent workers employed in these new forms of work.

Scheduling

Alternate forms of work scheduling include **flextime** (workers are allowed to partially or completely determine their own work hours), **compressed workweeks** (workers are allowed to work longer shifts in exchange for more days off), and **job sharing** (two employees share one full-time job). Work arrangements like these are becoming more common in organizations where job tasks can accommodate this sort of flexibility. In 2005, approximately 45 percent of Canadian workers had access to at least one of these forms of alternate scheduling, with the majority of those workers employed in non-manufacturing industries or services.[60] Employees tend to favour flexible scheduling because it allows them to adjust their work arrangements to accommodate non-work commitments such as child care or education. However, there are concerns that the option of flexible work arrangements might give the employer the power to impose work hours that meet the employer's rather than the employees' needs. Flexible work arrangements may also lead to a lack of clarity about work expectations, which can then cause conflict between employers and employees.

Unions attempting to organize workers on flexible work schedules are often challenged by very practical matters, such as how to contact an employee whose hours or days of work are continually changing. Most labour codes specify that organizing campaigns must be conducted outside working hours, but determining when working hours start and end can be problematic when flexible work arrangements are in place. Organizers run the risk of contacting employees during working hours and thus committing an unfair labour practice. Unions may also have a hard time making a case for their usefulness if the employer has already responded to worker needs for flexibility without being motivated by the pressure of a union. However, employees may perceive that unions will help them achieve a lighter workload in situations where the availability of flexible work arrangements is not considered sufficient to compensate for excessive workloads or overtime.

Telecommuting

Another type of flexible work arrangement is **telecommuting** (or **telework**). An employee in this arrangement works partially or fully at home or at another location outside the office and communicates with the workplace through computers and telephones. Like flexible work schedules, telecommuting allows the employee some degree of freedom in determining how and when the work will be done. In telecommuting arrangements, the employer usually specifies the nature of the work and the time by which it must be completed, and lets the employee determine how these conditions will be met.

Despite the advantages that telecommuting offers, concerns have been voiced about it and other forms of flexible work that parallel some of the original reasons for unionization: namely, the possibility of abuse or exploitation by the employer. In telecommuting, for example, workers may find that the cost of upgrading their computer equipment or remodelling a work space at home exceeds any savings they realize by not working outside the home. In addition, telecommuters may have anticipated that they could work at home and also meet other commitments, such as caring for their children, but instead find that they are working extended or unreasonable hours to meet the demands of both employer and family.

Contract workers and telecommuters provide another challenge for union organizers who seek to provide a collective voice for a decentralized workforce.

Telecommuting arrangements are challenges for unions because these arrangements contradict one of the most basic implicit assumptions in labour and employment standards legislation: namely, that employees work at a centralized location outside their homes, and at that location the employer dictates the conditions and content of work. If employees are not working at the employer's workplace, and their communication with the workplace is solely through a supervisor or other manager and not through peers or co-workers, such basic union organizing activities as distributing information to potential union members suddenly become very difficult. And, as with workers in other forms of flexible work arrangements, selling the benefits of union membership to telecommuters may be difficult, since the employer has already permitted non-traditional work arrangements without having been pressured to do so by a union.

Different Employment Relationships

Unlike the traditional employment relationship, some alternative work arrangements do not presume an ongoing connection between the employer and the employee, or assume that an employee will pursue the same occupation or progress within the same industry throughout his or her working life. Frequent changes in employment used to be considered a sign of a worker's instability or unwillingness to commit to serious employment. Now workers may have multiple employers, multiple occupations, or even multiple careers during their lifetime.[61]

One major change in the workplace is the increasing availability of **non-permanent employment relationships** such as contract, term, or temporary work. Employment relationships such as these are no longer seen as inferior or supplemental to full-time permanent work. The availability of full-time permanent work in Canada has also been decreasing in recent years, with growth in the labour market occurring more in part-time jobs and different forms of non-permanent employment.[62] In fact, some career theorists have suggested that future career patterns will resemble the career patterns that already exist in industries such as filmmaking. In these industries, employees engage in temporary work arrangements for a series of employers; they focus on developing a range of different skills through their varied experiences rather than having a permanent employment relationship as their ultimate goal.[63] In addition, other changes in the work environment, such as decreasing numbers of "standard" employment opportunities and the desire to have more control over one's own working life, have led more workers to explore career and employment options such as self-employment, lateral or downward career progression, and voluntary absences from the workforce.[64]

Non-permanent employment relationships may allow greater opportunities for workers to gain a variety of skills and to change occupations or employers to match their own interests. However, the downside of these non-permanent relationships is that they offer employers more extensive power to terminate workers, sometimes for unjustified reasons, because there is no expectation of an ongoing relationship between employer and employee. Employers may also engage in such employment practices as continually renewing a temporary contract with the same employee. These practices give the employer the productivity equivalent of full-time employment but do not give the employee the benefits usually associated with a permanent job.

New Human Resource Management Practices

Changes in career patterns and in workers' attitudes toward employment have also led many employers to explore new ways of attracting and retaining valued employees.

These include, for example, increased career development and training opportunities[65]; "high commitment" practices focusing on teamwork, problem-solving groups, and direct forms of communication between employer and employee[66]; other employer practices that aim to give employees more opportunity for a "voice"[67]; and pay structures with differences in compensation more clearly linked to different performance levels.[68]

The research evaluating these practices has produced mixed results that do not definitively answer the question of whether these practices actually produce the desired outcomes.[69] However, the intent of these practices is usually to attempt to increase employee retention by making employees feel more valued and more fairly compensated, and to discourage traditionally adversarial employee-employer relationships in favour of a "mutual gains" approach. In this sense, these new practices can be seen as philosophically similar to the alternative approaches to the traditional collective bargaining process discussed in Chapter 8.

UNION RESPONSES TO CHANGING WORK ARRANGEMENTS AND PRACTICES

Some of Canada's largest unions have addressed the issue of non-traditional work by negotiating collective agreements that validate these arrangements but establish rules to regulate their use. To guard against employer exploitation, unions have often insisted that their acceptance of these arrangements be tied to the adoption of other conditions. For example, one Canadian Auto Workers local agreed to accept a reduction in work hours only if the employer promised a reduction in overtime and the retention of jobs that were targeted for elimination. However, one recent survey of Canadian collective agreements found that 60 percent of those analyzed contained no provisions for flexible work arrangements.[70] This rather significant omission suggests either that many Canadian unions do not yet perceive flexible work arrangements as a bargaining priority or that employers are not willing to negotiate the control or regulation of these arrangements.

The relatively low level of unionization in the types of organizations where telecommuting is often found—high-tech companies, for example—suggests that Canadian unions and legislators have not yet developed the means to facilitate effective union representation in non-traditional forms of work. Most Canadian collective agreements contain language restricting the excessive use of overtime or reliance on temporary workers, but beyond those basic provisions, they usually do not contain language relating to non-permanent work, even in those industries where such work is the norm rather than the exception.

An example of collective agreements that actively address issues related to non-traditional forms of work can be found in the British Columbia film industry. Unions representing workers in this industry have negotiated contract terms that attempt to balance flexibility in employment and alternative employment relationships with protection of their members' working conditions. One provision in these contracts allows members to accept wage and benefit reductions when working on productions that offer opportunities for skill development. Another provision allows members to take equity (a share in the eventual earnings of the production) rather than immediate wage payments when working on locally made films with small commercial potential. This provision increases union members' opportunities to work on productions that would not otherwise be able to afford to hire unionized workers. Another provision requires certain levels of Canadian staffing on productions funded by American-based companies; this ensures that Canadian union members have equal or preferred access to job opportunities generated by foreign productions.[71]

The use of technology in many forms of non-traditional work also offers new opportunities for unions as well as employers and employees. Unions and union supporters have created numerous locations on the Internet to disseminate information about unions and unionization. Unions have also turned to social media to reach potential members and to communicate with current members. There is even the potential for online labour action: in 2007, a group of 2,000 Italian IBM workers and supporters conducted a "virtual strike" in response to a pay offer from their employer. The workers logged on from home to avoid disciplinary action, and "occupied" IBM's virtual office on the Second Life website. The "virtual strike" resulted in the resignation of IBM's Italian president and a new pay deal for the union members.[72] It has been suggested that while labour legislation historically has been constructed on the assumption of traditional forms of work and workplaces, its scope is broad enough that it could be interpreted to cover any place where work and work arrangements take place, even if that "place" does not have a physical location.[73]

Generally, however, unions have been reluctant even to suggest any form of non-traditional work arrangement, preferring to place a higher priority on maintaining the standards associated with full-time permanent employment and its attendant benefits. They fear that agreeing to any form of flexible work arrangement or non-traditional employment relationship in one collective agreement will weaken the union's ability to protect full-time permanent work in subsequent rounds of bargaining. Unions have also generally resisted many of the new workplace practices described above, since these policies' outcomes, intentional or otherwise, are to reduce or eliminate the union's role in the workplace as the representative and voice of employees. Employees may even feel that direct communication with management is more effective for them than having the union represent them indirectly.[74]

Having outlined some of the implications of new forms of work arrangements and practices, we will now turn our attention to changes in the structure of the organization itself. This form of change can also cause changes in the relationships between employees and managers.

CHANGES IN ORGANIZATIONAL STRUCTURES

As we have learned, unions evolved within the context of traditionally structured industrial organizations with several distinctive levels of hierarchy, each of which has different amounts of power and decision-making authority. Authority and power increase at higher levels of the hierarchy, with the most power and responsibility concentrated at the top. Non-managerial workers are usually at the bottom of the hierarchy, which means that they have the smallest amount of power and responsibility in the organization. Figure 13-1 shows two examples of traditional organizational structures.

One of the motivations behind the formation of unions was dissatisfaction with the distribution of power and authority in traditionally structured organizations. Employees at the bottom of the hierarchy had little opportunity to participate in any decisions within the organization—even those that directly affected them. Unions became a means through which employees could be represented in the decision-making process for work-related issues (e.g., wages, hours of work). Previously, the formal organizational structure had excluded their representation in such decisions.

A number of environmental changes beyond the emergence of unions have revealed the limitations of traditional organizational structures. Changes, such as the emergence of global markets, have necessitated the creation of new forms of organization to accommodate companies that conduct business in multiple locations or cultures. Changes in the purpose of organizations, such as broadened product or service offerings, have

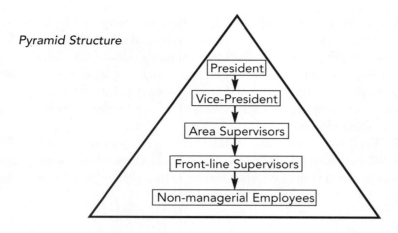

Pyramid Structure

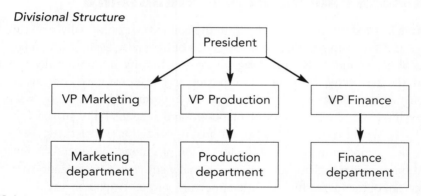

Divisional Structure

Figure 13-1 *Traditional Organizational Structures*

forced organizations to alter their structures so that new goals can be more easily achieved. The rate of change has increased in many industries and markets, which has increased the need for faster information flow and faster decision-making capability. This need has demonstrated the limitations of communication in traditional structures, in which information flows from the top down and takes a considerable amount of time to disseminate throughout the entire organization.

In summary, many organizations are realizing that traditional organizational structures no longer guarantee efficiency or effectiveness. Thus, organizations are exploring newer forms of structure that usually involve decreased levels of hierarchy—the so-called **flatter organization**—or more equitable distributions of power—the **matrix** and **network (or web) organizations**, where information and decision-making authority are shared laterally rather than vertically or are radiated throughout the entire organizational structure. Figure 13-2 depicts these new organizational structures.

Matrix Structure

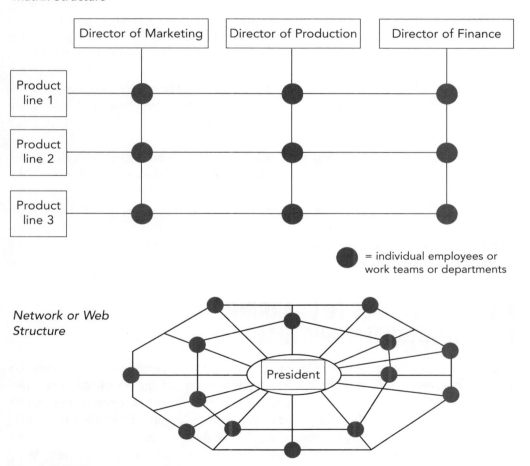

Figure 13-2 *New Organizational Structures*

The emergence of new forms of organizational structures may be beneficial for employers, but these structures are problematic for unions because they reduce or eliminate the traditional hierarchical distinctions between managers and employees. As we know from previous chapters, Canadian labour law makes clear distinctions between managerial and non-managerial employees, and usually excludes managers or individuals with managerial duties from membership in a bargaining unit. These distinctions may make it difficult to unionize within an organizational structure where there are few or no clearly defined boundaries between management and employees.

One often-cited advantage of new forms of organizational structures is that the historically adversarial relationship between employees and employers is somewhat diffused, as managers may no longer have the sole authority to direct workers, and workers are given much more autonomy in determining how their work will be conducted. However, this advantage can be problematic for unions. The union's function of representing workers' interests may be undermined if workers are allowed to have more formal input into decision-making or are able to work more cooperatively with other parts of the organization, including managers.

Unions may also have to deal with practical problems associated with the implementation of structural change, such as **downsizing** (the elimination of jobs or the reduction of work through such methods as changing full-time work to part-time), or changes in job content that reflect the new interrelationships or reporting responsibilities within the organization. These problems may be difficult to address effectively within the context of labour law or collective agreements that implicitly assume traditional organizational structures and traditional manager-employee relationships.

UNION RESPONSES TO CHANGING ORGANIZATIONAL STRUCTURES

Dealing with new forms of organization and new manager-employee relationships is a balancing act for unions. On the one hand, the structure of the organization is sometimes changed to a form that encourages more cooperative worker-employer relationships. In such situations, the control and direction of the organization still remains with the employer, even with the most progressive forms of organizational structure, and thus unions still have a role to play in ensuring that workers' issues are addressed. Many unions fear that compromising on structural issues will lead employers to expect similar compromises on more significant issues, and that will eventually lead to unions becoming ineffective as employees' advocates. Some unions thus feel compelled to resist structural change; if such change does not represent any fundamental alteration to the allocation of power and control within the organization, and if the union agrees to structural changes, its ability to influence the employer in the future may be diminished.

On the other hand, structural changes are often undertaken to ensure an organization's continued vitality. In these situations, a union's adversarial opposition to change may impair the organization's chances for long-term survival. The union also has an interest in seeing the company succeed, because success and survival mean that the union maintains its membership base and its revenues. Therefore, even within a traditionally adversarial relationship, the parties do have at least one long-term common goal, and a union's willingness to support structural change may facilitate the achievement of that goal.

Two brief examples will demonstrate some of the ways in which Canadian unions have attempted to balance these competing positions when faced with organizational restructuring. The Canadian Auto Workers (CAW) union has faced significant challenges in dealing with the restructuring of the Canadian automobile industry as a result of the economic downturn in 2009. The restructuring has involved plant closures, reductions in output, and significant job losses. In addition to representing the interests of its current members, the CAW has also had to consider the issue of maintaining the pensions and other benefits received by its retired or terminated members—the so-called "legacy costs" that represented a significant financial liability for the automobile industry.[75] An additional factor in the restructuring was the Canadian government, which, in exchange for providing financial subsidies to the struggling automobile industry, required certain structural changes, such as the retention of a certain amount of automobile production in Canada and a reduction in labour costs.[76] The CAW's responses to these pressures has been varied, but has involved renegotiating parts of collective agreements, agreeing to some concessions but rejecting others, and collaborating on issues related to the industry's new structure, such as ensuring that some subsidy funding is directed toward the ongoing cost of pensions and benefits. The CAW has acknowledged, however, that survival of the industry is key to its own survival, and that while it intends to continue advocating for its members' interests, it also recognizes that structural change is necessary for the industry's survival.[77]

The CAW has also developed strategies to deal with new forms of organizational structure. In 2007, it signed a "Framework of Fairness" agreement with Magna International, a large automobile parts maker based in Toronto. Magna's organizational structure emphasizes "labour-management cooperation and reciprocity, and individual responsibility"[78] through such mechanisms as small workgroups and informal decision-making by consensus. The agreement between the CAW and Magna allowed the CAW to conduct organizing campaigns in Magna's plants and to conduct representation votes, in exchange for the CAW agreeing to final-offer arbitration to resolve negotiating disputes.[79] As of 2009, workers at three Magna plants had voted to join the CAW under these terms, although some workers complained that their subsequent concerns in bargaining were ignored by a union eager to "push through" a deal with the company.[80] The framework has also been strongly criticized on the basis that it compromises the independence of the union, and that the union's agreement not to engage in strike action, considerably reduces its ability to successfully negotiate an acceptable contract.[81]

GLOBALIZATION

The way that the world does business is changing. The creation of large multinational organizations with huge amounts of resources, improvements in technology, new and faster forms of communication, expanded transportation routes, increased production capacities, and liberalized trade agreements have all combined to form a turbulent environment characterized by rapid change. This new environment has major implications for both workers and employers. Many organizations are no longer constrained by the availability of labour in their immediate geographic area, the skills or abilities of local workers, or the local cost of labour. Instead, they are able to locate the work where the appropriate skills are (or can be developed) or where the labour cost is such that their products can be competitively priced in the market. These changes challenge the traditional structure of the employer-employee relationship and, by creating a potentially worldwide labour market, also raise the issue of how that relationship can or should be regulated in this new environment.

Three models have been developed to explain the different ways that globalization might affect employment relationships in an individual region or nation.[82] The simple **globalization model** assumes that the pressures of globalization are so strong that there will eventually be little difference in how individual countries conduct or regulate employment relationships. From this perspective, workers' rights are threatened because individual nations will not have the power to maintain or justify employment standards that are significantly different from the norm or that fit the specific realities of a particular region or location. The **institutionalist model** assumes that existing differences in national frameworks and standards, including those related to employment relationships, will result in different responses to the pressures of globalization. This perspective suggests that because these differences are well established and have evolved over time to address the specific circumstances of each area, they will not be easily changed, even in the face of pressure from other parts of the world or from other forms of regulation. The third model, the **integrated approach**, suggests that both institutional and economic factors will influence the effects of globalization on a particular country, and that both factors must be considered in attempts to explain or predict globalization's effects on the regulation of employment relationships in specific countries.

While the impact of globalization on employment relationships in Canada may not be as extreme as it has been in other countries, globalization has become an increasing concern, particularly to unions, because of the potential job loss or reduced protection for employees. In other countries, many workers' rights that are taken for granted and guaranteed by law in Canada—such as safety and health standards, minimum-wage rates, the right to join a union, and the right to negotiate collectively with an employer—either do not exist or are not enforced. This is particularly true in countries that see international investment as essential to their economic development and thus want to discourage or ban any employee activity (such as unionization) that they perceive as detrimental to economic growth or as a deterrent to potential investment. In the opinion of some observers, this attitude leads to the "race to the bottom," where work is located in the countries with the weakest employment standards and lowest wage rates and there is no incentive to improve employment conditions as long as the countries are able to offer the economic advantage of low production costs. This results in a downward spiral of worsening work conditions and lower wages as countries struggle to keep that advantage.[83]

Unions also face specific challenges caused by globalization. Since unions are generally organized to represent workers in one industry or in one geographic area, it is not easy for them to counteract the power of a large multinational organization that may be operating in many locations or in many industries.[84] An example of this was the extended strike by the United Steelworkers union in Sudbury against the international mining company Vale Inco. The strike, which began in 2009, focused on the company's demands for contract concessions which, in its view, were necessary to bring the financial performance of the Sudbury nickel mine in line with the company's other operations around the world. While the union argued that it was unreasonable to expect a Canadian operation to meet the same performance measures as operations in other countries with lower pay rates or weaker environmental requirements, it also acknowledged, in the words of the union's district director, that the power of one local union against that of the multinational company was like "a pimple on an elephant's ass".[85]

A possible response to such pressures of globalization may include unions organizing workers in other locations or in other countries, but this can be extremely difficult. The challenge of organizing across distances that unions in Canada faced in their early days, as outlined in Chapter 3, is magnified when unions try to organize workers in other countries, since there are not only the challenges associated with distance but also the challenges of cross-cultural communication. Unions may also face legislative hurdles when they attempt to organize or to represent workers outside Canada. Canadian labour law does not address whether successorship exists when work is moved to other countries. Another very significant barrier may be labour legislation that is less supportive of organizing or that lacks the enforcement mechanisms that exist in Canadian labour law. In some countries, workers can only be organized by local unions, and this further restricts the ability of international unions to represent those workers. In others, the unions that do exist are controlled by the government and do little to meaningfully represent their members.[86]

For a specific example of how globalization affects unions and their members, we can look at the experience of the garment industry,[87] whose employees in North America were organized by strong unions that forced significant improvements in working conditions and wages in the early part of the 20th century. However, at the start of the 21st century, so-called sweatshop conditions are prevalent throughout the industry, both in North America and internationally, and union density in the domestic industry is rapidly declining. What factors led to this dramatic reversal?

The first is the evolving nature of the garment industry itself. Since the industry serves a highly price-sensitive market, there is constant pressure to produce goods at the lowest possible price and to find more cost-effective production methods. This pressure leads manufacturers to subcontract work if doing so will lower their production costs. It is not uncommon for parts of the production process in the garment industry to be subcontracted through two or three producers; this makes it very difficult for unions to organize or protect workers in the subcontracted firms, since they cannot easily identify or locate these firms or their employees.

The second factor in this reversal is the increasingly important role that imports and internationally based production are playing in the industry, partially facilitated by liberalized trade agreements. Manufacturers can now respond to the pressure for lower costs by subcontracting work domestically, elsewhere in North America, or by moving production out of North America entirely. In fact, they may have no alternative if they want to produce goods at prices comparable to the low-cost imports that are now a major part of the market because of relaxed trade regulations.

The third factor is the effect of automation in the workplace. The increased automation of the garment production process has made it easier for small producers or subcontractors to enter the industry with relatively low amounts of capital investment (in many cases, simply by purchasing a few industrial sewing machines and renting a work space). This means that many employers in the garment industry are small organizations that rely on high production volumes or low production costs for their competitive advantage, and thus have little incentive to pay their workers more or improve their working conditions. Automation has also reduced the amount of expertise needed to work in the industry, and as a result, many workers lack the linguistic or cultural ability to hold more skilled or better-paying jobs. Unfortunately, this situation has led to increased exploitation of the workforce (to the point where some employment arrangements have been characterized as akin to slavery). Employers are more demanding, and the workers are generally powerless to complain or are afraid to do so for fear of being fired or punished.

UNION RESPONSES TO GLOBALIZATION

Clearly, Canadian unions, and unions worldwide, face great challenges because of the forces of globalization. As the three models of globalization demonstrate, globalization can have varied effects, and consequently, unions have developed a number of different strategies to deal with these effects.

One strategy addresses the fact that many of the conditions or effects of globalization are regulated by international agreements, such as the North American Free Trade Agreement (NAFTA). Thus, Canadian unions, along with other unions in affected areas, have actively lobbied to have employment standards and labour rights included in such agreements, along with enforcement mechanisms to ensure that the terms of the agreements are followed. In the case of NAFTA, such lobbying resulted in employment labour standards being included in the North American Agreement on Labour Cooperation, a "side agreement" that stipulated 11 "labour principles" guaranteeing workplace conditions such as freedom of association, freedom from discrimination, and minimum wage standards. Although 23 labour-related complaints have been filed under this agreement since its implementation in 1994, none have resulted in sanctions against the alleged violators.[88] Because of this experience, unions pursuing this strategy now believe it is important to have such principles integrated into the main body of an agreement, rather than have them relegated to an addition or a secondary document, and they believe that meaningful enforcement mechanisms must also be included for the principles to have the desired effects. The Canadian Labour Congress has lobbied for the inclusion of these features in the proposed Free Trade Area for the Americas agreement and in proposed trade agreements between Canada and Singapore and between Canada and Central America.[89]

Another strategy involves attempting to overcome the legislative and cultural challenges of organizing foreign workers by partnering with or supporting locally based unions. This strategy usually involves a Canadian or international union providing organizing expertise or resources to new or smaller unions based in the region. One example of this strategy in action is occurring in the banana industry in Central America. International unions and other non-governmental associations assisted in the formation of a federation representing 42 unions in an area that is home to nearly 80 percent of the world's banana production.[90] The collective power of the federated unions was such that they were able to negotiate a framework agreement guaranteeing the rights of workers to join democratic and independent trade unions and to engage in collective bargaining, and that also required the banana producers to follow International Labour Organization guidelines against forced labour and child labour. Another example of this strategy is the Canadian Labour Congress's partnership with the Canadian International Development Agency in the Labour International Development Program. This program, which operates in the Americas, Asia, the Middle

East, and Africa, establishes partnerships between Canadian unions and local unions to support the work of the local unions in addressing their area's economic and labour issues.[91]

It should be noted that these strategies are not always used with the explicit goal of increasing the membership of the larger union or unions, which may seem somewhat counterproductive if these unions' membership is shrinking because work is being moved to other countries or contracted out to non-unionized employers that pay low wages. However, these strategies demonstrate the principle that "a rising tide lifts all boats." Since one of the original motivations for creating unions was the improvement of conditions for all workers, assisting other workers, unionized or non-unionized, is simply putting that belief into practice. More idealistically, it has also been suggested that these situations would be best addressed by a return to the concept of one worldwide union for all workers.[92]

On a more practical level, if unions can assist in improving the conditions and wages of other workers elsewhere, employers may be discouraged from moving work to other regions if there is a limited cost advantage in doing so. It has also been proposed that developing linkages with other unions in other areas, or with other activist organizations, assists individual unions in successfully managing the impacts of globalization in their region.[93] In addition to the international labour organizations and associations mentioned in Chapter 4, all of which are also examples of these types of linkages, we should note that, in many industries and trades, international federations or associations of unions have been formed to help their members collectively address the effects of globalization in their specific areas.[94]

Another strategy that unions use to deal with globalization involves addressing internal or domestic economic conditions to strengthen the union against the economic effects of globalization. An example of this strategy can be seen in the actions of UNITE, the union that has historically represented North American garment industry workers. UNITE initially responded to the impact of globalization with a strategy that has been labelled "boycott and exclusion,"[95] portraying the non-domestic industry as a "menace" and urging domestic producers to keep jobs in North America and thereby maintain the health of the North American economy. Clearly this strategy was not completely successful, and UNITE has undertaken other actions, such as merging with unions in related fields (after its merger with a major hospitality workers' union, the union is now known as UNITE-HERE) and organizing North American workers in industries related to garment manufacturing (e.g., laundries and uniform manufacturers) as the size of the North American garment industry declined. While these strategies have succeeded in maintaining the continued existence of the union, they have been criticized for not paying enough attention to the plight of non-domestic workers in the industries UNITE organizes; these workers work in substandard conditions and face significant barriers to collectively negotiating improvements.[96]

WHAT HAPPENS NEXT? FACTORS INFLUENCING THE FUTURE OF INDUSTRIAL RELATIONS IN CANADA

Earlier in the chapter, we described some of the ways in which unions and employers have adapted to changes in the workforce, work arrangements, and organizations. However, as we have seen, many of these changes are not widespread, and it would appear that the majority of Canadian unions and employers are still following the more traditional models of union-management relationships. This resistance to change, whether intentional or unintentional, generates questions about what the future holds for industrial relations in Canada.

The Canadian industrial relations system has certainly been successful in maintaining and improving working conditions for unionized workers in Canada as well as for many non-unionized workers, thanks to the influence unions have had on overall wage rates and employment standards legislation. However, the context within which this system has evolved is changing, and some researchers question whether a system based on an industrial and hierarchical model of organization can continue to be effective if that model is no longer dominant or practical. Other researchers point to the troubles faced by unions in the United States, which as we know has experienced a steep decline in unionization rates, and suggest that Canadian unions will soon encounter the same troubles. Still other researchers argue that the Canadian industrial relations system is healthy and will continue to be so in the future. We will conclude our discussion of future issues by outlining the factors that these researchers identify as being significant to the future of the Canadian industrial relations system, and speculating about the projected impact that these factors will have.

Legislation

As we know, one significant difference between the Canadian and American industrial relations systems is the allocation of jurisdiction over industrial relations and the effects of that allocation. In the United States, industrial relations legislation is the responsibility of the federal government, whereas in Canada there is a division of jurisdiction between the federal and provincial governments, with the primary responsibility for labour relations legislation assigned to the provinces. There is little consensus on whether the decentralization of Canadian labour legislation will help or hinder Canadian industrial relations in the future. Some researchers argue that decentralization is appropriate in Canada because the wide variations in labour markets and types of employment across the country make it more fitting to have different jurisdictions, each with the ability to create legislation appropriate for conditions in its area.[97] It has also been suggested that the centralized system of legislation in the United States has hindered the growth of unions in that country because centralized legislation cannot adequately address regional variations.[98] However, decentralization has also been characterized as hindering the growth of Canadian unions because of the need to change organizing, certification, and collective bargaining strategies to accommodate variations in legislation across multiple jurisdictions. While decentralized legislation is not a significant problem for employers or unions that work within a single jurisdiction in Canada, decentralization can become a major difficulty for employers or unions that operate in more than one jurisdiction—a situation that may become more common as businesses expand or merge to keep pace with regional, national, or international competition.

A more significant factor than jurisdiction over labour law, however, is the content of the laws themselves. The content of labour law is one area where American and Canadian industrial relations systems are very different, and this is one factor that is consistently identified as a reason why American union density rates have been lower than Canadian rates for the past four decades.[99] Canadian labour law is generally perceived as being more pro-union than American labour law because of differences in such areas as certification procedures, remedies available to labour relations boards in resolving disputes, protections for newly certified bargaining units, and the protection of striking workers.[100] Additionally, American labour law has evolved very slowly in comparison to other jurisdictions, with only one minor amendment (the extension of the *National Labor Relations Act* to cover hospital employees) since 1960. A major reform is proposed by the

Employee Free Choice Act (EFCA), originally co-sponsored in 2007 by President Barack Obama when he was a member of the United States Senate. The United States Congress is currently considering the EFCA, which would change American labour law by eliminating the need for a secret ballot vote if a majority of employees in a workplace have already expressed their support for a union; by requiring employers to begin collective bargaining with the union within 10 days of certification, and to reach a collective agreement within 90 days, with bargaining issues automatically referred to mediation and then binding arbitration if a collective agreement is not settled within this time frame; and by increasing the penalties for employers who commit unfair labour practices.[101] Supporters of the EFCA argue that these changes will remove many of the barriers that currently prevent American unions from expanding their coverage and increasing their effectiveness; for example, the mandatory timelines for collective bargaining and contract resolution address the fact that 44 percent of bargaining units certified in the United States never achieve a first collective agreement.[102] Opponents of the EFCA argue that removing the secret ballot vote deprives employees of their right to privately express their views on unionization, and that the mandatory timelines for collective bargaining and contract resolution, especially the required mediation and arbitration, will result in government interference in employment relationships.[103]

In the past, researchers have speculated whether Canadian legislators will come to perceive American laws as the more appropriate model to follow, and whether Canadian legislation will be modified to give employers more power than they have in the current Canadian industrial relations system. The eventual fate of the EFCA may give a clearer answer to this question, as its effect would be to alter American labour laws to be more similar to Canadian labour laws.

Nevertheless, in the recent past, several provincial governments in Canada have made alterations to labour legislation that suggest some Canadian legislators believe the current Canadian industrial relations system does not "create an environment for employees, employers and trade unions to build healthy enterprises that can compete on a world scale."[104] The Conservative government of former premier Mike Harris altered the *Labour Relations Act* in Ontario in several significant ways during the 1990s. For example, the legislation governing certification had previously only required that the application demonstrate support from a majority of workers in the proposed bargaining unit, but the Harris government's amendment introduced a mandatory certification vote, regardless of the level of support demonstrated in the certification application. The result was an immediate decline in the number of certification applications and in the number of successful union organizing campaigns.[105] More recently, the Liberal government of Ontario changed the legislation to permit certifications based on a demonstration of majority support, but only in the construction industry.[106]

In May 2002, the Liberal government of Premier Gordon Campbell made several major revisions to British Columbia's *Labour Relations Code*. The option of automatic certification was removed, as discussed in Chapter 5, and the code was modified to give the British Columbia Labour Relations Board eight specific duties that it must consider in its interpretation and application of the code. (The previous version of the code established five criteria as "purposes of the Code" and only stated that the board must exercise its powers "having regard to [these] purposes".) These duties are:

- to recognize the rights and obligations of employees, employers, and trade unions under the Code

- to foster the employment of workers in economically viable businesses

- to encourage the practice and procedures of collective bargaining between employers and trade unions as the freely chosen representatives of employees

- to encourage cooperative participation between employers and trade unions in resolving workplace issues, adapting to changes in the economy, developing workforce skills, and developing a workforce and a workplace that promotes productivity

- to promote conditions favourable to the orderly, constructive, and expeditious settlement of disputes

- to minimize the effects of labour disputes on persons who are not involved in those disputes

- to ensure that the public interest is protected during labour disputes

- to encourage the use of mediation as a dispute-resolution mechanism[107]

The British Columbia *Labour Relations Code* was also altered so that the language governing communication during an organizing campaign permits "a person [to have] the freedom to express his or her views on any matter, including matters relating to an employer, a trade union or the representation of employees by a trade union, provided that the person does not use intimidation or coercion."[108] This language is considerably broader than the previous language in the Code, which stated, "Nothing in this Code deprives a person of the freedom to communicate to an employee a statement of fact or opinion reasonably held with respect to the employer's business."[109]

In 2007, the newly elected Saskatchewan Party government in Saskatchewan introduced several changes to Saskatchewan's labour law, which included essential services legislation giving the employer the power to determine essential services levels if the employer and union cannot agree, eliminating automatic certification, allowing employers to communicate about union issues with employees during organizing campaigns, and raising the required level of employee support for certification applications from 25 to 45 percent.[110] In 2010, the same government further amended the labour legislation to allow all unions to organize construction workers, to allow unions to organize all workers on a construction job site instead of only those in a particular trade or occupation, and to automatically end a certification if a union has not represented workers at a company for three years.[111]

Changes in labour legislation are certainly not uncommon in Canada. However, their effect may be reduced by subsequent changes favouring a different policy direction. As one study of changes in Canadian employment legislation observes, "[A]djustments have usually been marginal, and they have often been offsetting, with reforms made by pro-labour governments subsequently offset by reforms from pro-business governments, and so forth."[112] Furthermore, changes to a single part of labour legislation may have a minimal effect if similar changes are not enacted in other parts of the legislation. For example, a change in the level of support required for certification applications may not have a major impact unless changes are also made in other regulations governing the certification process, such as regulations restricting employer or union conduct during the organizing campaign.

It is obviously difficult to predict what effect these changes will have and whether they will be copied in other jurisdictions. Another factor affecting the impact of the changes may be the way that the new legislation is being applied or interpreted, particularly in conjunction with the application or interpretation of existing legislation or case law. For example, after the Ontario government imposed the requirement for certification votes, the Ontario Labour Relations Board continued to enforce the existing sanctions against employer interference in organizing campaigns, and promptly held certification votes in situations where employer interference might have affected employees' voting intentions.[113] However, the interests of those appointed by a government to administer and interpret the law may also play a role. As we know, although the members of a labour relations board are appointed by government, they play a quasi-judicial role and are expected to be neutral and independent. When the Saskatchewan government enacted the first set of labour law changes described above, it also fired all the full-time members of the Saskatchewan Labour Relations Board and replaced them with new appointees. While the government argued that the reappointments were routine, the firings were widely criticized as poor public policy and as compromising the board's independence.[114]

It remains to be seen what the long-term effects of these changes will be, and whether Canadian labour law in general will follow these trends, remain the same, or reform in a different direction altogether.

Political Influence

Another factor that may affect the future of industrial relations in Canada is the amount of political power held or exercised by Canadian unions. As outlined in Chapter 3, the Canadian labour movement does not have a close formal relationship with a political party, as is the case in some other countries. However, the Canadian labour movement has a historical affiliation with the New Democratic Party (NDP). The declining political fortunes of this party have led some observers to question whether this affiliation threatens to damage the future of the Canadian labour movement. Less than 20 percent of the nationwide popular vote went to the NDP in the 2004, 2006, and 2008 federal elections, and the NDP has historically succeeded at forming provincial governments in only five Canadian provinces. In addition, provincial NDP governments have been accused of abandoning the party's basic social democratic principles in favour of more centrist policies that emphasize themes of fiscal prudence.[115]

The relatively low level of electoral support for the NDP and the apparent movement of the party away from its founding principles are not positive trends for the political influence of Canadian unions. In order to have a meaningful voice in shaping public policy, the Canadian labour movement needs to be aligned with a political party that has sufficient representation or support to be able to achieve labour-friendly goals. It appears that the NDP may not be able to fulfill that role, even in those provinces where the party has formed the government. No national political party has emerged as an adequate replacement for the NDP, according to the definition of being supportive of the labour movement's goals. Thus, unless the labour movement and the NDP are able to rebuild their formerly productive relationship, the labour movement may need to seek other allies through which to generate political influence.

For examples of these new kinds of alliances, we can start by looking at the experience of unions in the United States. The American labour movement has historically lacked a significant alliance with a major political party. The Democratic Party is the national party whose philosophy most closely matches that of the labour movement, but even when the Democratic Party has been in control of the American government, the labour movement has found it difficult to promote labour law reform. Former president Bill Clinton was elected with the help of funding from American unions, and in return Clinton convened a commission to review possibilities for labour-business compromises on new labour legislation. However, the commission's work failed because unions could not agree on appropriate strategies for compromise and few employers were interested in participating.[116] President Barack Obama was also elected with support from large American unions, but with the *Employee Free Choice Act* still going through the legislative process, the labour movement's support for Obama's government has diminished.[117] The American union movement has also had to contend with nearly two decades of so-called neo-liberal monetary and investment policies based on the assumptions that competitive markets are the most efficient form of economic regulation and that maximizing economic growth should be a primary goal of economic policy. Neo-liberalism, in the opinion of some researchers, has weakened union power by increasing unemployment and exacerbating income and wealth inequalities by reducing wages for low-skill workers.[118]

American unions have responded to their lack of political influence in several innovative ways. The American Federation of Labour-Council of Industrial Organizations (AFL-CIO), the American counterpart of the Canadian Labour Congress, has explicitly changed its strategic focus to include international issues such as global protectionism and international monetary policy. Rather than focusing on "narrow features," such as changes in labour law or the actions of a specific company, the AFL-CIO attempts to identify "systemic features" that affect all workers. This strategic direction acknowledges that the globalization of markets means that there will be competition between workers in all countries; hence, labour organizations should attempt to counteract this by promoting policies that benefit all workers rather than policies that foster competition.[119] The AFL-CIO has also formed alliances with groups that share its concerns about international policies, such as students, clergy, and social movement organizations.

The Canadian union movement has also taken steps in this direction, even though arguably it has faced as extensive and systematic opposition to its goals as American unions have. As described in Chapter 4, Canadian unions at the local, national, and international levels have formed alliances with other social activist groups. Canadian unions have been involved, for example, in community-based coalitions around such issues as health care,[120] public transit,[121] and privatization of utility services.[122] Many Canadian unions and labour federations have adopted policies similar to the AFL-CIO policies that address global and national trends affecting workers. Canadian unions have also been involved in mobilizing protests against perceived anti-labour and anti-worker policies at the federal and provincial levels (e.g., the B.C. Federation of Labour has been a key player in protests against provincial government cutbacks in social programs and the government's refusal to increase the province's minimum wage).

Some unions have also explored strategies that clearly link their own actions with larger social activism. For example, in 1999, the Canadian Auto Workers (CAW) executive board explicitly stated that achieving same-sex spousal benefits in its collective agreements is a bargaining priority. While this decision was met with strong resistance by some CAW members and locals, its impact is demonstrated by the results of a survey of Canadian collective agreements in 2002. This survey showed that 44 percent of the CAW's collective agreements included language addressing this issue, whereas only 16 percent of non-CAW collective agreements had such provisions.[123] It has been suggested that such internal strategies may have the effect of demonstrating "progressive leadership which will in turn appeal to new members and activists"[124] and thus give unions "the credibility and clout needed to have a broader impact on society."[125] Such alliances may also strengthen unions internally by encouraging members from diverse groups to work together and increasing the commitment to the union of members from marginalized groups.[126]

However, it is still debatable whether these sorts of alliances will create the degree of influence necessary for unions and other politically active organizations to significantly affect government policy and legislation in their favour. In the words of one author who examined the experience of American unions, "Refusal to rely exclusively on conventional political channels often provokes hostility on the part of economic and political elites."[127] In other words, alliances that attempt to exert influence in ways that do not follow the established processes for legislative or policy reform are often disregarded or marginalized, and they never succeed in achieving their goals. Canadian unions thus find themselves in a difficult situation; their existing political alliance is less effective as the influence of their primary political ally declines, yet alliances with other organizations may not generate sufficient influence to achieve desired outcomes.

Some Canadian unions have investigated another possible solution to this dilemma—"strategic voting," an option that uses the ability of unions to mobilize voters at election time.[128] The results of several studies of union influence on election outcomes have indicated that union members are more likely to participate in elections than non-union members. This phenomenon has been observed in most industrial democracies, including Canada and the United States.[129] In 1999, a coalition of unions attempted to build on this tendency by encouraging union members in key constituencies in the Ontario provincial election to vote for the opposition (non-Conservative Party) candidate with the best chance of winning. This strategy represented a major shift from the traditional union election strategy of automatically supporting the NDP candidate, and it was therefore criticized for weakening support for the already struggling NDP. While the strategy did not succeed in ousting the Conservative government, it did achieve some success in the targeted constituencies.[130] If the Canadian labour movement wishes to achieve legislative and policy changes through established political processes, it may have to choose between attempting to rebuild the NDP as a political entity and actively supporting labour-friendly candidates who may or may not represent the NDP.

Union Organizing

The future of Canadian industrial relations will also be affected by whether Canadian unions are able to maintain or increase their current membership levels. If union density significantly increases or decreases, the Canadian industrial relations system will have to adjust to the reality of more or less union membership.

As discussed in previous chapters, Canadian union density has remained at approximately 30 percent of the overall workforce for the past decade. In contrast, union density in the United States has sharply declined from 25 percent in the late 1970s to less than 13 percent in 2009.[131] A variety of reasons have been cited for this difference, including Canadian legislation that offers better protection against employer interference or intimidating during organizing campaigns, the inability of American unions to resist concession bargaining and the associated erosion of previously achieved standards, higher levels of unionization in the Canadian public sector, and stronger affiliations between unions and organized political parties in Canada than in the United States.[132] Better union security provisions in Canada, such as the Rand formula (discussed in Chapter 7), which requires all workers to pay union dues regardless of whether they actually join the union, have also been identified as a reason why Canadian union membership has not experienced the same drop as American union membership.[133]

However, Canadian unions cannot afford to become complacent simply because union membership in Canada has not declined while American union membership has dramatically decreased. Canadian union density has not decreased, but neither has it shown any significant increase for some time. This plateauing has been attributed to a number of factors, some of which have been described in detail in earlier chapters. The Canadian public sector is highly unionized, but this sector of the labour market is not growing and has in fact been reduced in many areas because of downsizing and privatization. Unions have also not succeeded in creating a noticeable presence in the sectors of the labour market that have been showing growth: retail, sales, and service occupations; and part-time, temporary, and other forms of non-permanent jobs. In addition, Canadian law, unlike American law, permits workplaces to operate non-union representation plans in which workers are elected by their peers to meet with management and mutually solve problems that in a unionized workplace would usually be addressed through collective bargaining. These plans are guided by a formal worker-management agreement that parallels a collective agreement in structure and function. While their use is not widespread in Canada, these plans do offer an alternative to unionization that may be attractive to workers who do not want to join a union but still wish to have a formal voice in workplace operations.[134]

Though global, societal, and technological changes provide new challenges, the strength and vitality of unions in the future still rests with the individual member.

Clearly, membership growth rather than membership maintenance is a preferable strategy for unions because of the increased power associated with larger membership and the increased revenues from union dues. But will Canadian unions be able to pursue a strategy of growth given the stagnation of the past two decades? Opinions on this issue are mixed. On the negative side, it is argued that Canadian unions have only achieved very modest increases in density rates over the past 20 years for part-time workers and, in the same period, have made almost no improvement in density rates for major parts of the private sector labour market, such as financial industries, accommodation, food services, and professional occupations. This suggests either that unions are not successful when they do attempt to organize these types of workers, or that their organizing attempts in these areas are minimal. Evidence indicates that the second scenario is the more accurate one. It appears that Canadian unions prefer to protect their bargaining successes rather than undertake organizing campaigns, and that they also prefer to organize in their traditional jurisdictions rather than venture into other industries and occupations.[135] This analysis suggests that a significant increase in union membership hinges on four conditions: unions should increase their commitment to the NDP; reciprocally, the NDP must make a commitment to support progressive labour laws; unions will have to commit considerable amounts of resources to organizing; and unions will have to "sell [their] attractiveness" to non-unionized workers.[136]

It has also been suggested that the "winner take all" structure of Canadian certification votes (i.e., that certification depends on the result of a majority vote) discourages those potential union members who are unable to persuade enough of their co-workers to also support the union, and who, if the certification vote fails, do not gain the union representation they seek. Similarly, unions may be weakened when all workers, including union opponents, are obliged to become union members when a certification is declared. It has been proposed that these problems could be avoided by developing some form of proportional voting structure in certification votes, allowing individual workers to support or oppose the union, and forming the bargaining unit only with those who support the union, regardless of their number.[137]

On the positive side, the major differences between American and Canadian labour law may at least ensure that Canadian union membership remains steady and that Canadian unions will therefore not have to direct their resources to addressing decreases in membership. Canadian labour law is also much stricter than American labour law in restricting or outlawing the use of replacement workers during strikes, which strengthens the ability of Canadian unions to gain desired outcomes in collective bargaining. Additionally, the process of certification is much easier in Canada because of the provisions in nearly every jurisdiction that certifications can be granted if sufficient membership support is demonstrated (American law requires a representation vote regardless of levels of support for the certification application) and because of strong sanctions against employers who interfere in organizing campaigns. These two forms of legislation have been cited as reasons why Canadian union membership has managed to remain relatively consistent while American union membership has declined.[138] The 2007 Supreme Court of Canada decision determining that collective bargaining is considered a right to association under the *Canadian Charter of Rights and Freedoms* may also serve as another form of legal protection for the continued functioning of Canadian unions.

In addition, while Canadian unions have not been completely successful in organizing some sectors of the Canadian labour market, there is evidence that Canadian unions are making attempts to adapt to changing workplace realities, as discussed earlier in this chapter. If unions are able to adapt their organizing, bargaining, and representation strategies to the changing needs of workers and workplaces, then it is entirely possible that union membership levels in Canada will grow. As an example of success with these sorts of adaptations, we can look at examples such as the UNITE-HERE Toronto hotel workers' union. This local union represents a large and diverse workforce in an industry with many national and international corporate employers. Despite these challenges, it has managed to maintain and even grow its membership through such strategies as sharing expertise in union operations across the workplaces where it represents workers; focusing on obtaining "master agreements" (a single agreement for multiple worksites); and "bargaining up" to common standards if a master agreement cannot be reached; conducting organizing campaigns even before new hotels open; and even such simple matters as conducting union demonstrations at times that fit as many members' work schedules as possible and at locations that are easy to reach by public transit. These multiple strategies have been collectively described as a "spatial circuit" of union renewal, in which unions acknowledge continual changes in structure and power and continually refine their strategies in response.[139]

Another possibility for Canadian unions to maintain or increase membership is through employee ownership of a company as a tactic to save unionized jobs. This is a somewhat non-traditional approach to union preservation in that it places the union, or its members, in the role of management or owners, which challenges the traditional opposition and division between union and management. However, some Canadian unions have used this strategy successfully when faced with the potential loss of jobs and membership if a workplace closes. In 2009, a group of unionized pulp mill workers in British Columbia formed a coalition with employers and investors to purchase the mill they worked at, which was threatened with closure because of a downturn in the worldwide pulp market and the cost of upgrades to the facility. A year after the court ruling permitting the sale, the mill was not only operating but was doing so with lower production costs and no outside debt. The union members also agreed to an 11-year collective agreement, with the flexibility for workers to perform any job they are quali-fied to do. One of the union members heading the coalition attributes the turnaround to a highly motivated workforce who, having personally invested in the purchase of the mill, want to see their jobs survive as well as their investment.[140]

A further example of adaptive strategies can be found, ironically, in the United States, in the case of unions in the entertainment industry. Work in this industry is char-acterized by many of the features cited as typical of modern employment practices: fre-quent changes of employer, non-permanent work arrangements, and job selection based on the opportunity to develop one's skills rather than on the potential for ongoing job security. Workers in these sorts of work arrangements are often considered too chal-lenging for unions to organize successfully. Nevertheless, the entertainment industry is one of the most heavily unionized industries in the United States, and it has remained so for nearly a century, in the face of opposition from powerful and wealthy employers, legislation that is unfavourable to unions, and changes in technology that have continu-ally transformed methods of film production and distribution.[141]

How have the American unions in the entertainment industry maintained their sta-tus despite such formidable challenges? Three major strategies have been used to adapt to these different forms of opposition. First, the entertainment unions do not focus on bargaining individualized agreements for each workplace or project, aiming instead to achieve standard or national agreements with major employers. This bargaining struc-ture forces unions to address major issues affecting overall employment rather than spe-cific issues pertaining to individual jobs. Second, entertainment unions have bargained not only for wages, but also for mechanisms that will protect their members' employ-ment prospects and skills development. An example of these mechanisms is the system of residual payments that provides compensation each time a production is presented or reissued in a new medium. Residual payments allow union members to receive a share of all profits from productions they have participated in and also provide income for members during periods of unemployment. Third, the entertainment unions place a high priority on providing services to members: for example, they notify them about auditions, give assistance in filing tax returns, provide systems for resolving disputes over production credits, and promote members' skills and experience to producers seek-ing workers with particular abilities.[142]

While this example is American-based, it holds important lessons for Canadian unions facing organizing difficulties. It is apparent that if unions take a long-term rather than a short-term perspective in bargaining, do not focus solely on wage issues, actively adapt to changes in workplace conditions in ways that benefit their membership, and serve the specific needs of the membership, they can survive and even expand in an unfavourable environment. As mentioned earlier in this chapter, Canadian unions in the film industry have followed the lead of their American counterparts in negotiating contract terms that facilitate members' skills development without compromising standards that have already been achieved. Other Canadian unions may benefit from considering similar initiatives in their own negotiations or planning.

SUMMARY

Several significant changes have been occurring in Canadian workplaces and within the Canadian workforce. These changes pose a number of different challenges for Canadian unions. Young workers, female workers, and workers from visible minorities have special workplace concerns that Canadian unions have not always addressed; in addition, the employment patterns of these groups of workers make them difficult to organize. New forms of work and employer-employee relationships are not always accommodated by traditional union-employer relationships, and unions face problems in organizing workers who are in these forms of work, both in actually conducting organizing campaigns and in proving the value or relevance of union representation. Finally, changing organizational structures reduce power and authority distances between employees and employers, which makes the traditional adversarial relationship between unions and employers less applicable. Canadian unions have responded in different ways to these multiple challenges, but it is not yet apparent how successful these responses will be in the long term. The future of the Canadian industrial relations system will be affected by trends in legislation, political influence, and union organizing, but it is unclear what the directions of these trends are or what impact they will have.

KEY TERMS FOR CHAPTER 13

compressed workweeks (p. 571)
downsizing (p. 580)
flatter organization (p. 579)
flextime (p. 571)
globalization model (p. 582)
institutionalist model (p. 583)

integrated approach (p. 583)

job sharing (p. 572)

matrix organizations (p. 579)

network (or web) organizations (p. 579)

non-permanent employment relationships (p. 574)

non-standard work (p. 557)

participation rate (p. 563)

reverse discrimination (p. 567)

salting (p. 571)

telecommuting (or telework) (p. 572)

underemployment (p. 566)

DISCUSSION QUESTIONS FOR CHAPTER 13

1. Why are some unions opposed to part-time, temporary, contract, and other forms of non-traditional work?

2. What difficulties do unions face in organizing workers in service occupations?

3. What difficulties do unions face in organizing female workers, young workers, and visible minority workers?

4. This chapter identifies some of the techniques that unions have used in organizing diverse workforces and occupations that have historically had low rates of unionization. Can you think of other techniques that could be used to organize these workers and occupations?

5. Explain some of the difficulties in applying traditional labour relations processes to telecommuting.

6. How do traditional forms of organizational structure distribute power and authority?

7. Why are newer forms of organizational structure a challenge to traditional union-employer relationships?

8. After reading the discussion of the future of Canadian industrial relations, what do you think will happen to the Canadian industrial relations system and why? Can you identify other factors that may affect the Canadian industrial relations system in the years to come?

CASE *13-1*

PINETREE LODGE AND RESIDENCE EMPLOYEES UNION

(Based on *Salvation Army in Canada and HEU*, 2003)

In this case, the employer is planning to contract out part of its operations. As required by the relevant labour legislation, the employer has given the union 60 days' notice of these changes, and the union and the employer are engaged in bargaining to adjust the terms of the collective agreement to address this situation. The union has filed an allegation that the employer has failed to bargain in good faith because it refuses to provide the information the union says it needs to negotiate revised contract terms. The union also alleges that the employer has engaged in surface bargaining by altering its bargaining position and requiring that the union make concessions if it wants to avoid some of the contracting out. The union also alleges that the employer has reneged on contract terms that the parties have already agreed to.

Case Facts

Pinetree Lodge is a residence for elderly individuals who can no longer live on their own. The Residence Employees Union (REU) represents the 80 workers employed at Pinetree. On June 10, as required by the relevant labour legislation, Pinetree provided the REU with 60 days' written notice that it intended to reorganize its workforce and that the reorganization could include contracting out some of the services performed by bargaining unit members. The reorganization was a result of Pinetree changing its operations to accommodate residents with complex medical problems. The notice said that a "significant number" of employees would be affected by the proposed changes. At the same time, all 80 REU members received layoff notices effective August 9.

The parties met to discuss the notice on June 16. At that meeting, the REU representatives stated that they needed to know what Pinetree's actual deficit was and what Pinetree needed to achieve in cost savings to offset that deficit. The REU also requested that Pinetree rescind the layoff notices.

The Pinetree representatives at the meeting stated that the projected deficit for the current fiscal year (which ended the following March) was $450,000. They stated that Pinetree was expecting to receive a one-time payment of $175,000 from the regional health authority, which would leave it with a shortfall of $275,000, and that it needed $200,000 in cost savings on an annual basis. The Pinetree representatives mentioned that the residence would have had those savings if the recent tentative collective agreement (which the membership had voted against ratifying in the previous month) had been accepted by the REU members. The representatives said that the remaining $75,000 in savings could be obtained from other sources. The lodge manager, Carlos Neiman, told the labour relations board that the $75,000 shortfall was worth it if it meant maintaining a stable relationship with the REU.

The REU wrote a letter to Pinetree on June 17 confirming the figures that had been discussed at the meeting and asking the provincial executive of the organization operating Pinetree to help it find ways to assist Pinetree in reducing its deficit. However, the letter erroneously stated that the Pinetree representatives had said they hoped to obtain $200,000 in savings by contracting out services.

On the same day, Pinetree sent a letter to the union in which it said, among other things, that its terms for negotiating cost savings were, at a minimum, equivalent to the terms in the unratified collective agreement.

The parties met again on June 23. At this meeting, the Pinetree representatives corrected the REU's statement that Pinetree would save $200,000 by contracting out services. They said that in fact the savings would be closer to $400,000, but reiterated that they hoped the REU would provide them with a sustainable plan to save $200,000. If Pinetree could not find $200,000 in savings from the REU, then it would proceed with contracting out.

The REU asked for Pinetree's costing calculations so that it could have some basis for developing a proposal, but the Pinetree representatives refused to provide that information. Neiman's explanation to the labour relations board regarding this refusal was that information being given to the media was creating a negative picture of events at Pinetree. He also said that in his opinion the REU was capable of doing its own costing calculations, and for this reason Pinetree was reluctant to share its costing figures or methodology.

The REU then asked Pinetree at least to provide its staffing estimates. The Pinetree representatives agreed to provide this information, and the REU agreed to prepare a proposal for the next meeting, which was scheduled for June 30.

The parties then discussed whether an agreement was possible at all and whether their respective parent organizations would sanction a specific local agreement.

(Pinetree management bargained as part of a group of health facility employers; the Pinetree REU local was represented in bargaining by the provincial REU negotiating team, which bargained for an agreement that would be shared by all REU locals.) The REU emphasized that it wanted the layoff notices rescinded, and the Pinetree representatives refused, saying they needed to be able to undertake layoffs to accomplish the reorganization.

On June 24, the REU confirmed the contents of the previous day's meeting in a letter to Pinetree. Pinetree sent a letter in response on June 25, saying that some of the REU's information in the June 24 letter was incorrect.

The parties met again on June 30. Pinetree asked the REU whether it was prepared to table a proposal that reflected $200,000 in sustainable cost savings. Pinetree then tabled draft job descriptions and schedules, which the parties discussed. The REU said it wanted more full-time and fewer part-time positions. The parties also discussed whether current employees would qualify for the new positions. The REU then asked Pinetree to provide a list of regular employees, current schedules, copies of the layoff notices, the current number of staffing hours, copies of all job descriptions, and copies of the current job postings for activity aides. The REU claimed that Pinetree had agreed to provide this information. Pinetree denied this, stating that it had agreed to provide only the number of staffing hours. Neiman told the board that he did not want to provide copies of the layoff notices because everyone had received them and the REU knew that everyone had received them. He also said that the REU already had copies of current job descriptions and that drafts of the new ones were provided at the meeting. He added that the REU had a copy of the seniority list and could reconstruct a list of employees on its own. He acknowledged that the collective agreement required him to provide copies of the layoff notices.

Chuck Young, the REU business representative who was at the June 30 meeting, told the board that some members had informed him that they had not received layoff notices and that the REU was entitled to copies of the notices for purposes of verification. He also said that the "current" job descriptions that the REU had were outdated and that the union needed accurate ones to understand the changes that Pinetree was proposing. He added that the REU could not construct a proposal without information on the current number of staffing hours.

The REU wrote to Pinetree on July 2 to confirm the content of the June 30 meeting and to reiterate that it was unable to provide a proposal until it received the current number of staffing hours. The union also confirmed that Pinetree had said that its bargaining group was not receptive to the idea of a local agreement but might reconsider if it received a "substantial" proposal from the REU.

On July 4, Pinetree wrote to the REU imposing a July 9 deadline for receiving a cost-savings proposal. The REU responded by letter the same day, stating that it had not yet received the information on staffing hours and that without that information it could not assemble a proposal. On July 7, Pinetree faxed the information to the REU. A handwritten note on the fax indicated that the fax had been sent once before, on July 2. The REU denies receiving the fax until the transmission on July 7. Upon examining the number of staffing hours provided by Pinetree, the REU concluded that the number was underestimated and alerted Pinetree to this fact.

The parties met again on July 10. At this meeting, the REU tabled an 11-point proposal. It offered a wage reduction of $1.25 per hour in all job classifications and offered to forgo wage premiums for weekend work. In return, the REU wanted Pinetree to not contract out any services provided by the REU bargaining unit members. The union also wanted Pinetree to accomplish its reorganization through the staffing provisions in the collective agreement and not through "cherry picking" by laying off and rehiring employees. The REU proposed that employees would be given an opportunity to qualify for the new job positions on the basis of their accumulated experience and seniority. It reiterated that it also wanted more full-time and fewer part-time positions. The proposal, if accepted, would expire on March 30 of the following year. The REU valued its proposal at just under $200,000 but felt it was close enough to that amount to make the plan viable.

The Pinetree representatives at the meeting left the meeting room briefly for a private discussion, and then returned and asked for more time to consider the union's proposal. They said they needed direction from their board of directors and their bargaining group, and offered to arrange another meeting to consider and discuss the proposal. The parties did agree to a joint review of the issue of full-time and part-time positions.

The next day, the REU sent a letter to Pinetree confirming the content of the meeting and emphasizing that some of the information it requested had still not been provided.

The parties met again on July 16. The day before, Pinetree had posted some part-time positions. At the start of the meeting, the issue of part-time and full-time positions was raised and discussed. The Pinetree representatives agreed to create more full-time positions if the REU bargaining unit members were willing to work shifts over nine hours, not including lunch breaks. The REU representatives said they would have to ask the membership about this proposal because the current collective agreement allowed only eight-hour shifts. If the membership agreed to waive this limitation, then Pinetree could move to nine-hour shifts. At the time of the hearing, the REU had not yet canvassed its membership on this issue.

The discussion at the meeting then turned to the REU's cost-savings proposal. The Pinetree representatives said that the proposal fell short of the $200,000 target and would produce savings of only $80,000 to $120,000 for the eight months the plan would be in effect. They then stated that their bargaining group was not willing to sanction local agreements and thus Pinetree would be proceeding with its contracting-out plans. They said that Pinetree needed savings to be sustained for at least the next three years if it was not going to contract out work currently performed by bargaining unit members.

In response, the REU representatives stated that their proposal had not been a final offer. They asked for a brief recess and after returning to the meeting, expressed concern about Pinetree's attitude in the talks. They pointed out that both parties had agreed to discuss the issue of part-time and full-time positions but that Pinetree had gone ahead and posted part-time positions.

The REU representatives then tabled a new cost-savings proposal. They now offered a wage reduction of $1.50 per hour in all job classifications. All other proposals remained the same except that the expiry date had been removed. The union representatives suggested that the plan would remain in effect until the parties negotiated something different. They estimated that the plan would save $221,000 per year.

The Pinetree representatives left the meeting briefly, but then returned and advised the REU representatives that their bargaining group disagreed with the proposal and felt that the savings were not substantial enough. Then, for the first time, they advised the REU representatives that in addition to the $200,000 savings from reduced wages, they expected the members of the bargaining unit to forgo the cost-of-living allowance increases and the pay equity increases included in the last ratified collective agreement. Neiman told the board that these increases were expected to cost $107,000 per year. Also for the first time, the Pinetree representatives stated that Pinetree was using a staffing figure of 140,000 paid staff hours per year as the basis for its estimates. Neiman told the board that the exact figure was 141,000 paid staff hours per year.

The REU representatives responded to these demands by telling the Pinetree representatives to table a counter-proposal in writing. Neiman claimed that the REU representatives invited him to table the tentative agreement that the bargaining unit members had voted to reject.

On July 17, the REU faxed a confirmation to Pinetree of the parties' agreement to create more full-time positions in one job category. On the same day, Pinetree faxed the REU, tabling the terms of the rejected collective agreement as its cost-savings proposal. This proposal was valued by Pinetree at just under $400,000. Neiman told the board that despite that value, Pinetree was still seeking only $200,000 in payroll savings in addition to the waiver of the cost-of-living increases and the pay equity increases, for a total of $307,000 in savings. He admitted that he had not informed the REU of this when he faxed the proposal. The REU estimated the cost savings of Pinetree's proposal at over $400,000.

On July 18, the REU sent two letters to Pinetree: one confirming the content of the July 16 meeting and the second rejecting the July 17 proposal. The next weekend, the bargaining unit members engaged in an unlawful work stoppage at Pinetree.

The Union's Position

The union argued that the employer had reneged on its promise to create more full-time positions when it posted the part-time positions. The union stated that the employer undertook this action before the parties had an opportunity to jointly address the question of part-time and full-time positions.

The union also argued that the employer had failed to bargain in good faith when it refused to provide the information the union needed to prepare its cost-savings proposal, and that some of the information it provided was inaccurate. The union stated that the employer had also refused to provide the methodology it used to arrive at the amount of cost savings it required, and that the union had found it difficult to develop a proposal to meet the employer's targets when it did not know how those targets had been calculated.

The union further argued that the employer had engaged in surface bargaining when it changed its bargaining position at the July 16 meeting and made new demands for concessions.

The Employer's Position

The employer argued that it had not bargained in bad faith because it regularly met with the union as requested, it exchanged proposals with the union and altered those proposals in response to bargaining discussions, and it had endeavoured to conclude an agreement. The employer stated that bargaining in bad faith cannot be declared simply because parties do not agree in negotiations.

The employer stated that its bargaining position had always been clear and had been communicated to the union: it wanted to achieve the terms in the collective agreement that the union membership rejected. The employer pointed out that this objective was clearly stated to the union in its letter of June 17. The employer also stated that it realized only at the July 16 that the union was fixated on the $200,000 figure and that the union did not realize that more was required. The employer indicated that it was willing to continue negotiations even after July 17.

The employer further argued that the union was capable of performing its own calculations to develop a proposal and that the employer had supplied the union with enough information to develop a proposal. The accuracy of some of the information provided is irrelevant because the union's costing figures were close to the employer's own, which proves that the information was ultimately unnecessary.

The employer argued that changing positions in bargaining is not evidence of surface bargaining and that whenever it changed its bargaining position, it had reasonable and rational explanations for doing so. The employer argued that its conduct must be assessed as a whole and that the overall pattern of the negotiations, with proposals being exchanged and with changes in one party's proposals in response to the other party's suggestions, shows that the employer had bargained in good faith and had not engaged in surface bargaining.

References

[1] Statistics Canada, CANSIM table 282-0087, data from June 2010.

[2] Statistics Canada, CANSIM tables 282-0014 and 282-0001, data from 2009.

[3] For example, Gallagher, D.G. (1998). Youth and labor representation. In Barling, J., & Kelloway, E.K. (Eds.), *Young workers: varieties of experience*. Washington, D.C.: American Psychological Association.

[4] Lowe, G. S. (1998). The future of work. *Relations Industrielles/Industrial Relations*, *53*(2), 235–257.

[5] Statistics Canada, 1996 census data; Canadian Council on Social Development (1999). *Youth at work in Canada: a research report*. Ottawa, ON: Canadian Council on Social Development; Statistics Canada, CANSIM tables 282-0008 and 282-0077, 2010 data.

[6] Statistics Canada, CANSIM table 282-0008, 2010 data,.

[7] Unionization. *Perspectives on Labour and Income* (Statistics Canada publication 75-001X), *10*(8), (2009, August) 32.

[8] Cited in Gallagher, *op. cit.*

[9] Barling, J., Kelloway, E.K., & Bremermann, E.H. (1991). Pre-employment predictors of union attitudes: the role of family socialization and work beliefs. *Journal of Applied Psychology*, *76*, 725–731.

[10] Puette, W.J. (1992). *Through jaundiced eyes: how the media view organized labor*. New York: St. Martin's Press.

[11] Gomez, R., Gunderson, M., & Meltz, N. (2002). Comparing youth and adult desire for unionisation in Canada. *British Journal of Industrial Relations*, *40*(3), 542–553.

[12] Lowe, G (2000). Organizing the next generation: influences on young workers' willingness to join unions in Canada. *British Journal of Industrial Relations*, *38*(2), 203–223.

[13] Statistics Canada, CANSIM tables 282-0087 and 282-0089, June 2010 data.

[14] Statistics Canada Labour Force Survey data, cited in Zukewich, N. (2000). Paid and unpaid work. In Statistics Canada, *Women in Canada 2000* (Statistics Canada, catalogue no.

89-503-XPE). Ottawa, ON: Statistics Canada; Statistics Canada, CANSIM tables 282-0087 and 282-0089, June 2010 data.

[15] Statistics Canada, CANSIM table 282-0002.

[16] Statistics Canada Labour Force Survey data, cited in Zukewich, *op. cit*; Statistics Canada, 2006 census data.

[17] Swimmer, G., & Thompson, M. (1995). Collective bargaining in the public sector: an introduction. In Swimmer, G., & Thompson, M. (Eds.), *Public sector collective bargaining in Canada*. Kingston, ON: Queen's IRC Press; Unionization, *op.cit*.

[18] Unionization, *op. cit*.

[19] Statistics Canada, CANSIM table 282-0077, June 2010 data.

[20] Yates, C.A.B. (2000). Staying the decline in union membership: union organizing in Ontario, 1985–1999. *Relations Industrielles*, *55*(4), 640–671.

[21] Yates, C.A.B. (2006). Challenging misconceptions about organizing women into unions. *Gender, Work and Organization*, *13*(6), 565–584.

[22] Yates (2000), *op. cit*.

[23] For example, Gordon, M.E., Philpot, J.W., Burt, R.E., Thompson, C.A., & Spiller, W.E. (1980). Commitment to the union: development of a measure and an examination of its correlates. *Journal of Applied Psychology Monograph*, *65*(4), 479–499; Yates (2006), *op.cit*.

[24] Creese, G. (1995). Gender equity or masculine privilege? Union strategies and economic restructuring in a white collar union. *Canadian Journal of Sociology*, *20*(2), 143–165.

[25] Marshall, K. (2010). Employer top-ups. *Perspectives on Labour and Income* (Statistics Canada catalogue no. 75-001-X), *11*(2), 5–12.

[26] Zukewich, *op. cit*; Girard. M. (2010). Effects of non-standard work on the work-family balance: a literature review. *McGill Sociological Review, 1*(1), 46–58.

[27] Sunter, D. (2001). *Demography and the labour market. Perspectives on Labour and Income* (Statistics Canada, catalogue no. 75-001-XPE), Spring 2001, 28–39.

[28] Statistics Canada, CANSIM table 282-0002, 2009 data.

[29] Sunter, *op. cit.*

[30] Sunter, *op. cit.*

[31] Dugan, B., & Robidoux, B. (1999). Demographic shifts and labour force participation rates in Canada. *Canadian Business Economist*, 7(2), 42–56. Cited in Sunter, *op. cit.*

[32] Sunter, *op. cit.*

[33] Mandatory retirement fades in Canada. CBC News. (2009, August 29). Available at <www.cbc.ca/canada/story/2009/08/20/mandatory-retirement-explainer523.html>.

[34] Unionization, *op. cit.*

[35] Palameta, B. (2001). Who contributes to RRSPs? A re-examination. *Perspectives on Labour and Income* (Statistics Canada, catalogue no. 75-001-XPE), Autumn 2001, 7–11.

[36] Visible Minority Population and Population Group Reference Guide, 2006 Census. Available at <www12.statcan.gc.ca/census-recensement/2006/ref/rp-guides/visible_minority-minorites_visibles-eng.cfm>

[37] Malenfant, É.C., Lebel, A., & Martel, L. (2010). Projections of diversity of the Canadian population. Statistics Canada catalogue number 91-551-X.

[38] Statistics Canada, Survey of Labour and Income Dynamics 1999. Cited in Jackson, A. (2002). *Is Work Working for Workers of Colour?* Ottawa: Canadian Labour Congress; Tran, K. (2004). Visible minorities in the labour force: 20 years of change. *Canadian Social Trends* (Statistics Canada, catalogue no. 11-008), Summer 2004, 7–11.

[39] Statistics Canada, 1996 census data. Cited in Statistics Canada, *Women in Canada 2000*, *op. cit.*

[40] Hou, F., & Coulombe, S. (2010). Earning gaps for Canadian-born visible minorities in the public and private sectors. *Canadian Public Policy, 36*(1), 29–43; Kelly, K. (1995). Visible minorities: a diverse group. *Canadian Social Trends* (Statistics Canada, catalogue no. 11-008-XPE), Summer 1995, 4–14.

[41] Jackson, *op. cit.*

[42] Malenfant, *op. cit.*

[43] Malenfant, *op. cit.*

[44] Jackson, *op. cit.*

[45] Jackson. A, & Schetagne, S. (2004). Solidarity forever? – an analysis of changes in union density. *Just Labour, 4*(2), 53–81.

[46] Creese, *op. cit.*, 144.

[47] Bourette, S. (1997, July 4). Organized labour lures growing number of youth. *The Globe and Mail*, p. B1.

[48] Hunt, G. (1995). Sexual orientation and the Canadian labour movement. *Relations Industrielles, 52*(4), 787–809.

[49] Brown, T. (2003). Sexual orientation provisions in Canadian collective agreements. *Industrial Relations/Relations Industrielles, 58*(4), 645–666.

[50] Hunt, *op. cit.*, 788.

[51] Gallagher, *op. cit.*

[52] Available at <www.canadianlabour.ca/human-rights-equality/youth>.

[53] Available at <www.csn.qc.ca/Jeunes/JeunesAcc.html>.

[54] Available at <www.gounion.ca/education/union.cfm#ywa>.

[55] Available at <www.bcfed.com/issues/young-workers>.

[56] Yates (2000), *op. cit.*

[57] Lowe, *op. cit.*; Yates (2000), *op. cit.*

[58] Galt, V. (1994, June 6). Reinventing the labour movement. *The Globe and Mail.* Cited in Craig & Solomon, *op. cit.*

[59] Kidd, K. (1994, June). Big Mac meets the McUnion Kid. *Report on Business Magazine*, 46–50.

[60] Lin, J. (2008). Trends in employment and wages, 2002 to 2007. *Perspectives* (Statistics Canada catalogue no. 75-001-X), *9*(9), 5–15.

[61] Ng. T.W.H., Sorenson, K.L,. Eby, L.T., & Feldman, D.L. (2007). Determinants of job mobility: a theoretical integration and extension. *Journal of Occupational and Organizational Psychology, 80,* 363–386.

[62] Gilmore, J., & Cote-Larochelle, S. (2009). Canada's employment downturn (October 2008 to October 2009). *Canadian Economic Observer*. Available at <http://www.statcan.gc.ca/pub/75-001-x/2009112/article/11048-eng.htm>

[63] Jones, C., & DeFillippi, R.J. (1996). Back to the future in film: combining industry and self-knowledge to meet the career challenges of the 21st century. *Academy of Management Executive*, *10*, 89–103.

[64] Sullivan, S.E., & Barach, Y. (2009). Advances in career theory: a critical review and agenda for the future. *Journal of Management, 35*(6), 1542–1571.

[65] Haines, V.Y., Jalette, P., & Larose, K. (2010). The influence of human resource management practices on employee voluntary turnover rates in the Canadian non-governmental sector. *Industrial and Labor Relations Review, 63*(2), 228–246.

[66] Godard, J. (2009). Institutional environments, work and human resource practices, and unions: Canada versus England. *Industrial and Labor Relations Review, 62*(2), 173–199.

[67] Benson, J., & Brown, M. (2010). Employee voice: does union membership matter? *Human Resource Management Journal, 20*(1), 80–99.

[68] Sturman, M.C., Trevor, C.O., Boudreau, J.W., & Gerhart, B. (2003). Is it worth it to win the talent war? Evaluating the utility of performance-based pay. *Personnel Psychology, 56*, 997–1035.

[69] Godard, *op. cit.*

[70] Provisions in Collective Agreements. (2005). Workplace Information Directorate, Labour Program, Human Resources and Skills Development Canada.

[71] Murphy, D.G. (1997). The entrepreneurial role of organized labour in the British Columbia motion picture industry. *Relations Industrielles*, *52*(3), 531–553.

[72] A video depicting the strike activities is available at <www.youtube.com/watch?v=dja5rlSGo0s>

[73] Cherry, M.A. (2010). A taxonomy of virtual work. *Georgia Law Review*, in press.

[74] Benson & Brown, *op. cit.*

[75] New GM boss calls CAW deal 'competitive'. (2009, March 31). *Toronto Star*, Available at <www.thestar.com/article/611089>.

[76] Keenan, G., McCarthy, S. & McFarland, J. (2009). Ottawa, Chrysler go public ahead of GM talks. (2009, April 17). *The Globe and Mail*. Available at <www.theglobeandmail.com/report-on-business/article1137599.ece>.

[77] Lewenza, K. (2009). Statement by CAW President Ken Lewenza on the Canadian and U.S. Auto Restructuring Announcements. Available at <www.caw.ca/en/7284.htm>.

[78] Lewchuk, W., & Wells, D. (2007). Transforming worker representation: the Magna model in Canada and Mexico. *Labour/Le Travail*, 60(3), 107–136, p. 113.

[79] Magna to let CAW organize in its plants. (2007, October 15) CBC News,. Available at <www.cbc.ca/money/story/2007/10/15/magna-caw.html>.

[80] Van Alphen, T. (2009, January 31). Magna deal spurs CAW infighting. *Toronto Star*. Available at <www.thestar.com/Business/article/580124>.

[81] See, e.g, The CAW-Magna Agreement: Not the Way Forward. (2008, January 12) *Canadian Dimension*. Available at <canadiandimension.com/articles/1768>.

[82] Bamber, G., Lansbury, D., & Wailes, N. (Eds.) (2005). *International and comparative employment relationships: globalization and the developed market economies* (4th edition). London: Sage Publications.

[83] For a discussion of how this process unfolds in one major international business, garment manufacturing, see Ross, R.J.S. (2005). *Slaves to fashion: poverty and abuse in the new sweatshops*. Ann Arbor, MI: University of Michigan Press.

[84] Briscoe, D.R., Rothman, M., & Nacamulli, R.C.D. (1993). *Industrial relations around the world: labor relations for multinational companies*. Berlin: de Gruyter.

[85] Gray, J. (2010, March 25). Nickelled and damned. *The Globe and Mail*. Available at <www.theglobeandmail.com/report-on-business/rob-magazine/nickelled-and-damned/article1509834>.

[86] Adams, R.J. (1994). State regulation of unions and collective bargaining: an international assessment of determinants and consequences. In Niland, J.R., Russell, D., & Verevis, C. (Eds.), *The future of industrial relations: global change and challenges*. Thousand Oaks, CA: Sage Publications.

[87] This discussion is summarized from Ross, *op. cit.*

[88] Human Rights Watch. (2001, April 16). NAFTA labor accord ineffective: future trade pacts must avoid pitfalls. Available at <hrw.org/english/docs/2001/04/16/global179.htm>.

[89] The CLC's involvement with lobbying efforts related to international trade agreements is described at <www.canadianlabour.ca/international-solidarity/acilla-program>.

[90] Riisgaard, L. (2005). International framework agreements: a new model for securing workers rights? *Industrial Relations: A Journal of Economy and Society, 44*(4), 707–737.

[91] Information on the program is available at <www.canadianlabour.ca/international-solidarity/labour-international-development-program>.

[92] Ward, O. (2005, June 26). The Wobblies are stirring—shrinking workforce, shrinking power: do we need 'one big union' in the global village? *The Toronto Star*, p. D04.

[93] Lévesque, C., & Murray, G. (2005). Union involvement in workplace change: a comparative study of local unions in Canada and Mexico. *British Journal of Industrial Relations, 43*(3), 489–514.

[94] Hammarström, O. (1994). Local and global: trade unions in the future. In Niland, Lansbury, & Verevis, *op. cit.*

[95] Quan, K. (2004). Trade union rights in China. *International Union Rights, 11*(4).

[96] Ross, *op. cit.*; Quan, *op. cit.*

[97] Weiler, P. (1993). Promises to keep: securing workers' rights to self-organization under the NLRA. *Harvard Law Review, 96*, 1769–1827. Quoted in Troy, L. (2000), U.S. and Canadian industrial relations: convergent or divergent? *Industrial Relations, 39*(4), 695–713.

[98] Lipset, S. (1989). *Continental divide: the values and institutions of the United States and Canada.* New York: Routledge.

[99] Logan, J. (2002). How "anti-union" laws saved Canadian labour: certification and striker replacements in post-war industrial relations. *Relations Industrielles, 57*(1), 129–158.

[100] Taras, D.G., & Ponak, A. (2001). Mandatory agency shop laws as an explanation of Canada-U.S. union density divergence. *Journal of Labor Research, 22*(3), 541–568.

[101] The text of the *Employee Free Choice Act* is available at <http://thomas.loc.gov/cgi-bin/query/z?c111:H.R.1409:>.

[102] See an example of the AFL-CIO materials supporting the EFCA at <www.aflcio.org/joinaunion/ voiceatwork/efca/whatis.cfm>.

[103] See an example of the U.S. Chamber of Commerce materials opposing the EFCA at <www.uschamber.com/issues/index/labor/cardchecksecrbal.htm>.

[104] British Columbia Ministry of Skills Development and Labour (2002). Backgrounder to the Labour Relations Code Amendment Act, 2002. Document no. 2002-006.

[105] Martinello, F. (2000). Mr. Harris, Mr. Rae, and union activity in Ontario. *Canadian Public Policy*, 26(1), 17–33.

[106] Brennan, R., & Benzie, R. (2005, June 14). MPPs pass slew of bills before break. *Toronto Star*, p. A.09.

[107] Section 1, Bill 42 (2002), *Labour Relations Code Amendment Act*. Victoria, BC: Crown Publications.

[108] Section 3, Bill 42, *op. cit.*

[109] Section 8, *British Columbia Labour Relations Code*, 1997. Victoria, BC: Crown Publications.

[110] Sask. labour law proposals slammed, praised. CBC News (2007, December 19). Available at <www.cbc.ca/canada/saskatchewan/story/2007/12/19/saskatchewan-labour.html>.

[111] Gilbert, R. (2010, July 31). Labour law change pleases open shop, irks Saskatchewan unions. *Daily Commercial News and Construction Record*. Available at <dcnonl.com/article/id39106>.

[112] Gunderson, M., & Riddell, W.C. (1999). The changing nature of work: implications for public policy. Paper prepared for the Institute for Public Policy.

[113] Logan, *op. cit.*

[114] Sova, G. (2008, July 2). Saskatchewan premier purges labour relations board, fires three. *Canadian HR Reporter*. Available at <www.canadianhrreporter.net/articleview.aspx?l=1&articleid=5952>.

[115] Rose, J.B., & Chaison, G.N. (2001). Unionism in Canada and the United States in the 21st century: the prospects for revival. *Relations Industrielles*, 56(1), 34–65.

[116] Robinson, I. (2000). Neoliberal restructuring and U.S. unions: toward social movement unionism? *Critical Sociology*, 26(1/2), 109–139.

[117] Thiessen, M.A. (2010, July 13). The fading embers of Obama's coalition. *The Washington Post*. Available at <www.washingtonpost.com/wp-dyn/content/article/2010/07/12/AR2010071202539.html>.

[118] Robinson, *op. cit.*

[119] Robinson, *op. cit.*

[120] Tattersall, A. (2009). A little help from our friends. *Labor Studies Journal, 34*(4), 485–506.

[121] <wemovetoronto.ca/?page_id=287>.

[122] <cupe.ca/deregulation/BE4627>.

[123] Eaton, J. & Verma, A. (2006). Does "fighting back" make a difference? The case of the Canadian Auto Workers union. *Journal of Labor Research, 27*(3), 187–212.

[124] Eaton & Verma, *op. cit.* p. 206.

[125] Eaton & Verma, *op. cit.,* p. 207.

[126] Briskin, L. (2008). Cross-constituency organizing in Canadian unions. *British Journal of Industrial Relations, 46*(2), 221–247.

[127] Robinson, *op. cit.,* p. 112.

[128] Rose & Chaison, *op. cit.*

[129] Radcliff, B., & Davis, P. (2000). Labor organization and electoral participation in industrial democracies. *American Journal of Political Science, 44*(1), 132–142.

[130] Rose & Chaison, *op. cit.*

[131] U.S. Bureau of Labor Statistics. (2009, January 22). Union Members in 2009. Available at <www.bls.gov/news.release/union2.nr0.htm>.

[132] Slater, Joseph E. (2005). *Public workers: government employee unions, the law, and the state, 1900–1962*. Ithaca, NY: Cornell University Press; Rose & Chaison, *op. cit.*; Logan, *op. cit.*

[133] Taras & Ponak, *op. cit.*

[134] Taras, D.G. (1998). Contemporary experience with the outlawed Rockefeller Plan. In Estreicher, S. (Ed.), *Employee representation in the emerging workplace: alternatives/supplements to collective bargaining*. Boston: Kluwer Law International.

[135] Rose & Chaison, *op. cit.*

[136] Harcourt, M. & Lam, H. (2007). Union certification: a critical analysis and proposed alternative. *WorkingUSA: The Journal of Labor and Society*, *10*, 327–345.

[137] Rose & Chaison; Slater, *op. cit.*

[138] Tufts, S. (2007). Emerging labour strategies in Toronto's hotel sector: toward a spatial circuit of union renewal. *Environment and Planning A, 39*(1), 2383–2404.

[139] Logan, *op. cit.*; Slater, *op. cit.*

[140] Worker-owned pulp mill dodges the scrap heap. (2009, February 27). *The Vancouver Sun.* Available at <www.canada.com/vancouversun/news/business/story.html?id=dc7518e1-8c74-43d7-84d0-9094d4b0c49e&k=64664>.

[141] Gray, L., & Seeber, R. (1996). The industry and the unions: an overview. In Gray, L., & Seeber, R. (Eds.), *Under the stars: essays on labor relations in arts and entertainment.* Ithaca, NY: IRL Press/Cornell University Press.

[142] Watanabe, R. (1996). The fat lady can't get a gig: the union movement is alive and well in show biz. In Estreicher, *op. cit.*

GLOSSARY

(Note: the number after each entry indicates the chapter in which the term is first discussed.)

Abandonment of bargaining rights   A reason for **decertification** based on a union's failure to commence bargaining for a first collective agreement. (12)

Accreditation   The legal process by which a group of employers (employers' council) is certified as a single entity for bargaining purposes. (7)

Adjudicator   An alternate term for **arbitrator**. (11)

Affiliates   A term used by the Canadian Labour Congress to describe its member organizations. (4)

Anti-union animus   The motivation to undertake an action solely to weaken or attack a union or its members. (6)

Application bar   Timelines in labour legislation that specify certain times when applications for certification can be filed with a labour relations board if a previous certification attempt has failed. (6)

Application for Certification   The application submitted to a labour relations board by a union wanting to represent a designated group of employees. (5)

Arbitral jurisprudence   Decisions in previous cases that deal with interpretation and/or applications of collective agreement language. (8)

Arbitration process   In **grievance arbitration**, a series of steps through which a resolution to an employer-union dispute is achieved. (11)

Arbitrator   An individual who makes a final and **binding** resolution to an employer-union dispute. (11)

Attitudinal structuring   A sub-process in bargaining that affects the parties' attitudes toward each other and toward their mutual relationship. (8)

Automatic certification   A process available in some Canadian jurisdictions allowing unions to be certified without a representation vote if a specified percentage of support is obtained from the members of the proposed bargaining unit. (5)

Back-to-work legislation   Legislation passed by a provincial or federal government to end a legal or illegal strike or lockout. (9)

Balance of probabilities   The standard of proof used in cases involving alleged unfair labour practices. (6)

Bargaining agent   After certification, the union's role as its members' representative in collective bargaining with the employer. (5)

Bargaining council   A group of unions who bargain as a single unit. (7)

Bargaining in good faith   The expectation that during collective bargaining, parties will bargain honestly and with the intention of concluding a collective agreement. (7)

Bargaining power   The ability of one side in bargaining to secure the other side's agreement to its terms. (8)

Bargaining unit   The group of workers represented by a union in collective bargaining. (5)

Beyond a reasonable doubt   The standard of proof used in criminal court cases. (11)

Binding   In the context of arbitration, an agreement by the parties that the arbitrator's decision will be final. (10)

Booking out   A mediator removing him or herself from the mediation process when he or she feels that his or her presence will no longer assist in solving the dispute. (10)

Bottom line   The absolute minimum that a negotiating team is prepared to accept as a settlement for a bargaining item. (8)

Boulwarism   The bargaining tactic of presenting a single offer, sometimes based on an employers' survey of union members' preferences, and refusing to negotiate any further. (7)

Boycott   A union request that its members not buy or use products or services from an employer whose employees are on strike or locked out. (9)

Business agent   A staff member of a union who administers the union's affairs. (4)

Business unionism   A type of unionism that focuses on protecting workers in a particular industry or occupation, or under a specific employer. (2)

Canadian Congress of Labour (CCL)   Founded in 1940 from a merger of the All-Canadian Congress of Labour and the American-based Council of Industrial Organizations, the second Canadian national labour federation after the Trades and Labour Congress. (3)

Canadian Labour Congress (CLC)   The largest national labour federation in Canada. (3)

Centrale des syndicats du Québec (CSQ)   A Quebec labour federation with membership primarily in the public sector. (4)

Certification order   An order issued by a labour relations board that names a union as the exclusive representative of the employees in a workplace and creates a collective bargaining relationship between the union and the employer. (6)

Charter of Rights and Freedoms   A part of Canada's constitution that guarantees certain basic rights to all Canadians. (3)

Chilling effect   In negotiations, the inability of parties to settle an agreement on their own because of continued reliance on third-party intervention. (10)

Clear and cogent evidence   The standard of proof used in grievance arbitrations involving serious employment offences. (11)

Closed shop   A union security provision requiring union membership as a condition of employment. Also known as a **union shop**. (7)

Common employer declaration   A declaration by a labour relations board that two separate businesses are a single entity. (12)

Commonwealth Trade Union Council An international labour organization representing unions and federations in the Commonwealth countries. (4)

Community of interest   Some form of commonality among workers in a proposed bargaining unit that must be present for a labour relations board to grant certification to the unit. (5)

Company union   A union controlled by the employer. (5)

Compressed workweek   A form of work scheduling in which longer hours are worked over fewer days than in a normal work schedule. (13)

Concessions   A party's willingness to agree to the other side's proposal in negotiations or to adjust their own bargaining position. (8)

Conciliation   A form of third-party intervention in which the third party investigates a bargaining dispute and makes a report on its findings. (10)

Conciliation Act   An act passed in 1900 that created a federal department of labour and gave the department the ability to appoint third-party intervenors or commissions of inquiry to assist in resolving labour disputes. (3)

Confédération des syndicats nationaux (CSN)   A Quebec labour federation with over 2,000 member locals in various industries. (4)

Confederation of Canadian Unions (CCU)   A national federation formed in 1973 for Canadian-based and controlled unions. (3)

Confederation of National Trade Unions (CNTU)   A Quebec-based labour federation formed in 1961. (3)

Congress of Industrial Organizations (CIO)   An American labour federation that affiliated with several unions and labour federations in Canada. (3)

Consensual adjudication   An alternate term for grievance arbitration. (11)

Continental movement   A movement of American-based international unions who solicited membership in Canada during the mid-1800s. (3)

Continuing grievance   A grievance involving an ongoing practice rather than a single incident. (11)

Continuity   In the context of successorship, the criterion deciding whether there is evidence indicating linkages between a former and current business. (12)

Control   (i) In the context of reasons for unionization, the ability of a union to allow workers some degree of control over their workplaces or jobs (2); (ii) in the context of successorship, the criterion deciding whether two businesses are owned and/or operated by the same party. (12)

Convention (or **congress**)   Regular meetings of union members or delegates where policies or a direction for the union are set through votes on motions. (4)

Craft union   A union that represents workers in a specific occupation, trade, or craft. (3)

Creature comforts   The ability of a union to improve its members' standards of living. (2)

Crisis   A bargaining stage in which parties decide whether to settle or to use economic sanctions to pressure an agreement. (8)

Cross-examination   An examination of one party's witnesses conducted by the other party during an arbitration hearing. (11)

Decertification   The process through which a union is removed as the legal representative of a group of employees. (12)

Deskilling   Management decisions that focus on designing a job to minimize the skills needed to perform it successfully. (2)

Device of restriction of numbers   Union structures such as apprenticeship that restrict the number of individuals employed in a craft or trade and control entrance to that craft or trade. (2)

Device of the common rule   Union structures that ensure the union's activities are guided by democratic principles and the vote of the membership. (2)

Direct examination   An examination of one party's witnesses by a representative of the same party during an arbitration hearing. (11)

Disputes inquiry board   A form of third-party intervention similar to conciliation that is available in some Canadian jurisdictions. (10)

Distributive bargaining   A sub-process in bargaining that consists of competitive behaviours intended to influence the distribution of limited resources. (8)

Downsizing   A temporary or permanent reduction in the size of a company's workforce. (13)

Dues check-off   A union security provision permitting union members to request that the employer automatically deduct union dues from their pay and forward the dues to the union. (7)

Duty of fair representation   The legal duty of a union to represent all its members fairly and without bias. (11)

Employer   An individual or organization that employs one or more individuals to carry out specified tasks, usually for pay. (1)

Employers' council   A group of employers who bargain as a single unit. *See also* **accreditation**. (7)

Essential service   A service whose provision is determined to be necessary to ensure public safety or health. (9)

Exempt employees   Non-management employees who may be excluded from a bargaining unit, usually because of access to confidential information. (5)

Expedited arbitration   An arbitration process which operates within predetermined timelines and which has the parties represent themselves in hearings. (11)

Fact finder   A form of third-party intervention similar to conciliation available in some Canadian jurisdictions. (10)

Final offer selection   A method of fashioning arbitration awards in which each party submits its final offer on each outstanding item and the arbitrator chooses some or all of the offer to create the award. *See also* **total-package final offer selection** and **item-by-item final offer selection**. (10)

Final offer vote   A method of resolving bargaining disputes in which members of one party vote on whether to accept the other party's final bargaining offer. (10)

Flatter organization   A redesigned organizational structure that has fewer hierarchical levels. (13)

Flextime   A form of work scheduling that allows employees to set their own working hours. (13)

Freeze   The requirement that working conditions established by a collective agreement remain in effect until a new collective agreement is completed. (7)

Friendly or uplifting unionism   A form of unionism that emphasizes the creation of social connections among the membership. (2)

Globalization model   Assumes globalization pressures are so strong that there will eventually be little difference in how countries conduct or regulate employment relationships. (13)

Grievance   A dispute between the union and the employer over the interpretation, application, or administration of the collective agreement language. (11)

Grievance arbitration   The process through which employer-union disputes during the term of the collective agreement are settled. (11)

Grievance mediation   A process of grievance resolution in which a third party assists the parties in reaching their own resolution to a dispute. (11)

Grievor   An individual or party alleging that misinterpretation, misapplication, or improper administration of the collective agreement language has occurred. (11)

Group grievance   A **grievance** alleging that actions have affected a group of employees rather than a single employee. (11)

Hiring hall   A union security provision in which the employer contacts the union with job opportunities and the union provides qualified union members as job candidates. (7) → No non- unionized workers.

Hot declaration   A declaration by a union that its members will refuse to work with any product or service from a company whose employees are on strike or locked out. (9)

Implied obligations   The philosophy that if a union and employer collectively bargain to determine workplace conditions, any workplace issues not addressed by the collective agreement should also be resolved by mutual negotiation. (12)

Individual grievance   A grievance submitted by an individual union member regarding an alleged violation of the collective agreement affecting that member. (11)

In good standing   A requirement for officers of most labour councils; officers must be full members of their own union and follow the union's rules and policies. (4)

Industrial action   *See* **strike**. (9)

Industrial conflict   *See* **strike**. (9)

Industrial Disputes Investigation Act   Federal legislation passed in 1907 requiring industrial disputes to be submitted to a third party for resolution. (3)

Industrial inquiry commission   A form of third-party intervention similar to conciliation that is available in some Canadian jurisdictions. (10)

Industrial union   A union that represents workers regardless of their occupation or employer. (3)

Industrial Workers of the World (IWW)   Also known as "Wobblies," an industrial union with socialist philosophies that recruited extensively in Canada during the early 1900s. (3)

Information   The ability of a union to improve its members' working lives by supplying information they would not otherwise receive. (2)

Institutionalist model   A model of the impacts of globalization on employment relationships, which assumes that different regions will respond differently to similar pressures from globalization. (13)

Instrumentality   The perception that a union will be able to help workers achieve desired outcomes in the workplace. (5)

Integrated approach   Suggests that both institutional and economic factors will influence the effects of globalization on a particular country and that both factors must be considered in attempts to explain or predict globalization's effects on the regulation of employment relationships in specific countries. (13)

Integrative bargaining   A sub-process in bargaining that consists of problem-solving behaviour focusing on common interests and joint gains. (8)

Integrity   The ability of a union to enhance its members' feelings of self-respect and fairness. (2)

Intentional discrimination   An action deliberately undertaken to deny opportunity to an individual on the basis of his or her personal characteristics. (1)

Interest arbitration   Arbitration that settles disputes during collective bargaining. (10)

Interests   The needs, wants, fears, concerns, desires, or other motivators of the parties in bargaining. (8)

International Trade Union Confederation (ITUC)   An international organization representing unions and federations throughout the world. (4)

International Labour Organization (ILO)   A labour organization based in Switzerland that provides research and information about unions and working conditions worldwide. (4)

International union   A union with membership in more than one country. (3)

Interprovincial component   The part of a business's operations that cross provincial boundaries; it is used to determine whether federal or provincial labour law applies to the employees of the business. (1)

Intra-organizational bargaining   A subprocess in bargaining during which negotiators for each side attempt to achieve consensus within the bargaining team on goals and objectives. (8)

Iron law of oligarchy   A principle suggesting that leadership of any organization will eventually be controlled by an elite whose actions are intended to maintain that control. (4)

Item-by-item final offer selection   A form of interest arbitration in which the arbitrator creates a collective agreement by selecting one party's final offer on each individual bargaining item. (10)

Job sharing   A work arrangement in which two workers share one full-time job. (13)

Jurisdiction   The legal responsibility for governance of an issue or area. (1)

Justification   In the terminology of the Canadian Labour Congress, a claim made by a member union to support its actions in attempting to certify another union's members. (4)

Key person doctrine   A criterion used in **successorship** that examines whether employees with highly specialized or difficult to replace skills or knowledge who were employed by the former employer are now employed by the current employer. (12)

Knights of Labor   An industrial union that recruited in Canada in the early 1900s. It distinguished itself by recruiting among previously unorganized workers and industries. (3)

Labour councils   Organizations composed of union representatives from unions in a specific geographic area. (4)

Labour relations board   A body established by a government to administer labour relations law. (1)

Libel   A statement of something untrue that would damage a person's reputation. (9)

Local union (or **local**)   The "smallest" unit of a union, representing workers in a particular industry or workplace. (4)

Lockout   An action by an employer barring employees' physical access to the workplace. (9)

Lost person-days   A calculation used to estimate the amount of working time lost because of strikes or lockouts. (9)

Make whole   The guideline used by labour relations boards in making decisions or remedies for unfair labour practices. It attempts to put the parties in the situation they were in before the unfair practices occurred. (6)

Management rights   The philosophy, often expressed in a clause in collective agreements, that management has the exclusive right to make decisions on workplace issues not addressed by the collective agreement. Also called the philosophy of **residual rights**. (12)

Management rights clause   A clause in a collective agreement giving management authority over any matters not specifically outlined in the agreement. (7)

Matrix organization   A form of organizational structure in which functional and productive departments are linked by sharing employees. (13)

Mediation   A form of third-party intervention in which the third party participates in bargaining and helps negotiators reach a solution on their own. (10)

Mediation-arbitration   A form of third-party intervention in which the third party acts first as a mediator, and, if negotiators are still unable to agree, then becomes an arbitrator who determines solutions to bargaining disputes. (10)

Method of collective bargaining   The method of achieving a union's goals through negotiating with the employer. (2)

Method of legal enactment   The method of achieving a union's goals by pressuring a government to pass legislation supporting unionism and workers' rights. (2)

Method of mutual insurance   The method of achieving a union's goals by using part of the union dues to support workers who are injured or sick. (2)

Monopoly laws   British laws passed during the late 1800s that were intended to counteract restraints of trade but were instead used to restrict the growth of unions. (3)

Narcotic effect   In negotiations, the parties' unwillingness or reluctance to settle disputes on their own because third-party intervention is available. (10)

Network (or web) organization   A form of organizational structure in which individuals or departments are linked by connections and not by hierarchical levels. (13)

Nine-Hour Movement   A movement in Central Canada during the late 1800s that lobbied for legislation to restrict the working day to nine hours. (3)

Non-permanent employment relationship Any form of employer-employee relationship where the employee is not indefinitely employed by the employer (e.g., contract work or temporary work). (13)

Non-standard work   Any work relationship other than full-time permanent employment. (13)

North American Free Trade Act (NAFTA) Legislation that reduces or removes trade barriers among North American countries. (3)

Notice to bargain   A formal notice issued by one party to the other after which collective bargaining must usually commence. (7)

One Big Union (OBU)   An American-based international union that recruited extensively in Western Canada during the early 1900s. (3)

Open periods   Times during which an application for certification can be filed with a labour relations board. (6)

Organizing campaign   The campaign undertaken by a union to persuade workers to express support for the union as their representative. (5)

Outsourcing   Removing jobs or tasks from an organization and contracting other organizations or individuals to perform those jobs or tasks. (5)

P.C. 1003   A Canadian order-in-council passed during World War II. It was the first piece of Canadian legislation to contain the principles of the American *Wagner Act*. (3)

Para-public/quasi-public sector   The labour market sector consisting of organizations funded by the government but not directly operated by the government (e.g., schools and hospitals). (1)

Parent union   A regional, national, or international union composed of locals. (4)

Participation rate   The number or percentage of individuals in a demographic group who are employed or otherwise in the labour market. (13)

Past practice   In the context of grievance arbitration, the acceptance of a previous or consistent violation of the collective agreement when a current occurrence of the same violation is now the subject of a grievance. (11)

Pattern bargaining   A bargaining strategy used when there are multiple employers in a single industry; the contract negotiated with one employer is used as a pattern for contract demands in negotiations with the other employers. Also known as **whipsawing**. (7)

Picket line   A demonstration outside the employer's place of business by employees on strike or locked out. *See also* **secondary picketing**. (9)

Policy grievance   A **grievance** filed by a union alleging that an employer's incorrect action has affected all employees. (11)

Position   The preferred outcome of one side in negotiations. (8)

Predatory unionism   A form of unionism in which unions are primarily concerned with increasing their power by any means possible. (2)

Primary industry   A resource-based industry such as mining or forestry. (3)

Procedural onus   In the context of an arbitration hearing, the expectation that one party to the alleged offence bears the responsibility of proving its actions were justified. (11)

Professional strikebreaker   An individual hired specifically to do the work of an employee on strike. The use of these individuals is illegal in some Canadian jurisdictions. (9)

Protected grounds   Personal characteristics (e.g., gender or ethnic background) defined in provincial and federal human rights legislation as factors which are forbidden from being used as the basis of discrimination. (1)

Provincial labour federation   A federation representing unions and labour councils in a specific Canadian province or territory. (4)

Psychology of the labourer   The principle underlying the idea that unions should be controlled by workers rather than intellectuals because workers are better able to understand the working-class experience. (2)

Public sector   The labour market sector consisting of municipal, regional, provincial, and federal government employment. (1)

Quasi-judicial   Having regulatory, enforcing, or interpretive powers similar to those of a civil or criminal court, but not operating in exactly the same manner. (1)

Quebec Federation of Labour (FTQ)   A Canadian Labour Congress-affiliated federation of Quebec unions. (4)

Raid   An attempt by a union to certify workers already belonging to another union. (6)

Rand formula   A collective agreement provision that permits workers to choose whether or not to join a union, but requires all workers in a unionized workplace to pay union dues regardless. (3)

Ratification   The bargaining stage in which the parties present the negotiated agreement to the constituencies they represent for approval. (8)

Ratification vote   A vote conducted by a union at the end of collective bargaining to determine whether bargaining unit members accept the negotiated agreement. (9)

Recognition strike   A strike intended to pressure an employer into recognizing a union as the legal representative of the employees. (9)

Re-examination   In a grievance hearing, the process in which one party's advocate can ask further questions of a witness supporting that party after the witness has been cross-examined. (11)

Relieve   In the context of grievance arbitration, the ability of the arbitrator to hear complaints that might otherwise be disqualified on procedural grounds (e.g., a complaint filed after a predetermined deadline). (11)

Religious exemption   A union security provision that allows workers whose religious beliefs discourage union membership to pay a sum equal to union dues to a mutually agreed upon charity. (7)

Reopener clause   A clause in a collective agreement permitting the union and management to renegotiate terms of the agreement before its expiry date without renegotiating the entire agreement. (12)

Replacement workers   Workers who carry out work usually done by union members who are on strike or locked out. (9)

Representation vote   A vote conducted by a labour relations board to determine whether employees wish to be represented by a union or not. (6)

Residual rights   *See* **management rights**. (12)

Reverse discrimination   When preference in access to services or employment is given to a designated demographic group, the discrimination that may result against individuals who do not belong to that group. (13)

Reverse onus   In unfair labour practice complaints against the employer, the expectation that the employer must prove its actions were not motivated by anti-union animus. (6)

Revolutionary unionism   A form of unionism in which unions are primarily agents for large-scale social change. (2)

Rights   The formalized powers of the parties in a negotiation. (8)

Rights arbitration   An alternative term to **grievance arbitration**, referring to the fact that grievance arbitration may deal with whether the employer or the union has the right to determine outcomes for matters not addressed in the collective agreement. (11)

Rotating strike   A strike action where different units of an employer's operation go on strike at different times. (9)

Salting   A union organizing technique which uses workers already employed in the bargaining unit as the primary campaign organizers. (13)

Scab   A slang term for an individual who does the work of employees on strike. (9)

Secondary industry   Industries such as manufacturing that process the products of resource industries. (3)

Secondary picketing   Picketing at a location of the employer which is not on strike, or picketing business associates of a struck or locked-out employer. (9)

Settlement orientation   An approach to **grievance mediation** in which grievance mediation is imposed by legislation and the parties are pressured to reach an agreement. (11)

Shop steward   A union member who acts as the union representative in the workplace. (4)

Single employer (**common employer**)   A declaration issued by a labour relations board when multiple businesses are under common control. The effect of the declaration is to treat all the businesses as a single employer for the purposes of certification. (5)

Social status   The ability of unions to improve their members' status in the community or workplace or within the union itself. (2)

Special mediator   A mediator appointed at any time during collective bargaining, generally with a wider range of powers than "regular" mediators. (10)

Standard of proof Guidelines to assist arbitrators in determining which party's case should be upheld or accepted. *See also* **reasonable doubt**, **clear and cogent evidence**, and **balance of probabilities**. (11)

Strike An action where bargaining unit members withdraw their labour. (9)

Strike mandate An indication by bargaining unit members that they are willing to undertake strike action. *See also* **strike vote**. (9)

Strike pay Payments given by the union to workers on strike to offset their loss of employment income. (9)

Strike vote A vote by bargaining unit members to authorize strike action by the union. It is required in most Canadian jurisdictions prior to a strike for the strike to be legal. (9)

Subpoena A legal order issued by an arbitrator for a party to testify or to provide evidence at an arbitration hearing. (11)

Successorship The legal obligation of an employer to continue its relationship with a union if the company undergoes changes. (12)

Surface bargaining Engaging in collective bargaining without any intention of concluding a collective agreement. (7)

Sweetheart agreement A collective agreement that unduly favours the employer's interests. (5)

Systemic discrimination Discrimination caused by policies or practices which have the effect of excluding particular individuals or groups, even if the policies or practices were not established with the intent to create discrimination. (1)

Technological change A change to the technology used to perform a job that may entail changes in the structure or content of the job itself. (12)

Telecommuting A work arrangement involving computers, fax, telephone, or any technology permitting a worker to work from someplace other than the employer's premises. (13)

Terminal date In some Canadian jurisdictions, the date by which all submissions related to an application for certification must be received by a labour relations board. (6)

Tertiary industry Service industries and other non-resource related industries. (3)

Time bar Restrictions in Canadian labour law that specify times when organizing campaigns can take place in a workplace. (6)

Total-package final offer selection A form of interest arbitration in which the arbitrator creates a collective agreement by accepting the entire final offer of one party. (10)

Trades and Labour Congress (TLC) Formed in 1883, the first truly representative national labour federation in Canada. (3)

Trades Union Advisory Committee of the Organization for Economic Co-Operation and Development (TUAC-OECD) An international committee of labour unions which provides information on labour-related issues to OECD members. (4)

Transformative orientation   An approach to **grievance mediation** in which the parties to the dispute are educated to resolve their own disagreements. (11)

Underemployment   When an individual is employed in a job requiring a lower level of training, experience, or education than that he or she possesses. (13)

Unfair labour practice   Any activity or behaviour by a union or employer that has the effect of unduly influencing employees. (5)

Union   A group established by and for workers to represent them in the workplace. (1)

Union dues   Membership fees paid to the union by its members. (5)

Union executive   A group elected by union members to run a local union. (4)

Union security   Structures and processes put into place after certification that assist the union in its ability to fully represent its members. (7)

Union shop   *See* **closed shop**. (7)

Voluntary recognition   When an employer accepts a union as the employees' representative in the workplace without the union having to go through the process of certification. (5)

Wagner Act   Federal legislation passed in the United States in 1935 that gave workers the right to unionize and legally strike, and compelled employers to bargain with unions. It was the basis for P.C. 1003 and subsequent labour legislation in Canada. (3)

Whipsawing   *See* **pattern bargaining**. (7)

Wildcat strike   A strike that occurs spontaneously without a strike vote or strike mandate. (9)

Winnipeg General Strike   A strike that occurred in 1919 and was the first long, large-scale general strike in Canadian history. (3)

Workplace restructuring   Changes to jobs or to an entire workplace or workforce (e.g., downsizing, relocation, or job redesign). (12)

Work-to-rule campaign   A form of industrial action in which bargaining union members rigidly adhere to collective agreement terms. (9)

Zone of agreement   A range of potential solutions to bargaining issues which are acceptable to both parties. (8)

PHOTO CREDITS

CP = Canadian Press
LAC = Library and Archives Canada

Chapter 1
2: PhotoDisc, Inc.; 5: (left) J.P. Moczulski/CP, (right) Courtesy British Columbia Ministry of Energy, Mines and Petroleum Resources; 11: J.P. Moczulski/CP; 13: Courtesy CN; 21: Library and Archives Canada/Credit: Robert Cooper/Office of The Prime Minister collection/e008300499

Chapter 2
36: Purestock/Jupiter Images; 38: TV Ontario, Visual Research Department; 41: Toronto Public Library (TRL), J. Ross Robertson Collection: T 10914; 45: LAC/C-030945; 58: W Harland/*Mail & Empire*

Chapter 3
70: Labourers Bell, Courtesy of Trustees of the Hatheway Trust; 79: W. Farmer/LAC/PA-103086; 86: Archives of Manitoba, Foote 1696 (N2762); 90: TV Ontario, Visual Research Department; 100: © *The Gazette* (Montréal), LAC/PA-163000;

Chapter 4
120: Grant Neufeld/Flicker.com; 127: Courtesy the Canadian Auto Workers Union. Reprinted by permission; 134: Tom Hanson/CP; 149: Wilson/Canadian Association of Labour Media; 154: Courtesy of International Trade Union Confederation

Chapter 5
162: Tom Galivan; 166: Tom Galivan; 177: Courtesy the Canadian Auto Workers Union. Reprinted by permission; 186: © James Martin/iStock; 194: Ryan Remiorz/CP

Chapter 6
214: John E. Lightfoot, Jr./CP; 221: Len Norris/Simon Fraser University Library Collection; 227: PhotoDisc/Getty Images; 236: British Columbia Archives/G-05174; 244: Mike Blake/Reuters

Chapter 7
258: Ron Sutherland; 265: Flat Earth; 267: Courtesy of Public Service Alliance of Canada (PSAC); 280: Courtesy Canadian Union of Public Employees; 283: PhotoDisc, Inc.

Chapter 8
302: Lance Anderson/Peterborough This Week; 310: Chris Young/CP; 322: Richard Buchan/CP; 327: Eric Parker

Chapter 9
352: Stephen C. Host/CP; 368: Dean Bicknell/CP; 370: Rene Johnston/Toronto Star/GetStock.com; 377: Larry MacDougal/CP; 391: Len Norris/Simon Fraser University Library Collection

Chapter 10
408: Yusuf Gomel/iStock; 415: Murray McKenzie/LAC/PA-120633; 436: Courtesy of Sun Media Corporation

Chapter 11
446: Matt Collingwood/iStock; 459: Weekend/LAC/PA-115252; 464: Tom Hanson/CP; 469: Wayne Glowacki/CP

Chapter 12
500: Courtesy of TransLink; 504: Bernard Weil/CP; 525: Eric Parker; 526: Dick Loek/CP; 531: Courtesy Air Canada

Chapter 13
554: Courtesy of CAW (Canadian Auto Workers union); 561: Courtesy CWIA (Canadian Women in Aviation); 569: PhotoDisc, Inc.; 573: Purestock/Jupiter Images; 597: Flores/Canadian Association of Labour Media.

INDEX